D0909788

Romanchuk '74

4th Chimney

Mathematics in the Archaeological and Historical Sciences

Mathematics in the Archaeological and Historical Sciences

Proceedings of the Anglo-Romanian Conference
Mamaia 1970, organized by The Royal Society of
London, and The Academy of the Socialist Republic
of Romania. Edited by F. R. Hodson,
D. G. Kendall FRS, and P. Tăutu

at the University Press, Edinburgh

© 1971
EDINBURGH UNIVERSITY PRESS
22 George Square, Edinburgh
ISBN 085224 213 1
North America
ALDINE·ATHERTON, INC.
529 South Wabash Avenue, Chicago
Library of Congress
Catalog Card Number 77-182901
Printed in Great Britain by
Aberdeen University Press

Contents

Seriation

Evolutionary tree structures in historical and other contexts
Parish register studies

Population genetics

Linguistics

Filiation of Manuscripts

Miscellaneous applications
Archaeology

Contents

Preface

When the organizers of the Anglo-Romanian Conference on Mathematics in the Archaeological and Historical Sciences embarked on their work in the autumn of 1968, they did so in the full knowledge that their task would not be an easy one, but encouraged by the warm support guaranteed at the outset by the Officers of the Academy of the Socialist Republic of Romania, and of the Royal Society of London. We were also fortunate in knowing that our own enthusiasm for the venture was shared by the then Secretary of the British Academy, Sir Mortimer Wheeler CH, FBA, FRS. Now that our work is finished we wish to record our deep gratitude to those who gave their unqualified support at the very beginning to what must have appeared a somewhat unusual project, as well as to all who, in participation, administration, and publication, are responsible for the appearance of this book.

It is believed that the reader will find the table of contents an adequate guide to the structure and content of the work. Papers dealing with cluster analysis come first, then those concerned with seriation, followed by papers attacking the problem of the identification of tree structures. In each of these three groups the theoretical papers are accompanied by others discussing the practical aspects of the problem and illustrating the use of some of the algorithms. Finally a miscellany contains a number of pioneer papers breaking new ground and cutting across the oversimplified tripartite structure imposed on the earlier sections of the book.

A marked feature of the Mamaia Conference was the vigour and depth of the formal Round Table Discussions and the no less important informal exchanges on the excursions (and on the beaches). It proved quite impossible to record these at all adequately, and in the book we have included only a very few of the more specially pertinent comments. We are delighted to know that the professional associations formed in this way between mathematicians, archaeologists, historians, and others are already leading to collaborative interdisciplinary studies, to provoke which was our primary intent.

Introductory Address

Introductory Address

Albert C. Spaulding
Some elements of quantitative archaeology

My purpose is to try to explain in general terms the kinds of entities that archaeologists count or measure and the behavioral relationships that are reasonably implied by comparison and ordering of the numerical data. My point of view is that of an Americanist prehistorian, which means one whose primary training is in anthropology rather than history. But I believe that the entities and relationships discussed are not altogether alien to the historians; I think that there is a substantial overlap of theoretical and methodological interests. Indeed, since historians have more direct access to human behavior through documents, I also hope that the historians can instruct and inform the prehistorians on the interrelationships between human behavior and the material results of that behavior. My original intention was to discuss the central problem of prehistorians conventionally labeled 'typology', but this problem is so closely related to the topic called 'seriation' and others that I have extended my remarks to a more general consideration of the patterning of numerical data provided by collections of archaeological objects. My present aspiration is to set out in the simplest possible manner the fundamental structure of numerical analysis in prehistoric archaeology as a foundation for subsequent discussion of specific quantitative methods and problems. In keeping with this aspiration, I will not attempt a catalogue of existing mathematical techniques that have been applied to archaeology nor will I try to present a history of archaeological methods. Further, I will concede at the outset that it is certain that my personal knowledge and analytical powers are hardly adequate to the task, and it may even be that our combined resources are deficient. But I do hope that we can succeed in giving the mathematicians a reasonably clear picture of what we think we are doing; if we do not succeed, we cannot expect effective help from them, and we need their help.

I have organized my discussion around certain intuitive notions underlying all archaeological research. I mean by the phrase 'intuitive notions' the seldom formalized, predefinitional, empirical, scientifically primitive awareness on the part of archaeologists (and others) of the major characteristics of human behavior and its material results. This awareness, sometimes called wisdom or common sense, is an implicit theoretical apparatus, and it has always been the intellectual background which gives primary meaning to the corpus of archaeological materials. In this respect prehistoric archaeology more than resembles history. It shares with history a common base of implicit understanding of human dispositions, and it frequently treats its data in a truly historical manner, that is, it solves an old puzzle by producing a new fact which is immediately illuminating because no reference to an explicit theory is required. In short, archaeologists and historians have a ready-made theory of past human behavior simply because they share the attributes of humanity with the people of the past. The methodological developments with which we are here concerned are an attempt to provide techniques for extending our understanding of the past beyond this common sense base; we do not concede that common human knowledge of common human properties exhausts the theoretical possibilities of prehistoric studies. However, the intuitive base has taken us quite a long way in the understanding of the past, and a consideration of its concepts is a logical beginning for our discussions.

The first concept, the artifact, provides the class of entities with which archaeology is concerned: the objects or remains of objects which exhibit the attributes of socially patterned human activity. One of the obvious and perhaps surprising aspects of this concept is its ease of application. For the most part, objects can be assigned to the classes 'artifact' or 'non-artifact' with confidence. There are puzzling cases, some of which are of great importance, but the area of disagreement on the artifactuality of particular objects or of classes of objects is small compared to the area of agreement. The characteristic agreement is produced, of course, by a widely shared knowledge of human neuro-muscular capabilities and motivations and of the physical properties of materials, assisted by experimentation and ethnographic comparison. The ability to recognize artifacts implies the ability to recognize those attributes of artifacts which represent patterned human modification, and we are brought to a fundamental collectivity, the set of culturally meaningful attributes bound together by their occurrence on a single object, the artifact. The culturally meaningful attributes may be discrete or qualitative—the presence or absence of handles on a pottery vessel, for example—or they may be expressions of the continuous or quantitative variables that are ordinarily called measurements. Qualitative attributes can be organized into dimensions (or variables) of mutually exclusive properties, and the measuring scale is a nominal one, simply a notation of which of the various discrete attributes of the variable is present on the artifact; for a crude example, is the artifact red, green, or some other color? Quantitative variables are measured by familiar scales of length, weight, and so on. Application of the quantitative and qualitative scales produces a list of attributes for each artifact, and artifacts are compared by comparing attribute lists.

The notion of the artifact as a list or assemblage of attributes selected by the archaeologist on an implicit theory of cultural relevance brings me to a second intuitive concept, that of the artifact type. Archaeologists, like other people, are aware that artifacts do not in fact exhibit innumerable combinations and recombinations of attributes; instead they exhibit a relatively small (although absolutely large) number of combinations. Combinations of attributes tend to be repeated rather than endlessly varied. The reasons for this tendency are matters of common knowledge. One reason has to do with the purpose for which the artifact was made. Certain purposes demand certain combinations of attributes; thus tools used for cutting wood must be made from hard and durable materials if they are to cut effectively. A second reason is simply a human predilection for patterned activity; repetition of attribute combinations occurs even when no criterion of efficient utilization can be applied. In our culture, table chinaware is often decorated with floral patterns; in western Canada, the bows of canoes have painted wolf designs. Rakes, shovels, and hoes are undoubted examples of three types of artifacts in our culture. Although manufactured from similar materials, each possesses its distinctive form and distinctive range of customary functions.

In the case of collections of archaeological artifacts, we cannot observe the mode of usage directly, and frequently there is no evidence other than the properties of the artifacts themselves to aid in the definition of types. But we can prepare attribute lists, note the attribute combinations exhibited by the collection, prepare a frequency distribution table for the combinations, and analyze the frequency distribution in terms of groups of associated attributes and clusters of similar artifacts. I present a simple example to illustrate the structure of the operation. In the example, the columns represent variables, the rows individual artifacts. To present the structure in ultimate simplicity, I suppose each variable to be discrete and dichotomous and adopt the convention of the incidence matrix; a notation of 1 signifies that the artifact exhibits one attribute of the dichotomy and a notation of 0 signifies that it does not exhibit this attribute (and consequently must exhibit the other attribute). The example in figure 1 is based on six artifacts (A_1 through A_6) and five variables (V_1 through V_5).

	V_1	V_2	V_3	V_4	V_5
A_1	0	0	1	1	0
A_2	1	1	0	0	1
A_3	1	1	0	0	1
A_4	0	0	1	1	0
A_5	1	1	0	0	1
A_6	0	0	1	1	0

Figure 1

From this matrix, we can construct an index or coefficient of similarity for each of the 15 possible pairs of artifacts simply by counting similarities (two 0s or two 1s), that is, by tallying the number of variables for which the pair scores 'same'. The coefficient can range from 0 (no similarities), as in the case of A_1 and A_2, to 5 for identity, as in the case of A_2 and A_3. In this example, each score is either 0 or 5; each pair of artifacts is either identical with respect to the five variables considered or the two artifacts of the pair have no attributes in common.

The similarity coefficients of the 15 pairs of artifacts can be represented by

	A_1	A_4	A_6	A_2	A_3	A_5
A_1	5	5	5	0	0	0
A_4	5	5	5	0	0	0
A_6	5	5	5	0	0	0
A_2	0	0	0	5	5	5
A_3	0	0	0	5	5	5
A_5	0	0	0	5	5	5

Figure 2

the square matrix formed by employing the row headings as the column headings also, a sort of half transpose. [For a mathematically sophisticated exposition of matrix operations in archaeology, see Kendall (1969).] We can also rearrange the order of the rows and columns in a search for patterning among the similarity coefficients. The result of transposition and rearrangement for our example is shown in figure 2.

This result is plainly a significant pattern. There are two clusters of artifacts defined by the two blocks of similarity coefficients of 5: the clusters are A_1, A_4, A_6; and A_2, A_3, A_5. Within each cluster, all relationships are identity relationships; outside the clusters, there is no discernible similarity. Two types of artifacts have been defined with respect to the five variables of the example. The operations described are a rudimentary illustration of the Q-technique of multivariate analysis.

The information provided by the original incidence matrix can also be used to investigate the association of the five variables (the R-technique of analysis). For this purpose, a coefficient of association for each pair of variables can be constructed by counting the instances in which the same attributes from each variable occur on the same artifact. Thus the coefficient of association for V_1 and V_2 is 6: both variables exhibit either two 0s or two 1s for each of the six artifacts. My example is so devised that the association coefficients are either 6 (complete association) or 0 (complete negative association). We can represent the 10 association coefficients of the 10 pairs of variables in a square matrix formed by a half transpose in which the column headings also become the row headings, and we can reorder the row and column headings of the transposed matrix in a search for patterning among the association coefficients. The result of the transpose and reordering is shown in figure 3.

	V_1	V_2	V_5	V_3	V_4
V_1	6	6	6	0	0
V_2	6	6	6	0	0
V_5	6	6	6	0	0
V_3	0	0	0	6	6
V_4	0	0	0	6	6

Figure 3

Again, the result is a significant pattern. There are two groups of associated variables defined by the two blocks of association coefficients of 6. Three variables, V_1, V_2, V_5, exhibit identical 'behavior' with respect to the six artifacts, as does the second group of two variables, V_3 and V_4. The significant grouping of variables is systematically related to the clustering of artifacts detected by the Q-technique. Two artifact types are also defined by the R-technique. One is characterized by the presence of V_1, V_2, V_5, and the absence of V_3 and V_4, the other by the presence of V_3 and V_4, and the absence of V_1, V_2, and V_5. The first group is composed of A_2, A_3, and A_5, the second of A_1, A_4, and A_6; these are the same clusters of artifacts evident in the A square matrix.

This relationship can be further illustrated by returning to the original incidence matrix. Since all of the information extracted by the reorderings of rows and columns was obtained by manipulation of information contained in the original incidence matrix, we can detect the patterning by simply rearranging its rows and columns, as in figure 4.

	V_1	V_2	V_5	V_3	V_4
A_1	0	0	0	1	1
A_4	0	0	0	1	1
A_6	0	0	0	1	1
A_2	1	1	1	0	0
A_3	1	1	1	0	0
A_5	1	1	1	0	0

Figure 4

Here the blocks of 1s and 0s reveal significant patterning in both rows and columns, the same patterning produced by the similarity coefficients in the A and V square matrices.

These simple operations illustrate the bare essentials of typology in the primary sense of identifying classes of artifacts that exhibit sets of associated attributes, or, alternatively, that exhibit consistently high internal similarity in some context of a matrix of similarity coefficients. On a less abstract plane, it is clear that questions on typology and the need for formal analysis arise only in a context of generally similar artifacts—I do not expect to see a formal analysis demonstrating that stone axes and clay vessels belong in different artifact types because the outcome of the analysis is self-evident. It is equally clear that my exemplary analysis is so purified as to be barely recognizable by a working archaeologist with a non-hypothetical problem in mind. In practice, our variables are frequently not dichotomies of two discrete attributes. How shall we treat a variable with three or more qualitative attributes? What of the quantitative variable, within which the measurements can be ordered as more or less similar in contrast to the 'same' or 'different' relationship of the qualitative variable? How can we best construct standardized coefficients of similarity and standardized measurements of clustering in order to compare analyses? How can we best incorporate sampling theory in our analysis so as to express our level of confidence in the results obtained from the finite and defective collections with which we always work? Can we find a typological meaning for other matrix operations, multiplication for example? The papers and discussions of this conference will, I am sure, assess the progress made in the solution of these and related problems and will point the way to further progress.

Before leaving typology, I cannot resist a short historical note on the endemic and sometimes acrimonious discussions on the subject in America for the past 25 years. In my perception of the controversy, there are two schools. One school (to which I belong) holds that the mathematically demonstrated cluster of similar artifacts is the essence of the matter and that once this concept is grasped, intellectual difficulties about artifact types vanish or are at least clearly defined. The second school argues that types are merely arbitrary creations of the archaeologist contingent on his immediate descriptive and comparative interests. In my view, the second school is simply confused; having failed to grasp that mathematical analysis of clustering and association provides a method of objectively defining types in non-obvious situations, they can define an artifact type only as any class of artifacts, and this definition leads in turn to the characterization of artifact types as subjective, or arbitrary, or narrowly hypothesis-oriented classes of artifacts. Secondary themes associated with this view include a philosophically naive emphasis on the observer side of the observer–observed relationship and a preoccupation with artifact classes as instruments for the comparison and seriation of collections of artifacts, reflecting a dominant research interest. It is interesting to note that the adherents of the second school in fact implicitly accept the cluster concept of artifact types; in practice they never place stone axes and clay pots in the same type. Their problem does not lie at the intuitive level; it is rather a matter of confounding such analytically distinct questions as (1) does the collection at hand exhibit well-defined clusters of similar artifacts? and (2) what artifact classes will best show a systematic relationship among collections A, B, and C? This analytical confusion has produced the mistaken notion that cluster analysis is somehow an alternative to a search for classifications effective in making systematic orderings among collections of artifacts; since the latter activity is obviously a worthy one, then cluster analysis must be unworthy. But in fact cluster analysis in no way precludes any number of additional hypothesis-oriented classifications, and the problem is a spurious one.

In discussing artifact types, I have of necessity introduced in a vague way the concept of a collection of artifacts. In practice, the collections usually are further examples of logically primitive or intuitive concepts; they are conceived as entities resulting from direct observation rather than products of explicit systematic analysis. Prehistoric and historic peoples did not distribute their activities randomly over space, and the archaeologist's record reflects this clustering. Artifacts are characteristically found in groups. The loci of these groups define the archaeological site. The social correlates of the artifact groups are plain; as everybody knows, prehistoric peoples lived in communities which were the spatial focus of the cultural activities producing the artifacts. The collection of artifacts representing a community is undoubtedly a fundamental, probably the fundamental, unit of archaeological analysis, but there are in addition intuitively meaningful subsets of associated artifacts within the including community group. These subsets may be the result of activities by special segments of the community (a nuclear family, for example), or they may be localized aspects of the cultural repertory of the entire community (materials from a ceremonial precinct for example), or they may be a combination of these factors. The segmentary or specialized character of the activity is expressed in spatial clusters. The clearest examples are those in which the spatial boundaries are themselves artifacts: a house floor with its associated artifacts; a grave with its funerary offerings; or a storage pit and its included material. Other examples are simply concentrations of artifacts and cultural debris whose spatial clustering corresponds to customary loci for particular kinds of activities: an area where flint was chipped; a cooking area with its hearths and food debris; or a cemetery. In addition to this within-community differentiation, there are extra-community archaeological sites—satellite sites—produced by extra-community activities of work groups: examples are the kill and butchering sites which are such an important component of our evidence for the early American Indians or the seasonally occupied small fishing camps of the Indians of western Canada. In some simple societies, the entire community is a set of specialized and spatially differentiated work teams on a seasonal basis as it moves through its accustomed yearly round of subsistence activities; here, rather than speaking of the site of a community with its satellite sites, we must think in terms of a set of sites, each of which represents the total activity of a community at a given time in a repetitive sequence. Finally, in more complex societies we have examples of permanently occupied and spatially segregated communities which are themselves specialized segments of a larger, multi-community society.

As I stated earlier, these artifact-horizontal space relationships are customarily treated as observables, which means in effect that boundaries are frequently definite enough to make a mathematical analysis seem superfluous. The major relationship is simply inclusion or exclusion with respect to some observed boundary, and the relationship of any pair of artifacts can be simply expressed in an incidence matrix. Put more simply, if the boundaries are given we are thereby given a collection of included artifacts which can be compared to other localized collections of artifacts with respect to artifact form and artifact class frequencies.

There do exist, however, situations in which easily observed boundaries are not present but in which, nevertheless, there seem to be tendencies toward spatial clusterings. In those situations, space must be defined in metrical terms—in x and y coordinates. Mathematical techniques for the description of this purely metrical clustering are not frequently applied in archaeology, and it is certain that culturally significant information has been lost from failure to employ the field procedures and mathematical analysis required to identify metrical clustering. The central problem is: given a list of x and y coordinates for the *loci* of some class or classes of artifacts, what is the most appropriate technique (or techniques) for detecting nonrandom spatial distribution of the *loci*? One thinks immediately of null hypotheses on a Poisson distribution basis and of the nearest neighbor analysis of geographers, but I believe that archaeologists are very much in need of mathematical instruction on this topic.

This discussion of *locus* has so far ignored the vertical dimension of space. Artifacts in fact have x, y, and z coordinates; archaeological deposits have superior and inferior as well as lateral boundaries. The vertical relationship is, of course, of fundamental interest to archaeologists because from this relationship time ordering can be inferred through the law of superposition. However, consideration of the vertical dimension does not in principle introduce new analytical problems, although adding the third dimension does complicate the description and analysis of metrical *loci*.

The foregoing discussion has attempted to set out the fundamental stock-in-trade of archaeologists, both old and new. Briefly, I have stated that archaeologists have a premathematical ability to recognize non-arbitrary collections of artifacts on the basis of spatial propinquity or inclusion within some well-defined boundary. The possession of these perhaps not very impressive abilities provides a logical foundation for a further step in the archaeological enterprise, the comparison of collections. I will discuss later the characteristics of collection comparison; it is necessary at this point only to acknowledge the existence of a plausible basis for describing pairs of collections as more or less similar with respect to the kinds and frequencies of artifacts and the internal spatial relationships of artifacts which they exhibit. But archaeological intuition is not confined to the abilities listed above; archaeologists also have some pervasive underlying ideas about relationships among the three broad variables of collection similarity (sometimes called formal similarity), space, and time. These ideas are that formal similarities between collections tend to be serially correlated with space and time and that the number of artifact types per collection tends to increase through time. Put in behavioral terms, societies which are in close communication are expected to exhibit close cultural similarity. Since both time and space impede communication, collections representing the cultures of societies distant in space or time, or both, are not expected to be closely similar. Serial correlation over time implies that the best prediction of the character of the culture of a society in one year from the present is that it will be very much like its present character. Over space, the concept implies that the culture of a community is usually very much like that of its neighbors. I will not attempt a serious discussion of the appropriate qualifications needed for these general statements, but we can inject a note of reality by mentioning that cultural space is in fact not mere space. Ecological circumstances, for example, vary at an irregular rate over space, and we know that cultural properties are systematically connected with environmental conditions. Nor does culture change proceed at a uniform pace over time; there are periods of relative stability and of rapid change. Nevertheless, the concept of serial correlation, properly qualified, has wide applicability to archaeological research. A third basic idea mentioned above is that culture change over time tends to be unidirectional: cultural complexity increases through time, or, in the simplest archaeological terms, later collections tend to exhibit more artifact types than do earlier ones. Again, qualifications are needed, but the concept is broadly useful. This concept is, of course, a much simplified version of the anthropological concept of cultural evolution; it focuses on the cumulative aspect of cultural evolution.

A prominent mode of comparison of collections is the process called 'seriation'. In broadest terms, seriation consists of arranging a set of collections in a patterned series with respect to similarity of the component artifacts either to infer ordering in some other dimension not directly observable or to demonstrate a relationship with ordering in another known dimension. The dimension not directly observable is usually time; most archaeologists would define seriation as a technique for inferring relative chronology, but one can visualize other applications. The inference on time ordering is drawn by application of the principle of serial correlation (other things being equal, the degree of similarity between two collections varies inversely with separation in time) or it may be drawn on evolutionary principles. Similarity is measured in practice by some sort of coefficient, explicit or implicit, for each pair of components based on the common presence or absence of selected classes of artifacts or on a comparison of the relative frequencies of the selected classes.

The earliest and simplest example of seriation of which I am aware is the Stone, Bronze, Iron Age classification of Danish antiquities made by C. J. Thomsen before 1820 (Rouse 1967). The underlying principle here is evolutionary: more efficient cutting tools replace less efficient ones. There was a period when only stone cutting tools were known. When bronze tools became available, they replaced the stone tools, and iron similarly replaced bronze. All collections with iron tools are later than collections lacking iron tools, all collections with bronze tools are later than collections lacking iron or bronze tools, and all collections lacking either iron or bronze tools are earlier than all sites possessing them. Assuming that the period of use of stone did not overlap with that of the use of iron, we would expect five kinds of collections on the basis of presence or absence of the three classes of cutting tools: (a) stone only; (b) stone and bronze; (c) bronze only; (d) bronze and iron; and (e) iron only. We can represent this relationship in an incidence matrix in which the rows are the five kinds of collections and the columns the three materials. (*See* figure 5.)

	Stone	Bronze	Iron
A	0	0	1
B	0	1	1
C	0	1	0
D	1	1	0
E	1	0	0

Figure 5

The pattern is evident: no 1s are separated by 0s in any column or row, and the cluster of 1s move steadily upward from left to right. The five classes are ordered, and they cannot be so simply ordered with any other significantly different row and column permutations.

We can also give meaning to the square matrices formed from the rows and columns respectively. For the row square matrix, I have computed coefficients of similarity for kinds of collections by counting each pair of 1s as 'same', and I have ignored the identity relationship. The resulting square matrix is shown in figure 6.

	A	B	C	D	E
A	–	1	0	0	0
B	1	–	1	1	0
C	0	1	–	1	0
D	0	1	1	–	1
E	0	0	0	1	–

Figure 6

Again a rudimentary pattern is evident: the entries assume the form called a Robinson matrix by Kendall in that the values increase (or at least do not decrease) toward the diagonal horizontally and vertically, suggesting that the pattern results from variation on a single dimension. The second square matrix also yields a Robinson matrix when the materials are placed in correct order, although here the matrix is so small as to convey little information. (*See* figure 7.)

	S	B	I
S	–	1	0
B	1	–	1
I	0	1	–

Figure 7

The result does not, at any rate, do violence to the interpretation of a stone–bronze–iron sequence; there is no kind of collection in which iron is associated with stone to the exclusion of bronze.

In the Thomsen case, we have a hypothetical scheme based on a highly plausible evolutionary principle, and the next step would be an examination of actual collections to test the fit between hypothetical expectations and reality. In a more usual situation, such a clear ordering principle is not available, and the archaeologist must resort to the serial correlation principle in his search for pattern. If the archaeological context is such that he can reasonably suppose change over time to be the chief factor involved in intercollection similarities and differences, then he can expect to find an arrangement of similarity coefficients which will assume the Robinson form, and he can interpret the collection ordering that produced this arrangement to be a chronological ordering, although the ordering will not of itself indicate which end of the sequence is the earlier. Various approaches to ordering of this sort have a long history in archaeological practice. It is commonly supposed that the sequence dating of pre-dynastic Egyptian graves by Flinders Petrie is the pioneer effort (Rouse 1967, Kendall 1969). A notable development in the United States is that particularly associated with the work of James A. Ford beginning in the 1930s (Ford 1936). Petrie ordered a large number of pre-dynastic Egyptian graves by means of the presence and absence of a number of classes of pottery used as burial furniture. Ford ordered collections of potsherds from village sites by graphical analysis of frequency distributions standardized as percentages. We are fortunate to have a mathematically competent analysis of the Petrie problem by Kendall (1969).

Kendall shows that the incidence matrix formed by notation of the presence or absence of each variety of pottery at each grave can under favorable circumstances reveal unidimensional ordering of the graves. This unidimensional ordering is expressed in the incidence matrix (in which individual graves are the rows, pottery varieties the columns) by 'bunching together the 1s in each separate column' in the manner I illustrated crudely with the Stone–Bronze–Iron Age example. He also explains the operation of forming the square matrices for, respectively, the pottery varieties and the graves and he discusses the archaeological interpretation of matrix multiplication. The major result of Kendall's work from my present point of view is that the seriation problem can be solved (if it is solvable with the data at hand) by row and column permutations of the square matrix for graves and that a successful solution puts the similarity matrix into the Robinson form.

The Robinson form is associated, in American archaeology, with the pioneer work of the statistician, W. S. Robinson, who collaborated with the archaeologist, George Brainerd, in ordering Maya pottery collections (Robinson 1951, Brainerd 1951). The similarity matrix here is a set of similarity coefficients between collections derived from the proportion of various classes of pottery present in the collections rather than the simple counting of common presences or absences that I have discussed above. Computation of the Robinson index is a simple matter, as shown in table 1.

	Class 1	Class 2	Class 3	Class 4	Class 5	Total
Collection A	10	25	35	20	10	100%
Collection B	0	40	30	25	5	100%
Difference	10	15	5	5	5	40%

Table 1

The total of percentage differences, taken without regard to sign, is 40 per cent, which is a measure of unlikeness. It can be converted to a measure of similarity simply by subtracting from 200, the maximum percentage difference possible for two collections, a similarity coefficient of 160 in the example. This particular similarity measure is not, of course, an essential feature of Robinson's method. Robinson's method was well received in America; the ground had been prepared by Ford's graphical seriation, also based on percentages of pottery classes, and by predecessors of Ford.

In subsequent years, much attention has been devoted in the United States to the development of computer programs for extracting order from Robinson matrices and to discussion of the archaeological meaning of such ordering. I will confine my remarks to one of the latest of these efforts, that of Craytor and Johnson (Craytor and Johnson 1968, Johnson 1968). Craytor has devised a refined computer program which incorporates a new definition of seriation and a new criterion for ranking success in seriation for the various row and column permutations of a given matrix. The essence of the new definition is the inclusion in the seriation model of all possible inequalities other than those involving identity scores. For example, in the half matrix in figure 8, which is a perfect Robinson form, all similarity scores below and to the left of a given score are equal to or smaller than the score in question. Thus score BC is higher than scores AC, AD, and BD. With this definition, relative success in ordering is measured by summing all score differences (coefficient H in Craytor and Johnson's terminology); the best ordering is the ordering which produces the highest sum of score differences. Here the magnitude of the differences contributes to the measure of success, thus conserving the relative distances implied by Robinson's index. Craytor has also devised a generalized coefficient (coefficient C) useful for comparing seriations of different sets of items. It is calculated by dividing the coefficient obtained by summing the score differences by the number of inequalities tested and then dividing this result by the standard deviation of the $n(n-1)/2$

similarity scores. It is stated that the coefficient C approaches a value of 2 as the inequality conditions are satisfied. However, these statistical niceties to be used in searching for an ordering reflecting the unidimensional relationship are not the main point of interest for my purpose. The main point here is that this elementary similarity scaling also arranges the matrix in the best manner for exhibiting clustering of the entities scaled—typology and seriation seem to have a common logical base in the search for order among a set of items, as Johnson (1968) illustrates. The square matrix of artifacts of my earliest typological example is also an example of searching for a matrix of Robinson form. Coefficient H for the example is 120, the highest possible for this matrix. The row and column permutation producing the best arrangement by the Robinson form criterion is also the best permutation for exhibiting clustering of entities. This happy relationship suggests that archaeologists should forget every approach to the seriation–typology problem other than the row and column permutation of the similarity matrix. Unfortunately, matters are not quite so simple as that; there are other approaches which are in some sense rivals.

	A	B	C	D
A	–			
B	180	–		
C	160	180	–	
D	140	160	180	–

Figure 8

The other approaches to cluster analysis or typology are associated with the development of numerical taxonomy (Sokal and Sneath 1963). These approaches represent cluster analysis in a pure or strict sense as opposed to the ordering (characteristically unidimensional ordering) of seriation: the clustering technique reduces 'the number of units of study by combining similar units into classes which will then form a new base for interpretation' (Hodson 1970, p. 300). In this mode of analysis, the square similarity matrix is not the object of analytical manipulation; it serves rather as a body of primary data, the analytical results being presented as a dendrogram or Venn diagram. We are very much in debt here to a happy pooling of archaeo-logical, mathematical, and computer expertize achieved in England and exemplified by the work of Hodson and others (Doran and Hodson 1966, Hodson 1969, 1970). I will not attempt to paraphrase the descriptions of techniques and results obtained; I am sure that these matters will be amply discussed by others. It is sufficient for my purpose to indicate that various techniques of similarity coefficient construction and procedures for defining clusters (including multi-dimensional techniques) have been explored with archaeological data, that there is good evidence of progress in appraising the merits and demerits of these techniques from both practical and theoretical points of view, and that a claim has emerged for the practical and theoretical superiority of this general approach as opposed to matrix ordering in the manner of Robinson and his successors (Hodson 1970, p. 305).

This last point illustrates my principle concern: it is hardly possible to doubt that explicit clustering techniques are the most efficient approach to the definition of clusters, as Hodson points out, but it is not clear (at least to me) whether or not this greater efficiency can be translated into greater archaeological insight. As an earnest devotee of the unity of knowledge, I will be keenly disappointed if it turns out that our theoretical base is too thin to support the analytical superstructure or, perhaps, that archaeological data simply do not exhibit the niceties of interrelationship that the most powerful analytical techniques have the capacity to reveal. But it is clear to me that the efforts to increase our analytical abilities should go forward. We need to try every plausible approach and to compare the results of the trials; the effort cannot fail to improve our understanding of techniques of archaeological research, and it just may provide the means for a richer understanding of the regularities of past human social behavior.

Continuing in this vein, I believe that we can and should pursue refinements in R-technique analysis, not only because of the symmetrical relationships between groups of associated attributes and clusters of more or less similar entities but also because the analysis of attribute interrelationships has a refreshingly direct connection with questions on past social behavior. When we can combine knowledge of clear attribute associations with knowledge of the sequence of operations performed in fashioning an artifact, we are in a position to offer a dynamic reconstruction of past behavior. If burned and crushed shell is added to the clay, then the vessel surface may be smoothed; and if the surface is smoothed, the shoulder is to be decorated with an incised design; and so on. We can make plausible behavioral inferences approach our professed goal of bringing to light past behavior. It is for this reason that I admire efforts such as those of Sackett (1966) to investigate attribute association (in his case, of certain attributes of Upper Paleolithic endscrapers) in all its complexity. Sackett proceeds to analyze his collection in the classical and direct manner by successive partitions to show that the primary association of variables A and B is increased in that part of the collection exhibiting attribute C_1, of the C variable. In short, he investigates all aspects of attribute association and interaction. I have heard Sackett's procedure criticized on the ground that (a) it is complicated, (b) there is not a computer program available, and (c) that it is not cluster analysis. These criticisms, it seems to me, illustrate a general difficulty which we must labor to overcome, the notion on the part of some archaeologists that someone will devise a perfect method, fully computerized, which will somehow painlessly extract the ultimate meaning from our counts and measurements. One R-technique, factor analysis, has sometimes been thought of as a universal sausage grinder, but some initial ventures in its application and subsequent comments have, I think, dispelled this idea.

My major conclusion from this survey of some elementary concepts and techniques of archaeology is that the present conference is very much needed. We are in a period of brisk activity, and we need to take stock of results achieved, classify these results in terms of their utility in attaining one or another of the basic objectives of archaeology, and, above all, convince the pre- or non-mathematical archaeologist that these techniques merely make explicit and extend the implicit mathematical reasoning that *all* archaeologists use.

REFERENCES

Brainerd, G.W. (1951) The place of chronological ordering in archaeological analysis. *Amer. Antiquity*, **16**, 301.

Craytor, W.B. & Johnson, L. (1968) Refinements in computerized item seriation. *Museum of Natural History, University of Oregon, Bulletin*, **10**.

Doran, J.E. & Hodson, F.R. (1966) A digital computer analysis of palaeolithic flint assemblages. *Nature*, **210**, 688.

Ford, J.A. (1936) Analysis of Indian village site collections from Louisiana and Mississippi. *Louisiana Department of Conservation, Anthropological Study*, **2**.

Hodson, F.R. (1969) Searching for structure within multivariate archaeological data. *World Archaeology*, **1**, 90.

Hodson, F.R. (1970) Cluster analysis and archaeology: some new developments and applications. *World Archaeology*, **1**, 299.

Johnson, L. (1968) Item seriation as an aid for elementary scale and cluster analysis. *Museum of Natural History, University of Oregon, Bulletin*, **15**.

Kendall, D.G. (1969) Some problems and methods in statistical archaeology. *World Archaeology*, **1**, 68.

Robinson, W.S. (1951) A method for chronologically ordering archaeology deposits. *Amer. Antiquity*, **16**, 293.

Rouse, I. (1967) Seriation in archaeology. *American Historical Anthropology*, pp. 153–95 (eds Riley, C.L. & Taylor, W.W.). Southern Illinois University Press.

Sackett, J.R. (1966) Quantitative analysis of Upper Paleolithic stone tools. *Amer. Anthropol.*, **68** (2), 356.

Sokal, R.R. & Sneath, P.H. (1963) *Principles of Numerical Taxonomy*, San Francisco: Freeman.

Taxonomy

General Survey

Cluster Analysis

Discrimination

Related Mathematical Topics

Abstracts

Discussion and Comments

General Survey

C. Radhakrishna Rao
Taxonomy in anthropology

There are three basic approaches to classification in anthropology.

Practical Taxonomy. This refers to a classification of individuals by specified class intervals of certain key measurements. For instance, the manufacturers of ready-made garments classify all individuals by neck size and arm length (for shirts) and chest girth (for suits), and so on. The choice of key measurements depends on how well they are related to all the measurements needed to produce garments giving a good fit. This area of study is known as applied anthropology, and is, perhaps, very useful from a purely practical point of view.

Pure Taxonomy. The second relates to a description of a taxonomic unit (TU), which may be an individual or a group of individuals or a set of groups, in terms of a chosen list of measurements (characters). In such studies the attempt is to find a few typical forms (or profiles defined by the measurements) into which a large number of TUs may be classified.

A typical profile may be specified in terms of original measurements or in terms of some simple functions of measurements indicating the 'size and shape' of an organism.

In pure taxonomy it is possible that different classifications are obtained by different choices of sets of measurements. Usually measurements are chosen in such a way that they provide an adequate description of a TU. For instance, anthropologists have standard lists of measurements for comparing and describing different populations.

Phylogenetic Taxonomy. The third is an attempt at phylogenetic classification which depends on genetic distance between groups, which may not be directly measurable but may be estimable from phenotypic measurements. Here the object is not just to describe a TU in terms of specified genetic characteristics but to study interrelationships between TUs taking into account *all relevant* genetic differences, with a view to reconstructing their evolution. This is, indeed, a very difficult problem and needs a cautious approach.

First, the choice of measurements is important. They must be true indicators of genetic differences and must represent all major genetic aspects in which the TUs differ. Second, a proper definition of genetic distance and its estimation using phenotypic measurements (which may be affected by environmental factors) have to be considered. Third and perhaps the most difficult problem is the construction of an evolutionary tree.

In this paper I propose to comment on some problems of taxonomic classification giving examples from the reports on two large-scale anthropometric surveys conducted in India. [These are Mahalanobis, Majumdar, and Rao (1949) and Majumdar and Rao (1958) which will be referred to in the text as the UP and Bengal reports respectively.]

STUDY OF INTERRELATIONSHIPS AMONG GROUPS

(1) *Mahalanobis Distance.* Let us examine how the problem of determining relationships between groups is approached when we have only a single measurement or a couple of measurements from which an index is computed. To begin with it is convenient to plot the group means on a line (we assume that the mean values are determined on sufficiently large samples so that the positions of the points are fairly stable). We may find that the points group themselves into a number of distinct clusters with intra-cluster distances of a smaller order than inter-cluster distances. Or it may turn out that there are no definite clusters and all the groups are located at more or less equidistant points in a continuous chain, or they may form into a number of clusters, some or all of which are linked by subclusters.

In principle the same thing can be done by considering two measurements. The mean positions of the groups could be located in a two-dimensional chart using two coordinate axes. As in the one-dimensional case one can look for clusters. There is, however, one difficulty since the angle of inclination of the coordinate axes needs to be specified; different angles may lead to different configurations. This is where, probably, theory helps.

It is reasonable to argue that the distance between any two groups represented on this chart should be an *index of discrimination* that is possible between individuals of the two groups. How far do the available measurements enable us to distinguish members of one group from another? It appears that whatever may be the criterion employed, so long as the distributions of measurements overlap, some individuals will be wrongly identified. The minimum attainable frequency of wrong identifications would provide us with an index of separation between groups. The higher this frequency the closer will be two groups and it seems reasonable to adopt it as a measure signifying different degrees of nearness. Assuming that the measurements have a bivariate normal distribution, it can be rigorously demonstrated (*see* Rao 1952, 1965) that the distance between two points on a two-dimensional chart is a monotone (decreasing) function of the frequency of wrong identifications between the groups defined by the points if the measurements are plotted in standard deviation units and the axes are inclined at an angle of $\cos^{-1} \rho$ (where ρ is the correlation between the measurements). The distance between two groups on such a chart is the same as the Mahalanobis distance (D^2) based on two measurements.

The visual representation is still available when we are considering three measurements although it may be necessary to resort to some mechanical means for representing points in a three-dimensional chart. The analysis is based essentially on mutual distances in a three-dimensional space.

When we are dealing with more than three measurements, a physical representation is no longer possible. We can, however, compute the distances among all pairs of groups; a table of such distances defines the configuration of points (groups) in a space of dimensions equal in number to that of the measurements. In the absence of a visual representation we have to develop other methods for determining clusters of groups. We shall discuss some of the methods employed for this purpose and examine their merits.

(2) *Canonical Analysis*. Canonical analysis is a method of fitting a lower-dimensional subspace to the conceptual configuration of points (representing group means) in the space of measurements. When a two or a three dimensional subspace provides a good fit, the projected points can be represented on a two or a three dimensional chart. In such a case we have again a visual representation for studying the configuration of groups.

The method is equivalent to reducing the original measurements to two or three or more, if necessary, linear functions of measurements called canonical variates and studying the configuration of groups based on them. Such an approach was developed in two previous publications by the author (Rao 1948, 1952) and later elaborated by Ashton, Healy, and Lipton (1957). To compute these linear functions we consider the matrix equation

$$|B - \lambda W| = 0 \quad . \tag{1}$$

where B and W represent between and within covariance matrices based on the original measurements. Let $(\mathbf{L}_i, \lambda_i)$ represent the ith eigenvector and eigenvalue obtained from eq. (1). If $\mathbf{X}$ is the vector of p original measurements, then $\mathbf{L}_1' \mathbf{X}$ (called the first canonical variate) is the best single linear function, $\mathbf{L}_1' \mathbf{X}, \mathbf{L}_2' \mathbf{X}$ (the first two canonical variates) are the best two linear functions, and so on. In earlier publications I have suggested that the goodness of fit of the best r functions may be judged by the ratio

$$\frac{\lambda_1 + \ldots + \lambda_r}{\lambda_1 + \ldots + \lambda_p} \tag{2}$$

where $\lambda_1, \ldots, \lambda_p$ are the p roots (eigenvalues) of eq. (1). In addition, it seems to be necessary to compute two sets of D^2 values, one based on the original measurements and the other on the chosen canonical variates in order to find out the extent and nature of distortion, if any, of the configuration of points in the reduced space.

Table 1 gives the D^2 values based on 9 characters (head length; head, bizygomatic, bigonial, and frontal breadths; nasal length, breadth, and depth; stature and sitting height) and on the first two canonical variates for 12 caste groups in the UP survey (designated by B_1, B_2, A_1, A_2, A_3, A_4, Ch, M, Bh, D, C_1, and C_2).

The total of all D^2 values based on 9 measurements is 159·89 and that based on the first two canonical variates is 98·07. The ratio

$$\frac{98 \cdot 07}{159 \cdot 89} = 0 \cdot 61 \tag{3}$$

is not high and the fit may not be considered adequate. However, a comparison of the two sets of D^2 values shows that a two-dimensional chart of the canonical variates provides a fairly good representation of the original configuration except for some distortion in the position of the groups C_1, C_2, and D. The cluster (C_1, C_2) is brought much closer to the (B_1, B_2) and (A_1, A_2, A_3, A_4) clusters in the chart of the two canonical variates. Further, the relationship of A_1, to A_2, A_3, A_4 on one hand, and to B_1, B_2 on the other, is also slightly distorted. In such a case we can use the two-dimensional chart of the canonical variates to study the configuration of the groups (cluster analysis) keeping in view the particular distortions revealed by the comparison of the D^2 values.

	B_2	A_1	A_2	A_3	A_4	Ch	M	Bh	D	C_1	C_2
B_1	0·27	1·17	1·48	2·13	3·30	3·05	2·86	4·45	2·86	3·48	2·23
	0·02	0·26	0·42	0·82	1·44	1·83	1·69	3·82	2·37	0·68	0·55
B_2		0·78	1·03	1·47	2·72	2·87	2·62	3·82	2·81	3·61	1·63
		0·16	0·28	0·61	1·19	1·78	1·53	3·31	2·00	0·65	0·60
A_1			0·30	0·49	1·52	3·38	2·45	2·53	2·91	2·68	1·26
			0·15	0·29	0·92	2·31	1·65	2·16	0·66	0·51	0·33
A_2				0·12	0·58	2·12	1·34	2·23	2·41	2·98	1·53
				0·07	0·35	1·44	0·82	1·81	0·85	1·21	0·91
A_3					0·43	2·72	1·45	1·75	2·31	3·35	1·67
					0·21	1·72	0·53	1·18	0·43	1·52	1·10
A_4						2·24	0·90	2·24	2·66	4·20	2·87
						1·13	0·34	1·26	0·51	2·79	2·24
Ch							0·40	5·02	3·84	5·25	4·68
							0·26	4·76	3·15	4·58	4·27
M								3·16	2·47	4·46	3·74
								2·83	1·66	3·92	3·44
Bh									1·15	5·08	3·47
									0·19	3·80	2·94
D										4·52	2·11
										2·75	2·05
C_1											1·32
											0·06

Table 1. Comparison of D^2s based on 9 original measurements (top value) and two canonical variates (lower value)

To summarize, the canonical analysis approach to classification involves the following: First, the choice of a number of canonical variates which provide a good fit to the original configuration judged by the overall criterion of (2) which is the same as eq. (3). Second, a comparison of D^2 values based on the original measurements and the chosen canonical variates to examine the nature of the distortions, if any, of the configuration of the groups in the reduced space. Third, a study of the charts based on two or three canonical variates supplemented by the information on the particular distortions revealed by a comparison of the D^2 values.

Thus, by an examination of figure 1 of two canonical variates and the D^2 values of table 1, we find that there are 5 distinct clusters consisting of (B_1, B_2), (A_1, A_2, A_3, A_4), (C_1, C_2), (Bh, D) and (Ch, M). On the basis of the chart alone, it would have been difficult to decide the cluster to which A_1 belongs or to discuss the relative positions of the clusters (inter-cluster comparisons).

(3) *The Use of a Dendrogram.* Methods for obtaining a dendrogram from a table of distances are given in a book by Sokal and Sneath (1963) while some

associated theoretical problems are discussed by Jardine, Jardine, and Sibson (1967). In constructing a dendrogram we start with a cluster or clusters at the lowest level, that is, select sets of groups with the smallest distance between groups within a set. If we consider each such cluster as one (compound) group we have a reduced number of what may be called second stage groups (which may consist of some single and some compound groups). With suitable definitions for distance between a group and a cluster and between two clusters we can obtain a table of distances for the second-stage groups. We repeat the process, that is, look for clusters of second-stage groups with the smallest distance. As before, all groups within a cluster are considered as one (compound) group so that the third-stage groups are still smaller in number. A new table of distances among the third-stage groups is computed and the process is repeated till all the original groups join in one cluster.

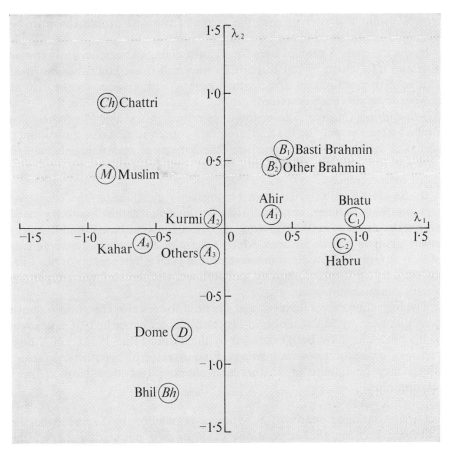

Figure 1. UP anthropometric survey group constellations in the $(\lambda_1 - \lambda_2)$ chart

This type of analysis forces a *tree* structure on the groups which may not always reveal the real nature of the configuration of the groups. The relative positions of the groups may be extremely complicated, as in the Bengal study, where there were no distinct clusters and the clusters formed on the basis of smallest distances overlapped with some common groups between clusters. A dendrogram does not allow for overlapping clusters which has some significance in studying relationships between biological populations. Jardine and Sibson (1968) have attempted to produce diagrams showing overlapping clusters which are too complicated when the number of groups is large. However, a dendrogram with a tree structure may serve a useful purpose in giving us a rough picture of the configuration of the groups, which has to be supplemented by closer studies of clusters formed at each stage. (4) *Profile Analysis*. The aim of profile analysis is to find out whether there exist a few physical types (profiles) to which many of the groups conform.

To determine typical profiles, we have to use the table of distances and look for distinct clusters at the lowest levels as was done in the UP study. A typical profile is specified by attaching to each measurement the average value for the groups in a cluster. The variation of the individual profiles of groups within a cluster around the typical (average) profile can also be examined as explained in the UP study.

In the UP study 5 profiles were found with definite characteristics of their own and into which 17 out of the 22 castes and tribes could be classified. The relative positions of the 5 other groups with respect to the typical profiles have also been described.

(5) *Stability of Clusters*. The methods described in sections (1)–(4) can be applied whatever may be the measurements chosen to describe a taxonomic unit. But the classifications based on different sets of measurements may be different. In such a case there may be special reasons for choosing a particular set of measurements.

If the classification is to have phylogenetic significance, the choice of measurements becomes important. Ideally the classification has to be based on genetic distance between groups, that is, a function based on differences in the ultimate genetic elements which determine the various measurements of an organism. Since a direct measurement of such differences is not possible, we may try to estimate them, if possible, on the basis of phenotypic (or observable) measurements.

The logical problems involved and the need for a stable classification have been discussed by Mahalanobis in his fundamental paper in 1936 and some of his postulates have been examined by the author (Rao 1954). Let $\mathbf{X}$ be a vector of p phenotypic measurements, $\mathbf{F}$ be a vector of hypothetical factors which may be infinite in number and suppose that they have a linear relationship

$$\mathbf{X} = \mathbf{AF} \quad . \tag{4}$$

Let the covariance matrix of $\mathbf{F}$ within a population be Σ, and δ be the difference between the expectations of $\mathbf{F}$ in two populations. Then the Mahalanobis D^2 based on the hypothetical factors is

$$\Delta^2 = \delta'\Sigma^{-1}\delta \quad , \tag{5}$$

which we may assume to be finite. Since the covariance matrix of $\mathbf{X}$ is $\mathbf{A}\Sigma\mathbf{A}'$ and the difference in the expectation of $\mathbf{X}$ between the populations is $\mathbf{A}\delta$, the Mahalanobis D^2 based on p phenotypic measurements $\mathbf{X}$ is

$$D_p^2 = \delta'\mathbf{A}'(\mathbf{A}\Sigma\mathbf{A}')^{-1}\mathbf{A}\delta \quad . \tag{6}$$

It can be shown that

$$\delta'A'(A\Sigma A')^{-1}A\delta \leqslant \delta'\Sigma^{-1}\delta \qquad (7)$$

so that the distance based on phenotypic measurements does not exceed the hypothetical distance. However $D_p^2 \leqslant D_{p+q}^2$, where D_{p+q}^2 is computed from $(p+q)$ phenotypic measurements including the first p, which suggests the possibility that $D_p^2 \rightarrow \Delta^2$ as $p \rightarrow \infty$, that is, as the number of measurements is increased. Thus by a judicious choice of the nature and number of measurements we may obtain a good approximation to the hypothetical distance.

The expression (5) for Δ^2 will represent the genetic distance between populations if all the hypothetical factors in eq. (4) affecting the phenotypic measurements are genetic in nature or if the non-genetic factors, such as environmental, are common to the populations under comparison.

CLASSIFICATION BY SIZE AND SHAPE

(1) *Computation of Size and Shape Factors.* A hierarchical classification by individual measurements results in too many classes if the number of measurements is large, and further the description of each class becomes complicated. For this reason biologists consider a smaller number of compound measurements (functions of original measurements) and use them for classification. Compound measurements chosen for this purpose should provide an adequate description of a taxonomic unit and should preferably have a physical interpretation. For instance, anthropologists classify individuals by cephalic index (head breadth/head length), nasal index (nasal breadth/nasal length), which are simple functions indicating shape. Another compound measurement usually employed is a simple sum of standardized measurements indicating size. It is generally found that size and shape factors, suitably defined, provide good discrimination between biological populations and are, therefore, suitable for purposes of classification. We give the following intuitive definitions of size and shape factors.

A *size factor* is a function of a set of measurements such that an increase in its value results on the average in an increase in each of the individual measurements. Similarly a *shape factor* is a function such that an increase in its value results on the average in an increase in each of a given subset of the measurements and a decrease in the rest.

Let X represent a vector of p standardized measurements with a correlation matrix R and $s = L'X$ be a linear function representing size. On the assumption of linear regression, the average change in X due to a unit increase in s is proportional to RL. To determine L such that $L'X$ represents size we solve the equation.

$$RL = \xi \qquad (8)$$

where ξ is a vector with all positive components specifying the ratios of increases in the individual standardized measurements. The value of L is $R^{-1}\xi$ giving the size factor

$$s = \xi'R^{-1}X \ . \qquad (9)$$

In practice one may choose each component of ξ to be unity, when X represents standardized measurements.

To determine a shape factor $h = M'X$, we solve the equation $RM = \eta$, where η is a vector of changes with some specified components having positive sign and others negative sign. The value of **M** is $R^{-1}\eta$ giving the shape factor

$$h = \eta' R^{-1} X. \tag{10}$$

In practice, the absolute values of each component of η may be chosen to be unity, when **X** represents standardized measurements.

The functions s and h defined by eqs (9) and (10) can be standardized to have unit (or some specified) standard deviation. They may be correlated, in which case the shape factor can be corrected for size by the formula

$$h' = h - \rho s \tag{11}$$

where ρ is the correlation coefficient between h and s. The values of s and h' for given populations can be plotted on a two-dimensional chart with rectangular axes and the configuration of points can be studied.

The configuration of castes and tribes belonging to three different states in

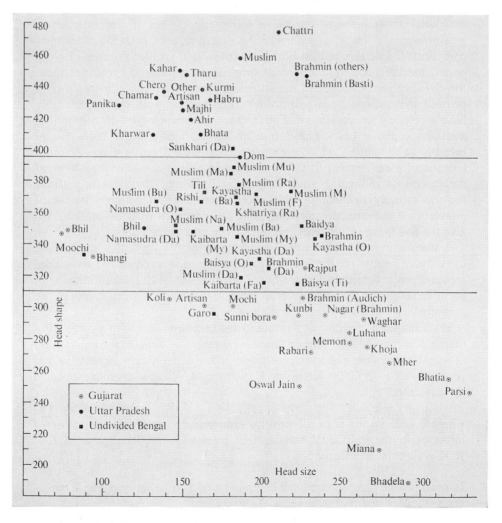

Figure 2

India are shown in figure 2 using the size factor based on HL (head length), HB (head breadth), FB (frontal breadth), BZB (Bizygomatic breadth), BB (Bigonial breadth), and ST (stature), and the shape factor based on HL, HB, FB, BZB, and BB (with a positive sign for change in HL and negative sign for the others to define shape of the head). It is interesting and somewhat surprising to note that horizontal lines at about the values 310 and 395 for head shape would almost completely separate the positions of the groups belonging to the different states, indicating clearcut differences between states in head shape. This is intriguing since all these states are situated in north India with Gujarat in the west, Bengal in the east, and UP in between. The groups in UP are narrow headed, and those in Gujarat are round headed, while in Bengal the shape is in between. The round-headedness does not show any regular pattern with respect to geographical location of the groups. If a common origin is claimed for Gujaratis and Bengalees on the basis of brachycephaly it may be difficult to explain the presence of long-headed people in the region between Gujarat and Bengal.

(2) *Comment on the Use of Indices.* It is sometimes the practice to replace two linear measurements by their ratio (called an index) in an attempt to reduce the number of measurements or to provide for a measurement of shape. For instance, in an investigation by Roe (1968) and Graham (1970) a number of indices have been chosen as basic measurements for statistical analysis. This seems to be unfortunate since replacing a pair of linear measurements by their ratio may not be the optimum way of reducing the number of measurements. Further, as demonstrated in the previous section, linear functions of measurements can represent shape. Multivariate methods applied on the original linear measurements seem to provide better information than when applied on a reduced number of some ratios and linear measurements. Further, many multivariate methods used in practice have certain optimum properties when the measurements follow a multivariate normal distribution. Linear measurements, with suitable transformations if necessary, are more likely to have an approximate multivariate normal distribution than indices.

WHAT IS A RELEVANT CLASSIFICATION IN A GIVEN PROBLEM?

The question is particularly important with the advent of computers providing routine programs for classification. Biological or archaeological data fed into a computer may provide us with a table of distances between groups, a cluster analysis by one of many available techniques, graphs based on canonical variates, and so on. I have advocated these methods and applied them in earlier publications (Rao 1948, 1952). These are indeed very efficient methods of reduction and summarization of multivariate data and might reveal interesting features which could not be discovered by a univariate approach. But such an analysis remains in an abstract form if attempts are not made to interpret results biologically or archaeologically, depending on the data under analysis, using previous evidence and other non-metrical data that might be available. In the UP and Bengal reports ethnographic notes, previous findings and other historical evidence available on the castes and tribes in India were used to interpret the statistical results and to draw new inferences.

However, it should not be claimed that the multivariate approach to cluster analysis as described above is the only method which will answer *all* questions. I may quote as an example the statistical analysis of handaxe data undertaken by Graham (1970) using canonical variates (multivariate approach) and by Roe (1968) examining individual variates. Both analyses have produced interesting results and it would not be surprising if the classifications differed. Roe was apparently looking for an archaeologically interpretable classification in terms of pointedness of handaxes. This might reveal some interesting features about the people using these handaxes. If the metrical characters describing pointedness of handaxes are not well represented in the battery of characters (measurements) chosen for study, the canonical analysis might provide an entirely different classification, as it might be comparing the handaxes in some other aspects. (Indeed, it might be possible to choose a set of measurements which would yield Roe's classification on canonical analysis.) The difference between the two analyses should not be regarded as inconsistent. One may be a supplement to the other and both seem to be important.

It would also be of some interest to examine what classification of handaxes would result by the size and shape analysis described in the section above. New questions may arise such as the following: Would differences in handaxe size indicate differences in palm size of the people who used them?

I strongly believe that available data should be examined from different points of view and analyzed by different approaches to reveal, possibly, different features of real significance.

I would like to comment briefly on the attempts that are being made to define distance between populations using observations on different systems of blood groups, ABO, MN, Rh, and so on. Useful results may be achieved by a classification of populations on the basis of such a distance as shown by Cavalli-Sforza and Edwards (1967). However, there seems to be no satisfactory justification for the particular distance function used by them.

In *addition* to the combined analysis it would pay to study individual blood group systems which may reveal interesting genetic features of different populations and throw some light on their evolutionary history. For instance, the geographical variation in the B-gene frequency (of the ABO system) in the populations of Europe and Asia has led to several anthropological speculations.

REFERENCES

Ashton, E. H., Healy, M. J. R. & Lipton, S. (1957) The descriptive use of discriminant functions in physical anthropology. *Proc. Roy. Soc. B*, **146**, 552–72.

Cavalli-Sforza, L. L. & Edwards, A. W. F. (1967) Phylogenetic analysis: models and estimation procedures. *Evolution*, **21**, 550–70.

Graham, J. M. (1970) Discrimination of British lower and middle Palaeolithic handaxe groups using canonical variates (with a note by Derek Roe). *World Archaeology*, **1**, 321–42.

Jardine, C.J., Jardine, N. & Sibson, R. (1967) The structure and construction of taxonomic hierarchies. *Math. Biosci.*, **1**, 173–9.

Mahalanobis, P.C. (1936) On the generalized distance in statistics, *Proc. Nat. Inst. Sci.*, **2**, 49–55.

Mahalanobis, P.C., Majumdar, D.N. & Rao, C.R. (1949) Anthropometric survey of the United Provinces, 1941: A statistical study. *Sankhya*, **9**, 90–324.

Majumdar, D.N. & Rao, C.R. (1958) Bengal anthropometric survey, 1945: a statistical study. *Sankhya*, **19**, 203–408.

Rao, C.R. (1948) The utilization of multiple measurements in problems of biological classification. *J. Roy. statist. Soc. B*, **10**, 159–93.

Rao, C.R. (1952) *Advanced Statistical Methods in Biometric Research.* New York: Wiley.

Rao, C.R. (1954) On the use and interpretation of distance functions in statistics. *Bull. int. statist. Inst.*, **34**, 90.

Rao, C.R. (1965) *Linear Statistical Inference and its Applications.* New York: Wiley.

Roe, D.A. (1968) British lower and middle palaeolithic handaxe groups. *Proc. prehist. Soc.*, **34**, 1–82.

Sokal, R.R. & Sneath, P.H. (1963) *Principles of Numerical Taxonomy.* San Francisco: Freeman.

Cluster Analysis

F. Roy Hodson
Numerical typology and prehistoric archaeology

This paper falls into three parts: first, a discussion of the relationship between numerical clustering techniques and certain basic archaeological concepts; second, an indication of which available numerical procedures seem most promising after trials on simple, archaeological test data; third, a pilot study that begins with these results and attempts to tackle a real archaeological problem: the definition of major 'types' of British handaxes.

NUMERICAL METHODS OF RECOGNIZING ARCHAEOLOGICAL STRUCTURE

The prehistoric archaeologist starts from material remains and attempts to interpret them in terms of the life and development of early man. Although not often explicitly stated, the method of proceeding from the relevant raw material to a useful interpretation depends on the basic, simple axiom that patterns or regularities in material remains may be expected to reflect patterns in the agency that produced them. The basic tasks of the prehistorian, then, are to recognize and interpret regularities in the known surviving material relevant to his field of study.

One kind of patterning that is useful for the prehistorian to recognize is a connected series showing a progression from one configuration to another—a 'seriation'. Another important kind of pattern to discover is the existence of relatively distinct groups of material, related to but separated from other comparable groups—'clustering'.

Corresponding with these patterns that are familiar to archaeologists, numerical procedures exist that are able to reveal such regularities in the more general situation. Ordering ('seriation') is indicated by those procedures that provide 'maps' of the material in a space of few (often for simplicity two) dimensions. Multi-dimensional Scaling and Principal Components are probably the best-known relevant procedures. The second kind of patterning is sought by 'cluster analysis'. Here, although not so well understood, a range of numerical procedures is available.

Although this paper is really concerned with clustering patterns, the archaeologist is generally faced with a problem where a combination of both ordering and clustering are of interest. It is quite feasible with a numerical approach to treat the two procedures as complementary and to produce a single diagram that combines the results of both, and so in the following discussion ordering will not be completely ignored.

In prehistory, there are two main levels at which patterns may be sought and recognized. First, at the level of individual objects: a group of objects morphologically alike and distinct from other objects may be expected to have a group significance (functional, chronological, 'tribal', and so on). A very extreme example would be the difference between a 'sword' and a 'safety-pin'. However, within each of these categories some examples will be relatively large or small, broad or narrow, decorated or plain, and it may well be possible to define groups further down a continuous hierarchy. At this more detailed level too, groups may be expected to have a group significance. Such groups at various levels are considered as 'types' by archaeologists and there is a clear relationship between this and the concept of 'clusters' in numerical taxonomy.

The second main level at which patterns may be recognized is at the *assemblage* level (that is, at the level of groups of types). At this level, assemblages that are related by sharing specific types of sword, pin, vase, and so on, may be expected to owe this to a higher level group relationship: they could, for example, represent the same tribe, or sect, or level of subsistence, or chronological stage. Interpretation of the patterning can, of course, come only after its recognition. Groups of types of this kind, again at various levels of a possible hierarchy, were called by Childe (1956) 'industries' if narrowly defined or 'cultures' if more comprehensive. 'Complex' is a term in current use that can cover the full range of the hierarchy. Its relationship with 'clustering' in numerical taxonomy is again clear.

A simple palaeolithic example may be given to demonstrate these concepts in action. Within the vast range of flint tools found in caves and open sites, certain morphological clusters or types have been recognized—for example, points and *racloirs* of specialized form. Assemblages related by containing a range of these specialized types have been recognized to form a 'Mousterian' complex, which is able to form the starting point for interpretation. In this instance one interpretation stresses the physical type (Neanderthal) sometimes associated with this complex, although other kinds of evidence are available for consideration. Here, then, clustering at the two basic levels may be seen as the first stage in studying a major archaeological problem.

There will clearly be many situations where clustering is self-evident: swords as against safety-pins, for example. Numerical clustering is likely to be of value at a more refined hierarchical level where controversy may exist, and where it is of value to state explicitly the evidence and assumptions on which a classification is based.

DEVELOPMENTS IN *K*-MEANS CLUSTER ANALYSIS

As a result of previous analyses of small sets of test data (Hodson 1970), the *K*-means method of cluster analysis seems the most promising general approach to follow for large quantities of data, provided that relatively few variables are concerned and a relatively small number of groups is suspected. This section presents the results of further experiments with this method. Two main sets of test data are again used: Fisher's well-known iris data (fifty irises of each of three species measured on four variables) and thirty La Tène fibulae (described by thirteen variables). The main ideas behind this work are taken from a research report by Ball (1967) and a paper by Friedman and Rubin (1967). The aim is to develop methods that can deal satisfactorily with large quantities of data without requiring an unrealistic amount of computation.

The *K*-means approach involves the following stages, and the current program will be discussed under these headings:

(1) A suitable number of clusters is chosen.

(2) The total data set is split up into this number of clusters as a starting point for improvement. Each cluster is characterized by the average scores of its members on each variable.

(3) A criterion of clustering is calculated for this partition (typically a ratio between the dispersion of units around their cluster centres and around the overall average for the whole sample).

(4) An iterative search procedure is required for transferring units from one cluster to another progressively until the clustering criterion is maximized.

(5) The final 'best' clustering must be reported.

Each of these aspects will be considered in turn.

1. THE NUMBER OF CLUSTERS TO BE INVESTIGATED

In most situations it is unlikely that the investigator will know *a priori* how many clusters are appropriate—the analysis will itself be expected to provide this information. And so usually a number of solutions will be required from which the 'best' may be picked by studying the value of the clustering criterion for different numbers of clusters. Initially, then, the analyst will have to set a maximum rather than a specific number of clusters to be investigated and a number of different results will be available for assessment. Consequently, the choice of a final number of clusters will come towards the end rather than at the beginning of the analysis and this problem will be deferred to the section on 'the presentation of results'.

2. THE INITIAL PARTITION OF THE SAMPLE INTO
A GIVEN NUMBER OF CLUSTERS

A major difficulty when attempting to maximize the clustering criterion in a *K*-means analysis is that the search may terminate when a local maximum rather than the global maximum has been found [rather as though the procedure had digressed into a cul de sac (a *local* maximum) from which it cannot continue towards the main objective (the *global* maximum) without some major reorientation]. The approach recommended by Friedman and Rubin is to obtain a number of different results from a number of different, random starting configurations, and to choose the 'best'. Table 1 presents the results of searching for a best six-cluster partition of the thirty fibulae starting from twenty-four different random partitions. The 'best' result was found only three times out of twenty-four runs (by the 'hill-climbing' procedure described in section 4). For any large-scale problem, this approach would seem to be unrealistic.

A more practical solution is to start from a partition that has been already engineered to approximate a final 'best' result. A promising strategy of this type is described by Ball as the 'Singleton–Kautz' algorithm (Ball 1967, section 7.04). First a 'splitting cycle' partitions the data successively into 2, 3, 4, . . . clusters up to a set maximum. Each of these partitions is derived directly from the preceding one: a search is made for the unit whose removal from its cluster will maximally improve the clustering criterion; this then forms the starting point for a new cluster. At each level of clustering an attempt is made to reach a global maximum by iteration (by the 'hill-climbing' procedure to be described in section 4). When the set maximum number of clusters is reached, a 'fusing' cycle is entered: at each stage a fusion is made between those two clusters whose fusion minimally affects the global criterion.

Criterion (%SSE)	Number of occurrences
38·44*	3
38·46	2
39·18	3
39·40	1
39·43	1
39·94	2
40·18	1
40·69	3
40·74	1
40·79	1
40·96	1
41·02	1
41·03	1
41·59	1
42·38	1
46·10	1
	Total 24

* It is assumed that this represents the global minimum.
Table 1. Results from random starting partitions. For each analysis, thirty fibulae were randomly divided between six clusters. A hill-climbing routine was then used to search for an optimal partition.

After this fusion and modification by 'hill-climbing', the current criterion is compared with the best previously obtained for this number of clusters. If this represents an improvement, the splitting cycle is re-entered and followed up to the level where no improvement on previous results is achieved. At this point the best result for that level is substituted and the 'fusing cycle' resumes. The procedure stops when a two-cluster partition is reached which does not represent an improvement on a previous two-cluster result. When this strategy was applied to the data on thirty fibulae, the best six-cluster result found from twenty-four random starts was in fact recovered. Further confidence in this strategy is given by results described in section 5, where very similar criteria were achieved for six successive 'shufflings' of these same data at cluster levels from two to eight. As a practical short cut then, likely to provide good solutions at a series of cluster levels from two to a set maximum, this strategy seems most promising, and has been used for the author's current program.

3. THE CRITERION OF CLUSTERING

In the previously reported archaeological application a relatively simple clustering criterion based on Euclidean (or rather 'Pythagorean') distance was used—the 'Sum Squared Error'. This is a percentage ratio of the sum of squared distances between units and their cluster centres relative to their summed distances from the overall data mean (and in this form is of course a criterion to be minimized). This is a very simple, fast criterion to compute, and in the reported application gave a useful result (Hodson 1970, p. 315). However, Friedman and Rubin have emphasized the two main drawbacks to Pythagorean distance: that it does not compensate for correlations between variables and that it is very sensitive to the scaling chosen for different variables. In the example which Friedman and Rubin report in most detail, Fisher's data on three species of iris, this criterion performed very badly, not only failing to separate the two closer species (*virginica* and *versicolor*), but not even exclusively separating the quite distinct *Iris setosa*. The scaling difficulty is often reduced by standardizing the variables of a study (dividing the score on each variable by its standard deviation). In experiments with the iris data I found that standardization immediately allowed *setosa* to be exclusively separated from the other two species at the two-cluster level. However, at the three-cluster level the separation between the three species was still far inferior to that achieved by Friedman and Rubin when a criterion for clustering related to Mahalanobis rather than Pythagorean distance was used. To judge by available results, then, situations exist where it is highly advantageous to use a criterion based on Mahalanobis distance, which compensates for linear correlations and differences in scale between variables. However, this will necessarily involve a very considerable increase in computation.

4. HEURISTICS FOR MAXIMIZING THE CHOSEN CRITERION

The previously reported program (Hodson 1970, p. 311) used a rapid but rather crude search procedure for improving the clustering criterion at any level of clustering (the 'reassignment pass' in Friedman and Rubin's terminology). For the SSE criterion based on Pythagorean distance, Friedman and Rubin's other main search procedure by 'hill-climbing' passes does not require much, if any, further computation. This involves, for any partition, taking each unit in turn and calculating whether its transference to another cluster will improve the global clustering criterion. If so, the best move is made directly and the two relevant cluster averages are recalculated. Successive runs through the data are made until a stable partition is reached. In experiments with test data, this search procedure has consistently found 'better' partitions than 'reassignment passes' and it has been incorporated in the current program for use when a 'Pythagorean' criterion is chosen. However, for large bodies of data and a Mahalanobis-related criterion, the successive computations required in hill-climbing seem excessive, and the 'reassignment pass' has been provisionally retained: an initial approximation based on the SSE criterion is 'improved' by reassignment based on Mahalanobis distance. This relatively fast combination of procedures tested on the iris data did in fact recover exactly the same optimal three-cluster partition that Friedman and Rubin report from hill-climbing and their 'determinant criterion'.

5. THE PRESENTATION OF RESULTS

In the previous archaeological report, K-means results were presented in two
forms: by a dendrogram (although a hierarchical presentation of this
essentially non-hierarchical procedure is not really appropriate), and by a
Venn diagram of clusters at a chosen level of clustering, that is, where the
units of the analysis are projected as points onto a plane with clusters indicated by boundaries. For this example, the dimensions of the plane were
defined by the first two principal components (Hodson 1970, figure 8). This
meant that ordering relationships between individual units and between
clusters could be at least approximately indicated as well as cluster membership. Other two-dimensional representations could be used and Friedman
and Rubin have emphasized the appropriateness of plotting units against the
first two discriminant functions for the clusters, that is to say, in a space
closely linked to Mahalanobis-type clustering criteria.

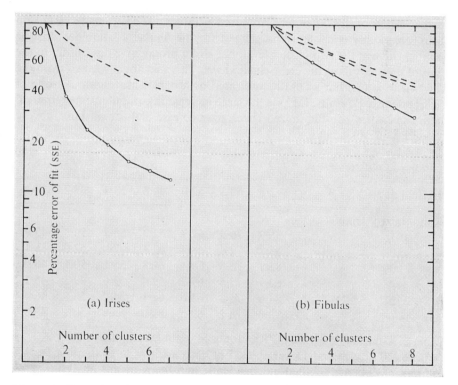

Figure 1. Clustering characteristics for two sets of test data. Solid lines
indicate results from original data, dashed lines after 'randomization' by
shuffling columns of scores. (For the fibulae, the dashed lines indicate the
extreme values found after six analyses of shuffled data. See table 2.)

For this non-hierarchical kind of representation the choice of a level of
clustering, or of a few levels, has to be made. As an aid to this choice, Ball
(1967) has emphasized the importance of studying a graph of the clustering
criterion against the increasing number of clusters. Any obvious level of
clustering in the data should give a pronounced shoulder to this curve at the

level of clustering where the progressive improvement of the configuration falls off. For the iris data, a pronounced shoulder of this kind is suggested after the two and three cluster levels, as would be expected [figure 1(a), solid line]. However, without any reference curve for comparable *non-clustered* data, picking out such a shoulder is likely to be difficult with archaeological data where gross clustering is not to be expected [compare figure 1(b), solid line]. J. MacQueen, reported by Ball (1967), has suggested one possible solution for this difficulty: he suggests random shuffling of the data by columns (that is, retaining the mean and standard deviation for variables) and repeating the analysis on sets of such 'randomized' data. The cost in computing paid for this increase in confidence is severe, since, in effect, the entire analysis has to be repeated for each 'randomized' check. For small quantities of data this is not serious and for the thirty fibulae six 'Singleton–Kautz' runs have been made after different shufflings. The ranges of values of the six runs are plotted as dotted lines on figure 1(b), and further details of the SSE criteria are given as table 2. The successive results do seem remarkably consistent and suggest for the fibulae a 'shoulder' for the original curve at the two-cluster level, but also a progressive descent up to the limit of the analysis at the eight-cluster level. This was not suspected from the 'raw' curve alone, but would be indicated by a comparison with any one of the 'randomized' results. Despite the large increase in computer time required, then, some form of randomized check may be essential for all but the very grossest *K*-means analyses.

Number of clusters	2	3	4	5	6	7	8
Original data	72·8	60·3	52·0	44·8	38·4	33·7	29·4
'Randomized' trials							
1	88·9	76·9	67·9	62·3	55·7	50·3	45·9
2	88·7	77·4	68·7	62·1	57·0	52·0	48·1
3	85·9	76·5	68·4	61·8	55·1	50·1	46·0
4	83·9	75·5	67·7	59·4	53·0	49·3	45·1
5	84·6	75·8	68·6	61·1	54·2	50·0	46·4
6	90·0	78·2	69·5	61·0	55·3	50·1	46·0

Table 2. *K*-means Analyses of 'Randomized' data [*See* figure 1(b).] Data for 30 fibulae and 13 variables. For each analysis after the first, columns of data are shuffled independently and the *K*-means analysis repeated. Stabilized partitions for 1 to 8 clusters are indicated by their percentage SSE (minimized by the Singleton–Kautz algorithm)

SUMMARY OF THE *K*-MEANS EXPERIMENTS
As a result of these experiments, the following procedure for analyzing realistic quantities of archaeological data seems to provide a reasonable compromise between computer time and confidence in the result:
(a) Initially, the SSE criterion is used after standardization of the data. The 'Singleton–Kautz' algorithm with 'hill-climbing' passes allows a graph of

SSE versus the number of clusters to be drawn up to a set cluster maximum.
(b) Unless a very obvious shoulder is seen to this curve, at least one and preferably more (a) type analyses are made on column-shuffled data. By comparing the original with randomized results it should be possible to concentrate interest on one or relatively few levels of clustering, or to decide that no evidence for clustering has been found.
(c) Using information from (b) the possibly crude 'Pythagorean' result may be refined by reassignment passes using Mahalanobis distance.
(d) The units are plotted against the first two discriminant functions for the clustering chosen.

This is essentially the procedure used for the handaxe problem described in the next section.

A Pilot Study of British Handaxes

The data used for this cluster analysis have kindly been made available by D. Roe, who has already studied them in some detail (Roe 1964, 1968).

THE PROBLEM

Of the many thousands of handaxes found in the British Isles, some five thousand from thirty-eight sites were chosen by Roe for detailed study. He judges these sites the most likely to represent genuine assemblages of material and so to be by far the most informative. Roe's chief interest, and that of Graham (1970), who has analyzed these data by canonical variate analysis, is centred on the sites themselves. Attempts are made to study relationships between the thirty-eight assemblages by reference to the measurements of their handaxes. For example, Roe has investigated differences between the mean values of such handaxe dimensions as length, thickness, and so on, from the sites using a *t*-test, and has plotted a scatter diagram for each site of its handaxes against selected measurements. Graham has treated the assemblages as 'groups' for a canonical variate analysis, each group characterized by the average values and dispersions of measurements of its handaxes. The analysis provides a 'map' of the sites on coordinates defined by pairs of canonical variates, and an indication of which original handaxe measurements best differentiate between sites.

A different problem concerns the taxonomy of the handaxes themselves without initial reference to their origin. Are there in fact discrete 'types' of British handaxes within the general handaxe category? If so it would be reasonable to ask their significance, whether functional, chronological, stylistic, technological, or a combined significance. Archaeologists have in fact tended to refer to different 'types' of handaxes since the last century, although with no marked consensus (Brézillon 1968). Roe is not primarily concerned with this problem and does not formally define 'types', although his contrast between handaxe groups of 'pointed' and 'ovate' tradition with further subdivisions hints at a possible taxonomy (Roe 1968, p. 54). The most systematic taxonomy *per se* is probably that suggested for French handaxes by Bordes (1961). A classification for British handaxes has been put forward by Wymer (1968), another for African handaxes by Kleindienst (1962). As in many archaeological classifications, the distinction is not always clear whether the suggested 'types' of handaxe are intended as arbitrary partitions of a continuous distribution, or as the recognition of discrete densities of related handaxes. In the former case, such 'types' cannot be expected *a priori* to have any immediate significance, while in the latter they can.

Roe's measurements on handaxes and a program for K-means cluster analysis seem to provide one possible starting point for an enquiry into the existence of types of this latter kind among British handaxes, and this pilot study attempts to ask whether discrete types are suggested by the evidence.

THE DATA

For this initial pilot study a random sample of 500 handaxes was chosen from Roe's total series by a random number generating routine. Twelve of the sample were later found to have missing data (scored as 0) and were discarded, leaving 488, or roughly a tenth of the total. Roe's data comprise information on six variables for all handaxes. The first variable, weight, is likely to be subsumed by the dimensions and was omitted, leaving the following (*see* Roe 1968):

(1) L: length (in millimetres)

(2) B/L: relative breadth (maximum breadth over length)

(3) Th/B: relative thickness (maximum thickness over maximum breadth)

(4) $B_1/B_2(P1)$: pointedness at the tip (width one fifth the length from the tip over width one fifth the length from the base)

(5) $L_1/L(P2)$: general pointedness (height of the maximum width relative to total length).

Many other handaxe features *could* be included in a quantitative description of this type, for example

(a) the presence or absence of flake scars from soft as well as hard hammer technique

(b) the quantity of cortex surviving on the finished implement

(c) an 's-twist' profile

(d) marked asymmetry.

Feature (a) has in fact been used for the definition of a major 'Abbevillian' type of handaxe [for example, by Bordes (1961, p. 69)]. But major sub-types have generally been defined as basic 'shape' variants and the dimensions (1)–(5) above should be sufficient to describe this kind of variability. For instance, the three major diagnostic measurement ratios suggested by Bordes are equivalent to variables (2), (3), and (5) [in the form of reciprocals], and variable (4) approximates Bordes' remaining 'pointedness' ratio. And so, although selected by Roe primarily for a purpose other than handaxe taxonomy, these five variables may be accepted as a provisional basis for defining major shape variants, or 'types' of handaxe. They should certainly be adequate for assessing K-means analysis as a general technique for the classification of flint tools.

THE K-MEANS ANALYSIS

As in Graham's study (1970), the data were first logarithmically transformed. Correlations between the transformed variables are shown in table 3.

For a first analysis using the SSE criterion based on 'Pythagorean' distance, variables were standardized, and solutions for two to six clusters were computed using the Singleton–Kautz algorithm and hill-climbing routines. This entire analysis was then repeated after shuffling the data by columns. The relevant plots of SSE criterion versus number of clusters are given on figure 2: a solid line represents the real result, a dotted line the comparative 'randomized' result.

	1 (L)	2 (B/L)	3 (T/B)	4 (P1)	5 (P2)
1 (L)	1·00				
2 (B/L)	−0·57	1·00			
3 (T/B)	0·26	−0·64	1·00		
4 (P1)	−0·19	0·24	−0·18	1·00	
5 (P2)	−0·24	0·26	−0·21	0·78	1·00

Table 3. Correlations between handaxe variables

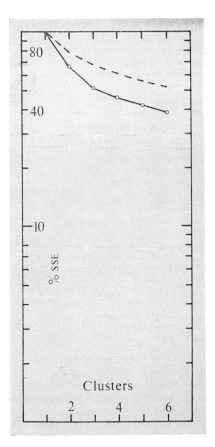

Figure 2. Clustering characteristics for 488 handaxes (bifaces). The solid line refers to original data, the dashed line to randomized data.

Final configurations for the real data for two to five clusters were then each taken as the starting point for further refinement by a routine combining Mahalanobis distance and reassignment passes. After stabilization, discriminant functions and coordinates for the handaxes on these functions were calculated. Values for Friedman and Rubin's determinant criterion were also calculated for each level of clustering. These results are summarized as table 4. Configurations for the two- and three- cluster results are plotted as figures 3 and 4. For the former, grouped frequencies of the handaxes are plotted as a histogram; for the latter, each handaxe is projected as a dot onto a plane defined by the two discriminant functions. For comparison, a scatter-diagram of the handaxes plotted against two original variables is given (figure 5). Consideration of the correlation matrix (table 3) and of the weightings for variables on discriminant functions (table 4) suggests that the best variables for this purpose are relative thickness (variable 3), and pointedness as indicated by the relative height of maximal width (variable 5).

Discriminant function	Latent root		2 Groups	3 Groups	4 Groups	5 Groups
	1		100%	79·4%	64·6%	77·6%
1		Length	2·5*	0·4	2·4	1·5
		Breadth/L	−0·5	−1·4	−0·7	−1·2
		Thickness/B	3·0	1·9	2·8	2·0
		Pointedness 1	−1·0	−1·5	0·2	−0·4
		Pointedness 2	−1·2	−2·0	0·1	−1·7
	2			20·6%	33·9%	19·8%
2		Length		1·6	0·5	−1·1
		Breadth/L		−1·3	1·4	1·5
		Thickness/B		2·0	−0·2	−0·1
		Pointedness 1		1·8	−2·0	−2·4
		Pointedness 2		1·5	−2·5	−1·0
3	3				1·6%	1·4%
4	4					1·1%
Determinant criterion: $LN(|T|/|W|)$			1·26	2·00	2·51	2·90

* Tabulated values represent the relative importance of the different variables for discriminating between groups. They are computed by multiplying the appropriate elements of the normalized latent vectors of $W^{-1}B$ by the square root of the corresponding diagonal element of W, where B represents the between-groups dispersion matrix, W the pooled-within-groups dispersion matrix. [*See* Friedman and Rubin (1967) and Cooley and Lohnes (1962, p. 118)].

Table 4. Discriminant analyses of 488 handaxes. The 'groups' are clusters defined by the K-means analysis.

DISCUSSION OF THE RESULTS

The main purpose of this pilot study was to see if these data implied clustering of handaxes and so the main interest centres on the plot of clustering characteristics for the sample (figure 2). This result does suggest a slight, but perceptible, difference between the real curve and the 'randomized' curve, but this is only evident at the two and three cluster levels. This hints at the existence of three 'natural' clusters for this particular sample. Figures 3 and 4 give more information about clusters at the two- and three- cluster levels, and emphasize how tenuous this clustering is. However, more structure is evident than would be guessed from studying a direct scatter diagram, even when the two most informative variables are used as coordinate axes (compare figure 5). To sum up, this pilot study suggests the possibility that a relatively small number of 'densities' of British handaxe shapes ('types') may exist, and that this K-means procedure may be able to reveal them. Because the suggested structure is (as would be expected) so slight, little if any confidence can be placed in this result until it is replicated using more of the available data. These results do seem to suggest that computer time devoted to such further analysis would not be wasted.

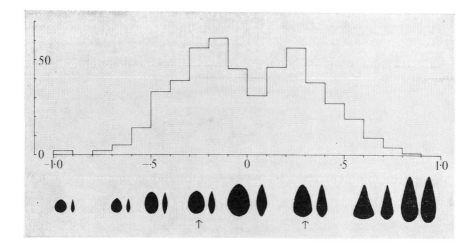

Figure 3. Two clusters of handaxes (bifaces): frequency of 488 handaxe scores on the discriminant function plotted as a histogram.
Arrows mark the position of cluster averages.
Silhouettes of a range of shapes located on the function are given below; they include the two cluster averages and the overall sample average (scoring 0).
The weight of the variables ($L=2\cdot5$; $B=-0\cdot5$; $T=3\cdot0$; $P(1)=-1\cdot0$;
$P(2)=-1\cdot2$; see also table 4) shows that the two clusters are basically of thin, small; and thick, large handaxes.

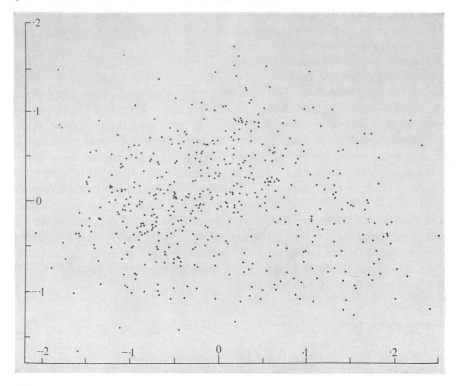

(a)

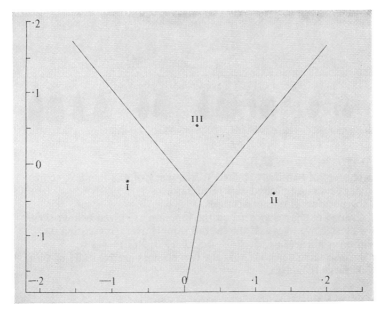

(b)

Figure 4. Three handaxe clusters. (a) 488 handaxes plotted against the two
discriminant functions for three clusters (*see* table 4). (b) The partition suggested
by *K*-means analysis. Asterisks mark the location of cluster centres (averages).

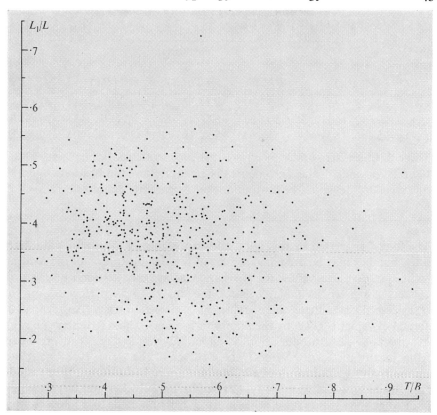

Figure 5. Scatter diagram of 488 handaxes against two original variables: relative thickness (T/B) and pointedness (L_1/L). Compare figures 3 and 4.

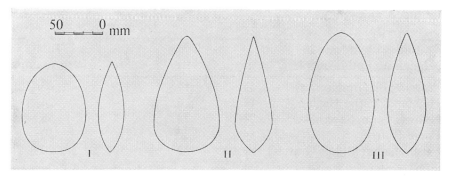

Figure 6. Three 'types' of British handaxe: outlines suggested by the K-means analysis (*see* table 5).

ARCHAEOLOGICAL COMMENTS

Cluster	Variables				
	1 (length)	2 (B/L)	3 (Th/B)	4 (P1)	5 (P2)
1	92 (73, 116)	·73 (·65, ·82)	·42 (·36, ·49)	·78 (·64, ·94)	·41 (·35, ·48)
2	120 (90, 160)	·58 (·50, ·67)	·57 (·47, ·69)	·46 (·38, ·55)	·25 (·21, ·30)
3	125 (96, 162)	·57 (·51, ·64)	·58 (·49, ·68)	·75 (·63, ·90)	·39 (·33, ·45)

Table 5. Characteristics of 3 'types' of British handaxe. For each variable the relevant mean value (geometric) is given, followed in brackets by units one standard deviation below and above. Apparently diagnostic values are in italic.

The 'types' suggested by this pilot study are evidently of provisional interest only, but they may be presented as part of this demonstration of the K-means technique. Average values for the handaxes assigned to each of the three clusters are given as table 5. Since the analysis was performed on log-transformed data, these values represent geometric means. An idea of the spread of values is given by the figures in brackets. These represent the range of values one standard deviation below and above the mean, converted back from logarithms to raw values. The outlines of the three 'types' suggested by the analysis are drawn out as figure 6. In very broad terms, type I is relatively thin, broad and small; types II and III are thicker and larger; type II is distinguished from III by being more sharply pointed. In a more comprehensive, future analysis a great deal of interest would centre on the relative frequency of different types in different contexts, and as an illustration only of this aspect, handaxes from the richer sites are presented in these terms (table 6). Even in this preliminary study the differential occurrence of types by sites is apparent.

Sites with at least 20 handaxes in this sample	Types			Total in this sample
	I	III	II	
Warren Hill (fresh series)	55	14	—	69
Highlands Farm, Henley	18	6	—	24
Knowle Farm, Savernake	28	24	4	56
Furze Platt	4	30	16	50
Swanscombe (Middle Gravels)	2	2	16	20

Table 6. Three handaxe types at different sites. For details of sites *see* Roe (1968).

CONCLUSIONS

A good deal of effort has recently been expended on the presentation and analysis of measurements of flint artifacts. These studies illustrate the general difficulty of dealing with multivariate archaeological data but in an extreme form because of the intractable nature of flint compared with, say, bronze, clay, or wood. This paper makes no attempt to review these approaches, which all too often have seemed rather confused in aim and method, but presents one possible way to establish taxonomies of flint tools. This reported analysis does not claim to present any definitive result of great archaeological import, but to illustrate an extremely powerful and promising technique. One reason for hesitating to accept the result is the relatively small sample size, combined with the indistinctness of the result achieved (even if this is to be expected from the nature of the problem). However, another reason for caution in this and any other quantitative taxonomic study is the basic difficulty of describing artifacts adequately prior to their analysis. It is hoped in future studies to concentrate on these problems.

ACKNOWLEDGMENTS

I would like to express sincere thanks to D. A. Roe for making available his handaxe data and to J. E. Doran and J. M. Graham for help in translating them into a form acceptable to my programs. I would also like to thank the following for their most helpful advice in conversation: J. E. Doran, J. C. Gower, D. G. Kendall, M. H. Newcomer, I. Olkin, and D. A. Roe. I gratefully acknowledge the computer facilities given to me at the Atlas Computer installation of London University and the SRC Laboratory, Chilton. This project is supported by a research grant from the Leverhulme Foundation.

REFERENCES

Ball, G. H. (1967) *A comparison of two techniques for finding the minimum sum-squared error partition.* Stanford Research Institute, California.

Bordes, F. (1961) *Typologie du Paléolithique Ancien et Moyen.* (2 vols). Bordeaux: Delmas.

Brézillon, M. N. (1968) La dénomination des objets de pierre taillée. *Gallia Préhistoire,* Supplément 4.

Childe, V. G. (1956) *Piecing together the past.* London: Routledge & Kegan Paul.

Cooley, W. W. & Lohnes, P. R. (1962) *Multivariate Procedures for the Behavioral Sciences.* New York: Wiley.

Friedman, H. P. & Rubin, J. (1967) On some invariant criteria for grouping data. *J. Amer. statist. Ass.,* **62,** 1159–78.

Graham, J. M. (1970) Discrimination of British lower and middle Palaeolithic handaxe groups using canonical variates. *World Archaeology,* **1,** 321–42.

Hodson, F. R. (1970) Cluster analysis and archaeology: some new developments and applications. *World Archaeology,* **1,** 299–320.

Kleindienst, M. R. (1962) Components of the East African Acheulian assemblage: an analytic approach. *Actes due 4ᵉ Congrès Panafricain de Préhistoire,* pp. 81–112.

Roe, D. A. (1964) The British Lower and Middle Palaeolithic: some problems, methods of study and preliminary results. *Proc. prehist. Soc.,* **30,** 245–67.

Roe, D. A. (1968) British Lower and Middle Palaeolithic handaxe groups. *Proc. prehist. Soc.,* **34,** 1–82.

Wymer, J. (1968) *Lower Palaeolithic Archaeology in Britain.* London: John Baker.

Cluster Analysis

Ralph M. Rowlett and Richard B. Pollnac
Multivariate analysis of Marnian La Tène cultural groups

The purpose of this paper is to describe a method which can be used to classify archaeological data, to contrast this method with other methods, and to provide a concrete example of this application contrasted with a more commonly used technique. The data which will be used in this analysis come from the Marne Culture, of northern Champagne, France. (*See* figure 1.)

The Marne Culture has long been recognized as constituting a distinctive variant of the widespread La Tène Culture of central, west-central, and east-central Europe. Although originally distinguished by a rather informal discussion of the evidence, the Marnian variant nevertheless does possess enough distinctiveness to be easily differentiated from other La Tène manifestations. Marnian sites are distinguished above all on the basis of fairly large cemeteries with consistent westward orientation of the graves, black earth grave fill (in an area where the prevailing soil color is light brown), almost universal burial of weapons with adult males, lineal village layout consisting of one or more parallel rows of houses, distinctive rectilinear carinated pottery with frequent incised or painted decoration, frequent chariot burials with occasional inclusions of trade vessels from the Etruscans or Greeks of classical antiquity, as well as a myriad of special types of jewellery and fibulae which are exclusively or predominantly found in the Marnian district of northern Champagne.

The distinctiveness of the Marne Culture persists clearly through four chronological horizons (La Tène Ia through II) from about 480 BC to 100 BC. There are hardly any students of prehistoric Europe who question the validity of the concept of a separate Marne Culture within the broader La Tène world, and, indeed, there are those who implicitly treat the Marne Culture as one main socio-cultural unit. Those who have worked closely with the Marne Culture, however, such as Bretz-Mahler (1957) or Rowlett (1968) have noted by inspection that certain cultural traits seem to occur more frequently in some parts of northern Champagne than in others, and that there may be other slight cultural differences within the easily perceived Marnian variant. However, virtually none of these elements was exclusively confined to one or the other geographic regions within the Marnian area, and in any case one would be interested to know if any of the different cultural traits tended to associate together when considering this problem of determining if there was any truly significant internal variation which would cluster geographically within the Marne Culture. One could see, for example, that when the geographic distribution of the spatial relationship of village area to cemetery was plotted on a map (figure 2), the eastern Marnian district tended to have virtually all of those sites where burials were planted among the

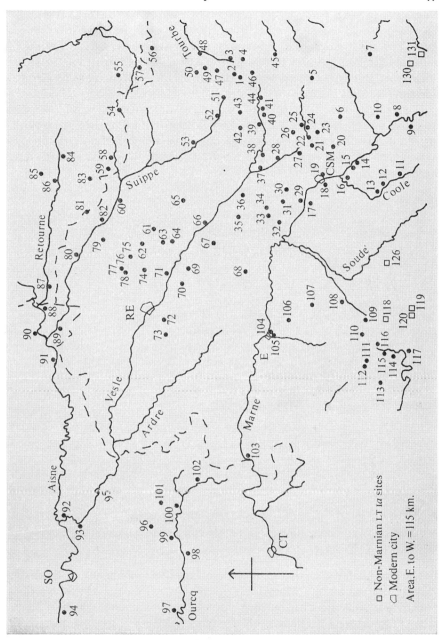

Figure 1

houses; in the more northern parts cemeteries are adjacent to village areas, while on the western side of the Marnian district, cemeteries are so far away from settlements that the particular cemeteries which go with any particular settlements have seldom been found or at least recognized as such. The choice of cemetery location with respect to the areas of the living were assuredly matters involving many other aspects of culture. Therefore, it seemed necessary to use some sort of multivariate analysis in order to determine if there was any consistent patterning at all in the varying distributions of cultural elements within the Marne Culture. To control for temporal differences, this study analyzes only data from the La Tène ɪa (480–400 BC) horizon (Rowlett 1968).

The analysis was initiated with two major objectives in mind. The first objective was to determine the geographical distribution of sites demonstrating similar assemblage items and the degree to which the site assemblages were similar. The second objective was to determine which assemblage items were those which were shared.

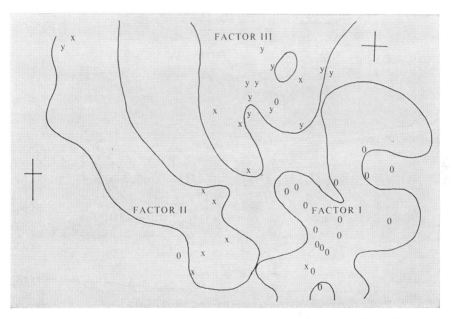

Figure 2. Spatial distribution of factors. Boundaries are factor loading of +0·30. 0=graves among houses; y=houses adjacent to cemetery; x=houses distant from cemetery.

The data analyzed consist of 104 assemblage items which are distributed in varying degrees among 77 archaeological sites within the above described area. These sites are distributed in an area approximately 100 by 75 kilometers (*see* figure 1). The assemblage item categories reflect mainly stylistic traits such as location of vessel in grave; vessel shape, color, and decorative motif; jewellery, knife and scabbard styles, and chariot pit shape. (*See* table 1, *on pages* 49–52.)

| | Factors | | |
Assemblage items	I	II	III
1. Vases chiefly to right, at foot	−1·22	0·28	0·39
2. Lances chiefly to the left	−0·50	−0·34	0·26
3. a°–1a bowls	−0·37	−0·07	−1·76
4. A°–1a jar	−1·12	3·48	−1·30
5. A° jar with neck cordon	0·04	−0·53	0·65
6. B vase with flat, everted rim	−0·82	−0·06	−0·40
7. B vase with vertical rim	−0·11	−0·18	0·20
8. Rimless B and b vases	−0·41	−0·13	0·44
9. Bi-conic plates with foot	−0·29	−0·70	0·66
10. Footless carinated cup	−0·19	−0·71	0·63
11. Footless ovoid cup c°–2b	0·06	−0·72	0·68
12. Rectilinear conical cist predominant form	−0·89	−0·87	0·74
13. Orange-yellow pottery at least 10% of ceramic colors	−4·32	−0·25	0·07
14. Thin red paint	−4·21	0·22	−0·10
15. Wide-band painting technique	−4·56	0·21	−0·00
16. Triple chevron ceramic motif	−0·88	0·52	0·12
17. Inverted chevron ceramic motif	−1·29	0·12	0·14
18. Zig-zag line ceramic motif	−0·58	−0·45	0·09
19. Reticular ceramic motif	−1·17	0·16	0·05
20. Circular ceramic motif	0·33	0·20	0·54
21. Vertical wavy combmarks on ceramics	−0·35	0·75	0·57
22. Less than 50% twisted torcs	−1·50	−0·31	0·21
23. Majority of twisted torc hooks in the plane of the torc	−1·54	−0·50	−0·48
24. Bird torcs and bird vases, and other bird images (except on fibulae)	−0·19	−0·57	0·36
25. Torcs with exterior annelets	−0·38	−0·21	0·59
26. Bracelet with continuous series of incised lines	−0·61	−0·09	0·62
27. Bracelet with serpentine decoration around the exterior	0·33	−0·67	0·17
28. Pin-and-socket bracelet with flattened wire section	−0·56	0·05	0·48
29. Multiple-node bracelet	0·03	−0·99	0·43
30. Fibula terminal semi-hemispherical (as at La Gorge Meillet)	0·48	−0·70	0·48
31. Fibula with false spring on foot	0·24	−0·98	0·81
32. Disc fibula	−0·23	−0·69	0·69
33. Bronze sword scabbards	0·62	−0·86	0·56
34. Predominantly high arc on scabbard mouth	0·00	−1·16	0·09

Table 1 (*cont.*)

Assemblage items	Factors		
	I	II	III
35. Knife with complete handle and rectangular pommel	−0·35	−0·48	−0·08
36. Knives with convex dorsal lines and short riveted handles (*D*–1 and *D3e*)	−1·15	−0·20	0·48
37. Narrow felloe clamp	−0·00	−1·16	0·71
38. Trapezoidal chariot burial pit	0·81	−1·06	0·82
39. Vases chiefly to the left side, not at foot	0·29	−0·75	−1·92
40. Black piriform wheelmade urns	0·20	−0·62	−1·57
41. *A–3c* urn with short, flat upper shoulder	0·48	−1·06	−0·66
42. Spheroid jars *A°–3*	−0·17	0·52	−3·82
43. *b°–3* spherical pots	0·72	−0·18	−1·09
44. *Ta°* chalice with flaring rim	0·80	−0·25	−1·02
45. *Tc°–3* conical chalice	0·25	−0·17	−1·43
46. Black pottery predominant (50% or more)	0·21	−0·41	−5·09
47. Relief decorative technique	0·45	−1·01	−1·59
48. Nested serial lozenge ceramic motif	0·78	−0·27	−0·60
49. *A* vases with rounded bellies	0·64	−0·35	−1·05
50. Concentric semi-circle decorative motif	0·60	−0·81	0·06
51. Vertical comb marks with top section curved	0·46	0·09	−0·39
52. Punctate decoration with relief margins	0·30	−0·57	−0·96
53. Pyramidal ceramic motif	0·35	−0·74	−0·89
54. La Tène curvilinear designs on wheel-made pottery	0·41	−0·76	−0·73
55. Bracelet of flattened wire with square-chipped ends (*B2a*)	0·03	0·22	0·09
56. Knife with complete handle with splayed butt	0·65	−0·80	−0·67
57. Knife with concave dorsal line, short handle	0·71	−0·28	−0·20
58. Wide felloe clamp	0·83	−0·48	−0·03
59. Square or rectangular chariot pit	0·43	−0·34	−0·32
60. Cremations as well as inhumations	0·63	0·82	0·34
61. Pots chiefly at the head	0·99	0·71	0·68
62. *A–3b* urn with short cylindrical neck, wide flat rim	0·67	0·56	−0·10
63. *A–2b* vase with drooping upper shoulder	0·57	1·22	0·67

Assemblage items	Factors		
	I	II	III
64. $b°$–2 vase	0·65	0·56	0·60
65. Cylindrical cist predominant cist form	0·66	0·99	0·57
66. Many grey pots (over 33%)	0·51	1·81	0·44
67. Triplet parallel lines on ceramic cists	0·72	0·30	0·66
68. Single and stacked lozenges ceramic motif	0·01	1·70	0·95
69. Left-oriented step ceramic motif	−0·41	1·59	0·46
70. Solid dot ceramic motif	0·15	0·65	0·46
71. Over 50% twisted torcs	0·67	3·00	−0·41
72. Plaque catch-plate on torcs	0·59	2·02	0·68
73. Majority of torc hooks perpendicular to the plane of the torc	0·48	3·29	−0·28
74. Bracelet with alternate band decoration with lines at right angles to the bands	0·36	0·55	−0·27
75. Rectangle and triangles bracelet motif	0·04	2·09	1·00
76. Pointed-ended bracelet with flattened section, overlapping ends	0·79	0·94	0·36
77. Predominantly low arc scabbard mouth	0·70	1·94	−1·18
78. Knife with arched back, stepped pommel	0·84	−0·13	0·32
79. Knife with short, stepped handle	0·86	0·55	0·57
80. Red piriform wheel-made urns	0·56	−1·15	0·56
81. Piriform flasks	0·06	−0·75	0·50
82. $B°$–3 jar (high rounded shoulder)	0·20	−0·08	0·48
83. $b°$–1 bowl (high rounded shoulder)	−0·35	−0·72	0·31
84. Rimless chalice $Tc°$–2a	0·23	−0·21	0·95
85. Triangle ceramic motif	−0·38	−0·70	0·26
86. Asymmetrical rectangular meander ceramic motif	−0·04	−0·93	0·50
87. La Tène curvilinear designs on handmade pottery	0·46	−0·80	0·40
88. Bracelet of ribbon twist with pointed ends	0·32	−0·77	0·62
89. Pointed oval design on fibula bow complemented by tick marks	0·56	−0·57	0·83
90. Knife with pointed handle	0·09	−1·01	0·71
91. Spear with long socket	0·18	−0·83	0·34
92. Lances chiefly at the feet	0·82	0·34	0·24
93. $B°$ vase with incurvate upper shoulder ($B°$–3)	0·84	−0·20	−1·20
94. $B°$ rimless ceramic situla	0·23	−0·79	−0·79
95. Cross-hatched decoration on fibula bows	0·11	−0·33	−0·57
96. Lances chiefly at the right	0·61	0·47	0·48

Table 1 (*cont.*)

Assemblage items	Factors		
	I	II	III
97. Symmetrical reactangular meander ceramic motif	0·30	0·15	−0·20
98. Pin-and-socket bracelets with round section	0·43	−0·31	−0·14
99. Flat rectangular fibula terminal with *X*-design incised	0·82	0·53	0·68
100. Vases chiefly at foot, no side preference	0·68	−0·27	0·55
101. Orange-brown pottery over 10%	0·42	0·45	0·77
102. Thick paint predominant technique of ceramic decoration (50% plus)	0·37	0·03	0·57
103. Double chevron design	−0·66	0·87	0·34
104. Series of small circles decorating bronzes	0·18	1·06	0·46

Table 1. Assemblage items and factor scores

There are several ways these data can be analyzed to achieve our objectives mentioned above. One would be to perform sorts on the various assemblage items until sets of co-occurring items were found and then plot the geographical distribution of the sites that manifest these sets.

Another method would be to first inter-correlate the assemblage items, and then select those items which are highly correlated. One could then determine the geographical distribution of the sites which manifested all the highly correlated items, all the highly correlated items minus one, and so on. This would result in charts of the spatial distribution of traits similar to those presented by Driver in his 1956 paper, *An integration of functional, evolutionary, and historical theory by means of correlations.*

These two methods would succeed in giving us an idea of the geographical distribution of co-occurring assemblage items, but they would fail to indicate the total degree of shared assemblage items between the sites.

One possible solution to this problem is to correlate the sites on the basis of assemblage items. This is the *Q*-Technique as outlined by Tugby (1965). This would give us a measure of the degree of association between the sites based on the patterns of occurrence of assemblage items. One could then select a site from the correlation matrix which manifests a fair number of high correlations with other sites and plot for each site its correlation with the selected site. Another site could then be selected which had a low correlation with the first site selected but high correlations with a set of sites which were not highly correlated with the first selected site. The degree of association between this second selected site and all the other sites could then be plotted as was done in the first instance. This process could be repeated until it appeared that all groups of sites which were closely associated with each other on the basis of shared assemblage items were plotted. A spatial analysis of these plots such as trend surface analysis could be used to outline the areal grouping of sites which are closely associated due to a shared pattern of assemblage items. The results of this type of analysis would be similar to that presented by Milke (1949) in an article on the quantitative distribution of cultural similarities and their cartographic representation. In his paper he plotted the coefficients of similarity of a number of American Indian tribes with one point-of-reference tribe, and connected their areas by isoplethes of cultural similarity. His conclusions have a significance beyond merely exemplifying the application of the technique and should be consulted.

Although this method would give us a quantitative spatial description of assemblage similarity, it has one weakness with regard to our objectives. The weakness of this method is that we would not easily be able to determine from the great number of artifacts and their relationships the set of specific assemblage items responsible for the clustering of the sites and the degree to which each item contributed to the inter-correlation of the sites.

A type of analysis which would produce all the needed information is factor analysis with factor scores. In the analysis presented here, this technique is used (1) to group the sites on the basis of patterns of occurrence of assemblage items, (2) to provide a value for each site that indicates its degree of association with the pattern or factor underlying each grouping of sites, and (3) to provide a score for each assemblage item which makes it possible to determine the assemblage items responsible for each grouping of sites.

The first step in the factor analysis was to correlate sites on the basis of assemblage items, as discussed earlier. A factor analysis of the resultant correlation matrix was then performed to determine the regularities that underlie its complex inter-relationships. The factor analysis model used was that of common factor analysis. Squared multiple correlations were used as the initial communality estimates and iterations were performed on this estimate until the mean absolute deviation of the communalities was reduced to less than 0·0001. Since the goal here was to define the distinct clusters of relationships that were present in the data, the factors were rotated to orthogonal simple structure, utilizing the varimax criterion. The first three factors rotated grouped the sites into three distinct groups. All of the factors beyond three accounted for very small increments of total variance explained and thus were considered irrevelant to our objective of determining the major groupings of sites.

The factor loadings for each site on each factor were then plotted on maps of the spatial distribution of the sites. The loadings for each factor were plotted on separate maps. The factor loading measures the degree to which a variable (in this case a site) is involved in a factor pattern. Its interpretation is similar to that of a correlation coefficient except that in this case the site is not being measured for its degree of association with another site, but is instead being measured for its degree of association with a cluster of sites that were determined on the basis of similarity of variation with regard to assemblage items.

The plotted factor loadings were then analyzed in a manner similar to that used for weather maps. Lines of equal factor loadings, which we call isoloads, were drawn, and the resultant configurations are presented in figures 3, 4 and 5.

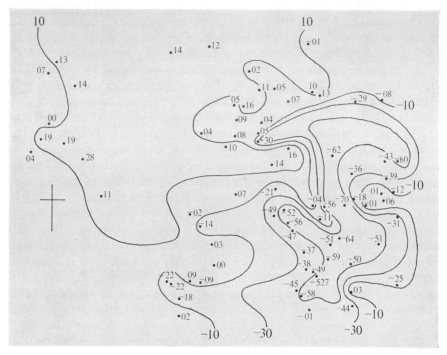

Figure 3. Spatial distribution of factor I. Plotted figures indicate factor loadings of sites.

In order to determine which assemblage items were those which were shared we took advantage of the fact that one can calculate a score for each case on a factor. In this instance, the cases are assemblage items. To calculate this score the regression estimate technique was used. The list of traits and their factor scores are presented in table 1.

In interpreting the analysis it should first be pointed out that the three factors explained 9·3, 6·0, and 5·2 per cent of the variance respectively, summing to a total of 20·5 per cent of the total variance in the data set. This low percentage of variance explained was not unexpected in light of the stylistic heterogeneity present in this area. Stylistic elements seemed to flow quite readily between the various sites. In another study, in which a hypothesis concerning residence pattern was tested, it was found that with regard to ceramic stylistic attributes, the degree of intra-community heterogeneity was about as great as the inter-community heterogeneity within five adjacent communities in the factor I area. (Pollnac, unpublished).

As can be seen in the figures, this analysis neatly grouped the sites into three geographical areas. The configurations of the isoloads for the various factors graphically display the general decrease in stylistic similarity as one moves away from a point of reference. The rate of decrease in similarity differs depending on the direction taken from the point of reference, a

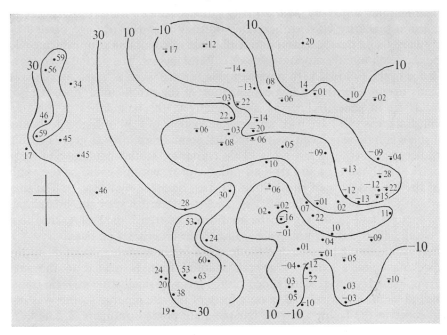

Figure 4. Spatial distribution of factor II. Plotted figures indicate factor loadings of sites.

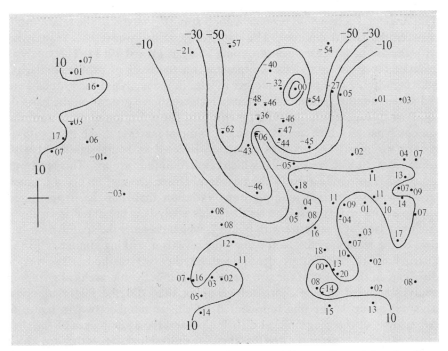

Figure 5. Spatial distribution of factor III. Plotted figures indicate factor loadings of sites.

phenomenon noted by Milke (1949) in his study of the distribution of cultural similarity cited earlier. This differential rate of change of stylistic similarity doubtless reflects a differential rate of communication which could be the result of either topographic or cultural factors. The partial correspondence of the isoloads with physiographic features such as rivers in the area leads one to infer that it is a combination of the two factors. Since the isoloads are in general clustered more tightly at the boundaries of the sub-cultural areas (we have used an absolute loading of 0·30 or higher to bound a sub-cultural area) it can be inferred that communication was greater within rather than between the areas. This clustering at the boundary is more marked with factors I and III than with factor II, but this could be the result of the lower density of sites within the area bounded by factor II. The sites which fall between the boundaries, such as those between the boundaries of factor I and factor III can be considered as transitional sites, sites that belong fully to neither group according to the criteria set up here.

It is interesting to note that the location of the burials in relation to the dwelling units, a rather large-scale cultural trait, is related to the sub-groupings which were determined on the basis of small scale stylistic traits. Burial location was entered in only forty of the site reports, so this was not included in the factor analysis, but these are plotted on figure 2. The fit is not perfect but it is surprisingly good.

Cluster analysis as well as factor analysis has been suggested as a method for determining the patterns of covariation within a large archaeological data set (Cowgill 1968, Hodson, Sneath, and Doran 1966). We felt that the data presented here would provide a good applied analysis of the relationship between the two techniques. The data set described above was reanalyzed with the use of a hierarchical grouping analysis (Ward 1963). This analysis grouped the sites, in a step-wise manner, on the basis of profile similarity. Starting with 77 groups (the number of sites in the analysis) the groups were reduced in number in a series of steps which combined groups on the basis of total assemblage similarity. The criteria used for reduction at each step was the combination which would provide a minimal increase in the total within-groups variation. The level of reduction selected as being significant with regard to our objective was that which resulted in four groups. This level was selected because reduction to the next level (three groups) involved a much larger increase in total within-groups variation than had been associated with previous reductions. The result of this analysis is presented in figure 6. A comparison of this figure with figure 2, which presents the spatial distribution of the results of the factor analysis, reveals a striking similarity in the distribution of the groups determined by the two methods. The major difference in the results of the two techniques is that the hierarchical grouping analysis resulted in one more sub-grouping than did the factor analysis. This sub-group is the one represented by cluster number two in figure 6. An analysis of the geographical distribution and the assemblages of the sites involved in cluster two indicated that these are the residual sites—the sites which are intermediate between the other sub-groups. It thus seems that one of the advantages to be gained by using factor analysis is that more of these intermediate sites can be classified with one or another group. The factor loading of the site in question can be used to indicate to the investigator the degree to which the site is associated with a specific sub-group. Over all, it seems that the use of the Q-technique factor analysis with plotted factor loadings (or the converse: R-technique factor analysis with the factor scores being plotted if the data is standardized) provides a more refined analysis of cultural similarity than does cluster analysis. This is especially true when the overall relationship between the variables is rather weak, which is common in large archaeological assemblages. We thus suggest using factor analysis in archaeological analyses such as the one presented here.

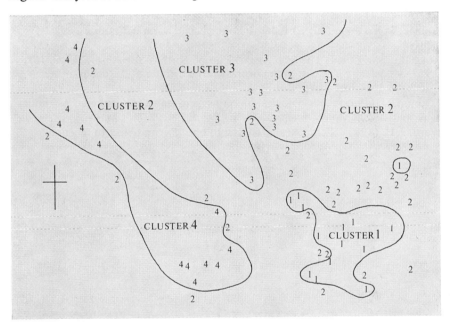

Figure 6. Spatial distribution of clusters. Plotted figures indicate cluster within which site is grouped.

In summary, it can be seen that we have achieved our objectives of determining the geographical distribution of the sites demonstrating similar assemblage items, the degree to which the site assemblages were similar, and the assemblage items responsible for these patterns. Isarithmic maps of the three major factors which underlay the data set were constructed, and their correspondence with topographical features was explored to determine whether the vectors representing differential rates of change in stylistic similarity from a reference point corresponded with any topographic features. Correspondence was slight but some was noted, thus leading to the inference that the variance in communication inferred from these vectors was due partially to topography and partially to cultural factors. The utility of constructing such isarithmic maps of multivariate measures of cultural phenomena and comparing them with other isarithmic maps, either cultural or non-cultural, as an exploratory technique or as a technique of testing hypotheses, is one that should prove to be extremely valuable in anthropology.

REFERENCES

Bretz-Mahler, D. (1957) Observations sur quelques cimetières de La Tène I. *Bulletin de la Société Archéologique Champenoise*, **44**, 3–5 (Reims).

Cowgill, G. L. (1968) Archaeological applications of factor, cluster, and proximity analyses. *Amer. Antiquity*, **33**, 367–75.

Driver, H. (1956) An integration of functional, evolutionary, and historical theory by means of correlations. *Indiana Publications in Anthropology and Linguistics, Memoir*, **12**, 1–35.

Hodson, F. R., Sneath, P. H. A. & Doran, J. E. (1966) Some experiments in the numerical analysis of archaeological data. *Biometrika*, **53**, 311–24.

Milke, W. (1949) The quantitative distribution of cultural similarities and their cartographic representation. *Amer. Anthropol.*, **51**, 237–51.

Pollnac, R. B. (unpublished) Relative homogeneity as an indicator of social processes in archaeological data: an old world example.

Rowlett, R. M. (1968) The Iron Age of Europe north of the Alps. *Science*, **161**, 123–34. *See also* The east group of the Marne Culture at the debut of the La Tène Iron Age. (In press).

Tugby, D. J. (1965) Archaeological objectives and statistical methods: A frontier in archaeology. *Amer. Antiquity*, **31**, 1–16.

Ward, J. H. (1963) Hierarchical grouping to optimize an objective function. *Amer. statist. Ass. J.*, **58**, 236–44.

Cluster Analysis

Robin Sibson
Computational methods in cluster analysis

This paper reviews from the computational viewpoint some methods of extracting clusters from a measure of similarity or dissimilarity. A measure of dissimilarity is assumed to take the value zero between an object and itself, and to be non-negative otherwise. The order of elements in a pair is not relevant; that is, $d(x, y) = d(y, x)$. Such a function d is called a *dissimilarity coefficient* (DC). It will be convenient to work with this as the data in cluster analysis. Most of the coefficients of similarity which are suitable for use in cluster analysis can be converted to a DC, usually by subtraction from a fixed number.

A DC on n objects can take up to $n(n-1)/2$ distinct values, one for each pair of objects. These values are normally read sequentially by the computer from an input stream or device. It is convenient, for reasons indicated below, to read the values in the following standard order.

$$2-1; 3-1, 3-2; 4-1, 4-2, 4-3; 5-1, 5-2, 5-3, 5-4; 6-1, \ldots$$

The regions between the semicolons are the strictly subdiagonal sections of the rows of the dissimilarity matrix, and when the input stream has been read as far as the appropriate semicolon the entire DC on the first i objects is known.

From the computational point of view methods of cluster analysis fall into four distinct groups; or, to be more precise, algorithms for carrying out cluster or clump methods fall into these groups, since it is quite possible for the same method to be realized by algorithms falling into different groups.

Group I algorithms are those which can process the DC value-by-value; that is to say, once a value in the input stream has been dealt with, it need not be referred to again and can be discarded from the computation. The only known cluster algorithms of this type are certain similar methods for carrying out the single-link (nearest-neighbour) method of cluster analysis; we mean here by the single-link method the process of constructing the entire single-link dendrogram, not just the determination of the clusters at some fixed threshold level. If the DC is available in the standard form described above, then the Group I algorithms for single-link are rather less efficient than the Group II algorithm described below; their real value is in cases where the DC is processed as it is generated, rather than created in its entirety and then processed, since for these algorithms the actual order of the DC values is not relevant. Group I algorithms tend to find their main applications in problems of document retrieval.

It will be convenient next to deal with the other extreme, Group IV algorithms. These are algorithms which require random access to the entire DC throughout their operation; the DC must thus be loaded into core storage, and the actual order in which it is presented is a matter of convention. Algorithms for carrying out the average-link and complete-link cluster methods are of this type; these methods are in any case deceptive and in most circumstances are better avoided. Methods for producing overlapping clusters, for example B_k (Jardine–Sibson) and C_u (Sibson) are also realized by Group IV algorithms. For some of these algorithms, in particular the reasonably efficient algorithm for B_k devised by C. J. Jardine and J. K. M. Moody, the DC values are accessed in ascending order, and only a flag-setting is needed on locations other than the one being considered; this can speed up the process, but it is still necessary to use $n(n-1)/2$ locations to store the DC.

The algorithms which are perhaps most attractive computationally are the Group II algorithms. These are algorithms which read the DC a part-row at a time and require only random access within a part-row. Two very important techniques can be realized by Group II algorithms: the single-link method; and the process of finding all maximal complete subgraphs of the graph associated with the DC at some fixed level. A Group II algorithm makes use of only up to n locations (which are re-used repeatedly) for storing the DC values. The author has developed a Group II algorithm for carrying out the single-link method; this algorithm, known as SLINK, has been programmed in standard FORTRAN. When the first i part-rows of the DC have been processed the single-link dendrogram on the first i objects is held in $2i$ storage locations (i real and i integer) as a tree structure. The vector of integers consists of pointers; $\mathbf{NA}(J)$ is the number of the highest-numbered object in the cluster which the jth object joins when it is no longer the highest-numbered object in a cluster as we go up the dendrogram. $\mathbf{HA}(J)$ is the level at which this happens. This sounds extremely complicated, but it is an easy data-structure to store and maintain. The $(i+1)$th part-row is read into the vector $\mathbf{HB}$, and it is fast and easy to generate in the vectors $\mathbf{NA}$ and $\mathbf{HA}$ a new tree-structure representing the dendrogram on the first $(i+1)$ objects. The main difference between this algorithm and one of the Group I algorithms is that certain book-keeping operations need to be done once each part-row for the SLINK algorithm and once each value for the Group I algorithm. When the tree-structure is complete for all n objects it is converted by a chaining routine into a packed form from which it is easy to draw the dendrogram, the objects being disposed automatically along the baseline in an order which allows the dendrogram to be drawn without crossovers. An extra vector of integers is used by the chaining routine as working store, so the total store requirement of the program is $4n$ locations plus overheads. Computation time increases as n^2 and is (on C. U. Titan) about 25 seconds for 100 objects, much of this being consumed by I/O processes. The practical limitation on the use of the program is the size of the largest DC which can be generated and handled as a whole.

The Group II algorithm MCSFIND which finds the maximal complete subgraphs of a graph has quite a long history. It was first programmed in Titan machine-code by J. K. M. Moody and J. Hollis, who based their algorithm on a suggestion by R. M. Needham. The current version of the algorithm incorporates modifications suggested by the author to improve efficiency, and is realized as a SNOBOL4 demonstration program by the author and BCPL working program by M. Richards. The algorithm finds all maximal complete subgraphs on the first $(i+1)$ objects from those on the first i objects and information about the links from the $(i+1)$th object; this makes it a Group II algorithm. Lists of *a priori* indeterminate length are generated by any process of finding maximal complete subgraphs, and much use is made of binary strings; both of these considerations make it essential to avoid the use of FORTRAN in programming the MCSFIND algorithm.

Certain types of clump or cluster are related to the single-link clusters. A subset of the set of objects in which for every object the remaining objects in the subset are strictly nearer neighbours to it than every object not in the subset has been called an *L*-cluster by Jardine (1969). Every *L*-cluster is a single-link cluster at some level; it is possible to find whether a single-link cluster is an *L*-cluster by a further scan of the data. Processes involving some specified number of scans of the DC after the first, but not needing random access to the DC, form Group III, so the process of finding *L*-clusters falls into this group. Van Rijsbergen has defined *L**-clusters to be subsets of the set of objects in which every within-subset link is smaller than every link from within the subset to outside it. Every *L**-cluster is an *L*-cluster (and hence a single-link cluster), but the converse is not true. The *L**-clusters are even more coherent than the *L*-clusters, and tend to be few in number or non-existent, but of great significance if they do exist. All *L**-clusters can be found from the single-link clusters in one further scan of the DC, so finding the *L**-clusters is also possible by a Group III algorithm.

Thus we see that the form of access to a standard input DC provides a convenient classification of cluster methods from the computational point of view. The two main Group II methods are very important: the single-link method because of its efficiency and because its exact mathematical properties are known; and the process of finding maximal complete subgraphs because this provides the most coherent possible clumps and is also part of the output process for various Group IV methods. The methods falling into Group III are mainly techniques for selecting good single-link clusters. The Group IV methods such as B_k are much more laborious, consuming vastly greater amounts both of space and time, but they may provide information about not-too-large-scale data which cannot readily be obtained by any simpler method.

REFERENCE

Jardine, N. (1969) Towards a general theory of clustering, *Biometrics*, **25**, 609–10.

Cluster Analysis

Herbert Solomon
Numerical taxonomy

In this paper we discuss and analyze several clustering procedures. The emphasis is strictly on multivariate data analysis and we expand only on those procedures that rely completely on the data set to obtain a grouping of individuals or elements or variables. There are three major approaches:

(1) total enumeration of all data partitions and the subsequent selection of a good or optimal clustering configuration;

(2) a step-wise clustering scheme that selects for each number of clusters the best available groupings with the realization that it may ignore some good clustering configurations in the process;

(3) reduction of multivariate data to two or three orthogonal dimensions producing a graphic or pictorial representation that permits visual clustering.

These three approaches are developed in this report and then described by application to the clustering of a data set obtained from responses to 19 socio-economic variables employed in a questionnaire submitted to approximately 225 individuals. Application of the step-wise clustering scheme is then made to several data sets that are now briefly described: (a) grouping of 82 children under observation in an aphasia clinic on the basis of 27 measurement variables applied to each child and subsequent checking of the groups with clinical prediction; (b) grouping of 560 nouns in the Russian language on the basis of their frequency of usage in each of the six grammatical cases of that language and association of groups so formed with the semantic features of the nouns in each group; (c) clustering of 238 individuals convicted of first-degree murder in California over a recent ten-year period on the basis of 25 measurements related to each defendant and the judicial process in his particular case, to study any association between these characteristics and the jury decision of death or life imprisonment for each individual; (d) clustering of 150 irises on the basis of four measurements related to petal and sepal dimensions made on each flower from Fisher's famous classification paper and subsequent checking against the three groups of irises that produced the data set; (e) the clustering of 63 measurement variables related to the characteristics of candy and association of groups so formed with the substantive meaning of variables in each group.

The socio-economic variable data set and the candy study data set may be viewed differently from the other four data sets. In those two sets we are interested in clustering measurement variables on the basis of responses made by individuals. In the other four data sets we are interested in clustering individuals or elements on the basis of responses to measurement variables. This difference will receive some discussion in the paper in so far as it affects clustering techniques.

INTRODUCTION

Data analysis has undergone a resurgence in the last two decades. In the main, this is due to the advent and development of the electronic computer and its extraordinary capacity to ingest data and spew out its product in accordance with instructions supplied by the appropriate algorithm. The eager and voluminous collection of data in the nineteenth century, especially by the British school of scholars, was denied the additional analysis it merited by the lack of a computer technology. In a very specific and substantive way, the desire of Francis Galton, Karl Pearson, and their contemporaries to analyze data, and some of the frustrations they encountered, led to mathematical modeling and the modern school of statistics.

One important aspect of data analysis that occupied the British empiricists of the last century is the subject of this exposition and constitutes the major reason for preparing this paper. Scientists and scholars have long been concerned with 'sorting things into groups' and numerical taxonomy either does this directly or serves to guide those who make such decisions. Under numerical taxonomy, we can list two categories: (1) clustering of data; (2) classification of data. The latter can be viewed as a subset of the former. In the former category, we require the data to produce both the number of groupings or clusters and the assignment of each element or individual to these groupings. In the latter category, the number of groups or clusters is pre-determined, each group is labeled, and rules are desired on the basis of which an assignment of each element is made to one of the fixed groups. Classification procedures may also be termed assignment procedures.

It is not prudent to convey a sharp distinction between clustering and classification in an operational sense. If a classification procedure is not producing meaningful groups through the assignments that are made, then changes are called for—namely, revising the pre-determined groupings either in number, or in shape, or in both on the basis of the new information. This sequential revision of groups on the basis of the data available at any one time suggests that one is indirectly engaging in clustering procedures. On the other hand, it is wise to keep in mind the conceptual differences just mentioned between attempts at clustering and attempts at classification.

DATA SUMMARIZATION AND REPRESENTATIONS

An essential step in numerical taxonomy is the representation of the associations among the variables on which data has been collected. Among other important steps, there are the processes of developing numbers to measure phenomena, making decisions on the employment of nominal, ordinal, or continuous data, and subsequent coding of this data for analysis. In this paper, we do not review these issues but we are mindful of their impact on the data analysis that will undergo investigation. Thus we return quickly to clustering and classification techniques and the basic summarizations of data for these purposes.

There are several ways to begin the data summarization. All give a picture of data inter-relationship but each has special reasons for its employment by an investigator. One representation is that of the scatter matrix. Here we portray the total scatter or dispersion displayed by n individuals or elements each measured on p variables (n points in a p-dimensional space) by a matrix with p rows and p columns where an element in the ith row and jth column, say t_{ij}, is the sum of the n cross products of measurements (taken around the mean) on variable x_i with measurements (taken around the mean) on variable x_j. In brief,

$$t_{ij} = \sum_{i<j=2}^{p} \sum_{k=1}^{n} (x_{ik} - \bar{x}_i)(x_{jk} - \bar{x}_j), \quad t_{ij} = t_{ji}, \quad \bar{x}_i = \frac{\sum_{k=1}^{n} x_{ik}}{n} .$$

Let us label this matrix T. Naturally an element in the main diagonal, say ith row and ith column, is the sum of the squares of the deviations of x_i from its mean. If $p=1$, then T is a scalar, namely

$$\sum_{k=1}^{n} (x_k - C)^2 \quad \text{where} \quad C = \frac{\sum_{k=1}^{n} x_k}{n} .$$

If each element in the scatter matrix T is divided by n, the resulting matrix is the covariance matrix with cell entries s_{ij} and we label this K. Now if we also divide each element, s_{ij}, in K by the standard deviations of x_i and x_j, the resulting element $r_{ij} = s_{ij}/s_i s_j$ is the correlation coefficient between x_i and x_j and the resulting matrix is now the correlation matrix which we label R.

An important advantage of T is the manner in which it can be decomposed into two matrices that are especially pertinent in clustering and classification studies. In a classification study, the n elements will be assigned to k pre-determined groups. Each group with, say, n_i elements can be viewed as a universe with its own scatter matrix formed as before and labeled W_i. If we sum all the W_i scatter matrices, we get $W = \sum_{i=1}^{k} W_i$ and let this represent the within scatter or homogeneity of the groupings. Likewise, if for each of the k groups, we compute the group mean (a p-dimensional vector where the rth coordinate is the mean value based on the n_r observations for x_r) and then produce the $(p \times p)$ scatter matrix for these group mean values each taken about the grand mean value (a p-dimensional vector where the rth coordinate is the mean value for x_r based on all n observations) we obtain a $(p \times p)$ matrix that we label B, for it expresses a measure of the 'betweenness' or heterogeneity of the k groups. The central point in this development is the existence of the fundamental matrix equation

$$T = W + B .$$

This result suggests immediately an index by which classification (pre-determined number of groups) can be evaluated and, by extension, how clustering can be terminated at some cluster size. For any given data set T is fixed. Thus measures of 'groupiness' or 'clusteriness' as functions of W and B are thrust forth for examination.

For $p=1$, the matrix equation reduces to an equation about scalars. Thus a good grouping index is one which minimizes W or equivalently maximizes B. We may also consider maximizing either the ratio B/W or

$T/W = 1 + B/W$. An added benefit is that this ratio is invariant under linear transformations of the data. Statisticians have long exploited this fact, for B/W multiplied by an appropriate constant is the familiar F ratio in the analysis of variance.

When the number of measurements per element is two or more ($p > 1$), grouping criteria are not so straightforward. Several possibilities suggest themselves and have been developed and studied by investigators. One criterion suggested by several authors that is a quite natural index is the minimization of the trace of W (sum of all elements in the main diagonal of the matrix) over all possible partitions into k groups. This is equivalent to maximizing trace B because

$$\text{Trace } T = \text{Trace } W + \text{Trace } B \quad .$$

However Trace W is invariant only under an orthogonal transformation and not under non-singular linear transformations.

Another criterion that may be employed for $p > 1$ is the ratio of the determinants

$$|T|/|W| = |1 + W^{-1}B| \quad .$$

We can use $|T|/|W|$ as a criterion for grouping and select that grouping for which this index is maximized, or equivalently $|W|$ is minimized. Also we may employ $\log(|T|/|W|)$ since it is a monotonic function.

Another criterion for grouping is the trace of $W^{-1}B$ and we select the grouping that maximizes this index. This index has been used as a test statistic in multivariate statistical analysis as has the ratio $|W|/|T|$. The latter was employed by Wilks to test whether groups differ in mean values, and the former has been put forth by Hotelling in some situations and by Rao as a generalization of the Mahalanobis distance between two groups for $k > 2$ groups. We will shortly define and discuss the implications and uses of the Mahalanobis distance in clustering procedures.

Both Trace ($W^{-1}B$) and $|T|/|W|$ may be expressed in terms of the eigenvalues, λ_i, of the matrix $W^{-1}B$. We write

$$|T|/|W| = \prod_{i=1}^{n}(1 + \lambda_i)$$

and $\quad$ Trace $W^{-1}B = \sum_{i=1}^{p} \lambda_i$

where λ_i are the roots of the determinantal equation, $|B - \lambda W| = 0$. The characterization of these ratios in terms of eigenvalues is helpful in data representation especially when the effects of some reduction in dimensionality is desired. All the eigenvalues of this equation are invariant under non-singular linear transformations of the data. It can be proved that these eigenvalues are the only invariants of W and B under non-singular linear transformations.

DISTANCE MATRIX

Thus far we have discussed some summarization of multivariate data in matrix form, either T (scatter), K (covariance), or R (correlation) and the kinds of grouping criteria that are suggested by the T format. Intuitively, we see that any grouping criterion is a function of homogeneity within groups,

5

and heterogeneity between groups and the indexes already described are specific quantities embodying these notions. We shall discuss other indexes as we proceed but each will be a function of homogeneity within groups and heterogeneity between groups in which attempts will be made to minimize the former, maximize the latter, or do both. For the correlation coefficient index, large values indicate homogeneity; small values indicate heterogeneity.

Another method of summarizing data that is more appropriate on occasion is to find the distance between each pair of the n points in p-dimensional space. This leads to a representation in matrix form of an $n \times n$ matrix where each element, in the ith row and the jth column, say d_{ij}, is the distance in the p-dimensional space between the ith element or individual and the jth element or individual. All the elements in the main diagonal are zero. The distance matrix is akin to the correlation matrix in that both may be viewed as similarity matrices—the jumping-off place for clustering and classification attempts.

The decision as to whether correlation matrices or distance matrices are to be employed is usually determined by the problem at hand. If n individuals or n elements are to be grouped on the basis of p measurements on each, then the $n \times n$ distance matrix is the natural summarization; if the p measurement variables are to be grouped on the basis of the measurements on n individuals or n elements, then the $p \times p$ correlation matrix is the natural summarization of the data. This latter matrix is the natural beginning point in factor analysis where parsimony in the number of latent measurement variables is the desired goal. We will return to factor analysis and its place in clustering in subsequent sections. In some taxonomic situations the question of which measure of similarity to employ, whether it is of the association or distance type, will require some thought. While we will touch on these points, these inquiries will not be featured in this exposition.

The issue of choice of correlation matrix or distance matrix will be placed in sharper focus by the six specific data bases on which we will attempt clustering. Before this is done, there still remains some discussion of appropriate distance measures. Because we will normally think of our data bases in clustering individuals or elements as n points in a p-dimensional space, the distance measures usually appropriate and available are Euclidean distance and Mahalanobis distance. The Euclidean distance between individuals or elements with respect to all p measurement variables may be written in vector notation

$$d_{ij}^2 = (\mathbf{P}_i - \mathbf{P}_j)'(\mathbf{P}_i - \mathbf{P}_j)$$

where d_{ij} is the Euclidean distance between individual i and individual j, $\mathbf{P}_i$ and $\mathbf{P}_j$ are column vectors each with p rows listing the p measurements on the ith and jth individuals respectively. The product of the difference row vector $(\mathbf{P}_i - \mathbf{P}_j)'$ by its transpose is a scalar. This is the distance function with which most of us are familiar. The Mahalanobis distance may be written as in the notation above as

$$_M d_{ij}^2 = (\mathbf{P}_i - \mathbf{P}_j)' W^{-1} (\mathbf{P}_i - \mathbf{P}_j)$$

where W^{-1} is the inverse matrix of $W = \sum_{i=1}^{k} W_i$ and W_i is obtained for each of the $i = 1, 2, \ldots, k$ groups by

$$W_i = \sum_{m=1}^{n_i} (P_{mi} - C_i)(P_{mi} - C_i)' \; .$$

Note that a grouping of elements is necessary to compute W_i and W. Thus the Mahalanobis distance takes into account the associations or inter-relationships in the measurement variables. If two measurement variables are highly correlated, the Euclidean distance can be misleading because of the equal weight it imposes inaccurately on each measurement variable, but this will not be so with the Mahalanobis distance. The Mahalanobis distance is more tedious to compute and for a long time it was avoided for this reason alone but the computer has brought it within reach. Actually if each of the correlations between the measurement variables is low, the error in employing the Euclidean distance is not damaging. As a rule of thumb, correlations as high as 0·5 will not produce Euclidean distances that lead to operational difficulties.

Other distance measures appear in the literature. The Minkowski distance is the name applied to all distance measures that are of the form

$$d(i, j) = \left\{ \sum_{m=1}^{p} |x_{im} - x_{jm}|^n \right\}^{1/n} \; .$$

We have discussed the case $n = 2$. When $n = 1$, the label 'city-block' distance is sometimes employed and it may be relevant for some distance situations.

DEVELOPMENT

The major thrust of this exposition will be the application to six specific data sets of the concepts discussed previously and the development of several clustering procedures. Before we get to the data sets, let us examine several clustering procedures. Recall that we are dealing with n points in a p-dimensional space and trying to group the n points except when we are interested in grouping the p measurement variables. In the former situation, we begin with an $n \times n$ distance matrix, and in the latter the $p \times p$ correlation matrix is the basic summarization. Conceptually we can list all the possible clustering configurations achieved by dividing the n points (individuals or elements) into k clusters each containing at least one element. If for each clustering configuration an appropriate index for grouping could be computed—some have already been mentioned and discussed—we could then list and rank all the configurations by this index and select the best one. Operationally we could do this for each value of k as $k = 1, 2, \ldots, n$. For example, $k = 1$ means putting all elements in one cluster and $k = n$ means considering each point as a cluster with one element. However this is an impossible task even for a computer when n and p are only moderate in size.

A TOTAL ENUMERATION PROCEDURE

In a paper by Fortier and Solomon (1966) an attempt was made, for one specific data set, to look into total enumeration of all clustering partitions and then to select the best clustering by the use of an appropriate index. The data set consisted of 19 socio-economic measurement variables for which responses were available from approximately 225 individuals. The investigators of this study, Kahl and Davis (1955), were interested in replacing the 19 variables by a set of fewer measurement variables, and intended accomplishing this by a cluster analysis of the data employing Tryon's technique (Tryon 1939). In this technique clustering is begun by inspection of the correlation coefficients to achieve an initial clustering partition and the process ends after a number of iterations of the initial partitioning. Each iteration, including the first, is examined by an index that is essentially the ratio of the heterogeneity between groups and the homogeneity within groups, and the clustering (or iterations) stops when no appreciable gain is registered by the index. Note that inspection looms very large in clustering and this has ramifications for computer usage.

Employing this technique Kahl and Davis (1955) terminated the process with a partitioning that placed the 19 variables into 8 clusters as listed in table 1. (Variables 5 and 7 are omitted.) This table also presents the results obtained by Fortier and Solomon employing a modification of the concept of total enumeration. We now offer some discussion of the latter procedure.

Clusters*	Kahl–Davis results employing Tryon's method	Fortier–Solomon C^* method
1	12. Area rating 14. House rating	The same variables
2	15. Subject's father's education 9. Subject's mother's education	The same variables
3	2. Friend's occupation 17. Wife's education	The same variables
4	4. Subject's occupation, Census 1. Subject's occupation, Warner 10. Source of income	The same variables
5	16. Wife's father's occupation, North-Hatt 6. Wife's father's occupation	Not a cluster
6	11. Census tract 18. Income	Not a cluster
7	3. Subject's education 8. Subject's self identification	The same variable
8	19. Subject's father's occupation, North-Hatt 13. Subject's father's occupation, Census	Not a cluster

* The clusters are ordered by decreasing values of Tryon's index.

Table 1. Results of clustering procedures

If we were to examine all possible partitions of 19 variables into 8 clusters we would soon give up the attempt for there are 1,709,751,003,480 distinct partitions. In addition we should also look at the partitionings obtained when 19 variables are allocated to $k = 2, 3, ..., 7, 9, ..., 18$ clusters and this also would be most formidable. Actually the number of distinct partitions of n elements into k groups, say $P_{n,m}$ is a Sterling number of the second kind and obeys the recursion formula

$$P_{n,m} = mP_{n-1,m} + P_{n-1,m-1} \quad .$$

This permits easy construction of a table, and one appears in Fortier and Solomon (1966) for $m = 2, 3, \ldots, 18$; $n = 3, 4, \ldots, 19$.

To overcome the large universes generated by total enumeration of clustering partitions, Fortier and Solomon tried random sampling. Using a computer, they obtained 10,000 clusterings by unrestricted random sampling for each fixed size of number of clusters $k = 2, 3, \ldots, 18$ (170,000 clustering configurations in all). These results were disappointing. In fact, the specific Kahl and Davis clustering result of 19 variables in 8 clusters, obtained through Tryon's method of constructing clusters sequentially, had a value for their clustering index larger than the best value of that clustering index obtained from our 10,000 partitions for $k = 8$. The clustering index employed was essentially the Holzinger 'coefficient of belongingness'—an index that measures the ratio of heterogeneity between groups to homogeneity within groups, by employing the ratio of the average correlation of all pairs of variables not in the same group to the average correlation of all pairs of variables that are in a group (over all groups).

Fortier and Solomon proposed a new clustering index and this was employed on the Kahl–Davis data. It is developed in the following way. Let two variables be clustered if the correlation coefficient, say ρ, is greater than some preassigned constant ρ^*. The gain (positive or negative) incurred by taking an action a could be expressed by $G_{ij}(a)$. Suppose we let $\rho^{*2} = 0.50$ for purposes of exposition since $\rho \geq 0.7$ signifies a close relationship. Then we may write

$$G_{ij}(a) = (\rho_{ij}^2 - 0.5)[g_{ij}(a)]$$

where

$$g_{ij}(a) = \begin{cases} +1 & \text{if the } i\text{th and } j\text{th variables are put in same cluster} \\ -1 & \text{otherwise.} \end{cases}$$

Now sum over all pairs once a clustering configuration is fixed, and we obtain a value, call it C, where

$$C(A) = \sum_{i<j} G_{ij}(a_{ij}) \quad ,$$

a_{ij} is the specific action taken for the pair (i, j), and A is the matrix of those a_{ij}s. Observe that some a_{ij}s depend on others. For instance, if the pair (X_2, X_3) is in the same cluster and this is so for the pair (X_3, X_4), then the pair (X_2, X_4) is also in the same cluster.

Let us now consider as foci of clusters only those pairs where $D_{ij} = (\rho_{ij}^2 - 0.5)$ are positive, or in other words the pair of variables are closely associated. In this way we may eliminate a large number of clustering partitions from evaluation — those that should not be examined because they never could produce optimal values of the clustering index C.

For the Kahl–Davis 19×19 correlation matrix, the resulting D matrix has 16 positive values. This suggests an examination of from one to 16 clusters. There may be less than 16 clusters, as we shall see soon, even if one chooses to include all 16 pairs in the analysis. Before we do this, a closer examination of the index C, shows

$$C(A) = 2 \sum_{(i,j \in S)} D_{ij} - \sum_{i<j} D_{ij}$$

where S is the set of pairs of variables that belong to the same cluster. Thus the critical quantity is

$$C^* = \sum_{(i,j \in S)} D_{ij} \quad .$$

This is so because $\sum_{i<j} D_{ij}$ is a constant for any fixed data set. It is the sum of the elements of the lower half of the D matrix and each element is fixed when ρ_{ij} and ρ^* are given.

We would like C^* to be as large as possible and we hope to achieve this maximum value by a quick selection of positive D_{ij}s. In general, the choice of, say, r of the D_{ij}s leads to $k \leqslant r$ clusters and to $s \geqslant r$ elements in the summing evaluation of C^*. If $k<r$, then $s>r$, since at least two pairs (three or more variables) are grouped together, introducing one or more new D_{ij} values.

In mathematical terms one must maximize C^*, but choosing the appropriate partition of the n variables into k clusters is a matter of judicious selection more by inspection procedures than by algebraic techniques. For the Kahl–Davis data, the set of partitions to be investigated consists of all r pairs out of the 16 positive D_{ij}s. Each time, D_{ij}s will be chosen implicitly and these must be summed together with the r D_{ij}s already chosen. There are $\binom{16}{r}$ possible combinations for each value of r and these represent a heavy work-load for all values of r from 2 to 15. However, this was done for all the combinations associated with each value of r from the Kahl–Davis data and the maximum C^* was obtained for each r.

If we plot the maximum C^* as a function of r, we find for the Kahl–Davis data that the optimal value of r is 6 and, for this data set, leads to five clusters. The curve depicting max C^* as a function of r rises sharply as r increases, then reaches a plateau, and then decreases sharply. The plateau stage is reached where the marginal gain due to clustering no longer increases with added clusters and this is the value of r that is optimal. This feature is typical of clustering indexes when the optimal value of the index for each cluster size is plotted against number of clusters. These clusterings are listed in table 1 where we see that five out of the eight clusters obtained by Kahl–Davis employing the Tryon technique are reproduced. There is a striking resemblance between the two listings—one obtained by expertise and iteration, the other by strict enumeration of an admissible set of partitions evaluated by an objective index based on gain (or loss) incurred by an assignment action of variables to a cluster.

The Kahl–Davis data set of 19 measurement variables can serve as a base for examination of other clustering techniques, and we continue along these lines before examining other data sets. A rapid clustering technique has been provided by King (1967). It does not guarantee optimal or sub-optimal clusterings but is done rather quickly on a computer. When King applied it to the Kahl–Davis data, it provided clusterings very similar to the one produced in that paper and to the cluster listing obtained from the C^* method. This is a staggering development because the computer time involved for the King procedure is infinitesimal compared with that for the Fortier–Solomon technique.

A STEP-WISE CLUSTERING PROCEDURE

The procedure proposed by King is a step-wise clustering procedure. This is its principal asset because it leads to a simple and quick algorithm that involves $(n-1)$ scannings of a correlation matrix based on n variables. At each scanning or pass, the variables are sorted into a number of groups that is one less than at the previous pass. In this way, we obtain $(n-k)$ groups of variables at the kth scanning. The $(n \times n)$ matrix can also be a distance matrix. In that case, we sort individuals or elements into groups.

The procedure operates as follows. We will employ the correlation matrix as our similarity matrix for expository purposes, and bring in the distance matrix when appropriate to highlight differences.

As a start, we can view the n variables as n groups, one variable to each group. Now scan the correlation matrix for the maximum cell entry (naturally without regard to sign). In a distance matrix we would seek the minimum distance cell entry. Suppose the maximum correlation is between variables X_i and X_j. Label it $r_{i'j'}$. We place X_i and X_j in the same group and we now have $(n-1)$ groups $X_1, X_2, ..., (X_i, X_j), ..., X_{n-1}, X_n$. This produces an $(n-1) \times (n-1)$ correlation matrix, all pairs of correlation coefficients over the original $(n-2)$ variables plus the correlations obtained by pairing each of these with the concocted variable $X_i + X_j = Y_{ij}$. Essentially, we are representing the group of two elements by its centroid.

On the second pass of what is now an $(n-1) \times (n-1)$ correlation matrix, a third variable may join the group of two variables formed on the first pass if the correlation between it and Y_{ij} is maximum, or the maximum correlation value in the reduced correlation matrix may again involve two individual variables. Thus we would get either one group of three variables and $(n-3)$ groups each containing one variable, or two groups each containing two variables and $(n-4)$ groups each containing one variable. In either situation we merge variables and revise the correlation matrix as on the first pass. In the former case, the centroid of the group of three variables represents its group, and in the latter case, each group with two variables is represented by its centroid. Recall that we do not have to divide the sum of the variables by the number of variables to obtain the centroid because the correlation coefficient is invariant when one variable of the pair is always multiplied by the same constant.

Thus, at each pass, the two groups with the highest correlations are merged and the total number of groups to that point is reduced by one. After a variable has joined a group of variables it cannot be removed from that group. In this way it is possible to miss an optimal grouping. This is very similar to selection of predictors in step-wise linear regression. It should also be mentioned that a group can lose its identity by merging with another group on a later pass. By the time all the scanning is completed we have produced successively $(n-1), (n-2), (n-3), ..., 3, 2$ groupings.

The clustering index employed by King for measuring the worth of the grouping is that of minimum correlation (or maximal distance) between the group centroids when the scanning has placed the n variables into two groups. He also reviews another index, suggested originally by Wilks for testing the mutual independence of k subsets of n multivariate normal random variables. In terms of what we described earlier in the paper, the index is the ratio of the determinants

$$Z = \frac{|T|}{\prod_{i=1}^{k} |W_i|}$$

where T is the scatter matrix defined previously and each W_i is the scatter matrix for each of the k groups.

This index has some nice geometrical and statistical properties. For example, when $k=2$,

$$Z = \frac{|T|}{|W_1| \cdot |W_2|} = \prod (1 - r_i^2)$$

where r_i is the ith canonical correlation between the two sets of variables. This index may be viewed as a 'generalized alienation coefficient' since it is an extension of $1 - R^2$, where R is the multiple correlation coefficient occurring when two groups have one variable in one group and $(n-1)$ in the other. However it is not too useful in some data analyses, especially in social science, because a number of data sets lead to quasi-singular correlation matrices and truncation error can give ridiculous results. For this reason, and possibly others, negative determinants appear and make it impossible to employ the Wilks index. The Kahl–Davis data, where tetrachoric correlations were employed, produces a negative determinant. This will present a slight problem we will discuss later when we do a factor analysis on this data set in connection with the use of factor analysis as a clustering tool.

Thus, King employed his first clustering index in examining the $(n-1)$ scannings of his step-wise clustering procedure on the Kahl–Davis data. He then compared his results with those of the original authors and with the Fortier–Solomon C^* method. In his article, we note that, on his sixth pass, he obtains 13 clusters that reproduce exactly the Fortier–Solomon results if we count the isolates in their results as clusters with one member.

We will employ this clustering technique on other data sets but, as mentioned previously, we continue first with other clustering techniques that we will apply to the 19 socio-economic variables in the Kahl–Davis data. At this point we turn to an older technique originally proposed for quite another purpose. Factor analysis was developed in the early years of this century to provide a conceptual model for mental measurement. This was the intent of Spearman, Thomson, and the early workers in the field. However, the extensions by Thurstone, Kelley, and others into multiple common factor analysis brought it somewhat afield from the designs of the initiators. Their work in multiple linear common factor analysis, coupled with Hotelling's fundamental papers (Hotelling 1933a,b) on principal component solutions and the computational algorithm to make that method feasible, have brought us to what we term 'factor analysis' today. In effect, what we now have is a research tool for achieving parsimony by expressing the total variation found in n correlated variables in terms of $m \leqslant n$ orthogonal variables with the added hope that m is much smaller than n. Thus by factor analysis we secure another representation of the data, and if this can be done economically, say by reducing the n oblique dimensions to two or three orthogonal dimensions, it becomes easier to group data.

The coming of the computer has made it possible to do principal component factor analyses rather quickly. A computer program for this technique exists in many computation centers. Even if the number of orthogonal dimensions produced by principal components is more than two, we can employ the first two dimensions to represent the data, and measure the error in doing this. Principal component factors are produced in order of their contribution to the total variation in the data—the first is the largest, the second the next largest, and so on. Moreover, the contribution that the ith factor makes to the total variation is equal to the ratio of the ith largest eigenvalue of the correlation matrix to n, the number of variables. Thus if we employ only the first two principal components, we know how much of the total variation in the data is still unexplained when the representation of n correlated variables in two orthogonal dimensions is attempted.

The Kahl–Davis data was subjected to factor analysis. No principal

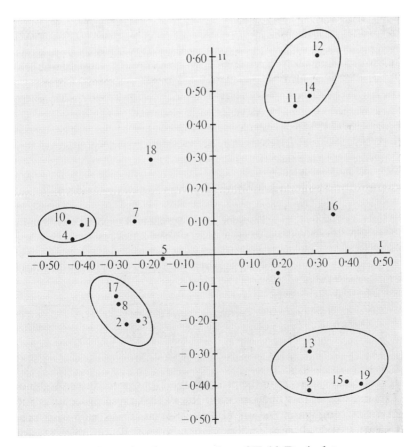

Figure 1. Two-dimensional representation of Kahl–Davis data

component solution was attempted because, as mentioned previously, the data correlation matrix is not positive definite. It was possible, however, to do a Thurstone centroid solution. This was then followed by a simple structure rotation. The reader is referred to Thurstone's text (1947) for an account of these techniques. Suffice it to say that once this is accomplished, the first two factor loadings (coefficients of the linear form in the m factors) can now serve to represent the 19 variables. These are plotted on a graph in figure 1. By eye, the points (variables) are grouped as follows (11, 12, 14), (9, 13, 15, 19), (1, 4, 10), (2, 3, 8, 17), and 5, 6, 7, 16, and 18 remain as isolates or groups of one element. Naturally we can still assign these to one of the four groups. In table 2, this clustering is compared with the Kahl–Davis results, the Fortier–Solomon C^* results, and the King step-wise clustering procedure results.

Clusters*	Tryon's method Variables	Fortier–Solomon C^* method	King step-wise procedure	Two-dimensional representation
1	12. Area rating	The same variables	The same variables	The same variables merged with 11
	14. House rating			
2	15. Subject's father's education			
	9. Subject's mother's education	The same variables	The same variables	The same variables merged with 13, 1
3	2. Friend's occupation	The same variables	The same variables	The same variables merged with 3, 8
	17. Wife's education			
4	4. Subject's occupation Census		The same variables	
	1. Subject's occupation, Warner	The same variables	merged with variables 3, 8, 5, and 7	The same variables
	10. Source of income			
5	16. Wife's father's occupation, North-Hatt	Not a cluster	Not a cluster	Not a cluster
	6. Wife's father's occupation, Census			
6	11. Census tract	Not a cluster	Not a cluster	Not a cluster
	18. Income			
7	3. Subject's education			
	8. Subject's self-identification	The same variables	*See* cluster 4 above	*See* cluster 3 above
8	19. Subject's father's occupation, North-Hatt	Not a cluster	Not a cluster	*See* cluster 2 above
	13. Subject's father's occupation, Census			

* The clusters are ordered by decreasing values of Tryon's index.

Table 2. Clustering of the 17 of 19 variables in Kahl–Davis data (variables 5 and 7 are omitted) by 4 clustering procedures

There is remarkable overlap in the product of all four procedures. A glance at table 2 demonstrates this phenomenon. Recall that these procedures run the gamut from total enumeration (Fortier–Solomon) to step-wise procedures (King) to two-dimensional representation of 19 variables (factor analysis) to expertise followed by sequential modification (Tryon). All this suggests that, for exploratory purposes, an investigator should try the simplest or most economical procedure since in many cases these will give meaningful clusters. These can then be adjusted by expertise, other methods, or both.

We have omitted a host of other methods that employ expertise in the clustering scheme. The methods we have described in detail force the data to tell the clustering story. Thus we are captives of both the actual clustering configurations we are trying to assess from the data and the coarseness of the measurement variables, or both. Our exploratory clustering procedures can be viewed as providing an initial partitioning for those who then wish to employ their own knowledge or conjectures to modify the clustering configuration. There are several papers in the literature and no doubt more will appear that deal principally with sequential modification of a specific clustering partition. Each modification is checked by the value of the clustering index employed by the investigator and naturally he seeks partitionings whose index values suggest that a good or optimal clustering has been achieved. As we mentioned earlier, we are not featuring any of these techniques in this paper. For those investigators who wish to begin with a partitioning and do not employ the techniques we have discussed in detail or do not attempt guesses, a random partitioning can serve as a beginning. Sequential modifications may take longer until a desirable partitioning is achieved, but if several random starts lead in a majority of the cases to the same or roughly the same clustering, one has more confidence in the results.

OTHER DATA SETS

Total enumeration (Fortier–Solomon), step-wise clustering (King), and factor analysis as a tool to achieve parsimony in data representation have been discussed in detail and applied to the Kahl–Davis data set of 19 socioeconomic variables. Each of these techniques relies only on the data to achieve a clustering partition as contrasted with, say, the Tryon technique employed by Kahl and Davis, which employed sequential modification of an initial partitioning.

With the total enumeration results for the Kahl–Davis data set made available by Fortier and Solomon as a base, we noted that the King technique and the factor analysis approach gave very good results. This was true for the Tryon procedure also, but we emphasize the others because they rely only on the data and thus do not require any expertise except for the clustering algorithms.

Let us now try these on other data sets that were identified briefly at the start of the paper. In the spirit of exploratory analysis and because of limitations on space we will report only on the employment of the King step-wise clustering procedure on these data sets. We will see how informative clusterings are obtained for each data set with a nominal amount of computer time, although the pre-computer preparation effort may take some time, as it would for any clustering procedure.

Children from an Aphasia Clinic. 82 children under observation at the Aphasia Institute, Stanford School of Medicine, were placed in one of 7

```
P= 78        B= 3            M= 23
CORR. COEF. = 0.2754D 00
  1  35004 72024 40300 32005 30330 03310 00320 02002 30300 30320 03060 06302 06030 00633 00303 26360 0000
  3  00720 00100 05014 00110 01001 10007 17001 30730 01017 04003 50003 70000 30106 30000 11030 00001 1000
 59  00000 00000 00000 00000 00000 00000 00000 00000 00000 03000 00000 00030 00000 00000 00000 00000 0000
 67  00000 00000 00000 00000 00000 00000 00000 00000 00000 00000 00000 00000 00000 06000 00000 00000 0000
 82  00000 00000 00000 00000 00000 00030 00000 00000 00000 00000 00000 00000 00000 00000 00000 00000 0300
 84  00000 00000 00000 00000 00000 00000 00000 00000 00000 00000 00000 00000 00000 00000 00000 00000 0006

P= 79        B= 1            M= 84
CORR. COEF. = 0.2619D 00
  1  35004 72024 40300 32005 30330 03310 00320 02002 30300 30320 03060 06302 06030 00633 00303 26360 0006
  3  00720 00100 05014 00110 01001 10007 17001 30730 01017 04003 50003 70000 30106 30000 11030 00001 1000
 59  00000 00000 00000 00000 00000 00000 00000 00000 00000 00000 00000 00030 00000 00000 00000 00000 0000
 67  00000 00000 00000 00000 00000 00000 00000 00000 00000 00000 00000 00000 00000 06000 00000 00000 0000
 82  00000 00000 00000 00000 00000 00000 00000 00000 00000 00000 00000 00000 00000 00000 00000 00000 0300

P= 80        B= 1            M= 67
CORR. COEF. = 0.1782D 00
  1  35004 72024 40300 32005 30330 03310 00320 02002 30300 30320 03060 06302 06030 06633 00303 26360 0006
  3  00720 00100 05014 00110 01001 10007 17001 30730 01017 04003 50003 70000 30106 30000 11030 00001 1000
 59  00000 00000 00000 00000 00000 00000 00000 00000 00000 00000 00000 00000 00000 00000 00000 00000 0000
 82  00000 00000 00000 00000 00000 00000 00000 00000 00000 00000 00000 00000 00000 06000 00000 00000 0300

P= 81        B= 1            M= 82
CORR. COEF. = 0.1814D 00
  1  35004 72024 40300 32005 30330 03310 00320 02002 30300 30320 03060 06302 06030 06633 00303 26360 0306
  3  00720 00100 05014 00110 01001 10007 17001 30730 01017 04003 50003 70000 30106 30000 11030 00001 1000
 59  00000 00000 00000 00000 00000 00000 00000 00000 00000 00000 00000 00030 00000 00000 00000 00000 0000

P= 82        B= 1            M= 3
CORR. COEF. = 0.9966D-01
  1  35724 72124 31331 45314 32115 13317 17321 32732 31317 34323 53063 76302 36136 36633 11333 26361 1306
 59  00000 00000 00000 00000 00000 00000 00000 00000 00000 00000 00000 00030 00000 00000 00000 00000 0000

P= 83        B= 1            M= 59
CORR. COEF. =-0.4269D-01
  1  35724 72124 31331 45314 32115 13317 17321 32732 31317 34323 53063 76332 36136 36633 11353 26361 1306
```

Table 3. Step-wise clustering for 82 aphasic children. Computer printout

diagnostic categories by the staff. On the basis of 27 physiological, psychological, and biographical measurements of each child, the 82 children were clustered by King's step-wise procedure. In this case, the summarization was an 82×82 distance matrix. Each cell entry was the Mahalanobis distance in 27-dimensional space between a pair of children. From the clustering printout in table 3 it appears that there are two clusters of children. One contains those classified clinically as 2, 3, and 6 and the other cluster contains those classified clinically as 1 and 7. The number of children in categories 4 and 5 are too small to give information. The categories are shown in table 4.

Category	Diagnosis	No. of children
1	Mentally retarded	17
2	Severe hearing impairment	10
3	Neurologically handicapped/aphasic	30
4	Oral apraxia	5
5	Dysarthric	4
6	Maturational lag	9
7	Autistic	7
	Total	82

Table 4

Thus it appears that the 24 children in categories 1 and 7 are alike and the 49 children in categories 2, 3, and 6, are alike, a conclusion accepted subsequently by the staff as more in line with suggested treatment. This effort was aided in large measure by my colleague, Professor Jon Eisenson of the Stanford Medical School, who brought the data to my attention.

Nouns in Russian. 590 nouns in the Russian language for which frequency of usage in each of six grammatical cases was available were studied for any association between such usage and the semantic content of the nouns. The data come from a frequency study of Russian by Shtejnfeldt (1963). The work contains information on 961 common nouns but the linguistic study of this data by my colleague, Professor Joseph M. Greenberg, Stanford Anthropology Department, was reduced to 590 nouns, mainly because of the limitations of the computer. In this situation, we computed the Mahalanobis distance between all pairs of nouns in the six-dimensional space created by the relative frequency of usage of a noun in each of the six cases. A King step-wise clustering procedure was employed on this data set and produced meaningful clusters for Professor Greenberg. The grouping of personal individual nouns as against all others appears quite convincingly. For example, after the 400th pass, there are, of course, 160 groups. Of these 102 have only one or two nouns. In the remaining 58 groups with 3 or more members, there are 8 groups which contain 69 of the 86 personal individual nouns in the set. Nineteen of the place words appear in three groups along with ten other nouns most of which have, however, a 'place feature' such as class, ship, conference. A group of 4 has the membership: window, table, desk, chair.

PASS=137   B= 1   M= 15
DISTANCE BETWEEN B,M = 0.318019E 01

```
          1 11111 11111 11111 11110 11111 11111 11111 11111 11111 10111 11111 11111

   25  00000 00000 00000 00001 00000 00000 00000 00000 00000 00000 01000 00000 00000   48
   42  00000 00000 00000 00000 00000 00000 00000 00000 00000 00000 00000 00000 00000    1
   51  00000 00000 00000 00000 00000 00000 00000 03000 03000 00000 00000 20000 00000    1
   52  22200 00000 00000 00200 00300 30330 00000 03000 20202 30000 00000 00000 02002   23
   54  00000 00000 00000 00000 00003 00330 30333 00200 30003 03033 00300 00000 03000   24
   56  00002 22200 00220 00020 00000 00000 00000 00020 00020 03033 00000 20020 00300   17
  101  00020 00022 22002 03030 00000 00000 00030 03000 00030 00000 00003 00300 00003   24
  107  00000 00000 00000 00000 00000 03000 00000 00000 00000 00000 00000 00000 00030    3
  118  00300 00000 30000 00000 00000 00000 00000 00000 00000 00000 00000 00000 00000    1
  135  00000 00000 00000 00000 00030 00000 00000 00030 03000 30000 00300 00030 00000    4
  136  00000 00000 00000 00000 00000 00000 00000 00000 00000 00000 00003 00000 00000    1
  142  00000 00000 00000 00000 30000 00000 00000 00000 00000 00000 00000 30000 00000    1
        00000 00000 00000 00000 00000 00000 00000 00000 00000 00000 00000 03000 30000    2
```

TIME FOR THAT PASS WAS   0.37 SECONDS

```
PASS=138           B= 52           M= 56
DISTANCE BETWEEN B,M = 0.334658E 01
   1  11111 11111 11111 1.110 11111 11111 11111 10111 11111 00000 11111 00000 00000 00000 00000 00000    48

  25  00000 00000 00000 00000 00000 00000 00000 00000 00000 00000 00000 00000 00000 00000 00000 00000     1
  42  00000 00000 00000 00000 00000 00000 00000 01000 00000 00300 00000 00000 00000 00000 00000 00000     1
  51  22200 00000 02000 00000 00200 00000 00000 00000 00000 20202 00020 30000 20000 02002 02002 03000    23
  52  00000 03000 00000 22002 22002 30000 00000 00030 02000 22002 02000 22022 02200 02200 03000 20020    48
  54  00000 02202 00000 03033 00003 30333 00000 00000 02000 00333 00330 00200 00022 00022 00303 00290    17
 101  00002 22200 00202 00000 00000 00000 00000 00003 00003 00000 00000 00000 00000 00000 00000 00000     3
 107  00000 00000 00000 00000 30000 00000 03000 00000 00000 00000 00000 00000 00000 00000 00030 00030     1
 118  00000 00000 00000 00000 00000 00000 03000 30000 30000 03000 00000 00000 00000 00000 00000 00000     4
 135  00000 00000 00000 00000 00000 00000 00000 00300 00300 00000 00000 00000 00000 00000 00030 00030     1
 136  00000 00000 00000 00000 00000 00000 00000 00000 00000 00000 00000 30000 30000 00000 00000 00000     1
 142  00000 00000 00000 00000 00000 00000 00000 00000 00000 00000 00000 00000 00000 00000 03000 30000     2

TIME FOR THAT PASS WAS    0.34 SECONDS
```

Table 5. Step-wise clustering for Fisher data on 150 Irises. Computer printout for 137th and 138th passes

Another group consists of three members: foot, nose, ear. All in all there is a general impression of lawfulness in the manner in which the groupings of nouns appear. Certainly the distribution of frequency over the cases in Russian is far from random in relation to the semantic characteristics of nouns.

Individuals convicted of murder. 238 individuals convicted of first-degree murder in California over a recent ten-year period were studied on the basis of 25 measurements each as to whether an association existed between their 25-dimensional descriptions and the penalty decision that resulted in life imprisonment for 135 and capital punishment for 103. These 25 variables consisted of biographical information on the individual, description of the crime, information on defense counsel, the prosecution, and the judge. A King step-wise clustering procedure was employed to cluster the 238 individuals and then seek a substantive association, if any, between the characteristics of the individual, characteristics of the crime, the judicial process, and the penalty decision. My thanks for the data under analysis go to several Law Review students at Stanford with whom I worked on this study. One of their major concerns was to see if there were any association between the penalty decided upon by a jury, which under the law is given no instruction on standards to be employed in arriving at a decision, and socio-economic characteristics or racial and ethnic background of the individual. Either of these would be unconstitutional under the 14th Amendment to the US Constitution; a matter presently under review by the Supreme Court, where a petitioner has claimed that standardless sentencing violates the Constitution. The clustering printout did not reveal any significant associations between penalty and whether the defendant was black, Mexican–American, or white; or whether the defendant was a blue-collar worker or not. At the 58th pass, there was one significant group that contained 18 members, all of whom had received the life penalty. As the number of passes increased, this group remained the principal group until the last few passes. At the 75th step the group contained 34 members, of whom 30 received life imprisonment. At the 100th step the group contained 42 life cases out of 62 members and at the 125th step, the group contained 63 life cases out of 102 members—a 62 to 38 per cent composition which should be measured against the 55 to 45 per cent mixture for all 238 cases. What we seem to be getting is clustering indicating very little or no association of penalty with defendant and judicial characteristics. This may also have judicial implications; for a penalty jury is, in effect, tossing for each defendant a coin which lands head or tail in a 55 to 45 per cent ratio.

Irises. In Fisher's well-known paper on the linear discriminant function, he employed three groups of irises, each containing 50 members. Sepal width and length, petal width and length were obtained for each of the 150 irises— 50 *Iris Setosa*, 50 *Iris Virginica*, 50 *Iris Versicolor*. We will assume only that we have 150 irises represented as points in a four-dimensional space which we wish to cluster by the King step-wise clustering scheme. The results are interesting. The *Iris Setosa* are quite different from the other two, which overlap a great deal. Thus we find at the 137th pass that there is a cluster of

48 members, each an *Iris Setosa*, there are four clusters containing 23, 24, 17, and 24 members respectively, with 12, 4, 16, and 18 *Iris Versicolor* respectively, all demonstrating the natural overlap between *Iris Versicolor* and *Iris Virginica*. At the very next pass (138th) the two groups with 24 members each merge into a group with 48 members, 22 *Iris Versicolor* and 26 *Iris Virginica*. (The computer printout for these passes is shown in table 5.) Thus when there is real and decided overlap the step-wise clustering scheme reflects it; but if we did not know of the original three groups we would be hard-pressed for a decision, and obviously would have to resort to additional techniques, or expertise, or both.

Candy. In connection with a candy-marketing study, a questionnaire containing 63 items was given to four hundred teenagers. These items fell into queries on candy content, motivation for eating candy, and situations in which candy is eaten. As in the Kahl–Davis data, and in contrast to the other studies, an attempt was made to achieve fewer measurement variables by clustering the 63 items. Thus we have a 63×63 correlation matrix, each entry based on 400 observations, and we employ the King step-wise clustering scheme. At the 31st pass we get several clusters that appear to be quite meaningful. There is a cluster of eight members each having to do with the 'chocolateness' of the candy, a cluster of 20 members, each having to do with the packaging of the candy, a cluster of 5 members, each relating to the 'nuttiness' of the candy (whole nuts, chopped nuts, almonds, peanuts, nougat). Thus operationally meaningful groups are achieved and this will be helpful in obtaining economy in the number of variables to be employed in subsequent studies.

REFERENCES

Fortier, J.J. & Solomon, H. (1966) Clustering procedures. *Multivariate Analysis*, pp. 493–506 (ed. Krishmaiah, P. R.). New York: Academic Press.

Freidman, H.P. & Rubin, J (1967) On some invariant criteria for grouping data. *J. Amer. statist. Ass.*, **62**, 1159–78.

Hotelling, H. (1933a) Analysis of a complex of statistical variables into principal components, I. *J. educ. Psychol.*, **24**, 417–41.

Hotelling, H. (1933b) Analysis of a complex of statistical variables into principal components, II. *J. educ. Psychol.*, **24**, 498–520.

Kahl, J.A. & Davis, J.A. (1955) A comparison of indexes of socio-economic status. *Amer. sociol. Review*, **20**, 317–25.

King, B.F. (1967) Step-wise clustering procedures. *J. Amer. statist. Ass.*, **62**, 86–101.

Šteinfeldt, E. *Russian Word Count*. Moscow: Tallin.

Thurston, L.L. (1947) *Multiple-Factor Analysis*. Chicago: University of Chicago Press.

Tryon, R.C. (1939) *Cluster Analysis*. Ann Arbor: Edwards Bros.

Discrimination

Marius Iosifescu and Petre Tăutu
Bayesian inference in an archaeological problem

The present paper tries to advance a (perhaps) new solution to a problem frequently met with in archaeology: how can one infer the cultural origin of a group of artifacts when this origin is uncertain.

An example in this line is offered by the analysis of the ceramics of the Jugoslav–Romanian group within the Incrusted Pottery Culture of the Middle Bronze Age. Mention must be made here of the fact that during the Bronze Age a great number of Indo-European tribes occupied the whole area of the middle Danube and part of the lower Danube leaving there objects of the culture known under the generic term of 'Urnfield Culture'. The Jugoslav–Romanian cultural group is characterized by the existence of some vast cremation cemeteries, cremation being always an alternative rite to inhumation (Piggott 1965). This group has been divided by Dumitrescu (1961) into the following three subgroups by means of the features of the objects discovered:

(A) the Bjelo Brdo–Vîrşeţ (or Vatina–Bjelo Brdo–Vîrşeţ–Temes Kubin) subgroup;

(B) the Gîrla Mare–Cîrna–Zuto Brdo subgroup;

(C) the Kličevac–Dubovaţ subgroup.

In some cases there is a perfect correspondence between the artifacts belonging to the first two subgroups, but there are also obvious distinctions even with the typical urns. Thus numerous urns, more or less related to those from Cîrna in Oltenia, have been discovered in three of the four places of archaeological importance in Banat (Vatina, Vîrşeţ, Temes Kubin and Dubovaţ). Therefore objects belonging to the A and C cultural subgroups share a few characteristics with those of the B subgroup, so that the origin of a newly discovered object with features common to the three (or two) subgroups becomes uncertain (Dumitrescu 1961, p. 201).

We consider this situation to be similar to the authorship inference problem brilliantly studied by Mosteller and Wallace (1963, 1964), and named by them the Federalist problem. We are going to recall this shortly. *The Federalist* papers were published anonymously in 1787–1788, exhorting the citizens of the state of New York to ratify the Constitution of the United States. Nowadays the papers are known to be the work of Alexander Hamilton, James Madison, and John Jay, and it is also firmly established that among the first 77 papers Jay wrote 5, Hamilton 43, and Madison 14. Twelve papers are disputed between Hamilton and Madison, while 3 are considered to be the joint work of Hamilton and Madison. Applying 'a 200-year-old mathematical theorem to a 175-year-old historical problem', Mosteller and Wallace decided that the author of the 12 disputed papers is Madison.

The two mathematicians (*see also* Särndal 1967, Sedelow and Sedelow 1967) start from the study of word distribution: some words vary considerably in their rates of use from one paper to another by the same author; others show remarkable stability for an author. Nevertheless, there are quite a series of words with a distinct status, because they betray the author's specialization. If the latter is, say, a statistician, then an abundance of words like distribution, frequency, probability, parameter, and so on, is to be expected, this abundance depending on the subject-matter of the text rather than on the author's style. These words with such variable rates have been called 'contextual', being 'dangerous for discrimination'. Consequently a list of the discriminating words must necessarily be drawn up; these are actually selected on the basis of only part of the known texts (the screening set), and the remaining part is used to validate the discriminating power of words selected from the screening set.

It is natural to consider an archaeological site a 'text' (or a 'paper') with each artifact standing for a 'sentence' and the features of the objects standing for 'words'. Correspondingly, we must set up a specific dictionary in archaeology and select the screening set. On analyzing the manner of describing pottery types in the south-west, Colton (1952) found that there are specific categories of words for pottery, for example: (1) construction; (2) firing (3) paste; (4) surface finish and color; (5) fire clouds; (6) form; (7) decoration; and that some of these categories are apt to be divided. Thus for the category of 'form', the tertiary division includes the following notes of detail: depth; bases; walls; shoulders; rims; jar necks; additional features; overall shape; and so on. In the case of the archaeological applications the creation of this pool of words requires a mathematical study as a preliminary. As shown by Gaines (1970), any classification of ceramic attributes must allow for the attributes to be continually subdivided into distinctive but not mutually exclusive characteristics. An example of this would be the attribute 'temper'. This attribute may be characterized by material (quartz, sherds, volcanic ash, and so on), size of temper, amount (number of particles per square unit, or general scale: abundant; moderate; scarce; and so on). The pool of words is thus obtained, in the knowledge that the words we want to use are nearly invariant under change of topic ('non-contextual'), and that we check the small filler words ('function' words).

The next step is to establish frequency distributions for the words of the dictionary. It is to be expected that all words will have low rates per hundred words, say, so that the frequencies of any word would be well represented by Poisson distributions.

Suppose that for a certain word the parameter of the Poisson law fitting its frequencies of occurrence in subculture i is $v\lambda_i$, $i = 1, 2$ where v is the size of the sample expressed in suitable units. (Thus λ_1 and λ_2 are the rates per unit.)

Suppose next that our word appears v times in the group of objects considered whose size is v. What are the odds that it belongs to 1?

Let H_i be the hypothesis that our group belongs to subculture i, $i = 1, 2$. Let p_1 and p_2 be the probabilities before the observations that H_1 and H_2

respectively are true. Denote by *odds* $(1, 2 | v)$ the odds for H_1 relative to H_2 given observation v. Bayes' theorem yields

$$odds\,(1, 2 | v) = \frac{P(H_1 | v)}{P(H_2 | v)} = \frac{p_1\,e^{-v\lambda_1}\,\lambda_1^v}{p_2\,e^{-v\lambda_2}\,\lambda_2^v} \,,$$

whence

$$\log odds\,(1, 2 | v) = \log p_1 - \log p_2 - v(\lambda_1 - \lambda_2) + v(\log \lambda_1 - \log \lambda_2).$$

For one observation on each of n independent words appearing $v_1, \ldots, v_n$ times the total log *odds* will be

$$\text{total log } odds\,(1, 2 | v_1, \ldots, v_n)$$

$$= \log p_1 - \log p_2 + \sum_{i=1}^{n} v_i \log (\lambda_1 | \lambda_2) - nv(\lambda_1 - \lambda_2) \quad .$$

A practical application of this method would need, perhaps, a more sophisticated treatment as has been done by Mosteller and Wallace. We intend to do such an application in the near future.

REFERENCES

Colton, H.S. (1952) Pottery types of the Southwest. Unpublished.

Dumitrescu, V. (1961) *The Cremation Necropolis of Cîrna in the Bronze Age* (Romanian; Russ. Fr. Abstr.) Bucharest: Ed. Academiei R P R.

Gaines, S.W. (1970). Computer ceramics. *Newsletter of computer Archaeology*, **5**, 3.

Mosteller, F. & Wallace, D.L. (1963) Inference in an authorship problem. *J. Amer. statist. Ass.*, **58**, 275–309.

Mosteller, F. & Wallace, D.L. (1964) Inference and disputed authorship. *The Federalist*. Reading: Addison–Wesley.

Piggott, S. (1965) *Ancient Europe: From the Beginnings of Agriculture to Classical Antiquity*. Edinburgh: Edinburgh University Press.

Särndal, C.E. (1967) On deciding cases of disputed authorship. *Appl. Statist.*, **16**, 251–68.

Sedelow, S.Y. & Sedelow, W.A. (1967). Stylistic analysis. *Automated Language Processing*, pp. 181–213. (ed Borko, H.) New York: Wiley.

Related Mathematical Topics

Mario Borillo and Peter Ihm
Une méthode de classification d'objets archéologiques
dont la description est structurée et incomplète

To our knowledge, little attention has so far been paid to the problem posed when rigorous classification is sought for individuals or objects which are incompletely described. This situation is surprising because in archaeology it often happens that objects are damaged or that their description is not complete. The methodological study here presented arose largely from research on G. A. M. Richter's work on *Kouroi. Archaic Greek Youths*, where these two factors contribute to a very fragmentary description of the material.

The usual practice in this situation is to calculate for each pair of objects a coefficient of similarity based only on those traits that are known to both objects. Subsequently, in general, one of the methods is applied that has been designed for completely described objects. It therefore seemed of interest to investigate whether methods based on the properties of vector spaces could be employed in a theoretical study of the validity of these approaches.

The description of our material is incomplete partly because of damage to the statues and partly because of omissions and the non-exhaustive description of each individual. These individual sculptures exhibit a definite arrangement of their parts, so that the specification or non-specification of descriptive traits is to a certain extent systematic (for example, the absence of the arm makes observations on the hand impossible). Omissions due to non-exhaustiveness, on the other hand, could be random, as has been verified from several descriptive traits in the material studied. A general method suitable for both types of incomplete data is presented; and the treatment of random omissions is dealt with. Naturally, the structure suggested here with respect to missing data differs from that where a logical relationship between the recognition or non-recognition of certain traits exists. The latter case does not present any special problem and may be expressed simply by linear relationships between variables, which reduce the dimensionability of the vector space under consideration, but do so without any essential modification in the method.

INTRODUCTION

Les méthodes de classification automatique—ou taximétriques—comprennent des procédures de deux types. Celles du premier type consistent en une représentation des individus à classer dans un espace n-dimensionnel pour lequel on cherche à déterminer un sous-espace de dimension réduite contenant toute l'information nécessaire à l'identification des groupes. Les méthodes du deuxième type reviennent à analyser les coefficients de similarité ou les distances entre les individus. Le premier type de méthodes exploite les propriétés des espaces vectoriels normés et consiste spécialement dans la détermination des solutions propres de certaines équations matricielles. Celles du deuxième type se fondent seulement sur l'existence d'un espace métrique et sont de nature agglomérative (les individus de plus grande similarité sont successivement rassemblés). Malgré les différences des procédures de calcul utilisées dans l'un et l'autre cas, les résultats peuvent être très proches pour des raisons dont certaines sont exposées ci-après.

A notre connaissance, peu d'attention a été accordée jusqu'ici au problème que pose la recherche de classifications rigoureuses lorsque les individus ou objets à classer sont incomplets ou incomplètement décrits. Cette situation est d'autant plus paradoxale que ce cas se présente très fréquemment en archéologie, que les objets soient mutilés ou que leur description souffre d'irrégularités qui la rendent incomplète. Le travail méthodologique que l'on trouvera ici a été suscité dans une certaine mesure par une étude entreprise sur l'ouvrage de Richter (1960): *Kouroi. Archaic Greek Youths*, dans lequel ces deux phénomènes se conjuguent pour donner une description très fragmentaire du matériel (Borillo 1970).

L'usage dans ce cas est de calculer pour tout couple d'objets un coefficient de similarité déduit des seuls traits connus pour l'un et l'autre. A la suite de quoi on applique généralement une des méthodes du deuxième type définies pour des objets complètement décrits. Il était donc intéressant d'explorer les possibilités d'utilisation des méthodes basées sur les propriétés des espaces vectoriels en étudiant d'un point de vue théorique les conditions de validité de ces méthodes. Il faut observer que la description de notre matériel se trouve incomplète du fait d'une part des mutilations subies par les statues, d'autre part des omissions dues à la non-exhaustivité de la description de chaque individu. Ces individus sont munis d'une certaine organisation de leurs parties, ce qui impose que la *spécification* et la *non-spécification* de traits descriptifs soient munis d'une certaine systématique (l'absence des bras rend l'observation de la main impossible). Les omissions dues à la non-exhaustivité, par contre, pourraient avoir un caractère aléatoire, ce qui a été vérifié à propos de certains traits descriptifs du matériel étudié. On trouvera ci-après une méthode générale applicable aux deux types de données incomplètes. Bien entendu, la structure évoquée ici à propos des données manquantes est différente de celle qui découle d'une dépendance logique entre *vérification* et *non-vérification* de certains traits. Cette dernière ne pose aucun problème particulier et s'exprime simplement par des relations linéaires entre variables, ce qui réduit la dimension de l'espace vectoriel étudié sans modifier l'essentiel de la méthode.

PROCÉDURES DE CLASSIFICATION DANS LES
ESPACES VECTORIELS NORMES

Etant donné un échantillon de N individus à classer, divisés en g groupes inconnus, on représente chaque individu par un vecteur dans un espace vectoriel euclidien à n dimension, où n est le nombre de traits du système descriptif. L'objectif est la détermination d'un 'hyperplan' passant par le centre de gravité de chaque groupe. Cet hyperplan $\mathbb{H}^r$ est lui-même un espace euclidien à $r \leqslant g - 1$ dimensions. On projette ensuite les points représentant chaque individu perpendiculairement (en général) sur $\mathbb{H}^r$ et on essaie d'identifier les groupes dans $\mathbb{H}^r$. Chaque individu est représenté par un point ou vecteur $\mathbf{x}$ qui se décompose de la manière suivante:

$$\mathbf{x} = \bar{x} + \varepsilon$$

où $\bar{x}$ est le centre de gravité du groupe auquel l'individu appartient et où ε représente la variation aléatoire de x autour du centre de gravité. Nous écrivons $\mathbf{x}_k$ pour le k-ième individu, $k = 1, 2, ..., N$. Pour simplifier et sans perte de généralité nous supposons que

$$\sum_{k=1}^{N} \mathbf{x}_k = 0$$

ce qui correspond à l'utilisation de la déviation de chaque composante par rapport à sa moyenne générale. Au facteur $N - 1$ prés, on calcule la matrice de covariance d'ordre n:

$$S = \sum_{k=1}^{N} \mathbf{x}_k \mathbf{x}_k' \tag{1}$$

où $\mathbf{x}_k'$ est le vecteur-ligne correspondant au vecteur-colonne $\mathbf{x}_k$. Pour la matrice

$$X = (\mathbf{x}_1 \mathbf{x}_2 ... \mathbf{x}_N)$$

d'ordre $n \times N$, dont la k-ième colonne représente le k-ième individu, on a également

$$S = XX'$$

S se décompose en une matrice intragroupe et une matrice intergroupe

$$S = S_\varepsilon + \bar{S}$$

avec

$$\bar{S} = \sum_{i=1}^{g} N_i \bar{x}_i \bar{x}_i'$$

où $\bar{x}_i$ est le centre de gravité du i-ième groupe, N_i le nombre d'individus dans ce groupe. $\bar{S}$ est de rang $r \leqslant g - 1$ et $\mathbb{H}^r$ est engendré par les r vecteurs propres dominants u_i de $\bar{S}$, c'est-à-dire les vecteurs propres dont les valeurs propres correspondantes μ_i sont les plus grandes. Nous les ordonnons de la manière suivante: $\mu_1 \geqslant \mu_2 \geqslant ... \geqslant \mu_r$. Lorsque les variables sont indépendantes avec la même variance à l'intérieur de chaque groupe nous avons:

$$S_\varepsilon = CI, \quad C > 0 \quad ,$$

ou I est la matrice unité. On montre facilement que les r vecteurs propres dominants de S sont ceux de $\bar{S}$ et les valeurs propres dominantes de S sont alors $\lambda_i = \mu_i + C$ pour $i \leqslant r$ et $\lambda_i = C$ pour $i > r$ (Ihm 1965). Il est donc possible de déterminer $\mathbb{H}^r$ à partir de S sans connaître les $\bar{x}_i$. Définissons la matrice U_p, $p \leqslant n$ dont les colonnes sont les p vecteurs propres dominants de S normés à la longueur 1

$$U_p = (u_1 u_2 ... u_p), \quad |u_i| = 1 \quad .$$

Pour $p = n$ on obtient la matrice des projections y_k des x_k sur $\mathbb{H}^r$ par

$$U_r' X = Y \quad . \tag{2}$$

La matrice de covariance des y_k est, au facteur $N - 1$ près, $YY' = \Lambda_r$ où Λ_r est la matrice diagonale des $\lambda_1, ..., \lambda_r$.

Cette méthode présente certaines ressemblances avec l'analyse des composantes principales en analyse factorielle. Pour $|u_i| = \sqrt{\lambda_i}$ on obtient en effet des vecteurs u_i dont les composantes constituent les saturations (*factor loadings*) du i-ème facteur. Y est alors la matrice des *factor scores* avec $YY'=I$. Une différence réside dans le fait qu'on emploie généralement dans l'analyse des composantes principales la matrice de corrélation R (au lieu de la matrice de covariance S). C'est la raison pour laquelle cette méthode est parfois appelée R-technique. Malgré cette différence, la méthode exposée ci-dessus est aussi appelée parfois une R-technique.

On sait que dans le domaine de l'analyse factorielle certaines Q-techniques correspondent aux R-techniques. Dans les Q-techniques, on intervertit variables et individus pour calculer les coefficients de corrélation entre les individus et non entre les variables, ce qui donne une matrice d'ordre N. Quelques arguments théoriques s'opposent à l'emploi des Q-techniques en taxinomie (Ihm 1962). Nous proposons ici de partir de

$$Q^* = X'X = (q_{kl}^*)$$

c'est-à-dire la matrice d'ordre N dont les éléments sont égaux à

$$q_{kl}^* = \mathbf{x}_k'\mathbf{x}_l \quad .$$

L'intérêt de la matrice Q^* est que ses v vecteurs propres dominants v_i donnent la matrice Y. En effet, si pour $p \leqslant n$

$$V_p = (v_1 v_2 \ldots v_p), \quad |v_i| = \sqrt{\lambda_i}$$

on a pour $p = r$

$$V_r' = Y = U_r'X \quad . \tag{3}$$

Cette propriété se déduit du fait que V_r vérifie l'équation

$$Q^* V_r = V_r \Lambda_r \quad .$$

En substituant $X'U_r$ à V_r on voit que

$$Q^*(X'U_r) = (X'U_r)\Lambda_r$$
$$X'XX'U_r = X'U_r\Lambda_r$$
$$X'(SU_r) = X'(U_r\Lambda_r)$$
$$X'(U_r\Lambda_r) = X'(U_r\Lambda_r)$$

on a aussi

$$\Lambda_r^{-1}V_r'X' = \Lambda_r^{-1}U_r'XX'$$
$$= \Lambda_r^{-1}U_r'S$$
$$= \Lambda_r^{-1}\Lambda_r U_r'$$
$$= U_r' \tag{4}$$

ce qui montre qu'on obtient U_r et Y par le traitement de Q^* aussi bien que par celui de S.

Pour des raisons pratiques, on se limite souvent à une projection sur $\mathbb{H}^p$, au lieu de $\mathbb{H}^r$, avec $p < r$; par exemple, $p = 3$. Dans ce cas U_p remplace U_r. Désignant par $\bar{y}_i$ la projection de $\bar{x}_i$ sur $\mathbb{H}^p$, on prouve que

$$\sum_{i=1}^{g} \sum_{j=1}^{g} N_i N_j |\bar{y}_i - \bar{y}_j|^2$$

est maximisée lorsque $\mathbb{H}^p$ est engendrée par les p vecteurs propres dominants.

UTILISATION DES DISTANCES OU DES COEFFICIENTS DE SIMILARITÉ

Le fait que l'élément q_{kl}^* de Q^*, produit scalaire de $\mathbf{x}_k$ et $\mathbf{x}_l$, puisse être lié à un coefficient de similarité d_{kl} par les relations

$$d_{kl}^2 = (\mathbf{x}_k - \mathbf{x}_l)'(\mathbf{x}_k - \mathbf{x}_l) = |\mathbf{x}_k|^2 + |\mathbf{x}_l|^2 - 2q_{kl}^*$$
$$q_{kl}^* = \tfrac{1}{2}(|\mathbf{x}_k|^2 + |\mathbf{x}_l|^2 - d_{kl}^2)$$

suggère d'employer également la méthode déjà exposée dans les cas où on remplace q_{kl}^* par un coefficient de similarité quelconque a_{kl}, ou mieux

$$\alpha_{kl} = a_{kl} - \bar{a}_k - \bar{a}_l + \bar{a}$$

avec

$$\bar{a}_k = \frac{1}{N} \sum_{l=1}^{N} a_{kl}$$

$$\bar{a} = \frac{1}{N} \sum_{k=1}^{N} \bar{a}_k$$

ceci pour rendre la somme de chaque ligne et de chaque colonne de la matrice $\alpha = (\alpha_{kl})$ égale à zéro (ce qui était aussi le cas de Q^*). A chaque α_{kl} on fait correspondre une distance d_{kl}

$$d_{kl} = (\alpha_{kk} + \alpha_{ll} - 2\alpha_{kl})^{\frac{1}{2}} \tag{5}$$

Etant donné un échantillon d'objets θ_k, $k = 1, 2, \ldots, N$, et une matrice α de coefficients de similarité, on cherche une application de l'ensemble des θ_k sur un ensemble de points y_k dans un espace euclidien de dimension minimale égale à d tel que $|y_k - y_l| = d_{kl}$, d_{kl} étant calculé selon (5). Cette application existe si et seulement si la matrice α est semi-définie positive et de rang d (Gower 1966). Dans ce qui suit, cette condition sera appelée condition $\mathscr{C}$. On peut d'ailleurs partir directement des distances d_{kl} qu'on remplace par δ_{kl} selon la formule

$$\delta_{kl}^2 = d_{kl}^2 - \bar{d}_k^2 - \bar{d}_l^2 + \bar{d}^2$$

avec

$$\bar{d}_k^2 = \frac{1}{N} \sum_{l=1}^{N} d_{kl}^2$$

$$\bar{d}^2 = \frac{1}{N} \sum_{k=1}^{N} \bar{d}_k^2$$

on montre que

$$\alpha_{kl} = -\tfrac{1}{2}\delta_{kl}^2 \quad .$$

Nous n'entrerons pas ici dans le détail des méthodes à employer lorsque α n'est pas semi-définie positive. On emploie souvent dans ce cas la méthode de Messick et Abelson (Torgerson 1958) qui consiste à remplacer d_{kl} par $d_{kl} + C$ où C est déterminé de façon telle que la condition $\mathscr{C}$ soit vérifiée. Ce procédé se justifie dans le cas de la mesure des distances par la méthode des triades (Torgerson 1958). Dans les autres cas, elle conduit à des déplacements perturbateurs des images y_k. Lorsque dans nos expériences α n'est pas semi-définie positive mais qu'elle possède des valeurs propres négatives de valeur négligeable, on attribue ce phénomène à des approximations dans la détermination des a_{kl} ou d_{kl}. Si les valeurs propres négatives ne sont pas négligeables, il faudra douter de ce que les d_{kl} correspondent à des distances dans un espace euclidien et vérifier si les d_{kl} ne correspondent pas à la norme p de Minkowski avec $p \neq 2$; cette vérification s'effectue à l'aide d'un programme due à Kruskal. Une expérience de sériation chronologique a été publiée (Ihm 1970) dans laquelle les objets O_k ont été représentés par des vecteurs $\mathbf{x}_k$, la distance mesurée dans la norme $p = 1$ par

$$d_{kl}^{(1)} = \sum_{v=1}^{n} |x_{kv} - x_{jv}|$$

et les $\mathbf{x}_k$ projetés sur des points y_k dans un espace euclidien tel que en norme euclidienne $|y_k - y_l| = d_{kl}^{(1)}$. Dans cette même publication ont été définis les cas dans lesquels cette méthode est valide.

Le Traitement des Données Incompletes

Supposons maintenant que $\tilde{\mathbf{x}}_k$ soit le vecteur représentant le k-ième individu pour lequel une composante au moins est inconnue pour l'une ou l'autre des raisons exposées dans l'introduction. Le nombre et la qualité des composantes inconnues varient d'un vecteur à l'autre. On se souvient que les k_l étaient normés avec une somme égale au vecteur nul, $\mathbf{0}$. La même propriété est exigée pour la somme des $\tilde{\mathbf{x}}_k$ et de plus chaque composante absente est remplacée par zéro.

L'espérance mathématique de notre matrice de covariance S, pour des données complètes, s'écrit

$$E\,S = (N-1)\Sigma = (N-1)(\sigma_{ij})$$

Cette propriété n'est plus valable pour des données incomplètes où on obtient

$$ES = (N-1)\tilde{\Sigma} = (N_{ij}-1)(\sigma_{ij})$$

N_{ij} représente le nombre de vecteurs dans lesquels la i-ième et la j-ième composantes sont simultanément connues. Si l'on calcule par contre une matrice $\tilde{S}$ d'élément

$$\tilde{s}_{ij} = \frac{N-1}{N_{ij}-1}\ \ s_{ij} = \frac{N-1}{N_{ij}-1}\sum_{k=1}^{N}(x_{ik}-\bar{x}_i^{(j)})(x_{jk}-\bar{x}_j^{(i)})\quad,$$

où $\bar{x}_i^{(j)}$ et $\bar{x}_j^{(i)}$ sont les moyennes de $\mathbf{x}_i$ et $\mathbf{x}_j$ calculées pour les mêmes N_{ij} vecteurs, nous obtenons comme précédemment

$$E\tilde{S} = (N-1)\Sigma\quad.$$

$\tilde{S}$ n'est plus nécessairement semi-définie positive. S'il existe des valeurs propres négatives non négligeables, la méthode n'est pas applicable.

On détermine sans difficulté la matrice $\tilde{U}d$ à partir de $\tilde{S}$ (d désigne le rang de $\tilde{S}$); par contre les $\mathbf{y}_k = \tilde{\mathbf{y}}_k$ ne sont plus calculables comme précédemment. La méthode, plus complexe, passe par la résolution d'un système d'équations linéaires.

$\mathbf{x}_k$, avec des données complètes, s'écrit

$$\mathbf{x}_k = y_{1k}u_1 + y_{2k}u_2 + \ldots + y_{dk}u_d$$
$$= U_d\mathbf{y}_k\quad.$$

La transformation $U_d'\mathbf{x}_k$ donne, à cause de l'orthonormalité des $\mathbf{u}_i$, le vecteur $\mathbf{y}_k$:

$$U_d'\mathbf{x}_k = U_d'U_d\mathbf{y}_k = \mathbf{y}_k\quad.$$

Cette relation n'est plus valable avec les vecteurs $\hat{\mathbf{x}}_k$ qui contiennent $n_k < n$ composantes connues. Soit $\hat{U}_d^{(k)}$ la matrice à n_k lignes déduite de $\tilde{U}_d$ par suppression des lignes correspondant aux composantes inconnues de $\tilde{\mathbf{x}}_k$. Nous avons

$$\hat{\mathbf{x}}_k = \hat{U}_d^{(k)}\tilde{\mathbf{y}}_k$$

et

$$(\hat{U}_d^{(k)})'\hat{\mathbf{x}}_k = (\hat{U}_d^{(k)})'\hat{U}_d^{(k)}\tilde{\mathbf{y}}_k \tag{6}$$
$$= C_d^{(k)}\tilde{\mathbf{y}}_k$$

c'est-à-dire un système de d'équations linéaires dont la solution est le vecteur cherché $\tilde{\mathbf{y}}_k$. La condition nécessaire et suffisante est que pour tout k les matrices $C_d^{(k)}$ soient non-singulières.

Puisque d est le rang de $\tilde{S}$ et non plus celui de $\bar{S}$ (la matrice de covariance intergroupes) on obtiendrait une projection de chaque $\tilde{\mathbf{x}}_k$ sur $\mathbb{H}^d$. En fait, on se contente dans les problèmes taximétriques d'une projection sur $\mathbb{H}^p$ où $p \leqslant r \leqslant g-1$. On ne cherche donc que p variables y_{ik}. Dans ce cas, on emploie $\hat{U}_p^{(k)}$ à la place de $\hat{U}_d^{(k)}$ et le vecteur $\hat{\mathbf{y}}_k$ n'a que p composantes. La solution de (6) minimise

$$|X_k - \hat{U}_p^{(k)}\tilde{\mathbf{y}}_k|^2 \quad.$$

Cette solution est donc la solution obtenue par la méthode des moindres carrés.

Il n'existe pas pour $\tilde{R}$ un dual $\tilde{\mathbf{Q}}^*$ qui se déduise aussi simplement que Q^* dans le cas de R. Si l'on voulait utiliser une méthode de type Q, on pourrait employer en première approximation, à la place de q_{ij}, la valeur $n\hat{q}_{kl}/n_{kl}$ où n_{kl} est le nombre de traits spécifiés simultanément pour les objets k et l, et $\hat{q}_{kl}$ le produit scalaire des vecteurs $\mathbf{x}_k$ et $\mathbf{x}_l$ pour ces traits. Cette matrice sera appelée Q^* *corrigée*.

APPLICATIONS

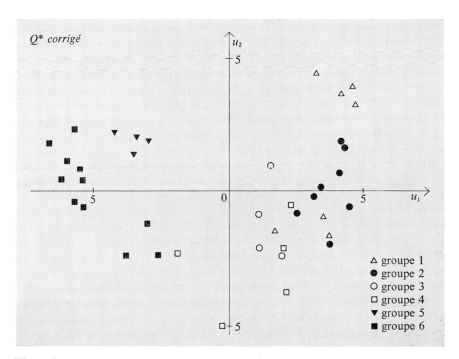

Figure 1

Les méthodes décrites ci-dessus ont été appliquées à un échantillon de 40 statues, choisies parmi les moins mutilées. Malgré cela, le nombre de traits non-spécifiés, pour l'une ou l'autre des raisons exposées dans l'introduction, est en moyenne voisin pour chaque individu de la moitié des 259 traits que comporte le système descriptif. Par conséquent, les valeurs de l'expérience sont $n=259$, $N=40$. Ces 40 statues, selon Richter, se répartissent en 6 groupes ($g=6$) et la représentation sur $\mathbb{H}^r$ exigerait $r \leqslant 5$; pour des raisons pratiques, nous avons choisi $\mathbb{H}^p$ avec $p=3$. Q^* *corrigé* a été calculé ainsi que les trois premiers vecteurs dominants normalisés à la longueur $\sqrt{\lambda}$. Les k-ièmes composantes de chaque vecteur représentent le k-ième individu dans H^3. Les figures 1 et 2 montrent les projections des individus respectivement dans les plans (u_1, u_2) et (u_1, u_3).

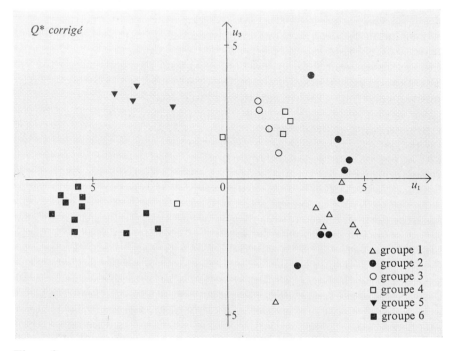

Figure 2

METHODE Q^* CORRIGÉ

La figure 1 (dimensions 1 et 2) montre une nette séparation entre les groupes 1 à 4 d'une part, 5 et 6 d'autre part. Si l'on observe la figure 2 (axes 1 et 3) on relève une franche distinction entre les groupes 5 et 6. A un niveau de distinction plus fin, le groupe $1+2$ est également séparé du groupe $3+4$. Les groupements qui ont été observés jusqu'ici présentent trois exceptions très nettes; un premier objet appartenant au groupe 4 est tout-à-fait séparé de l'ensemble des groupes; un autre se trouve en fait plus près du groupe 6; enfin le groupe 2 comprend un objet pour lequel il serait, sur la figure, difficile de choisir entre les groupes 2 et $3+4$. Ces anomalies, se répétant sur les deux projections (figure 1 et figure 2) pourraient conduire à se poser la question de savoir si l'affectation de ces trois objets à leurs groupes nominaux est bien correcte.

En ce qui concerne l'interprétation des axes de projection, il est clair sur la figure 1 comme sur la figure 2 que l'axe u_1 correspond à la dimension temporelle puisque les groupes sont numérotés de 1 à 6 selon l'ordre chronologique et que cet ordre se retrouve bien sur chaque figure. Pour les groupes 1 à 4, qui ont une dimension importante selon l'axe u_2, il est beaucoup plus difficile d'établir une interprétation archéologique de ce phénomène.

METHODE $\tilde{R}$

Les figures 3 et 4 constituent les projections obtenues par la méthode $\tilde{R}$ décrite déjà. Elles offrent pratiquement les mêmes configurations que celles de la méthode Q^* *corrigé*. La seule différence réside dans la disparition de deux des anomalies signalées ci-dessus. Il est cependant notable que l'une d'elles persiste. Il y a là un travail de vérification qui doit être effectué en collaboration avec l'archéologue, en ce qui concerne les données intrinsèques (morphologie) aussi bien qu'extrinsèques (origine, inscriptions, connaissances historiques etc.). Les commentaires au sujet de l'interprétation archéologique des axes u_1 et u_2 sont identiques à ceux qui ont été faits à propos de la méthode Q^* *corrigé*.

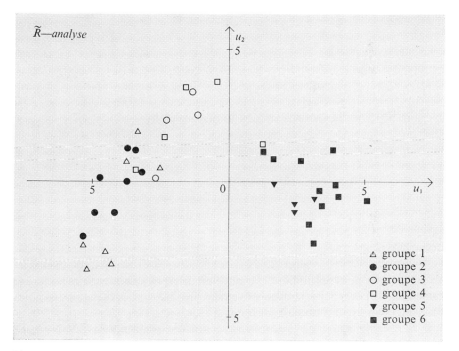

Figure 3

Remarque. La méthode Q^* *corrigé* a également été appliquée aux mêmes objets décrits par 265 traits. Ces traits comprenaient les 259 traits précédents plus un certain nombre d'autres concernant les accessoires (plinthe, base) de la statue. Les résultats dans ce cas sont hautement comparables aux précédents, ce qui coincide avec l'exigence fondamentale en matière de taxinomie qu'une variation modérée dans le nombre des éléments descriptifs ne doit pas provoquer des modifications importantes de la classification.

METHODE Q (classique)

Parallèlement aux méthodes déjà mentionnées, la même population a été soumise à une analyse Q classique. Deux expériences ont été conduites. Dans la première, les traits non-spécifiés ont été remplacés par les valeurs moyennes de ces traits calculés sur l'échantillon. Dans la deuxième a été effectuée une correction analogue à celle de Q^*. Les résultats sont dans les deux cas moins clairs que ceux obtenus par les méthodes précédentes. Cependant trois groupements sont également identifiables ici : le premier comprend les groupes 1 à 4, les deuxièmes et troisièmes sont formés respectivement des groupes 5 et 6.

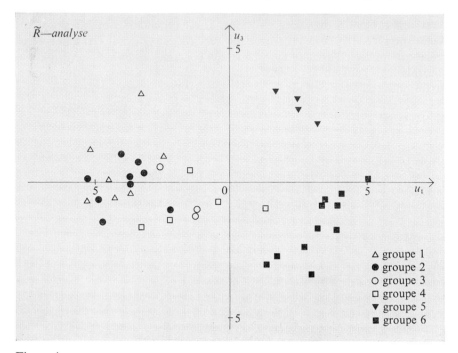

Figure 4

CONCLUSION

Les méthodes Q^* *corrigé* et $\tilde{R}$, dans la mesure où elles séparent mieux les divers groupes dont se compose l'échantillon peuvent légitiment être préférées. Cependant, si ces groupes sont effectivement bien marqués, des méthodes moins spécifiques suffisent à obtenir un premier résultat.

Il faut également faire une remarque d'ordre pratique : la nombre n de variables étant considérable et N relativement petit, les calculs afférents à $\tilde{R}$ exigent une grande capacité de mémoire et de préférence un calculateur rapide. La faible différence entre les résultats de Q^* *corrigé* et de $\tilde{R}$ suggèrent que l'on commence par une application de Q^* ou de Q^* *corrigé*.

RÉFÉRENCES

Borillo, M. (1970) La vérification des hypothèses en archéologie : deux pas vers une méthode. *Archéologie et Calculateurs*. Paris : C.N.R.S.

Gower, J.C. (1966) Some distance properties of latent root and vector methods used in multivariate analysis. *Biometrika*, **53**, 325–38.

Ihm, P. (1962) *Methoden der Taxometrie*. Tagunsbericht des IBM World Trade European Education Center. Blaricum. Nederland Reprint Euratom no. EUR 1671. d. Brussel 1964.

Ihm, P. (1965) Automatic classification in anthropology. *The Use of Computers in Anthropology* (ed. Dell Hymes). The Hague: Mouton.

Ihm, P. (1970) Distance et similitude en taximétrie. *Archéologie et Calculateurs*. Paris: C.N.R.S.

Torgerson, W.S. (1958) *Theory and Methods of Scaling*. New York: Wiley.

Richter, G.A.M. (1960) *Kouroi. Archaic Greek Youths*. London: Phaidon Press.

Related Mathematical Topics

Silviu Guiaşu
On an algorithm for recognition

Problems of recognition occur in practically every field of human activity: for example, in medical diagnosis, in chemical analysis, in recognition of a failure in a complicated mechanism, in classification problems, in recognition of an entity in archaeology, and so on. The problem of recognition dealt with in this paper can be described by the following simple model, similar to the Rényi model for the theory of random search (Rényi 1965). (*See* Guiaşu 1968).
    Let

$$E_n = \{x_1, x_2, ..., x_n\}$$

be a finite set having $n \geqslant 2$ distinguishable elements—called entities—and suppose that we want to recognize an unknown entity x of the set E_n. The set E_n itself is supposed to be known to us. Let us suppose further that it is not possible to observe the entity x directly, but that we may choose some functions from a given set F_N of functions defined on E_n,

$$F_N = \{f_1, f_2, ..., f_N\}$$

(called the set of the characteristics of the entities from the set E_n) and observe the values $f_1(x), f_2(x), ..., f_N(x)$ taken on by these functions at the unknown entity x. We suppose that the number of different values taken on by every function f belonging to the set F_N is much smaller than n. Let

$$V_{r_k} = \{f_k^{(1)}, f_k^{(2)}, ..., f_k^{(r_k)}\}$$

be the set of the values taken on by the characteristic $f_k \in F_N$. For many particular problems we are especially interested in the case when each characteristic $f \in F_N$ takes on only two values (that is, the respective characteristic occurs or does not occur in x). When n is a large number it is necessary, of course, to observe the value of a large number of characteristics $f \in F_N$ at the entity x. Each such observation gives us only partial information on the entity x, namely it specifies a subset of E_n to which x must belong. But, after making a fairly large number of such observations the information obtained enables us to recognize x without an excessive number of observations.
    Landa (1962) proposed such a strategy of recognition giving his 'most rational' algorithm of recognition and applying it to the problem of recognition of sentences in Russian syntax. Also, Manolescu (1970) applied this algorithm of recognition in sociology. According to this algorithm, it is necessary at every moment to choose and to observe, first, such a characteristic f from the set F_N supplying the largest amount of information, that is, eliminating the largest degree of uncertainty.
    For a good understanding of this algorithm let us give an example. Thus we suppose that we have five possible entities $E_5 = \{x_1, x_2, x_3, x_4, x_5\}$ and four characteristics $F_4 = \{f_1, f_2, f_3, f_4\}$. We suppose also that each characteristic takes on only two values, namely the characteristic f_1 takes on the values

$\{a, \bar{a}\}, f_2$ takes on the values $\{b, \bar{b}\}, f_3$ takes on the values $\{c, \bar{c}\}$ and finally f_4 takes on the values $\{d, \bar{d}\}$; where, for instance, b means that the characteristic f_2 occurs and $\bar{b}$ means that the same characteristic f_2 does not occur. Let us suppose that the entities of the set E_5 are defined by

$$x_1 = a \wedge d, \quad x_2 = a \wedge \bar{d}, \quad x_3 = \bar{a} \wedge c, \quad x_4 = \bar{a} \wedge b, \quad x_5 = \bar{a} \wedge \bar{b} \wedge \bar{c}$$

where the sign $\wedge$ represents the conjunction **and**. Let also

$$c \wedge \bar{d} = \varnothing, \quad b \wedge \bar{d} = \varnothing,$$
$$\bar{a} \wedge d = \varnothing, \quad b \wedge c = \varnothing,$$

be the incompatibility relations between characteristics, where $\varnothing$ is the impossible event. Using Boole's classical formalism the explicit expressions of the respective entities as functions of the values of the characteristics are

$$x_1 = (a \wedge \bar{b} \wedge c \wedge d) \vee (a \wedge b \wedge \bar{c} \wedge d) \vee (a \wedge \bar{b} \wedge \bar{c} \wedge d),$$
$$x_2 = a \wedge \bar{b} \wedge \bar{c} \wedge \bar{d}, \quad x_3 = \bar{a} \wedge \bar{b} \wedge c \wedge d, \quad \quad (1)$$
$$x_4 = \bar{a} \wedge b \wedge \bar{c} \wedge d, \quad x_5 = \bar{a} \wedge \bar{b} \wedge \bar{c} \wedge d.$$

We suppose that all the entities of the set E_5 have the same *a priori* probabilities, that is,

$$p(x_1) = p(x_2) = p(x_3) = p(x_4) = p(x_5) = 1/5 \quad . \quad (2)$$

Let now x be an arbitrary entity, which we want to recognize by a reasonable number of observations. Obviously, we have

$$x = x_1 \vee x_2 \vee x_3 \vee x_4 \vee x_5 \quad \quad (3)$$

where the sign $\vee$ represents the conjunction **or**.

According to the equalities (1)–(3), we obtain for the probabilities of the characteristics' values

$$p(a) = 2/5, \quad p(\bar{a}) = 3/5; \quad \quad p(b) = 4/15, \quad p(\bar{b}) = 11/15;$$
$$p(c) = 4/15, \quad p(\bar{c}) = 11/15; \quad p(d) = 4/5, \quad p(\bar{d}) = 1/5 \quad .$$

Now, without any difficulty, it is possible to estimate the amount of uncertainty contained by each characteristic, according to Shannon's entropy. Indeed, the entropy of the first characteristic f_1 is given by the formula

$$H_1 = -p(a) \log p(a) - p(\bar{a}) \log p(\bar{a}) = 0.9710 \quad .$$

Similarly, the entropy for the other characteristics will be

$$H_2 = 0.8375; \quad H_3 - 0.8375, \quad H_4 = 0.7219 \quad .$$

Thus, it is necessary to verify first the characteristic f_1, supplying the largest amount of information. If we verify this characteristic we may obtain only two possibilities, a and $\bar{a}$ respectively.

(a) Suppose now that we have found the value a. Then, according to the expression (1), it follows that

$$x = x_1 \vee x_2$$

with the probabilities

$$p(x_1) = p(x_2) = \tfrac{1}{2} \quad .$$

Taking into account the entities x_1 and x_2 of expression (1) we now obtain

$$p(a) = 1, \quad p(\bar{a}) = 0; \quad \quad p(b) = \tfrac{1}{6}, \quad p(\bar{b}) = \tfrac{5}{6};$$
$$p(c) = \tfrac{1}{6}, \quad p(\bar{c}) = \tfrac{5}{6}; \quad \quad p(d) = \tfrac{1}{2}, \quad p(\bar{d}) = \tfrac{1}{2} \quad .$$

Then

$$H_1 = 0; \quad H_2 = 0.6508; \quad H_3 = 0.6508; \quad H_4 = 1.000 \quad .$$

Of course, in this case it is necessary to verify the characteristic f_4; and if we obtain the value d it results that $x = x_1$, and if we obtain the other value $\bar{d}$ it results that $x = x_2$.

7

(*b*) Let us suppose that verifying the characteristic f_1 we have found the value $\bar{a}$. Then it follows from expression (1) that we may have the possibilities

$$x = x_3 \vee x_4 \vee x_5 \tag{4}$$

with the probabilities

$$p(x_3) = p(x_4) = p(x_5) = \tfrac{1}{3} \ . \tag{5}$$

From the expression (1) of the entities x_3, x_4, x_5 we have

$$p(a) = 0, \quad p(\bar{a}) = 1; \quad p(b) = \tfrac{1}{3}, \quad p(\bar{b}) = \tfrac{2}{3};$$
$$p(c) = \tfrac{1}{3}, \quad p(\bar{c}) = \tfrac{2}{3}; \quad p(d) = 1, \quad p(\bar{d}) = 0 \ , \tag{6}$$

and we obtain from expressions (4)–(6)

$$H_1 = 0; \quad H_2 = 0 \cdot 9189; \quad H_3 = 0 \cdot 9189; \quad H_4 = 0 \ .$$

It is necessary to verify at this step the characteristic f_2 (or f_3). If for the characteristic f_2 we obtain the value b then $x = x_4$, but if we obtain the other value, $\bar{b}$, there are still two possibilities

$$x = x_3 \vee x_5$$

with the probabilities

$$p(x_3) = p(x_5) = \tfrac{1}{2} \ .$$

In this new situation, using the same techniques as above, we obtain

$$p(a) = 0, \quad p(\bar{a}) = 1; \quad p(b) = 0, \quad p(\bar{b}) = 1;$$
$$p(c) = \tfrac{1}{2}, \quad p(\bar{c}) = \tfrac{1}{2}; \quad p(d) = 1, \quad p(\bar{d}) = 0,$$

and therefore

$$H_1 = 0; \quad H_2 = 0; \quad H_3 = 1; \quad H_4 = 0 \ .$$

Verifying the characteristic f_3 we may obtain the value c, and then $x = x_3$, or the value $\bar{c}$, when $x = x_5$ results.

Synthesizing all these results we obtain the diagram of the most rational algorithm of recognition in the form shown in figure 1 (the number in the circle represents the number of the characteristic which must be verified at every step).

The most rational algorithm of recognition (*see* figure 1) neglects one very important fact. As a matter-of-fact we want to recognize the entity x without an excessive number of observations, but, at the same time, without too large a cost. Indeed, we may suppose, for example, that each observation is connected with a certain cost, and we want to keep the cost of the whole procedure of recognition relatively low. At the same time, to verify one characteristic may be much more difficult from a practical point of view than to verify another. Or, it is possible that to verify, for example, the characteristic f_k having the value, $f_k(x) = f_k^{(i)}$, may be more expensive, or more difficult, than to verify the same characteristic f_k when it has another value, $f_k = f_k^{(j)}$. Therefore, of course, to verify the characteristic f_k when it has the value $f_k^{(j)}$ is more useful from the point of view of cost, or of practical possibilities, than to verify the same characteristic when it has the value $f_k^{(i)}$.

According to this fact, the reinforcement of the most rational algorithm of recognition needs a measure of information which takes into account both aspects of the information, the quantitative and the qualitative. Now in Beliş and Guiaşu (1968) such a formula of information was proposed taking into account the two basic concepts of probability and utility with respect to all possible events.

Let $\omega_1, \omega_2, \ldots, \omega_n$ be a finite number of events and let $p_1, p_2, \ldots, p_n$ be the

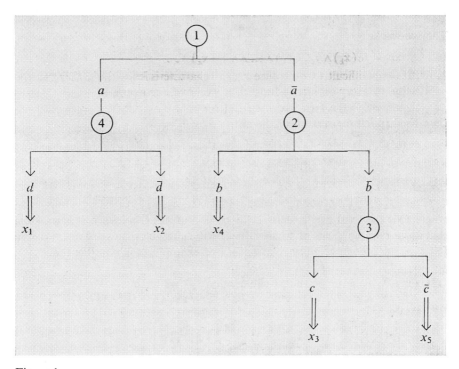

Figure 1

probabilities of occurrence of these events satisfying

$$p_i \geqslant 0, \quad (i=1, 2, ..., n); \quad \sum_{i=1}^{n} p_i = 1 \quad .$$

We suppose that the different events $\omega_1, \omega_2, ..., \omega_n$ are more or less relevant, depending upon the goal to be reached, that is, they have different utilities. Let $u_1, u_2, ..., u_n$ be the utilities of the events $\omega_1, \omega_2, ..., \omega_n$, that is non-negative real numbers. The amount of information supplied by an experiment having the events $\omega_1, \omega_2, ..., \omega_n$ is

$$I = I(u_1, ..., u_n; p_1, ..., p_n) = -\sum_{i=1}^{n} u_i p_i \log p_i \quad . \tag{7}$$

The axioms for this formula are given in the appendix at the end of the paper. Of course, the utility of an event is independent of its objective probability of occurrence; for instance, an event of small probability can have a utility equal to zero with regard to a given goal. Also, an experiment for which all useful events are not possible and all possible events are useless, supplies the information I equal to zero.

Let us consider the set of the entities E_n and we suppose that the set F_N is a complete $\updownarrow$ system of characteristics for the given set E_n, that is, for every entity $x_k \in E_n$ there are the indices

$$i_1^{(k)}, i_2^{(k)}, ..., i_{N_k}^{(k)} \quad (N_k \leqslant N)$$

such that x_k is completely determined by the values

$$f_{i_1^{(k)}}(x_k), f_{i_2^{(k)}}(x_k), ..., f_{i_{N_k}^{(k)}}(x_k)$$

where $\quad f_{i_j^{(k)}}(x_k) \in V_{r_{ij}^{(k)}} \qquad (j=1, \ldots, N_k)$.

Then we write

$$x_k = f_{i_1^{(k)}}(x_k) \wedge f_{i_2^{(k)}}(x_k) \wedge \ldots \wedge f_{i_{N_k}^{(k)}}(x_k) .$$

Now, it is not difficult to introduce all the characteristics $f_1, f_2, \ldots, f_N$ in the expression of every entity x_k. Indeed, if we have, for example,

$$x_k = f_1(x_k) \wedge f_2(x_k) \wedge \ldots \wedge f_{N-1}(x_k)$$

then the explicit expression of the entity x_k will be

$$x_k = [f_1(x_k) \wedge f_2(x_k) \wedge \ldots \wedge f_{N-1}(x_k) \wedge f_N^{(1)}] \vee$$
$$[f_1(x_k) \wedge f_2(x_k) \wedge \ldots \wedge f_{N-1}(x_k) \wedge f_N^{(2)}] \vee \ldots$$
$$\ldots \vee [f_1(x_k) \wedge f_2(x_k) \wedge \ldots \wedge f_{N-1}(x_k) \wedge f_N^{(r_N)}]$$

because always

$$f_k^{(1)} \vee f_k^{(2)} \vee \ldots \vee f_k^{(r_k)} = \Omega, \qquad (k=1, \ldots, N)$$

where Ω is the total event, that is, the certain event. Obviously, it is possible that some combinations of some values of the characteristics are not possible (that is, the incompatibility relations). For example, it is possible that

$$f_1^{(2)} \wedge f_2^{(1)} \wedge f_6^{(4)} \wedge f_N^{(3)} = \emptyset .$$

Of course, whichever be the possible value $f_k^{(j)}$ we have

$$f_k^{(j)} \wedge \emptyset = \emptyset, \quad f_k^{(j)} \vee \emptyset = f_k^{(j)}, \quad f_k^{(j)} \vee \Omega = \Omega, \quad f_k^{(j)} \wedge \Omega = f_k^{(j)} .$$

Let now

$$p(x_k) \geqslant 0, \quad (k=1, \ldots, n); \qquad \sum_{k=1}^{n} p(x_k) = 1$$

be the probabilities of all the possible entities. If we do not know anything about this *a priori* distribution of the entities we shall suppose all these entities with the same probability, that is, $1/n$. If we have written the explicit expressions of all the entities $x_1, x_2, \ldots, x_n$ taking into account the incompatibility relations, then it is very easy to count the probabilities of all the values of the characteristics. We denote by

$$p_{jk} = p(f_k^{(j)})$$

the probability of the value $f_k^{(j)}$ of the characteristic f_k. Let now u_{jk} be the utility in respect to a goal of the same value $f_k^{(j)}$ of the characteristic f_k. Then, according to expression (7), the amount of information supplied by the observation of the characteristic f_k will be

$$I_k = I(f_k) = - \sum_{j=1}^{r_k} u_{jk} p_{jk} \log p_{jk}, \quad (k=1, \ldots, N) \qquad (8)$$

Now, by the most rational algorithm of recognition, *it is necessary to choose and to observe first the characteristic f_{k_0} for which*

$$I_{k_0} = \max_{1 \leqslant k \leqslant N} I_k .$$

The observation of this characteristic specifies a subset $E'_m \subset E_n (m < n)$, to which x must belong and we will repeat the procedure described above.

Let us consider the example given above and let us suppose that each observation is connected with a certain utility with respect to a goal. From this point of view we suppose now that we have

$$u_{11} = 1, \quad u_{21} = 9, \quad u_{12} = 7, \quad u_{22} = 3, \quad u_{13} = 1, \quad u_{23} = 10, \quad u_{14} = 3, \quad u_{24} = 7.$$

Utilizing the measure of information (8), the diagram of the most rational algorithm of recognition in this case will be as shown in figure 2.

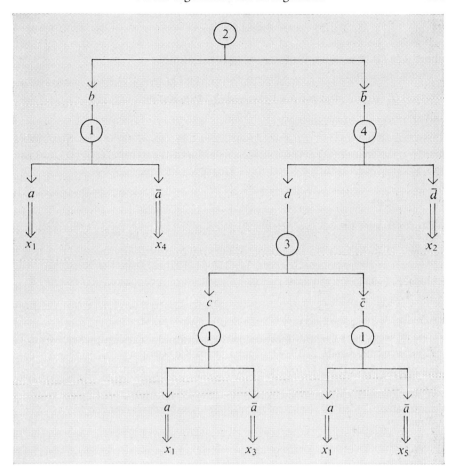

Figure 2

APPENDIX

In Guiaşu (1970) the following theorem is proved:

Let there be the functions $I_n(u_1, ..., u_n; p_1, ..., p_n)$, $(n=1, 2, ...)$ defined on the set

$$u_i \geqslant 0, \quad p_i \geqslant 0, \quad (i=1, ..., n); \quad \sum_{i=1}^{n} p_i = 1$$

such that

(a) $I_2(u_1, u_2; p, 1-p)$ is a continuous function of $p \in [0, 1]$;

(b) $I_n(u_1, ..., u_n; p_1, ..., p_n)$ is symmetric with respect to the pairs (u_i, p_i), $(i=1, ..., n)$;

(c) If $u_n = \dfrac{q'u' + q''u''}{q' + q''}$, $p_n = q' + q''$, $(q' \geqslant 0, q'' \geqslant 0, u' \geqslant 0, u'' \geqslant 0)$,

then $I_{n+1}(u_1, ..., u_{n-1}, u', u''; p_1, p_2, ..., p_{n-1}, q', q'')$

$$= I_n(u_1, ..., u_n; p_1, ..., p_n) + p_n I_2\left(u', u''; \frac{q'}{p_n}, \frac{q''}{p_n}\right);$$

(d) $\quad I_n\left(u_1, \ldots, u_n; \dfrac{1}{n}, \ldots, \dfrac{1}{n}\right) = L(n)\dfrac{u_1 + \ldots + u_n}{n}$

where $L(n)$ is a positive function of natural number n.

Then, the expression of $I_n(u_1, \ldots, u_n; p_1, \ldots, p_n)$ is given by

$$I_n(u_1, \ldots, u_n; p_1, \ldots, p_n) = -\lambda \sum_{i=1}^{n} u_i p_i \log p_i$$

where λ is a positive constant.

Remarks. If $u_1 = u_2 = \ldots = u_n = u$, $I_n(u_1, \ldots, u_n; p_1, \ldots, p_n)$ becomes Shannon's entropy, the axiom (d) is obviously satisfied and the axioms (a), (b), (c) are just Faddeev's axioms for Shannon's entropy (Faddeev 1956).

REFERENCES

Beliş, M. & Guiaşu, S. (1968) A quantitative–qualitative measure of information in cybernetic systems. *IEEE Trans. Inform. Theory*, IT–14, 593–4.

Faddeev, D. K. (1956) On the notion of entropy in probability theory. *Progress in mathematical Sciences*, 11, 227–31. (Trans. from the Russian.)

Guiaşu, S. (1968) On the most rational algorithm of recognition. *Kybernetik*, 5, 109–13.

Guiaşu, S. (1971) A generalization of Shannon's entropy. *Reports on Mathematical Physics* (to be published).

Landa, L. N. (1962) Logical-informational algorithm in learning theory. *Psychological Journal*, 2, 19–40. (Trans. from the Russian).

Manolescu, M. I. (1970) O metodă (logico-) matematică pentru diagnoza sociologică. în volumul: Metode şi tehnici ale sociologiei. *Editura didactică şi pedagogică* (ed. Constantinescu, M.) pp. 181–95. Bucuresti. [A (logico-) mathematical method for sociological diagnosis. *Methods and Techniques in Sociology.*]

Rényi, A. (1965) On the theory of random search. *Bull. Am. Math. Soc.*, 71, 809–28.

Related Mathematical Topics

Israël César Lerman
Sur l'analyse des données préalable à une classification automatique

For the purpose of classification a finite set A of attributes is supposed to be established in order to describe a finite population E of objects. For a given object x we have the subset $X(X \subset A)$ of its own attributes. The representation is thus defined by an application of E into the set $P(A)$ of the parts of A. Equivalently, to each object x we can associate the logic vector $\mathbf{a}(x) = (x_1, x_2, ..., x_i, ..., x_p)$ where x_i is equal to 1 if the object x has the attribute a_i and 0 otherwise, $\mathbf{a}(x)$ is a point of the cube $\{0, 1\}^p$. With regard to the same attribute a_i, two objects x and y arc said to have a positive association (or negative) if a_i is present (or absent) simultaneously for the two objects; that is, $x_i = 1$, $y_i = 1$ (or $x_i = 0$, $y_i = 0$). We suppose here that only positive association can be significant for similarity; this situation is in fact the most frequent one.

Let us call $s = \Sigma x_i y_i = |X \cap Y|$ the number of attributes owned in common by the two objects x and y; the main idea of this study is to adopt as a measure of similarity the probability $\Pr\{|X \cap Y| < s\}$ in the hypothesis N that X (or Y) would be taken out of the parts of A with l_x (or l_y) elements; each of these two sets being provided with a measure of similarity uniformly distributed. This idea allows us to specify the notion of polythetic class introduced by Beckner (1959), to determine *a priori* those neutral attributes or ill-typed objects which upset the classifiable nature of a population, to define finally in a natural way a measure of proximity between classes.

The basic information that we retain in our method is a total preorder upon the set of the pairs of distinct objects from E established from the choice of similarity measure. We have shown incidentally that this expression is sensitive to the choice of the similarity only if the variance of the number of attributes possessed by a single object is not negligible. In this last case, the measure of similarity proposed allows the preorder to be satisfactorily established.

Une idée qui permet de préciser la notion de classe polythétique introduite par Beckner (1959) nous autorise ici à intervenir sur deux questions importantes et liées de la Taxinomie: le choix des attributs de description et le choix de la mesure de similarité.

Représentation des Données

Relativement à une visée classificatoire on suppose établi pour la description d'une population finie E d'objets $(|E| = n)$, un ensemble fini A d'attributs; $A = \{a_1, a_2, ..., a_i, ..., a_p\}$, $(|A| = p)$.

On retient pour un objet donné x sa description; c'est-à-dire le sous-ensemble $X(X \subset A)$ des attributs qu'il possède. La représentation est ainsi définie au moyen d'une application de E dans l'ensemble $P(A)$ des parties de A. De manière équivalente on peut associer à chaque objet x le vecteur logique $\mathbf{a}(x) = (x_1, x_2, ..., x_i, ..., x_p)$ où x_i est égal à 1 si l'objet x possède l'attribut a_i et 0 sinon; $\mathbf{a}(x)$ est un point du cube $\{0, 1\}^p$.

De la sorte E nous est transmis comme un échantillon dans $P(A)$ ou dans $\{0, 1\}^p$. Cette information est généralement consignée dans un 'tableau de données' qui est une matrice d'incidence (ε_{ij}), $i = 1, 2, ..., p$ et $j = 1, 2, ..., n$; où $\varepsilon_{ij} = 1$ si l'attribut a_i est présent chez l'objet codé j et 0 sinon. Ainsi chaque attribut est représenté par une ligne de la matrice et chaque objet par une colonne.

Définition. Par rapport à un même attribut a_i, deux objets x et y sont dits avoir une association positive (resp. négative) si a_i est présent (resp. absent) simultanément chez les deux objets; c'est-à-dire $x_i = 1$, $y_i = 1$ (resp. $x_i = 0$, $y_i = 0$).

LES HYPOTHÈSES INITIALES

L'hypothèse fondamentale du spécialiste est que la population qu'il étudie a une aptitude suffisante à être organisée en une hiérarchie de classifications emboîtées de moins en moins fines qui respecte de manière satisfaisante les ressemblances entre objets; c'est-à-dire telle que deux objets se trouvent réunis à un niveau d'autant plus élevé que leur similarité est grande.

La ressemblance entre deux objets donnés sera perçue à partir des attributs de description que nous supposons établis de telle façon que seule une association positive contribue à la mesure de leur similarité. Cette circonstance correspond d'ailleurs à la situation la plus fréquente. Si, par exemple, les différents caractères de la population étaient bivalents, les deux modalités d'un même caractère étant telles que

(a) également significatives de la ressemblance ou bien

(b) l'une des deux modalités est significative de la ressemblance alors que l'autre ne l'est pas;

on définira l'ensemble A des attributs en retenant pour chacun des caractères la ou les deux modalités significatives. De cette manière la prise en compte des associations négatives peut être négligée.

LA NOTION DE CLASSE

Selon Beckner une classe polythétique G d'une classification 'naturelle' se réfère à un sous-ensemble B d'attributs tel que

(a) chaque élément de la classe possède une proportion importante (mais non fixée) d'attributs de B;

(b) chaque attribut de B est présent chez une proportion importante (mais non fixée) d'éléments de G;

(c) il n'y a pas nécessairement un attribut de B qui soit possédé par tous les éléments de G.

Restreignant notre attention aux paires d'objets de G où aux paires d'attributs de B, nous pouvons substituer à cette définition, la suivante:

(d) deux objets donnés de la classe G possèdent simultanément une proportion importante d'attributs de B;

(e) deux attributs donnés de B sont simultanément présents chez une proportion importante d'objets de G.

Si $(E_1, E_2, ..., E_k)$ est la partition de E en k classes qui définit la classification la plus significative, celle 'naturelle' que vise Beckner; puisqu'à chacune des classes E_i est associé un sous-ensemble A_i des attributs auquel elle se réfère, à la famille des classes $\{E_i | i = 1, 2, ..., k\}$ correspond bijectivement une famille $\{A_i | i = 1, 2, ..., k\}$ des parties de A. Chacune des parties étant plutôt spécifique d'une seule classe, on peut imposer à cette dernière famille d'être une partition. De plus dans la restriction de la matrice à $\bigcup_{1 \leqslant i \leqslant k} A_i X E_i$ (resp. au complémentaire de $\bigcup_{1 \leqslant i \leqslant k} A_i X E_i$) la fréquence des uns est significativement grande (resp. petite). Introduisons ici relativement à deux objets x et y le nombre $s = S(x, y)$ des attributs qu'ils possèdent en commun,

$$s = \sum_{1 \leqslant i \leqslant p} x_i y_i = |X \cap Y|$$

où X (resp. Y) est le sous-ensemble d'attributs possédés par x (resp. y).

De même relativement à deux attributs a_l et a_m définissons le nombre $\sigma = \Sigma(a_l, a_m)$ des objets possédant simultanément les deux attributs, $\sigma = |G \cap H|$, où G (resp. H) est l'ensemble des objets où a_l (resp. a_m) est présent. Omettant de préciser la classe et l'ensemble des attributs auquel elle se réfère, les conditions (d) et (e) deviennent

(f) Deux objets d'une même classe (resp. de deux classes distinctes) ont une valeur de s 'relativement' grande (resp. petite);

(g) Deux attributs d'une même classe d'attributs (resp. de deux classes distinctes) ont une valeur de σ 'relativement' grande (resp. petite).

Il nous reste à donner un sens plus précis à l'adverbe 'relativement' qu'on retrouve dans chacune des assertions ci-dessus. Ayant observé une valeur s associée à deux objets x et y ($s = S(x, y)$), comment juger si par exemple une telle valeur est assez grande?

Si X et Y sont les deux parties de l'ensemble A que définissent les deux objets x et y pour lesquelles on a $|X| - l_x$ et $|Y| - l_y$, considérons comme nous l'avions fait dans l'étude de la classificabilité, l'hypothèse N où X (resp. Y) serait pris dans l'ensemble des parties de A à l_x (resp. l_y) éléments; chacun de ces deux ensembles étant muni d'une probabilité uniformément répartie. La manière la plus objective pour répondre à la question posée est d'étudier dans l'hypothèse N la *vraisemblance* d'une valeur aussi grande que s; c'est-à-dire

$$\Pr\{|X \cap Y| \geqslant s\} \quad .$$

La valeur de s sera considérée d'autant plus grande que cette probabilité est plus petite; ou, ce qui revient au même, les deux objets x et y seront jugés d'autant plus proches que $\Pr\{|X \cap Y| < s\} = P(x, y)$ est plus grande. Dualement, on se placera dans l'ensemble des parties de E pour juger de la *vraisemblance* d'une valeur observée de $\Sigma(a_l, a_m)$ aussi grande que σ et on désignera par $\Pi(a_l, a_m)$ la probabilité $\Pr\{|G \cap H| < \sigma\}$ calculée dans une hypothèse M duale de N.

En remplaçant l'adverbe 'relativement' par $P(x, y)$ dans (f) et par $\Pi(a_l, a_m)$ dans (g) on aura achevé de donner un sens plus précis à ces énoncés.

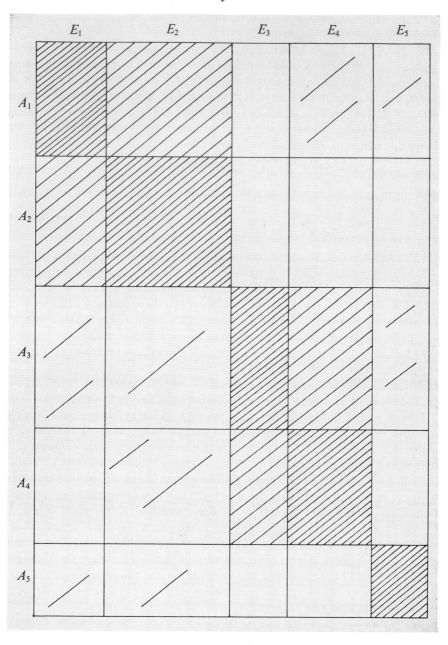

Figure 1

D'un point de vue calcul, n et p sont généralement assez grands pour admettre de manière sûre une distribution binomiale pour $|X \cap Y|$ (resp. $|G \cap H|$) dans l'hypothèse N (resp. M) de paramètres p et $u = |X|x|Y|/p^2$ (resp. n et $v = |G|x|H|/n^2$). En posant $\lambda = p.u$ et $\mu = n.v$, dans la mesure où λ (resp. μ) est trop petit vis à vis de p (resp. n) on adoptera pour la loi de la statistique $|X \cap Y|$ (resp. $|G \cap H|$) une approximation de type Poisson; sinon, une approximation par la loi normale.

Ces remarques nous conduisent à aborder le problème du choix des attributs.

Choix des Attributs

Définition. Soit $(E_1, E_2, ..., E_i, ..., E_k)$ une partition de E. Si **a** est un attribut donné, désignons par f_i la proportion des objets de la classe E_i qui possèdent l'attribut **a**. $(f_1, f_2, ..., f_k)$ définira la distribution de la fréquence relative de présence de **a** sur les différentes classes. L'attribut **a** discrimine d'autant mieux la classification que la dispersion de $i \rightarrow f_i$ est plus grande par rapport à la dispersion de la fréquence de présence de **a** dans E.

Nous appellons *signification* de l'attribut **a** par rapport à la classification $(E_1, E_2, ..., E_k)$ la quantité:

$$\frac{1}{(k-1)} \sum_{i=1}^{k} (f_i - \bar{f})^2 \left/ \frac{\bar{f}(1-\bar{f})}{n} \right. \tag{1}$$

où $\bar{f} = \frac{1}{k} \sum_{i=1}^{k} f_i$, le rapport de l'estimation de la variance inter-classes sur celle, globale.

Il en résulte une pondération sur l'ensemble A des attributs où à chaque attribut $a_i (i = 1, 2, ..., p)$ est attaché un coefficient tel que (1). Si le choix des objets constituant la population E peut s'imposer de manière plus ou moins évidente au spécialiste, il en est tout autrement du choix des attributs de description. À ce sujet deux questions se posent *a priori* au taxinomiste:
(1) Quels sont les attributs pertinents vis à vis du problème étudié?
(2) Quelle importance convient-il d'accorder à chacun d'eux pour définir au mieux la classification?

Nous nous proposons de montrer que (1) est un vrai problème alors que (2) en est un faux. Supposons pour cela découverte la classification recherchée et illustrons cette solution par le tableau d'incidence ci-joint où en la figure 1 la densité des hachures représente la densité des uns, la hiérarchie de classifications correspondante étant (la figure 2).

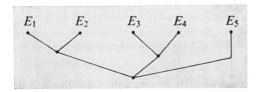

Figure 2

La première raison qui nous fait penser que (2) est une fausse question

est que l'importance d'un attribut ne peut être définie dans l'absolu; elle est
établie relativement à une classification comme nous l'avons exprimé ci-dessus
[compare (1)]. Par conséquent, il nous faudra connaître à l'avance la
classification visée pour définir la bonne pondération. D'ailleurs la connaissance de cette pondération diminue très sensiblement l'intérêt d'une classification automatique.

Si un attribut est important; c'est-à-dire s'il est assez caractéristique d'une
classe G relative à une classification 'naturelle', sa présence chez un objet
impliquera, en général, la présence de la plupart des attributs de la classe B
des attributs, à laquelle G se réfère; ainsi que l'absence chez cet objet de la
plupart des attributs du complémentaire de B dans A. Donc on peut s'attendre
à ce que l'importance d'un attribut donné apparaisse dans une classification
basée sur l'étude des ressemblances entre objets. Bien plus, la prise en
compte d'une bonne pondération des attributs dans l'établissement d'une
mesure de similarité accroît artificiellement l'importance propre de certains
attributs. Enfin, dans cette hiérarchie de classifications que recherche le
taxinomiste un même attribut peut être plus ou moins discriminant selon les
différents niveaux.

En établissant ses attributs de description le chercheur en Sciences Humaines
se rend tout à fait compte du caractère crucial du problème (1). On ignore
souvent si un attribut donné interviendra dans la formation des classes. Il en
résulte un alourdissement du tableau des données par un accroissement du
nombre d'attributs et, ce qui est plus grave, la présence d'attributs neutres qui
perturbent la nature classifiable de la population.

Nettoyage de la Matrice d'incidence des Données

Supposons le problème résolu et adoptons pour illustrer cette solution le
tableau d'incidence ci-dessus. Si $\{\mathbf{b}, \mathbf{c}\}$ est une paire donnée d'attributs,
on constate soit une nette proximité lorsque $\mathbf{b}$ et $\mathbf{c}$ sont relatifs à une même
classe; soit une franche opposition lorsque les deux attributs sont relatifs à
deux classes éloignées; donc une valeur de $\Pi(\mathbf{b}, \mathbf{c})$ soit trop grande soit trop
petite. Dans ces conditions, considérons pour un attribut donné $\mathbf{a}$ l'ensemble
des paires d'attributs dont l'une des composantes est $\mathbf{a}(A\mathbf{a} = \{\{\mathbf{a}, \mathbf{c}\} \mid \mathbf{c} \in A -
\{\mathbf{a}\}\}, |A\mathbf{a}| = p - 1)$ et examinons l'allure de la distribution $\Pi(\mathbf{a})$ des valeurs
de $\Pi(\mathbf{a}, \mathbf{c})$ pour $\mathbf{c}$ parcourant $A - \{\mathbf{a}\}$. Pour cela, on portera sur un axe
horizontal du plan l'intervalle $[0, 1]$ des valeurs possibles de $\Pi(\mathbf{a}, \mathbf{c})$ et sur
un axe vertical le nombre d'éléments $\mathbf{c}$ pour lesquels on aura observé une
valeur donnée de $\Pi(\mathbf{a}, \mathbf{c})$. Une telle distribution sera portée vers les
extrémités de l'intervalle $[0, 1]$ comme essaie de la suggérer la figure 3.
Si par exemple il s'introduit dans notre tableau d'incidence un attribut α
neutre pour la classification, on devra généralement s'attendre à ce que la
distribution $\Pi(\alpha)$ associée soit plus uniformément répartie entre 0 et 1 que
celle $\Pi(\mathbf{a})$ attachée à un attribut pertinent pour la classification. Par conséquent, dans un tableau correspondant à un ces réel, en étudiant pour chacun
des attributs $\mathbf{a}$ la distribution $\Pi(\mathbf{a})$, il nous sera possible de détecter ceux des
attributs pour lesquels $\Pi(\mathbf{a})$ n'est pas suffisamment *dispersée* (et ce, au
moyen d'un coefficient de dispersion) et de les éjecter de notre étude.

Figure 3

On pourra dualement, par une technique analogue nettoyer les colonnes du tableau d'incidence, on éliminera ainsi les objets les moins 'typés'. On se trouvera finalement devant des données bien classifiables.

Exemple géométrique. Considérons la figure formée par deux surfaces carrées se déduisant l'une de l'autre par translation horizontale et reliées par une très mince bande oblique comme l'indique la figure 4. Rapportons le plan de la figure à deux axes parallèles aux côtés de l'un des carrés et définissons une grille par un pavage du plan en petits carrés; a est une tranche horizontale de la grille, b, c, et b' sont des tranches verticales. L'ensemble des attributs sera défini à partir de l'ensemble des tranches horizontales ou verticales. Si h (resp. k) est le nombre de tranches horizontales (resp. verticales) la description d'un point de la surface étudiée se fera au moyen d'un vecteur logique à $(k+h)$ composantes indexé sur l'ensemble des tranches où le 1 exprime pour le point son appartenance à une tranche. On montrera que la technique précédente permet d'éliminer tous les attributs relatifs à des tranches telles que c.

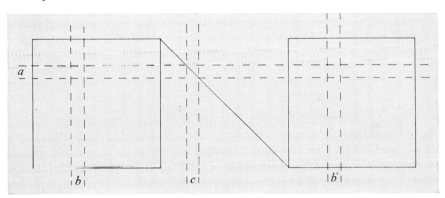

Figure 4

On se rend compte que cette purification des données permet d'éviter l'effet de chainage qu'on redoute dans l'application de l'algorithme 'lexicographique' (*cf.* Lerman 1970).

Mesure de Similarité et Préordonnance Associée

La mesure de similarité qui s'impose après l'analyse effectuée precedemment ('La notion de classe') peut être définie par une application de l'ensemble F des paires d'objets distincts de E dans l'intervalle $[0, 1]$ qui à chaque paire $\{x, y\}$ affecte le nombre $P(x, y)$ qui, rappelons-le, est la probabilité

$$\Pr\{|X \cap Y| < s\}$$

calculée dans l'hypothèse N, où s est la valeur observée de l'indice $S(x, y)$.

Pour calculer effectivement $P(x, y)$ on aura à se référer soit à une table de la fonction de repartition d'une loi de Poisson soit à celle d'une loi normale;

on sait que c'est chose facile que d'introduire ces deux tables dans la mémoire d'un ordinateur. Nous allons tenter de faire sentir le progrès que représente cet indice par rapport à ceux, connus. Reprenons pour cela notre point de vue qui a été introduit par Benzecri (1969) et qui trouve son origine dans les travaux de P. N. Shepard où on ne retient comme information relative à la ressemblance des objets qu'une préordonnance. Rappelons que cette donnée est un préordre total sur l'ensemble F des paires d'objets distincts de E pour lequel une paire p précède une paire q si les deux objets composant p se ressemblent davantage que ceux composant q.

Cherchant à synthétiser l'ensemble des indices de similarité proposés et à étudier l'influence du choix d'un indice sur la préordonnance associée, nous introduisions, relativement à deux objets x et y, en même temps que le paramètre s, les paramètres suivants:

t: cardinal du sous-ensemble des attributs non possédés par aucun des deux objets;

u(resp. v): cardinal du sous-ensemble des attributs possédés par l'objet x (resp. y) et non possédés par y (resp. x);

et nous définissions une mesure de similarité comme une fonction réelle positive S définie sur l'ensemble $E \times E$ qui se présente sous la forme $(x, y) \mapsto S(x, y) = \mathscr{S}(s, u, v)$ où la fonction $\mathscr{S}(s, u, v)$, définie sur le sous-ensemble de $\mathbb{N}^3$, $\{(s, u, v) \mid s + u + v \leqslant p\}$, est croissante par rapport à s, symétrique en u et v et décroissante par rapport à u, la croissance par rapport à s ou la décroissance par rapport à u étant stricte.

Nous montrions que si le nombre d'attributs possédés par un même objet était invariable dans E, tous les indices de similarité étaient équivalents. Dans le cas où deux indices S et S' n'étaient pas équivalents, nous exprimions l'écart entre les deux préordonnances respectivement associées, $w(S)$ et $w(S')$, par le nombre d'inversions que présente $w(S')$ par rapport à $w(S)$. Parmi les indices de similarité qui se présentaient sous la forme $\mathscr{S}(s, u+v)$, $S(x, y) = s$ et $S'(x, y) = s + t$ étaient les deux pour lesquels les préordonnances respectivement associées étaient les plus écartées. Si la variance du nombre d'attributs possédés par un même objet était petite le nombre d'inversions que présente $w(s+t)$ par rapport à $w(s)$ était également petit.

Ces résultats étaient décisifs dans la pratique lorsqu'on avait à traiter des questionnaires ou certains codes descriptifs d'objets pour lesquels le nombre d'attributs possédés par un même objet, dans la population étudiée, était sinon invariable du moins de faible variance. Cependant le problème restait entier lorsque cette variance n'était pas négligeable. Un calcul théorique nous a permis de nous en rendre compte ainsi qu'un exemple concret qui portait sur 'les caractéristiques des personnages-enfants à travers les contes d'enfants'. Dans le cadre de cet exemple, P. Achard, cherchant à neutraliser dans la statistique s les effets de taille (nombre d'attributs possédés) qui rendaient trop ressemblants les objets de grosse taille, nous avait proposé de centrer et de réduire s en se référant à l'hypothèse N; c'est-à-dire, avec les notations données déjà d'adopter comme indice

$$(s-pu)/\sqrt{(pu(p-u))} \quad . \tag{2}$$

Toutefois simulant l'hypothèse N nous avons remarqué une tendance de cet indice de similarité à rendre trop proches les objets de petite taille, remarque que nous allons confirmer par un calcul et un graphique.

Supposons $n = 1000$ et soient deux paires d'objets $\{x, y\}$ et $\{x', y'\}$ telles que les deux composantes de la première (resp. seconde) paire aient une taille commune égale à 50 (resp. 500). Les valeurs de l'indice s correspondant à une valeur égale à 1 pour la statistique (2) sont respectivement 4 pour la paire $\{x, y\}$ et 264 pour la paire $\{x'y'\}$. Or il semble intuitivement que deux objets de taille 500 qui ont 264 attributs communs se ressemblent davantage que deux objets de taille 50 qui n'ont que 4 attributs communs.

Calculons la vraisemblance dans l'hypothèse N de chacun de ces deux résultats. Pour la paire $\{x, y\}$, $\lambda = pu = 2\cdot5$ est trop petit devant $p = 1000$; utilisant la table de la loi de Poisson on a $P(x, y) = 0\cdot76$, tandis que pour la

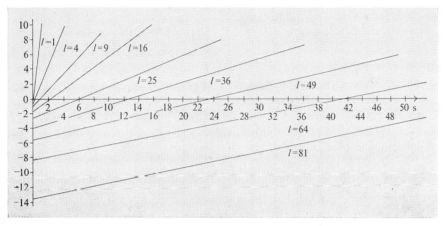

Figure 5

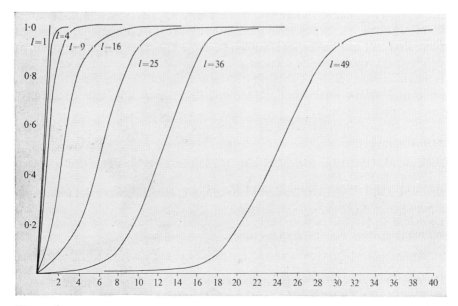

Figure 6

paire $\{x'y'\}$, $\lambda' = pu' = 250$ et la table de la loi normale fournit $P(x', y') = 0\cdot84$. Du point de vue de notre mesure de similarité les objets x et y sont moins proches que x' et y'.

La figure 5 représente une famille de segments de droite. Une même droite définit la variation de l'indice (2) lorsque s varie, pour une paire d'objets de même taille 1, ($p = 100$); alors qu'une courbe donnée dans la figure 6 définit, dans les mêmes conditions, la variation de la mesure $P(x, y)$. On notera que si le nombre d'attributs possédés par un même objet était constant dans E, la préordonnance associée à $P(x, y)$ est la même que celle associée à s qui est d'ailleurs la même que celle associée à tout indice de la forme $\mathscr{S}(s, u, v)$. De plus si la valeur du paramètre λ ne devenait pas trop petite par rapport à p dans E, la préordonnance associée à $P(x, y)$ est la même que celle associée à l'indice (2) ci-dessus.

Mesure de Similarité Entre Parties Disjointes de E

Cette nouvelle notion de mesure de similarité nous permet de définir, de façon naturelle, une mesure de similarité entre parties disjointes de E qui tient en particulier compte des cardinaux de ces parties.

Si G et H sont deux sous-ensembles disjoints de E de cardinaux respectifs g et h. Considérons l'ensemble des valeurs de $P(x, y)$ lorsque x parcourt G et y, H:
$$\{P(x, y) \mid x \in G, y \in H\} \tag{3}$$
et désignons la plus grande de ces valeurs par
$$P(G, H) = \max \{P(x, y) \mid x \in G, y \in H\}$$

On ne peut juger de la proximité des parties en cause en se référant uniquement à la valeur de $P(G, H)$, car une même valeur assez grande de $P(G, H)$ peut être naturelle si G et H sont de cardinal élevé et assez exceptionnelle si G et H sont de faible cardinal.

Par conséquent nous allons comme précédemment nous référer à l'hypothèse N où l'ensemble (3) des valeurs est un échantillon de $g.h$ points d'une variable aléatoire uniformément répartie entre 0 et 1. La probabilité d'observer pour $P(G, H)$ une valeur inférieure à t étant t^{gh}; si $\overline{\omega}$ est la valeur observée de $P(G, H)$, on retiendra comme mesure de similarité entre G et H, $\overline{\omega}^{gh}$. Il sera intéressant d'appliquer l'algorithme classique définissant une hiérarchie de classifications ascendante (Benzecri 1969) avec une telle mesure de similarité entre classes.

BIBLIOGRAPHIE

Beckner, M. (1959) *The Biological Way of Thought*. New York: Columbia University Press.

Benzecri, J.P. (1969) Classification automatique et reconnaissance des formes. *Cours I.S.U.P.* 1968–9.

Lerman, I.C. (1970) Les bases de la classification automatique. *Collection Programmation*. Paris: Gauthier-Villars.

Sokal, R.R. & Sneath, P.H.A. (1963) *Principles of numerical taxonomy*. London & San Francisco: Freeman.

De la Vega, W.F. (1970) Techniques de classification automatique utilisant un indice de ressemblance. *Rev. Fr. Sociologie*. (Dec.)

Abstracts

Mircea Manolescu and Gabriela Bordenache
Some mathematical aspects of taxonomy and diagnosis in archaeology
The possibility is investigated of applying certain mathematical methods and techniques to some archaeological problems. In particular, reference is made to a work on the mathematical modelling of 'scientific diagnosis' and the relationship between this and taxonomy (Manolescu 1970). The author here seeks to adapt mathematical methods (and models) to some specific aspects of archaeology (certain problems of taxonomy and diagnosis).
REFERENCE
Manolescu, M. I. (1970). Une méthode (logico-) mathématique pour la diagnose sociologique. *Méthodes et techniques de la sociologie*, pp. 181–95 (ed. Constantinescu, M.). Bucharest.

Gr. C. Moisil
The axiom systems of similarity relations
The propositions 'the object a is more similar to the object b than to the object c' and 'the object a is more similar to the object b than the object c is to the object d' introduce two similarity relations in the set of the objects. The author gives some axioms which make the set of objects a topological space.

Silvia Savu
Discrimination and classification of certain types of ancient pottery
The paper first presents the two usual procedures for the computation of R. A. Fisher's discriminant function. The analysis of variance, the Mahalanobis generalized distance, and Hotelling generalized ratio are then introduced.

Significance tests for the distances between samples are then reconstructed and applied to the particular problem of classifying a single observation into one of the samples.

Questions concerning the comparison of discriminant functions and testing the difference between them are then discussed.

The resulting comparison criterion allows a distinction to be made between useful variates to be included in, and insignificant ones to be excluded from the discriminatory analysis, thus removing the difficulty of reducing the number of variates.

As an application, the discrimination between two groups of pottery is treated.

We consider two groups of pottery, the styles of which are well determined: Rhodian style pottery (Wild goat style) and Black-figure style pottery (Attic).

Twenty vases (having the following shapes: amphora, oenochoe, cup and plate) are taken from each group.

For discrimination we use the criteria: shape, with special references to lip, foot, handle; clay; surface: slip, glaze, 'couverte'; ornament-colour, ground colour, accessory colours, incisions and filling motifs; exterior ornament-lip, neck, shoulder, belly, foot, handle; interior ornament.

The problem we solve is to classify a group of twenty vases.

Taxonomy

Discussion and comments

L. L. Cavalli-Sforza. Coming to some specific problems raised by Dr Rao, I would like to comment on his criticism of our measure of genetic distance. Observations on genetic differences have features that are not shared by phenotypic differences. The latter have important internal correlations that have a morphological or physiological basis, for instance, due to general size factors. The former do not usually show such correlations; they have instead negative correlations (between alleles at one locus) that can be removed by appropriate scaling. They also have correlations due to evolutionary process. Pairs of populations which have a long common history are more highly correlated than those which have a shorter one. These between population correlations involve correlations between characters, which should not be removed when computing distances. The penalty could be the loss of evidence desired for reconstructing phylogenics. For this reason, techniques commonly employed for morphometric distances are not to be recommended for genetic distance, and special methods have to be developed such as those used by Edwards and myself.

Another difficulty concerning morphometric, that is, phenotypic differences, is that one cannot state, in general, their relationship to genetic differences. Especially when comparing different populations, the genotype environment covariance can be zero, or can have a positive or a negative sign. It is possible to have a large phenotypic difference without any underlying genetic difference, but also the reverse is possible.

C. R. Rao. I am aware that environmental factors are important and in fact, in relationship (4) in my paper, some of the factors could be genetic and some environmental. I agree that some caution is necessary in comparing populations living in different environments, whether we are using morphometric characters or blood groups. But as I have mentioned in my paper (*see* 'Stability of clusters'), this difficulty does not arise in comparing groups of individuals living under the same environmental conditions. In the UP and Bengal surveys, the groups studied belonged to a state or to a sub-region of a state.

It is well known that certain blood group gene frequencies can be altered by environment due to selection. In such a case even the genetic distance based on certain blood groups is not a suitable measure for studying relationships and tracing the evolution of groups living under different environmental conditions.

I do not understand how the existence of internal correlations between morphometric characters, referred to by Dr Cavalli-Sforza, makes them unsuitable for phylogenetic classification. If correlations exist, they are taken care of in the measure of distance employed, where each character gets its due weight depending on its importance in relation to genetic and possibly environmental factors.

It is true that we know more about the genetics of blood groups than that of the morphometric characters. But it cannot be denied that the latter have a genetic basis and that differences in their values between populations reflect genetic differences. Morphometric characters probably reflect differences in wider genetic material than blood groups alone, in which case it would not be wise to neglect the former. Ideally one should consider the combined evidence if classification has to cover all genetic aspects (*see* Sangvi 1953). However, the existing methods for this purpose do not seem to be very satisfactory.

V.Liveanu. One must consider carefully whether it is possible to use correlation coefficients for clustering procedures if the data are not normally distributed.

From the historian's point of view the important matter in comparing the results of different clustering procedures is the meaning of the clusters obtained.

C.A.Moberg. In the paper by Drs Tăutu and Iosifescu an important and often-met type of archaeological problem has been considered. Of course, the real structure of what we call archaeological 'cultures', 'sub-cultures', and so on, is much discussed; but we do in fact use these concepts, and we do ask such questions as 'to which sub-culture, and so on, does this group of objects belong'. Provided the mathematical basis of the approach of Dr Iosifescu and Dr Tăutu is firm, the approach must be welcomed. It will be interesting to compare this study with the ideas on a partially related topic, expressed by B.I.Marshak (1965), who uses concepts from information theory.

REFERENCES

Marshak, B.I. (1965) In *Archeologija i estestvennye nauki* (ed. Koltchin, B.A.). Moscow: Akademia nauk S.S.S.R., Institut archeologii. Nauka.
Sangvi, L.D. (1953) Comparison of genetic and morphological methods for a study of biological differences. *Amer. J. phys. Anthrop.*, **11**, 385–404.

Multi-dimensional scaling and related procedures

General Survey

Special Topics

Discussion and Comments

General Survey

Joseph B. Kruskal
Multi-dimensional scaling in archaeology: time is not the only dimension

SERIATION AND SCALING

Suppose we know the dates of various events, artifacts, or objects, as in figure 1. Then it requires only simple arithmetic, subtraction, to make a table showing the time intervals between events. Conversely, if we start with a table showing the time intervals (or time 'distances') between objects, it is not hard to reconstruct the dates, though with two important limitations: (1) the dates are only relative to each other; (2) since time intervals are always positive numbers, we cannot tell from the intervals alone which way time flows along the series of events. The reconstruction process can be considered a kind of seriation, based on information about the intervals between objects.

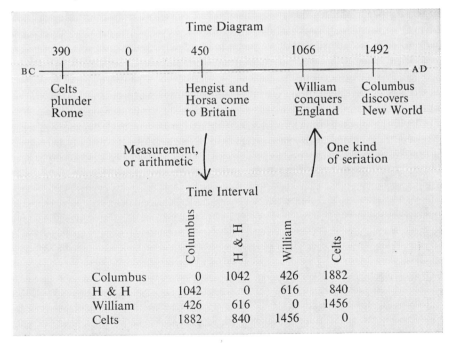

	Columbus	H & H	William	Celts
Columbus	0	1042	426	1882
H & H	1042	0	616	840
William	426	616	0	1456
Celts	1882	840	1456	0

Figure 1. Time diagram

This process is not of course restricted to the time variable. Given the distances between stations on a straight railroad, we can reconstruct the positions of the stations. In fact, we can reconstruct the values for any variable, without even knowing what it refers to or means, if we are given the distances. If the distances are expressed not in years or kilometers but in arbitrary units, then of course the reconstructed values will also be in arbitrary units. In geometrical terms, the values can be thought of as a configuration of points on a line. All we are saying is that such a configuration may be reconstructed from the interpoint distances.

If the distances are contaminated by random errors (as all real data are), it is still often possible to reconstruct the underlying values approximately, though some of the methods used for this purpose are very complex, and some may serve better than others. Elsewhere in this volume, Gelfand (1971) proposes two methods of seriation based on information about the distances between objects. In psychology, techniques for this purpose have been widely used and studied under the name 'scaling', see, for example, Torgerson's book *Theory and Methods of Scaling* (Torgerson 1958).

In Archaeology One Dimension may not be Enough

Suppose we start with several artifacts or collections of artifacts (such as grave sites), which appear to vary in date of formation. There are many ways in which we can form the distance, or dissimilarity, between objects of this type, based purely on internal evidence, such as presence or absence of features, abundance of various types, and so on. Papers by Kendall (1971), Gelfand (1971), Hodson, Sneath, and Doran (1966), all present examples of this. With the idea in mind that these dissimilarities reflect time intervals between objects (in arbitrary units, and contaminated by random errors, of course), we can reconstruct the underlying values by whichever method we prefer, and then hope that we have obtained the dates of formation (with the previously mentioned limitations).

However, the dissimilarities may reflect other variables in addition to time—for example, social class, wealth, climate, and so forth. If the dissimilarities reflect more than one variable to a substantial degree, we may discover that a satisfactory reconstruction of the kind we have been discussing is just not possible. In other words, there may be no way of arranging points on a line so that the interpoint distances satisfactorily match the dissimilarities.

One way to allow two variables into the reconstruction is to permit the points to be anywhere in a plane, rather than restricting them to a line. In other words, two dimensions may be required if one dimension is not enough. Later we shall present an archaeological example where this happens. First, however, we shall explain how scaling works in two dimensions.

Two-dimensional Scaling

Suppose we have a map of Europe with various cities marked on it (*see* figure 2). To describe the position of each city on the map requires two coordinates, such as latitude and longitude, or the classical x and y coordinates of geometry. It is a simple matter to form the table of map distances, for example, by measuring them with a ruler. Alternatively, we can calculate the distances d_{ij} from the classical coordinates by the well-known Pythagorean formula

$$d_{ij} = distance\,(city_i,\, city_j) = \sqrt{((x_i - x_j)^2 + (y_i - y_j)^2)}$$

Conversely, if we start with a table of accurate map distances, it is possible

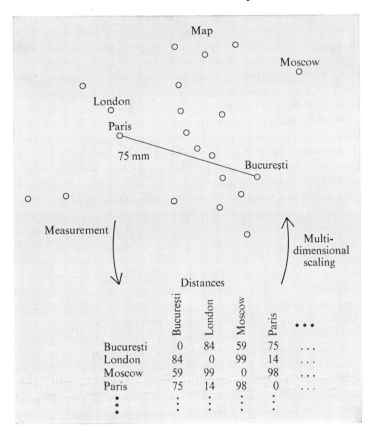

Figure 2. Map of Europe

to reconstruct accurately the positions of the cities. We illustrate one simple method in figure 3. (This method is for illustrative purposes only, since it does not work well in the presence of error.) First place $city_1$ anywhere. Then place $city_2$ anywhere on the circle of radius d_{12} around $city_1$. Then place $city_3$ where a circle of radius d_{13} around $city_1$ intersects a circle of radius d_{23} around $city_2$ (either point of intersection may be used). After this, use the first three cities as reference points for all the rest. For each value of $i = 4$ to n separately, place $city_i$ where these three circles all intersect:

radius d_{1i} around $city_1$,
radius d_{2i} around $city_2$,
radius d_{3i} around $city_3$.

It is easy to see that there are two limitations on the reconstruction, regardless of what method is used. They parallel the two limitations we mentioned for seriation. First, the reconstructed positions are only relative to one another: the entire configuration of points can be rigidly translated (shifted) from one place in the plane to another. Second, but more important, the compass directions North, East, South, and West are not determined: the entire configuration can be rigidly rotated and 'reflected'. (If the reconstructed map has been drawn on transparent paper, a reflection can be

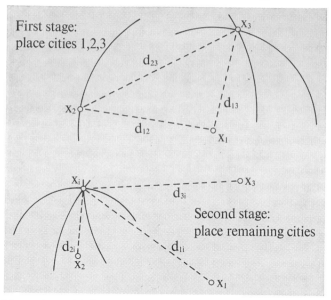

Figure 3. Multi-dimensional scaling: a simple method

accomplished by turning the paper over.) It is quite important to remember that any solution is subject to rotation and reflection.

Suppose we are given not the accurate distances d_{ij} but rather imperfect distances, which we call dissimilarities, $\delta_{ij} = d_{ij} + e_{ij}$, where the e_{ij} are random errors, not too large. Then it is still possible to reconstruct the map approximately, though the method of figure 3 cannot be used. Although the random errors e_{ij} must not be too large, it is amazing how large they can be and still permit reasonably accurate recovery of the original map, particularly if there are many cities. Here too, of course, the solution is subject to translation, rotation, and reflection.

MULTI-DIMENSIONAL SCALING

Regardless of the number of dimensions—one, two, three, or more—procedures much like two-dimensional scaling can be carried out. Regardless of dimensionality, multi-dimensional scaling means reconstructing a configuration of points from information about the distances between them.

In three or more dimensions, everything is much the same as in two dimensions. Each point x in R dimensions can be described by R coordinates $(x_1, x_2, ..., x_R)$. The distance between two points x and x' is given by

$$d(x, x') = \sqrt{((x_1 - x'_1)^2 + ... + (x_R - x'_R)^2)}$$

From a configuration of points, it is easy to calculate the table of distances by using this formula. Given the table of accurate distances, it is possible to reconstruct the original configuration accurately, though the solution is subject to translation, rotation, and reflection. Of course the meaning of rotation and reflection is not so obvious in R-dimensional space. However, such matters are fully discussed in many books on matrix theory.

Suppose we are given, not the distances, but rather dissimilarities $\delta_{ij} = d_{ij} + e_{ij}$ where the e_{ij} are random errors. Then it is possible to reconstruct the original configuration approximately, still subject to translation, rotation, and reflection.

Deciding how many dimensions to use is seldom obvious. Typically, the analysis is done for several different dimensionalities, and the results are compared, before a decision is reached as to which one to use. This subject is further discussed later.

Multi-dimensional scaling is almost always done on computers. Many programs have been written for this purpose. There are three major groups of programs: by Shepard and Kruskal (MDSCAL), by Guttman and Lingoes (SSA, for Smallest Space Analysis), and by Torgerson and Young (TORSCA, for Torgerson Scaling). Further information about the various programs is available in a book by Green and Carmone (1970), and from the various workers in this field, including the present author.

It is clear that multi-dimensional scaling generally deals with a single matrix of dissimilarities (or similarities—*see below*). If several matrices are available (relating to the same objects), a valuable new method described in this volume by Wish and Carroll (1971) can often take advantage of the differences among them in a very significant way. Until recently, it was necessary either to treat the several matrices as totally unrelated (by scaling them separately), or to treat them as mere replicate measurements which differ only by random error (by averaging them before scaling, or by scaling with replicate values explicitly present).

NON-METRIC MULTI-DIMENSIONAL SCALING

In many cases, the imperfect distances reach us in distorted form. Thus we may not be able to assume that $\delta_{ij}=d_{ij}+e_{ij}$, but only that $f(\delta_{ij})=d_{ij}+e_{ij}$, where f is some *order-preserving* function, such as

$$f(\delta)=e^{\delta}, \quad f(\delta)=\delta^{3}, \quad \text{or} \quad f(\delta)=\sqrt{\delta} \quad .$$

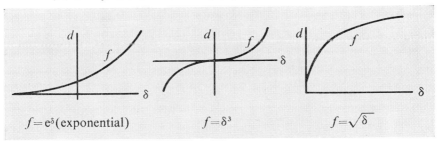

$f=e^{\delta}$ (exponential) $f=\delta^{3}$ $f=\sqrt{\delta}$

Figure 4

If we know what function f is, this offers no new difficulties, since we can calculate $\delta'_{ij}=f(\delta_{ij})$, and use the δ'_{ij} instead of the δ_{ij}. However, if we do *not* know what function f is, merely that it is order-preserving, it is still possible to reconstruct the configuration approximately, and simultaneously construct a graph which approximates the curve of f! This type of reconstruction, which is called non-metric multi-dimensional scaling, is in fact used far more commonly than the simpler type described earlier.

Suppose that f is not order-preserving, but rather order-reversing (for example, $f(s)=e^{-s}$ or $f(s)=1/s$). Then it is natural to call the observed values similarities (rather than dissimilarities) and use s instead of δ, since a large value indicates that the objects are very alike, rather than very different. Non-metric scaling can be carried out equally well in either case (but we must know which case it is!).

Configurations which arise from non-metric scaling are subject not only to translation, rotation, and reflection, but also to uniform expansion (or contraction). We are using information only about which distances are larger than others, and this is preserved under uniform expansion.

AN EXAMPLE FROM PSYCHOLOGY

An example from psychology will illustrate how multi-dimensional scaling works. [The data are from Rothkopf (1957) and the analysis from Shepard (1963).] In this example, the objects were the 36 well-known signals of International Morse code (for example, A · –, B – · · ·, 2 · · – – –, 3 · · · – –). Subjects (who did not know Morse code) heard two of these signals in succession, separated by an interval of 1·4 seconds, and declared whether

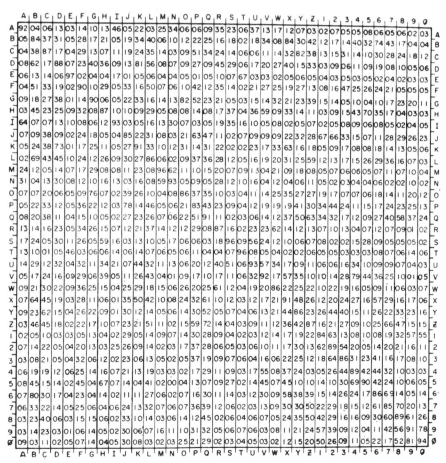

Figure 5. Table of similarities of Morse code signals

the two symbols were the 'same' or 'different'. Since the signals (produced by machine) were quite rapid, there were a substantial number of confusions (incorrect responses). The frequency with which two signals were declared the same was used as the measure of similarity. In particular, each pair of symbols was heard once by approximately 150 subjects, and the percentage of 'same' responses was used as the similarity value. The table of these similarities (essentially as published by Rothkopf) is shown in figure 5. It is not easy, by direct examination of this table, to get deep insight into what governs the confusions. The analysis described below threw substantial new light on the auditory process.

When Shepard scaled these data in two-dimensional space, the configuration in figure 6 resulted. At this point, the substantial problem of interpretation arises: what does this configuration mean? In archaeological seriation a corresponding problem sometimes arises: does the series really reflect time, and if not, what does it reflect?

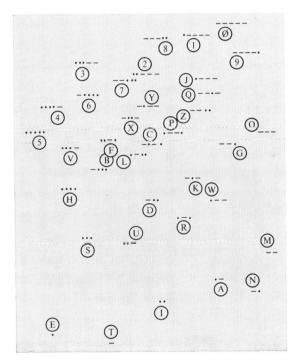

Figure 6

In this case, a very convincing interpretation becomes clear to many people who simply examine the figure for several minutes. Before looking at Shepard's interpretation, you may wish to make your own.

Shepard's interpretation is shown in figure 7. A more or less vertical direction corresponds to the length of the signal. Slightly curved horizontal lines completely separate the signals according to whether they have 1, 2, 3, 4, or 5 components. Within the sections formed by these lines, a more or less horizontal direction corresponds to the ratio of dots to dashes in the signal.

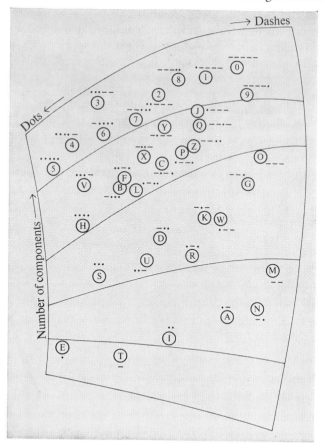

Figure 7. Shepard's interpretation of the configuration in figure 6

GOODNESS-OF-FIT

Whenever we attempt to explain data by some theory or model, such as seriation or scaling, the question always arises as to how convincing the results are. Do the data really support the explanation? For example, it is always possible to place artifacts in a series somehow or other, but whether we find the series convincing is another matter. This question overlaps with interpretation, but is not the same. For example, we may find a series convincingly supported by some data, while the interpretation of the series (time?, social class?) is still unclear.

To illustrate the comparison between the input data for scaling and the configuration that is produced, we use the Morse code example. In this case the data are in figure 5, and the configuration in figure 6. The relationship which was assumed to connect them is $f(s_{ij}) = d_{ij} + e_{ij}$, where f is some order-reversing function and e_{ij} random errors, not too large. *Ex post facto*, does this assumption seem reasonable? To see, we examine the plot of d_{ij} (as measured or calculated from figure 6) against s_{ij}. This is displayed in figure 8 (but for historical reasons, d_{ij} is on the horizontal axis, s_{ij} on the vertical axis, and the graph should be looked at sideways).

In general, a scatter diagram (like figure 8) is ideal if the points lie very close to some uphill curve or some downhill curve (for dissimilarities and similarities, respectively). The curve is interpreted as the graph of f, and the scatter of points away from the curve is ascribed to the random errors e_{ij}. In figure 8, the points do clearly indicate a downhill curve, but based on experience the scatter is rather larger than we like. The jagged line indicates an estimate $\hat{f}$ of f (in fact, the least-squares estimate).

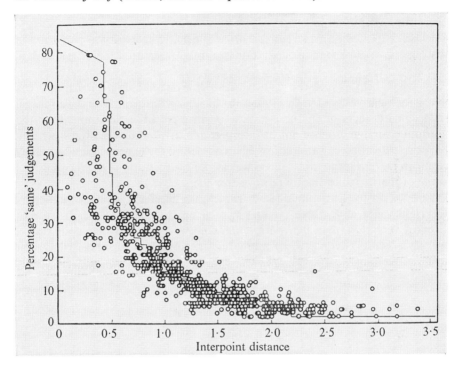

Figure 8

To get some measure of scatter in numerical form, we estimate the individual errors by solving the equation

$$\hat{f}(s_{ij}) = d_{ij} + \hat{e}_{ij},$$

for $\hat{e}_{ij}$. We then combine the estimated errors $\hat{e}_{ij}$ into a single number called stress:

$$s = \text{stress} = \sqrt{(\Sigma \hat{e}_{ij}^2 / \Sigma d_{ij}^2)} \geqslant 0 \quad.$$

(Since uniform expansion or contraction of the configuration would not change anything essential, but does change the $\hat{e}_{ij}$, the denominator is necessary to make stress meaningful.) If stress is large, the scatter is large, which is undesirable. Small values are good.

Small stress, and hence small values of $\hat{e}_{ij}$, suggests *ex post facto* that the assumption of small e_{ij} was reasonable. But how small is small? To determine this we can use published tables, as yet extremely limited, which are analogous to χ^2, t, and F tables. These tables must be heavily supplemented by good judgement and experience.

It should be remembered that stress is substantially affected by n (the number of objects) and many other things (such as the number of replicated measurements for each dissimilarity, whether the scaling is non-metric or metric, if non-metric by the way that equal dissimilarities are handled, if metric by which type of metric scaling is used, and so on). The tables available so far cover an extremely limited set of cases.

HOW MANY DIMENSIONS?

From one set of data, scaling can produce a configuration in R-dimensional space for any value of R. It is always necessary to decide which value of R is appropriate.

In order to reach a sensible decision, it is usually necessary to perform the scaling for several values of R. For example, Shepard tried $R = 1, 2, 3, 4$, and 5 with the Morse code data. Once this has been done, there are several clues which help us pick the right value of R. For one thing, we examine the maps for each value of R, and attempt to interpret them. If R is too large, then some aspects of the configuration will have been determined by the random errors, and hence not be interpretable. If R is too small, it may well happen that different variables will be competing for expression, which may result in an uninterpretable mess (unless the competition is so unequal that some of the variables simply fail to show themselves).

In addition to these valuable but sometimes unreliable clues for choosing the right value of R, there are clues based on the stress values. If we plot stress S versus R, as in figure 9 (which comes from the Morse code data), we get a 'curve' (actually, just a few points, connected together by straight

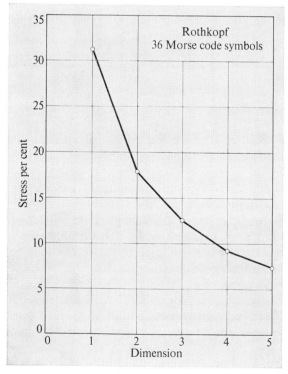

Figure 9

lines for convenience). The shape of this curve, and the actual stress values, can be very helpful in indicating the appropriate value of R. We shall discuss briefly the interpretation of this curve, based on common sense and experience, and then touch briefly on the statistical approach of Wagenaar and Padmos (1971), which is quite useful though their tables cover a very limited range of values.

For any data, S always decreases as R increases, because an extra dimension can help only in matching the data values. Suppose we have data without any random error, that is, dissimilarities for which $f(\delta_{ij})=d_{ij}$ with no error terms e_{ij} present, where the distances arise from an underlying configuration in R_0-dimensional space. Then the S versus R curve drops to 0 at R_0, and thereafter stays 0. Typically, a rather abrupt change in direction occurs at R_0, so this corner or 'elbow' in the curve indicates the true dimension. If the data contains fairly small errors, typically an elbow is visible at R_0 (where the stress has a small positive value): S decreases sharply to R_0, and very slowly thereafter. If the data contain larger errors, which is common, then no sharp elbow may be visible. However, with experience it is possible to make a good guess at the appropriate value of R, based not only on shape but also on the actual stress values.

Wagenaar and Padmos (1971) have made a systematic study (using the Monte Carlo technique) of how stress values are influenced by R_0 and the size of the random errors (represented by a single parameter σ). Using their results, it is sometimes possible to match the S versus R curve (from the data) to particular values of R_0 and σ. In several cases, this has yielded well-determined and quite convincing estimates of R_0 and σ. We present an archaeological example below. Unfortunately, their results are usable only for a few values of n (the number of objects) up to 12.

SOME ARCHAEOLOGICAL EXAMPLES

Gelfand's paper on seriation (Gelfand 1971) discusses three sets of archaeological data, which we shall refer to as the first Robinson matrix, the second Robinson matrix, and the Meggers and Evans matrix. (For further information, see his paper.) Myron Wish and I have applied scaling to all three sets, and I display the stress values in table 1.

	Stress (as a percentage value)		
	First	Second	Meggers and
R	Robinson matrix	Robinson matrix	Evans matrix
	$n=8$	$n=17$	$n=8$
1	7·9	16·5	16·7
2	0·6*	9·3	1·7
3	1·0*	5·2	0·8*
4		2·7	

*Convergence was not complete. Ultimate stress would be smaller.

Table 1

9

Since the original data, on which the matrices were based, were not available to us, we could make no interpretation, nor do any significant analysis of the data. For this reason, I do not wish to suggest that our analyses have any real archaeological meaning, but include them purely to illustrate the process of estimating dimension based only on stress values. (In practice, many other considerations should be used also.) It is interesting to compare the following conclusions with Gelfand's discussion.

I plotted the S versus R curves, and based on my experience reached the following conclusions. The first Robinson matrix seemed quite possibly one-dimensional despite the apparently sharp elbow at $R=2$. The reason I felt this way is that a stress of 7·9 is not very large under these circumstances, so the elbow is not really as sharp as it seems. On the other hand, the Meggers and Evans data has an elbow that really is very sharp at $R=2$, and seemed as clearly two-dimensional as any real data matrix I have seen. The second Robinson matrix does not have a clear elbow, but appears to be two- or three- dimensional.

This brings us to an important point: even if the underlying situation truly involves more dimensions, we may not have sufficient observations to find them all. Thus a decision that a particular matrix is, say, two-dimensional is *not* the same as a decision that the entire underlying situation is two-dimensional: it merely means that all we can hope reasonably to make sense of from *this matrix* is two dimensions.

After making these interpretations, I applied the Wagenaar and Padmos method to the two matrices for which $n=8$ (their tables do not include $n=17$). The stress values for the first Robinson matrix make a very satisfying match to their results for $R_0=1$ and $\sigma=0·19$ (certainly $0·16 \leqslant \sigma \leqslant 0·22$). Furthermore, $R_0=2$ seems unlikely, since for $n=8$ truly two-dimensional data yield typical stress values which never dip below 14 per cent, regardless of σ. The Meggers and Evans matrix makes a fair match with $R_0=2$ and $0·06 \leqslant \sigma \leqslant 0·14$. $R_0=1$ is unlikely, since in this case a one-dimensional stress of 16·7 per cent would be matched by a two-dimensional stress of roughly 4 or 5 per cent. $R_0=3$ is unlikely, because for truly three-dimensional data the typical stress value never dips below 20 per cent in one dimension, nor below 4 per cent in two dimensions.

In using the Wagenaar and Padmos results this way, it is necessary to realize certain facts which they do not emphasize. Use of MDSCAL to do one-dimensional scaling is hazardous, since the local minimum problem is severe. This probably accounts for the curious non-monotonic curves for $R=1$. (Some of the other programs are distinctly better in this respect.) Just looking at their results, furthermore, it seems likely that the local minimum problem for MDSCAL in one dimension may be particularly severe if σ is small. Regardless of program, the stress values (for fixed R and σ) have a rather narrow distribution if $R \geqslant 2$, and a rather broader distribution if $R=1$.

Figure 10 displays the two-dimensional solution for the Meggers and Evans matrix. Possibly an archaeologist with access to the original data (which we are told appears in Meggers and Evans, *Bureau of American*

Ethnology Bulletin, **167**, table 52 and figure 201), may be able to find some significance in it.

Figure 10. Configuration for Meggers and Evans data

SUMMARY AND CONCLUSIONS

One kind of seriation starts with dissimilarities which are intended to represent the time 'distances' between the objects. However, these dissimilarities may in fact reflect more than one variable in a substantial way, so that a one-dimensional representation like seriation is not adequate. A 'multi-dimensional series', that is, a configuration of points in several dimensions, may be necessary.

Multi-dimensional scaling is the name for a well-developed class of methods and computer programs which recover a configuration of points from information about the distances between them. Sometimes this information consists of the distances contaminated by random error. Fortunately for practical use, a large degree of random error can be tolerated. Often the contaminated distances have been distorted by an *unknown* order-preserving (or order-reversing) transformation. The configuration can frequently be reconstructed quite effectively in this case also, which is described as non-metric multi-dimensional scaling.

The configuration generally requires an interpretation to be useful. In archaeology, we would naturally ask how (or if) time, social class, and so on. are related to position in the configuration. Providing the interpretation is a very significant step. An example from psychology provides a striking illustration of interpretation, and of how the configuration can provide insight.

In most applications, it is not at all obvious in advance how many dimensions to use. Some examples from archaeology illustrate the methods for deciding this, including a recently introduced method which relies on the statistical distribution of stress.

REFERENCES

Gelfand, A.E. (1971) Rapid seriation methods with archaeological applications. *Mathematics in the Archaeological and Historical Sciences*, pp. 186–201 (eds Hodson, F.R., Kendall, D.G., & Tăutu, P.). Edinburgh: Edinburgh University Press.

Green, P. & Carmone, F. (1970) *Multi-dimensional Scaling*. Boston, Mass: Allyn & Bacon.

Hodson, F. R., Sneath, P. H. A. & Doran, J. E. (1966) Some experiments in the numerical analysis of archaeological data. *Biometrika*, **53,** 311–24.

Kendall, D. G. (1971) Seriation from abundance matrices. *Mathematics in the Archaeological and Historical Sciences*, pp. 215–52 (eds Hodson, F. R., Kendall, D. G., & Tăutu, P.). Edinburgh: Edinburgh University Press.

Kruskal, J. B. (1964a) Multi-dimensional scaling by optimizing goodness to a nonmetric hypothesis. *Psychometrika*, **29,** 1–27.

Kruskal, J. B. (1964b) Nonmetric multi-dimensional scaling: a numerical method. *Psychometrika*, **29,** 115–29.

Rothkopf, E. (1957) A measure of stimulus similarity and errors in some paired-associate learning tasks. *J. exp. Psych.*, **53,** 94–101.

Shepard, R. N. (1963) Analysis of proximities as a technique for the study of information processing in man. *Human Factors*, **5,** 19–34.

Torgerson, W. S. (1958) *Theory and Methods of Scaling.* New York: Wiley.

Wagenaar, W. A. & Padmos, P. (1971) *J. Math. stat. Psych.*, **24,** 101–10.

Wish, M. & Carroll, J. D. (1971) Multi-dimensional scaling with different weighting of dimensions. *Mathematics in the Archaeological and Historical Sciences*, pp. 150–67 (eds Hodson, F. R., Kendall, D. G., & Tăutu, P.). Edinburgh: Edinburgh University Press.

Special Topics

A. J. Ammerman
A computer analysis of epipalaeolithic assemblages in Italy

This study is part of a series of analyses being carried out on epipalaeolithic flint assemblages in Italy. The assemblages found at the end of the Italian Upper Palaeolithic possess a diversified tool kit consisting of various types of burins, end-scrapers, and backed blades. The method employed in this analysis follows that described by Doran and Hodson (1966). It permits the relationships between a large number of assemblages, considered as units, to be clearly and conveniently expressed in the form of a 'map'.

The aim of this particular study was to compare assemblages from sites in different regions of Italy to see whether or not regional complexes or traditions could be observed. A marked regional tradition would be expected to produce a definite grouping of assemblages on the maps. As shown in

Figure 1. Distribution map of epipalaeolithic sites in Italy

figure 1, twenty-seven assemblages were selected from different parts of Italy. Since the intention was to compare assemblages on a geographic basis, it was essential to have as much control over chronology as possible in order to insure that, if a chronological pattern did emerge from the analysis, it could be identified. To increase the likelihood that some of the assemblages from one region would belong to the same time periods as those from other regions, an intentional selection was made of those assemblages at the upper end of the epipalaeolithic sequence at sites where more than one level had been distinguished. Stratigraphy offered a further check against the possible confusion of time factors with geographic ones. At three sites where there was a strong element of cultural continuity, two, and in one case three, assemblages in stratigraphic sequence were chosen. On the computed maps, stratigraphic position would indicate the 'direction' of the time relation between assemblages from the same site. A third control over chronology stemmed from the fact that eight of the assemblages could be associated with C_{14} dates falling in the period from roughly 7,000 BC to 11,000 BC.

Those concerned with the Upper Palaeolithic in Italy owe a considerable debt to Laplace for the work he has done on the comparative study of flint assemblages (Laplace 1966). The data used in this analysis were drawn largely from Laplace. The data for Ponte di Pietra, a site now being prepared for publication, were made available by Broglio, while those for Paglicci were published by Mezzena and Palma di Cesnola (1967). Thirty-six types were selected from the eighty-five primary types in the full Laplace type-list. Each type not included in the set represented, with few exceptions, less than one per cent of the total number of tools in a given assemblage. The full type-list, although somewhat more awkward to handle, could have been used in the analysis, but this was found to be unnecessary, as is explained below. The thirty-six types covered about 90 per cent of the tools in each assemblage; 24 assemblages fell within the 84 to 96 per cent range. Multiple tools, which present their own special problems of classification, were included under a primary type whenever they occurred as a double of that type; otherwise, they were placed with the tools not in the set. Fortunately, the proportion of multiple tools in the assemblages was small and the total percentage of multiple tools not included in the set for each assemblage was likewise small. In terms of sample size, the poorest assemblage, Santa Croce, had only 114 among the 36 types. The majority had well over 200 tools. It is perhaps worth pointing out here that the analysis was carried out under the two-fold set of assumptions: that the Laplace type-list provides a reasonably detailed description of the full range of tools in the assemblages; and that the actual process of classification had been performed properly.

As an initial step in the procedure, the percentage values of the 36 types were replaced with their arcsine square-root equivalents, an accepted transformation for improving the characteristics of binomial and similar data. Similarity coefficients were then computed between each pair of assemblages according to the formula:

$$d_{ij} = (\sum_k [x_{ik} - x_{jk}]^2)^{\frac{1}{2}}$$

where i and j are assemblages and x_{ik} is the transformed value of the percentage of the kth tool-type in assemblage i. As a check on the suitability of representing the assemblages in terms of the abridged list of 36 types, similarity coefficients were generated in the same manner between several of the assemblages using the full Laplace type-list. Comparison of the similarity coefficients generated by the two means for the same pairs of assemblages showed only a small order of difference which meant that an analysis based on the abridged list would produce essentially the same results as one based on the full type-list.

The second step in the procedure involved the use of a multi-dimensional scaling program to translate the matrix of similarity coefficients into a 'map' in a prescribed number of dimensions. Here each assemblage is expressed as a point on the map and the distance between points is made to reflect the degree of similarity between assemblages so that 'like' (small coefficient) is close and 'unlike' (large coefficient) far away. The computer is programmed to generate a random configuration of points to start with. It then proceeds iteratively to rearrange the points of the configuration attempting to achieve a progressively better fit. A 'strain' value is calculated for each configuration as a measurement of the goodness of fit. Full details of the method have been given by Hodson, Sneath, and Doran (1966). The analysis was run on the Atlas computer of the University of London. A configuration with a consistent pattern of relations and low strain values was obtained from several different random starts in both three and two dimensions.

The interpretation of a computed 'map' depends on a careful consideration of the various factors possibly determining the pattern of the configuration. This involves the consideration of a wide range of factors: both those belonging directly to the structure of the data, such as particular tool-types in this case, and those, such as geographic or ecological factors, influencing the structure of the data in a more indirect way. Only the main results of the attempt to interpret the configuration, shown in figure 2, can be presented here. An initial point to make is that on close examination the configuration revealed no clear time trend. In terms of the tool-types themselves, a definite relation could be seen between the relative abundance of denticulates in an assemblage and its general position along the horizontal axis. In figure 2, the six assemblages on the left (1, 2, 3, 14, 16, 18) each have a total of 4 per cent or less of denticulates. Those on the right side (6, 7, 13, 17, 19, 20, 21, 24, 25, 27) each contain at least 20 per cent of denticulates. The remaining assemblages in the centre have a value that falls between 5 and 19 per cent. An interesting counterpart to this pattern was observed with respect to geometric microliths. Unlike denticulates, they occur only in small numbers and do not play a significant role in determining the pattern of the configuration. Geometric microliths accounted for more than 1 per cent of an assemblage in only four cases. Examined in terms of presence and absence, the six assemblages on the left with few denticulates all possessed geometric microliths. Of the assemblages on the right with a high percentage of denticulates, only three out of ten exhibited geometric microliths. Six of the remaining eleven assemblages showed their presence. While the inverse relationship suggested here is obviously far from perfect, there is a definite indication that geometric microliths are most likely to be encountered where there are relatively few denticulates and least likely to be found where denticulates are particularly abundant.

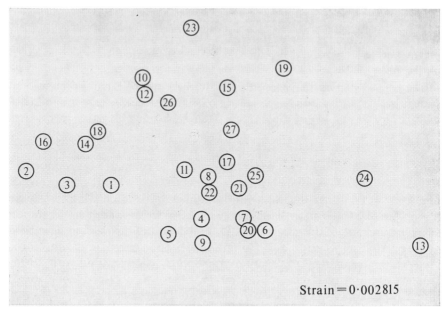

Figure 2. Two-dimensional configuration of 27 assemblages

The analysis revealed no marked regional trends. No clear separation or segregation of assemblages on a regional basis could be observed. The opposite appears to be the case. There are a number of places in figure 2 where assemblages from different regions are found in close proximity. A notable example of this is seen in the relation between Cavallo (6, 7, 8) in southern Italy and Arene Candide (20, 21) in northern Italy. Evidence for a much less well-defined regional tradition can perhaps be seen in the tendency of assemblages from Puglia in southern Italy (1 through 11) to be located on the left side and lower half of the configuration. But this general tendency cannot be equated with a distinct regional tradition. The analysis then seems to support the conclusion that marked regional traditions did not characterize the flint assemblages of this phase of Italian prehistory. It is important to emphasize that this conclusion is put forward only as a first level of approximation to the fundamental question raised. This interpretation will undoubtedly need to be re-examined as further evidence and better methods of analysis become available.

ACKNOWLEDGMENTS
I would like to thank Dr F. R. Hodson of the Institute of Archaeology for his helpful advice and Dr J. E. Doran of the Atlas Computer Laboratory whose multi-dimensional scaling program was used in the analysis. The data for Ponte di Pietra were generously provided by Prof. A. Broglio of the University of Ferrara.

List of assemblages

1. Cipolliane, level 1	15. Palidoro, level 2
2. Romanelli, levels A–B	16. Ponte Lucano, level 2
3. Romanelli, level C	17. Ortucchio, levels A–D
4. Taurisano, levels 1–5	18. Tane del Diavolo
5. Ugento, Pozzo Zecca	19. Ponte di Pietra
6. Cavallo, level B I	20. Arene Candide, level I
7. Cavallo, level B II a	21. Arene Candide, level II
8. Cavallo, level B II b	22. Arma dello Stefanin, levels I V
9. Mura, upper level	23. Riparo Mochi, level A
10. Santa Croce	24. Ponte di Veia C, levels IV–VI
11. Paglicci, level 4	25. Battaglia
12. Cala delle Ossa, level 5	26. Corrugi
13. Blanc, upper level	27. San Teodoro, level A
14. Sezze Romano	

REFERENCES

Doran, J. E. & Hodson, F. R. (1966). A digital computer analysis of palaeolithic flint assemblages. *Nature*, **210**, 688–9.

Laplace, G. (1966) *Recherches sur l'origine et l'evolution des complexes Leptolithiques*. École française de Rome. Suppléments 4.

Mezzena, F. & Palma di Cesnola, A. (1967) L'Epigravettiano della Grotta Paglicci nel Gargano (Scavi F. Zorzi 1961–63). *Rivista di Scienze Preistoriche*, **22**, 23–156.

Hodson, F. R., Sneath, P. H. A. & Doran, J. E. (1966) Some experiments in the numerical analysis of archaeological data. *Biometrika*, **53**, 311–24.

Special Topics

John C. Gower

Statistical methods of comparing different multivariate analyses of the same data

This paper considers how to compare two sets of distances d_{ij} and d_{ij}^* $(i, j = 1, 2, ..., n)$ amongst the same n samples. Rather than correlate the $\binom{n}{2}$ distance pairs (d_{ij}, d_{ij}^*) it is suggested that each set of distances be represented by n points P_i, P_i^* $(i = 1, 2, ..., n)$ which are rotated to best fit defined by minimizing $R^2 = \sum_{i=1}^{n} \Delta^2(P_i P_i^*)$. The mathematical technique required is useful with many different multivariate problems. It is illustrated with a new type of analysis using anthropological data on skulls from six hominoid populations with eight recognizable constellations of characters. A canonical variate analysis for each constellation gives eight sets of canonical variate means and each pair (u, v) is rotated to best fit R_{uv}^2. The elements of the 8×8 symmetric R^2 matrix can themselves be treated as distances and represented by points in three dimensions, allowing examination of how the descriptions of the populations are related when analyzed by different constellations of characters. Some of the statistical distributional problems raised by this and similar types of analysis are discussed.

INTRODUCTION

The sort of problem I shall discuss is well illustrated by the long standing dispute over the relative merits of Mahalanobis's D^2 statistic and Karl Pearson's Coefficient of Racial Likeness (CRL) in anthropometry. With k populations there are $\frac{1}{2}k(k-1)$ derived distances for each of the two measures. Many authors have noted that when these $\frac{1}{2}k(k-1)$ pairs of values are plotted against each other, a strong linear relationship expressible as a large positive correlation is often found. From this they deduce that whatever theoretical advantages D^2 may have, the more simply computed CRL is, for all practical purposes, just as good.

That the $k(k-1)$ distances are not independent may well produce a specious correlation, but this is usually overlooked. The effect of non-independence can be seen by considering k populations, $k-1$ of which form a homogeneous set, all of which are very different from the single remaining population. With both D^2 and CRL we shall have $k-1$ long distances and $\frac{1}{2}(k-1)(k-2)$ short distances, and the correlation between D^2 and CRL must therefore be large (*see* figure 1).

This paper describes some preliminary work on a statistic (R^2) for comparing different sets of distances, without using dependent values. The example cited above is only one of many ways that a distance matching problem arises, but before outlining other examples it will be convenient to examine some of the different types of distance used in multivariate analysis.

Many multivariate methods may be regarded as two-step processes. First a set of distances $d_{ij}(i, j = 1, 2, ..., n)$ between n points, representing samples or populations, is defined. Examples are D^2, CRL, Hiernaux's Δ_g, Penrose's C_Q^2, Sanghvi and Balkrishnan's B and G, and various dissimilarity coefficients all discussed by Gower (1970). Second, these distances are mapped onto a set of n points (preferably in few dimensions) with Euclidean distances d_{ij}^*. The techniques used here include canonical variate analysis, principal components, multi-dimensional scaling, and so on, where d_{ij}^* is chosen to minimize some function of d_{ij} and d_{ij}^*. Alternatively, the mapping is onto a dendrogram (scaled hierarchical representation) using some form of nested cluster analysis. In this case, the dendrogram can be regarded as defining ultra-metric distances d_{ij}^+ ideally chosen to minimize some function of d_{ij} and d_{ij}^+.

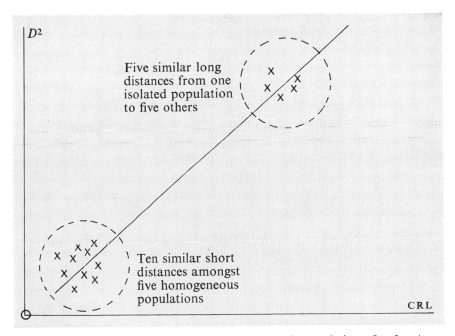

Figure 1. Relation of D^2 to CRL distances between six populations, five forming a homogeneous set and one being an outlier

The derivation, described below, of ultra-metric distances from a dendrogram seems first to have been suggested by Sokal and Rohlf (1962) when defining co-phenetic correlation, but was first set out more formally by Hartigan (1967).

Figure 2 is a simple dendrogram illustrating the hierarchical representation of 5 populations by points A, B, C, D, E, with a scale labelling the branching points or nodes. The distance between any two points is given by the scale value corresponding to the node where they first join. Thus, in figure 2 the distance A, B is 1 and the distance A, D is 7. Also from figure 2, concentrating on the points A and C, we can see that for any point X between A and C (B, for example) that

$$AC = \max(AX, XC) \quad .$$

However, for any point X outside A and C (D, for example) then $AX = XC$ and

$$AC < \max(AX, XC) \quad .$$

Thus, for all points ABC

$$AC \leqslant \max(AB, BC) \quad .$$

This is the main property defining ultra-metric distances. Clearly $AB + BC \geqslant AC$, the triangle rule for Euclidean distances. This is insufficient to show that with a finite set of points ultra-metric distance is a special case of Euclidean distance, but I conjecture that ultra-metric distances are also Euclidean distances. [This conjecture has now been proved true (Buneman and Gower 1971).]

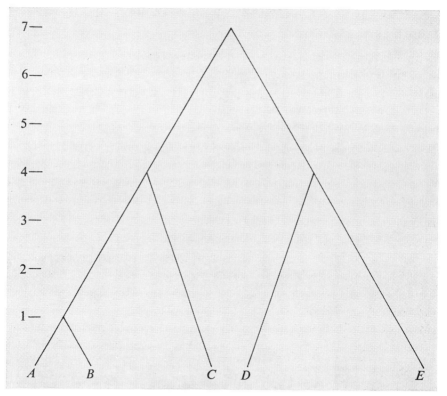

Figure 2. Simple dendrogram illustrating properties of ultrametric distances: $d_{AB} = 1; d_{AC} = d_{BC} = 4; d_{AD} = d_{CD} = 7; d_{AC} = \max(d_{AB}, d_{BC}); d_{AC} < \max(d_{AD}, d_{CD})$

Thus, many forms of multivariate analysis can be regarded as mapping computed distances d_{ij} on to Euclidean distances d_{ij}^* or ultra-metric distances d_{ij}^+. As there are many ways of computing d_{ij} and of analyzing it, we are constantly coming across problems of comparing two different sets of distances pertaining to the same samples or populations. The following are important practical problems of this type.

(1) Comparing different distances derived from the same observations on the same samples (as with D^2 and CRL discussed above). An archaeological example is where an archaeologist (or two different archaeologists) have scored hand-axe data in different ways or decided to examine different measures of distance based on the same hand-axe data.

(2) Comparing different distances (possibly using the same statistical formulae) derived from different observations on the same samples. For example, comparing D^2 as evaluated on one set of variates (say concerned with the jaw-bone) with D^2 evaluated on another set (say from the frontal region of the skull). An analysis of this kind is given below in the section 'Anthropometric example'. In archaeology we may wish to compare different criteria (or graves), first on biological properties (skeletal measurements), and secondly on artifacts.

(3) Comparing the original distances d_{ij} with those obtained by analysis, say d_{ij}^* or d_{ij}^+. That is to say, we want to see how well the distances derived from the analysis agree with the original values. In fact d_{ij}^* or d_{ij}^+ are often defined by optimizing a function of d_{ij} with these fitted values.

(4) Comparing distance d_{ij}^* and d_{ij}^{**} derived from two different analyses of the same distances. For example, a set of D^2 values may be expressed in two dimensions by (a) canonical variate analysis, giving d_{ij}^* and (b) non-metric multi-dimensional scaling giving d_{ij}^{**}. Under this heading we can include comparison of d_{ij}^* with d_{ij}^+ and comparison of d_{ij}^* with $d_{ij}^{+\,+}$. An analysis of this kind is given below in the section 'Anthropometric example'.

(5) Comparing distances derived from different samples from the same populations. Thus, we may evaluate D^2 from one set of samples and then re-sample to obtain a second set of D^2 values, pertaining to the same populations. Problems of this kind are theoretically important, for their solution forms the basis of any statistical inference.

Just as some authors have correlated d_{ij}^* with d_{ij}^{**} others have suggested correlating d_{ij}^+ with $d_{ij}^{+\,+}$ or with d_{ij}. I have already explained why I think this can be misleading and shall now outline the derivation of an alternative statistic.

ROTATIONAL FITS

Rather than concentrate on the distances themselves, consider geometric points $P_i(i=1, 2, ..., n)$ that give rise to all the inter-distances d_{ij}. With any Euclidean distance, the coordinates of these points can be evaluated by principal coordinates analysis (Gower 1967). The required coordinates are given by the canonical means in canonical variate analysis and by the data themselves in principal components analysis. Thus, the problem is to compare two sets of distances arising from points P_i and Q_i (say). Clearly we can move the points Q relative to P with translations and rotations. Reflection must also be considered as can be seen from figure 3, which shows how two congruent triangles best fit without reflection. The criterion of best fit adopted is to move the points Q_i relative to the points P_i until the 'residual' sum of squares $R^2 = \sum_{i=1}^{n} \Delta^2(P_iQ_i)$ is minimum. It can be shown that the best fit occurs when the two sets of points have the same centroid and this takes care of translation. To determine the required rotation, we need some matrix algebra.

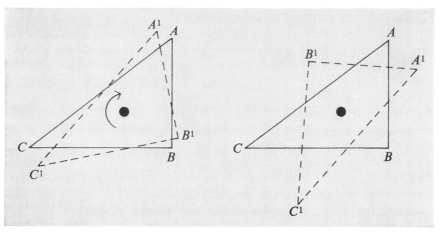

Figure 3. The effect of rotating two congruent triangles in a plane. The two triangles on the left hand side fit exactly. On the right hand side one triangle is a mirror image of the other and the best fit when rotating in a plane is poor; if one is allowed to rotate in three dimensions the fit is again exact

Let X be the $n \times p$ matrix of the coordinates of the points P_i (referred to orthogonal axes and with zero means) and Y the $n \times q$ matrix of the coordinates of the points Q_i (also orthogonal axes and zero means); where we have assumed that the ith row of both matrices refers to the same samples or populations. There is no loss of generality in assuming that $p \geqslant q$ and, to avoid discussing the cases $p = q$ and $p > q$ separately, I shall further assume that $p = q$; if necessary extra zero columns must be appended to Y until it has a total of p columns. Any rotation of Y relative to X can be expressed as an orthogonal matrix H. After rotation, the coordinates of Q_1 are given by the rows of YH. The best estimate of H requires $R = X'Y$ and the solutions to the equation $R = U\Sigma V'$ to be computed where U and V are orthogonal matrices and Σ is a diagonal matrix whose elements are known as the zeros of R. The values of U, V, and Σ are probably best computed by the method recently given by Golub and Reinsch (1970), but in the example given below they have been computed as the latent vectors of RR' and $R'R$. The required rotation is given by $H = VU'$.

After rotation we have
$$R^2 = \text{Trace}\,(XX' + YY' - 2YHX')\quad.$$
We have to consider the effect of the arbitrary signs of the latent vectors which are the columns of U and V. These signs determine different reflections of the rotated Y and the best out of the 2^n different possibilities is required. To find the best reflection suppose S is a diagonal matrix whose elements are all $+1$ or -1, in an order to be determined. To change the signs of the columns of V relative to those of U we can write $H = VSU'$. Thus, to minimize R^2 above, we must select S so that the Trace $(YVSU'X')$ is maximum.

This is the same as maximizing Trace $(U'X'YVS)$ (that is, Trace $[\Sigma S]$) which occurs when the elements of S have the same signs as those of Σ. The elements of S determine the signs to be associated with the columns of V and take care of reflection.

A reflection in n dimensions is the same as a rotation in $(n+1)$ dimensions. So it seems that the above method of dealing with reflections could be avoided merely by adding an extra zero column to X and Y, but the arbitrariness of the signs of the latent vectors still remains a problem; so nothing is gained.

A further complication must be considered when the scales of the two sets of distances are arbitrary. For example, in problem (5) above, d_{ij}^* and d_{ij}^{**} are on the same scales but this is not so in problem (1). To take care of scale changes, we could scale the coordinates in the matrix Y by a factor δ and estimate δ by Δ to get minimum R^2. Luckily this estimation proceeds independently of translation and rotation, to give Δ Trace $(YY')=$ Trace $(YHX)=$ Trace (Σ). It can be shown that after rotation:
$$\Delta^2 \text{ Trace } (YY')+R_{\min}^2=\text{Trace } (XX') \quad .$$
This may be used as the basis for an analysis of variance, interpreted as equating the total sum of squares amongst the variates of Y, after scaling, plus the residual sum of squares, to the total sum of squares amongst the variates of X.

Clearly the best system of scaling Y relative to X is not the inverse of the best system of scaling X relative to Y. This unfortunate property needs further investigation, but to avoid it in the numerical problem discussed below, I have scaled both sets of points to have unit total squared distance from their respective centroids, that is, Trace $(XX')=$ Trace $(YY')=1$. With this unit scaling, the analysis of variance simplifies to $\Delta^2+R_{\min}^2=1$ where $\Delta^2=$ Trace (Σ), a value independent of whether we rotate X to Y or vice versa.

A more difficult problem occurs when we do not know how the rows of X match with the rows of Y, that is, we believe that some permutation of the rows Y may match those of X. Suppose P is a permutation matrix such that YP matches X without regard to rotation. A permutation matrix has a single unit in every row and column, and zeros everywhere else. To estimate P, consider the class of doubly stochastic matrices (that is, those which have non-negative elements and whose rows and columns all sum to unity). A permutation matrix is a special case of this class. To maximize the sum of squares
$$R^2=\text{Trace } [(X-YP)'(X-YP)]$$
subject to the n^2+2n linear restrictions $0 \leqslant p_{ij} \leqslant 1$.
$$\sum_{i=1}^{n} p_{ij}=\sum_{j=1}^{n} p_{ij}=1$$
is a quadratic programming problem which can in theory be solved by the standard methods available. That the optimum must occur on a vertex of the feasible region ensures that a true permutation matrix is found. It seems worth mentioning this version of the problem in case it occurs in an archaeological or historical context.

The problem of seriating the u rows of a matrix X whose elements relate to presence/absence or frequencies of different grave articles can be put into the same framework. We require to find an $n \times n$ permutation matrix P which permutes the rows of X into an optimum for $Y = PX$. A suitable optimality criterion S might be to minimize the sum of squares of the differences between adjacent rows of Y, that is, choose:

$$S = \sum_{i=1}^{n-1} \sum_{j=1} (Y_{ij} - Y_{i+1,j})^2$$

subject to the same linear restrictions as before.

Even more complicated problems would occur if we were to combine permutations with rotation and scaling, and so on, but these problems are not considered any further here.

ANTHROPOMETRIC EXAMPLE

I am indebted to Mr A. Bilsborough, of the Department of Anthropology, Cambridge, for permission to use the extensive set of data he has collected on skull measurements of ancient human populations. To illustrate the methods discussed above, without giving a thorough anthropometric account here, I have selected six of the hominoid populations, namely:

1. Modern Homo Sapiens
2. Upper Palaeolithic Homo Sapiens
3. Middle East Neanderthal
4. European Würm Neanderthal
5. Late (Pekin) Homo Erectus
6. Australopithecus Africanus;

and measurements from eight different regions of the skull, namely:

1. Upper Face (16)
2. Upper Jaw (15)
3. Articular Region (8)
4. Balance (14)
5. Basicranial Region (12)
6. Cranial Vault (16)
7. Lower Jaw (16)
8. Overall (16).

Each region was characterized by a set of variates referred to as a constellation. The number of variates at each constellation is given in brackets in the above list. For each constellation the Mahalanobis D^2 distances were computed for all 15 population differences, giving eight such matrices in all. For each pair u, v of constellations, the best rotational fit can be found using the canonical variate means as the coordinates representing the populations; this gives the residential fit R_{uv}^2. The analysis is that required for problem (2) above. When all constellations have been rotated to fit all other constellations we have an 8×8 symmetric matrix of R^2 values, shown in table 1.

The present analysis has similarities to the INDSCAL method discussed by Wish and Carroll (1971). In their analysis, each individual constellation is represented relative to the axes of an overall analysis. In the above, each constellation is represented by its own canonical analysis and then combined in a separate constellation analysis. To get a metric equivalent to INDSCAL all that would be required is, first, to provide an overall (canonical) analysis using all the varieties (regardless of what constellation they belonged to), and then to rotate each separate constellation canonical analysis to fit this overall analysis. The R^2 analysis may be taken further, as described in the remainder of this section.

	1	2	3	4	5	6	7
1. Upper Face							
2. Upper Jaw	1·0012						
3. Articular Region	1·0753	0·5766					
4. Balance	1·0530	0·6324	1·0997				
5. Basicranial Region	0·3485	0·5736	0·6533	0·5486			
6. Cranial Vault	0·8332	0·5596	0·8034	0·2582	0·3466		
7. Lower Jaw	1·0275	0·8155	0·4385	0·5952	0·5541	0·3309	
8. Overall	0·8498	0·2147	0·5483	0·4580	0·3504	0·4155	0·5075

Table 1. Values of R^2 between eight constellations, based on best rotational fits of canonical variate means for six hominoid populations

These R^2 values may now themselves be regarded as squared distances. (In this example these distances turned out to be Euclidean but I have been unable to prove that this is necessary.) The R^2 distances were analyzed in two ways to give low-dimensional representations of the eight different constellations.

The first analysis using principal coordinates (Gower 1967) gave figure 4. Psychologists refer to this type of analysis as a metric multi-dimensional scaling.

The second analysis using non-metric multi-dimensional scaling (Kruskal 1964) gave figure 5.

Both methods needed three dimensions to express the distances of table 1 adequately (two and three dimensions accounted respectively for 62% and 84% of the total squared distance from the centroid with principal coordinates and gave respective stresses of 0·146 and 0·044 with multi-dimensional scaling). The third dimension is represented in the figures by a horizontal arrowed line of appropriate length (to the right if positive, to the left if negative). It is hard to say how figures 4 and 5 compare. Their general agreement becomes clearer when both figures are referred to their principal axes and it would ease such comparisons if all multi-dimensional coordinates of maps produced by whatever method of analysis were presented in this way. To get more information on this comparison, the coordinate values depicted in figures 4 and 5 were used as starting points for an analysis [of the type discussed in problem (4) above] rotating one analysis of the distances of table 1 (principal coordinates) to fit best another analysis of the same distances (non-metric scaling). This was done (see figure 6) and gave an R^2 value of 0·066. Although

10

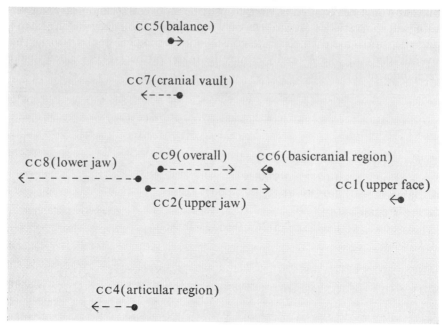

Figure 4. 3-dimensional principle coordinate fit of the R^2 matrix

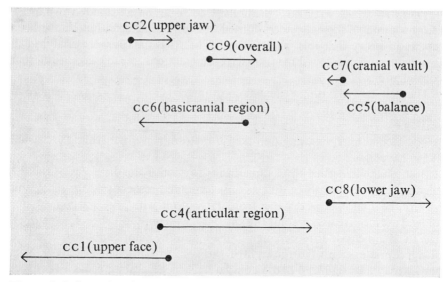

Figure 5. 3-dimensional MDSCAL ($r=3$) fit of the R^2 matrix. This figure does not obviously agree with figure 4

as yet we know nothing of the sampling properties of R^2, this value seems satisfactorily small.

The multi-dimensional scaling program when asked to give a fit in r dimensions also gives a fit in all lower dimensions, using the coordinates found at the sth stage as starting values for the solution in one fewer dimension at the $(s+1)$th stage. With this example I set $r=3$ and 4, and so

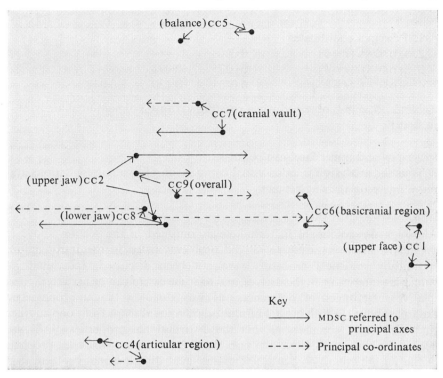

Figure 6. MDSCAL ($r=3$) rotated to fit 3-dimensional principal coordinates solution. The two solutions are seen to agree very well

got two different 3-dimensional solutions (and two 2-dimensional solutions too). Figure 5 is the solution for $r=3$. Although ideally the 3-dimensional solutions for $r=3$ and $r=4$ should fit each other exactly after a suitable rotation, they will differ because of the effects of whatever stopping rule is used to define convergence, and also because convergence may be to different local optima. In fact $r=3$ gave a 3-dimensional fit with stress 0·044 and $r=4$ gave a 3-dimensional fit with stress 0·042 which, although close, did not give obviously similar representations. When the two results were rotated to best fit, it was clear that both solutions were much the same, but the value 0·091 of R^2 was worse than the R^2 for figure 6, indicating that $R^2=0·066$ is satisfactory and that principal coordinates and non-metric scaling have given, effectively, the same results with these data. The 3-dimensional solutions for $r=3, 4, 8$ are compared with the principal coordinates solution in table 2. It is remarkable that each of the three MDSCAL solutions fit the principal coordinates solution better than any of the other 3-dimensional MDSCAL solutions.

From figures 4, 5, or 6 it seems that different constellations of characters give different interpretations of the differences between the six populations in terms of D^2. To be more precise we would like to be able to construct confidence regions about each point. Statements like 'the balance and cranial vault regions of the skull determine a set of D^2 values more alike than do the

	1	2	3	4
1. Principal coordinates	—			
2. MDSCAL $(r=3)$	0·066	—		
3. MDSCAL $(r=4)$	0·027	0·091	—	
4. MDSCAL $(r=8)$	0·043	0·120	0·048	—

Table 2. R^2 values obtained when rotating various 3-dimensional analyses to best fit

lower jaw and upper face' can be made.

Thus the analysis has aided visual comparison of two representations and put a figure on their agreement.

STATISTICAL PROBLEMS

Although the rotational fit technique as outlined in the section above is applicable mathematically to all the problems listed in the introduction, specifically statistical problems have not been discussed. Individual R^2 values are interesting in themselves, and to some extent can be used to express relative magnitudes of differences, as was done in the anthropometric example above. Rotating pairs of multi-dimensional maps to fit one another simplifies visual comparisons, but the distributional properties of R^2 are needed for a truly objective analysis. When it is realized that each problem in the introduction poses a different statistical distributional problem it is clear that much work remains to be done. Problem (5) seems most likely to yield to analytical treatment. Assuming multi-normal populations with equal covariance matrices, the distribution of R^2 is required when sample values of the canonical variate means are rotated to fit the true values of these means. The next step would be to find the distribution when canonical variate means obtained from two different samples are rotated to fit. Problem (2) requires an extension to consider the effect of using different or overlapping sets of variates for the different analyses. The latter problem would still be meaningful when assessing distances between individual samples drawn from a single multi-normal population.

Whether any of these distributional problems can be solved remains to be seen, but large sample asymptotic χ^2 approximations should be available. I am less hopeful of any analytical solution for distributional problems involving ultrametric distances, where it seems that the best hope is to get information from Monte Carlo sampling experiments. I hope to tackle some of these problems soon.

ACKNOWLEDGMENTS
I thank Mr A. Bilsborough for the data and Mr W. J. Krzanowski for programming the rotational fit technique and for seeing most of the calculations through the computer. The mathematical derivation of the results quoted in the section of this paper on 'Rotational fits' was largely worked out while the author was visiting the Bell Telephone Laboratories, Murray Hill, N.J.

REFERENCES

Buneman, P. & Gower, J.C. (1971) The representation of ultrametric distances in Euclidean space (in preparation).

Golub, C.H. & Reinsch, C. (1970) Handbook series linear algebra. Singular value decomposition and least squares solutions. *Numer. Math.*, **14**, 403–20.

Gower, J.C. (1966) Some distance properties of latent root and vector methods used in multivariate analysis. *Biometrika*, **53**, 325–38.

Gower, J.C. (1970) Measures of taxonomic distance and their analysis. *Proc. Symp. Assessment of Biological Affinity and Distance between Human Populations, Utrecht* 1969. London: Oxford University Press.

Hartigan, J.R. (1967) Representation of similarity matrices by trees. *J. Amer. statist. Ass.*, **62**, 1140–58.

Kruskal, J.B. (1964) Multidimensional scaling by optimising goodness-of-fit to a nonmetric hypothesis. *Psychometrika*, **29**, 1–27.

Sokal, R.R. & Rohlf, F.J. (1962) The comparison of dendrograms by objective methods. *Taxon.*, **11**, 33–40.

Wish, M. & Carroll, J.D. (1971) Multi-dimensional scaling with differential weighting of dimensions emphasizing interesting applications. *Mathematics in the Archaeological and Historical Sciences*, pp. 150–67 (eds Hodson, F.R., Kendall, D.G., & Tăutu, P.). Edinburgh: Edinburgh University Press.

Special Topics

Myron Wish and J. Douglas Carroll
Multi-dimensional scaling with differential weighting of dimensions

The earlier multi-dimensional scaling techniques, for instance the MDSCAL procedure (Kruskal 1964a, b) described by Kruskal (1971) in this volume, have been applied with great success in many fields. The basic input for these procedures is a single matrix of similarities or dissimilarities among objects or other stimuli. The output is a single map, or configuration, of points—one point for each stimulus. Distances between points reflect the relative similarities among objects; that is, objects which the data indicate to be more similar are in general closer to each other in the map than are less similar pairs.

In many applications of multi-dimensional scaling in the behavioral sciences, the similarities are obtained from several different subjects (individuals who participate in the study), or by the same subjects on different occasions or under different experimental conditions. This kind of data has generally been analyzed by means of (a) a single scaling (usually of averaged similarities), treating the data from different individuals as experimental replications, or (b) a separate scaling of each subject's data, treating the data from different subjects as unrelated (*see also* Tucker and Messick 1963). [Carroll and Chang (1970a) provide some comparisons between INDSCAL, Tucker and Messick's 'points of view' model (Tucker and Messick 1963), and Tucker's 3-mode factor analysis (Tucker 1964).] Although the latter alternative does make it possible for the experimenter to compare different multi-dimensional structures, this potential advantage is generally outweighed by other considerations—the reliability of a single subject's similarities is too low, and the cost of individual analyses and comparisons is too high.

Recently a new method was developed by Carroll and Chang (1970a) based on a model that relates structures from different sources in a strong way, yet also permits large differences among them. This method has been implemented in a computer program (Carroll and Chang 1969) called INDSCAL (for INdividual Differences SCALing). [*See also* Carroll 1971.]

The input to INDSCAL consists of many different matrices of similarities or dissimilarities, all pertaining to the same stimulus objects. Each matrix typically comes from one person, but it is also possible for it to be associated with one of several different experimental conditions, measures of similarity, time periods, or locations.

As in the earlier multi-dimensional scaling procedures, the output includes a map, referred to in INDSCAL as a *group stimulus space*, in which each point represents one object. For example, figure 1(a) shows a sketch of a hypothetical 2-dimensional group stimulus space. Another important part of

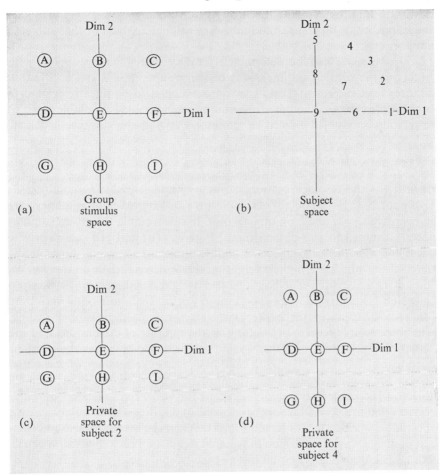

Figure 1. Hypothetical example of INDSCAL model. Weights from the subject space, (a), are applied to the dimensions of the group stimulus space, (b), to produce private spaces for subjects 2, (c), and 4, (d)

the INDSCAL output is a set of dimension weights for each subject which shows the relative importance of each stimulus dimension to him. Subject weights are usually plotted in a *subject space* (one point per subject) such as is illustrated for hypothetical data in figure 1(b). Hypothetical subjects 1, 2, and 6 have higher weights on dimension 1 than on dimension 2, while the opposite is true for hypothetical subjects 4, 5, and 8. The further a subject's point is from the origin of the subject space, the better his data can be accounted for by the dimensions of the group stimulus space. Thus, if figure 1(b) were based on real data, one would conclude that the similarities for subjects 1 through 5 could be predicted more accurately than could the similarities for the other four subjects. In fact, none of subject 9's data could be accounted for by those two dimensions since his point is precisely at the origin. [In order to determine whether a subject who has low weights on all dimensions responded in a random way or whether other dimensions were relevant to him, one could either do INDSCAL analyses in spaces of higher dimensionality or do a separate multi-dimensional analysis of that subject's similarities.]

A *private space* can be determined for any individual by applying his weights to the respective dimensions of the group stimulus space. Stimulus distances in a subject's private space are assumed to be linearly related to his similarities data (although a 'quasi-nonmetric' version is available in which the relation is assumed only to be monotonic). [Stimulus distance is defined by

$$d_{jk}^{(i)} = \sqrt{\left(\sum_{t=1}^{r} w_{it}(x_{jt} - x_{kt})^2 \right)} \quad ,$$

where $d_{jk}^{(i)}$ is the distance between stimulus j and stimulus k in subject i's private space, w_{it} is the weight of dimension t for subject i, and x_{jt} and x_{kt} are the coordinates of j and k on dimension t. In this formula the group stimulus space is assumed to be r-dimensional.] Figures 1(c) and 1(d) show private spaces for hypothetical subjects 2 and 4. Subject 2's space is horizontally stretched since he has a higher weight on the horizontal than on the vertical dimension. Since subject 4 has a higher weight on dimension 2 than on dimension 1, his private space shows more vertical than horizontal variation.

In INDSCAL, as in the earlier methods for multi-dimensional scaling, experimentation is required to determine the number of dimensions that are needed. For any specified dimensionality INDSCAL determines the stimulus coordinates, the subject weights, and the *unique orientation of axes* that account for the maximum total variance in the similarities data from all subjects. [The procedure actually accounts for variance in matrices of scalar products that are derived from the original similarities or dissimilarities by a procedure described in Torgerson (1958). When the dimensions are normalized in such a way that the sum of squared weights on each dimension equals 1·00, w_{it}^2 is approximately equal to (or exactly equal to if the dimensions of the group stimulus space are uncorrelated) the proportion of variance in subject i's matrix that can be accounted for by dimension t.] The (unrotated) axes, or dimensions, have a special status in INDSCAL, and might be assumed to correspond to fundamental psychological processes that have different saliences for different individuals. The remarkable fact is that in most cases the dimensions can be interpreted without rotation, as is necessary for solutions obtained from earlier multi-dimensional scaling procedures or from factor analyses. INDSCAL is therefore particularly valuable when the dimensions are not known in advance.

We shall now illustrate INDSCAL by applying it to data from three studies of human perception. In the first and third illustrations we re-analyze data from earlier experiments dealing respectively with 'psychological distances' among colors (Helm 1964, Helm and Tucker 1962) and with confusions among acoustically degraded English consonants (Miller and Nicely 1955). The data analyzed in the second example are from a recent study of individual differences in perception of rhythm and accent in English speech (Wish 1969). We conclude the paper with a discussion of potential applications of INDSCAL in archaeology.

PSYCHOLOGICAL DISTANCES AMONG COLORS

In a study of individual differences in color perception, Helm asked 14 individuals to judge the psychological distances among ten colors of constant saturation and brightness. Using a standard color discrimination test, Helm had determined that 10 of the subjects had normal color vision, while 4 of the subjects were deficient (in varying degrees) in red–green color vision. The matrices of perceived color dissimilarities for two of the subjects, one color deficient (CD1) and one with normal color vision (N7), are shown in table 1. One can readily see that these subjects differ markedly in their assessments of color differences. For example, in the matrix for CD1 red is closer to green than to any other color, whereas in N7's matrix red and green are perceptually far apart. Although systematic differences can be observed in the data for these and the other subjects, it takes more than inspection of these matrices to discover the dimensions of color vision and to determine quantitatively how important they are to each subject. We therefore used Helm's data as input to the INDSCAL procedure (*see also* Carroll and Chang 1970b).

A. Dissimilarity matrix for subject CD1

	1 RP	2 R	3 Y	4 GY1	5 GY2	6 G	7 B	8 PB	9 P1	10 P2
1. Red-Purple		9·9	13·2	12·3	11·1	8·7	5·6	7·4	6·4	5·8
2. Red	9·9		7·3	7·9	6·9	6·8	9·9	13·1	12·7	12·1
3. Yellow	13·2	7·3		4·5	5·3	9·7	11·5	13·7	14·1	13·4
4. Green-Yellow (1)	12·3	7·9	4·5		5·3	8·6	12·5	13·4	14·1	13·1
5. Green-Yellow (2)	11·1	6·9	5·3	5·3		6·9	9·0	12·2	12·5	13·4
6. Green	8·7	6·8	9·7	8·6	6·9		6·7	9·7	11·3	9·9
7. Blue	5·6	9·9	11·5	12·5	9·0	6·7		5·5	7·4	5·4
8. Purple-Blue	7·4	13·1	13·7	13·4	12·2	9·7	5·5		4·2	4·0
9. Purple (1)	6·4	12·7	14·1	14·1	12·5	11·3	7·4	4·2		4·3
10. Purple (2)	5·8	12·1	13·4	13·1	13·4	9·9	5·4	4·0	4·3	

B. Dissimilarity matrix for subject N7

	1 RP	2 R	3 Y	4 GY1	5 GY2	6 G	7 B	8 PB	9 P1	10 P2
1. Red-Purple		7·1	10·2	11·1	12·5	11·8	9·9	8·6	4·3	2·9
2. Red	7·1		5·7	11·5	10·7	11·8	11·2	12·5	9·2	8·2
3. Yellow	10·2	5·7		6·7	8·9	9·4	11·3	12·5	11·9	10·5
4. Green-Yellow (1)	11·1	11·5	6·7		3·7	5·9	10·3	11·6	10·9	11·5
5. Green-Yellow (2)	12·5	10·7	8·9	3·7		3·6	8·2	9·8	11·3	11·1
6. Green	11·8	11·8	9·4	5·9	3·6		5·1	8·1	10·2	10·6
7. Blue	9·9	11·2	11·3	10·3	8·2	5·1		4·9	8·7	9·7
8. Purple-Blue	8·6	12·5	12·5	11·6	9·8	8·1	4·9		6·3	7·5
9. Purple (1)	4·3	9·2	11·9	10·9	11·3	10·2	8·7	6·3		3·0
10. Purple (2)	2·9	8·2	10·5	11·5	11·1	10·6	9·7	7·5	3·0	

Table 1. Matrices of perceived distances among colors for two subjects in Helm's study. Standard color discrimination tests showed that subject CD1 was very deficient in red–green color vision while subject N7 had normal color vision

Figure 2(a), the 2-dimensional group stimulus space for these data, nicely reproduces the well-known color circle. It is interesting to note that the colors do not lie along a straight line as is the case for the uni-dimensional electromagnetic spectrum (whose visible portion ranges from a wavelength of about 400 to 700 millimicrons; that is, from violet to red). INDSCAL, in common with earlier multi-dimensional scaling methods (*see* Shepard 1962) makes it clear that psychologically we must bring the ends of the straight-line spectrum together to form a circle. Such a circular representation

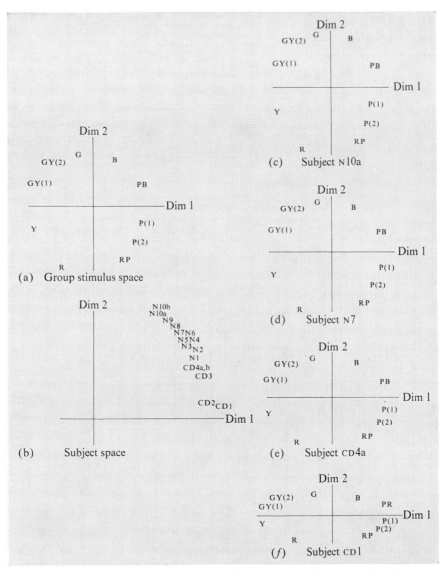

Figure 2. A 2-dimensional INDSCAL analysis of Helm's color perception data produced the group stimulus space shown in (a) and the subject space shown in (b). Private spaces for four subjects are shown in (c)–(f). The coding of the stimuli is as follows: R=red; Y=yellow; GY(1)=green yellow; GY(2)= green yellow with more green than GY(1); G=green; B=blue; PB=purple blue; P(1)=purple; P(2)=purple with more red than P(1); RP=red purple

shows that red and violet, which are at opposite ends of the physical spectrum, are perceived to be more similar to each other than, say, yellow and blue, which are physically closer together. The group stimulus space also reveals that the non-spectral purples, which cannot be produced by any light of a single wavelength, are perceptually between the violets and reds. Although only the ten colors used by Helm are shown in the diagram, it is fairly clear where others would fit.

The precise locations of the coordinate axes describing this 2-dimensional space are of particular interest since, unlike the earlier multi-dimensional scaling procedures, the orientation of axes is *not* arbitrary in INDSCAL. Dimension 1 could be interpreted as a 'yellow-blue' dimension, since yellow is at one extreme and a purplish blue is at the other. Dimension 2, whose extremes are red and green, could be called a 'red-green' dimension.

The dimension weights for all of the subjects (2 of whom gave complete sets of dissimilarity judgments on 2 different occasions) are plotted in figure 2(b), the subject space. Individual differences in the importance of the red-green dimension are particularly large. It is interesting to note that all four color-blind subjects have lower weights on this dimension than any of the subjects with normal vision. Furthermore subjects CD1 and CD2, whom Helm reports to be the most color deficient, have the lowest weights on the red-green dimension.

Private spaces for four subjects, two of whose matrices appear in figure 2, are shown in figures 2(c) to 2(f). (Comparisons between these private spaces and the associated matrices can be quite illuminating.) Due to low weights on the second dimension, the private spaces for CD1 and CD4 (and the other color-deficient subjects) deform the 'color circle' into figures that are approximately ellipses, whose major and minor axes are the blue-yellow and red-green dimensions, respectively. Subject N10, whose private space is stretched vertically, appears to border on blue-yellow color deficiency (which is much rarer than red-green deficiency).

This analysis shows how INDSCAL can accommodate considerable perceptual variations among subjects in a very simple, easily comprehensible, and economical way. The appropriateness of the INDSCAL model for the color data is indicated by the fact that the group stimulus space and the subject space in combination account for over 90% of the variance in the data for all subjects.

PERCEPTION OF RHYTHM AND ACCENT IN ENGLISH WORDS

The stimuli used in the second study (*see* Wish 1969) were 21 words and phrases selected to represent most of the 3-syllable rhythm and accent patterns that occur in English. Every subject who participated in the experiment gave dissimilarity ratings for every possible pair of stimuli. One of the pages from the 21-page response booklet in which subjects recorded their ratings is shown in table 2. The subjects were instructed to circle a low number in a row if the rhythm and accent of the word (or phrase) in that row differed very little from that of the word (or phrase) at the top of the page (in this case, 'Pink Grapefruit'). Greater differences in rhythm and accent (between row stimuli and the stimulus at the top) were to be indicated by circling higher numbers in those rows.

After the subjects had responded to every stimulus pair they indicated how much musical and phonetics training they had had and what their native language was. The native speakers of English were divided into two subgroups: (1) 6 subjects with musical or phonetics training; and (2) 7 subjects without musical or phonetics training. A third subgroup was comprised of the 5 subjects whose native language was not English.

	Pink grapefruit									
	No difference									Very different
1. personal	0	1	2	3	4	5	6	7	8	9
2. ice machine	0	1	2	3	4	5	6	7	8	9
3. garage door	0	1	2	3	4	5	6	7	8	9
4. aquaplane	0	1	2	3	4	5	6	7	8	9
5. enfranchise	0	1	2	3	4	5	6	7	8	9
6. teaspoonful	0	1	2	3	4	5	6	7	8	9
7. pineapple	0	1	2	3	4	5	6	7	8	9
8. big parade	0	1	2	3	4	5	6	7	8	9
9. string quartet	0	1	2	3	4	5	6	7	8	9
10. twilight zone	0	1	2	3	4	5	6	7	8	9
11. hot cross buns	0	1	2	3	4	5	6	7	8	9
12. field hockey	0	1	2	3	4	5	6	7	8	9
13. timbuctoo	0	1	2	3	4	5	6	7	8	9
14. creative	0	1	2	3	4	5	6	7	8	9
15. long meeting	0	1	2	3	4	5	6	7	8	9
16. the papoose	0	1	2	3	4	5	6	7	8	9
17. reduced fee	0	1	2	3	4	5	6	7	8	9
18. first-aid kit	0	1	2	3	4	5	6	7	8	9
19. aroma	0	1	2	3	4	5	6	7	8	9
20. interrupt	0	1	2	3	4	5	6	7	8	9

Table 2. A page from the response booklet in which 18 subjects rated differences in rhythm and accent among 21 English words and phrases

The first two dimensions of the group stimulus space from a 5-dimensional INDSCAL solution for these data are plotted in figure 3(a). Both of these dimensions are based on the degree of accent, or stress, on different syllables. The first dimension contrasts stimuli (such as 'Aróma' and 'Creátive') that have the strongest accent on the middle syllable with stimuli (such as 'Áquapláne' and 'Bíg Paráde') that are most strongly stressed at the beginning or end. The second dimension separates stimuli whose major stress is on the

Figure 3. Planes of dimensions 1 and 2, (a), and dimensions 3 and 4, (b), from 5-dimensional INDSCAL analysis of rhythm and accent dissimilarities data

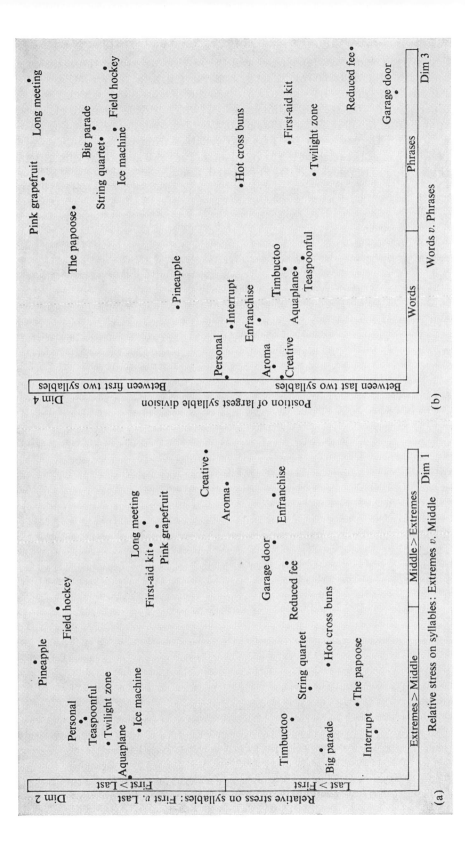

(a)

Dim 2 Relative stress on syllables: First *v.* Last

First > Last | Last > First

Relative stress on syllables : Extremes *v.* Middle
Extremes > Middle | Middle > Extremes **Dim 1**

Pineapple

Field hockey

Personal
Teaspoonful
Twilight zone
Aquaplane • Ice machine

Long meeting
First-aid kit •
Pink grapefruit

Creative •
Aroma •
Enfranchise

Garage door
Reduced fee

Timbuctoo
String quartet
Big parade • Hot cross buns
Interrupt • The papoose

(b)

Dim 4 Position of largest syllable division

Between first two syllables | Between last two syllables

Words *v.* Phrases
Words | Phrases **Dim 3**

Pink grapefruit   Long meeting

The papoose •
String quartet •
Ice machine • Field hockey

Big parade •

Pineapple •

Personal • Interrupt
Enfranchise

Aroma • Timbuctoo •
Creative • Aquaplane •
Teaspoonful •

Hot cross buns •

First-aid kit •

Twilight zone •

Reduced fee •

Garage door •

first syllable (such as 'Píneápple' and 'Field Hóckey') from those that are most strongly accented on the last syllable (such as 'Interrúpt' or 'The Papóose'). Figure 3(b) shows two other dimensions along which subjects differentiated the stimuli—dimension 3, which divides the single-word stimuli from the phrases, and dimension 4, which separates phrases that have a word division between the first two syllables from phrases whose word division comes between the last two syllables. The third and fourth dimensions of the group stimulus space for the rhythm and accent data might also have been based in part on subjects' perceptions of the relative duration of the intervals between adjacent syllables. Thus, since intervals between syllables of a word appear to be shorter than intervals between words, the third dimension could be said to distinguish stimuli whose inter-syllabic intervals are quite different in duration (the two-word phrases) from stimuli whose inter-syllabic intervals do not differ much in duration (the single-word stimuli). Likewise, the fourth dimension could be said to distinguish phrases that appear to have a shorter interval between the first and second syllables

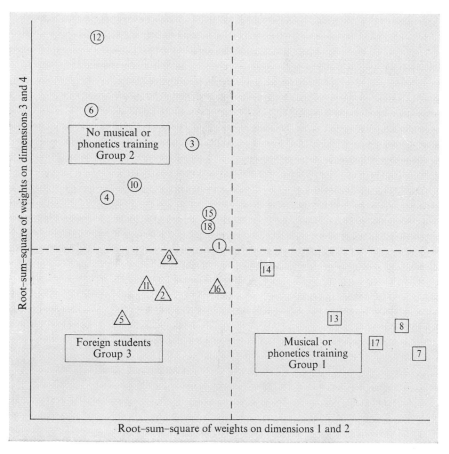

Figure 4. Plot of combined (root-sum-square) weight on dimensions 1 and 2 (horizontal axis) v. dimensions 3 and 4 (vertical axis) for 18 subjects.

(those whose first word has two syllables) from phrases that appear to have a shorter interval between the second and third syllables (those whose second word has two syllables).

Figure 4 shows the relative importance of dimensions 1 and 2 versus dimensions 3 and 4 for all 18 subjects. The fifth dimension, interpreted as 'number of stressed syllables', was weighted about equally on the average by subjects in all three subgroups. The projection of a subject's point on the horizontal axis is equal to his combined weight (the square root of the sum of his squared weights) on the first two dimensions, while the projection of his point on the vertical axis shows his combined weight on the third and fourth dimensions. While all of the native English speakers with musical or phonetics training have high weights on the first pair of dimensions and low weights on the second pair, the opposite is true for native English speakers without such training. Since the first 2 dimensions are the only ones that deal with the relative stress on different syllables, we can conclude that the impression which appropriately trained subjects have of rhythm and accent has much in common with most linguists' conception of stress. In contrast these results show that distinctions among stimuli associated with conventional stress markings (as, for example, in Chomsky and Halle 1968) are not perceptually salient to 'naive' subjects. Since the foreign subjects have low weights on both pairs of dimensions, their dissimilarity judgments must have been based on criteria different from those relevant to the native speakers of English. It appears from this result and other analyses not reported here that a person's perception of rhythm and accent in speech depends in part on the stress rules appropriate to his own language. Since each of the foreign students had a different native language, no 'common dimension' appeared for them.

Dimensions analogous to those for the rhythm and accent data were obtained in an earlier study of perceptual confusions among Morse Code and related signals (*see* Wish 1967). The correspondence of dimensions for the verbal and non-verbal stimuli, despite great differences in the experimental procedures, shows that the dimensions most salient to the perception of rhythm and accent in speech are also relevant to the perception of other kinds of auditory stimuli.

3. Perceptual Confusions among English Consonants

In the final application (*see* Wish 1970a) the matrices used as input to INDSCAL are associated with different experimental conditions rather than with different individuals. The data are from a classical study of confusions among some English consonants under each of 17 degradation conditions (Miller and Nicely 1955). In the experiment, female speakers read one-syllable stimuli, such as *pa*, *ta*, *ka*, from long randomized stimulus lists. Each stimulus consisted of the vowel *a* (as in *ah*) preceded by one of 16 consonants—*p*, *t*, *k*, *f*, *θ* (as in *thin*), *s*, *ʃ* (as in *show*), *b*, *d*, *g*, *v*, *ð* (as in *the*), *z*, *ʒ* (the *zh* sound in *azure*), *m*, or *n*. (Figure 5 may be of interest to those who are familiar with spectrograms.) After each syllable was read, the subjects wrote down the consonant they thought was spoken.

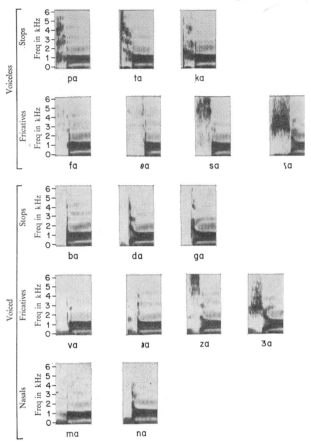

Figure 5. Sound spectrograms of a typical utterance of the 16 stimuli by a female speaker. In each spectrogram time runs from left to right (about a half second per stimulus), while frequency in kilohertz (thousands of cycles per second) increases from bottom to top. The consonant portion occupies approximately the left-most third of each spectrogram

There were 17 experimental sessions, in each of which the speech transmission circuit was degraded in a different way. Table 3, which lists the degradation conditions, shows that there were several degrees of noise (relative to signal level), low-pass filtering (in which only the sound energy below a specified frequency was audible), and high-pass filtering (in which only the sound energy above a specified frequency was audible). More severe degradations of each type are denoted by higher numbers.

The data, then, consist of 17 matrices of consonant confusions. Each matrix is based on 4,000 responses given in a particular degradation condition. E.g., matrices derived from the responses in conditions N5, L6, and H5 are shown in table 4. Each row corresponds to the consonant that was spoken, while each column corresponds to the consonant that was perceived by a listener. The values in a row of a matrix indicate, for the particular condition, the number of times each of the consonants was written down when the consonant associated with that row was spoken.

Degradation condition	Signal-to-noise ratio	Frequency response in HZ	Observed proportions of confusions
Added noise			
N1 (=L1)	12 db	200–6500	0·092
N2	6 db	200–6500	0·158
N3	0 db	200–6500	0·260
N4	−6 db	200–6500	0·535
N5	−12 db	200–6500	0·730
N6	−18 db	200–6500	0·922
Low-pass filtering			
L1 (=N1)	12 db	200–6500	0·092
L2 (=H1)	12 db	200–5000	0·167
L3	12 db	200–2500	0·272
L4	12 db	200–1200	0·428
L5	12 db	200–600	0·505
L6	12 db	200–400	0·592
L7	12 db	200–300	0·735
High-pass filtering			
H1 (=L2)	12 db	200–5000	0·167
H2	12 db	1000–5000	0·268
H3	12 db	2000–5000	0·494
H4	12 db	2500–5000	0·619
H5	12 db	3000–5000	0·728
H6	12 db	4500–5000	0·787

Table 3. Degradation conditions in Miller and Nicely's study of consonant confusability. Higher numbers are associated with more severe degradations of each type (noise, low-pass filtering, and high-pass filtering)

Six dimensions, 4 of which will be discussed here, account quite well for the patterns of confusion under all degradation conditions. Although the other 2 dimensions could clearly be interpreted, a discussion of them would require too many technical details. [The fifth and sixth dimensions were interpreted as 'voiceless stops v. voiceless fricatives' and 'second formant transition after voiced consonants', respectively.] Figures 6(a) and 6(b), respectively, show dimensions 1 and 2 and dimensions 3 and 4 of the group stimulus space. The first dimension separates the voiceless consonants (those which when spoken produce no vocal cord vibration, and which therefore are acoustically aperiodic or noisy) from their voiced counterparts. Dimension 2 distinguishes the nasals, *m* and *n*, from all of the other consonants. The third dimension divides the sibilants as a class from the non-sibilants, while the fourth dimension contrasts the higher frequency sibilants, *s* and *z*, with the lower frequency sibilants, ʃ and ʒ.

Figures 6(c) and 6(d) show plots of weights for conditions on the same pairs of dimensions. (Since the points are associated with different experimental conditions, this could be referred to as a *condition space* instead of a

A. Condition N5: s/n = −12 db; 200–6,500 hz

	p	t	k	f	θ	s	ʃ	b	d	g	v	ð	z	ʒ	m	n
p	51	53	65	22	19	6	11	2		2	3	3	1	5	8	5
t	64	57	74	20	24	22	14	2	3	1	1	2	1	1	5	1
k	50	42	62	22	18	16	11	4	1	1	1	2			4	2
f	31	22	28	85	34	15	11	3	5		8	8	3		3	
θ	26	22	25	63	45	27	12	6	9	3	11	9	3	2	7	2
s	16	15	16	33	24	53	48	3	5	6	3	1	6	2		1
ʃ	23	32	20	14	27	25	115	1	4	5	3		6	3	4	2
b	4	2	2	18	7	7	1	60	18	18	44	25	14	6	20	10
d	3		1	4	7	4	11	18	48	35	16	24	26	14	9	12
g	3	1	1	1	4	5	7	20	38	29	16	29	29	38	10	9
v		1	1	12	5	4	5	37	20	23	71	16	14	4	14	9
ð		1	4	17	2	3	2	53	31	25	50	33	23	5	13	6
z	6	1	2	2	6	14	8	23	29	27	24	19	40	26	3	6
ʒ	3	2	2	1		6	7	7	30	23	9	7	39	77	5	14
m		1			1	1		11	3	6	8	11		1	109	60
n	1				1		1	2	2	6	7	1	1	9	84	145

B. Condition L6: s/n = +12 db; 200–400 hz

	p	t	k	f	θ	s	ʃ	b	d	g	v	ð	z	ʒ	m	n
p	72	68	90	20	15	4	1	2	4	1		1				2
t	73	72	74	20	8	6	3	1	2	2		2		1		
k	63	74	127	9	7	5	2			1		1	1	1		1
f	7	7	10	63	69	41	8	3	1	1	1	3		1	1	
θ	5	8	11	60	85	45	14	2	4	2	6	5	1			
s	1	6	5	19	49	125	60	5	2	1	2	9	4			
ʃ	2	6	8	8	22	69	89	2	4	1		3	5	1		
b		1	1	19	14	5		134	20	13	14	11	4	1	2	1
d			2		1	6	4	19	120	23	2	3	11	3		2
g			2	1		5	1	11	116	59	8	7	11	4	1	2
v		1		1	1	2		25	4	8	111	55	18	2	2	2
ð		1	1	6	5	1		43	16	15	75	66	23	11	1	4
z	2		2	1	5	5	2	21	20	17	18	33	91	25	1	1
ʒ						4	2	1	27	29	11	16	83	78	1	
m								12	3		1				219	57
n					1	1		12	3		1	2			99	120

C. Condition H5: s/n = +12 db; 3,000–5,000 hz

	p	t	k	f	θ	s	ʃ	b	d	g	v	ð	z	ʒ	m	n
p	31	15	15	15	14	11	6	19	11	8	15	15	5	9	12	19
t	11	184	16	6	5	5	5	8	9	3	4	2	5	3	6	4
k	15	35	50	7	16	7	2	14	14	24	7	9	8	9	8	7
f	19	12	12	15	19	8	2	25	16	25	15	12	6	2	17	11
θ	15	14	13	13	30	15	3	15	24	12	14	17	10	3	14	20
s	4	4	8	11	8	140	4	7	8	6	6	11	35	7	2	7
ʃ		6	2	3	1	4	177	1	2	2	1	6	1	23	7	
b	17	13	11	25	23	8	1	27	13	19	25	13	5	6	17	13
d	14	23	15	11	11	4	3	15	63	25	14	10	13	6	19	14
g	14	15	17	17	12	8	1	23	39	45	14	10	13	7	17	16
v	19	19	22	18	20	8	10	35	18	16	19	21	7		28	16
ð	19	13	12	12	24	8	6	22	24	15	24	21	10	5	33	16
z	9	21	9	7	17	59	6	6	11	13	10	15	41	4	10	14
ʒ	4	6	1	5	1	11	51	3	3	7	1	10	9	128	7	5
m	16	7	14	11	19	5	4	31	16	17	17	10	10	6	58	19
n	16	7	12	6	16	7	6	14	29	16	13	22	7	4	19	58

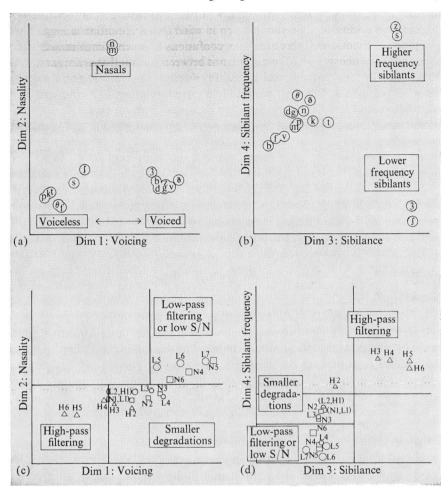

Figure 6. Planes of dimensions 1 and 2, (a), and of dimensions 3 and 4, (b), of group stimulus space from a 6-dimensional INDSCAL analysis of the Miller–Nicely data. Planes of the corresponding dimensions of the 'condition space' (in which each point represents a degradation condition) are shown in (c) and (d). Noise, low-pass filtering, and high-pass filtering conditions are denoted by squares, circles, and triangles, respectively. The three most severe degradations of each type are represented by larger symbols

subject space.) In these figures the noise, low-pass filtering, and high-pass filtering conditions are represented by squares, circles, and triangles, respectively. Larger symbols are used to denote the three most severe degradations

Table 4. Confusion matrices for three of the Miller–Nicely degradation conditions. Each row of a matrix corresponds to the consonant that was spoken, while each column corresponds to the consonant that was perceived by a listener. The value in row i and column j of a matrix shows, for the particular condition, the number of times that the consonant associated with column j was written down by subjects when the consonant associated with row i was spoken

of each type. In comparing the patterns of dimension weights for different degradation conditions, one should keep in mind that a condition has a high weight on a dimension if there are many confusions between stimuli near each other on that dimension and few confusions between stimuli that are far apart.

Weights on the 'voicing' and 'nasality' dimensions are highest for the extreme noise (N4, N5, and N6) and low-pass filtering (L5, L6, and L7) conditions, and lowest for the extreme high-pass filtering (H4, H5, and H6) conditions. This shows that discrimination between voiced and voiceless consonants and discrimination between nasals and non-nasals is much better in the low-frequency range than in the high-frequency range. The relative weights for conditions on the third and fourth dimensions [figure 6(d)] is almost the reverse of that shown for the first two dimensions; that is, the high-pass filtering conditions have the highest weights while the extreme noise and low-pass filtering conditions have the lowest weights on the sibilance dimensions. The patterns of dimension weights for different kinds of degradations make sense since the acoustical information which distinguishes voiced from voiceless consonants and which distinguishes nasals from non-nasals is primarily in the lower frequency range, while most of the acoustical information which distinguishes sibilants from each other and from non-sibilants is in the higher frequency range.

This example, which illustrates the possibility of using data sources other than individuals, shows that the dimensions obtained and their relative importance may depend on the experimental conditions as well as on the subjects and stimuli. Moreover, the information about dimension weights for various degradation conditions contributes to the interpretation of dimensions and to a better understanding of consonant perception.

CONCLUSIONS

Much of what we have reported in these examples could have been discovered by using one of the earlier multi-dimensional scaling procedures. The major contributions of INDSCAL in these analyses were:

(1) unique determination of dimensions which could be interpreted without first rotating the axes;

(2) a parsimonious representation of widely varying perceptual structures; and

(3) information regarding the weights, or saliences, of the dimensions to different subjects, or under different conditions, which could be related to other important differences among them.

In concluding this paper we would like to suggest some ways in which INDSCAL might be applied in archaeology. Suppose that there are a number of archaeological sites, each of which contains several categories of artifacts such as tools, pottery, clothing, jewelry, and so on. Suppose also that an archaeologist has divided each category into types. A sites-by-types abundance matrix could then be made for each artifact category. (The value in row j and column k of an abundance matrix would indicate how many artifacts of type k there are in site j.) A matrix of similarities (or dissimilarities) among sites could be derived from each abundance matrix in many different ways, for example, by correlating the frequency values for each pair of sites.

The input to INDSCAL would then be a number of different matrices of similarity among sites, one for each category of artifacts. The output would be a group stimulus space (whose points correspond to sites) which would reveal the primary dimensions along which the sites could be distinguished, and a 'category space' (analogous to a subject space) which would show the relative importance of each dimension for each category of artifacts. For example, a dimension interpreted as 'time' might be the most important one for distinguishing tools from different sites, while a 'geography' dimension might be most important for pottery.

A less conventional procedure for obtaining several matrices of similarities among sites would be simply to ask a skilled archaeologist to make direct numerical ratings of similarity, for example, on a scale from 1 to 9. These ratings could be made in a table, such as table 5, whose rows are associated with pairs of sites [$n \times (n-1)/2$ rows if there are n sites] and whose columns indicate the categories of artifacts (one column per category). (It is assumed in this simple example that there are only four sites: $A, B, C,$ and D.)

Sites	Categories				
	Tools	Pottery	Clothing	Jewelry	
A and B					
C and D					
B and D					
B and C					
A and D					
A and C					

Table 5

For example, if the archaeologist felt that the *tools* in sites C and D were very different from each other, he would write a low number in the second row and first column. Higher numbers would be used to express greater degrees of similarity. The first column of the table would lead to a matrix of similarities between sites based only on tools, the second column to a similarity matrix pertaining only to pottery, and so on.

Although the form of the INDSCAL input and output would be the same as described in the previously suggested application, the results might differ considerably. In fact, a comparison between the spaces from the analyses of the derived and direct similarities might prove to be quite illuminating (*see* Wish 1970b, Wish, Deutsch, and Biener 1970).

Still another potential way of collecting data suitable for an INDSCAL analysis would be to ask several archaeologists to rate directly the overall similarity between the entire archaeological contents from each pair of sites. In this case the group stimulus space would indicate the dimensions used by the archaeologists to distinguish among sites, while the subject space would show the relative importance of these dimensions to each archaeologist.

Due to our lack of experience in archaeology, we realize that we may have overlooked other possible applications which might be of greater interest to archaeologists. We trust, however, that we have communicated to you the basic aims of INDSCAL, how it has been applied in psychology, and how it might be used in archaeology. We hope that it may prove to be as valuable in your field as it has been in ours.

ACKNOWLEDGMENT

The authors wish to thank Joseph Kruskal for many helpful comments and suggestions.

REFERENCES

Carroll, J.D. (1971) Individual differences and multidimensional scaling. *Multi-dimensional Scaling: Theory and Applications in the Behavioral Sciences* (eds Shepard, R.N., Romney, A.K. & Nerlove, S.). New York: Seminar Press. In press.

Carroll, J.D. & Chang, J.-J. (1969) How to use INDSCAL, a computer program for canonical decomposition of N-way tables and individual differences in multi-dimensional scaling. Bell Telephone Laboratories, unpublished report.

Carroll, J.D. & Chang, J.-J. (1970a) Analysis of individual differences in multi-dimensional scaling via an N-way generalization of 'Eckart-Young' decomposition. *Psychometrika*, **35**, 283–319.

Carroll, J.D. & Chang, J.-J. (1970b) Reanalysis of some color data of Helm's by INDSCAL procedure for individual differences multidimensional scaling. *Proceedings, 78th Annual Convention, APA*, pp. 137–8.

Chomsky, N. & Halle, M. (1968) *The Sound Pattern of English*. New York: Harper & Row.

Helm, C.D. (1964) A multi-dimensional ratio scaling analysis of perceived color relations. *J. optic. Soc. Amer.*, **54**, 256–62.

Helm, C.D. & Tucker, L.R. (1962) Individual differences in the structure of color perception. *Amer. J. Psychol.*, **75**, 437–44.

Kruskal, J.B. (1964a) Multi-dimensional scaling: A numerical method. *Psychometrika*, **29**, 1–27.

Kruskal, J.B. (1964b) Multi-dimensional scaling by optimizing goodness of fit to a nonmetric hypothesis. *Psychometrika*, **29**, 115–29.

Kruskal, J.B. (1971) Multi-dimensional scaling in archaeology: time is not the only dimension. *Mathematics in the Archaeological and Historical Sciences*, pp. 119–32 (eds Hodson, F.R., Kendall, D.G., & Tăutu, P.). Edinburgh: Edinburgh University Press.

Miller, G.A. & Nicely, P.E. (1955) An analysis of perceptual confusions among some English consonants. *J. acoust. Soc. Amer.*, **27**, 338–52.

Shepard, R.N. (1962) The analysis of proximities: Multi-dimensional scaling with an unknown distance function. I, II. *Psychometrika*, **27**, 125–40; 219–46.

Torgerson, W.S. (1958) *Theory and Methods of Scaling*. New York: Wiley.

Tucker, L.R. (1964) The extension of factor analysis to three-dimensional matrices. *Contributions to Mathematical Psychology*, pp. 109–27 (eds Fredriksen, N. & Gulliksen, H.). New York: Holt, Rinehart & Winston.

Tucker, L.R. & Messick, S. (1963) An individual differences model for multi-dimensional scaling. *Psychometrika*, **28**, 333–67.

Wish, M. (1967) A model for the perception of Morse-code like signals. *Human Factors*, **9**, 529–40.

Wish, M. (1969) Individual differences in perceived dissimilarity among stress patterns of English words. Paper presented at Psychonomic Society Meetings, St. Louis, October 1969.

Wish, M. (1970a) An INDSCAL analysis of the Miller–Nicely consonant confusion data. Paper presented at meetings of the Acoustical Society of America, Houston, November 1970.

Wish, M. (1970b) Comparisons among multi-dimensional structures of nations based on different measures of subjective similarity. *General Systems*, **15**, pp. 55–65 (eds Rapoport, A. & von Bertalanffy, L.).

Wish, M., Deutsch, M. & Biener, L. (1970) Differences in conceptual structures of nations: An exploratory study. *J. Personality & social Psychol.*, **16**, 361–73.

Multi-dimensional scaling and related procedures

Discussion and comments

V. Liveanu. Non-quantified data are not necessarily not objective data. The grouping by INDSCAL of the subjects' answers along two axes is a mathematical relation (or structure) that belongs to the data and not to the investigator. But the sense assigned to these axes by the investigator is a matter of interpretation, based on concepts of the investigator.

Seriation

Seriation

Liliana I. Boneva
A new approach to a problem of chronological seriation associated with the works of Plato

CLASSICS AND STATISTICS

In each field and each epoch, ever since science began, past, present and future, which hide so many tempting secret and unknown curiosities, have been and will be a matter of no little interest.

To keep in chronological order let us begin with the past, or rather with the remote past. Among the names of the most famous learned Greeks, whose works have survived for more than 22 centuries, is that of Plato. His philosophical ideas and elegant style have been carefully studied and used as a model ever since. Unfortunately, nobody mentioned or, perhaps, nobody knew, the true chronological order in which his 35 dialogues, 6 short pieces, the *Definitions* (if genuine), and 13 letters appeared.

About a century ago (1867) L. Campbell first proposed this question, interesting but difficult to solve. He published a work in which he tried to discover an approximately true chronological order of just two of the dialogues—*Sophist* and *Politicus*. Since then numerous authors (mostly German) have done much work in an effort to find out some satisfactory method of putting Plato's works in their sequence of composition. One can imagine how onerous such work must be—to study all the works, and all sources connected with them, to try to find out some features which might give a basis for making guesses about the chronological seriation. Little by little it became quite clear that without the help of statistics no agreement on this question could ever be reached. But what sort of statistics and which statistical methods to use?

W. Kaluscha (1904), a German philologist, first hit on the idea that one can follow changes in style and rhythm by studying the sentence-endings. Seeking to obtain more objective data, he decided to investigate the so-called *clausula* (that is, end of a sentence or clause), for it was considered by Greek and Latin philosophers as the part of the sentence most important with regard to rhythm. [According to Cicero the sentence-endings (clausulae) are rhythmically the most important, although the remaining part of the sentence should not be neglected completely.] The clausula was taken to consist of the 5 last syllables, and the following conditions applied:

(1) Clausulae concluding with a long vowel before a vowel at the beginning of the next word should be omitted.

(2) Clausulae in which a short vowel is followed by a combination of mute and liquid consonants should also be omitted.

(3) The last syllables of the clausula are not to be regarded as 'anceps'.

(4) Two short syllables should not be reckoned as the equivalent of a long one in the same place.

Since there are only two possible types of syllable (long and short), Kaluscha divided all sentence-endings into $2^5 = 32$ distinct classes of clausulae. He then studied a large sample of Plato's works, investigating 25 of the *Dialogues*, of which the *Republic* and the *Laws* consist respectively of 10 and 12 separate books, that is, 45 different books altogether. In this way he constructed the frequency distribution of clausula-types for each of these 45 dialogues.

Kaluscha's main purpose was, not to arrange this whole set of books in chronological order, but to establish which dialogue had a clear rhythm and, moreover, to check and if possible to establish the hypothesis that Plato wrote his last books in accordance with the precepts of Isocrates' school (that is, with strict rules of rhythm). It seems that he was able to reach definite conclusions by interpreting the frequency distributions. For he not only regarded the last 6 books as belonging to a separate period, but also concluded that their chronological order should be: *Timaeus*, *Critias*, *Sophist*, *Politicus*, *Philebus*, and *Laws*.

Sixteen years later, another German philologist, L. Billig (1920), trying to show that Kaluscha's statistical investigations had 'in many ways' not been satisfactory (but failing to explain why) came to the same conclusions about the order of the last 6 works of Plato.

Although both Kaluscha and Billig obtained the same chronological seriation, using slightly different approaches (for Billig (1) counted the clausulae only before a full-stop and not before a colon, (2) used one and the same (Burnet's) edition, and (3) assumed *a priori* that the final syllable of the clausula is always 'anceps'), their results were largely neglected for a long time. Obviously the time was still 'too early' for applying statistics in linguistic investigations. Only 12 years ago the first positive echo of Kaluscha's idea rang out with the appearance of Cox and Brandwood's paper concerning Plato's works (Cox and Brandwood 1959). This was followed immediately by Brandwood's PhD thesis (Brandwood 1959). Both were based on Kaluscha's idea, but improved upon the statistical approach, to a great extent.

Plato's rhythmical preferences, expressed in preferring some and neglecting other clausulae, show considerable evolution. That is why his works have been such a tempting object for linguistics study. This fact, however, attaches great importance to Kaluscha's idea of basing the statistical approach on the clausulae.

The present paper is based on Kaluscha's data (taken with the permission of Dr Brandwood from the tables included in his thesis): first because of the fact mentioned above, and secondly because his data form the largest available group of frequency distributions of clausulae. According to Brandwood the weakest point in Kaluscha's work was that he did not mention from which of the numerous editions he took his data, and whether he used the same or different editions for the whole collection of observations; therefore it was difficult to check if the data had been accurately recorded.

The second volume of Brandwood's thesis consists of Kaluscha's tables, together with tables of his own, showing that the frequencies do differ from edition to edition, but one can also see that the frequencies obtained from the same edition depend on which philologist carried out the calculation. Hence it seems reasonable to choose the largest amount of data obtained by the same person, hoping that this will make the random error relatively smaller.

STATISTICS AND CLASSICS

Most of the scholars who have studied Plato's works, and the chronological order in which he wrote them, used a sort of elementary statistics. They either counted how many times a particular word or syllable appeared in each of the books, or calculated percentages of appearance of some carefully chosen features on which they tried to base their hypotheses. Obviously they could not rely only on these, so their conclusions had to be in some way subjective, that is, they had to be connected with their previous knowledge about the conditions in which Plato lived and worked, and about the influence of different schools and philosophers on him. Cox and Brandwood carried out the first wholly statistical investigation. They used a new approach (constructed by Cox) related to the well-known discriminatory analysis. In fact Karl Pearson and Mahalanobis developed an interest in that subject around 1920. But the direction they both took was, more or less, to find a suitable coefficient which would measure in some sense the distance between two populations. Pearson denoted his coefficient of population likeness by C^2, while Mahalanobis, after considering that C^2 varied too much with the sample size, and did not measure, practically, the *value* of the difference between the two groups observed, proposed another more satisfactory measure, D^2. Since then not only Mahalanobis but the whole Indian statistical school (including C. R. Rao), as well as other mathematicians in different parts of the world, have tried to improve this method of classification. The first to introduce the so-called discriminant function was R. A. Fisher (1936) who in 1936 switched on the green light for those who wanted to assist the theoretical development of this subject.

Many such workers (mostly anthropometricians) made satisfactory use of C^2 and D^2 as well as of some generalizations suggested by Hotelling, Wilks, Bartlett, Rao, and so on, based on the famous Neyman–Pearson likelihood-ratio method. In 1939 Welch showed in a brief note that if we have two populations P_1 and P_2 with probability distributions p_1 and p_2 then, without making any assumptions of normality or equality of variances and covariances, the optimum discrimination between P_1 and P_2 can certainly be based on the likelihood ratio (Welch 1939). Cox and Brandwood chose Welch's opinion as a starting point for their work. They studied the last six books of Plato, adding for comparison the *Republic*, which was accepted as having been written earlier. *Assuming* the *Rep.* to be the earliest (of these seven works) and the *Laws* to be the latest, they employed a parametric model in estimating the linear order in which the five other dialogues lay between these two. For that purpose Cox suggested the use of combined probabilities for the five middle works. In their results they obtained a linear seriation differing by only one 'inversion' from the Kaluscha–Billig seriation, namely: *Rep., Tim., Soph., Crit., Pol., Phil., Laws.*

Although Cox and Brandwood's procedure seems quite natural it has some disadvantages, as was shown by A. C. Atkinson (1970). In his elegant and comprehensive analysis based on Cox's method of combining two tested hypotheses in one single model (of which they will both be special cases) Atkinson shows that to take a *one*-parametric family (formed by $\lambda_1 + \lambda_2 = 1$) and to assume that the combined probabilities lie on a line through the two basic populations, is not satisfactory. In order to avoid some undesirable anomalies (like obtaining negative probabilities) he recommended a model involving, so to speak, a *multi*-parametric family to be used for constructing the combined probability distribution function. Although the improvement proposed by Atkinson was well motivated, his estimations in fact gave exactly the same chronological order for the last 6 works of Plato. The fact that the same order has also been established by several philologists almost without any statistics gave rise to the present paper. Why not try another method, and why not try to bring in some of Plato's works about which no agreement has yet been reached?

A variety of numerical methods of classification and seriation has been developed and much discussed recently. What one has to do is either to work out and to develop some new method, or to choose one of the known methods and to try to adapt it, if possible. Of course it is very important to make clear first what purpose one is after. For instance, the purpose in this present paper is not to find out the exact year in which each of the studied 45 works of Plato was written (or published) but to arrange them in a chronological *series*. This means that we are not interested in, so to speak, an absolute chronology which will give us the dated order, but only in the correct order in time. It is clear now why the choice of the method used here fell on the well-known 'horse-shoe' approach to seriation developed recently by D. G. Kendall (1970). It will be a waste of time to repeat here the details of the method, which is one of the main problems lectured on and discussed at the present conference. The only remarks necessary are:

(1) The data (frequencies) have been arranged in a matrix with as many rows as there are books, and as many columns as there are types of clausulae. By the help of a simple FORTRAN program the similarities were obtained by summing up the minima of compared pairs of frequencies (that is, if p_{ik} and p_{jk} denote the frequencies of clausula k in two different books i and j, then

$$SIM_{ij} = \sum_{k=1}^{n} \min\,(p_{ik}, p_{jk}), \text{ where } n = \text{number of clausulae} = 32).$$

(2) CIRCLEUP was not used in the experiments described here, but the effects of introducing this variation in the 'horse-shoe' program are now being studied.

(3) The distinction between PTT and STT is not really relevant to us because there are only a few 'ties' in the data.

But it is high time to acquaint the reader with some actual results, and he is therefore now invited to turn his attention to the two accompanying figures.

Figure 1 represents the 'horse-shoe' final configuration for the 7 works of

Plato studied by Cox and Brandwood; that is, *Republic* (*R*), *Critias* (*C*), *Philebus* (*F*), *Politicus* (*P*), *Sophist* (*S*), *Timaeus* (*T*) and *Laws* (*L*). The only differences are that:

(1) Cox and Brandwood took three books of *Rep.* (namely R_8, R_9, R_{10}) added together and treated as a single book, and three books of *Laws* (L_1, L_2, L_3) similarly added together, while we treated *all* ten *R*s and *all* twelve *L*s, and moreover regarded them *as separate books*.

(2) *No* assumptions about *R* and *L* have been used, all the 27 books being treated by us in the same manner. The reason for this was that we wished to see if the *R*s and *L*s were written one after another or whether there were, in fact, some other books written during the *R* or *L* periods, and also to establish if the labels attached to the *R*s and *L*s are in the right order.

Looking at the picture (Figure 1) drawn by the TITAN plotter (TITAN is the name of the computer in the Computer Laboratory of Cambridge University) one can easily see that:

(1) the *R*s come together at one end (presumably the early end) of the sequence;

(2) the *L*s come together at the other end (presumably the late end) of the sequence;

(3) the mutual arrangement of the *L*s shows no obvious pattern;

(4) apart from the placing of R_{10}, one might conclude that the *R*s were written in the order R_6–R_9 (and R_{10}) followed by R_1–R_5;

(5) *F* and *P* appear to be contemporary with the *L*s;

(6) *S*, *C*, and *T* come between the *R*s and the *L*s.

Figure 2 shows the 'horse-shoe' picture of *all* 45 books (*see* table 3). The only one not linked with the other books is *Critias* and the cause of this could be the small number of clausulae in it—only 150 (*see* table 4). The most important remarks concerning this figure are:

(1) There are two very well distinguished periods in Plato's style. Obviously, the philologists were right to consider that in most of his works, that is, in the earlier period, he was influenced by the style of Socrates, and in the later period (*T*, *C*, *S*, *P*, *F* and all *L*s) he was influenced by the strict rhythm of the school of Isocrates.

(2) The *R*s were written during the 'early' period. [This is clear from the calculations, although the *L*s and *R*s are not labelled in figure 2. All the unlabelled books in the group containing *P* and *F* are L_1–L_{12}. (See the 'Notes' at the foot of table 2.)]

For the convenience of the reader we also give several tables, of which the first two correspond to figures 1 and 2 respectively. They give the coordinates of the points in the final configuration and the corresponding names of the books. Table 3 gives the alphabetic list of all books, and table 4 gives the clausula frequency distributions for all 45 works.

We hope that these preliminary results will be of some help to philologists and philosophers, and before publishing our further results we should very much welcome their opinion.

REFERENCES

Atkinson, A.C. (1970) A method for discriminating between models. *J. Roy. stat. Soc. (Ser. B)*, **32**, 313.

Billig, L. (1920) Clausulae and Platonic chronology. *J. Philology*, **35**.

Brandwood, L. (1959) *The Dating of Plato's Works by the Stylistic Method— Historical and Critical Survey*. PHD. thesis. University College, London.

Cox, D.R. & Brandwood, L. (1959) On a discriminatory problem connected with the works of Plato. *J. Roy. stat. Soc. (Ser. B.)*, **21**, 1.

Fisher, R.A. (1936) The use of multiple measurements in taxonomic problems. *Ann. Eugen.*, **7**, 179–88.

Kaluscha, W. (1904) Zur Chronologie der platonischen Dialoge. *Wiener Studien*, pp. 25–7.

Kendall, D.G. (1970) Seriation from abundance matrices. *Mathematics in the Archaeological and Historical Sciences*, pp. 215–52 (eds Hodson, F.R., Kendall, D.G., & Tăutu, P.). Edinburgh: Edinburgh University Press.

Welch, B.L. (1939) Note on discriminant functions. *Biometrika*, **31**, 218–19.

Final configuration			Name
1	−0·192	−1·198	R_1
2	0·063	−1·277	R_2
3	−0·729	−1·271	R_3
4	0·118	−1·489	R_4
5	−0·050	−1·215	R_5
6	−0·180	−1·778	R_6
7	0·346	−1·815	R_7
8	−0·183	−2·178	R_8
9	−0·662	−2·050	R_9
10	−0·402	−1·340	R_{10}
11	0·096	0·753	L_1
12	0·562	1·388	L_2
13	−0·419	1·048	L_3
14	0·010	1·336	L_4
15	0·008	1·648	L_5
16	−0·273	1·457	L_6
17	−0·068	1·136	L_7
18	−0·567	1·504	L_8
19	−0·576	1·235	L_9
20	−0·115	1·607	L_{10}
21	0·775	1·284	L_{11}
22	−0·233	1·039	L_{12}
23	1·058	−0·313	C
24	0·295	1·061	F
25	0·181	0·571	P
26	0·217	−0·246	S
27	0·919	−0·898	T

Table 1 Coordinates of points in figure 1

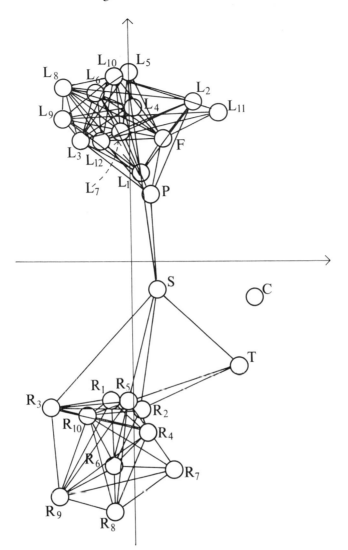

Figure 1

	Final configuration		Name
1	0·179	1·020	*Charm*
2	−0·292	0·662	*Lach*
3	1·513	0·108	*Lys*
4	0·706	0·483	*Euthyp*
5	0·248	0·463	*Gorg*
6	1·177	0·395	*Hipp II*
7	0·443	1·144	*Euthyd*
8	0·346	0·167	*Crat*
9	0·310	0·990	*Meno*
10	1·119	1·344	*Menex*
11	0·811	1·046	*Phaedr*
12	0·195	0·774	*Symp*
13	0·323	0·524	*Phaedo*
14	0·237	0·428	*Theaet*
15	0·874	0·613	*Parm*
16	0·339	0·812	*Prot*
17	−0·335	1·125	*Crito*
18	0·641	1·137	*Apol*
19	0·194	0·645	R_1
20	0·561	0·597	R_2
21	−0·295	0·956	R_3
22	0·647	0·826	R_4
23	0·403	0·635	R_5
24	0·301	1·238	R_6
25	−0·019	1·494	R_7
26	0·178	1·681	R_8
27	0·316	1·639	R_9
28	−0·009	0·892	R_{10}
29	−0·566	−1·158	L_1
30	−0·799	−1·893	L_2
31	−1·053	−1·449	L_3
32	−0·348	−2·040	L_4
33	−0·489	−2·301	L_5
34	−1·404	−1·643	L_6
35	−0·851	−1·569	L_7
36	−1·323	−1·707	L_8
37	−1·438	−1·351	L_9
38	−1·176	−1·899	L_{10}
39	−1·824	−1·040	L_{11}
40	−1·096	−1·257	L_{12}
41	0·945	−1·009	*C*
42	−0·584	−1·802	*F*
43	−0·335	−1·162	*P*
44	0·232	−0·327	*S*
45	0·997	−0·232	*T*

Table 2 (*see notes on p.* 181)

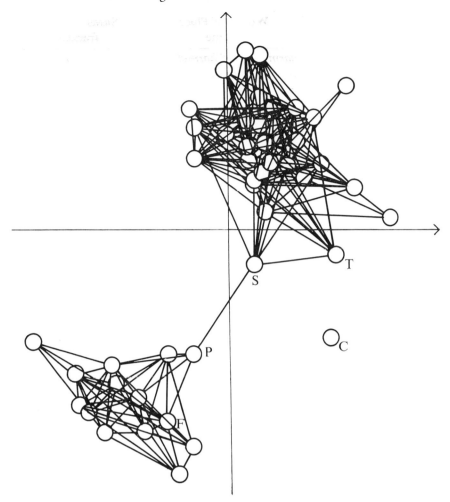

Figure 2

Notes. (1) Apart from *C*, *S*, and *T*, the books fall into two well-marked groups defined thus: (a) those for which *both* coordinates are negative (i.e. *F*, *P*, and all *L*s); (b) those for which the *second* coordinate is positive. *This group contains all R*s.

(2) The 'horse-shoe' output can fortuitously undergo a reflection, and this has happened here; we have to reflect (and rotate) figure 2 to match it with figure 1. There is a fifty per cent chance of such a reflection occurring with every use of 'horse-shoe'.

No	Works of Plato		Sums of clausulae frequencies
	Name		
1	*Charm*	*Charmides*	415
2	*Lach*	*Laches*	376
3	*Lys*	*Lysis*	347
4	*Euthyp*	*Euthyphro*	245
5	*Gorg*	*Gorgias*	1185
6	*Hipp II*	*Hippas Minor*	198
7	*Euthyd*	*Euthydemus*	672
8	*Crat*	*Cratylus*	899
9	*Meno*	*Meno*	487
10	*Menex*	*Menexenus*	184
11	*Phaedr*	*Phaedrus*	713
12	*Symp*	*Symposium*	742
13	*Phaedo*	*Phaedo*	824
14	*Theaet*	*Theaetetus*	1026
15	*Parm*	*Parmenides*	601
16	*Prot*	*Protagoras*	522
17	*Crito*	*Crito*	158
18	*Apol*	*Apology*	363
19	R_1	*Republic*	511
20	R_2	*Republic*	369
21	R_3	*Republic*	393
22	R_4	*Republic*	355
23	R_5	*Republic*	476
24	R_6	*Republic*	373
25	R_7	*Republic*	334
26	R_8	*Republic*	311
27	R_9	*Republic*	307
28	R_{10}	*Republic*	349
29	L_1	*Laws*	341
30	L_2	*Laws*	266
31	L_3	*Laws*	319
32	L_4	*Laws*	281
33	L_5	*Laws*	243
34	L_6	*Laws*	367
35	L_7	*Laws*	450
36	L_8	*Laws*	252
37	L_9	*Laws*	333
38	L_{10}	*Laws*	358
39	L_{11}	*Laws*	267
40	L_{12}	*Laws*	304
41	*C(Crit)*	*Critias*	150
42	*F(Phil)*	*Philebus*	955
43	*P(Pol)*	*Politicus*	770
44	*S(Soph)*	*Sophist*	919
45	*T(Tim)*	*Timaeus*	764

Table 3

Type of ending	1 Charm	2 Lach	3 Lys	4 Euthyp	5 Gorg	6 Hipp II	7 Euthyd	8 Crat	9 Meno	10 Menex	11 Phaedr	12 Symp	13 Phaedo	14 Theaet	15 Parm
	5	4	3	10	16	2	8	29	5	1	9	10	17	19	22
	4	7	7	7	18	5	11	27	4	1	13	11	16	23	18
	6	4	10	3	24	2	10	17	8	6	17	11	15	18	17
	8	1	11	5	19	8	11	17	9	1	18	16	10	20	9
	11	8	17	14	22	4	13	23	11	3	10	27	21	21	19
	6	5	14	3	27	6	9	26	5	3	9	11	15	20	15
	4	8	11	2	22	1	9	25	5	3	14	12	16	16	14
	9	8	13	8	21	3	17	21	6	6	29	10	19	23	13
	10	12	5	5	30	4	20	18	13	4	25	25	10	38	25
	10	16	6	10	42	5	12	22	25	6	22	20	41	28	12
	14	14	15	7	36	7	12	38	21	5	18	19	15	39	15
	17	6	17	6	29	10	35	28	18	5	23	16	21	32	21
	17	16	15	10	38	6	21	29	23	17	33	28	38	25	26
	8	6	4	4	27	1	21	13	8	6	10	13	23	29	7
	20	8	15	10	39	9	37	25	14	9	28	33	32	39	23
	11	11	17	9	44	15	24	42	11	0	23	26	30	35	31
	9	10	13	5	39	2	16	27	14	6	20	18	26	42	13
	8	22	16	5	32	8	20	52	13	4	17	26	28	34	19
	17	9	11	9	59	2	32	22	19	8	39	23	28	39	24
	16	7	9	5	34	5	12	17	16	4	18	26	18	37	13
	31	22	19	9	61	11	51	35	26	4	29	48	44	36	24
	14	13	16	12	52	11	20	36	24	6	42	29	43	43	28
	15	13	6	11	45	6	27	32	27	6	21	22	30	40	15
	9	9	10	10	40	7	25	34	23	6	40	39	34	35	30
	19	19	19	9	73	8	26	47	22	8	26	35	32	37	16
	6	6	3	3	24	3	18	9	12	3	9	22	15	17	9
	20	24	10	9	42	11	28	39	24	11	26	27	30	37	26
	20	18	5	12	58	7	21	25	17	6	19	24	34	45	18
	21	12	8	10	43	5	26	31	15	6	37	25	33	37	26
	23	30	14	11	46	9	36	34	18	14	39	45	47	55	21
	8	8	4	3	37	6	16	21	11	9	11	13	11	18	7
	19	20	4	9	46	9	28	38	20	7	19	32	32	49	25
Total	415	376	347	245	1185	198	672	899	487	184	713	742	824	1026	601

Table 4 Frequency distribution of sentence endings

Type of ending	16 Prot	17 Crito	18 Apol	19 Rep 1	20 Rep 2	21 Rep 3	22 Rep 4	23 Rep 5	24 Rep 6	25 Rep 7	26 Rep 8	27 Rep 9	28 Rep 10	29 Laws 1	30 Laws 2
⏑⏑⏑⏑⏑	9	2	2	12	3	2	3	5	5	3	2	1	5	6	6
	11	0	3	15	9	2	3	10	7	3	1	5	5	5	7
	12	1	8	10	8	6	4	13	5	6	5	2	6	11	4
	10	1	2	10	7	6	4	13	10	6	5	1	10	5	7
	14	4	11	10	9	4	9	9	9	6	9	6	8	13	10
	13	2	10	11	6	2	13	13	8	8	5	4	4	13	11
	8	2	6	11	16	7	10	9	4	9	3	3	7	16	5
	11	3	5	7	7	9	8	9	10	10	6	8	7	5	6
	21	5	14	13	6	9	10	17	13	5	12	12	8	3	0
	9	3	10	17	12	13	17	19	19	24	17	17	19	25	17
	20	5	7	28	12	15	10	19	7	8	5	13	9	14	10
	14	6	11	15	9	7	7	9	12	12	9	6	12	4	3
	15	4	14	27	23	10	24	22	16	15	11	16	9	3	4
	15	4	11	13	11	14	7	10	19	3	5	7	11	6	3
	11	5	13	15	13	19	16	19	13	16	23	19	14	10	3
	8	6	13	9	11	12	10	14	11	8	9	3	6	21	20
	12	3	6	11	15	21	14	14	8	6	8	6	6	13	11
	18	3	16	11	13	10	6	15	13	6	11	16	13	8	6
	25	6	16	11	12	11	11	19	16	18	7	11	11	3	2
	17	6	16	7	5	19	8	7	6	7	5	5	8	13	8
	31	9	22	30	20	25	22	27	22	29	21	21	23	8	6
	17	6	17	26	10	12	18	23	16	14	15	16	9	3	3
	21	6	12	22	12	13	11	15	7	8	6	8	5	15	5
	19	9	13	20	18	13	12	18	17	15	18	13	15	4	1
	16	10	13	23	13	19	18	18	21	15	15	15	23	24	17
	13	3	17	10	5	19	11	10	5	3	7	11	8	5	1
	24	8	11	25	19	15	11	15	6	5	8	12	15	15	19
	25	5	15	14	12	13	11	16	18	16	25	8	19	13	6
	22	7	11	18	15	18	18	18	17	12	12	9	19	12	10
	28	13	14	18	13	22	6	22	10	21	9	20	15	27	26
	13	1	9	13	10	4	6	11	6	11	7	4	5	8	8
	20	10	15	29	15	22	17	18	17	6	10	9	15	10	21
	522	158	363	511	369	393	355	476	373	334	311	307	349	341	266

Table 4 (cont.) Frequency distribution of sentence endings

Table 4 (concl.) Frequency distribution of sentence endings

Type of ending	31 Laws 3	32 Laws 4	33 Laws 5	34 Laws 6	35 Laws 7	36 Laws 8	37 Laws 9	38 Laws 10	39 Laws 11	40 Laws 12	41 Crit	42 Phil	43 Pol	44 Soph	45 Tim
)))))	8	7	8	9	13	4	10	4	8	7	5	24	13	26	18
)))) |	16	13	11	22	13	8	17	13	7	12	3	27	19	33	30
)) |))	6	4	6	4	9	3	4	8	4	8	3	20	24	31	46
))) |)	8	10	11	6	10	8	7	14	6	8	2	25	20	24	14
) |)))	10	12	9	12	13	10	6	9	3	8	10	38	25	22	26
)))))	19	11	14	20	17	10	7	9	6	8	6	46	22	23	27
|))) |	6	9	9	11	11	3	7	8	9	8	5	41	25	30	26
)) | | |	4	9	5	4	12	5	7	4	2	4	3	14	18	37	26
))) | |	2	3	5	1	3	1	3	2	1	2	2	7	3	19	13
) |)))	37	20	19	30	43	23	31	40	20	28	9	62	31	21	25
|) |))	13	7	5	15	12	3	15	11	13	12	4	64	41	30	26
)))))	3	3	2	1	7	2	3	3	1	4	4	6	7	15	17
| |)))	7	2	3	1	1	1	5	6	3	5	3	7	8	28	20
)) |))	7	5	1	9	7	3	3	4	5	5	4	30	24	28	23
)) | |)	11	9	8	13	11	8	11	9	8	12	5	18	23	28	17
) |) | |	11	17	15	32	24	10	19	21	13	12	10	52	33	47	30
|) |) |	15	15	13	12	21	11	8	19	7	12	4	53	53	48	23
| |)))	5	5	3	3	5	6	2	8	2	0	3	7	21	24	25
))) | |	1	4	1	3	1	3	2	3	7	3	1	4	5	21	25
)) | | |	14	1	3	8	6	3	4	9	9	9	3	11	26	34	23
) | | | |	5	6	9	7	13	4	9	11	7	7	2	27	14	19	21
|)) | |	3	2	1	5	3	1	1	3	0	1	7	7	6	28	23
) | | |)	8	3	5	2	20	11	7	8	5	9	2	25	35	31	25
| | | |)	3	5	0	14	6	3	6	2	5	6	4	12	8	12	17
|) | | |	22	22	18	3	46	21	36	28	17	29	8	51	34	42	18
| | | |)	7	5	5	29	9	6	9	3	13	5	5	32	19	23	23
| | | | |	14	8	3	5	17	17	15	9	13	11	3	32	29	27	49
| | | | |	8	15	10	15	13	14	14	9	9	12	7	32	38	32	29
| | | | |	5	2	6	16	11	6	8	7	4	4	9	23	16	38	17
) | | | |	22	17	15	5	32	28	28	46	40	29	3	86	52	43	25
|) | | |	7	17	13	22	12	4	16	8	5	7	5	28	22	24	23
| | | | |	12	13	11	22	29	12	13	20	15	17	6	47	56	31	14
Total	319	281	243	367	450	252	333	358	267	304	150	958	770	919	764

Seriation

Alan E. Gelfand
Rapid seriation methods with archaeological applications

This paper considers new seriation techniques useful in handling the problem of temporally ordering archaeological materials. Part of this material has been taken from a previous paper (*see* Gelfand 1969). In dealing with the above problem, numerous seriation, scaling, and cluster analysis methods have been discussed. The literature on seriation alone is extensive (*see* Sterud 1967).

In particular we offer two rapid seriation methods for multivariate data vectors reduced to a similarity matrix through the choice of an appropriate similarity function. The techniques are presented in detail and are applied to several sets of archaeological data considered by earlier researchers. In addition we give several new related theorems as well as a more general discussion of the sequencing problem.

INTRODUCTION

In a one-dimensional setting, given a collection of n objects, seriation techniques try to order these objects on a one-dimensional scale in the sense of assigning to each object a rank from 1 to n. Scaling techniques attempt to do more by assigning a numerical value to each object so that not only is order achieved but also some quantitative measure of relative closeness is computed.

Problems of seriation arise in various fields of research. For example, an important problem in archaeology is the sequencing in temporal order of collections of deposits or graves in which archaeological artifacts have been located. An issue in political thought is the ordering of a group of individuals on a scale from 'Liberal' to 'Conservative' on the basis of their responses to political questionnaires. An example of a psychological application is the attempt to order a group of children on an intelligence scale through IQ tests. In these and in many other situations scaling may be desirable as well.

Among previous published investigations on seriation, Kendall (1963), Robinson (1951), and Sternin (1965) have considered the archaeological problem in particular with respect to sequencing collections of graves.

Kendall's method treats the problem entirely as one of estimation. He assumes the observed graves, Y_i, are independent with independent components, Y_{ij}, indicating the number of occurrences of the jth variety of pottery or artifact in the ith grave, and that each Y_{ij} has a Poisson distribution with mean μ_{ij} where μ_{ij} is a function of several other parameters indicating abundance, centrality and dispersion. He also lets P, the permutation of the Ys yielding the true temporal order, be a parameter. Employing a maximum likelihood approach he is able to maximize over the μ_{ij}s independently of P

and thus obtain a scoring function $S(P)$ which must be maximized over all P. However, for n of any reasonable size the number of permutations becomes prohibitive. We remark that this same difficulty will occur in a Bayesian approach to the problem and motivates the need for approaches other than an exhaustive search through all possible permutations. In particular Kendall suggests a two-stage reduction procedure through the use of similarity functions.

Robinson, in an earlier, less technical, paper, also suggests the use of similarity functions. His technique depends to some extent on archaeological expertize and still requires the checking of a large number of permutations. Sternin points this out in his paper and offers an interesting although not precisely defined solution using properties of the first and second eigenvectors of certain types of similarity matrices.

Several psychologists such as Guttman (1954) and Coombs (1964) have mentioned particular problems in psychological seriation.

The problem of scaling (or multi-dimensional scaling, as it is more generally labeled) once again considers the pairwise similarities between the n vectors of our collection. Taking these as given, there is an attempt to reconstruct n points in a lower-dimensional space whose distances 'match' as well as possible, in some sense, the observed experimental similarities. In our case, of course, the lower-dimensional space is one dimensional. A discussion of scaling theory and methods up through 1958 is contained in a book by Torgerson (1958). A major advance was made by Shepard (1962) which first enabled one to find solutions through an iterative procedure requiring a computer. The methods of Kruskal (1964) and Shepard and Carroll (1966) seem to be the most appealing solutions available at present. Additionally, the work of Beals, Krantz, and Tversky (1968) is of interest.

In the interest of clarity let us state our problem more precisely.

We observe n k-dimensional vectors $\mathbf{Y}_1, \mathbf{Y}_2, ..., \mathbf{Y}_n$. Let us assume some flexibility in the choice of the size of k and in the interpretation of the components. In other words $\mathbf{Y}_i$ is a suitably chosen attribute vector for the ith person or object. For instance, in the archaeological problem the $\mathbf{Y}$s refer to the different graves or deposits and the components of the $\mathbf{Y}$s might be the occurrence of or the number of a particular type of variety of artifact.

On the basis of comparison of the components of the $\mathbf{Y}$s within and between vectors we seek 'good' methods for associating with each $\mathbf{Y}_i$ a rank $r(\mathbf{Y}_i)$, 1, 2, ..., n and thus ordering these vectors on a one-dimensional scale. The question of whether this scale corresponds in any sense to the scale of interest will be deferred to the last section. For the moment let us assume that it does do so, in which case it makes sense to speak of a true underlying order for the $\mathbf{Y}$s which we will denote by $\mathbf{X}_1, \mathbf{X}_2, ..., \mathbf{X}_n$.

SIMILARITY FUNCTIONS

Since similarity functions are basic to our work, a few remarks are in order. The discussion follows the ideas of Shepard and Carroll.

For a collection $\mathbf{Y}_1, ..., \mathbf{Y}_n$, each $\mathbf{Y}$ being a k-dimensional vector, a measure of similarity between a pair $\mathbf{Y}_i$ and $\mathbf{Y}_j$ should reflect the closeness of the components of $\mathbf{Y}_i$ and $\mathbf{Y}_j$, and in particular the similarity between $\mathbf{Y}_i$ and $\mathbf{Y}_j$ should decrease as the discrepancy between their corresponding components increases and vice versa.

Thus we shall consider a similarity function in our case as a mapping F where

$$F: R^k \times R^k \to R \text{ (usually } R^+) \quad . \tag{1}$$

Given $\mathbf{X} = (X_1, ..., X_k)$, $\mathbf{Y} = (Y_1, ..., Y_k)$ we want to compute a 'discrepancy' for each pair X_t and Y_t: $t = 1, ..., k$, and then to combine these discrepancies suitably, in accordance with the above remarks. A very general class of measures of this kind, F, may be written in the form

$$F(\mathbf{X}, \mathbf{Y}) = g\left\{ \sum_{t=1}^{k} f_t(X_t, Y_t) \right\} \tag{2}$$

where we assume that for the f_t:

(a) $f_t(x, y) = f_t(y, x)$ (symmetry property);
(b) $f_t(y, y) = 0$ (not essential);
(c) $f_t(x, y) \geqslant f_t(x, z)$ if $x \leqslant z \leqslant y$ or $y \leqslant z \leqslant x$.

As for g we assume:

(d) $g(x) \leqslant g(x')$ if $x' < x$ (monotone decreasing property);
(e) $g(x)$ is bounded from above on R^+, i.e. $g(0) = c$;
(f) $g(x) \geqslant 0$ (not essential).

As a result of the above assumptions we have

$$c = g(0) = F(\mathbf{X}, \mathbf{X}) \geqslant F(\mathbf{X}, \mathbf{Y}) \geqslant 0 \quad . \tag{3}$$

Defining $G(\mathbf{X}, \mathbf{Y}) \equiv c - F(\mathbf{X}, \mathbf{Y})$, G is called the dissimilarity between $\mathbf{X}$ and $\mathbf{Y}$. We note that while

$$G(\mathbf{X}, \mathbf{X}) = 0 \leqslant G(\mathbf{X}, \mathbf{Y}) \quad \text{and} \quad G(\mathbf{X}, \mathbf{Y}) = G(\mathbf{Y}, \mathbf{X}) \tag{4}$$

G is not necessarily a metric but rather a semi-metric. It is easy to see that the triangle inequality need not hold.

Nonetheless $G(\mathbf{X}, \mathbf{Y}) \leqslant G(\mathbf{X}, \mathbf{Z})$ means $\mathbf{Y}$ is less dissimilar or more similar ('closer') to $\mathbf{X}$ than $\mathbf{Z}$ is, so that G retains an intuitive interpretation as a distance.

F will usually be scaled down to the interval $[0, 1]$ where $F(\mathbf{X}, \mathbf{Y}) = 1$ implies $\mathbf{X} \equiv \mathbf{Y}$, that is $X_t = Y_t$ for all t. $F(\mathbf{X}, \mathbf{Y}) = 0$ means $\mathbf{X}$ and $\mathbf{Y}$ are as dissimilar as possible. In particular some examples of frequently used measures that satisfy assumptions (a)–(f) are given below.

For vectors whose components exist on $(-\infty, \infty)$ we can use

$$F(\mathbf{X}, \mathbf{Y}) = \frac{1}{1 + \sum_{t=1}^{k} w_t |X_t - Y_t|^p} \tag{5}$$

where the w_t are non-negative weighting constants and $p > 0$. Then $0 \leqslant F \leqslant 1$.

For vectors whose components sum to 1 (percentages) we can use

$$F(\mathbf{X}, \mathbf{Y}) = \frac{2 - \sum_{t=1}^{k} |X_t - Y_t|^p}{2}, \quad p > 0 \quad . \tag{6}$$

Then again $0 \leqslant F \leqslant 1$. This measure was suggested for the archaeological problem by Robinson (1951).

For dichotomized data (vectors with 0s or 1s as components) we can use

$$F(\mathbf{X}, \mathbf{Y}) = \frac{1}{k} \sum_{t=1}^{k} \max\{X_t Y_t, (1-X_t)(1-Y_t)\} \tag{7}$$

$$= \frac{1}{k} \sum_{t=1}^{k} \{1 - |X_t - Y_t|\} = 1 - \frac{1}{k} \sum_{t=1}^{k} |X_t - Y_t| \quad,$$

which again implies that $0 \leqslant F \leqslant 1$.

In particular if we have n observation vectors and if we calculate $F(\mathbf{Y}_i, \mathbf{Y}_j)$ for all i and j we can arrange these numbers in a symmetric $n \times n$ matrix with constant diagonal, which we *define* as a similarity matrix.

METHODS

At this point we shall assume that we are given the set of $n(n-1)/2$ calculated similarities $F(\mathbf{Y}_i, \mathbf{Y}_j)(1 \leqslant i < j \leqslant n)$ obtained from $\mathbf{Y}_1, ..., \mathbf{Y}_n$, and arranged in a similarity matrix. From them we seek an easily obtainable 'good' estimated serial order for the $\mathbf{Y}$s. The question of handling ties among the Fs will be discussed separately for each method.

Additionally we must mention that through similarities the best we can hope to do is obtain an estimated order up to reversibility. This is clear from the fact that an estimated order and its reverse have the objects in the same relative order and it is up to us to interpret or determine the direction of the underlying scale for each particular problem. Realistically this should present no difficulty since expertize should enable us to distinguish oldest from youngest, most liberal from most conservative, and so on, once we have a 'good' estimated order. Of course, in situations where all our objects are located within a small segment of the ordering scale, such as the case of excavating a collection of graves all, say, only a hundred years apart, this 'reversibility' difficulty may not be so easily handled. We will assume this problem can be resolved by expertize.

METHOD I

If $\mathbf{X}_1, \mathbf{X}_2, \mathbf{X}_3, ..., \mathbf{X}_n$ is the assumed underlying true order then our first technique attempts to pick out $F(\mathbf{X}_1, \mathbf{X}_2), F(\mathbf{X}_2, \mathbf{X}_3), ..., F(\mathbf{X}_{n-1}, \mathbf{X}_n)$.

In other words, from the F-matrix arrange the $n(n-1)/2$ terms, $F(\mathbf{Y}_i, \mathbf{Y}_j)$, in decreasing order assuming no ties. We then select the $n-1$ largest Fs successively subject to the following conditions:

(1) $n-2$ subscripts appear exactly twice and 2 subscripts appear exactly once among the $2(n-1)$ subscripts of the $(n-1)$ Fs picked.

(2) All subscripts 'communicate' in the sense that given i and j there exists $k_1, ..., k_p$ for some p such that among the $(n-1)$ Fs are included

$$F(\mathbf{Y}_i, \mathbf{Y}_{k_1}), F(\mathbf{Y}_{k_1}, \mathbf{Y}_{k_2}), ..., F(\mathbf{Y}_{k_p}, \mathbf{Y}_j) \quad.$$

These two conditions ensure that we can construct an estimated order. We label one of the subscripts that appears once as α_1, the other as α_n. Since they communicate and appear only once and all other pairs communicate, for this pair the set $k_1, ..., k_p$ must have $p = n-2$; and labeling k_1 as α_2, k_2 as α_3, and so on, we obtain the order

$$\mathbf{Y}_{\alpha_1}, \mathbf{Y}_{\alpha_2}, ..., \mathbf{Y}_{\alpha_n} \quad. \tag{8}$$

Let us illustrate the method. First consider the following unordered F

obtained for Aurignacian end-scrapers by Sackett (1966). The entries were computed using the measure given by eq. (6).

	$1=CA$	$2=HH$	$3=LF$	$4=CC$	$5=FL$	$6=FF$	$7=FH$
$1=CA$	—	122·7	150·2	*198·8*	129·8	172·2	141·6
$2=HH$	122·7	—	*172·5**	122·9	*192·2*	150·5	*181·1**
$3=LF$	150·2	172·5	—	150·4	*177·3**	178·0	*179·0*
$4=CC$	198·8	122·9	150·4	—	130·0	*172·4*	141·8
$5=FL$	129·8	192·2	177·3	130·0	—	154·6	*188·2*
$6=FF$	172·2	150·5	178·0	172·4	154·6	—	169·4
$7=FH$	141·6	181·1	179·0	141·8	188·2	169·4	—

Table 1

We must pick the six largest Fs successively such that neither condition A nor B is violated. Using the numerical coding as indicated, the first F selected is $F(\mathbf{Y}_1, \mathbf{Y}_4)=198\cdot8$. Next is $F(\mathbf{Y}_2, \mathbf{Y}_5)=192\cdot2$ and then $F(\mathbf{Y}_5, \mathbf{Y}_7)=188\cdot2$. The next largest is $F(\mathbf{Y}_2, \mathbf{Y}_7)=181\cdot1$ but it is not acceptable since its inclusion would violate condition B, that is, the subscripts 2, 5, and 7 would form a cluster and will fail to 'communicate' with the subscripts 1, 3, 4, and 6. Next is $F(\mathbf{Y}_3, \mathbf{Y}_7)=179\cdot0$ and then $F(\mathbf{Y}_3, \mathbf{Y}_6)=178\cdot0$ both of which are acceptable. The next is $F(\mathbf{Y}_3, \mathbf{Y}_5)=177\cdot3$ which is unacceptable since its inclusion would violate condition A, that is, the subscript 3 will have been included more than two times. Similarly the next F, $F(\mathbf{Y}_2, \mathbf{Y}_3)=172\cdot5$, is eliminated, and lastly we include $F(\mathbf{Y}_4, \mathbf{Y}_6)=172\cdot4$. This set of six Fs produce the $\boldsymbol{\alpha}$ vector, $\boldsymbol{\alpha}=(1, 4, 6, 3, 7, 5, 2)$, and the estimated order $CA, CC, FF, LP, FH, FL, HH$. Table 2 shows the F_α-matrix corresponding to this estimate.

	CA	CC	FF	LP	FH	FL	HH
CA	—	198·8	172·2	150·2	141·6	129·8	122·7
CC	198·8	—	172·4	150·4	141·8	130·0	122·9
FF	172·2	172·4	—	178·0	169·4	154·6	150·5
LP	150·2	150·4	178·0	—	179·0	177·3	172·5
FH	141·6	141·8	169·4	179·0	—	188·2	181·1
FL	129·8	130·8	154·6	177·3	188·2	—	192·2
HH	122·7	122·9	150·5	172·5	181·1	192·2	—

Table 2

Similarly let us apply the method to the following unordered F obtained for Aurignacian burins by Sackett (1966). [*See* table 3.]

For this set of data the set of Fs selected successively is easily seen to be $F(\mathbf{Y}_4, \mathbf{Y}_7)$, $F(\mathbf{Y}_1, \mathbf{Y}_6)$, $F(\mathbf{Y}_1, \mathbf{Y}_5)$, $F(\mathbf{Y}_3, \mathbf{Y}_7)$, $F(\mathbf{Y}_2, \mathbf{Y}_5)$, $F(\mathbf{Y}_6, \mathbf{Y}_8)$, $F(\mathbf{Y}_3, \mathbf{Y}_8)$. This set produces the $\boldsymbol{\alpha}$ vector, $\boldsymbol{\alpha}=(4, 7, 3, 8, 6, 1, 5, 2)$ and the estimated order $FG, AC, LP, FF, FH, HH, DL, FL$. The corresponding F_α-matrix is given in table 4.

	1=HH	2=FL	3=LP	4=FG	5=DL	6=FH	7=AC	8=FF
1=HH	—	*183·6**	144·6	125·9	*190·8*	*191·5*	130·2	*171·1**
2=FL	183·6	—	128·3	109·6	*184·6*	*177·2**	113·9	159·2
3=LP	144·6	128·3	—	*181·3**	143·6	150·7	*185·6*	*169·1*
4=FG	125·9	109·6	181·3	—	124·9	141·2	*194·3*	150·4
5=DL	190·8	184·6	143·6	124·9	—	*182·3**	129·2	159·8
6=FH	191·5	177·2	150·7	141·2	182·3	—	136·3	179·6
7=AC	130·2	113·9	185·6	194·3	129·2	136·3	—	154·7
8=FF	171·1	159·2	169·1	150·4	159·8	179·6	154·7	—

Table 3

	FG	AC	LP	FF	FH	HH	DL	FL
FG	—	194·3	181·3	150·4	*141·2*	125·9	124·9	109·6
AC	194·3	—	185·6	154·7	*136·3*	130·2	129·2	113·9
LP	181·3	185·6	—	169·1	150·7	144·6	143·6	128·3
FF	150·4	154·7	169·1	—	179·6	171·1	159·8	159·2
FH	*141·2*	*136·3*	150·7	179·6	—	191·5	182·3	177·2
HH	125·9	130·2	144·6	171·1	191·5	—	190·8	183·6
DL	124·9	129·2	143·6	159·8	182·3	190·8	—	184·6
FL	109·6	113·9	128·3	159·2	177·2	183·6	184·6	—

Table 4

In the case of ties we suggest the following. First, they may not matter; that is, both may be included or both may be excluded. If it is the case that including one excludes the other then we suggest calculating both resulting estimated orders and comparing them via the criterion to be introduced at the end of this section.

Several remarks are in order. Success for this method will come from an assumption that the data exhibit a kind of 'local' one-dimensionality. In other words, if the X_i are not well spaced and tend to form clusters on the underlying scale then for some X_is the similarities on one side will tend to be larger than those on the other side. Furthermore, this method does not necessarily consider all the entries in the F matrix. Thus, in just being concerned with the largest of the F_{ij}s, this method may lose some of the overall perspective in the relationships between the Ys which is contained in the whole F-matrix.

The above comments suggest that this method may be strongly affected by error. However, it should provide a fairly good approximate solution in most 'well-behaved' practical situations. Additionally, we note that the estimated order is invariant under the observed order of the Ys, and that this technique has been easily programmed and can be done by hand for small n.

Lastly this method seems to provide a fairly good approximate solution to what is called the 'minimum length path', that is, to the linear order having minimum sum of distances between adjacent points. This problem is, of course, related to the famous 'traveling salesman' problem which requires the path to be closed.

METHOD II

This method seems to be preferred to Method I, especially in the light of its success in application to actual data.

For each $\mathbf{Y}_i$ we construct an estimated order as follows. Consult the F matrix and arrange the similarities containing $\mathbf{Y}_i$ in decreasing order, assuming no ties. Without loss of generality we put the $\mathbf{Y}$ most similar to $\mathbf{Y}_i$ to the right, and order each subsequent $\mathbf{Y}$ in the following way. Suppose that when we get to the kth $\mathbf{Y}$ the order of the previous $k-1$ is

$$\mathbf{Y}_{\beta_1}, ..., \mathbf{Y}_{\beta_{k-1}} \quad . \tag{9}$$

Then if for this Y,

$$F(\mathbf{Y}, \mathbf{Y}_{\beta_1}) > F(\mathbf{Y}, \mathbf{Y}_{\beta_{k-1}}) \quad ,$$

put Y on the left in eq. (9), while if

$$F(\mathbf{Y}, \mathbf{Y}_{\beta_1}) < F(\mathbf{Y}, \mathbf{Y}_{\beta_{k-1}}) \quad ,$$

put Y on the right in eq. (9). If

$$F(\mathbf{Y}, \mathbf{Y}_{\beta_1}) = F(\mathbf{Y}, \mathbf{Y}_{\beta_{k-1}}) \quad ,$$

compare $\mathbf{Y}$ with $\mathbf{Y}_{\beta_2}$ and $\mathbf{Y}_{\beta_{k-2}}$.

Suppose at stage k there are two Ys, $\mathbf{Y}'$ and $\mathbf{Y}''$, such that $F(\mathbf{Y}_i, \mathbf{Y}') = F(\mathbf{Y}_i, \mathbf{Y}'')$. Then if they are assigned to different sides of (9) there is no problem. If they are assigned to the same side (say the left) then a comparison of $\mathbf{Y}'$ and $\mathbf{Y}''$ with $\mathbf{Y}_{\beta_1}$ (or even with $\mathbf{Y}_{\beta_2}$ if necessary) will resolve the tie, with a similar resolution on the right.

Thus, in this way we obtain an estimated order for each i, where $i = 1, ..., n$,

$$\mathbf{Y}_{\alpha_1}^{(i)}, \mathbf{Y}_{\alpha_2}^{(i)}, ..., \mathbf{Y}_{\alpha_n}^{(i)} \quad . \tag{10}$$

At this point it is necessary to orient these n rank orders 'in the same direction'. For reasonably well-behaved data this should not present much of a problem since the $\boldsymbol{\alpha}$ vectors will tend to be quite similar up to reversibility. In all our data applications no difficulty was encountered, nor was any archaeological expertize required.

Having accomplished this orientation we now let $R^{(i)}(\mathbf{Y}_j)$ be the rank of Y_j in the ith estimated order. Calculate

$$T_j \equiv \sum_{i=1}^{n} R^{(i)}(\mathbf{Y}_j), j = 1, ..., n \quad . \tag{11}$$

Note. $\sum_{j=1}^{n} T_j = n^2(n+1)/2$ (as a check).

Arrange the T_j in increasing order and thus obtain the following final estimated order:

$$\mathbf{Y}_{\alpha_1}, ..., \mathbf{Y}_{\alpha_n}, \tag{12}$$

where $\mathbf{Y}_{\alpha_j}$ is that $\mathbf{Y}$ which corresponds to the j smallest T. In the case of ties amongst the Ts each possible order should be constructed. They can be compared by the criterion at the end of this section.

Again we illustrate the method using the same two sets of data from Sackett (1966). For the first set, using the numerical coding as before, we list for each $\mathbf{Y}_i$ the order obtained.

$$\mathbf{Y}_1: \mathbf{Y}_1^{(1)}, \mathbf{Y}_4^{(1)}, \mathbf{Y}_6^{(1)}, \mathbf{Y}_3^{(1)}, \mathbf{Y}_7^{(1)}, \mathbf{Y}_5^{(1)}, \mathbf{Y}_2^{(1)}$$
$$\mathbf{Y}_2: \mathbf{Y}_1^{(2)}, \mathbf{Y}_4^{(2)}, \mathbf{Y}_6^{(2)}, \mathbf{Y}_3^{(2)}, \mathbf{Y}_7^{(2)}, \mathbf{Y}_5^{(2)}, \mathbf{Y}_2^{(2)}$$
$$\mathbf{Y}_3: \mathbf{Y}_1^{(3)}, \mathbf{Y}_4^{(3)}, \mathbf{Y}_6^{(3)}, \mathbf{Y}_3^{(3)}, \mathbf{Y}_7^{(3)}, \mathbf{Y}_5^{(3)}, \mathbf{Y}_2^{(3)}$$
$$\mathbf{Y}_4: \mathbf{Y}_1^{(4)}, \mathbf{Y}_4^{(4)}, \mathbf{Y}_6^{(4)}, \mathbf{Y}_3^{(4)}, \mathbf{Y}_7^{(4)}, \mathbf{Y}_5^{(4)}, \mathbf{Y}_2^{(4)}$$
$$\mathbf{Y}_5: \mathbf{Y}_1^{(5)}, \mathbf{Y}_4^{(5)}, \mathbf{Y}_6^{(5)}, \mathbf{Y}_3^{(5)}, \mathbf{Y}_7^{(5)}, \mathbf{Y}_5^{(5)}, \mathbf{Y}_2^{(5)}$$
$$\mathbf{Y}_6: \mathbf{Y}_1^{(6)}, \mathbf{Y}_4^{(6)}, \mathbf{Y}_6^{(6)}, \mathbf{Y}_3^{(6)}, \mathbf{Y}_7^{(6)}, \mathbf{Y}_5^{(6)}, \mathbf{Y}_2^{(6)}$$
$$\mathbf{Y}_7: \mathbf{Y}_1^{(7)}, \mathbf{Y}_4^{(7)}, \mathbf{Y}_6^{(7)}, \mathbf{Y}_3^{(7)}, \mathbf{Y}_7^{(7)}, \mathbf{Y}_5^{(7)}, \mathbf{Y}_2^{(7)}$$

and thus $T_1 = 7$, $T_2 = 49$, $T_3 = 28$, $T_4 = 14$, $T_5 = 42$, $T_6 = 21$, $T_7 = 35$, so that the final estimated order is $\mathbf{Y}_1$, $\mathbf{Y}_4$, $\mathbf{Y}_6$, $\mathbf{Y}_3$, $\mathbf{Y}_7$, $\mathbf{Y}_5$, $\mathbf{Y}_2$; that is, CA, CC, FF, LP, FH, FL, HH.

For the second set, again using the numerical coding, we see that for $\mathbf{Y}_i$, $i \neq 6$, the estimated order is
$$\mathbf{Y}_4^{(i)}, \mathbf{Y}_7^{(i)}, \mathbf{Y}_3^{(i)}, \mathbf{Y}_8^{(i)}, \mathbf{Y}_6^{(i)}, \mathbf{Y}_1^{(i)}, \mathbf{Y}_5^{(i)}, \mathbf{Y}_2^{(i)}$$
while for $i = 6$ the order obtained is
$$\mathbf{Y}_7^{(6)}, \mathbf{Y}_4^{(6)}, \mathbf{Y}_3^{(6)}, \mathbf{Y}_8^{(6)}, \mathbf{Y}_6^{(6)}, \mathbf{Y}_1^{(6)}, \mathbf{Y}_5^{(6)}, \mathbf{Y}_2^{(6)} \quad .$$
Thus $T_1 = 48$, $T_2 = 64$, $T_3 = 24$, $T_4 = 9$, $T_5 = 56$, $T_6 = 40$, $T_7 = 15$, $T_8 = 32$, so that the final estimated order is, $\mathbf{Y}_4$, $\mathbf{Y}_7$, $\mathbf{Y}_3$, $\mathbf{Y}_8$, $\mathbf{Y}_6$, $\mathbf{Y}_1$, $\mathbf{Y}_5$, $\mathbf{Y}_2$; that is, FG, AC, LP, FF, FH, HH, DL, FL.

We remark that for both sets of data both methods give the same estimate and these estimates agree with Renfrew and Sterud (1969).

Several remarks concerning Method II are in order. Since we use all the information contained in the F-matrix and since 'we average over i' we would expect this technique to 'smooth out' possibly spurious similarities and produce a reasonably good estimate. Additionally it is invariant with respect to the observed order of the $\mathbf{Y}$s. Lastly, for small n, hand computation can be done, while for larger n the technique can be readily programmed.

The following remarks will prove, for both methods discussed, an optimality property which though 'weak' is certainly desirable.

Consider a matrix $A = \{a_{ij}\}$ satisfying the following monotonicity property

a_{ij} increases in j for $j < i$, $i = 1, 2, ..., n$,

a_{ij} decreases in j for $j > i$, $i = 1, 2, ..., n$.   (13)

Additionally, suppose

$a_{ij} = a_{ji}$,

$a_{ii} = c$ and thus $c \geqslant a_{ij}$.   (14)

If a matrix satisfies assumptions (13) and (14), then it is said to be a Robinson matrix.

In view of the interpretation attached to similarity measures, given an observed similarity matrix, F, it seems reasonable that the goal of any seriation method should be to permute the rows of F to obtain 'as nearly as possible' a Robinson matrix. The resulting permutation would be an estimate of the true order. In fact this was the aim of Robinson's approaches when he first considered the problem. Furthermore, if there exists a permutation which will transform F to an exact Robinson matrix, then we would certainly want to accept the corresponding permutation as the true underlying order. How to manipulate F to this general sort of goal is not immediately clear. However, by way of supplying additional support for our proposed methods we can show that, if there exists a permutation of the observed $\mathbf{Y}_1, ..., \mathbf{Y}_n$ that will

13

transform our observed F into a Robinson matrix, then both of our methods will produce this permutation.

We use the notation of this section with $\mathbf{X}_1, ..., \mathbf{X}_n$, the 'true' order, taken as the one which will have its F-matrix in Robinson form. We also assume no ties among the Fs since, if there are ties and our method produces more than one estimate, then one of these estimates will put F in the desired form.

Theorem

If F can be transformed into a Robinson matrix, then Method I will provide this transformation.

Proof. We must show that Method I will pick out the set $\{F(\mathbf{X}_1, \mathbf{X}_2), ..., F(\mathbf{X}_{n-1}, \mathbf{X}_n)\}$. It suffices to show that for each i, $i = 2, ..., n-1$, $F(\mathbf{X}_{i-1}, \mathbf{X}_i)$ and $F(\mathbf{X}_i, \mathbf{X}_{i+1})$ must be chosen.

Suppose we proceed to pick our set of Fs until we arrive for the first time at an F whose inclusion will make one of the subscripts appear twice. Let this subscript be j. (Note that j cannot be 1 or n by our assumptions.) Then up to this point we must have included only Fs of the form $F(\mathbf{X}_i, \mathbf{X}_{i+1})$ since F has a Robinson form.

Suppose without loss of generality that $F(\mathbf{X}_j, \mathbf{X}_{j+1})$ was the first F included with subscript j. (A similar argument will hold if it was $F(\mathbf{X}_{j-1}, \mathbf{X}_j)$.) Then the new F at this point can be either $F(\mathbf{X}_{j-1}, \mathbf{X}_j)$ or $F(\mathbf{X}_j, \mathbf{X}_{j+2})$. If $F(\mathbf{X}_{j-1}, \mathbf{X}_j) > F(\mathbf{X}_j, \mathbf{X}_{j+2})$ we are done; the desired pair will have been chosen. If $F(\mathbf{X}_j, \mathbf{X}_{j+2}) > F(\mathbf{X}_{j-1}, \mathbf{X}_j)$ then since $F(\mathbf{X}_{j+1}, \mathbf{X}_{j+2}) > F(\mathbf{X}_j, \mathbf{X}_{j+2})$, $F(\mathbf{X}_{j+1}, \mathbf{X}_{j+2})$ has been included already. Thus the addition of $F(\mathbf{X}_j, \mathbf{X}_{j+2})$ to a set including $F(\mathbf{X}_j, \mathbf{X}_{j+1})$ and $F(\mathbf{X}_{j+1}, \mathbf{X}_{j+2})$ would mean that the subscripts j, $j+1$, and $j+2$ fail to communicate with the others and thus $F(\mathbf{X}_j, \mathbf{X}_{j+2})$ must be rejected. Similarly, if $F(\mathbf{X}_{j-1}, \mathbf{X}_j) < F(\mathbf{X}_j, \mathbf{X}_{j+k})$, $k > 2$, the addition of $F(\mathbf{X}_j, \mathbf{X}_{j+k})$ will isolate the subscripts $j, j+1, ..., j+k$.

Now proceeding on in this fashion we see that for each i the pair $F(\mathbf{X}_{i-1}, \mathbf{X}_i)$ and $F(\mathbf{X}_i, \mathbf{X}_{i+1})$ must have been selected.

The next theorem offers a characterization of those matrices that can be permuted to Robinson form.

Theorem

A necessary and sufficient condition that F can be transformed into a Robinson matrix is that the estimated orders given by eq. (10) when oriented in the same direction be identical for each i. This order will produce the Robinson form.

Before proving the theorem we note the obvious corollary relating to our second technique.

Corollary. If F can be transformed into a Robinson matrix, then Method II will provide this transformation.

Let us denote by $\boldsymbol{\alpha}^{(i)} = (\alpha_1^{(i)}, ..., \alpha_n^{(i)})$ the permutation obtained in eq. (10) for the ith row.

Proof of theorem. For the necessity it suffices to apply our second method to F already in Robinson form and show that for all i, $\boldsymbol{\alpha}^{(i)}$ is the identity permutation, that is, $\alpha_j^{(i)} = j$. Since F is in Robinson form

$$F_{1i} < F_{2i} < ... < F_{i-1,i}, \quad F_{ij} < F_{i,n-1} < ... < F_{i,i+1}$$

and for both $j, k < 0$ or both $j, k > 0$

$$F_{i+j,i+j+1} > F_{i-k,i+j+1}$$

it is clear that the estimated order will be $\mathbf{Y}_1, ..., \mathbf{Y}_n$ for each i.

For the sufficiency if we apply $\boldsymbol{\alpha}^{(i)}$ to our observed F matrix then by the very definition of our second method it is clear that the transformed ith row will satisfy the monotonicity property (13). However, since $\boldsymbol{\alpha}^{(i)}$ is the same for each i, each row of the transformed F-matrix will have the monotonicity property, that is, F will be a Robinson matrix.

Let us recall the applications of our methods to Sackett's data in light of the above remarks and theorems. We note that table 2 is exactly a Robinson matrix (as expected) while table 4 is very nearly so (but not exactly, again as expected).

Given an estimated order one would like to compare it with other estimates, particularly to see if minor rearrangements in the order improve the estimate. As we have seen, it is reasonable to judge the 'goodness' of an estimated order by 'how well' its correspondingly permuted F-matrix assumes a Robinson structure. We would like to measure this 'goodness' quantitatively in order to be more precise about the question of improvement. In particular we would like to define an index of fit for a particular permutation of the $\mathbf{Y}_i$s and the observed set of F_{ij}s. We employ the ideas of Shepard and Carroll.

Recalling that the dissimilarities G_{ij} have an intuitive interpretation as 'distances' and letting $\mathbf{Y}_{\alpha_1}, \mathbf{Y}_{\alpha_2}, ..., \mathbf{Y}_{\alpha_n}$ be an estimated order, we define the continuity index of a particular permutation $\boldsymbol{\alpha} = (\alpha_1, \alpha_2, ..., \alpha_n)$ with respect to the similarity measure F as

$$C(F; \boldsymbol{\alpha}) = \sum_{i<j} \frac{G_{ij}}{|\boldsymbol{\alpha}^{-1}(i) - \boldsymbol{\alpha}^{-1}(j)|^{p+r}} = \sum_{i<j} \frac{G_{\alpha_i,\alpha_j}}{|i-j|^{p+r}} \qquad (15)$$

where $p > 0$ is chosen appropriately for the particular $G(F)$ being, used as indicated by the examples in the section on 'Similarity Functions', and the choice of $r \geqslant 0$ is a pragmatic one (that which works best). The motivation for this criterion is that for each pair of vectors $\mathbf{Y}_i, \mathbf{Y}_j$, it compares the given 'distances', G_{ij}, and the 'distances' associated with them by $\boldsymbol{\alpha}$, $|\boldsymbol{\alpha}^{-1}(i) - \boldsymbol{\alpha}^{-1}(j)|^p$ and cumulates these comparisons. The rationale behind the addition of the 'r-factor' is to enable us to 'weigh' the terms in the summation by factors which are non-increasing as elements become further apart in our estimated order. In other words, one would consider the larger similarities as more important and informative than the smaller ones. The choice of $r=0$ provides a constant weighting. Employing $r=1$ or $r=2$ has worked well in practice.

With respect to eq. (15), the permutation that minimizes $C(F; \boldsymbol{\alpha})$ for fixed F will be said to have the best 'fit' with the data. Thus this index provides a way of comparing estimated orders. However, this criterion cannot be converted into a sequencing method since we run into the old problem of having too many permutations to consider.

One criticism of this index is that it compares a non-metric order vector to the 'metric' quantities G_{ij}. In other words, perfectly ordered sets of points on the real line can give rise to infinitely many different values of this index. However, in light of our purpose for this index, the criticism seems invalid as the following theorem indicates.

Theorem

If there exists a permutation, α_0, that will transform our matrix F into a Robinson matrix then $C(F; \alpha_0) = \min C(F; \alpha)$ as α runs over all permutations of the integers $1, 2, ..., n$.

Proof. Without loss of generality let us assume that F has already been transformed to a Robinson matrix. Then $\alpha_0 = (1, 2, 3, 4, ..., n)$. If $\alpha^{(k)} = (1, 2, 3, ..., k-1, k+1, k, k+2, ..., n)$, that is, k and $k+1$ interchanged, then it suffices to show that $C(F; \alpha_0) \leqslant C(F; \alpha^{(k)})$, $k = 1, 2, ..., n-1$. But

$$C(F; \alpha^{(k)}) - C(F; \alpha_0) = \sum_{i<j} \frac{G_{\alpha_i^{(k)} \alpha_j^{(k)}}}{|i-j|^{p+r}} - \sum_{i<j} \frac{G_{ij}}{|i-j|^{p+r}} \quad .$$

After cancelling common terms the difference can be written as

$$\sum_{t=1}^{m} \left[\frac{1}{t^{p+r}} - \frac{1}{(t+1)^{p+r}} \right] \left[G_{k-t,k+1} + G_{k,k+t+1} - G_{k-t,k} - G_{k+1,k+t+1} \right]$$

where $m = \max(k-1, n-k-1)$ and if either $k-t<1$ or $k+t>n-1$ then $G=0$. However, by the assumption that F is a Robinson matrix each term of the summation must be non-negative, and the result follows.

In the next section we consider applications of our methods and 'goodness of fit' index. Claims of success for these methods must be viewed with respect to the preceding discussion.

APPLICATIONS TO ARCHAEOLOGICAL DATA

In Robinson's paper he discusses two examples in which archaeological deposits are to be ordered chronologically. One case produced the 8×8 similarity matrix given in table 5 in initial form and in table 6 according to Robinson's estimated final order, that is, Robinson's α vector for $Y_{\alpha_1}, Y_{\alpha_2}, ..., Y_{\alpha_n}$ would be

$$\alpha = (1, 6, 7, 4, 8, 5, 2, 3) \quad .$$

	Y_1	Y_2	Y_3	Y_4	Y_5	Y_6	Y_7	Y_8	$\sum_{j=1}^{8} F(Y_i, Y_j)$
Y_1	2·00	0·05	0·01	0·39	0·04	0·66	0·67	0·11	3·95
Y_2	0·05	2·00	1·96	1·08	1·95	0·03	0·29	1·14	8·50
Y_3	0·01	1·96	2·00	1·07	1·96	0·01	0·26	1·15	8·42
Y_4	0·39	1·08	1·07	2·00	1·10	0·50	0·82	1·72	8·68
Y_5	0·04	1·95	1·96	1·10	2·00	0·04	0·30	1·19	8·58
Y_6	0·66	0·03	0·01	0·50	0·04	2·00	1·01	0·27	4·52
Y_7	0·69	0·29	0·26	0·82	0·30	1·01	2·00	0·66	6·03
Y_8	0·11	1·14	1·15	1·72	1·19	0·27	0·66	2·00	8·24

Table 5. 8×8 matrix (Robinson): initial order

The other case produces a 17×17 similarity matrix which is given in table 7 and indicates a late, perhaps final stage of rearrangement according to Robinson.

Meggers and Evans (1957) produced an 8×8 matrix as a result of findings at 8 sites (cemeteries) in the Amazon region. The matrix is given in table 8 reflecting the final estimated order achieved by Meggers and Evans.

In all the above cases the choice of similarity measure F was twice eq. (6) with $p = 1$.

	Y_1	Y_2	Y_3	Y_4	Y_5	Y_6	Y_7	Y_8	$\sum_{j=1}^{8} F(Y_i, Y_j)$
Y_1	2·00	0·66	0·69	0·39	0·11	0·04	0·05	0·01	3·95
Y_2	0·66	2·00	1·01	0·50	0·27	0·04	0·03	0·01	4·52
Y_3	0·69	1·01	2·00	0·82	0·66	0·30	0·29	0·26	6·03
Y_4	0·39	0·50	0·82	2·00	1·72	1·10	1·08	1·07	8·68
Y_5	0·11	0·27	0·66	1·72	2·00	1·19	1·14	1·15	8·24
Y_6	0·04	0·04	0·30	1·10	1·19	2·00	1·95	1·96	8·58
Y_7	0·05	0·03	0·29	1·08	1·14	1·95	2·00	1·96	8·50
Y_8	0·01	0·01	0·26	1·07	1·15	1·96	1·96	2·00	8·42

Table 6. 8×8 matrix (Robinson): final order

In addition, since Sternin applied his procedure to the above three cases we compare our best (second) method with Sternin's, and with the above estimates in these cases. We consider several other reasonable orders in each case. We assume that tables 6, 7, and 8 respectively represent the *observed* order of the Ys. We let α_R be Robinson's estimate, α_M be Meggers and Evans', α_S be Sternin's, and α_G be ours.

For each estimated order we calculate $C(F; \alpha)$ given by eq. (15) with $p = 1$ and $r = 1$ (although the choice of r did not seem to affect the conclusions).

For table 6:

$$\alpha_R = (1, 2, 3, 4, 5, 6, 7, 8), \quad C(F; \alpha_R) = 2 \cdot 592$$
$$\alpha_S = (1, 2, 3, 4, 5, 6, 7, 8), \quad C(F; \alpha_S) = 2 \cdot 592$$
$$\alpha_G = (1, 2, 3, 4, 5, 6, 7, 8), \quad C(F; \alpha_G) = 2 \cdot 592$$
$$\alpha_1 = (1, 2, 3, 4, 5, 6, 8, 7), \quad C(F; \alpha_1) = 2 \cdot 587$$
$$\alpha_2 = (1, 3, 2, 4, 5, 6, 7, 8), \quad C(F; \alpha_2) = 2 \cdot 739$$
$$\alpha_3 = (1, 3, 2, 4, 5, 6, 8, 7), \quad C(F; \alpha_3) = 2 \cdot 734$$

Thus $\alpha_R = \alpha_S = \alpha_G$ and α_1 is possibly slightly better. Interestingly, Method I produced the order α_1 and Method II is a toss-up between α_G and α_1, since $T_7 = 59$ and $T_8 = 60$. [T_j is defined by eq. (11).]

For table 7:

$$\alpha_R = (1, 2, 3, 4, 5, 6, 7, 8, 9, 10, 11, 12, 13, 14, 15, 16, 17), \quad C(F; \alpha_R) = 4 \cdot 146$$
$$\alpha_S = (1, 2, 3, 4, 9, 5, 6, 7, 8, 10, 11, 12, 13, 14, 15, 16, 17), \quad C(F; \alpha_S) = 4 \cdot 092$$
$$\alpha_G = (1, 2, 4, 3, 5, 9, 6, 7, 8, 10, 11, 12, 13, 14, 15, 16, 17), \quad C(F; \alpha_G) = 3 \cdot 933$$
$$\alpha_1 = (1, 2, 4, 3, 5, 6, 7, 8, 9, 10, 11, 12, 13, 14, 15, 16, 17), \quad C(F; \alpha_1) = 4 \cdot 061$$
$$\alpha_2 = (1, 2, 4, 3, 9, 5, 6, 7, 8, 10, 11, 12, 13, 14, 15, 16, 17), \quad C(F; \alpha_2) = 4 \cdot 045$$
$$\alpha_3 = (1, 2, 3, 4, 5, 9, 6, 7, 8, 10, 11, 12, 13, 14, 15, 16, 17), \quad C(F; \alpha_3) = 4 \cdot 018$$

Clearly α_G seems the best as is further indicated by the fact that α_1 is better than α_R, α_2 is better than α_S, and α_G is better than α_3.

	Y_1	Y_2	Y_3	Y_4	Y_5	Y_6	Y_7	Y_8	Y_9	Y_{10}	Y_{11}	Y_{12}	Y_{13}	Y_{14}	Y_{15}	Y_{16}	Y_{17}	$\sum\limits_{j=1}^{17} F(Y_i, Y_j)$
Y_1	2·00	0·92	1·32	1·04	1·01	0·84	0·95	0·88	0·94	0·92	0·81	0·72	0·55	0·46	0·44	0·51	0·49	14·80
Y_2	0·92	2·00	1·05	1·24	1·07	1·16	1·08	1·13	1·06	0·91	1·07	0·92	0·84	0·82	0·60	0·78	0·64	17·29
Y_3	1·32	1·05	2·00	1·53	1·45	1·35	1·46	1·38	1·50	1·28	1·35	1·26	1·10	1·00	0·91	1·02	1·05	22·01
Y_4	1·04	1·24	1·53	2·00	1·44	1·42	1·50	1·51	1·68	1·40	1·34	1·21	1·07	1·13	1·00	0·76	0·99	22·26
Y_5	1·01	1·07	1·45	1·44	2·00	1·47	1·66	1·67	1·54	1·59	1·49	1·50	1·39	1·47	1·33	1·31	1·14	24·53
Y_6	0·84	1·16	1·35	1·42	1·47	2·00	1·64	1·69	1·66	1·57	1·55	1·54	1·42	1·32	1·29	1·19	1·31	24·38
Y_7	0·95	1·08	1·46	1·50	1·66	1·64	2·00	1·81	1·70	1·68	1·67	1·64	1·48	1·40	1·38	1·39	1·37	25·81
Y_8	0·88	1·13	1·38	1·51	1·67	1·69	1·81	2·00	1·68	1·58	1·67	1·60	1·51	1·43	1·40	1·43	1·33	25·70
Y_9	0·94	1·06	1·50	1·68	1·54	1·66	1·70	1·68	2·00	1·53	1·46	1·49	1·29	1·29	1·28	1·20	1·21	24·51
Y_{10}	0·92	0·91	1·28	1·40	1·59	1·57	1·68	1·58	1·53	2·00	1·47	1·59	1·49	1·48	1·43	1·34	1·39	24·65
Y_{11}	0·81	1·07	1·35	1·34	1·49	1·55	1·67	1·67	1·46	1·47	2·00	1·53	1·52	1·43	1·27	1·52	1·57	24·72
Y_{12}	0·72	0·92	1·26	1·21	1·50	1·54	1·64	1·60	1·49	1·59	1·53	2·00	1·78	1·54	1·64	1·49	1·52	24·47
Y_{13}	0·55	0·84	1·10	1·07	1·39	1·42	1·48	1·51	1·29	1·49	1·52	1·78	2·00	1·71	1·72	1·66	1·61	24·14
Y_{14}	0·46	0·82	1·00	1·13	1·47	1·32	1·40	1·43	1·29	1·48	1·43	1·54	1·71	2·00	1·75	1·52	1·45	23·20
Y_{15}	0·44	0·60	0·91	1·00	1·33	1·29	1·38	1·40	1·28	1·43	1·27	1·64	1·72	1·75	2·00	1·45	1·39	22·28
Y_{16}	0·51	0·78	1·02	0·76	1·31	1·19	1·39	1·43	1·20	1·34	1·52	1·49	1·66	1·52	1·45	2·00	1·54	22·11
Y_{17}	0·49	0·64	1·05	0·99	1·14	1·31	1·37	1·33	1·21	1·39	1·57	1·52	1·61	1·45	1·39	1·54	2·00	22·00

Table 7. 17×17 matrix (Robinson): a late order

For table 8:

$$\alpha_M = (1, 2, 3, 4, 5, 6, 7, 8), \quad C(F; \alpha_M) = 2\cdot712$$
$$\alpha_S = (2, 3, 1, 4, 5, 6, 7, 8), \quad C(F; \alpha_S) = 2\cdot705$$
$$\alpha_G = (2, 3, 1, 4, 6, 5, 7, 8), \quad C(F; \alpha_G) = 2\cdot653$$
$$\alpha_1 = (1, 2, 3, 4, 6, 5, 7, 8), \quad C(F; \alpha_1) = 2\cdot663$$
$$\alpha_2 = (1, 2, 3, 6, 4, 5, 7, 8), \quad C(F; \alpha_2) = 2\cdot671$$
$$\alpha_3 = (2, 3, 1, 6, 4, 5, 7, 8), \quad C(F; \alpha_3) = 2\cdot769$$

Once again α_G seems best, in particular when compared with α_S and α_1.

	Y_1	Y_2	Y_3	Y_4	Y_5	Y_6	Y_7	Y_8	$\sum\limits_{j=1}^{8} F(Y_i, Y_j)$
Y_1	2·00	1·29	1·11	1·21	1·11	1·26	1·13	0·95	10·06
Y_2	1·29	2·00	1·15	0·95	0·72	0·79	0·84	0·60	8·34
Y_3	1·11	1·15	2·00	0·90	0·95	0·95	0·91	0·78	8·75
Y_4	1·21	0·95	0·90	2·00	1·10	1·49	1·30	1·14	10·09
Y_5	1·11	0·72	0·95	1·10	2·00	1·44	1·36	1·02	9·70
Y_6	1·26	0·79	0·95	1·49	1·44	2·00	1·63	1·32	10·88
Y_7	1·13	0·84	0·91	1·30	1·36	1·63	2·00	1·45	10·62
Y_8	0·95	0·60	0·78	1·14	1·02	1·32	1·45	2·00	9·26

Table 8. 8×8 matrix (Meggers and Evans): final order

DISCUSSION

The success of any seriation method depends largely on the assumption that there is a single dimension underlying the data. Furthermore, we must assume that this scale is related to the scale we are interested in *via* a continuous and strictly monotone transformation, for then, since rank orders are invariant under this group of functions, we can consider the scales as equivalent.

For example, the application of seriation techniques to archaeological problems is very appealing, since the assumption of a true underlying order for the objects on a one-dimensional (temporal) scale is reasonable. However, in addition to time, there may be geographic, cultural, or other dimensions accounting for differences in various archaeological materials, and a resultant estimated order may not actually represent the desired time dimension.

These remarks suggest that it may be appropriate to apply a multi-dimensional scaling technique to determine the feasibility of a one-dimensional analysis. In any case it seems clear that the choice of components for our object vectors for a particular problem should be such that the investigator really believes they reflect or contain information regarding the 'true' order of these objects on the scale of interest. Additionally the choice of an appropriate similarity function may be important as well. In other words, we presume some sort of 'continuity' (alternative words are 'alignment' or 'collinearity') between the observed vectors and the scale of interest, in the sense that one object is 'close' to another (in terms of our similarity measure) if and only if their ranks are 'close' on the scale.

It is easy to see that, if a given set of vectors are such that they can be ordered on a one-dimensional scale *via* our similarity measure, then the corresponding F will be a Robinson matrix. Thus if we considered our observed vectors as random, and hence the calculated F-matrix as random, we might assume that the expected value of F when permuted to the 'true' underlying order is a Robinson matrix. An 'alignment' assumption of this sort motivates our seriation methods. Of course it is also clear under such an assumption that for particular sets of data no reasonable technique can hope to reconstruct the true order. For example, if $n = 3$, X_1, X_2, X_3 is known to be the correct order, and $F(X_1, X_2) = 0.7$, $F(X_2, X_3) = 0.5$ and $F(X_1, X_3) = 0.6$, then the best any rational method can hope to conclude is an order $X_2 X_1 X_3$ or $X_3 X_1 X_2$.

Even transcending these difficulties a further problem may arise. If the objects are strongly clustered on the underlying scale, then good seriation is not possible. Some discussion of this difficulty in the archaeological problem is given in Renfrew and Sterud (1969).

Lastly we note that if one-dimensional scaling is desired, a good starting permutation is required. Thus our methods can provide a good starting solution for a scaling program.

ACKNOWLEDGMENT

This research was supported in part by the Office of Naval Research.

REFERENCES

Beals, R., Krantz, D.H. & Tversky, A. (1968) Foundations of multi-dimensional scaling. *Psychol. Rev.* **75**, 127–42.

Coombs, C.H. (1964) *A Theory of Data.* New York: Wiley.

Gelfand, A.E. (1969) Seriation of multivariate observations through similarities. *Stanford Technical Report No. 146.*

Guttman, C.H. (1954) A new approach to factor analysis: The radex. *Mathematical Thinking in the Social Sciences*, chapter 6 (ed. Lazarsfeld, P.). New York: The Free Press.

Kendall, D.G. (1963) A statistical approach to Flinders Petrie's sequence-dating. *Bulletin of the ISI, 34th Session, Ottawa*, 657–80.

Kruskal, J.B. (1964) Multi-dimensional scaling by optimizing goodness of fit to a non-metric hypothesis. *Psychometrika*, **29**, 1–27.

Meggers, B.J. & Evans, C. (1957) Archaeological investigation in the mouth of the Amazon. *Bulletin* 167. Smithsonian Institution, Bureau of American Ethnology.

Renfrew, C. & Sterud, G. (1969) Close-proximity analysis: A rapid method for the ordering of archaeological materials. *Amer. Antiquity*, **34**, 265–77.

Robinson, W.S. (1951) A method for chronologically ordering archaeological deposits. *Amer. Antiquity*, **16**, 293–301.

Sackett, J.R. (1966) Quantitative analysis of upper paleolithic stone tools. *Amer. Anthropol.*, **68**, 356–94.

Shepard, R.N. (1962) The analysis of proximities: Multi-dimensional scaling with an unknown distance function. *Psychometrika*, **27**, 219–46.

Shepard, R.N. & Carroll, J.D. (1966) Parametric representation of non-linear data structures. *Proc. int. Sympos. Multivariate Analysis* (ed. Krishnaiah, P.R.). New York: Academic Press.

Sternin, H. (1965) Statistical methods of time sequencing. *Stanford University Technical Report No.* 112.

Sterud, G. (1967) *Seriation techniques in archaeology.* Master's thesis, Department of Anthropology, University of California at Los Angeles.

Torgerson, W. S. (1958) *Theory and Methods of Scaling.* New York: Wiley.

Seriation

Klaus Goldmann
Some archaeological criteria for chronological seriation

Bronze-age material, ranging in date from 2000 to 1400 BC and coming chiefly from South-Eastern, Central, and Northern Europe, was examined in order to place about 4,000 finds into chronological order more accurately than previously (Goldmann 1970).

As a result of preliminary theoretical considerations it was possible to reduce this material to about 900 assemblages of primary relevance to the setting up of a chronological framework. In co-operation with the 'Rechenzentrum der Universität zu Köln' (Kammerer 1968) the material of 404 types in 790 key-finds was *petrified* in one seriation (Kendall 1969). By means of 51 different stratigraphies of finds, containing representatives of types from the petrified system, we were able to prove that the system itself could only be a chronological one.

Two computer programs, both written in FORTRAN, were used independently: these are called ARCH and GGG. They were tested in numerous runs with an interchanging material (50 types in 100 finds) on an IBM 360-30 computer. Finally, the complete data-set was seriated on an IBM 360-75 (run-time about 65 minutes).

In this paper I need not go into the details of the methods or programs we used (these will be given in a published version of Goldmann 1970); here we shall discuss only the methodological basis of chronological seriation.

The key-question in this connection would appear to be: what data pertaining to a given set of archaeological material will permit a reconstruction of its relative chronology? Only if there is a specific relation of archaeological data to the course of time, which can be formalized, can a seriation be expected to give chronological results.

FORMAL SIMILARITY-CLASS AND TYPE

There are two concepts relevant here, 'similarity' and 'type'. For our purpose it is necessary to differentiate the terms, as shown in figure 1.

The main reason for making this differentiation is the phenomenon, well-known to the archaeologist, of convergence, that is, formal similarity of different objects not belonging originally to one single type. So long as the presence of such convergence cannot be excluded, the archaeologist cannot take formal similarity alone as direct proof of chronological coherence in similar objects. It then follows that the term 'type', as well as the methodological inferences connected with its use, should not be applied unless it can be shown by independent means that the majority of objects grouped into one 'class of similarity' stems from a clearly delimited prehistoric period. Defined in this manner, a type set up by the archaeologists will probably correspond to a 'genuine' type as it was understood and produced by prehistoric man. Formal similarity can be related to different factors of time.

Similarity of objects having an identical function. Examples are swords, axes, halberds. This may be called 'production-similarity'.

At the outset, the archaeologist will list the attributes of his individual objects. If he notices specific attributes common to several objects, he can try to make a seriation, that is, to order all the objects according to their degree of similarity to each other. This seriation should be a qualitative one (using only presence and absence), for the degree of similarity between objects of like function does not increase with the number of attributes they have in common, but depends on the relevance of the attributes. However, there is no standard by which to measure this relevance in a more or less objective manner.

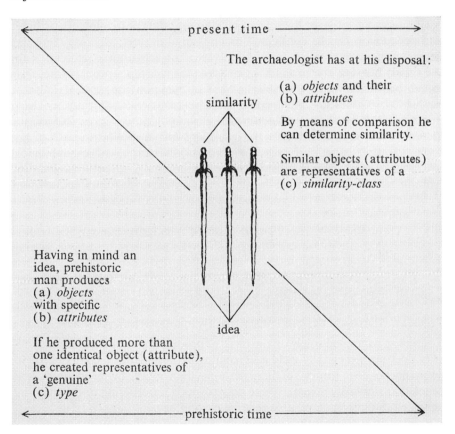

present time

The archaeologist has at his disposal:

similarity

(a) *objects* and their
(b) *attributes*

By means of comparison he can determine similarity.

Similar objects (attributes) are representatives of a
(c) *similarity-class*

Having in mind an idea, prehistoric man produces
(a) *objects*
with specific
(b) *attributes*

idea

If he produced more than one identical object (attribute), he created representatives of a 'genuine'
(c) *type*

prehistoric time

Figure 1

As every archaeological object has an infinite number of attributes, any selective limitation with a view to codification is bound to be subjective. Provided that a seriation of objects on the basis of formal similarity of attributes can be shown, on independent grounds, to be in approximately chronological order, it can furnish us with a sequence of production-dates.

However, it cannot be established beyond doubt, either in advance or afterwards, whether all objects included in this seriation belong to a 'genuine' type.

Find-combinations or Assemblages Displaying a Similarity of another Kind.
We may call this 'deposition-similarity'. In this case, similarity of different assemblages is determined by two factors, viz. (a) the presence of like objects, that is, objects of one 'class of similarity', in different find-combinations; and (b) the frequency of such objects in various assemblages.

Any single combination of objects forming an assemblage can be regarded as a unit in itself; the attributes are supplanted by the objects as the smallest component parts, permitting the archaeologist to compute a presence-absence seriation of this data. Provided this seriation can be interpreted in a chronological sense, it will reflect not the changes in manufacture but the sequence in which each batch of objects was deposited. There is an additional risk of error involved; the attributes of an object are most likely to have been integrated with it at the time of production; thus possession of attributes and production can be considered as contemporaneous; whereas there can be a considerable time-lag for the individual object in an assemblage (not the type!) between the production phase (that will most probably be close to the period in which the objects were in common use) and its date of deposition. It does not seem possible to overcome this difficulty by using frequency-distributions as an additional chronological criterion. In fact, the archaeologist very rarely knows the cause by which a specific assemblage has come about; furthermore, even a rare object can be of chronological relevance. Again, there is no sure way of determining, either beforehand or later, if all the objects used in the seriation are true representatives of 'genuine' types or if some were obsolete at the time of deposition.

To sum up:
(1) A chronologically relevant degree of similarity among individual objects supposedly of the same function cannot be determined by weighting or counting the attributes.
(2) The same is valid for assemblages, with the additional difficulty that even a 'closed find' can include objects out-of-date at the time of deposition.

FORMAL SIMILARITY-CLASSES AND TYPES IN RELATION TO TIME

A seriation computed solely on the basis of production or of deposition similarity does not necessarily yield a chronological result. But a combination of both independent groups of information (data given by production and deposition similarity) will pave the way towards an ordering of the material on which to establish a reliable relative chronology.
We start with two hypotheses:
(1) The 'similarity-class' is identical with the corresponding 'type'.
(2) All representatives of a type belong to a period of time relatively short in relation to the total span of time undergoing investigation.

In order to find out how far the different types overlap or not, we need an independent criterion once more. This is given by assemblages or 'closed finds'. There are now two different and independent relations of archaeological objects to the factor 'time': (a) the proximity in time of all representatives of every type (in figures 2 and 3, dots on a vertical line); (b) the proximity in time of those types whose representatives were found together in closed finds in one or more instances (in figures 2 and 3, dots on a horizontal line).

A seriation of vertical and horizontal dots can prove the congruence of both statements. If seriation gives a fairly clear arrangement of dots, the sequence will automatically be a chronological one.

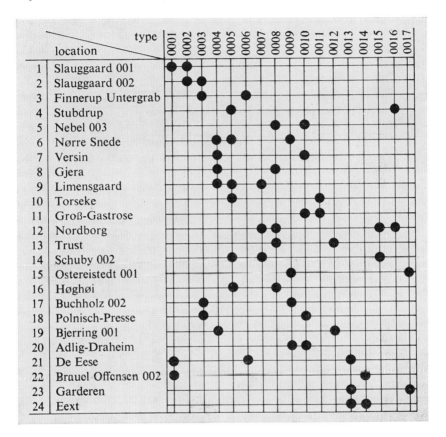

Figure 2

THE CRITERION OF 'KEY-FINDS'

For the archaeologist, there is one limitation to computing this seriation: not all assemblages will provide novel information in a qualitative sense. We have learned that frequency of repeated combinations must not be traced back to the factor time. Therefore it is advisable to reduce the number of closed finds examined up to now, and to seriate only those assemblages containing representatives of different types in varying combination. Such assemblages we name 'key-finds'.

All assemblages with several representatives of one type and all with representatives of several types known already to be represented by a key-find, will not necessarily give data of relevance for a chronological seriation

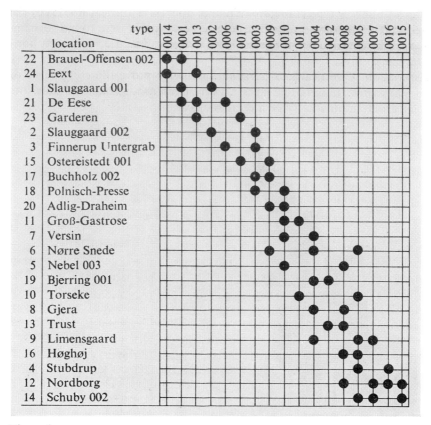

Figure 3

itself. (However, they will be useful later on as a means of control.)

The definition of key-finds depends on the archaeologist's choice of the similarity-classes (or types) which he regards as being relevant to his investigation. Every alteration of these data will involve a new inspection of the complete data-set to determine the key-finds. Further factors relevant to this inspection preparatory to chronological seriation are that each type intended for use must be represented in at least two key-finds; and that different types, always to be found together in the same key-finds, provide identical information and hence must be handled as *one* type.

This data-retrieval can be done economically only by a computer. We used the computer program SORT, written in FORTRAN by Christiane Klatt, Rechenzentrum der Universität zu Köln. By using an open code (*see* Goldmann 1968), it was possible to record on a single punch-card for each assemblage all data thought relevant in chronological seriation. The terminal register of the SORT-output is input for a chronological seriation computed with our programs ARCH and GGG. Input and output in the form of a diagram is given in figures 2 and 3.

It can be demonstrated by stratigraphic finds, which include the same types used in the previous seriation, that the order generated by the computer really is a chronological one (*see* figure 4). Find-numbers 14–16 may show

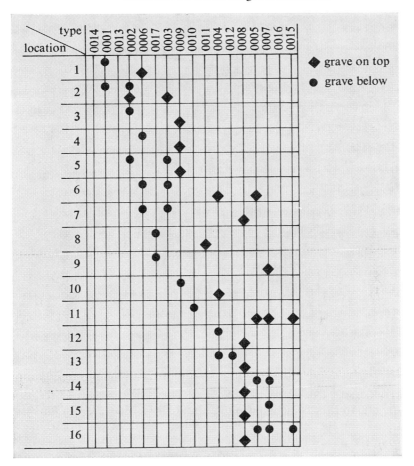

Figure 4. Stratigraphic finds: type numbers are identical with those in figures 2 and 3, but the finds (location 1–16) are not. The seriation in figure 3 must be read from left to right (older to younger)

a contradiction, but all types in these 3 finds can all occur together in one assemblage, too. Therefore overlay of these types was to be expected.

THE CRITERION OF TOTAL REPRESENTATION

The example of a seriation given in figures 2 and 3 could be proved to be truly chronological. Nevertheless, at the outset every computed sequence must be regarded with reserve. All assemblages used above derive from the same cultural context, yet several seriations have shown that an individual sequence obtained in this manner may be misordered. This possible error can be demonstrated by figures 5 and 6, the first showing a correct relation between two cultures, having had contact only for a short phase, the second displaying an order as simulated by seriation.

An error of this kind can be avoided, but only if the archaeologist has at his disposal all assemblages observed hitherto. This calls for 'total representation' of archaeological material in a computerized data bank.

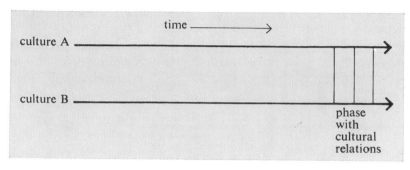

Figure 5

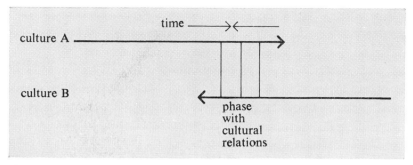

Figure 6

ACKNOWLEDGMENTS

Thanks are due to Mrs Derchain, Cologne, and Dr G. Mahr, Berlin for their help in translating the text. I also wish to thank the Deutsche Forschungsgemeinschaft for a travel grant.

REFERENCES

Goldmann, K. (1968) Zur Auswertung archäologischer Funde mit Hilfe von Computern. *Die Kunde*, **19**, 122 ff.

Goldmann, K. (1970) Chronologische Gruppierung in der älteren Bronzezeit. (Thesis, Univ. of Köln, 1970) *Fundamenta Series* (ed. Schwabedissen, H.). In press.

Kammerer, E. (1968) University of Cologne Yearbook.

Kendall, D. G. (1969) Some problems and methods in statistical archaeology. *World Archaeology*, **1**, 71.

Seriation

Henry T. Irwin
Effects of excavation on seriation at a Palaeo-Indian site

In evaluating cultural assemblages from archaeological excavations we usually lack any proof of the exact contemporaneity of the materials. Most often the best control is a geologically identifiable level or an artifactual layer. However, it stands to reason that we may have many occupations during an interval of sedimentary deposition. Some further refinements may be made by dividing any depositional unit into arbitrary sections which will, to some degree, improve our units of interpretation, as in Modoc Rockshelter, Illinois (figure 1).

However, we are still operating with a mixture of cultural materials resulting from the exigencies of excavation procedure. In attempting to discover the actual cultural isolates at the Palaeo-Indian Site of Hell Gap, recourse was made to mechanical models involving the distribution patterns of known chronological equivalents, that is, fragments of artifacts which could be reassembled, and plotted horizontally and vertically (figure 2).

This necessitated the use of a 3-dimensional model at approximately one-quarter scale, where points indicating matching fragments of broken artifacts are hung by magnetic hooks to an overhead metal sheet (figure 3). This produces a model of an archaeological site upon which one can perform various experiments, presuming all the data from the site are properly collected. The units isolated may be thought of as representing individually synchronous events which in reality represent the living site surface at the time of deposition. All artifacts falling within the planes created by these surfaces can be treated as part of single complexes. Artifacts whose relationship to one or another of these units is obscure should be left aside in initial studies. From our data we can realize the significance of this approach if we consider chronological seriation. In studying projectile point types, for example, it can be seen that, by actual occupational units proven by the above method, we have at Hell Gap a sequence of Plainview (projectile point type of Clovis occupation), Midland, Agate Basin, Hell Gap, Alberta, Cody, and Frederick types, in that chronological order.

Let us now assume that we had excavated the site in arbitrary metrical units, as in Modoc Rockshelter cited above (*see* figure 1), or in geological levels, for in essence either method will result in similar, although slightly different, interpretations. Here we will illustrate what happens with the first approach, as it is the easier to visualize. Passing an artificial plane horizontally through the model and recording artifacts which lie in this plane will produce excavation units which are the result of the blending of material from various different occupational horizons, as can be seen in figure 4.

In figure 5 projectile points from the Hell Gap Site are represented as if it were hypothetically excavated in 100 mm intervals. This shows a chronological seriation of materials from various composite cultures. These follow, in part, the proven real succession (as discussed above). However, it would appear that, at any particular point in time, several types of projectile points were in simultaneous use; this was not the case, as we have seen when actual occupational units were established. Further, the seriation itself reflects the actual

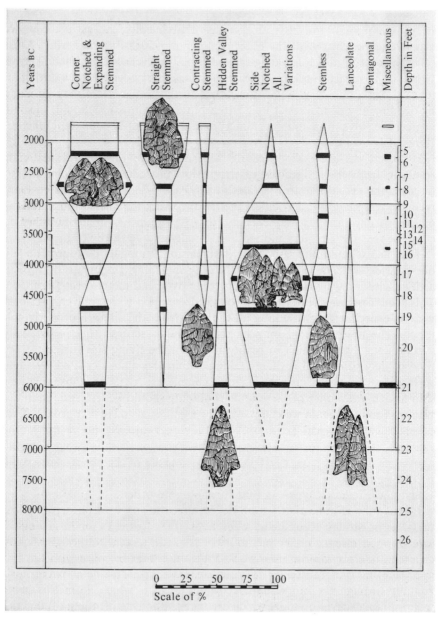

Figure 1. Distribution of projectile points at Modoc Rockshelter, Illinois (Fowler 1959)

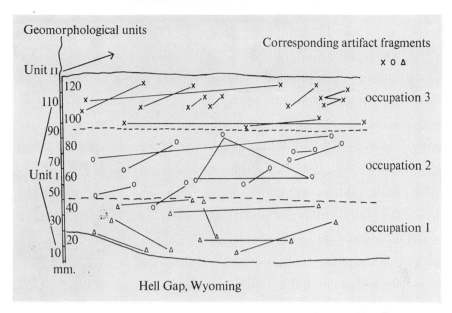

Figure 2. Establishing cultural units at the Hell Gap Site by matching fragments

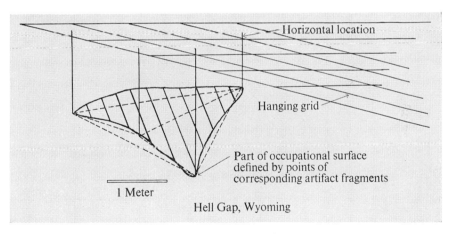

Figure 3. Model established for Hell Gap materials

chronology only when the various horizons more or less coincide in their horizontal distributions, or the occupational surfaces throughout the sequence lie in a horizontal plane and are of uniform thickness. For instance, in this configuration, projectile points of the Folsom and Plainview (Clovis) types are correctly shown as the two oldest. However, it would appear from the seriation that Folsom preceded Plainview and then lasted longer. This misrepresentation of the data can be understood by an examination of figure 6, where we see that the Folsom camp was more scattered, and that the diversity represented in the seriation as *temporal* is actually due to horizontal dispersion. One type that completely fails to fall into place in

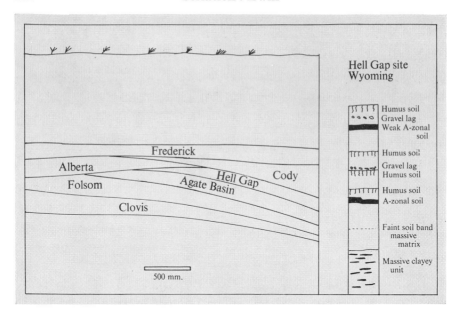

Figure 4. Order of components at the Hell Gap Site, showing inclined surfaces

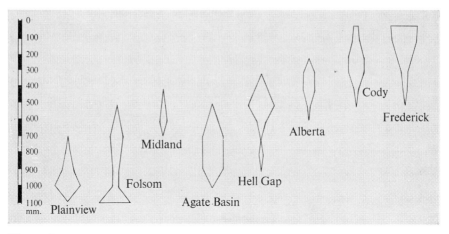

Figure 5. Frequency of projectile points, by type, at the Hell Gap Site as reconstructed by arbitrary (100 mm) units (sample 100)

the seriation is that of Midland, which in reality lies chronologically between Folsom and Agate Basin. The reason for this failure of seriation to reflect the chronological situation is that the Midland materials lie in a very small area, concentrated in one location in the site. Using the model, if, hypothetically, you move Midland into a more central horizontal location keeping the same vertical position, its locus in the seriation more accurately reflects its actual chronological position.

It follows that in chronological ordering of materials from a site, groups of like artifacts should be plotted according to horizontal location even when excellent stratigraphic control exists.

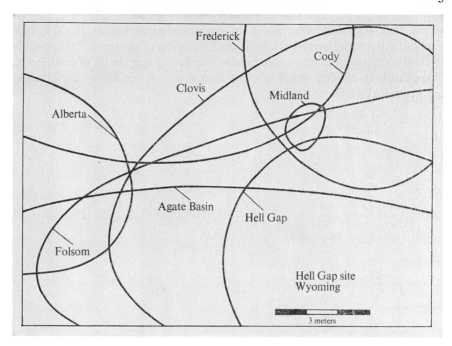

Figure 6. Horizontal distribution of cultural materials at the Hell Gap Site, disregarding vertical location

Models must then be constructed which will allow examination of the relationships existing between the various artifacts. Realistic devices such as the matching of broken artifact fragments should then be employed to establish natural units of occupation. Only at this point would it seem advisable to employ more complicated mathematical techniques, such as correlation involving horizontal locations of artifact types. The latter purport to shed light upon artifact co-function. However, if correlations are based upon a mixture of cultural assemblages known to be temporally discrete, it stands to reason that the information provided by them will be, at best, imperfect.

In a survey or salvage operation where one must make excavation decisions before a full and close analysis can be made, or where data is imperfectly gathered, it is possible to anticipate errors introduced by arbitrary excavation. We can imagine another site like Hell Gap only excavated in arbitrary units. Locating the materials horizontally as we have done in figure 6, a number of projectile point types nonrandomly distributed may be noted. The object of our analysis is then to determine if the results of our seriation of the projectile point types by arbitrary units at the site is correct. For this we can construct an index which can be of help. Presuming a grid of 100 meter squares we might note that type 1 occupies 10 squares in common with type 2, but no others. The latter occupies an additional 40 squares which contain no type 1. We may say we have a coefficient of disagreement in location of 40/100. Now suppose we had type 3 which occupies no squares in common with type 2, but itself occupies 10 squares. This gives us a coefficient of 60/100. In this approach we have found that any coefficient as high as 80% is very likely to give a false seriation, whereas, if the coefficient is as low as 10–20% it is likely that the seriation reflects the correct ordering of the types. It is possible to treat such an index in a more precise manner, giving limits of confidence. Complications arising from relative frequency of artifacts can also be mathematically adjusted.

Seriation

David G. Kendall
Seriation from abundance matrices

The object of this paper is to present a self-contained account of what has come to be known as the 'horse-shoe' method of sequencing, or seriation, in archaeology, but I shall sketch only very briefly those aspects of the method which have been discussed at length in my earlier papers (Kendall 1963, 1969a,b, 1971a,b), in order to make room for a detailed account of some recent developments now presented in a practical context for the first time.

GENERAL REMARKS ABOUT 'SEQUENCING'

Although this basic concept could conceivably be traced back to earlier writers, the idea that a set of 'closed finds'—graves, tombs, and so on— could be sequenced solely on the basis of the incidence or abundance of the objects found in them appears to have been first clearly formulated by Flinders Petrie (1899). While his writings are not easy to follow, they make fascinating reading for a mathematician, because they are so obviously written by a *mathématicien malgré lui*, and in my view Petrie should be ranked with the great applied mathematicians of the nineteenth century. He makes use of many sophisticated statistical ideas which, it seems—despite sporadic correspondence with Karl Pearson—he must have invented for himself; and his writings also contain what must surely be the first fully developed 'mathematical model' (a mechanical analogue of his sequencing process) in the literature of archaeology. It is most appropriate, therefore, that we should pay tribute to him in the present conference, which might be quite properly regarded as an efflorescence of his ideas.

Petrie's object was to establish a basis for prehistoric Egyptian chronology by a process involving at least three distinct stages:

(a) the construction of a typology for the objects and varieties of object (principally pottery) found in the 900 graves studied by him;

(b) the sequencing (hopefully chronological) of the graves into 50 successive groups of 18 graves each (labeled 31, 32, . . ., 80);

(c) the assignment of each variety of pottery to a *range* of 'sequence-dates' by noting the labels of the grave-groups in which the variety was found. Thus

        B11*a*: S.D.35–51 (61)

means that variety B11*a* occurred in the grave-groups labeled 35 and 51, and also intermediately, and that in addition there was an isolated instance of the variety in a grave in the group labeled S.D.61.

Once stage (c) had been reached, Petrie was in a position to transfer his typology and the associated sequence-date-*ranges* to other Middle Eastern cultures, and so a great ordinal chronology was built up, by no means confined to Egypt alone.

The typology at (a) was, of course, of a highly subjective kind and might nowadays (if we could agree upon the principles to be employed) be replaced by some sort of computer taxonomy; but to change from a personal to a computerized taxonomy is not to eliminate subjectivity altogether. Whatever the computer program employed, there remains the choice (and sometimes the weighting) of the characters considered to be significant for the end in view. This is still a subjective matter, and in the last resort must be left to the good sense of the archaeologist (who may also, from one investigation to another, vary, for good reasons, his choice of method).

Petrie's procedure at (b) would now be regarded as a hybrid one, involving both subjective and objective elements, and also a 'feedback' from (c) to (b), because his personal opinion about the most likely way and direction in which a style of decoration would develop was used in stage (b) (especially in the case of the so-called 'wavy-handled' pots) in order to make deductions about grave-sequencing.

It may be worth making the following general comment on 'subjectivity *versus* objectivity' in problems such as these. If we desire the 'best' set of inferences which can be derived from the observed data at the time of writing, then subjective judgments will necessarily enter in at least two ways:

(1) in the choice of site and strategy of excavation (normally influenced, however covertly, by a motivation special to the archaeologist, or by the views current in the archaeological world), and in the construction of the typology ['stage (a)'] whether or not this is carried out with the assistance of the computer;

(2) in the ultimate 'editing' of the 'output' of whatever mathematical seriation processes have been employed—the treatment of anomalous cases, the arrangement of graves not mutually sequenced by the mathematical resolving power available, and (most important of all) the assessment of the status of the sequencing eventually obtained: is it a time-sequence, a geographical sequence, a social sequence, or a combination of all three? Are the assumptions on which the method is based satisfied in this special case? Do 'repeat' analyses yield comparable results, and what does 'comparable' actually mean in this context? To what extent has the sequencing-objective been realized by the sequencing obtained and was this objective well chosen? And so on.

These *essential* 'subjective' judgments are the exclusive preserve of the archaeologist, who should resist all attempts which might be made by mathematicians to wrest them from him. At the same time he must recognize their dependence on personal factors (his own, perhaps gradually developing, opinions) and on factors special to the age in which he happens to be working (the unquestioned assumptions accepted by all archaeologists of his time, possibly later to become explicit and then abandoned as further knowledge and understanding is obtained). The role of the mathematician with his 'objective' methods is, in my view, to carry out quickly, efficiently, and in a permanently non-controversial way, those aspects of the analysis which are, or can be made, *purely* mechanical, thus separating what may require continual review and revision, from what can be done once and for all. When this role has been played to his archaeological colleagues' satisfaction, the mathematician should retire from the scene and go about his own affairs, leaving all further decisions to his betters; unless in the excitement of the chase—as might happen—he finds himself converted into mathematician-*and*-archaeologist, in which case his 'betters' become (hopefully) his 'peers'; but *even in this case* he must split apart, with the most scrupulous honesty, the decisions taken by the two halves of his personality. In general, the motto for the mathematician trying to work in this area should be, maximal participation and maximal humility.

I have attempted (Kendall 1963) to give an account of Petrie's own methods, and I have been told that this account is unreadable. I am happy to invite such critics to wrestle with Petrie's own writings, and see if they find them more comprehensible. The truth is that Petrie used every method he could think of (many of them extremely novel) in an order to some extent arbitrary, and the unravelling of his analysis is no simple matter, especially now that all the evidence which he used has been destroyed. From among these methods, however, we can extract what I have called Petrie's 'Concentration Principle': this asserts that:

if the typology is 'chronologically significant', and when the graves have been correctly ordered (or anti-ordered), then the 'sequence-date'-*ranges* for the individual types will be found to have been individually *or in some communal way* minimized.

This principle lies at the root not only of his own methods, but also of those of his successors. Its implementation is difficult in two respects; what do we mean by a 'chronologically significant' typology, and what sort of 'communal minimization' is to be adopted (for one cannot expect to obtain simultaneous minimization on behalf of some 800 varieties of pottery, not to mention objects of other types found in the graves)?

The decision, whether a typology is or is not expected to be 'chronologically significant' is, of course, one of those things which must be left to the archaeologist, but he can be given some guidance in arriving at this decision by more clearly expounding the basis of the sequencing method to be employed. Petrie's 'Concentration Principle' might indeed be reversed so as to yield a criterion for 'chronological significance'.

As for 'communal minimization', variants of this abound in the literature. Petrie himself imagined a mechanical model with elastic strings pulling together graves containing a common variety, and reaching some sort of static equilibrium (possibly not unique, and possibly not stable). If we try to make this idea more precise, and to set up a 'potential energy function' which is to be minimized, we can do so at the (heavy) cost of committing ourselves to a highly specific mathematical model of the innovation and obsolescence of types. Such an idea is followed through in the later sections of Kendall (1963), but I have little use for it now, for three reasons.

(1) The method is impracticable. For example, one such model introduced (among others) in Kendall (1963) led to the following 'potential energy function', $S(\Pi)$. Let Π denote a permutation (linear rearrangement) of the graves, let N_i denote the total number of representatives of the ith

variety, and let R_i denote the *range* for the ith variety when the rearrangement Π is accepted (so that if the variety occurs in just one grave then $R_i = 1$, if it occurs in just two adjacent graves then $R_i = 2$, and so on). Then

$$S(\Pi) = \sum_i N_i \log R_i,$$

and Π is to be chosen so as to make this number S as small as possible. We must therefore scan through all possible permutations Π, and note when S is least; but even with the fastest computer physically imaginable, run for a thousand million years (the 'age of the universe'), this program could not be carried out in full unless the number of graves was no more than 33. Variants of such methods involving only *restricted* searching (local searches, random searches, searches involving only transpositions and relocations, 'branch-and-bound' methods, and so on) have been proposed by a series of authors commencing with Hole and Shaw (1967) and concluding with numerous contributors to the present conference. These suggestions are of the very highest importance in enabling one to 'polish' 'rough' permutations found by other methods, but they do not resolve the difficulty just mentioned, which might be re-expressed thus: how among the myriads of possible permutations can one choose a 'rough' permutation which is sufficiently close to the optimum for it to be worth while 'polishing'?

(2) The model is highly artificial, and it is far from clear how sensitive the method would be to variations in the model. (Some other possible models are considered in Kendall (1963), but all are subject to the same criticism.)

(3) As long as we work solely with permutations, the method, or any variant of it, will of necessity yield a linear ordering as an answer, and so will be given no opportunity to 'fail'. I attach great importance to methods which are capable of failure, because it is obvious that in some ill-chosen problems a method ought to fail, and thus warn us that we are taking too simple-minded a view of the data.

THE 'HORSE-SHOE' METHOD

What is (fortunately now rather inappropriately) called the 'horse-shoe' method of sequencing takes as its starting point the assumption (not always valid) that the material and the typology imposed upon it are such as to make Petrie's 'Concentration Principle' applicable, at least in some approximate sense. The decision, whether this assumption can safely be made or not, must in the first instance be made by the archaeologist, although (as we shall see) there are at least two distinct ways in which the method can (but need not) confirm the applicability of the principle. If such confirmation is not obtained, the method has failed and the status of the material and of the typology imposed upon it must be reconsidered.

The major component of the program is the Shepard–Kruskal MDSCAL algorithm (Kruskal 1964), variants of which, of differing degrees of complexity, are now available in FORTRAN at most computer installations. If MDSCAL is available in some form (modified if necessary so that it will accept zero as a 'similarity' value), and if a computer-plotting device is also available, then the implementation of the 'horse-shoe' procedure is very simple and will present no difficulty. The Cambridge prototype was evolved by a process of aggregation and is therefore inefficient both as regards time and storage. It will, however, sequence assemblages of about 100 graves in five minutes or so of computing time, using a storage of 32K. I have no doubt at all that a clever programmer could very appreciably improve on both these figures.

In the following paragraphs I shall describe the ideas lying behind the 'horse-shoe' method, and in the following section I shall discuss and illustrate its use in relation to the *La Tène* cemetery at Münsingen-Rain in Switzerland.

In its original form (Kendall 1969a,b) the method was evolved to sequence data presented in the form of an *incidence matrix*; that is to say, a table of double entry in which each row represents a grave, and each column a 'variety' (of pottery, jewellery, or whatever), and in which the (i, j)th *cell* (that in which row i and column j meet) contains:

1   if the jth variety *is* present in the ith grave,
0   if it is *not*.

All excavation records can be forced into this form, usually at the cost of some loss of information, but there are occasions when it is preferable to work with what I shall call an *abundance* matrix; here the (i, j)th cell contains a non-negative number specifying the frequency of occurrence of the jth variety in the ith grave. Thus this number a_{ij} may be the *actual number* of occurrences, or may be the *proportion* of the contents of the ith grave which happen to belong to the jth variety. In the latter case the proportion may be computed in relation to all the contents of the ith grave, or in relation to some appropriate subset of these. [For examples of these two last alternatives, though in contexts where the objects being sequenced are not graves, but rather (respectively) manuscripts or inscriptions, see Boneva (1971), Ştefan (1971) and Kivu-Sculy (1971).]

It came as a complete surprise to me to find, after a rather elaborate study of the incidence-matrix case, that by a very slight generalization of one part of the construction the whole procedure could be adapted without further change to abundance matrices, and it is in this improved form that I shall present it here. This will suffice, because the generalized procedure contains the original one as a special case, whenever the data are presented in the form of an incidence matrix.

Let A be the abundance matrix, with components a_{ij}. Now let us set up an (archaeologically unreal) problem of pure mathematics (which does however have immediate applications to molecular biology), for the sake of a rather close and instructive analogy between the archaeological problem ('Problem A') on the one hand, and the mathematical problem ('Problem M') on the other.

We formulate 'Problem M' thus: let us call A a *Q-matrix* when in each individual column either, *the elements increase to a maximum and then decrease*, or *the elements increase*, or *the elements decrease*.

Here 'increase', 'decrease', and 'maximum' are to be understood in the 'weak' sense; thus the following is a Q-matrix:

4	2	0
1	3	0
1	4	2
0	4	2
0	1	3
0	1	5

Now suppose that someone in possession of a Q-matrix has rearranged the rows, and has communicated the matrix to us in this row-scrambled form (in mathematical terms, we have been presented not with A itself, but with ΠA, where Π is a permutation matrix); our problem is to recover the original form of A, i.e. to 'queuetrify' the scrambled matrix ΠA.

Note that there is at least one solution to the problem, namely A itself, but there may be more than one. Ideally we should like to know all solutions, but here we shall consider 'Problem M' to have been solved if we can find any one solution.

If A is an incidence matrix, then ΠA is a matrix of zeros and ones and the task (now called that of 'petrifying' it) is simply that of rearranging the rows of ΠA so that simultaneously in every column the ones are brought together (i.e. the matrix is given the pattern P demanded of it by a strict form of Petrie's 'Concentration Principle'). (Explication of the notation: P is for Petrie; and Q is just the next letter after P.)

It will I think be agreed that the pattern Q possessed by a Q-matrix represents a natural generalization of the Petrie pattern P to the 'abundance' case. We shall return to this matter in a moment; for the time being we are still concerned with the mathematical problem, 'Problem M'.

I have proved (Kendall 1971b) the following theorems (and the reader can find more elegant proofs, as well as valuable generalizations, in the contribution by Wilkinson).

Theorem 1

Let the numbers w_h be strictly positive, but otherwise arbitrary, and let the square symmetric matrix S be defined by requiring its (i, j)th element to be

$$s_{ij} = \sum_h w_h \min(a_{ih}, a_{jh}) \quad .$$

Then S contains all the information relevant to the solution of 'Problem M'.

Moreover, if Π is any permutation matrix, then ΠA will have pattern Q if and only if

$$\Pi S \Pi'$$

has pattern Q.

Note that the symmetric matrices S and $\Pi S \Pi'$ both necessarily have a dominant diagonal, so that pattern Q *for these two matrices* reduces to the pattern studied in a classical paper (Robinson 1951) from quite another point of view.

Theorem 2

If S is the matrix introduced in theorem 1, let a new matrix $S \circ S$ be defined by requiring its (i, j)th element to be

$$(S \circ S)_{ij} = \sum_h w_h \min(s_{ih}, s_{jh}),$$

and similarly define $(S \bigcirc S) \bigcirc (S \bigcirc S)$, etc. Then any one of $S \bigcirc S$, $(S \bigcirc S) \bigcirc (S \bigcirc S)$, etc., contains all the information relevant to the solution of 'Problem M', and the appropriate generalizations of the statement at the end of theorem 1 are still true.

Note that in forming $S \bigcirc S$, etc., there is no need to retain the original values of the 'weights' w_h.

It should be mentioned at this point that Fulkerson and Gross (1965) gave a different solution to 'Problem M' in the incidence-matrix case, and expressed this in algorithmic form; this algorithm has been generalized to the abundance-matrix case by Wilkinson. Another algorithmic solution was described to me informally by Olkin during the conference. All these algorithms are of great importance in the molecular-biological context to which 'Problem M' properly belongs (and which Fulkerson and Gross had explicitly in mind), but they are useless for archaeological purposes. Why is this so?

The point to be appreciated here is that in 'Problem A', (the archaeological problem) we do not know that an exact recovery of pattern Q is possible. We only hope, believe, tentatively suppose that an approximate realization of pattern Q may be achieved by row-rearrangements, and (what is worse) we do not know what we mean here by 'approximate'.

The basis for our belief, hope, or supposition is that, relative to the assigned typology, relative to the form in which the matrix is computed [i.e. whether it is built up out of actual numerical abundances, or—in some appropriate sense—relative abundances (i.e. frequencies)], and relative to the choice of the quite arbitrary 'weights' w_h, Petrie's Concentration Principle will approximately apply, in the extended sense that: a 'correct' (temporal, spatial, or social) sequencing will yield a pattern approaching pattern Q. Even in the most favourable circumstances we shall not expect to get pattern Q exactly. This being so, algorithmic solutions to 'Problem M' will inevitably break down during their application, if transferred to 'Problem A'. Perhaps interactive versions of such algorithms (in which the user is invited to intervene subjectively at each breakdown) might be of value, but none have, so far as I know, been devised, and they would in any case have the defect, by their very nature, of subjective intervention in what it was hoped would be an objective calculation.

We must therefore approach 'Problem A' from an entirely different standpoint, but may yet derive some help from theorems 1 and 2, even though these apply strictly only in the case of 'Problem M'.

I am concerned here only with the sequencing of 'closed finds', not with the sequencing of types, or of finds and types together, as practised with great success by Goldmann in his contribution to this conference. In this context, a wide range of sequencing methods reduce to some specific member of the class of procedures consisting of the following three stages:

Stage (i): construct a similarity-matrix for the graves, i.e. a diagonally dominant square symmetric matrix Σ having as many rows (and columns) as there are graves, and having non-negative elements chosen in such a way that four graves correctly sequenced in one of the orders

$$(i, j, k, l) \text{ or } (l, k, j, i)$$

would 'approximately' be expected to produce the inequality,

$$\sigma_{jk} \geqq \sigma_{il}$$

(we later refer to these as the 'tetrad' inequalities);

Stage (ii): construct a measure of discrepancy $D(\Sigma)$ for the matrix Σ, which will be the less, the more nearly these inequalities are fulfilled, and which will vanish if and only if they are fulfilled exactly;

Stage (iii): construct a search procedure which, starting from a chosen or randomly selected linear rearrangement, will progressively improve the sequencing until a local (hopefully global) minimum value of the discrepancy $D(\Sigma)$ is attained.

In a strict formulation of any one of these procedures (i.e. in a formulation intended for use with 'Problem M') the above set of 'tetrad' inequalities is redundant, and may be reduced to the following 'triad' inequalities:

whenever (i, j, k) or (k, j, i) are correctly sequenced, then $\sigma_{ij} \geqq \sigma_{ik}$.

If we combine this fact with the symmetry and diagonal dominance of Σ, we see that the procedure can be rephrased thus: simultaneously permute the rows and columns of Σ until it most nearly displays pattern Q. It is relevant to note that for such symmetric and diagonally dominant matrices, pattern Q becomes identical with what we may call pattern R of Robinson (1951). Thus the procedure reduces to Stage (i): the choice of a similarity matrix Σ, Stage (ii): the choice of a measure $D(\Sigma)$ of the extent to which Σ is not of the Robinson form, and Stage (iii): the choice of a search algorithm whose object is to find a permutation Π which will reduce

$$D(\Pi \Sigma \Pi')$$

to the least possible value.

In practice the choice of such a procedure involves some degree of arbitrariness both at Stage (i) (in the selection of Σ), and at Stage (ii) in the selection of $D(\Sigma)$; it also involves the heavy penalties associated with the necessarily local character of the search at Stage (iii), unless we are using the procedure to 'polish' a 'rough' permutation obtained by other methods; in that case such 'local' procedures are invaluable and probably essential.

We are here, however, confining our attention to the special difficulties presented by 'Problem A' when (a) the number of graves is large and (b) no prior sequence is available. Thus our methods are simply intended to be used as a means of securing 'rough' sequencing-permutations for subsequent 'polishing' by refined methods of the type just described.

Even in the context of the refined 'polishing' methods, however, it is interesting to note that our theorems 1 and 2 suggest natural candidates for the similarity matrix Σ, viz.

$$\Sigma = S$$

or $\Sigma = S \circ S$,

etc. It is easily verified that any of these choices of Σ will yield a diagonally dominant symmetric matrix having (in relation to 'Problem M') the required inequality properties (this is part of the content of the final statement of theorem 1, and of the final statement implicit in theorem 2).

Our theorems do not make any suggestion about the way in which $D(\Sigma)$ should be constructed, but the generalizations of these theorems given by

Wilkinson have much to offer in this direction.

In practice we shall also have to choose between $\Sigma = S$, $\Sigma = S \circ S$, etc. How is this to be done? Let us note that, in the incidence case, and with all 'weights' $w_h = 1$, s_{ij} is just the number of varieties represented in *both* the graves i and j. Now it may be the case that 'most' of the numbers s_{ij} are equal to zero, and yet S contains almost enough (in 'Problem M', certainly enough) information to permit sequencing. In such a case the use of $S \circ S$ would seem to be indicated, because this links a pair of graves via the graves with which each has something (perhaps different) in common. We shall return to this point in more detail when we come to deal with a concrete example, while referring the reader to Wilkinson's article for some valuable theoretical ideas on the choice of Σ.

We must now turn to a quite different and more basic matter: the replacement of Stages (ii) and (iii) of the 'polishing' procedures by something at once cruder and yet more powerful; cruder in that a steam hammer will replace the electric 'polishing' apparatus, more powerful in that the steam hammer will be heavy enough to chip the major rugosities off even mountain-sized pebbles.

We know (strictly only for 'Problem M') that the choice $\Sigma = S$ (or $S \circ S$, etc.) involves no loss of sequencing-relevant information, and so we can take advantage of this fact, keeping our strategy in line with the requirements of the tetrad or triad inequalities, and (most important) putting ourselves in possession of an algorithm which cannot fail to 'run', but which *can* fail to yield an interpretable solution,

by taking $\Sigma = S$ (or $S \circ S$, etc.) as the similarity matrix initiating a MDSCAL analysis in two dimensions.

The decision to use two dimensions would in any case be desirable in order to avoid too great a probability of becoming trapped in local minima, but it is of greater significance than that: it allows the computer program to present us with a nonsense-answer, if the question we put to it is badly posed. To put the matter another way; we know that the whole analysis rests on a series of subjective initial judgments about the appropriateness of the typology, etc. If the computer program were allowed to produce only a permutation as its principal output, we should lose a most valuable control on these judgments; as, however, it is here required to produce a two-dimensional configuration, which may or may not be interpretable as a 'twisted one-dimensional object', we shall have a means of checking the validity of our basic suppositions. Another (always available) check will of course be to read off the prescribed or implied permutation and rearrange the rows of the matrix A accordingly, in order to see whether in fact, to some satisfactory degree of approximation, pattern Q has been produced.

The method is in practice very laborious unless a computer-plotting device is available, and when that is so its effectiveness can be immensely enhanced by a very simple piece of additional programming.

We know that all the relevant information (at any rate so far as 'Problem M' is concerned) resides in the order-structure of the non-diagonal elements of Σ, but this is not fully contained in the MDSCAL picture, which merely arranges, as far as may be, that distances (in two dimensions) and similarities (in the sense of Σ) shall be oppositely ordered (and this ordering will *not* be perfect). We can feed into the picture further valuable and relevant information by telling the machine to link by linear segments each pair of points (=pair of graves) whose similarity-value exceeds some stated critical level.

Our judgment, whether the diagram so produced can be interpreted as a 'twisted one-dimensional object', must be made with reference to the local structure provided by these segments; in fact, we look at the output and see whether the links drawn by the computer define in some loose sense a Hamiltonian arc through all the points, and then we take the derived sequence (or anti-sequence) to be that corresponding to progression along the Hamiltonian arc. (The relevance of Hamiltonian arcs to this problem was first realized by Wilkinson, and is more fully exploited in his own paper. I borrow his terminology here, with acknowledgment, because it enables me to say clearly what I have on previous occasions said only very obscurely.)

Evidently the choice of the right critical-similarity-value-for-links will be important; this (in the first analysis) is a matter of trial and error, facilitated in the Cambridge 'horse-shoe' program by the option of receiving a series of two-dimensional outputs with the critical similarity progressively lowered from one such output to the next.

I deliberately say, 'in the first analysis', because I recommend the use of a random initial configuration for each MDSCAL run (with, say, 50 iterations), and the execution of, say, 5 independent such runs before any conclusions are drawn. The analysis will be judged to have 'failed' (and I have already stressed the importance I attach to the possibility of such failure) if the 5 Hamiltonian arcs fail to have much the same 'vertices', and to pursue much the same course between these vertices. The 5 sequencings so obtained can be pooled by familiar techniques (e.g. by using the customary solution to 'the problem of m rankings'). This pooled ranking can then be taken as the starting point of a 'polishing' procedure.

One point calls for comment here. We saw that in 'Problem M' the tetrad inequalities could be reduced to the triad inequalities. I do not think that this reduction should be relied upon in a 'horse-shoe' analysis (though it might perhaps be introduced at the 'polishing' stage), because, in an imperfect situation, information otherwise redundant may still be of value. In fact the procedure recommended above goes too far in the opposite direction; not content with the tetrad inequalities (which are restricted by the requirement that (i, j, k, l) or (l, k, j, i) are to be compatible with the current ordering) it makes use of *derestricted* tetrad inequalities, of the form,

$s_{ij} > s_{kl}$ implies distance$(G_i, G_j) \leqslant$ distance(G_k, G_l),

for *all* tetrads (i, j, k, l). Of course, not all such implications will be true of the map produced, but the aim to achieve each one of them will have contributed to it. As, however, there is no 'current ordering' during the operation of the two-dimensional MDSCAL run, there is no obvious way in which the tetrad inequalities can be 'de-derestricted'.

A similar point is that if we wished to use only the triad inequalities, we should have to derestrict these in a similar way. The later versions of MDSCAL in fact permit this option, but I have already given reasons for not using it save at the 'polishing' stage (where it is particularly valuable because of the smaller number of comparisons which have to be made, with consequent saving of time). However, 'polishing' will usually be done by special sequencing-oriented procedures, and then the restricted-triads condition can be used as it stands.

By this time the reader new to the method will be troubled by the terminology; *why 'horse-shoe'?* We proceed to answer this question.

Our aim is to recover a linear structure which we hope may be present in the data, and so we begin (as in Kendall 1971a) with a synthetic example in which the data have a genuinely one-dimensional origin but suffer from the sort of 'noise' which we should be prepared to encounter also in the archaeological application. Let us try to sequence 51 points $O_1, O_2, ..., O_{51}$ which in fact lie in that order on a straight line, with next neighbours exactly one unit of distance apart. We shall construct a similarity matrix Σ for these 51 objects, and then carry out a two-dimensional MDSCAL analysis in the manner recommended above. We set up Σ by defining its elements σ_{ij} as follows:

$$\sigma_{ij}=0 \text{ if } |i-j|\geq 25 \quad ;$$
$$\sigma_{ij}=1 \text{ if } 24\geq |i-j|\geq 22 \quad ;$$
$$\sigma_{ij}=2 \text{ if } 21\geq |i-j|\geq 19 \quad ;$$
$$. \quad . \quad . \quad . \quad . \quad . \quad .$$
$$\sigma_{ij}-8 \text{ if } 3\geq |i-j|\geq 1 \quad .$$

Obviously the tetrad inequalities are satisfied by this choice of Σ, which moreover is square and symmetric, and will have a dominant diagonal if we agree to set $\sigma_{ii}=9$. It is important to notice that among the effective (non-diagonal) elements of Σ (2550, in number) nearly one third (in fact, 702) are equal to zero. This is, therefore, pretty 'thin' as similarity matrices go. The topologist will notice that there is an alternative and very illuminating way of describing this feature of Σ; the values of σ_{ij} are related to the familiar 'bounded' metric $d(O_i, O_j)$ for the line, which coincides with the (topologically equivalent) everyday euclidean metric when O_i and O_j are sufficiently close to one another, but which treats as equidistant *all* pairs (O_i, O_j) for which the euclidean distance $|i-j|$ is 25 or greater.

This last feature of Σ is certainly one which we must expect to encounter if in the archaeological problem we use the similarity matrix $\Sigma = S$ suggested by theorem 1, because pairs of fairly remote graves will then be lumped together with pairs of extremely remote graves by reason of the fact that in general neither such pair of graves will have any 'varieties' in common. Thus any peculiarities we may notice in the artificial example now being studied must be expected to manifest themselves in the archaeological situation also.

The results of (a) 45 and (b) 50 MDSCAL iterations, using a random starting configuration, and Σ as similarity matrix, are shown in figure 1 (reproduced from Kendall (1971a)). It will be seen that the correct order has been almost recovered after 45 iterations, and perfectly recovered after 50 iterations. This is an extremely encouraging result, and yet it also brings

15

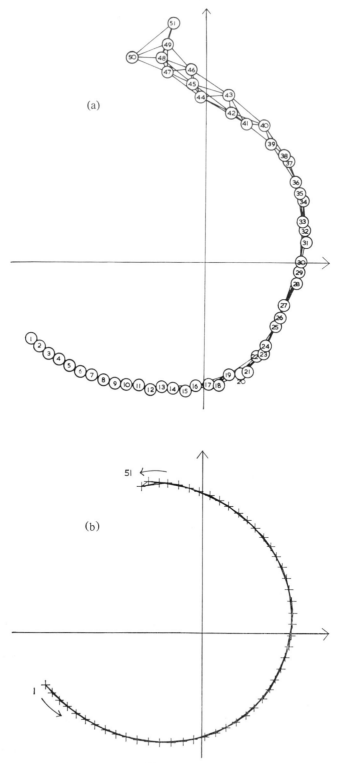

Figure 1. MDSCAL reconstructions of linear data: (a) 45 iterations; (b) 50 iterations

us a warning: the objects have been arranged in the two-dimensional output, not linearly, but in the form of a 'horse-shoe' (hence the name of the method.)

I am told (E.C.Zeeman: personal communication) that this is to be expected on general Lie-group-theoretical grounds. I believe that it should be possible to predict the angle of the 'sector' missing from the 'horse-shoe' in terms of some features of the similarity matrix (proportions of zeros, etc.), but so far as I am aware this question has not been studied in any detail. It is of course quite easy to vary the example described here by varying the critical value (here 25) at which the euclidean metric is 'flattened', and this has been done; a more (less) extreme flattening produces a more (less) nearly closed 'horse-shoe'. Further studies of this phenomenon are proceeding, but for the moment it has served its turn, and we shift our attention to real archaeological data.

APPLICATION TO THE MÜNSINGEN–RAIN DATA

It will be quite unnecessary to describe the origin of the data because the *La Tène* cemetery at Münsingen–Rain has been referred to over and over again in this book; full details of it will be found in the definitive work by Hodson (1968). To its author I am very much indebted; he supplied me with an incidence matrix relating 59 'closed find' graves with 70 varieties of fibulae, anklets, bracelets, etc. If we refer to his Plate 123, these are the 59 graves corresponding to the first 59 rows (starting at the *top*), and the 70 'types' corresponding to the first 70 columns (starting at the *left*). The graves had already been seriated by Hodson, and are also seriated geographically by reason of the elongated shape of the cemetery—but both seriations were concealed from me by a thorough encoding of the row and column labels of the incidence matrix. It was therefore impossible to cheat. A similarity matrix $\Sigma = S$ was chosen in the manner suggested by theorem 1 (with all $w_h = 1$), and many two-dimensional MDSCAL analyses were carried out with different random initial configurations (normally with 50 iterations per run). The questions one should ask of such an analysis are as follows.

(1) Is the two-dimensional output, when appropriately supplied with links as explained in the preceding section, roughly in the form of a 'horse-shoe'?

(2) If we read round the 'horse-shoe' from one vertex to the other do we obtain approximately the same sequencing for the graves (in direct or reverse order) irrespective of the random initial configuration?

(3) Is the order so obtained in reasonable agreement with that previously arrived at by Hodson?

(4) Is the order so obtained in reasonable agreement with the geographical sequencing implied by the almost linear form of the cemetery?

(5) If we use the order so obtained to rearrange the rows of the incidence matrix, do we obtain a good approximation to Pattern P of Petrie (the 1s in each column bunched together)?

The answer to each one of these five questions is, *yes*.

That this is so for questions (1) and (3) can be seen by looking at figure 2 (reproduced from Kendall (1971a)). Here each grave is represented by a circle, and the number inside the circle is the rank order assigned to that

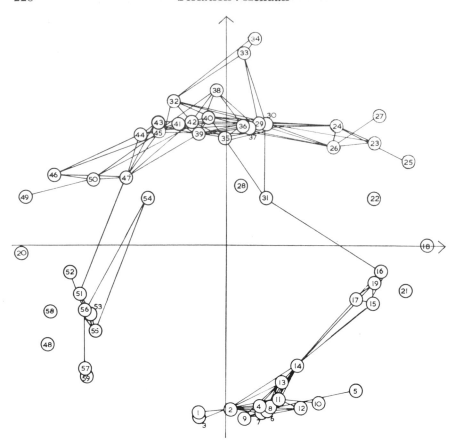

Figure 2. Hodson's order used to label tombs. Critdiss=6. (MUNS: HORSHU/ 1802; 50 iterations; 0·84371)

grave in the earlier seriation carried out by Hodson. It will be observed that we have in this example a very nearly closed 'horse-shoe', and indeed if the 'links' were not drawn we should not have recognized the 'horseshoe' form at all. This therefore underlines the paramount importance of link-drawing and of considering different levels of linkage (for the choice of too high a level would have given a complete loop, while the choice of too low a level would have given a number of isolated bunches). The almost-closed character of the 'horse-shoe' is to be associated with the very large number of zero values for s_{ij}; in fact, of the 3422 non-diagonal elements of S, there are 2628 for which the entry $s_{ij}=0$. Thus our archaeological incidence matrix is even 'thinner' than the artificial one which we studied in the preceding section of this paper. It will also be observed that Hodson's grave number 1 lies at one vertex of the 'horse-shoe', that his grave number 59 lies at the other vertex, and that intermediately the graves lie on the 'horse-shoe' almost in the order which he ascribed to them.

The two axes are of interest only for reference purposes (the computer also prints out the cartesian coordinates of the points representing the graves, relative to this pair of axes, and this is how the graves are identified on the computer-plot). The two axes meet in the centroid of the 'horse-shoe', and the Cambridge program arranges for the polar coordinates of the points representing the graves to be printed out also; these polar coordinates are formed with reference to the centroid just mentioned, in such a way that the forward direction of the 'horizontal' axis is given the angular coordinate 180°. Once the angular coordinate of a ray passing through the 'gap' in the 'horse-shoe' has been found, this polar-coordinates table provides a very simple way of reading off the implied permutation of the graves, these being identified by the coded labels used in the analysis.

We defer giving the evidence in favour of an affirmative answer to question (2) for the moment, because it will be more convenient to present a portion of that in a later context.

The 'yes' to question 4 can be justified by looking at figure 3 (also reproduced from Kendall (1971a)). This shows an exact plan of the Münsingen–Rain cemetery, with the position of each grave once again marked by a circle. This time, however, the number inside the circle is *not* the rank order in the Hodson seriation. On the contrary, it is the rank order of the grave in the seriation derived by reading counter-clockwise round the 'horse-shoe' in figure 2, starting at one vertex and finishing at the other. What is significant now is that the low values 1–9 all occur at the NW end of the cemetery, while the large values 51–59 all occur at the SE end of the cemetery. We are here using only one computer run, and nevertheless there is an approximate sense in which we can say that the computer, knowing only S, has reconstructed the map of the cemetery.

The answer to question (5), again affirmative, will also be deferred until some preliminaries have been dealt with.

FURTHER DEVELOPMENTS

The Cambridge 'horse-shoe' program consists of a very much simplified version of the Kruskal MDSCAL program transcribed into a local autocode by Jessie McWilliams and by Kruskal himself, preceded and followed by a large number of fairly simple-minded additional facilities, most of which are very briefly listed in Appendix A to this paper. Only two of these call for mention here. One is the subroutine CIRCLEUP, which replaces a square symmetric matrix S by $S \circ S$ (as defined in theorem 2). The other is an option which permits, as in the major editions of the Kruskal program, a choice between the 'primary treatment of ties' (PTT) and the 'secondary treatment of ties' (STT). Readers who wish to know the difference between the two are referred to Kruskal's articles (Kruskal 1964). All that need be remembered in practice is that PTT is probably much to be preferred when any one value (for example, zero) occurs frequently in the similarity matrix, together with the fact that a PTT analysis is always slower than an STT analysis, although the difference need not be too serious if an efficient sorting procedure is employed within the MDSCAL program (the Cambridge version uses SHELLSORT).

Now let us reflect for a moment on the great inconvenience of being

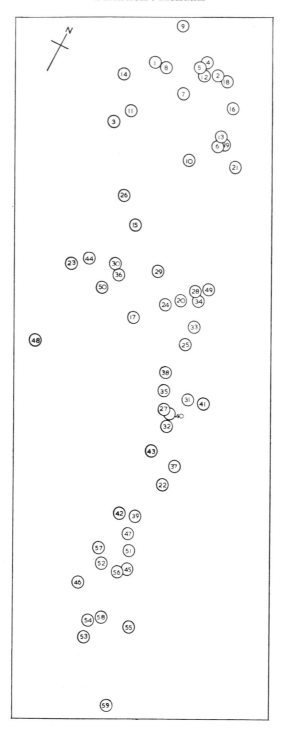

Figure 3. Map of the cemetery

presented (as in figure 2) with a 'horse-shoe' that is almost a complete circle.

There are two distinct reasons why this is irritating. In the first place, with such a 'horse-shoe', it is essential to look at the computer-plot and decide for one's self where the gap in the 'horse-shoe' lies; that is, subjective intervention is required before we are able to pass from the computer-plot to a seriation. If the missing arc in the 'horse-shoe' were larger—say of the order of 90°—we could trust the computer to locate it for us, and then this residual subjectivity could be removed.

In the second place, the closed-up form of the 'horse-shoe' is frustrating because it presents us with a two-dimensional picture from which one could not possibly derive a meaningful one-dimensional seriation by projection on the principal component. From the standpoint of a principal components analysis, indeed, figure 2 is virtually circularly symmetric, and we should wind up with a projection of the diagram on some rather arbitrary diameter of it, which would be utterly valueless.

There is therefore everything to be said for trying by one means or another to *unbend* the horse-shoe. Admirers of Mr Sherlock Holmes will recall an incident in April 1883, when Dr Grimesby Roylott 'stepped swiftly forward, seized the poker, and bent it into a curve with his huge brown hands. "See that you keep yourself out of my grip", he snarled, and hurling the twisted poker into the fireplace, he strode out of the room.' Holmes, however, 'picked up the steel poker, and with a sudden effort straightened it out again'. This is what we must do with the 'twisted one-dimensional object' with which S and MDSCAL have presented us.

We have already noted that CIRCLEUP (i.e. the use of $S \circ S$ rather than S itself) may be of value, and should lose us no relevant information, when S is very full of zeros; on the other hand we know that PTT is to be preferred to STT (which was used in the analysis leading to figure 2) when any single value (and zero here is certainly one such) occurs over-frequently in a similarity matrix. Now figure 2 shows the result of using S and STT with an initial randomizer value (determining the initial configuration) of 0·84371, MDSCAL being run for 50 iterations. In figures 4 to 6 we show the effects of introducing our 'unbending' devices, separately and together, the initial randomizer value and the number of iterations being kept the same throughout. The choices corresponding to the three analyses are as follows:

figure 4 : $S \circ S$, and STT
figure 5 : S , and PTT
figure 6 : $S \circ S$, and PTT.

There is no doubt that figure 6 represents a dramatic improvement, but we may have been lucky here with our initial configuration. Accordingly we have applied $S \circ S$ and PTT together to two other (still random) initial configurations, and in each case (figures 7 and 8) we find a result which is even more startlingly satisfactory. The 'twisted one-dimensional object' has here been straightened out as if the fingers of Holmes himself had been at work on it. As all the many 'S with STT' analyses gave almost-closed 'horse-shoes' like that in figure 2, there seems to be no doubt that the treatment '$S \circ S$ with PTT' is very greatly to be preferred, and for this fortunate result

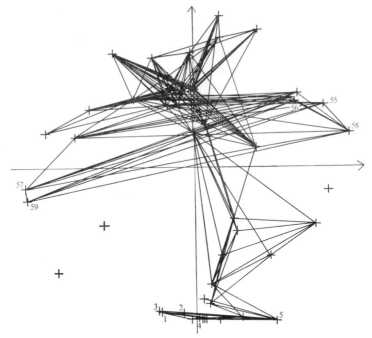

Figure 4. MUNS : STT, SIMSQ, 84371, 50, $\sigma = 0.2476$***

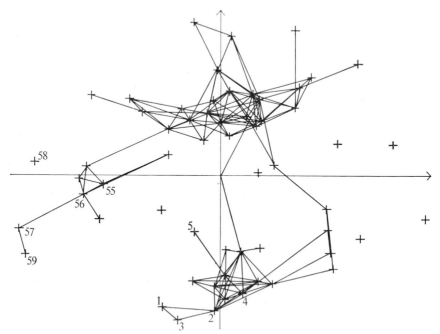

Figure 5. PTT, SIM, 84371, 50, $\sigma = 0.0377$***

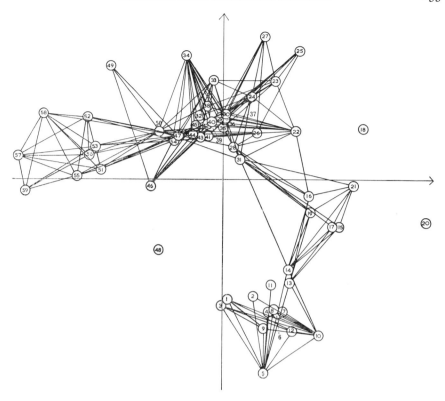

Figure 6. MUNS: PTT, SIMSQ, 84371, 100 (The number labelling the grave indicates its position in Hodson's order.)

we are, of course, indebted to theorem 2. Wilkinson's work suggests that even better results might be obtained by using

$$(S \circ S) \circ (S \circ S), \text{etc.,}$$

but we have not explored these possibilities yet in relation to the Münsingen data.

As two of the three '$S \circ S$ with PTT' analyses gave us almost linear outputs, and the third gave us what might be called a semi-circular output, it is now very natural to take these three two-dimensional computer-plots and project them severally onto their principal components (using a straightforward subroutine called DIM/DROP); the one-dimensional plots thus obtained are then each used as initial configurations for a 50-iteration *one*-dimensional MDSCAL analysis, and in this manner we have obtained the one-dimensional plots shown in figure 9 ((i)–(iii)). The seriations derived from these are listed in table 1, the graves being here identified by their rank orders (H) in the Hodson seriation. This table confirms our statement that the seriations are reasonably robust under a change of the starting configuration ('yes' to question (2)), and, what is more important, they are computer-seriations obtained without any human intervention whatsoever; the subjective identification of the 'vertices' of the 'horse-shoe' has been rendered unnecessary, and indeed the very name of the procedure has become an archaism.

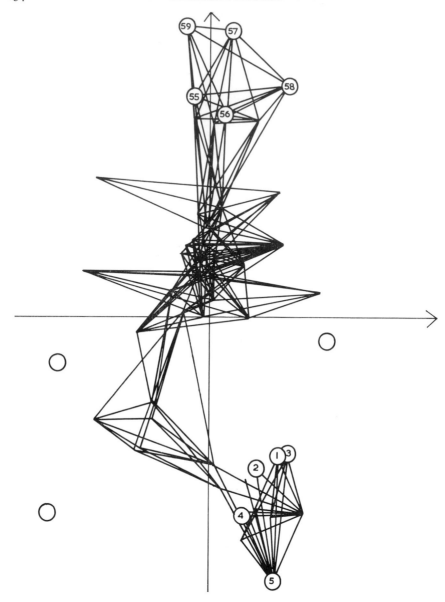

Figure 7. MUNS: PTT, SIMSQ, 96329, 75, $\sigma = 0.0886$

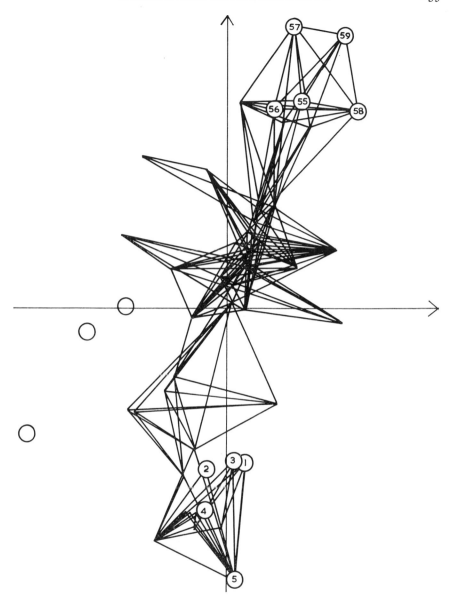

Figure 8. MUNS: PTT, SIMSQ, 73430, 50, $\sigma = 0\cdot1005$**

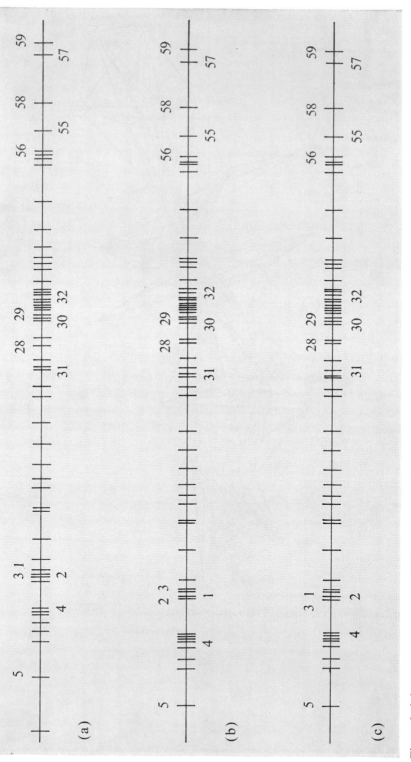

Figure 9. (a) MUNS: PTT, SIMSQ, 84371, DIMDROP (Labels indicate Hodson's order.) $\sigma = 0.1442$; (b) MUNS: PTT, SIMSQ, 96329, DIMDROP (Labels indicate Hodson's order.) $\sigma = 0.1420$; (c) MUNS: PTT, SIMSQ, 73430, DIMDROP (Labels indicate Hodson's order.) $\sigma = 0.1419$

Inspection of table 1 shows how the computer seriations fluctuate from one random initial configuration to another; it is obvious, as might be expected, that some graves are better fixed in the sequence than others, and that some of them (graves $H=20$ and 27) are not really adequately located at all; even here, however, the median rather than the mean ranking agrees well with Hodson. Reference back to figure 9 brings out the further fact that the computer-seriation tells only a part of the story; the actual placing of the graves in the one-dimensional MDSCAL arrays suggests that some graves should really be regarded as contemporary. This is shown a little more clearly in table 2, where the MDSCAL coordinates of the graves are listed, following first *Hodson*'s order, and then rearranged according to the *mean* grave-coordinates.

This seems to be a good point at which to ask: what do we mean by the degree of accuracy of a seriation? This question was touched on briefly in (Kendall 1963), where it was pointed out that answers might be based on any one of a number of quite different invariant metrics which have been proposed from time to time for the symmetric group. There is however no reason why the archaeologist should plump for any one of these, and perhaps the answer to our question is one which only an archaeologist can give, after he has considered and possibly dismissed as unsuitable all the possibilities which naturally suggest themselves to a mathematician. It might be better to pose our question in a different way, and to ask: what do we mean by a *good* seriation? Do we mean (a) one in which *no* grave is out of place by more than a few steps; (b) one in which the *average* displacement of a grave only amounts to a few steps; (c) one in which *only a small number of graves* are seriously out of place; or (d) one in which certain *graves of key importance* are placed as accurately as possible, at the cost of major misplacements of other less significant graves?

Presumably the right answer is: it all depends on what the seriation (or sequencing, if that word be preferred) is *for*. But I think that we are here broaching an aspect of the subject which has so far received far too little attention.

Another question is: how should we pool the results of several seriations? Should we combine ranks by the method of m rankings (as in table 1), or should we take arithmetic means of the positions in the one-dimensional outputs (as in table 2)? By calculating the arithmetic means given in table 2, and then ranking these arithmetic means, we obtain a pooled seriation ($\hat{r}$) which has been used to rearrange the rows of the Münsingen incidence matrix: the result, with Hodson's original tomb numbers shown in the extreme left-hand column, will be found in table 3. This justifies our affirmative answer to question (5), and also provides the reader with a version of the raw data on which he can, if he wishes, perform yet further analyses. The columns have been rearranged in table 3 so as to improve the appearance of the matrix, in such a way that each variety appears in the matrix in the order of its first appearance (relative to the pooled computer-seriation of the graves). The varieties ('types') are identified by the entries in the top row, so that co-ordination with Hodson's work (his plate 123) is possible. Tables 4 and 5 will be found useful when working with table 3. (See Hodson's note on p. 285).

Table 1

	Randomizer				
H	84371	96329	73430	Σr	r̂
1	13	10	12	35	12/13
2	12	9	10	31	9
3	11	12	9	32	10/11
4	9	5	8	22	7/8
5	2	1	1	4	1
6	8	7	5	20	6
7	7	8	7	22	7/8
8	6	6	6	18	5
9	5	4	4	13	4
10	3	2	2	7	2
11	14	13	13	40	14
12	4	3	3	10	3
13	10	11	11	32	10/11
14	15	14	14	43	15
15	16	15	16	47	16
16	20	20	20	60	20
17	17	16	15	48	17
18	21	21	21	63	21
19	19	19	19	57	19
20*	1	17	17	35	12/13
21	18	18	18	54	18
22	23	23	23	69	23
23	27	28	28	83	27
24	29	30	30	89	29
25	24	24	24	72	24
26	26	25	25	76	25
27*	49	27	26	102	33/34
28	28	29	29	86	28
29	34	34	34	102	33/34
30	32	31	31	94	30

Table 1 (*contd.*)

H	Randomizer			Σr	$\hat{r}$
	84371	96329	73430		
31	25	26	27	78	26
32	41	42	42	125	42
33	42	36	36	114	38
34	48	49	49	146	49
35	33	35	35	103	35
36	30	33	33	96	32
37	31	32	32	95	31
38	37	39	39	115	39
39	36	38	38	112	36/37
40	38	37	37	112	36/37
41	35	41	41	117	40
42	39	40	40	119	41
43	40	43	43	126	43
44	43	44	44	131	44
45	44	45	45	134	45
46	50	50	50	150	50
47	45	46	46	137	46
48	22	22	22	66	22
49	51	51	51	153	51
50	47	48	48	143	48
51	52	52	52	156	52
52	53	54	54	161	54
53	54	53	53	160	53
54	46	47	47	140	47
55	56	56	56	168	56
56	55	55	55	165	55
57	58	58	58	174	58
58	57	57	57	171	57
59	59	59	59	177	59

Table 1. (i) Hodson's serial order (*H*); (ii) 3 independent *fully automatic* computer seriations; and (iii) the pooled computer seriation ($\hat{r}$), obtained by ranking the values of Σr

Table 2

| | Graves arranged (i) in Hodson's order | | | | | | (ii) In $\bar{x}$-order | | |
| | Randomizer | | | | | | | | |
H	84371	96329	73430	Σx	$\bar{x}$	$\hat{r}$	$\hat{r}$	$\bar{x}$	H
1	$-1\cdot14$	$-1\cdot26$	$-1\cdot22$	$-3\cdot62$	$-1\cdot21$	12	1	$-1\cdot87$	5
2	$-1\cdot17$	$-1\cdot28$	$-1\cdot26$	$-3\cdot71$	$-1\cdot24$	9	2	$-1\cdot65$	10
3	$-1\cdot18$	$-1\cdot22$	$-1\cdot28$	$-3\cdot68$	$-1\cdot23$	10	3	$-1\cdot59$	12
4	$-1\cdot37$	$-1\cdot52$	$-1\cdot48$	$-4\cdot37$	$-1\cdot456$	8	4	$-1\cdot52$	9
5	$-1\cdot78$	$-1\cdot92$	$-1\cdot92$	$-5\cdot62$	$-1\cdot87$	1	5	$-1\cdot48$	8
6	$-1\cdot39$	$-1\cdot50$	$-1\cdot52$	$-4\cdot41$	$-1\cdot47$	6	6	$-1\cdot47$	6
7	$-1\cdot39$	$-1\cdot48$	$-1\cdot50$	$-4\cdot37$	$-1\cdot458$	7	7	$-1\cdot458$	7
8	$-1\cdot41$	$-1\cdot51$	$-1\cdot51$	$-4\cdot43$	$-1\cdot48$	5	8	$-1\cdot456$	4
9	$-1\cdot45$	$-1\cdot56$	$-1\cdot56$	$-4\cdot57$	$-1\cdot52$	4	9	$-1\cdot24$	2
10	$-1\cdot56$	$-1\cdot69$	$-1\cdot69$	$-4\cdot94$	$-1\cdot65$	2	10	$-1\cdot23$	3
11	$-1\cdot07$	$-1\cdot16$	$-1\cdot16$	$-3\cdot39$	$-1\cdot13$	14	11	$-1\cdot22$	13
12	$-1\cdot51$	$-1\cdot63$	$-1\cdot63$	$-4\cdot77$	$-1\cdot59$	3	12	$-1\cdot21$	1
13	$-1\cdot21$	$-1\cdot23$	$-1\cdot23$	$-3\cdot67$	$-1\cdot22$	11	13	$-1\cdot18$	20
14	$-0\cdot96$	$-0\cdot98$	$-0\cdot98$	$-2\cdot92$	$-0\cdot97$	15	14	$-1\cdot13$	11
15	$-0\cdot78$	$-0\cdot82$	$-0\cdot81$	$-2\cdot41$	$-0\cdot803$	16	15	$-0\cdot97$	14
16	$-0\cdot52$	$-0\cdot50$	$-0\cdot50$	$-1\cdot52$	$-0\cdot51$	20	16	$-0\cdot803$	15
17	$-0\cdot77$	$-0\cdot81$	$-0\cdot82$	$-2\cdot40$	$-0\cdot800$	17	17	$-0\cdot800$	17
18	$-0\cdot39$	$-0\cdot39$	$-0\cdot39$	$-1\cdot17$	$-0\cdot39$	21	18	$-0\cdot66$	21
19	$-0\cdot59$	$-0\cdot59$	$-0\cdot59$	$-1\cdot77$	$-0\cdot59$	19	19	$-0\cdot59$	19
20*	$-2\cdot11$	$-0\cdot71$	$-0\cdot71$	$-3\cdot53$	$-1\cdot18$	13	20	$-0\cdot51$	16
21	$-0\cdot66$	$-0\cdot66$	$-0\cdot66$	$-1\cdot98$	$-0\cdot66$	18	21	$-0\cdot39$	18
22	$-0\cdot10$	$-0\cdot06$	$-0\cdot07$	$-0\cdot23$	$-0\cdot08$	23	22	$-0\cdot27$	48
23	$0\cdot12$	$0\cdot15$	$0\cdot15$	$0\cdot42$	$0\cdot14$	27	23	$-0\cdot08$	22
24	$0\cdot25$	$0\cdot27$	$0\cdot27$	$0\cdot79$	$0\cdot26$	29	24	$-0\cdot03$	25
25	$-0\cdot05$	$-0\cdot02$	$-0\cdot02$	$-0\cdot09$	$-0\cdot03$	24	25	$0\cdot06$	26
26	$0\cdot07$	$0\cdot05$	$0\cdot05$	$0\cdot17$	$0\cdot06$	25	26	$0\cdot07$	31
27*	$0\cdot79$	$0\cdot09$	$0\cdot06$	$0\cdot94$	$0\cdot31$	30	27	$0\cdot14$	23
28	$0\cdot20$	$0\cdot25$	$0\cdot25$	$0\cdot70$	$0\cdot23$	28	28	$0\cdot23$	28
29	$0\cdot38$	$0\cdot39$	$0\cdot39$	$1\cdot16$	$0\cdot39$	34	29	$0\cdot26$	24
30	$0\cdot35$	$0\cdot36$	$0\cdot36$	$1\cdot07$	$0\cdot36$	31	30	$0\cdot31$	27

Table 2 (*contd.*)

| | Graves arranged (i) in Hodson's order | | | | | | (ii) in $\bar{x}$-order | | |
| | Randomizer | | | | | | | | |
H	84371	96329	73430	Σx	$\bar{x}$	$\hat{r}$	$\hat{r}$	$\bar{x}$	H
31	0·06	0·07	0·09	0·22	0·07	26	31	0·36	30
32	0·47	0·51	0·51	1·49	0·50	42	32	0·359	37
33	0·51	0·43	0·43	1·37	0·454	38	33	0·360	36
34	0·72	0·75	0·76	2·23	0·74	49	34	0·39⁻	29
35	0·37	0·40	0·40	1·17	0·39	35	35	0·39⁺	35
36	0·35	0·37	0·37	1·09	0·360	33	36	0·44	40
37	0·35	0·37	0·37	1·09	0·359	32	37	0·45⁻	39
38	0·43	0·47	0·47	1·37	0·455	39	38	0·454	33
39	0·42	0·46	0·46	1·34	0·45	37	39	0·455	38
40	0·43	0·45	0·45	1·33	0·44	36	40	0·47⁻	42
41	0·41	0·50	0·50	1·41	0·47	41	41	0·47⁺	41
42	0·44	0·48	0·48	1·40	0·47	40	42	0·50	32
43	0·46	0·54	0·54	1·54	0·51	43	43	0·51	43
44	0·52	0·57	0·57	1·66	0·55	44	44	0·55	44
45	0·53	0·57	0·57	1·67	0·56	45	45	0·56	45
46	0·89	0·88	0·88	2·65	0·88	50	46	0·61	47
47	0·59	0·62	0·62	1·83	0·61	46	47	0·69	54
48	−0·26	−0·27	−0·27	−0·80	−0·27	22	48	0·72	50
49	1·05	1·05	1·05	3·15	1·05	51	49	0·74	34
50	0·69	0·73	0·73	2·15	0·72	48	50	0·88	46
51	1·28	1·26	1·26	3·80	1·27	52	51	1·05	49
52	1·31	1·33	1·33	3·97	1·32	54	52	1·27	51
53	1·33	1·31	1·31	3·95	1·32	53	53	1·32⁻	53
54	0·66	0·70	0·70	2·06	0·69	47	54	1·32⁺	52
55	1·48	1·48	1·48	4·44	1·48	56	55	1·36	56
56	1·36	1·36	1·36	4·08	1·36	55	56	1·48	55
57	1·93	1·92	1·92	5·77	1·92	58	57	1·65	58
58	1·64	1·65	1·65	4·94	1·65	57	58	1·92	57
59	2·01	1·99	2·00	6·00	2·00	59	59	2·00	59

Table 2. (i) Hodson's serial order (H), together with 3 independent *fully automatic* computer seriations (actual MDSCAL coordinates), and the seriation ($\hat{r}$) obtained from averaging the latter; (ii) the results rearranged in order of increasing average MDSCAL coordinates, with (H) shown again for comparison.

The $\hat{r}$-order is the order of the graves (ROWS) in table 3. Thus the 37th row in table 3 is the grave $H=39$, and table 4 then tells us that this is the grave $T.130$ in the notation used in Hodson's book.

16

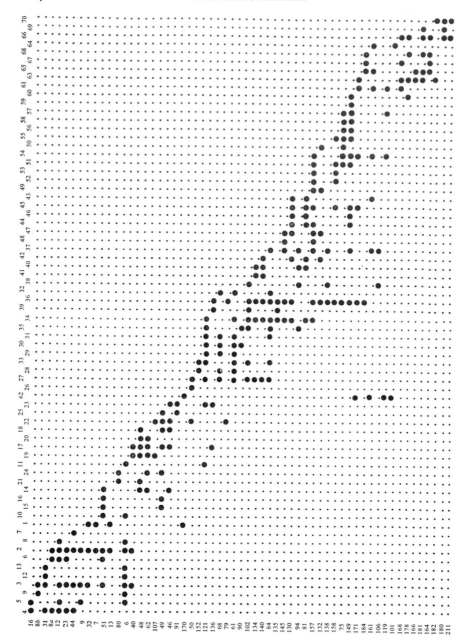

Table 3. A computer-rearrangement (based on table 2) of the Münsingen-
Rain incidence matrix

H	T	H	T
1	13	31	136
2	32	32	138
3	7	33	94
4	9	34	106
5	16	35	135
6	23	36	140
7	44	37	134
8	12	38	81
9	8a	39	130
10	8b	40	145
11	6	41	132
12	31	42	157
13	51	43	158
14	40	44	75
15	48	45	149
16	46	46	119
17	62	47	171
18	91	48	170
19	49	49	101
20	80	50	161
21	107	51	168
22	50	52	166
23	68	53	178
24	61	54	184
25	152	55	164
26	121	56	181
27	90	57	180
28	79	58	182
29	84	59	211
30	102		

W	V	W	V
1	4	36	39
2	5	37	36
3	9	38	32
4	3	39	38
5	12	40	41
6	13	41	40
7	6	42	42
8	2	43	37
9	8	44	48
10	7	45	47
11	1	46	44
12	10	47	46
13	15	48	45
14	16	49	43
15	14	50	49
16	21	51	52
17	24	52	53
18	11	53	51
19	19	54	54
20	17	55	50
21	20	56	55
22	18	57	56
23	22	58	58
24	25	59	57
25	23	60	59
26	62	61	60
27	26	62	61
28	27	63	63
29	28	64	65
30	33	65	67
31	29	66	68
32	30	67	64
33	31	68	66
34	35	69	69
35	34	70	70

Table 4. The 59 Münsingen tombs. *T* is the tomb-identifier used in Hodson's Plate 123, and in pages 42–65 of his text. *H* is the ordinal number given to these tombs in *his* seriation (1 = earliest, 59 = latest); it thus is the ordinal number of the corresponding ROW of *his* matrix (plate 123), counting from the top.

Table 5. The 70 Münsingen 'varieties'. The varieties ('types') are those identified in the top row of Hodson's plate 123, where they are arranged in the order $V=1$, $V=2$, ..., $V=70$ ($V=71$, 72, and 73 are not used here). In the computer's rearrangement of this matrix (table 3) the varieties (COLUMNS) occur in the order $W=1$, $W=2$, ..., $W=70$.

We conclude this paper by mentioning two problems which are still being investigated, and which seem to me to be likely to prove to be of major importance.

The first problem arises when the number of graves in the cemetery becomes so large that the space and/or time limitations of the computer program are exceeded. In practice it is the space limitation which is the only really serious one, because a very long 'horse-shoe' analysis can be broken down into a sequence of 50-iteration runs, the output-configuration of the mth run being used as the (now assigned, not random) initial configuration of the $(m+1)$st run. The Cambridge program contains facilities which permit this to be done very easily, and which ensure that the 'step-size' used at the commencement of the $(m+1)$st iteration is equal to the last step-size used in the mth iteration, instead of being set to the customary initial value 0·2.

Space limitations are however very serious. The storage required is proportional to the square of the number of graves in the cemetery, and for the Cambridge program in its current form this implies a restriction to not more than 90 graves, if the storage required is not to exceed 32K. Now this program can certainly be made much more efficient, but it is obvious that, after all possible improvements have been introduced, we are unlikely to be able to handle the Petrie collection of 900 graves when (as now begins to seem possible) the lost incidence matrix has been recovered by using the reconstruction of Petrie's excavation records currently being made by Mrs Elise Baumgartel. It is therefore not too early to consider how such a vast cemetery should be handled by 'horse-shoe' methods.

For definiteness, suppose that we have a program which can handle 100 graves and no more, and that we are confronted with a cemetery of 150 graves. How should we proceed?

Very much depends on whether it is of archaeological importance that all graves should be treated in an entirely symmetrical manner. If this is not considered to be important then it is likely that there will exist some rational basis for selecting a subset of graves for primary seriation; the present problem only appears in its most severe form when no such prior selection can be justified. We may then decide to split the original set of 150 graves randomly into three subsets of 50 graves each, which we shall denote by E_1, E_2, and E_3, and then to seriate by 'horse-shoe' methods each one of the 100-grave-collections

$$E_2 \cup E_3, \ E_3 \cup E_1, \ E_1 \cup E_2 \ .$$

As each seriation is not in principle any more or less acceptable than its direct reverse, we shall first have to accept the seriation of $E_2 \cup E_3$, and then decide whether the seriation for $E_3 \cup E_1$ (and similarly, for $E_1 \cup E_2$) is to be taken in direct or reverse order. There need be no difficulty at this stage; it would suffice, for example, to compare the rank correlations between the orders for E_3 implied by

$$E_2 \cup E_3 \quad \text{and} \quad E_3 \cup E_1$$

on the one hand, and between the orders for E_3 implied by

$$E_2 \cup E_3 \quad \text{and} \quad (E_3 \cup E_1)\text{-reversed},$$

on the other, in order to establish the 'sense' (forward, or reverse) in which the seriation for $E_3 \cup E_1$ was to be taken; similarly for $E_1 \cup E_2$.

Once these ambiguities of direction have been removed, the real problem faces us. We have seriations for each of the three mutually overlapping subsets $E_2 \cup E_3$, $E_3 \cup E_1$, and $E_1 \cup E_2$ of the original cemetery, and we have to fit these partial sequences together by a symmetrical and terminating procedure. What is needed here is an extension of the usual solution to the problem of m rankings in the direction of the theory of partially balanced incomplete blocks. So far as I am aware, no such extension exists as yet.

We might sidestep the lacuna in ranking theory by noting that our recipe for obtaining seriations yields a one-dimensional configuration at the penultimate stage (as in figure 9). It might be easier to combine the partial solutions at this level, rather than at the ranking level. We have, however, the awkward difficulty that the three one-dimensional configurations have each been normalized so as to have zero mean and unit variance, and it is far from clear how this should be taken into account in adapting the classical PBIB analysis. We therefore leave this as an open problem, for the present.

The second problem arises when it is possible to assess the statistical fluctuations present in the original data, i.e. in the matrix A, and one wishes to take this possibility into account. This question does not seem to arise in the incidence-matrix situation: at any rate I do not know how I would try to formulate it there, without recourse to an artificial 'model' of the type employed in Kendall (1963) and discredited by my earlier remarks on p. 217 above. But it can arise quite naturally in the abundance-matrix situation. For example, if we are given and wish to use the actual number n_{ij} of objects of type j found in the ith grave, we could (recalling the properties of the Poisson distribution) put

$$a_{ij} = \sqrt{n_{ij}}$$

and apply the 'horse-shoe' method to the matrix $S = A \circ A'$ where $A = (a_{ij})$. Taking the square root is legitimate, because it is a monotone-increasing operation, and so if Petrie's principle could be applied to (n_{ij}) then it must be applicable to (a_{ij}). It is also desirable, because if, as seems natural, we think of n_{ij} as a Poisson random variable, then this procedure will stabilize the sampling variance for each element of the matrix A to a value of (approximately) $\frac{1}{4}$.

Similarly if (as in the problem of Platonic chronology investigated by Miss Boneva) the basic data are proportions p_{ij} (this being the proportion of the clausulae of the ith book which are of type j, where $j = 1, 2, \ldots, 32$), then we may wish to set

$$a_{ij} = \sin^{-1}(\sqrt{p_{ij}}) \quad ,$$

for this once again is a monotone-increasing operation with variance-stabilizing properties.

In either case, reflection will show that we are faced with a new situation which cannot be handled by either the primary or the secondary treatment of ties, when MDSCAL is to be applied to $S = A \circ A'$. In order to explain this point it will be necessary to give rather more detail about PTT and STT than I at first intended.

A basic component of the MDSCAL algorithm is the antimonotone regression sub-algorithm of Brunk and others. This arises as follows. At each iteration of the MDSCAL algorithm one has the original matrix Σ of similarities, and the current matrix D of interpoint distances for the current two-dimensional configuration. It is then required that one should fit an *anti*monotone regression of the nondiagonal components of D on the non-diagonal *ranked* components of Σ. In STT, MDSCAL carries this out by producing a best-fitting step-function such that,

$$\sigma_{ij} \geqq \sigma_{kl} \text{ implies } \hat{d}_{ij} \leqq \hat{d}_{kl} \quad . \tag{1}$$

In PTT, however, MDSCAL carries out the regression under the much weaker restriction that,

$$\sigma_{ij} > \sigma_{kl} \text{ implies } \hat{d}_{ij} \leqq \hat{d}_{kl} \quad . \tag{2}$$

This is much weaker because whenever $\sigma_{ij} = \sigma_{kl}$ then no order-relation is imposed on $\hat{d}_{ij}$ and $\hat{d}_{kl}$. (This description, incidentally, makes it clear why PTT and STT only differ appreciably when there are many equalities between the elements of the similarity matrix.)

Now, in both the situations envisaged above it would normally happen that there would be some such equalities, because one would expect occasionally to find that $a_{ij} = 0$ (because $n_{ij} = 0$, or because $p_{ij} = 0$); thus, at first sight, PTT might seem to be the right type of analysis. But this is not so because we should surely replace (1) and (2) by the still *weaker* restriction, that

$$(\sigma_{ij} > \sigma_{kl}, \text{ and } \sigma_{ij} \text{ significantly different from } \sigma_{kl}) \text{ implies } d_{ij} \leqq d_{kl}. \tag{3}$$

What do we mean by 'significantly different'? In the straight abundance case $(a_{ij} = \sqrt{n_{ij}})$ I should be inclined to take this to mean something like $|\sigma_{ij} - \sigma_{kl}| > \frac{1}{2}$, because one would presumably be anxious to continue to distinguish between a σ-value of 1 (implying *something* in common between the graves) and a σ-value of 0 (implying *nothing* in common). A better criterion could perhaps be constructed after studying the joint distribution of the σ-values, and in the 'proportions' case (when $a_{ij} = \sin^{-1}(\sqrt{p_{ij}})$) the criterion would of course involve the numbers of instances on which the proportions were based. In all cases an extremely liberal 'significance level' should be used; the five per cent level, for example, would be far too severe. Our business here is not to carry out a series of significance tests, but simply to decide which pairs of similarities are to be regarded as 'distinct' for the purposes of the antimonotone regression.

It is important to notice that 'insignificantly different from' is *not* an equivalence relation. It is reflexive and symmetric, but *not* transitive. (We are in fact concerned here with a tolerance space in the sense of Zeeman.) Thus we cannot simply collapse 'insignificantly different' similarities into an equivalence class of 'almost equal' similarities, and therefore the required modification to the usual antimonotone regression will be a very radical one. It is hoped that it will prove possible to report in further detail on this question elsewhere.

CONCLUDING REMARKS

Unfortunately it was not possible to record in full the extremely stimulating 'round-table' discussion on seriation and sequencing which took place at Mamaia, and I have therefore incorporated many of the remarks which emerged in that and in other open discussions into the revised text of this paper, in order that they should not be overlooked. I regret that I have not been able to attribute them to their original authors.

In conclusion it only remains for me to thank Roy Hodson, Joseph Kruskal, David McLaren, Robin Sibson, and Martin Wilkinson for helpful discussions of all these problems, to acknowledge gratefully the computing space and time generously assigned to me by the Director of the Cambridge University Computer Laboratory, and to thank Mary Brooks for redrawing all the diagrams in a form suitable for printing.

APPENDIX A: THE HORSHU PROGRAM

In this appendix to the paper I shall simply note very briefly those modifications to and additions to MDSCAL which convert it into the main HORSHU program, unless they have already been discussed in the main body of the paper. I shall also describe the form in which data should be encoded for use on the Cambridge program in the simplest (incidence matrix) case. It will be unnecessary to describe the details of the very simple sister-programs PREP/HORSHU, CIRCLEUP, and DIM/DROP which complete the 'package'.

It has been mentioned that we have the option of a random initial configuration (initiated by a randomizer given in the form $U=0.84371$), or a prescribed configuration together with a prescribed initial step-size (each of which may be taken from an earlier analysis). Normally several repeat analyses will be carried out with different values of U. It is wasteful of time to sort the similarity matrix again and again, and so it is arranged that this need only be done on the first such run; the sorted similarity matrix is then sent to an output and used in future, the preliminary sorting being discontinued thereafter by appropriate setting of a switching parameter.

From one step of the algorithm to the next the current configuration has to be normalized in scale and location. In some versions of MDSCAL the scale norming is done on a cartesian basis. For 'horse-shoe' purposes this is usually undesirable, and by setting a switching parameter to zero the scale norming will be carried out isotropically.

The program will accept (possibly zero) similarities or dissimilarities, but will always *work* with the latter, a linear antimonotone transformation being applied if similarities form the input. The printed sorted dissimilarity table usually forming part of the output of MDSCAL is very bulky and will not normally be required after the first run; this option can therefore be 'switched off', or alternatively a very much compressed version (essentially a histogram of the dissimilarity values) can be obtained in its place.

There is a facility for sampling randomly from the similarity matrix; this may be useful in supplying a greater degree of random replication. It has not yet been tested, and should be used with care, because it is important that enough similarities be used to link all the graves into a connected graph.

We have explained in the text that links are drawn joining pairs of points representing graves having similarities above some critical (ranked) level; this level must be stated as a parameter. Several other facilities are related to this one. For example, especially when $\Sigma = S \circ S$, the strongest links may be very numerous and largely redundant in defining the 'horse-shoe'; if this happens to be the case then the program offers one the option of not drawing the K strongest links. In figures 4 and 6, for example, this option has been used with $K=287$ (and similarly in figures 7 and 8).

It may occasionally be of interest to see how the configuration develops as the iterations proceed. Another facility causes the configuration to be plotted and the desired links to be drawn whenever the ordinal number of the last iteration is a member of an arbitrarily prescribed terminating arithmetical progression.

If points in the final (or other to-be-plotted) configuration lie 'out of range' on the plotter, they are omitted from the plot, but this fact is recorded in the printed output.

Normally the program employs STT, but it will exchange this for PTT if the parameter defining the number of graves is prefixed by a minus sign. With STT, the 'final block sizes' in the last antimonotone regression are sent to the printed output. With PTT, this output is curtailed because there will normally be a very large number of final 'blocks'; only blocks containing one of the 300 most similar pairs will then be recorded in this way.

Even in two-dimensional applications of MDSCAL it is surprising, but true, that 'collisions' can occur; i.e. the points representing two graves can approach one another so closely that the division by their mutual distance causes an overflow. To avoid this, MDSCAL has here been modified in such a way that if two points are about to 'collide', they are made to 'pass through one another' and follow the tangential directions in which each one was respectively moving prior to the 'collision'. In most other versions of MDSCAL, 'collisions' stop the run. Another way of dealing with 'collisions' has been devised by Sibson.

'Collisions' are of course even more likely to occur in one dimension. In the one-dimensional case all those of the above remarks which continue to make sense, do in fact still apply. A one-dimensional configuration is drawn by the plotter, and of course also printed out (both in the forward and in the reverse direction).

Finally we describe how an incidence matrix should (in most cases) be coded before conversion to a similarity matrix. For each row separately, starting with the first, one records the ordinal numbers (in order) of those columns which contain the entry 1, following these with the number $C+1$ (where C is the number of columns in the incidence matrix) in order to show that a row has been completely recorded. One then proceeds to the next row, etc. Thus the incidence matrix

$$
\begin{array}{cccccc}
0 & 1 & 0 & 0 & 0 & 1 \\
1 & 0 & 0 & 0 & 1 & 0 \\
0 & 0 & 1 & 1 & 0 & 0
\end{array}
$$

would be coded as   2, 6, 7, 1, 5, 7, 3, 4, 7.

As most incidence matrices are very 'thin' (contain many zeros) this method of coding is particularly convenient. A pre-program PREP/HORSHU will then compute the similarity matrix S and store its elements in the form

$$
\begin{array}{ccc}
s_{12} & 1 & 2 \\
s_{13} & 1 & 3 \\
s_{14} & 1 & 4 \\
\cdot\ \cdot\ \cdot\ \cdot \\
s_{1N} & 1 & N \\
s_{23} & 2 & 3 \\
s_{24} & 2 & 4 \\
\cdot\ \cdot\ \cdot\ \cdot \\
s_{N-1,N} & N-1 & N,
\end{array}
$$

where N is the number of graves, this list being automatically prefixed by the integer 121 to indicate that it contains a *similarity* matrix. *Dissimilarity* matrices, if for some reason preferred as an input, are to be set out in a similar manner and prefixed by the integer 49 to identify them as such. Whenever any part of the program (or of its sister programs) sends a similarity/dissimilarity matrix to an output, the appropriate prefix 121/49 is automatically placed at the beginning. This remark applies, in particular, to the subroutine CIRCLEUP which *must* be given a similarity matrix as input and which will stop at once if the first number read is 49 instead of 121. The current version of CIRCLEUP (and the usual form of the preprogram PREP/HORSHU for computing $S = A \bigcirc A'$) use 'weights' w_h which are all equal to unity, but PREP/HORSHU also contains four optional other ways of choosing these weights, and is moreover constructed in such a way that it will handle abundance or incidence matrices, and will accept these in coded or in conventional form.

The Münsingen incidence matrix supplied to me by Hodson (in its original unscrambled form) is given in Appendix B; the conventional code defined above has been used to present this information; the matrix has 59 rows and 70 columns, both being arranged as in his plate 123.

Appendix B

Hodson's Münsingen (incidence) matrix is here encoded in the manner described at the end of Appendix A. Note that the entries '71' merely serve to indicate the end of each row. The rows and columns here occur in the same order as in Hodson's plate 123.

In the experiments with HORSHU described in this paper, a row- and column- scrambled version of this incidence matrix was used, and the inverses of the two scrambling codes were then applied to the solutions generated automatically by the computer. This was done to prevent unconscious cheating. Those wishing to do further work on Hodson's matrix are recommended to use the unscrambled version given above; the computer cannot cheat, so that scrambling serves very little purpose, and the unscrambling process is very laborious.

APPENDIX B—*contd.*

```
 1   2  71
 1   2   3   71
 1   2  71
 2   3   5  71
 4   5  71
 2   3   4   6  71
 2   3   4   7  71
 2   3   4   5   6   8  71
 2   4   6  71
 3   9  71
 2   3   5   8   9  10  11  12  13  71
 3   4  12  13  71
 2   3   6  10  14  15  16  71
 2   3  17  19  71
14  17  18  19  20  21  71
14  17  18  22  23  71
14  17  19  20  24  71
23  25  71
15  16  17  18  22  24  25  71
21  24  71
19  22  71
22  26  27  71
27  28  29  30  31  32  71
27  28  29  30  31  32  33  34  71
28  33  71
11  23  27  29  30  31  33  34  35  71
30  35  71
22  36  71
27  31  32  33  34  35  36  37  71
27  33  34  35  36  38  39  71
17  23  36  39  71
36  37  38  71
35  37  38  40  71
37  38  71
34  36  39  71
27  34  36  40  41  42  71
27  34  36  40  41  71
34  40  42  43  44  45  46  71
34  36  42  43  44  45  46  47  71
34  36  37  47  48  71
36  42  47  49  50  71
34  36  37  44  45  47  48  49  51  52  53  54  71
36  45  51  52  53  55  71
36  50  51  54  55  56  57  58  71
36  37  44  45  46  51  54  55  56  57  58  59  60  71
54  57  61  62  71
36  45  54  61  62  63  71
 1  62  71
62  64  71
37  43  54  61  62  64  65  71
61  63  66  67  71
63  65  71
60  63  66  68  71
36  65  67  68  71
65  66  67  68  71
63  65  66  68  69  71
66  69  70  71
63  70  71
66  70  71
```

REFERENCES

Boneva, L.I. (1971) A new approach to a problem of chronological seriation associated with the works of Plato. *Mathematics in the Archaeological & Historical Sciences*, pp. 173–85 (eds Hodson, F.R., Kendall, D.G., & Tăutu, P.). Edinburgh: Edinburgh University Press.

Fulkerson, D.R. & Gross, O.A. (1965) Incidence matrices and interval graphs. *Pacific J. Math.*, **15**, 835–55.

Hodson, F.R. (1968) *The La Tène Cemetery at Münsingen-Rain*. Berne: Stämpfli.

Hole, F. & Shaw, M. (1967) Computer analysis of chronological seriation. *Rice Univ. Studies*, **53**, 1–166.

Kendall, D.G. (1963) A statistical approach to Flinders Petrie's sequence dating. *Bull. int. statist. Inst.*, **40**, 657–80.

Kendall, D.G. (1969a) Incidence matrices, interval graphs, and seriation in archaeology. *Pacific J. Math.*, **28**, 565–70.

Kendall, D.G. (1969b) Some problems and methods in statistical archaeology. *World Archaeology*, **1**, 68–76.

Kendall, D.G. (1971a) A mathematical approach to seriation. *Phil. Trans. Roy. Soc. London* (A), **269**, 125–35.

Kendall, D.G. (1971b) Abundance matrices and seriation in archaeology. *Zeitschrift für Wahrscheinlichkeitstheorie*, **17**, 104–12.

Kivu-Sculy, I. (1971) On the Hole-Shaw method of permutation search. *Mathematics in the Archaeological & Historical Sciences*, pp. 253–4 (eds Hodson, F.R., Kendall, D.G., & Tăutu, P.). Edinburgh: Edinburgh University Press.

Kruskal, J.B. (1964) Multidimensional scaling. *Psychometrika*, **29**, 1–27 and 28–42.

Petrie, W.M.F. (1899) Sequences in prehistoric remains. *J. anthropol. Inst.*, **29**, 295–301.

Robinson, W.S. (1951) A method for chronologically ordering archaeological deposits. *Amer. Antiquity*, **16**, 293–301.

Ștefan, A. (1971) Applications of mathematical methods to epigraphy. *Mathematics in the Archaeological & Historical Sciences*, pp. 267–75 (eds Hodson, F.R., Kendall, D.G., & Tăutu, P.). Edinburgh: Edinburgh University Press.

Seriation

Ileana Kivu-Sculy

On the Hole–Shaw method of permutation search

The principal idea of the methods of solving seriation problems is to define a function on the set of permutations of the n objects to be seriated, so that its extreme value will be reached at the permutation corresponding to the true chronological order. To apply this idea, one would have to calculate the values of the function for the $n!$ permutations of the n objects to be seriated.

Hole and Shaw (1967) have proposed that one should choose a subset of the whole set of permutations, that gives a reasonable chance of containing the right order. The number of permutations of the subset proposed is $n(3n+1)/2$. This is a substantial reduction, and the current problems of seriation in archaeology then becomes solvable with actual computers.

As far as concerns the definition of the function whose extreme corresponds to the right chronological order, we choose two variants:
(a) the variant introduced by Robinson (1951) for deposits, and improved by Hole and Shaw (the raw data are percentages), with the modifications proposed by David Kendall (1969) for graves, consisting in replacing the percentage values by presence-absence and in the deduction of a matrix of similarity;
(b) a variant proposed by David Kendall (1963), as a development of Flinders Petrie's method, based on the following hypotheses:
    (1) the numbers of objects (for example, of the variety i found in the grave j) are independent random variables having Poisson distributions;
    (2) there is a constant probability for a variety of pottery to appear in the time-interval (t_i, t_{i+1}), and this probability is zero outside that interval.

To solve this problem, we have elaborated a program for the computer IBM 360/30 in the Computing Center of the University of Bucharest (64K) written in FORTRAN IV. The program contains two parts. The first part (main program) consists in performing the permutations proposed by Hole and Shaw on: first, the rows and columns of the matrix of similarity in variant (a) above; and then rows of the matrix $A = (a_{ij})$, where a_{ij} is the number of occurrences of the variety j in the object i to be seriated.

The second part of the program, which consists of two variants corresponding to the two definitions of the score function, contains two subroutines: (i) that which calculates the values of the score function in variant (a) by

$$\delta = \sum_{i,j} |a_{ij} - a_{i,j+1}| \Delta(i,j)$$

where $\Delta(i,j) = 0$ if passing from a_{ij} to $a_{i,j+1}$, the Robinson form of the matrix
              A is respected,
        $= 1$ if not.
(ii) that which calculates the log likelihood [variant (b) above].

The raw data for the program are integers; this permits the seriation of a greater number of objects, because in FORTRAN IV the integers can also be expressed in 2 bytes. Using this trick, the program can seriate about 60 objects, using only the internal memory of the computer mentioned, thus reducing the computation time. The use of the external memory on disks considerably increases the number of objects which can be seriated but leads to a prohibitively long computation time.

The variants of the program could not be applied to the seriation of graves, because the necessary data was not available in time.

At the proposal of the epigraphist Alexandra Ştefan, we applied these 2 variants of the program to the seriation of certain inscriptions of the Hellenistic epoch. We applied the program in variant (a) to the inscriptions, starting with the chronological order proposed by the epigraphists. The results led to a partially-changed order, but these changes can be justified from the epigraphic point of view. Details about these results are expounded by Alexandra Ştefan in her contribution to the present volume (Ştefan 1971).

In applying the program for version (b) to the inscriptions, and in view of the specific character of the objects we wanted to seriate (in which the abundance of the various letters depends on the text of the inscription), I decided to change the raw data, as follows. Let $A_1, ..., A_n$ be n variants of the same letter and $a_{i1}, ..., a_{in}$ be the numbers of occurrences of them in the inscription i. Then the values of the elements of the modified raw matrix are:

$$a'_{ij} = a_{ij} \bigg/ \sum_{j=1}^{n} a_{ij} \ .$$

The results of this experiment with version (b) were unsatisfactory, as even the inscriptions absolutely dated were wrongly ordered. This fact demonstrates that the various hypotheses used in the elaboration of algorithm (b) are not justifiable here. We think that the specific character of the inscriptions is such that methods based on quantitative evaluations are not suitable. This could explain why method (b) failed. On the other hand, method (a) led to interesting results and—after further improvements—even better results could be obtained.

REFERENCES

Hole, F. & Shaw, M. (1967) Computer analysis of chronological seriation. *Rice Univ. Studies*, **53**, 1–166.

Kendall, D.G. (1963) A statistical approach to Flinders Petrie's sequence dating. *Bull. Int. statist. Inst.*, **40**, 657–80.

Kendall, D.G. (1969) Some problems and methods in statistical archaeology. *World Archaeology*, **1**, 68–76.

Robinson, W.S. (1951) A method for chronologically ordering deposits. *Amer. Antiquity*, **16**, 293–301.

Ştefan, A. (1971) Applications of mathematical methods to epigraphy. *Mathematics in the Archaeological and Historical Sciences*, pp. 267–75 (eds Hodson, F.R., Kendall, D.G., & Tăutu, P.). Edinburgh: Edinburgh University Press.

Seriation

Jeannette Landau and Fernandez de la Vega
A new seriation algorithm applied to European protohistoric
anthropomorphic statuary

This paper deals with the application of a new seriation algorithm to the
establishment of a scheme of development for protohistoric anthropomorphic
statuary in Western Europe (France, Sardinia and the Iberian Peninsula).
The paper is divided into two parts: the material and the results are presented
in the first part, and the seriation algorithm is described in the second.

ARCHAEOLOGICAL STUDIES

PRINCIPLES

Our purpose is to establish a scheme for tracing the development of proto-
historic anthropomorphic statuary. It covers 200 statues from the third to the
first millennium BC, from the Western Mediterranean [France, Italy, Corsica,
Sardinia and the Iberian Peninsula] to Eastern Europe and the Near East
[Anatolia, Bulgaria, Greece, Irak, Romania, Russia and Syria] (Landau
1971). We will present here only the results obtained for France, the Iberian
Peninsula and Sardinia.

The study was carried out in three successive steps. First, we brought
together a body of documents, as complete as possible, presented in the form
of a punched-card index. [The corpus and punched-card index will be presented separately. They have been established according to the methods
developed by the Centre d'Analyse Documentaire pour l'Archéologie (*see*
Gardin 1963, 1967). For the modes of application of documentary analysis in
the case of objects, see Christophe and Deshayes (1964).] Second, the
application of a rigorous formal procedure (seriation) allowed us to induce
an order from the descriptions, which conformed with the internal criteria
(formal validity). Third, in order to test the archaeological validity of the
groups, we examined the extent to which a hypothesis, established previously
for other countries, proved applicable here. According to this hypothesis,
the more recent the origin of the figures, the richer they will prove to be in
iconographic elements. All the evidence indicates that in each of the sets
studied (we use the term here to designate a grouping of figurations of common
origin—in this case the Iberian Peninsula), the material progress of the
culture, related to the passage of time, was evidenced by an increasing
complexity in the anatomical representation (increase in the number of
figurative elements of the anatomy) and/or by a progressive diversification
of the non-anatomical elements (objects, ornamentation, garments).

We obtained an estimate of the validity of this hypothesis by comparing
the formal sequence, deduced from the morphological data, with the temporal
sequence, deduced from the archaeological data. Each time a concordance

occurred between the formal order and the chronological evolution, the probability increased. [The theoretical justification for this procedure is given by Borillo (1969).] In other cases we may impute other factors, notably a difference in 'atelier', and so explain the fact that some of the monuments do not follow the general law of evolution.

PRESENTATION OF RESULTS

The seriation algorithm led to the differentiation of six groups based on points of resemblance between the monuments, as shown in table 1.

Group	Face	Bust	Ornament	Weapons-tools	Garments	Lower part of body
I	geometric nose eyes					
II	geometric nose eyes	arms and/or breasts	necklace	crozier		
III	geometric nose eyes	arms	necklace	crozier pendant-dagger	'nervures'	
IV	geometric nose eyes	arms breasts	necklace	pendant-dagger	folds belt	lower extremities
V		breasts	necklace			
VI			necklace	crozier pendant-dagger		

Table 1

We assigned a number from I to IV, representing increasing iconographic complexity, to the four groups which verify the hypothesis concerning stylistic evolution. Thus number I has been given to the simplest figurations, being limited to the face, number II to those figurations including elements of the torso and diverse objects. Group III shows clothing or garments, and Group IV, which is the richest of them, represents the elements of the lower parts of the body.

The number V has been attributed to a group characterized by the elements of the torso and objects of decorative ornamentation. The hypothesis of evolution has not been verified for this group. In fact, the algorithm placed it at the beginning of the seriation, even though it is clearly more recent in date. Group VI, which the algorithm placed between Group V and Groups I, II, III, and IV, does not seem to be of any historical significance. It is made up of some rather simplified monuments which include objects or ornaments figuring in II, III or IV.

HISTORICAL INTERPRETATION OF RESULTS

Only the chronological conclusions concerning the French monuments (66 out of 72) have been developed here. We may note that the conclusions reached for the foreign monuments (from Sardinia or the Iberian Peninsula) confirm the schema of development suggested for Groups I and V. Thus the similarity between the figurations of Asqueroza and Moncorve, which belong to Group I, and the idols of Los Millares, confirms the early date of this group.

The assignment of the *Is Araus* figuration to a tomb from the end of the third millennium is in accordance with the recent dating of Group v to which it has been attached. The Iberian figurations of Group II, being without context (Quinto do Couquinho, Crato) or re-used (Soto) have remained impossible to date.

The groups, thus determined, enable us to establish the stages in the evolution of these monuments, despite the geographical disparity between some of them (Groups I, II and v bring together monuments of diverse origin). In fact the diffusion of the figurations is not related to the limited colonization of a given territory, in our opinion, but is rather the work of a restricted number of individuals (tradesmen or metal-workers), undoubtedly natives of the Iberian Peninsula, who were to be found in many places simultaneously, and worked within divergent cultures which had no link between them. The transmission of other elements of the magico-religious life to France (funeral rites, types of tomb) may also be attributed to the latter.

Even should this interpretation of the geographical disparity between the groups prove invalid, their chronological validity would remain. In fact, it has been demonstrated (*see* Appendix) that Group I is the most ancient, Groups v and iv being the most recent. Group II appears to be more recent than Group I and older than Groups III and iv. Group III seems later than I and II and earlier than iv.

CLASSIFICATION AND SERIATION

Classification and seriation techniques are often used on the same material by archaeologists. It is easy to see that these two types of technique are closely related. Their first common feature is that they start with some set of units, and some numerical measure of similarity or resemblance between every possible pair of units. We do not wish to discuss, here, the choice of the attributes or artifacts upon which the similarity measures are computed, nor the particular form of similarity coefficient to be selected, though of course these choices critically determine the relevance of the whole process.

The similarity coefficients form a matrix. Classification and seriation techniques both try to extract, in a handy fashion, information about the structure of this matrix. Classification techniques attempt to find a division of the units into clusters, such that the coefficients corresponding to units belonging to the same cluster tend to be larger than the coefficients corresponding to units belonging to distinct clusters. Seriation techniques, on the other hand, try to arrange the units in that sequence which comes closest to being such that the similarity coefficient of one unit to another unit invariably decreases as we compare the first unit to units farther away in the sequence.

Thus, while, in a classification, units with high similarity coefficients tend to belong to the same clusters, in a seriated sequence such units tend to lie close to each other. This suggests the use of cluster analysis as a subroutine in a seriation algorithm.

THE BRAINERD–ROBINSON MODEL OF SERIATION

An ordered matrix of similarity coefficients takes the Robinson form (Robinson 1951) if the following condition is fulfilled. In each row of the

17

matrix the coefficients always decrease when one moves from the main diagonal either to the left or to the right. Experience shows that a similarity matrix almost never fits this ideal model perfectly. One is therefore faced with the problem of finding the order or the orders of the units which most nearly conform to this model, when a notion of proximity has been specified. Given a similarity matrix, let us consider two coefficients $S(i, j)$ and $S(i, l)$ belonging to the same row and to the upper (lower) half of the matrix, with the second coefficient standing to the right (left) of the first. If these co-efficients satisfy the inequality $S(i, l) > S(i, j)$ then a deviation from the ideal model has taken place and the magnitude of this deviation is the difference $S(i, l) - S(i, j)$. We use as an overall measure of deviation from the Robinson model the total sum F of these differences. Together with this sum F, we use the quotient FR obtained by dividing F by the total number of possible deviations ($\simeq N^3/3$). FR allows the comparison of results obtained with matrices of different sizes.

We require the following definition: Given an order 0 and a classification P of the set of units, the classification P is consistent with the order 0 if there exists an order between the classes of P such that the induced order in the set of units is consistent with 0. This amounts to saying that each class of P is an interval in the order 0.

The possible success of a seriation program which uses classification as a subroutine rests clearly on the extent to which the classifications obtained satisfy the above consistency condition with the best order 0 (which is generally unknown). It is easy to check however, in the case where the similarity matrix can be put in the Brainerd–Robinson form, that the following algorithm gives classifications which possess the required consistency property with the order 0 (or with its reverse) for which the matrix is in the Brainerd–Robinson form; in fact any sensible clustering algorithm possesses the consistency property in this very special case.

THE CLASSIFICATION ALGORITHM

The classification algorithm which is a subroutine in our seriation algorithm is used to produce a classification of a subset a of the set of units into two classes α and β. It starts with the classification of the subset a in which each unit is a cluster by itself and constructs a sequence of classifications each of which is obtained from the preceding one by merging the two clusters with the highest average similarity. [This process is known in the literature as the 'average linkage' method.] This process is stopped when the average size of the clusters obtained exceeds the half of the size of the set being classified. Then the two clusters of higher sizes are selected and each of the remaining units is merged into the cluster with which its average similarity is the highest.

THE SERIATION ALGORITHM

We define the function f, from the reals to the non-negative reals, by

$$f(r) = r \text{ if } r \geqslant 0 \quad ,$$
$$f(r) = 0 \text{ if } r < 0 \quad .$$

Let E be the set of units, N its cardinality, $S(i, j)$ the similarity coefficients of the pair (i, j). Let w be a partial order relation defined in E. We consider the function $F(w)$ defined by

$$F(w) = \sum_{xwy,ywz} f[S(x,z)-S(x,y)]+f[S(x,z)-S(y,z)] \quad .$$

Notice that if w is a total order relation, this definition of F is the same as the one given before, when w is interpreted as the order corresponding to the seriation of the units. F differs from the norm used by Küzara, Mead, and Dixon (1966) and Hole and Shaw (1967). Our choice of F is due to the fact that F extends naturally to the case were w is a partial order while the usual norm does not.

The seriation algorithm finds a sequence of partial orders $w_0, w_1, ..., w_t$ each of which corresponds to an ordered classification of the set of units. By an ordered classification we mean a classification plus a total order w^* defined between the classes. w is the partial order induced on E by w^*: $xwy \Leftrightarrow C(x)w^*C(y)$ where $C(x)$ and $C(y)$ are the classes of x and y. w_0 is the empty relation; for each i we have $w_{i+1} \supset w_i$; w_t is a total order (the final seriation).

Let $\{a_1, a_2, ..., a_k, ... a_h\}$ be the ordered classification P_i corresponding to w_i. The ordered classification P_{i+1}, corresponding to w_{i+1}, is computed as follows:

(1) A class of P_i, say a_k, is selected.

(2) The classification algorithm (see above) is applied to a_k, producing a classification of a_k into two subsets α and β.

(3) Call u the partial order corresponding to the ordered classification
$$U = \{a_1, ..., a_{k-1}, \alpha, \beta, a_{k+1}, ... a_h\} \quad ,$$
and v the partial order corresponding to the ordered classification
$$V = \{a_1, ..., a_{k-1}, \beta, \alpha, a_{k+1}, ... a_h\} \quad .$$

If $F(u)-F(v) \leqslant 0$, set $w_{i+1} = u \; P_{i+1} = U$

If $F(u)-F(v) > 0$, set $w_{i+1} = v \; P_{i+1} = V$

(4) If w_{i+1} is a total order (representing the final seriation) stop. Otherwise set $i = i+1$ and go to (1).

This algorithm is easily seen to possess the following properties:

(1) The results are independent of the numbering of the units (there is no initial sequence involved).

(2) The results are independent of the selection of the 'next class to be processed' in the step (1) of the algorithm: the difference $F(u)-F(v)$ is independent of the classifications of the sets $A = a_1 \cup a_2 ... \cup a_{k-1}$ and $B = a_{k+1} \cup a_{k+2} ... \cup a_h$ lying respectively at the left and at the right of the class a_k being processed.

(3) If the data are amenable to the Brainerd–Robinson form, the algorithm will find the corresponding order. This results from the stated consistency property of the classification algorithm used, and from the fact that given a 'consistent' classification of a_k into two classes α and β, either $F(u)$ or $F(v)$ (*see* step (3) of the algorithm) vanishes in this case.

THE COMPUTER PROGRAM

A computer program for this algorithm was written in the FORTRAN V language. The program can seriate a hundred units on a 64K computer. Minor modifications could allow the treatment of two hundred units.

Particular attention has been paid to provide the user with all the information which governs the successive steps in the construction of the seriation.

The program prints for each basic iteration (steps 1 to 3 of the algorithm):
(a) the classification of the class being processed;
(b) the values of the increments of F corresponding to the prospective orders u and v; and
(c) the value of F for the order retained.

The user can thus grasp the sharpness with which each partial seriation takes place by comparing the increments of F. If one of the increments is much smaller than the other the partial seriation is well defined. If the increments are almost equal the partial seriation is not well defined.

This program is particularly suitable for the treatment of large sets of units. The computation time which depends on the factor $N^3 \log N$ (where N is the number of units) is 90 seconds for a set of 76 units on a moderately fast computer (UNIVAC 1106).

AN APPLICATION: QUANTITATIVE RESULTS

This algorithm was used to seriate a collection of anthropomorphic, proto-historic figurines. The following similarity coefficient was used:

$$S(i,j) = \frac{n_{i,j}}{\sqrt{n_i n_j}}$$

where $n_{i,j}$ is the number of attributes present in both units i and j; n_i and n_j are the total number of attributes present in i and j respectively.

The algorithm was used first to seriate the whole collection of 76 figurines. The values of the parameters for the final seriation were

$$F = 3233 \cdot 073 \quad FR = 0 \cdot 024 \quad .$$

(Recall that FR is obtained by dividing F by the total number of individual differences from which F is defined.)

Next, two groups of figurations, numbered v and vi, which departed from the general pattern of evolution, were left apart and the groups of identical figurines were each reduced to a single unit. The algorithm was used to seriate the 46 remaining figurines. The values of the parameters were:

$$F = 619 \cdot 236 \quad FR = 0 \cdot 019$$

The description of this material and the possible archaeological significance of one particular ordered classification given by the algorithm are discussed at the beginning of this paper.

APPENDIX

The figurations of Group I have been discovered in non-megalithic tombs, (cists and *tholoi*) older than the middle of the third millennium, which are found to the East of the Hérault region, in the Bouches-du-Rhône, the Var and the Vaucluse. To the East of the Hérault, the figurations belong to the culture of Ferrières, beginning in the middle of the third millennium, where they appear to occupy rather archaic tombs (*tholoi*). In the Bouches-du-Rhône, the Var and the Vaucluse, they are associated with the Lagozzian civilization, by certain observations concerning funeral rites (for example, the practice of cremation), allowing us to situate them slightly before the middle of the third millennium.

The figurations of Group v have been discovered in megalithic tombs (gallery graves, in some cases, tombs with a lateral entrance and a v-configuration), dating from the very end of the third millennium, which may be found in the Paris region on the left bank of the Seine, and in the Armorican Peninsula (Ile-et-Vilaine, Côtes-du-Nord, Finistère). In these two regions they belong to the 'Seine-et-Oise-et-Marne' culture. They seem to be later than the figurations of Group II which also belong to this culture. In fact, the type of tomb is more recent. The representations of archaic objects have disappeared. On the other hand, in the tombs of the Armorican Peninsula, we find the Cypriot dagger which dates from the Early Minoan III, that is, from *circa* 2300 BC.

The figurations of Group IV have been found standing in the Aveyron, the Tarn and the western part of the Hérault. They date from the end of the third millennium and the beginning of the second millennium. They are later than the figures of Group II, belonging to the Grandes Causses culture, which is derived from that of Fontbouisse. They are contemporary, in the beginning, with those of Group III, but they continue until a rather advanced date in the Bronze Age, as is shown by the presence of metallic objects (belt buckles and ornaments).

The figurations of Group II were discovered in the hypogea (with or without dried stone or slab constructions), dating from the middle of the third millennium, which are found in the Gard and in the Marne. A single figuration, coming from a gallery grave situated on the right bank of the Seine, was associated with a representation of an axe and occupied the separating slab as seen in the representations of hypogea in the Marne. The archaic character of the type of tomb (hypogeum) and that of the objects represented (axe and crozier) allows us to attribute the figures from the Gard to the beginnings of the Fontbouisse culture and those from the Marne to the beginning of that of Seine-et-Oise-Marne, which may be situated, respectively, in the middle of the third millennium.

The figurations of Group III were found to the west of the Gard figurations of Group II. They date from the end of the third millennium just as the first figurations of Group IV. They appear to be later than the Gard figurations of Group II, although they do belong to the same culture. In fact, their location is peripheral and they include some specific elements of Group IV, which is more recent. Still, the absence of metallic objects shows that they lasted less time than the figurations of Group IV, as is confirmed also by the rather small number of finds. It would seem, then, that we may consider Group III as a landmark between Groups II and IV.

REFERENCES

Borillo, M. (1969) Le problème de la vérification d'hypothèse en archéologie. *Colloque International du CNRS sur l'Emploi des Calculateurs en Archéologie: Problèmes Sémiologiques.* (7–12 April 1969).

Christophe, J. & Deshayes, J. (1964) Index de l'outillage sur cartes perforées. *Outils de l'âge du Cronze des Balkans à l'Indus.* CNRS.

Gardin, J.-C. (1963) Problèmes d'analyse descriptive en archéologie. *Etudes archéologiques* (ed. Sevpen).

Gardin, J.-C. (1967) Methods of descriptive analysis of archaeological material. *Amer. Antiquity*, **32**, 13–30.

Hole, F. & Shaw, Mary (1967) Computer analysis of chronological seriation. *Rice Univ. Studies*, **53**, 1–166.

Küzara, R. S., Mead, G. R., & Dixon, K. A. (1966) Seriation of anthropological data: a computer program for matrix ordering. *Amer. Anthropol.*, **68**, 1442–55.

Landau, J. (1971) *Reliefs sur pierre de Mediterranée du 4 eme ou 1er millénaire av. J.-C.* In preparation as a thesis for 'doctorat d'état'.

Robinson, W. S. (1951) A method for chronologically ordering archaeological deposits. *Amer. Antiquity*, **16**, 293–301.

Seriation

Robin Sibson
Some thoughts on sequencing methods

A *sequence* in this context is a pair of orderings of a set of objects (say, 1, ..., n), the two orderings in the pair being related by total reversal; thus
$$((a_1, a_2, ..., a_i, ..., a_n), (a_n, ..., a_i, ..., a_2, a_1))$$
is a sequence. Informally I shall speak of $a_1, ..., a_n$ as a sequence, but it is essential to remember that this is just a representative ordering for the sequence, the ordering $a_n, ..., a_1$ being an equally valid representative.

A *dissimilarity coefficient* (DC) on a set P of objects is a function d on $P \times P$ which takes real non-negative values, and is such that $d(x, x) = 0$ and $d(x, y) = d(y, x)$. Thus a DC is rather like a distance function, but $d(x, y) = 0$ need not imply $x = y$ and the essentially geometrical 'triangle inequality' need not hold.

If d is a DC on P, and $a_1, ..., a_n$ is a sequence composed of the elements of P, then the sequence fits the DC well if, roughly speaking, wide separation in the sequence corresponds to large values of the DC and small separation to small values. A sequencing method is a process which, given a DC d and a measure δ of the discordance between a sequence and a DC, seeks a sequence $A = a_1, ..., a_n$ such that $\delta(d, A)$ is minimal.

It is important to distinguish between a sequencing method in this formal mathematical sense and a seriation method in archaeology. For example, the HORSHU method developed by Kendall is a seriation method which gives an overall picture of the layout of a system through time without, except by an artifice, attempting to yield a sequence as such. Sequencing methods can however be very valuable in seriation problems as a supplement to such techniques as HORSHU, since they are capable of tidying up the approximation provided by HORSHU, and in many cases the sequencing method described in what follows does not even need the assistance of HORSHU and the two methods provide a valuable mutual cross-check.

Hole and Shaw (1967) have given an extensive account of sequencing methods. They list a considerable number of different measures of discordance, all of which seem to me to be more or less unsatisfactory. All but one of their discordance measures make use of arithmetical operations on the values of the DC, and this is a process of very dubious merit, since in effect it amounts to saying that there is something very special about the scale on which the dissimilarities are measured, and that their properties would be altered by, say, squaring them. Whilst this is true of ordinary geometrical distances, it is a very strong assumption to make about dissimilarities in general, and is best avoided. What we may be able to say meaningfully is that one dissimilarity is smaller or larger than another. Multi-dimensional scaling, and in particular the HORSHU method, depends only on the ordering of the values of the DC, and our confidence in a sequencing method might properly be increased if the discordance measure which it was attempting to minimize also depended only on the ordering. The only one of Hole and Shaw's list of discordance measures which has this property is the simple error count ε. This is defined as follows. Let d be the DC, $a_1, \ldots, a_n$ the sequence. Define $\Delta(i, j)$ to be

$$
\begin{array}{ll}
1 & \text{if } j < i \text{ and } d(a_i, a_j) < d(a_i, a_{j+1}) \\
0 & \text{if } j < i \text{ and } d(a_i, a_j) \geqslant d(a_i, a_{j+1}) \\
1 & \text{if } j \geqslant i \text{ and } d(a_i, a_j) > d(a_i, a_{j+1}) \\
0 & \text{if } j \geqslant i \text{ and } d(a_i, a_j) \leqslant d(a_i, a_{j+1}) \quad .
\end{array}
$$

Then

$$
\varepsilon(d, A) = \sum_{i=1}^{n} \sum_{j=1}^{n-1} \Delta(i, j) \quad .
$$

We may express $\varepsilon(d, A)$ in words by saying that it is the sum for all i of the number of times when, moving away from a_i in the sequence A, we encounter a dissimilarity smaller than the preceding one. The analogous measure of how well a set of numbers is sorted is unable to distinguish between the magnitudes of the departures from correct sorting in the following two cases:

$$
\begin{array}{cc}
1\ 2\ 3\ 5\ 4\ 6 & 2\ 3\ 4\ 5\ 1\ 6 \quad .
\end{array}
$$

Obviously the second example is more in error than the first, but in each case as we move from left to right there is only one step at which we encounter an out-of-order number. It is difficult to have much confidence in a distortion measure which cannot make a distinction of this kind.

To remedy this situation we now construct an order-based discordance measure which measures rather sensitively how well a sequence fits a DC. If $a_1, \ldots, a_n$ is a sequence, we cannot in general expect to be able to compare, say, $d(a_1, a_3)$ with $d(a_5, a_9)$, because they occur in different parts of the sequence. In the archaeological seriation problem, for example, we usually have little idea of the relative density of sampling in different parts of the time-scale, and even less idea about the relative values of the possibly varying rate of increase of dissimilarity with time. Thus to say '$d(a_5, a_9) \geqslant d(a_1, a_3)$ because $(9-5) \geqslant (3-1)$' is not usually very meaningful in this context. We can, however, reasonably expect that $d(a_1, a_9) \geqslant d(a_3, a_5)$, because one interval is wholly contained within the other; moreover, this is the *only* kind of comparison we can make with any immediate justification. Thus we are led to consider the number $\mu(d, A)$ of the inequalities $d(a_i, a_l) \geqslant d(a_j, a_k)$ which are not satisfied, where $i \leqslant j \leqslant k \leqslant l$. The calculation of this measure of discordance involves making $O(n^4)$ comparisons—a very laborious procedure, prohibitive if combined directly with a permutation search. μ also contains certain redundancies, for if $d(a_i, a_l) < d(a_j, a_k)$ then

either $d(a_i, a_k) < d(a_j, a_k)$ or $d(a_i, a_l) < d(a_i, a_k)$

and either $d(a_j, a_l) < d(a_j, a_k)$ or $d(a_i, a_l) < d(a_j, a_l)$.

In both cases the 'either . . . or . . .' is not exclusive. Thus it seems reasonable to consider instead the number $\lambda(d, A)$ of inequalities $d(a_i, a_j) \leqslant d(a_i, a_k)$ and $d(a_j, a_k) \leqslant d(a_i, a_k)$ which fail ($i \leqslant j \leqslant k$). Calculation of λ involves only $O(n^3)$ comparisons, which is rather better from the computational point of view. The use of λ also has the merit that we need only concern ourselves with the accuracy of judgments of the form 'W and X are more unlike than W and Y' and we do not need to say directly 'W and X are more unlike than Y and Z' (W, X, Y, Z all different), although this may be implied *via* the redundancy discussed above. Thus a reasonable goal would seem to be to develop a method for finding a sequence A to minimize $\lambda(d, A)$ for given d.

The technique suggested by Hole and Shaw for minimizing a discordance measure, and called by them 'Permutation Search', is as follows. Start from some sequence as a first approximation. Test against this a set of permutations, applying a permutation to the sequence if the resultant sequence has lower discordance with the DC than the sequence from which it is obtained. Continue until all the permutations fail—this may need several scans of the set, since a permutation which was previously unprofitable may produce a gain after some other change has been made. The resultant sequence is a local optimum with respect to this set of permutations. If many different initial configurations lead to the same local optimum, then provided that the set of permutations through which searching was carried out is large enough, we can reasonably hope to have found a global optimum. If we search through too few permutations, we shall often find local but non-global optima: if we search through too many, the task takes too long. A reasonable compromise is that suggested by Hole and Shaw of searching through the $n(n-1)/2$ transpositions and/or the $n(n-1)$ relocations. A transposition is of course the interchange of two objects in the sequence. A relocation (called a 'rotation' by Hole and Shaw) is the process of picking up one object and dropping it into a gap between two others. It looks on the face of it as if searching through relocations is less likely to yield local but non-global optima than searching through transpositions, and tests support this view. In searching through relocations it is desirable to adopt a slight modification of the basic permutation search process: at each stage all possible relocations of one object are considered, and the most profitable one is selected. So we now focus attention on the following process: generate or read in an initial sequence A_0; calculate $\lambda(d, A_0)$; relocate object 1 to the best available position, giving a new sequence A_1 with a discordance $\lambda(d, A_1)$; relocate object 2 ...; ...; relocate object n ...; relocate object 1 ...; ...; continue until there is no object which can profitably be relocated; output the final sequence and value of the discordance. This process has $O(n^2)$ steps per cycle, and the calculation of $\lambda(d, A)$ takes $O(n^3)$ steps, so the entire process appears to have an $O(n^5)$ dependence, which severely limits its applicability. Fortunately, we can improve substantially on this. If we have a sequence $A = a_1, ..., a_n$ and we know $\lambda(d, A)$, then we can calculate $\lambda(d, A')$ for the sequence $A' = a_1, ..., a_{i-1}, a_{i+1}, a_i, a_{i+2}, ..., a_n$ from $\lambda(d, A)$ in only $O(n)$ steps, since only $O(n)$ triples are affected by a_i having jumped over a_{i+1}. Thus when we wish to relocate a_i, we can determine λ for all sequences obtainable from the current one by relocations of a_i in only $O(n^2)$ steps, by moving a_i first to the right one jump at a time from its current position, and then to the left. So one object can be relocated to the best currently available position and the resultant new value of the discordance calculated in $O(n^2)$ steps rather than $O(n^4)$. This means that the entire relocation cycle has an

$O(n^3)$ rather than an $O(n^5)$ dependence—the same order of magnitude as a single complete calculation of the discordance. We usually want to know the value of the discordance as well as the best sequence, so we now have a process which is as follows: read in or generate the initial sequence; calculate the initial discordance ($O(n^3)$ steps); relocate until no further relocations are profitable ($O(n^3)$ steps per cycle); output the final configuration and discordance. The number of cycles is affected by how near the initial configuration is to an optimum, but in any case rarely seems to exceed 3 including the final cycle in which no moves are made, this figure being independent of the number of objects. The entire process consequently has $O(n^3)$ time-dependence, and is very much a practicable proposition. I have written a FORTRAN program to carry it out, and will conclude by reporting briefly on its practical results. The program has been run on data collected by Hiernaux on 15 African tribes and by Mahalanobis on 23 Indian castes. In each case other evidence, including multi-dimensional scaling plots, suggests that there is a fairly clear cline. The sequencing method picks this out, taking 1·5 seconds in the first case and 4·5 in the second (CU Titan Computer) and does not have any trouble with local but non-global optima. The program was run on a DC for the Münsingen Graves (for access to which I am indebted to Professor D. G. Kendall). This is a DC on 59 objects, which must in this context be considered to be quite large-scale data. The DC has a large number of equalities, and takes only about 10 distinct values. Starting from an internally generated sequence the program found in 112 seconds a local optimum which the HORSHU output and the other evidence suggested was non-global, the time-sequence being folded. A sequence obtained from the HORSHU output was fed in, and in 88 seconds the program improved this (in terms of the value of the discordance) to an optimum which corresponds well to the external evidence and differs mainly by 'tidying' operations from the HORSHU approximation. Values of the discordance (as a percentage of the total number of inequalities considered) are as follows.

Internally generated sequence	10·03%
Local non-global optimum from this	2·12%
HORSHU sequence	2·19%
Optimum from this	1·75%

It is noteworthy that in this case the 'untidiness' of the HORSHU approximation leads to a *larger* value of discordance than the folding in the non-global optimum. This effect is no doubt caused by the large number of equalities in the data, and it is likely that the non-global optimum arose for the same reason.

These tests indicate that the discordance measure λ is not only appealing from the theoretical point of view, but also meaningful in practice, and further that the form of permutation search technique suggested here for use with it is efficient enough to provide a workable sequencing method which is a valuable complement as a method of seriation to the HORSHU method.

REFERENCE

Hole, F. & Shaw, M. (1967) Computer analysis of chronological seriation. *Rice Univ. Studies*, **53**, 1–166.

Seriation

Alexandra Ştefan
Applications of mathematical methods to epigraphy

Starting from the application of mathematical methods to archaeology I
suggested and, in December 1969, achieved, the adaptation and application
of one of these methods to epigraphy. My researches in this new direction
have always been encouraged by Professor Gr. C. Moisil and Professor D. M.
Pippidi, to whom I express once more all my gratitude. [An extended text
of the paper I delivered in May 1970 at the Institute of Archaeology,
Bucharest, will appear in *Studii Clasice*, 13, Bucharest.]

The mathematical methods of chronological seriation used until now only
in archaeology can be applied to epigraphy as well, because inscriptions
(like ancient sites and graves) are monuments that belong to certain historical
epochs and consist of variable elements: I mean the letters of the inscriptions,
which took different forms, over the centuries, each form being used in a
limited period. Thus, except for archaisms, local aspects of the script, and
casual variations due to the masons, we find that letters in contemporary
inscriptions have similar forms, which differ from those in inscriptions of
other periods. This criterion of the degree of resemblance in the character of
the script is usually used by epigraphists to date inscriptions. The same
criterion may be expressed in terms of numerical indices of similitude (or
dissimilitude), as used in certain mathematical methods.

As the dates of the majority of the inscriptions are still to be determined,
and as a palaeographical analysis is often the only means available, of all the
possible criteria, to determine chronology, I adapted a mathematical method
of chronological seriation to the study of Greek inscriptions. The following
were my aims:

(a) to establish the chronological order of the inscriptions belonging to a
common site, on the basis of their letter-forms;

(b) to establish the chronological order of the forms of each letter individually and of the alphabet as a whole, in order to draw up and then to
compare tables showing the evolution of local scripts.

First, I adapted to epigraphy the method elaborated by Hole and Shaw
(1967) for archaeological sites; I considered as variables the particular forms
of the letters of different inscriptions, and I noted in the incidence matrix
only the presence (shown in the figures by a triangle), instead of the percentages of the occurrences of every variable. In this way I set up several
incidence and agreement matrices for a few dozen Greek inscriptions discovered in Romania.

I take this opportunity to thank again Ileana Kivu-Sculy for having, since
May 1970, complied with my request to analyze on a computer the epigraphi-
cal data I had already gathered, using the mathematical program she had

developed—for graves—according to the Hole–Shaw method (Kivu-Sculy 1971).

My experiments took into account both the rules of traditional palaeographical analysis and the recommendations of the authors of the mathematical method with regard to the preparation of the data. (*See* Hole and Shaw 1967).

The advantages that epigraphy offers us in comparison with archaeology as a field for the application of mathematical methods are as follows.

(1) We have to do with variables of a limited set of elements, always the same, namely, the letters of the alphabet. As their morphological evolution is already known in general, it is easy to select and to designate the variables of the incidence matrix, so as to put the inscriptions beforehand in a roughly correct order and to recognize the proper chronological orientation ('backwards' or 'forwards') of the final order (Kendall 1969).

(2) Usually these elements (the letters) are all to be found in every inscription, with two exceptions: the 'unusual' letters (Z, Ξ, Φ, X, Ψ), which may be excluded as variables from the outset, and the inscriptions which do not include all the letters because of their shortness or of their fragmentary condition. Apart from these exceptions, the agreement-coefficients, and the comparison, can be based on a quite complete analysis and consequently should lead to far more accurate results than in archaeology.

My attempts deal with the Greek inscriptions discovered at Histria.

SET OF 15 INSCRIPTIONS, RANGING FROM 3RD CENTURY BC TO 2ND CENTURY AD

These include 99 variables (that is, varieties of all the letters of the alphabet, except for the five 'unusual' letters).

For the first run, the input order of the inscriptions (1, 2, 3, 4, 5, 6, 7, 8, 9, 10, 11, 12, 13, 14, 15) was that corresponding to the dates stated by the epigraphists; the corresponding 'norm' (or score) was 381. The best (=minimum) 'norm' calculated was 54, and the final order so obtained was: 14, 12, 13, 15, 11, 2, 10, 9, 8, 6, 7, 5, 3, 4, 1.

First of all we have to point out that this output order largely agrees with the inverted chronological sequence of the inscriptions. Indeed, this order can be considered to be a good one, even better than the initial, as the occurrence of the 'presences' in the columns of the variables is now quite regular in comparison with the occurrence corresponding to the input order (*see* figure 1). Thus the computed sequence confirms the dates proposed by the epigraphists, but with some exceptions:

(a) Inscription 2, dated 'in the third century BC' is shifted in the output order to the second century BC.

(b) Inscription 15, dated 'in the second half of the second century or at the beginning of the third century AD' is shifted to the late second century BC, a date that agrees both with its palaeography and with its content (honorary decree).

(c) Inscription 13, dated 'about the beginning of our era' now turns out to be earlier than inscription 12, dated 'of the second half of the first century BC'.

In addition, automatic seriation brought further minor alterations to the input order, by diminishing the uncertainty of the dates stated by the epigraphists and by specifying the chronological relations of inscriptions otherwise dated as being of the same period. [For the third century BC we got the sequence: 1, 4, 3, 5; the numbers 6 and 7, both dated 'from the late third to the early second century BC' were now put in the order 7, 6; for the second century BC the sequence remains: 8, 9, 10, (2), 11.]

Besides the chronological order of the inscriptions, the automatic seriation also gives us a chronological sequence of the letter-forms found in the observed time interval. This is to be seen by looking at the incidence matrix constructed according to the final order of the inscriptions [see figure 1(b)].

The same data were run once more with the same program, but starting from a random input order: 1, 7, 12, 5, 11, 14, 3, 8, 10, 4, 13, 2, 6, 15, 9. The 'norm' corresponding to this order is 694. The best norm found is once more 54, and it corresponds to a final computed order identical with the former computed one: 14, 12, 13, 15, 11, 2, 10, 9, 8, 6, 7, 5, 3, 4, 1. Thus it seems it is not always necessary to establish beforehand a roughly correct input order, and that the method is sometimes able to reach the best result inherent in the data even when starting from a random input order.

Once the incidence matrix was constructed according to the output order, I tried to increase the regularity of the occurrences on the columns of variables; in this way, from this 'final' computed order two other input orders were established for the new runs:

(a) 1, 3, 5, 4, 7, 2, 6, 10, 8, 9, 11, 15, 13, 12, 14;
(b) 1, 5, 3, 7, 4, 6, 2, 8, 10, 9, 15, 11, 13, 12, 14.

For order (a) the 'norm' was 77, for (b) it was 101. In both cases the best 'norms' calculated after analysis were again 54, and the output order was the same as in the preceding experiments, but this time the correct and not the inverted chronological sequence of the inscriptions was obtained: 1, 4, 3, 5, 7, 6, 8, 9, 10, 2, 11, 15, 13, 12, 14.

A SET OF 25 GREEK INSCRIPTIONS OF THE CLASSIC, HELLENISTIC AND ROMAN PERIODS

As the letters B and Γ were missing from some inscriptions, I excluded their varieties from the set of variables (125). As input order I took 1, 2, 3, 4, 5, 6, 7, 8, 9, 10, 11, 12, 13, 14, 15, 16, 17, 18, 19, 20, 21, 22, 23, 24, 25, corresponding to the dates assigned by the epigraphists; the 'norm' is 630. The best 'norm' found was 337, and the computed output order was 1, 2, 3, 5, 6, 12, 7, 9, 8, 10, 13, 14, 16, 24, 11, 4, 17, 19, 20, 22, 18, 21, 15, 25, 23.

In order to diminish the anomalies noticed in the incidence and correlation matrices corresponding to this final order, it was modified so as to obtain an input order for another run, as follows: 1, 2, 3, 5, 6, 12, 7, 9, 8, 10, 13, 14, 16, 11, 4, 17, *24, 25, 21, 15,* 19, 20, 22, 18, 23. At the beginning the 'norm' is 237: the best 'norm' calculated was 148 and the computed order was: 1, 2, 3, 5, 6, 12, 7, 9, 8, 10, 13, 14, 11, 4, 17, 24, 16, 15, 25, 21, 19, 20, 22, 18, 23.

Fifteen inscriptions of this set have in fact formed the first set (see table 2), seriated by an analysis using all the letters. The order obtained in the absence of *B* and *Γ* was the same for most of these 15 inscriptions common to the two sets, and varied only for the numbers 5, 6, and 24, 16, which were inverted (6, 5, and 16, 24) when compared with the final order obtained for the first set.

I therefore proposed the following order for another run: 1, 2, 3, *6, 5*, 12, 7, 9, 8, 10, 13, 14, 11, 4, 17, *16, 24*, 15, 25, 21, 19, 20, 22, 18, 23. The 'norm' was first 170, and the best 'norm' calculated was 156. Three different final orders corresponded to this 'norm':

(a) 1,2,3,5,6,12,7,9,8,10,13,*14,17,4,11*,16,24,15,25,21,19,20,22,18,23;
(b) 1,2,3,5,6,12,7,9,8,10,13,*14,4,17,11*,16,24,15,25,21,19,20,22,18,23;
(c) 1,2,3,5,6,12,7,9,8,10,13,*11,17,4,14*,16,24,15,25,21,19,20,22,18,23;

Consequently, for this set of 25 inscriptions we have to accept as the best result the order corresponding to the smallest 'norm' 148, although this order offers some differences as against the result based on the analysis and comparison of all the letters (in fact, the differences only involve the succession of almost contemporaneous inscriptions, as both the number 5 and 6 are to be dated in the third century BC, and both the numbers 24 and 16 are to be dated in the late second century BC).

In the main, however, the result is correct and, as in the corresponding incidence matrix we have a greater regularity of the occurrences on the columns of variables, we can accept the following modifications to the dates formerly accepted by the epigraphists:

(a) Inscription 12, dated 'in the first half of the second century BC' is shifted to the third century BC; from the matrix (figure 2b), I think it must date from the end of this century.

(b) Inscription 4 dated, 'in the third century BC' is removed to the second century BC.

(c) Inscription 24, dated 'in the second half of the second century AD or at the beginning of the third century AD' is shifted to the late second century BC, just as in the analysis of the first set of inscriptions.

(d) Inscription 25, dated 'in the second half of the second century AD or in the first half of the third century AD' is shifted to the first half of the first century BC, a date indeed suitable to its palaeography.

(e) As in the final order reached for the first set of data, inscription 21, dated 'about the beginning of our era', reveals itself to be earlier than number 20, dated 'in the second half of the first century BC'.

(f) Inscription 18, dated 'in the second–first centuries BC' is to be brought near to those of the beginning of the first century AD, whose palaeography is very similar.

Apart from this, this automatic seriation sharpened the accuracy of the dates of inscriptions belonging to the same century (*see* numbers 6, 7, 11, 17, 15).

A SET OF 15 GREEK INSCRIPTIONS FROM THE
LATE HELLENISTIC AND ROMAN PERIODS

As it frequently happens that not all letters occur in the texts of inscriptions, I tried other experiments with the view to examining the accuracy and value of the results attained in this case. I therefore considered a set of 15 Greek inscriptions from the late Hellenistic and Roman periods, with 63 variables (varieties of the form of 16 letters: I, N and T were struck out). The dates of the inscriptions 3, 6, 7, 9, 11, 13, 14 are known (*see* table 1).

Input order	Dates assigned by epigraphists	Output order	Dates assigned according to the output order
1	2nd half of 1st C. BC	2	Third quarter of 1st C. BC
2	About the beginning of our era	1	2nd half of 1st C. BC
3	Late 1st C. BC to AD 14	3	Late 1st C. BC to AD 14
4	Mid–2nd C. AD	4	Early 2nd C. AD
5	Around AD 138	5	Around AD 138
6	AD 138	6	AD 138
7	AD 156–158,	7	AD 156–158
8	2nd half of 2nd C. to early 3rd C. AD	9	AD 198–200
9	AD 198–200	15	Early 3rd C. AD
10	Late 2nd C. to early 3rd C. AD	8	Early 3rd C. AD
11	AD 215	12	Early 3rd C. AD
12	Early 3rd C. AD	11	AD 215
13	AD 218	13	AD 218
14	AD 235–238	10	Between 218–235
15	1st half of 3rd C. AD	14	AD 235–238
	Norm 158		Norm 52

Table 1

The input order (1, 2, 3, 4, 5, 6, 7, 8, 9, 10, 11, 12, 13, 14, 15) was that corresponding to the dates accepted by epigraphists; the 'norm' for this is 158. The best 'norm' found by the computer was 52 and the corresponding output order was 2, 1, 3, 4, 5, 6, 7, 9, 15, 8, 12, 11, 13, 10, 14. We can accept it as being the right order, on taking into account the following arguments:

(a) The seven inscriptions whose dates are known occur in the final order according to their correct chronological succession.

(b) The other eight inscriptions are inserted among these seven so that they follow closely the dates formerly assigned by the epigraphists, with only some small corrections (to the dates of inscriptions 4, 8, and 10) and an increase of precision for some of the dates (for inscriptions 2, 1 as against 3; for inscriptions 15 and 12, now placed between 9 and 11).

(c) Inscriptions 1 and 2, which are identical with inscriptions 12 and 13 of the first set of data and with inscriptions 20 and 21 of the second set of data (*see* table 2) are consistently placed in the order 2, 1.

Thus, when we are dealing with inscriptions which do not contain all the letters, we can obtain a largely correct seriation by giving up some letters. But the selection has to be very judicious: it has to observe certain qualitative, as well as quantitative considerations concerning the degree of morphological variability of the removed letters. Such a result is in some degree approximate and it follows that, in order to obtain a better chronological order, it is advisable to seriate inscriptions that contain all the letters to be compared.

The utility of applying mathematical methods to epigraphy, and the advantages this application presents as against the traditional methods of dating the inscriptions, lie in the facts that the results are improved, and at the same time the task of the epigraphist is facilitated. By means of the computer a rigorous and objective palaeographical comparison is obtained. It relies on the correlation coefficients, through which a simultaneous comparison is obtained and through which it becomes possible to use an analysis, quite complete with regard to the number of the letters, and far more developed with regard to the palaeographical particularities. The dates previously accepted by epigraphists are verified, and their uncertainty diminished. In a very short time we can obtain chronological series covering some dozens of inscriptions. By a comparison with these chronological series, it then becomes easier to establish the date of any newly-discovered inscriptions. In addition to the rigorous chronological seriation of the inscriptions, the computer also gives us indications which are valuable for establishing the chronological order of the varieties of the form of each letter; it thus becomes easier to set up comparative tables to synthesize the development of the script in various geographical areas.

Table 2

Figure 1	Figure 2	Table 1	
	1		Epigram, Menecharmos, son of Eusthenes: I. Stoian (1954) *SCIV*, **5** (8) 94; W. Peek (1956) *SCIV*, **7**, 199–203.
	2		Epigram, Hediste, daughter of Euagoras: W. Peek (1960) *Griechische Grabgedichte*, 89; D. M. Pippidi (1966) *St. Cl.*, **8**, 45.
1	3		Decree of Milet: V. Parvan (1923) *Histria*, **7** (6) 13 Pl. II, 1; *Id.* (1925) *Dacia*, **2** (7) 203, Fig. 9–10; S. Lambrino (1927–32) *Dacia*, **3–4** (2) 398, Fig. 14–15.
2	4		Decree: V. Parvan (1923) *Histria*, **7**, Pl. I, 2.
3	5		Decree, Zalmodegikos: D. M. Pippidi (1960) *SCIV*, **11**, 39–54; *Id.* (1967) *Contributii la istoria veche a României*[2] 167–85, Pl. 5–6.
4	6		Decree: V. Parvan (1925) *Dacia*, **2** (8) 204, Fig. 11–12; D. M. Pippidi, Em. Popescu (1959) *Dacia*, *N.S.*, **3** (2) 237, Fig. 2.
5	7		Decree, Diogenes, son of Diogenes: D. M. Pippidi (1954) *Histria*, **1** (1) 476, Fig. 1.
6	8		Decree, Hephaistion, son of Matris: D. M. Pippidi (1954) *Histria*, **1** (2) 487, Fig. 2; *Id.* (1967) *Contributii la istoria veche a României*[2], 32–67, Pl. 1.
7	9		Decree, Dionysios, son of Strouthion: D. M. Pippidi (1961) *Dacia*, *N.S.*, **5**, 305–16, Fig. 1; *Id.* (1967) *Contributii la istoria veche a României*[2], 242–59, Pl. 9.

Table 2 (*contd*)

Figure 1	Figure 2	Table 1	
8	10		Decree, Agathocles, son of Antiphilos: S. Lambrino (1960) *Rev. des Etudes Roumaines*, **5–6**, 180–217, Fig. 1, Pl. I, II, III; D. M. Pippidi (1967) *Contributii la istoria veche a României*[2], 186–221.
	11		Decree, Diocles, son of Artemidoros: Em. Popescu (1956) *SCIV*, **7**, 347 sq, Fig. 1.
	12		Decree, The merchant from Carthage: S. Lambrino (1927–32) *Dacia*, **3–4** (3) 400, Fig. 16–17.
9	13		Decree: D. M. Pippidi (1954) *Histria*, **1** (4) 498, Fig. 4.
10	14		Decree, Hegesagoras, son of Monimos: D. M. Pippidi, Em. Popescu (1959) *Dacia*, *N.S.*, **3**, 235–58, Fig. 5. = (1960) *St. Cl.*, **2**, 203–24.
	15		Decree: V. Pârvan (1923) *Histria*, **7** (11) 17, Pl. III, 1.
11	16		Decree of the *Neoi*: Em. Popescu (1956) *SCIV*, **7**, 349 sq. Fig. 2; I. Stoian (1967) *SCIV*, **18**, 235–42; L. Robert (1968) *St. Cl.*, **10**, 77–85.
	17		Decree: D. M. Pippidi (1954) *Histria*, **1** (7) 505, Fig. 7 = D. M. Pippidi, Em. Popescu (1959) *Dacia*, *N.S.*, **3** (3) 237, Fig. 3.
	18		Decree, Moschion, daughter of Diogenes: D. M. Pippidi (1968) *SCIV*, **19** (2) 430, Fig. 2.
	19		Decree: V. Pârvan (1923) *Histria*, **7** (16) 23, Pl. v, 1.
12	20	1	Decree, Aristagoras, son of Apatourios: Gr. Tocilescu (1882) *AEMO*, **6** (78) 36, Pl. III; (*Syll.*[2], 325); O. Fiebiger (1911) *O. Jahresh*, **14** Beibl., 67–71; (*Syll.*[3], 708). For the dates proposed, *see* D. M. Pippidi (1967) *Contributii la istoria veche a României*[2], 270–86, Pl. 12–13.
13	21	2	*Album*, The second foundation of Histria: D. M. Pippidi (1967) *St. Cl.*, **9**, 153–66, Fig. 1–5; *Id.* (1968) *Bulletin de Correspondance Hellenique*, **92** (1) 226–40, Fig. 1.
	22	3	Augustus' temple: D. M. Pippidi (1954) *Histria*, **1** (9) 511, Fig. 9; *Id.* (1969) *Studii de istorie a religiilor antice*, 157–63, Pl. XXII.

18

Table 2 (*contd*)

Figure 1	Figure 2	Table 1	
14	23		*Album*: D.M.Pippidi (1954) *Histria*, **1** (33) 559, Fig. 33.
15	24		Decree: D.M.Pippidi (1954) *Histria*, **1** (19) 540, Fig. 19.
	25		Decree: D.M.Pippidi (1954) *Histria*, **1** (30) 553, Fig. 30.
		4	*Album*, Priests of Dionysos Karpophoros: D. M. Pippidi (1954) *Histria*, **1** (22) 546, Fig. 22; *Id.* (1969) *Studii de istorie a religiilor antice* (1) 238.
		5	Decree, Aba, daughter of Hecataios: Em. Popescu (1954) *SCIV*, **5,** 449–66; *Id.* (1960) *Dacia, N.S.*, **4,** 273–96.
		6	*Album*, Members of the Gerusie: V.Pârvan (1916) *Histria*, **4** (20) 64, Pl. x–xi.
		7	Dedication to Antoninus Pius: V.Pârvan (1923) *Histria*, **7** (47) 60.
		8	Laberius Maximus' Horothesy: V.Pârvan (1916) *Histria*, **4** (16) 26, Pl. v; D.M. Pippidi (1967) *Contributii la istoria veche a României*[2], 349 sq. Pl. 20.
		9	Dedication to Caracalla: S.Lambrino (1927–32) *Dacia*, **3–4** (5) 407, Fig. 19–20.
		10	*Album*, Priests of Dionysos Karpophoros: D.M.Pippidi (1954) *Histria*, **1** (15) 524 Fig. 15; *Id.* (1969) *Studii de istorie a religiilor antice* (4) 239 Pl. xxxi.
		11	Dedication to Caracalla: D.M.Pippidi (1954) *Histria*, **1** (16) 530, Fig. 16.
		12	Agonistical Inscription: I.Stoian (1954) *SCIV*, **5** (6) 93; D.M.Pippidi (1967) *Contributii la istoria veche a României*[2], 445–63, Pl. 26.
		13	Dedication to Elagabal: D.M.Pippidi (1954) *Histria*, **1** (17) 533, Fig. 17; *Id.* (1969) *Studii de istorie a religiilor antice*, (5) 246, Pl. xxx.
		14	Honorary inscription: V.Pârvan (1916) *Histria*, **4** (39) 125.
		15	Funerary altar: V.Pârvan (1925) *Dacia*, **2** (30) 232, Fig. 51–52.

Table 2. Correspondence table and selected bibliography of the studied inscriptions. *Note*. For each inscription I have mentioned only the first and the most recent editions, usually accompanied by photograph; I have added papers important with regard to its dating

REFERENCES

Hole, F. & Shaw, M. (1967) Computer analysis of chronological seriation. *Rice Univ. Studies*, **53**, 1–166.

Kendall, D.G. (1969) Some problems and methods in statistical archaeology. *World Archaeology*, **1**, 70.

Kivu-Sculy, I. (1971) On the Hole–Shaw method of permutation search. *Mathematics in the Archaeological & Historical Sciences*, pp. 253–4 (eds Hodson, F.R., Kendall, D.G., & Tăutu, P.). Edinburgh: Edinburgh University Press.

Seriation

E. Martin Wilkinson

Archaeological seriation and the travelling salesman problem

This study of Petrie matrices shows the importance of minimal Hamiltonian circuits; indeed the main problem of petrifying matrices is an example of the travelling salesman problem that has been discussed in operations research. Many of the results have practical applications in seriation, and in multi-dimensional scaling in particular.

INTRODUCTION

D. R. Fulkerson and O. A. Gross have discussed a problem, belonging to molecular biology, which in mathematical terms becomes a graph theoretic question about the identification of interval graphs (Fulkerson and Gross 1965). They developed a matrix formulation for this problem, which is the basis for this paper. The relevance of these results to the seriation of archaeological data was noted by D. G. Kendall (1969a,b, 1971a,b) who, in a series of papers, has extended and generalized the original work. I want to give a new interpretation to the problem, which will have practical as well as theoretical implications.

STATEMENT OF PROBLEM

I start with a discussion about matrices whose elements are 0s or 1s. Let A be such a matrix, then I say that it is:

Definition. A *P matrix* if and only if in each column all the 1s occur consecutively, or a *pre-P matrix* if and only if there is a permutation matrix T such that TA is a P matrix.

This follows the notation of Kendall, who uses P in recognition of Flinders Petrie's original work. The problem is to find necessary and sufficient conditions for a matrix A to be pre-P and to determine, when A is known to be pre-P, what information is required to construct a permutation T such that TA is a P matrix.

THE FULKERSON AND GROSS APPROACH

They considered interval graphs and arrived at the present matrix problem by considering the 'dominant-clique *versus* vertex' matrix A. In particular they investigated the properties of the 'overlap matrix' $A'A$ (where A' denotes the transpose of matrix A) and proved their main theorem:

Proposition 1 (Fulkerson and Gross)

Let A and B be $(0, 1)$ matrices. If A is a pre-P matrix and $A'A = B'B$ then B is also a pre-P matrix. If, further, A and B have the same number of rows, then there is a permutation T such that $TA = B$.

The proof follows by adding zero rows if necessary, and by induction on the number of columns.

So $A'A$ contains enough information to decide whether A is pre-P. In fact, if A is pre-P, a knowledge of $A'A$ also allows us to construct all P matrices that can be formed from A; however the row order of A is lost in the multiplication and so a knowledge of A itself is required for a simple search operation to calculate row permutations T. I have available a fast FORTRAN program which will perform this type of seriation.

MATRIX CONVENTIONS

It will simplify later work if matrices are in a standard form. Let A be an $(0, 1)$ matrix, then we modify A by performing the following operations:

(1) Add, if there is not one already, a row consisting of 0s.

(2) Delete all columns consisting of 0s.

(3) Delete all but one of each set of identical rows.

I shall assume that the resulting matrix has more than three rows (the problem is trivial otherwise).

It is perhaps helpful to see the rows as generators of a cylinder. In this form, the problem of constructing consecutive 1s is identical with that of constructing consecutive 0s. One can always construct a matrix from a cylinder by unzipping along the generator containing all 0s. I will in fact assume that the first row of A is always the zero row. I call this the *unzipping convention*. It is clear that these operations and assumptions lose us no generality. I will assume henceforth that all $(0, 1)$ matrices are in this standard form.

MAIN THEOREM

Let A denote an $(0, 1)$ matrix with m rows and n columns. I now consider the m distinct rows of A to be m distinct points in n-dimensional space. They are vertices on a hypercube. I impose the 'city block' metric on this space, so that the distance between the rth and the sth point is equal to the number of 1s in the rth row, not in the sth row, plus the number of 1s in the sth row not in the rth row. I now recall the definition of what will be an important concept in this paper.

Definition. A *Hamiltonian circuit* is a re-entrant path (loop) passing through each of these m vertices precisely once.

The minimum length for a Hamiltonian circuit through the m points is $2n$, since each column contains at least one 0 and at least one 1. If A is a P matrix, then the length of the circuit formed by going through the points in row order is $2n$. If A is not a P matrix, the length of this circuit is strictly greater than $2n$. Thus I have proved the

Proposition 2

A is a pre-P matrix if and only if there exists a Hamiltonian circuit of length $2n$.

Each Hamiltonian circuit will give two P-forming permutations. The ambiguity arises from the two directions possible for each circuit. (Note that the two are distinct since $m > 3$.) So we also have the

Proposition 3

If A is pre-P, then there is a one-to-one correspondence between the minimal directed Hamiltonian circuits and the permutations T such that TA is a P matrix.

If A is pre-P, then sufficient information to construct a permutation T is contained in the inter-point distance matrix D. We then have the classical travelling salesman problem of finding the shortest Hamiltonian circuit; a solution to this will give us T. If A is an arbitrary matrix, we can again construct the shortest circuit from D, and if we have in addition n, the number of columns, then we can decide whether A is pre-P from the above condition on the circuit length.

ALTERNATIVE FORM OF THE MAIN THEOREM

The distance matrix D is closely related to the matrix, $S = AA'$. We have the identity

$$d_{ij} = s_{ii} + s_{jj} - 2s_{ij}$$

Hence S contains all the information held in D. However we can say more than that. If this identity is summed over a Hamiltonian circuit given by $i_1, i_2, \ldots i_m, i_{m+1} = i_1$, we have an equation for the circuit length L:

$$L = 2(U - Z),$$

where $U = \text{trace}(S)$, and

$$Z = \sum_{r=1}^{m} s_{i_r i_{r+1}} .$$

Each circuit can be uniquely associated with a row permutation T, in such a way that the circuit corresponds to taking the row order of TA.

Proposition 4

Given n and $S = AA'$, we can determine whether A is pre-P and also which are the P-forming permutations. In fact a permutation T will be such that TA is a P-matrix iff the sum of the elements of $TST' = (TA)(TA)'$ lying immediately beneath the principal diagonal is equal to

$$\text{trace}(S) - n.$$

This follows trivially from proposition 2 and the fact that $s_{1i} = s_{i1} = 0$.

The value of $\text{trace}(S) - n$ is the maximum value attainable for this sub-diagonal sum. So if we treat S as a distance matrix we have an equivalent travelling salesman problem of finding the longest Hamiltonian circuit. Thus if A is pre-P, then S by itself contains sufficient information to construct T (this was Kendall's first result); while if A is arbitrary, S and n together contain sufficient information to decide if A is pre-P and to construct the P-forming permutations. (This is a considerable generalization of Kendall's result.)

HAMILTONIAN CIRCUITS

Rarely in archaeological data will a matrix be pre-P. Rather will it be almost pre-P. I want to discuss this point briefly. The Fulkerson and Gross approach can be used to construct possible seriations even with non pre-P data. However it is not always possible to interpret the results satisfactorily.

Consider the Hamiltonian circuit ideas relating to the standard 'graves *versus* artifacts' matrix. The length of a circuit represents the sum of the changes in neighbouring graves. Hence we have a measure for the overall rate of change of fashions during a given period, based on a particular seriation. Certainly it would seem reasonable that a seriation that gives a minimal value to this measure is of interest. I feel therefore that the search for a shortest Hamiltonian circuit is of value, even with non pre-P data. I will give further results, below, which show that this is a generalization of an idea due to W. S. Robinson (1951).

TECHNIQUE APPLIED TO KENDALL'S WORK

I now want to recall some of Kendall's further results (Kendall 1969a, 1971a,b) and to prove these afresh from our present point of view. I make the

Definition. A matrix S is called an R *matrix* if and only if the columns and the rows are unimodal and attain their maximal values on the principal diagonal.

A sequence of numbers is here said to be *unimodal* if and only if it increases (in the weak sense) to a maximum (weak sense) and then decreases (weak sense). R is used because W. S. Robinson introduced this type of matrix into seriation theory.

Proposition 5 (Kendall)

If A is a P matrix then $S = A A'$ is an R matrix.

It is sufficient to prove this for a column vector **x**. This is trivial, however, as **x** is unimodal.

Proposition 6 (Kendall)

If A is pre-P and $S = A A'$ is an R matrix, then A is a P matrix.

It suffices to show that the sum of the terms of S immediately beneath the principal diagonal takes a maximal value. We use induction on the number of rows to show that the sum of the terms excluding the last is maximal. Because the last row of S is unimodal with maximal value on the diagonal, it is clear that the addition of the last term retains the maximality of the sum.

FURTHER RESULTS

If S is an R matrix then it is not generally true that A is a P matrix. However we can prove an important new result along these lines. First, make the

Definition. A matrix A is called an H *matrix* if and only if the Hamiltonian circuit defined by the order of the rows is of minimal length.

Proposition 7

If $S = A A'$ is an R matrix then A is an H matrix.

The proof of this follows identically the lines of the proof for proposition 6.

The converse of this proposition is, in general, false. This shows that the concept of Hamiltonian circuits is a generalization of those associated with property R.

Another result along these lines is

Proposition 8

If $S = A A'$ and the sum of the terms immediately beneath the principal diagonal of S is trace$(S) - n$, then A is a P matrix and S is an R matrix.

This is an amalgamation of propositions 4 and 5. We can use this in an elementary check on whether A is pre-P; in fact we have

Proposition 9

Let $E = \sum_{j=1}^{m} (s - \max_{i \neq j} s_{ij})$; if $E > n$, then A is not pre-P.

The converse of this is in general false.

GENERALIZATION

I now want to generalize the problem by considering abundance matrices instead of $(0, 1)$ matrices, following Kendall (1971b).

Definition. A matrix A is called an *abundance matrix* if and only if all its elements are non-negative.

An example of such a matrix would be where a row gave a percentage distribution amongst pottery styles for the contents of a grave. It should be clear that these matrices are a natural subject to study. A pattern that one might expect for such matrices in correctly seriated archaeological data is that in which the values in each column are (weakly) unimodal; that is, a fashion increases to a peak and then decreases. This is Kendall's reason for defining the next type of matrix.

Definition. An abundance matrix is called a Q *matrix* if and only if each column is unimodal. An abundance matrix is called a *pre-Q matrix* if and only if there is a permutation T such that TA is a Q matrix.

We now have the problem of finding necessary and sufficient conditions for an abundance matrix A to be pre-Q, and of determining what information is necessary to construct a permutation T such that TA is a Q matrix (Kendall (1971b) has solved only the second of these two problems). Before tackling this, I want to point out some features of pre-Q matrices. Consider a particular column of a Q matrix with values $x_1, x_2, ..., x_m$. If w is a positive number then if we replace the column by $wx_1, wx_2, ..., wx_m$, the resulting matrix is pre-Q. Thus we see that the weighting of columns becomes feasible. Clearly if the resulting matrix is pre-Q, then the original matrix was pre-Q.

A much stronger statement is true in fact. If we have a column y given by $y_1, y_2, ..., y_m$, such that $x_i > x_j$ if and only if $y_i > y_j$, then replacement of column y does not alter the pre-Q character, and vice versa. In other words only the rank order of the terms in each column determines the pre-Q nature of the matrix. This is of great interest; and I will say more about it later in the section on 'Practical details'.

THE FULKERSON AND GROSS APPROACH EXTENDED

I now describe a method of translating the Q problem into the P problem, so that the methods of Fulkerson and Gross can then be applied. I will replace an abundance matrix by a $(0, 1)$ matrix which will have the same Q properties. I carry out this replacement in two steps. First, since the rank order of the terms in each column is the only relevant information, I can replace a column (say the jth one) by integers between 0 and $h-1$, where h is the number of distinct elements in the column. Secondly, I replace this single column x by $h-1$ columns, which contain only 0s and 1s. Define $y^{(k)}$ to be the column of numbers $z_1, z_2, ..., z_m$, such that

$z_i = 1$ if $x_i \not< k$

$z_i = 0$ if $x_i < k$.

I replace x by $y^{(1)}, y^{(2)}, ..., y^{(h-1)}$. It is clear that this replacement will not alter the pre-Q nature of the original matrix. If all the columns are replaced in this way, then we will have a $(0, 1)$ matrix as required. (Note that h will in general vary with j).

Although this translation has effectively answered all the questions, it is rather an elaborate method of tackling them.

GENERALIZED RESULTS

It turns out that the technique of the Hamiltonian circuit in m space goes through in the new problem with very little change. I will described only the minor alterations necessary to facilitate the statement of the generalized propositions. Let A be an abundance matrix, which has been standardized as before. I introduce the new quantities

$$m_j = \max_i a_{ij}$$

$$M = \sum_{j=1}^{n} m_j \ .$$

Proposition 10

A is pre-Q if and only if there is a Hamiltonian circuit with length $2M$ and there is a one-to-one correspondence between these minimal directed circuits and the Q-forming permutations for A.

We replace $S = AA'$ by a new binary operation introduced by Kendall (1971b) and defined by

$$(A \circ A')_{ij} = \sum_{k=1}^{n} \min (a_{ik}, a_{jk})$$

Then we have

Proposition 11

Given M and $S = A \circ A'$, we can determine whether A is pre-Q and also which are the Q-forming permutations. In fact a permutation T is a Q-forming permutation if and only if the sum of the elements of $TST' = (TA) \circ (TA)'$ lying immediately beneath the principal diagonal is equal to trace $(S) - M$.

Proposition 12 (Kendall)

If A is a Q matrix, then $A \circ A'$ is an R matrix.

Proposition 13 (Kendall)

If A is pre-Q and $A \circ A'$ is an R matrix, then A is a Q matrix.

Proposition 14

If $S = A \circ A'$ and the sum of the terms immediately beneath the principal diagonal is trace $(S) - M$, then A is a Q matrix and S is an R matrix.

Let E be defined as in proposition 9 in relation to the matrix $S = A \circ A'$. Then we have

Proposition 15

If $E > M$, then A is not pre-Q.

Proposition 16

If $A \circ A'$ is an R matrix then A is an H matrix.

CAUTIONARY NOTE

Because an R matrix is a Q matrix, it would seem reasonable to investigate the sequence of matrices obtained from A by powering up in the above fashion. Define $A \circ k$ in the following inductive way.

$$A \circ 1 = A \circ A'$$
$$A \circ (n+1) = (A \circ n) \circ (A \circ n)'$$

Kendall has noted that if A is pre-Q, then the information required to construct a Q-forming permutation is contained in $A \circ n$ for any one number n. However proposition 16 is the strongest possible converse to this. It is not true that if $A \circ (n+1)$ is a Q matrix then the same is true for $A \circ n$. Nor is it true that if $A \circ (n+1)$ is an H matrix then $A \circ n$ is an H matrix. Hence multiplying up matrices seems to have little mathematical justification as yet, except possibly when A is known to be pre-Q or almost pre-Q.

PRACTICAL DETAILS

I want to differentiate between various types of data that require seriating.

First, there is the data that is pre-Q or is extremely close to being pre-Q. Molecular biologists might hope to measure this type of information from the fine structure of genes. The best way to tackle this form of the problem is to transform the data into a $(0, 1)$ matrix by using the method outlined in the extension of the Fulkerson and Gross approach, and to use the fast computer program that I mentioned in its discussion. The ratio of E/M may prove useful as an index for judging the Q-formability of a matrix, because of proposition 15. However more practical experience of the index will be needed before its true value can be assessed.

Secondly, there is the data that is almost pre-Q. I feel that some method for finding a shortest Hamiltonian circuit is the best technique to apply. I want to mention that the general form of column replacement, preserving the rank order in each column, mentioned in the section on 'Generalization', that can be used on pre-Q matrices, is dangerous in this case, as it may accentuate the non pre-Q-ness of the data. At most I would recommend column weights to be applied. One possible weighting for the columns could be the dispersions of the values in each column. Several seriations with different weightings would give an idea of the stability of the chronologies.

Kendall has used multi-dimensional scaling, taking $S = A \circ A'$ as a similarity matrix. If the 2-dimensional map obtained from this procedure looks like a horseshoe then the order around it is taken to be the chronological order. In order to emphasize the shape of the map, points with s-values above a certain critical level are joined up by lines on the graph. My work suggests the following points.

(a) The critical level for s-values should be of the order of
$$(\mathrm{trace}(S) - M)/m.$$

(b) The whole technique may be seen as squashing the n-dimensional space down to a 2-dimensional space, preserving the order of the distances as well as possible, and then observing if there is any clear Hamiltonian arc.

(c) If there are ambiguities in the order to be taken for the map, then that which gives the shortest Hamiltonian arc on the map should be taken.

(d) $S = A \circ A'$ is undoubtedly the correct matrix of similarity to be used. Multi-dimensional scaling only uses the ordering of the terms, and when A is pre-Q the ordering of the terms of S is sufficient. Note that this is not the case with the inter-point distances of matrix D.

(e) Note that only the individual column orderings of S are really needed. I have written a small fast FORTRAN program that performs multi-dimensional scaling using only this information. It is particularly suited for on-line use on a computer.

It should be noticed that when A is not pre-Q, then the rank order of the terms of the matrix S is not in general sufficient to find a shortest Hamiltonian circuit. Indeed the ordering of the terms only permits a good seriation if the correct circuit passes between closest neighbours. However this multi-dimensional scaling technique is a useful qualitative method when the data is almost pre-Q.

Lastly, if the data does not give good results when used with either of these two methods, then a brute force method of solving the travelling salesman problem is called for. I repeat that my reason for adopting the shortest Hamiltonian circuits is that they correspond to slowly changing fashions for a society. Methods, such as finding local minima with respect to a set of elementary operations, are fast and provide helpful information. Indeed it would provide a method of checking seriations produced by MDSCAL if the initial circuit were taken from the horseshoe order.

ACKNOWLEDGMENTS

I would like to thank Professor D. G. Kendall and Mr. C. E. Thompson for many helpful discussions, and to thank the Scientific Research Council for financing my research.

REFERENCES

Fulkerson, D. R. & Gross, O. A. (1965) Incidence matrices and interval graphs. *Pacific J. Math.*, **15**, 835–55.

Kendall, D. G. (1969a) Incidence matrices, interval graphs, and seriation in archaeology. *Pacific J. Math.*, **28**, 565–70.

Kendall, D. G. (1969b) Some problems and methods in statistical archaeology. *World Archaeology*, **1**, 68–76.

Kendall, D. G. (1971a) Abundance matrices and seriation in archaeology. *Zeits. f. Wahr.* **17**, 2, 104–12.

Kendall, D. G. (1971b) A mathematical approach to seriation. *Phil. Trans. R. Soc. Lond.*, A, **269**, 125–35.

Robinson, W. S. (1951) A method for chronologically ordering archaeological deposits. *Amer. Antiquity*, **16**, 293–301.

Seriation

Discussion and comments

R. W. Hiorns. Some ten years ago I was presented with a seriation problem concerning a series of Wessex Bronze Age graves, around 90 in number, in which 21 types of grave object were represented. This data had been skilfully compiled by Professor R. J. C. Atkinson. In the light of the highly-developed seriation techniques now known, and which have been described so fully at this conference, my attempt with Professor Atkinson to make a seriation by means of mathematical techniques was no doubt premature. Professor Kendall will, I very much hope, be ready to take up my challenge to produce a better seriation with his programs than we obtained and, if so, I will present him with these data at the earliest opportunity. However, there is a distinct feature of this data which needs special consideration and which proved to be the key to my own solution to this seriation problem.

The graves are of two types, inhumation and cremation, and the prevalence of these two types overlapped in time to a considerable degree and many object types were common to both. In statistical terms, the graves of the two types may be seen to constitute samples from two distributions, one for each type, and this form of data is familiar in the context of discriminant analysis. Such an analysis provides a score for any grave, computed from coefficients for each object type which are estimated from the two samples. This score for an assemblage of unknown origin may be compared with the two mean scores for the samples, in order to classify the assemblage as an inhumation or cremation, that is, early or late. However, the individual scores for the graves in the two samples permit a relative ordering of the graves, and also, in a crude manner, a simple chronology, if at least two of the graves could be dated by other means. All this would be, in the usual sense, subject to certain technical assumptions upon which discriminant theory rests. The fact that these are seldom found to operate in other situations should reassure archaeologists that this technique has often proved useful if the significance tests and standard errors which do require the assumptions are foregone. At worst, the technique provides, in the situation I have described, an immediate seriation requiring only a matrix multiplication followed by an inversion which nowadays is almost the simplest thing a computer could be entreated to provide.

Perhaps Professor Rao would care to comment upon this kind of application in view of his very considerable experience of the multivariate techniques and, in particular, of discriminant analysis.

F. R. Hodson (later, in writing). I should like to comment on Professor Kendall's seriation of the Münsingen data. The only major difference between the HORSHU and Hodson seriations appears to be the treatment of grave 170. This grave is anomalous, containing two types: a bracelet-type otherwise found in early graves, and a fibula-type otherwise found in late. The mechanized procedure has evidently sought the best compromise, giving equal weight to each object, and has placed grave 170 relatively early. My published archaeological solution has given much greater chronological weight to the fibula because of its more detailed and delicate construction. The simple, massive type of bracelet was considered likely to have been in fashion over a greater period of time than the fibula, and also likely to have survived as an heirloom, and so grave 170 was located late in the sequence to conform with the fibula evidence. The position of grave 170 in the horizontal sequence of cemetery development also suggested a late rather than an early date.

The use of column weights in the mechanized procedure (*see* the section on 'The horse-shoe method') would help in this kind of situation.

D. G. Kendall (in reply). Tomb *T* 170 is *H* 48 (*see* my table 4), and was placed by the three computer runs given here in position *C* 22 (*see* my table 1). In the enciphered coding with which I worked originally, this was grave *G* 39. Some of the points made by Dr Hodson (with which I fully agree) are illustrated by my figure 2 (look at *H* 48—and note that it is unlinked, indicating that its position is uncertain), and by my figure 3 (look at *C* 22).

Some readers may have seen the earlier HORSHU analysis which was used in the construction of the model exhibited at the British Museum, and now permanently on exhibition in the Statistical Laboratory, Cambridge. Here the *G*-labelling is employed and it is noticeable that *G* 39 is there located by the computer at *C* 10, and in the diagram is placed halfway between the centre and the perimeter of the 'horseshoe', once again indicating uncertainty in its seriation.

At about the same time I compared 5 early horseshoe analyses, and it may be of interest to note here the five corresponding computer orders assigned to *T* 170 = *H* 48 = *G* 39; these were

$$C = 3, 44, 10, 59, 52 \quad .$$

Such divergence between the five computer orderings was very unusual. Note however that, even here, the median ordering was *C* 44, which is quite close to Hodson's *H* 48. Thus on that occasion the computer gave a good median order, but also indicated correctly the ambiguities inherent in the situation.

Dr Hodson's explanation of the anomaly is very convincing, and the whole discussion illustrates well what I think should now be the correct order of events; first an 'objective' seriation (or far better, set of seriations), followed by a return to the data and an intensive scrutiny of anomalous cases.

A relevant technical point is that the three HORSHU runs used to illustrate the present paper gave almost identical results and probably represent different convergent approaches to the same solution. It may in future be good practice to continue repeating the analysis until at least one clearly different solution is obtained, because the differences then revealed will point to latent ambiguities requiring special attention.

Alexandra Ştefan. As for the question raised by Professor D.G.Kendall about the importance of the number of the analyzed variables (letters of the alphabet), experiments I have already carried out show that the greater this number of variables is, the more precise the result becomes. As brief inscriptions are very frequent, I soon encountered the problem of determining to what extent the result of automatic seriation of inscriptions from which some letters are missing is correct. It seems preferable to omit either the very brief inscription, or the variable that is lacking in the text of one or more inscriptions of the set. The result will otherwise lean upon inexact data and will itself be incorrect, at least according to Hole and Shaw's method of basing the degree of agreement (whence the order) of the inscriptions upon the *number* of the variables they have in common. I tried an experiment upon a set of 15 inscriptions, eight of which had known dates and, although the letters Π and Ω were missing from one of these inscriptions, I had not omitted them. Consequently, the result of the automatic seriation put not only this inscription but two more in an incorrect order. On the other hand, two of the experiments (numbers 2 and 3) I described in my paper concern seriations done in the absence of some letters which I had omitted from the variables just because they were missing from some inscriptions. As they were letters with a scanty variability (namely *B, Γ* or *I, N, T*), the results were only slightly affected (*see*, however, the discussion in the paper).

On the other hand we have to take heed of both the number and the chronological importance of the dropped variables. On the set mentioned above 1 tried another experiment, omitting the letters Π and Ω from the variables, as they were missing from one inscription; as a result of this, the automatic seriation assigned an incorrect order to seven of the fifteen inscriptions of the set. Therefore, by leaving aside the letters whose chronological variability is great, the risk is run of using insufficient information and, consequently, of getting a wrong result.

At the same time, the result is affected not only by the number of letters analyzed but also by the fineness with which the varieties (=particular forms) of each letter are distinguished. The information obtained from a more rough discrimination of these varieties may prove itself insufficient and the consequences I met with in my experiments were, either, a somewhat incorrect final order, or the impossibility of discerning the best order; in this last case I got six different final orders corresponding to the same minimum 'norm', and each of them was partly wrong. Thus the chronological order was proved to be more correct when leaning upon the comparison of the varieties of all the letters of the alphabet, a comparison which only the computer is able to carry out with accuracy for a great number of inscriptions.

Evolutionary tree structures in historical and other contexts

Parish Register Studies

Population Genetics

Linguistics

Filiation of Manuscripts

Discussion and Comments

Parish Register Studies

Robert W. Hiorns
Statistical studies in migration

The genetic consequences of various migration patterns between populations have been investigated in terms of the effects of movements, for marriage purposes, on the relatedness of these populations. The particular measure of relatedness used is the proportion of the total ancestry which is common to all populations, and this may be determined from a mathematical model using a migration matrix. This method is applied to a few idealized systems to give some general results, and to a group of parishes in the Otmoor region of Oxfordshire, using data from marriage registers for the period 1600 AD to the present time. In addition to the spatial relatedness, the relatedness of the social classes has been investigated, using the occupations of the grooms, their fathers, and the brides' fathers, recorded in the marriage registers. Thus, the effects of social class change for marriage purposes and of father-to-son social mobility are studied separately and in combination. In view of the short periods required for almost complete relatedness to be achieved from a starting point of no relatedness, it is concluded that there is unlikely to exist any stratification, in the parishes or in the social classes, for genes other than those affecting behavioural traits, which are taken into account during mate selection.

INTRODUCTORY REMARKS

Migration, both by its amount and its character, is of prime importance in determining the characteristics of populations. Whether expressed in genetic terms or otherwise employing social, economic, or cultural descriptions, these characteristics are subject to changes caused by internal forces, such as selection, mutation, and drift, as well as by external migration. These internal forces are respectively attributable to the nature of the environment in which a population finds itself, the particular characteristics under consideration, and the size of the population. The study of population systems by means of a model which takes account of the internal and external forces and the interactions between them proves, not surprisingly, to be exceedingly complex.

Closed form mathematical solutions to models, in the above terms, which have meaning and value in actual systems, are unattainable; and more restricted models had to be considered as a consequence. The customary restriction is to think of systems in equilibrium where differences between populations are constant with time, being maintained by a balance between some of the forces already mentioned. A convenient and concise summary of the two most tractable examples is given for a single population in mathematical terms by Bartlett (1966, section 4.32). In this general stochastic formulation of the respective earlier work of Wright and Malécot, drift is considered, in turn, with mutation and selection. Models including migration have been developed for several systems, namely: a model for an island system (Wright 1943); a model for a spatially isotropic system with the migration rate a known function of distance, perhaps negative exponential (Malécot 1948); a nearest neighbour model for the dispersal of a gene along a linear array (Fisher 1937); a 'stepping-stone' model for an isotropic lattice system (Weiss and Kimura 1964); and models for a system whose migration rates are known in the form of a migration matrix (Bodmer and Cavalli-Sforza 1968, Smith 1969). Of these, the models of Malécot and of Weiss and Kimura were concerned with mutation and migration, the remainder with drift and migration only.

In the present paper, in contrast to all the work to which reference has so far been made, the models to be described refer to the situation in which the populations of a system are not in equilibrium. Actual populations have environments, population sizes, and migration rates, which change in the short term, before any equilibrium is reached. Having already alluded to the intrinsic difficulty in dealing with models sufficiently complex to include these temporal fluctuations, no comprehensive solutions will be expected here. Before turning to the present approach to a difficult problem, a remark may be in order concerning equilibrium treatments, fluctuating rates and environments. Because of the mathematical property of weak ergodicity for models with slowly changing components, some degree of change may be tolerable; and certain limit laws of restricted value are available.

In some situations of interest, however, it is valid to question the extent to which migration is the dominant force in a system. This extent will typically be a period of time, during which some equilibrium may be establishing itself in a system. After such a period, there is no question that population differences may be attributed to migration, or to any lack of it. In this way, the time needed to reach an equilibrium position may be defined, and this may readily be compared with historical knowledge concerning the establishment of any particular population system (Hiorns, Harrison, Boyce, and Küchemann 1969).

PHASES OF DEVELOPMENT OF POPULATION SYSTEMS

The several approaches to migration situations may be considered in relation to the phase diagram in figure 1. Four phases are shown representing four hypothetical situations in which a system of populations may exist. This is not intended to imply a consequential shift from one phase to another, or that all phases are ever experienced by any actual population system. In particular, many systems conceivably do pass through phase B and arrive in phase D without experiencing A or C. For present purposes, phase B proves particularly useful in establishing, under deterministic migration, the effective time scale involved in such a transition. In other words, there is a time limit for any population system in phase B; and after this time, if not sooner, the system must move into some other phase. Indeed, this time may be thought of as the absolute limit after which any genetic differences between populations must be ascribed to causes other than migration.

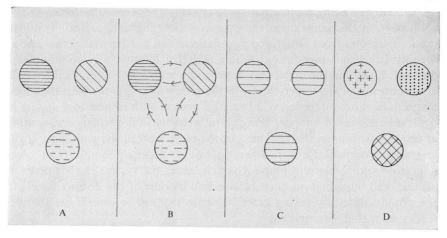

Figure 1. Phases of development for a system of populations. Four distinct phases are identified to assist reference to models. Not all phases are relevant to any actual population system and A and C may not be phases at all, only 'reference points' in time

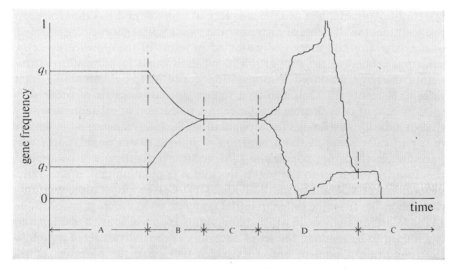

Figure 2. Gene frequencies in two populations. An artificial system with different forces acting at different times to produce the phases shown. The initial frequencies of the gene in the two populations are q_1 and q_2 respectively

The action of the various forces upon a system of populations to produce different phases is illustrated in figure 2.

The remainder of this paper will consider systems in phase B. First, however, a few remarks concerning the populations themselves and the type of migration to be envisaged are in order. It will be necessary to think of an unstructured population, that is, not partitioned in any way with respect to its genetic composition. Furthermore, the migration is non-selective in that the migrants, although fixed in number, and therefore in one sense deterministic, are random samples from the populations, and consequently have the property of being representative or typical. The term *selective migration* will apply, in this context, to the case in which migrants are not stratified random samples from structured populations. Such is inevitably the case in socially structured populations where selective migration is common and due to the fact that the upper classes are more mobile. This results in an over representation of the upper classes in the group of migrants. With the phase diagram in mind, migration will be called *neutral* with respect to a system if, by its own devices, it does not bring about a change in the genetic constitution of the populations in the system, and the term *neutralizing* will apply if the migration compensates for other forces to maintain equilibrium. Any migration taking place in phase A which leaves the system in that phase is *neutral*, and by definition must be selective in view of the distinctiveness of the populations; any taking place in phase C must be *neutral* or, if other forces are acting, *neutralizing*.

A MATHEMATICAL MODEL FOR RELATEDNESS

A migration matrix M is defined with elements m_{ij} representing the probability that a marriage settling into population i comprises one partner from j; the other partner is assumed to originate in population i. This matrix, for a system of N populations, will be a square of order N and has the stochastic property that the elements of each row sum to unity. The genetic consequences of the migration are more easily studied in terms of the *effective exchange rates* p_{ij}, defined as the proportion of all individuals in population i who, before marriage, belonged to population j. The matrix P containing these rates as elements will then also be a square stochastic matrix of order N.

A concept of considerable assistance in a discussion of relatedness will be that of ancestor frequencies for a population. Such a frequency a_{ij} is defined in a particular sense as the proportion of individuals in population i who have an ancestor from population j. More strictly, as these will be applied, the ancestry will refer to the initial stock of a population and, after several generations of migration, the individuals of a given population will have these ancestors from the different initial populations in different proportions. In the following analysis, in which all migration is non-selective and all mating is assumed to be random, the set of ancestors of the individuals of a population constitute a pool of ancestors which will serve the purposes of the analysis in exactly the same way as does a gene pool in the genetical theory of panmictic populations.

The ancestry of a population is thus denoted by a row of a matrix A with elements a_{ij} and under the above conditions, after one generation of migration and mating, the new ancestry of the system is denoted by the product PA. If I is the unit matrix and a suffix t is introduced to denote the time, in generations,

$$A_{(t)} = \tfrac{1}{2}(I+M)A_{(t-1)} = PA_{(t-1)} = P^t A_{(0)} \tag{1}$$

where $A_{(0)}$ are the initial ancestor frequencies. A convenient starting point is to assume distinct initial populations, and this implies that

$$A_{(0)} = I \tag{2}$$

and hence

$$A_{(t)} = P^t \quad . \tag{3}$$

A measure of relatedness between a pair of populations or total relatedness for a system may be defined in a number of ways. For any reasonable such definition the relatedness at any time will be a single-valued function of the time in generations n and the migration matrix P. This may be written
$$r=f(t, P)=f(P^t) \tag{4}$$
where the dependence of r upon time is through the accumulated migration over n generations; and this conforms with the vehicle of ancestral relatedness introduced above. Except in the case of trivial migration patterns, in which there is complete isolation of a population, the relatedness between populations will increase monotonically with time.

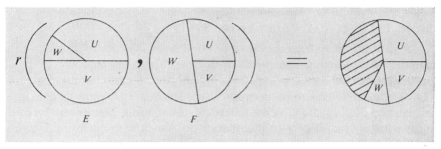

Figure 3. Relatedness diagram. Two populations E and F have ancestral proportions from U, V, and W. E has 0·4, 0·5, and 0·1 from the three respective parental populations and F has 0·3, 0·2 and 0·5. The unshaded proportion of the pie chart on the right is the relatedness between E and F, it equals 0·6

By using some specific value for relatedness, for example, r^*, it is possible to determine the time which a system would spend in phase B in order to achieve this amount of relatedness. This time, in generations, recalling the monotonicity of the relatedness function, is the solution for t of the equation
$$f(P^t)=r^* \ . \tag{5}$$
Such times may be calculated by iteratively solving equation (5) for a whole system and for every pair of populations in a system. The complexity of this calculation will depend upon the form of the function f and this in turn upon the definition of r. A suitably convenient and practically appealing definition was given by the present author (Hiorns et al. 1969), and this is illustrated here by an example, given in figure 3. At some point in time, two populations E and F have inhabitants descended from three distinct ancestral groups U, V, and W. Suppose that 40% of the ancestors of the inhabitants of E are descended from U ancestors, 50% from V and 10% from W, whereas the respective percentages for F are 30%, 20%, and 50%. A simple measure is the sum of the minimum of each pair of corresponding percentages, that is, $30+20+10=60\%$. As a proportion, 0·60 is called the ancestral relatedness between the populations E and F and has the physical interpretation that, for equal sized populations, it expresses the proportion of all ancestry which is common to both populations. In figure 3 this measure is represented in a natural way using a pie chart. This measure of relatedness may be extended to define the total relatedness of a complete system. For a pair of populations i and j, the relatedness between them is

$$r_{ij} = \sum_{s=1}^{N} \min_{s} (a_{is}, a_{js}) \tag{6}$$

where a_{is} and a_{js} are the elements in the sth column and ith and jth rows, respectively, of the matrix A, and represent at any time the respective proportions of ancestors of the present populations i and j who belonged to the initial population s.

The total relatedness r_r for a system is then

$$r_r = \sum_{s=1}^{N} \min_{s} (a_{is}) \tag{7}$$

and this may be shown to be not greater than the smallest value of relatedness between any pair of populations.

SOME THEORETICAL POPULATION SYSTEMS

Some generalized systems may now be considered in order to investigate the manner of developing relatedness with time. These systems will be based upon features of actual populations like those of the Otmoor region of Oxfordshire which are to be discussed later. The high endogamy rates in most actual populations are a consequence of these being themselves breeding units, that is, parish or city boundaries do function as enclosing barriers. Because of this high endogamy the pattern of the exogamy may not be of consequence. In one extreme such pattern, the exogamy for a given population will involve all other populations of that system to an equal degree; in another, it takes place with a single population. This latter model may be appropriate for a mainland-island system in which the mainland population serves as a centre with which all exogamy for the islands takes place. Hence, the former (symmetric) system will be known as system S, and the latter (mainland one) system M.

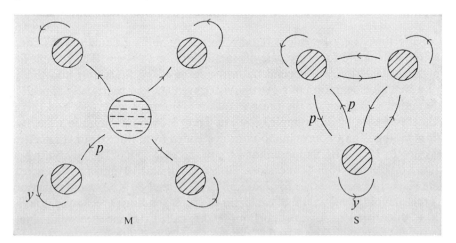

Figure 4. Two symmetric systems. In system M each island population has exogamy p with the mainland only and endogamy rate y, whereas in system S each population has endogamy rate y and exogamy rate p with each other population

By means of some analysis it transpires that although these extreme patterns produce different patterns of relatedness at any time, for systems with many populations these differences are small. This will be demonstrated by a consideration of these two symmetric systems.

Suppose, for system S, that each of N populations experiences a proportion y of endogamy and p is the effective proportion of marriage partners deriving from each of the remaining $(N-1)$ populations. This implies that $y+(N-1)p=1$. By straightforward arguments (Hiorns *et al* 1969) it may be shown that the relatedness between any pair of populations on this system at any time t (in generations) is given by

$$r_S(t) = 1 - (1 - Np)^t = 1 - \left(\frac{Ny - 1}{N - 1}\right)^t .$$

(8)

From the form of this expression, or directly, the relatedness will be seen to increase by an amount

$$\frac{N(1-y)}{(N-1)}\left(\frac{Ny-1}{N-1}\right)^{t-1}$$

in the tth generation.

For the system M, let the N populations be those of $N-1$ islands and one mainland, with the latter having a considerably larger population size than any of the islands. The particular pattern described above may then be represented by an island having endogamy rate y and effective exogamy rate $1-y=p$ with the mainland, and zero with the other islands. The mainland itself is reckoned to have effective endogamy rate unity and zero exogamy by virtue of its larger size, and this assumption results in the islands making no effective contribution to the mainland population. In this case, the relatedness between any pair of island populations concerns only their separate degrees of relatedness to the mainland and is independent of N, the number of populations. The relatedness between any pair of populations, whether both are islands or not, is

$$r_M(t) = 1 - y^t .$$

(9)

A comparison of eqs. (8) and (9) indicates that the difference between the relatedness for populations in these two extreme situations will be small if N or t is large. Suppose that N is large; and that t_S is the time at which the relatedness reaches the level $1-\alpha$ according to eq. (8), and t_M is the corresponding time according to eq. (9). Then to a first-order approximation, ignoring terms of order $1/N^2$ or less,

$$t_M = t_S\left(1 + \frac{1-y}{Ny}\right)$$

(10)

in which the second term in the bracket is less than $(1/N)$ so that t_S and t_M are identical for all practical purposes.

The symmetry of the models considered above is not their most unrealistic feature when compared with actual populations. More likely to be in question is the constancy of the endogamy rates with time. In real populations developing over several centuries, the increasing communications between them with time ensures that these rates will decrease considerably. For the particular system of parish populations in Oxfordshire to be considered later, the progression from foot or horseback as a means of travel to the bicycle or railway and later on to motor vehicles produces a large reduction in the endogamy rates in these rural parishes.

To take account of this reducing endogamy, it has been proposed (Hiorns *et al* 1969) that the rates may be presumed, as an approximation, to decrease in a simple manner with time. Furthermore, assuming only a small reduction per generation in actual endogamy rates, a first-order approximation suffices. Corresponding to the system S above, if each endogamy rate reduces by an amount c each generation,

$$r_S = 1 - \left(\frac{Ny-1}{N-1}\right)^t + \tfrac{1}{2}ct(t+1)[N/(N-1)]\left(\frac{Ny-1}{N-1}\right)^{t-1} \qquad (11)$$

and for the mainland system

$$r_M = 1 - y^t + \tfrac{1}{2}ct(t+1)y^{t-1} \qquad (12)$$

and eq. (11) approximates to eq. (12) where the number of populations is large.

The similarity between eqs. (11) and (12) indicates that the relatedness at any time between any one of a large number of populations and the remainder may be obtained using the system M above. In this case, where only the endogamy rate of one population is concerned, the time and the rate of the decrease in the endogamy rate would be required for the calculation of the relatedness.

The Application of Mathematical Models to some Oxfordshire Parishes

In this section, the models above will be applied to a system of parish populations in the Otmoor region of Oxfordshire. These parishes have been traditionally regarded as self contained, possessing a character of their own, and from the present point of view their attraction lies in the lack of major expansion or disturbance concerning their populations over some three or more centuries. The records used to provide data for the models are the marriage registers of the Anglican Churches in a group of eight adjacent parishes. From these registers it was possible to establish the places of residence of the marriage partners just prior to the marriage and, in the absence of other complete information over the period considered, these places have been taken to represent birthplaces. This information was then used for the purposes of classification of the marriages into two types, endogamous if both marriage partners resided in the same parish, and exogamous if not, that is, where just one partner comes from a place outside the parish in which the marriage is contracted. The exogamous marriages, it will be seen, more often than not involved one partner from outside the group, and the approximation to an island model will be considered. To make an analysis using such a model, an important feature of the present situation is that no means is available for estimating the effects of migrants leaving Otmoor upon the 'outside world' populations and, as in the theoretical model, an assumption will be made in view of the number of the migrants in relation to the size of these populations that these effects are negligible. The consequences of this assumption are that the outside world will be very slightly more closely related to the Otmoor populations than is stipulated in the model. However, since the determination of a maximal time to reach some level of close relatedness is of present interest, this consequence is an acceptable one.

In this investigation into the spatial relatedness of these populations, a sharp decline was noted in their endogamy caused by improvements in communications with the City of Oxford, notably the railway which began

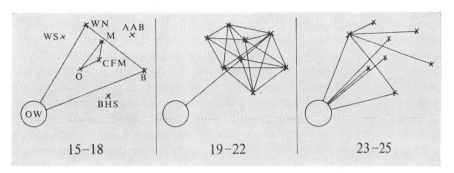

Figure 5. The pattern of developing relatedness of Otmoor parishes based upon marriage rates prior to 1850. The parishes are shown in their approximate geographical positions with the outside world (ow) being located in the position of the City of Oxford. (ws=Weston; wn=Wendlebury; o=Oddington; cfm= Charlton, Fencott and Murcott; m=Merton; aab=Ambrosden, Arncott, and Blackthorn; bhs=Beckley, Horton and Studley; b—Boarstall)

Three time periods are depicted during which the relatedness develops and the numbers represent the times (in generations) which have elapsed since an initial position of completely unrelated parishes. When a pair of populations has become related according to the criterion given in the text, a line joining the respective points appears, but, for clarity, only those new lines arising in the period are shown. The outside world may be seen, therefore, to become related to two of the parishes during the earliest period (15–18 generations) and to the remainder of the parishes in the latest period (23–25 generations).

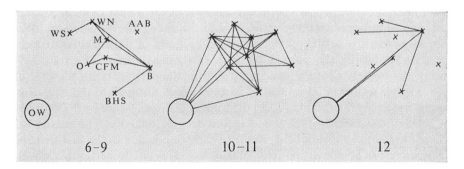

Figure 6. The pattern of developing relatedness of Otmoor parishes based upon marriage rates in the period 1851–1966

As in figure 5 three time periods are depicted during which the relatedness develops and the lines show the pairs of populations which become related during each period.

to operate in 1851. For this reason, it was decided to divide the data upon marriage movement into two periods on either side of that date. The effects of movement pre-1851 and from 1851 to 1966 were then studied in terms of ancestral relationship between the parishes and between them and the outside world. In the early period the rates of exchange were such as to produce ancestral homogeneity, in the sense indicated using 95 % as a critical value for the ancestral relatedness, in twenty-five generations as opposed to merely twelve generations for the late period.

The detailed pattern of developing relationship within the system for the two time periods is shown in figures 5 and 6. In each diagram, the period of developing ancestral relatedness is divided into three parts with the new links formed in each part being shown in three separate diagrams. This enables a distinction to be made between the two time periods, the later period depicted in figure 6 having the more rapid convergence, and also to indicate that the spatial patterns of this convergence are different. Whereas, in the early period, as shown in figure 5, two parishes become related to the outside world before any great amount of relatedness develops between the parishes themselves, it appears that this is not the case in the rapid development in the late period. The higher endogamy rate of one parish (AAB) in the late period has the expected effect of partly isolating that parish until all others are highly related.

As has already been noted, the assumption that the size of the outside world is considerably greater than that of each parish population at once implies that the migration from Otmoor to it does not affect the ancestral composition of the outside world, but the reverse effect is present. For this reason, the homogeneity within Otmoor is only brought about when all parish populations resemble the outside world. Since most of the exogamy for each population is with the outside world, the model for system M discussed earlier may be applied to give an approximate time for this to happen. If the outside world is regarded as an infinite system of populations each identical to one Otmoor parish, then system S is appropriate, giving in this case the same results as system M. In order to consider the total relatedness of an idealized system for comparison with the actual Otmoor system, the most appropriate value for the level of the endogamy would seem to be the largest in the actual system since the progress of ancestral relatedness will be limited by the population with smallest exogamy. From eq. (9), using the highest effective endogamy rate in the early period (Weston, of 0·875) gives a time of 23 instead of 25 generations using all of the migration rates, and in the late period (AAB) the highest endogamy rate ($=0·750$) gives 9 generations instead of 12 found in the detailed analysis. The reason for these approximate values being lower in each case is due to the fact that the exogamy is not all directly with the outside world, as is assumed in this model. This leads in the real system to a delay caused by ancestors being 'passed around' between other populations before reaching their destination. The approximation to the order of magnitude of the time required for ancestral homogeneity in each period is satisfactory, however, with regard to the extreme simplicity of this model.

As a further application of the model, the social class relatedness of the Oxfordshire parishes has been considered (Harrison, Hiorns, and Küchemann 1970). The marriage registers used for the analysis described above also contained, from 1837 onwards, data on the occupations of the groom, his father, and the father of the bride. In an approximate manner, using a Registrar General's key, social classes were determined from these occupations. Treating the five social classes as five breeding units of the Otmoor population, ignoring for this purpose spatial differences, two types of migration between the classes could be examined. First, the mobility of a son in relation to his father, this being formally known as 'social mobility', and secondly the change of class of a bride as a consequence of her marriage to a groom not belonging to her father's class, or 'migration for marriage purposes'.

When the social mobility alone is considered, the five social classes become related according to the above criterion after twenty generations, but after only five generations classes I and II are not distinct, neither are classes III and IV. Migration for marriage purposes produces by itself homogeneity of the classes in twenty-four generations, with a similar effect of clustering of I with II and III with IV after twelve generations. Combining the two kinds of movement additively to produce a maximal time for the homogeneity, assuming that the two patterns of migration are not negatively correlated, indicates that this time would be ten generations with a similar early clustering after five generations.

In principle an analysis of such data could be extended to take account of spatial and social class migration simultaneously. This requires the consideration of a number of smaller, spatially isolated, populations each of which represents one social class of a parish. There are certain methodological difficulties, in particular those arising from the definition of the social classes from occupations and the smallness of some of these new population units. However, a great deal is known concerning the social class composition of the parishes and of the 'outside world' populations which supplied marriage partners for Otmoor (Harrison, Hiorns, and Küchemann 1971). Furthermore, the presence of selective migration in this system, evident though it is, does not profoundly affect the developing relatedness with time as compared with an equivalent non-selective system (Hiorns 1970).

The applications of the models above indicate the high degree of relatedness between the Oxfordshire parishes and between the social classes within them which would have been achieved by the present time. It follows that no genetic stratification would be expected in the parishes or classes except for those genes affecting traits relevant to the choice of marriage partners. The consequences of assortative mating for such genes and the selective migration referred to above would, however, produce considerable heterogeneity.

REFERENCES

Bartlett, M.S. (1966) *An Introduction to Stochastic Processes* (2nd edn). Cambridge: Cambridge University Press.

Bodmer, W.F. & Cavalli-Sforza, L.L. (1968) A migration matrix model for the study of random genetic drift. *Genetics*, **59**, 565–92.

Fisher, R. A. (1937) The wave of advantageous genes. *Annals of Eugenics*, **7**, 355–75.

Harrison, G. A., Hiorns, R. W. & Küchemann, C. F. (1970) Social class relatedness in some Oxfordshire parishes. *J. Biosoc. Sci.*, **2**, 71–80.

Harrison, G. A., Hiorns, R. W. & Küchemann, C. F. (1971) Social class and marriage patterns in some Oxfordshire populations. *J. Biosoc. Sci.*, **3**, 1–15.

Hiorns, R. W., Harrison, G. A., Boyce, A. J. & Küchemann, C. F. (1969) A mathematical analysis of the effects of movement on the relatedness between populations. *Ann. Hum. Genetics*, **32**, 237–50.

Hiorns, R. W. (1970) Selective migration and relatedness in structured populations. Unpublished paper read at the Third Annual Mathematics in Population Conference, Chicago, 1970.

Malécot, G. (1948) *Les mathématiques de l'hérédité*. Paris: Masson.

Malécot, G. (1966) Identical loci and relationship. *Proceedings of the Vth Berkeley Symposium on Mathematical Statistics and Probability*, Vol. 4, pp. 317–32 (eds Le Cam, L. & Neyman, J.). Berkeley: University of California Press.

Smith, C. A. B. (1969) Local fluctuations in gene frequencies. *Ann. Hum. Genetics*, **32**, 251–60.

Weiss, G. H. & Kimura, M. (1965) A mathematical analysis of the stepping-stone model of genetic correlation. *J. Appl. Probab.*, **2**, 129–49.

Wright, S. (1943) Isolation by distance. *Genetics*, **28**, 114–38.

Parish Register Studies

David G. Kendall
Maps from marriages: an application of non-metric
multi-dimensional scaling to parish register data

1. For a thorough understanding of this paper, some familiarity with the
algorithm known as MDSCAL (multi-dimensional scaling) is essential, and
may be obtained by referring to the definitive papers by J. B. Kruskal (1964)
(following earlier work by R. Shepard), or to one of Kruskal's own papers
in this volume (Kruskal 1971). But I have tried to write in such a way that
the greater part of the present paper will be comprehensible to those without
prior knowledge of the mode of operation of MDSCAL. I begin, therefore,
with a very brief sketch of what MDSCAL does.

Suppose we have a group of N objects, which in the present context will be
ecclesiastical parishes, or smaller domiciliary units (villages, townships,
and so on). Suppose further that we have available some, perhaps quite
crude, measure of 'similarity' or 'proximity'; that is, associated with each
pair of parishes (P_i, P_j) we have a non-negative number S_{ij} which will be
the larger, the more 'similar' P_i and P_j are. Here 'similarity' is deliberately
being left as an undefined concept. All that is essential is that, by and large,
'similar' parishes will be expected to be readily inter-accessible, and 'dissimilar' parishes will be expected to be mutually remote or separated from
one another by substantial barriers (mountain ranges, unbridged rivers, or
other such obstacles). The actual numerical values of the numbers S_{ij} will
be unimportant, because we shall be concerned only with the relationship of
order between them. Thus it will make no difference whatsoever if we replace
S_{ij} by $\alpha S_{ij} + \beta$ (provided that $\alpha > 0$), or by $\sqrt{S_{ij}}$, or by S_{ij}^2, and so on.

We now take *any* set of N points in the plane (they may be chosen in some
special way, or may be chosen by a randomizing device). If we then make use
of the algorithm MDSCAL, these points will be progressively moved about in
the plane in such a way that eventually they take up a configuration in which,
so far as possible, the *distances* D_{ij} in this 'map' have an order-structure
inverse to that of the *similarities* S_{ij}. That is, for as many tetrads (i, j, k, l)
as possible we shall have

$$D_{ij} \geq D_{kl}$$
whenever
$$S_{ij} < (\leq) S_{kl} \quad .$$

It is characteristic of the algorithm (especially when N is small) that with
different initial starting positions it may settle down to different locally
stable terminal positions. However, with each of these there is associated a
number called the *stress*, σ, which will be zero when and only when the
ordering requirements stated above are exactly satisfied; otherwise it will be
positive, and it will be larger for Map A than for Map B if the desired

inequality-implications are broken more severely in Map A than in Map B. Another useful criterion of 'success' is provided by the *final number of blocks*, β. The algorithm initially lumps together pairs (P_i, P_j) with comparable 'similarities', and then systematically refines this rather coarse partitioning of the data. The extent to which such refinement is possible is measured by the size of the final number β of blocks into which the pairs are lumped. So, for a good solution, one would like σ to be small and β to be large.

Because the algorithm is an iterative one it is necessary to instruct the computer to carry out a specified number of iterations; 50 is a very usual number, and 100 may sometimes be preferred. The machine prints out the final configuration, and also draws it on transparent paper. It also prints out the values of σ and β, and much other diagnostic data, some of which is valuable in indicating whether a local optimum has been reached, or whether, alternatively, the stress was still in the process of being reduced when the algorithm was stopped (stopped because the required number of iterations had been completed). In the remainder of this paper we shall attach an asterisk (*) to the stress value whenever we wish to indicate that equilibrium appears *not* to have been reached.

As an example of the construction of maps from similarities we reproduce [from Kendall (1970)] figure 1, which shows a map of Romania constructed from similarities arrived at as follows. We put

$$S_{ij} = K - \delta_{ij},$$

where δ_{ij} is the distance in kilometres between two towns P_i and P_j by the recommended road-route, and K is a sufficiently large constant chosen so as to make all the S-values positive. Notice that in Romania, because of the magnificent wall presented by the mountainous boundaries of Transylvania, the recommended road-route is by no means necessarily that along which 'crows would fly'. In supplying these numbers S_{ij} to the computer we in effect merely tell the computer the following facts:

the quickest journey is that from Constanţa to Mamaia;

the next quickest journey is that from Braşov to Predeal;

. . . .

. . . .

the longest journey is that from Baia Mare to Mangalia.

With this knowledge alone, the computer produced a map shown in figure 1 in about one and a half minutes. It is a remarkably good map of Romania, and would enable one to find one's way about with only very slight and local confusion.

Perhaps it is needless to mention the following points, but we record them for completeness:

(1) the scale of the computed map is a standardized one and has no geographical significance;

(2) the orientation of the computed map is random, but, before printing, it has been roughly adjusted so that the northerly towns appear at the top of the figure;

(3) the computer may or may not (with probabilities equal to one half) produce a 'reflected' map, and if this happens then one has merely to turn the

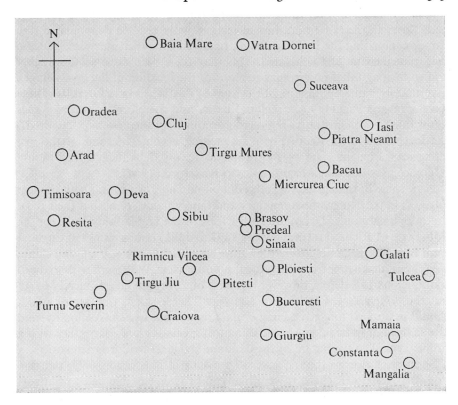

Figure 1. A MDSCAL map of Romania

(transparent) plotter-paper over and read through the back of it—this will then bring the westerly towns to the left in accordance with the customary geographical convention;

(4) the computer could, but does not, write the names of the towns on the map. These are added later by hand. This can easily be done because the computer also prints out the cartesian co-ordinates ('latitude' and 'longitude') which it assigns to the towns, and so these can be identified on the computer-drawn map and labelled, with the names reading from west to east as usual. Alternatively one can arrange for an approximate (because quantized) *printer*-map to be printed out by the computer, in addition to and on approximately the same scale as the accurate *plotter*-map. In the printer-map the rough locations of the towns will be shown by letters indicating also their identity. These 'names' can then quickly be traced on to the accurate plotter-map. (I am indebted to my friend John Lambert for this idea.)

2. The background information about MDSCAL given in the preceding section, and the experience gained by contemplating the problem of drawing the map of Romania shown in figure 1, should have given the reader enough knowledge of the techniques being used here to follow the new application which we wish to propose. We now proceed to introduce this.

It is a familiar fact to students of English history that many villages have been 'lost', in the sense that they have eventually become depopulated, the stones comprising the buildings being removed for other purposes, and the land ploughed up and cultivated. This may have been done so thoroughly and so long ago that no memory remains of the location of the 'lost village', save that its name appears in (for example) mediaeval taxation rolls. These were arranged roughly on a regional basis, and therefore one usually *does* know in what administrative region (for example, 'wapentake', or 'hundred') the lost village once stood. For a fascinating account of some of the lost villages of England, and of the problems involved in their identification, reference may be made, for example, to Beresford (1954).

Now some of the mediaeval rolls contain much information about the lost villages; in particular, the forenames and family names of all but their most destitute inhabitants. To be sure, at the time of the Lay Subsidy Rolls for the Poll Taxes of Richard II (in the years 1377 to 1381) family names in England were only just beginning to harden into heritable characters, and later data would be much better from the present point of view. We do not wish to dwell too much on this defect, however, because our purpose here is merely to set out the *principle* of a method of analysis. The decision, whether or not it should be applied to a given body of data, is one not to be taken lightly, and also is one not to be taken on mathematical grounds alone, but rather with a proper regard to the nature of the data and its general appropriateness.

Suppose, however, for the sake of a colourful illustration only, that the Poll Tax Rolls of Richard II were likely to provide suitable data; what sort of similarity measure could we construct? It would be very tempting to try to do this by evolving a measure of similarity between the stock of fore- and family- names in each pair of two villages P_i and P_j. One could then construct a MDSCAL map and, if the *surviving* villages and their spatial interrelationships could be seen to be more or less faithfully portrayed in the computed map, then the position assigned to a *lost* village in the computed map might be thought to constitute useful evidence concerning its actual geographical location. It is hardly to be supposed that the computer would come up with the command, 'dig at point Q and you will find the foundations of the village'. But it might, conceivably, enable one to decide between two sites to which the search had previously been narrowed on other grounds.

I must confess that I have grave doubts about the feasibility of such a program in England, but the principle seems one worthy of record, and there may well be analogous situations in other parts of the world in which the method could actually be used.

Notice that if an initial analysis yielded the degree of success outlined above, one would, of course, then proceed to a rather different kind of analysis. In this the surviving villages would be constrained to lie at their known positions, and only the positions of the lost villages would be left to the 'decision' of the computer. The first stage described above is however an essential one; we could have no confidence in the adequacy of a similarity measure for map reconstruction, unless it were first shown to be capable of reconstructing the known and indisputable positions of the surviving villages.

3. Some suitable data for a general check on the feasibility of the method are to be found in a recent paper by Hiorns, Harrison, Boyce, and Küchemann (1969); *see also* the contribution by Hiorns in this volume (Hiorns 1971). These authors studied 8 somewhat isolated Oxfordshire parishes which lie together near the formerly marshy region known as Otmoor; for a map [reproduced from Hiorns *et al.* (1969)] *see* figure 2. It will be noticed that these (ecclesiastical) parishes sometimes contain three townships, so that it is not quite sensible to speak of the parish as if it were located at a point.

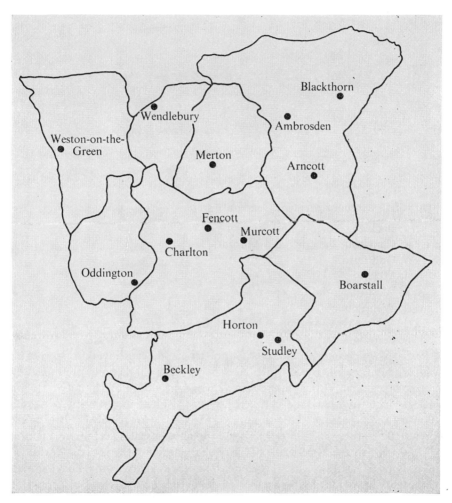

Figure 2. The Otmoor parishes

However, when we have to do this, we shall take the centroid of the triangle formed by three townships, as representing the centre of the parish. We thus arrive at the reduced map shown in figure 3; here parishes have been identified by the following code:

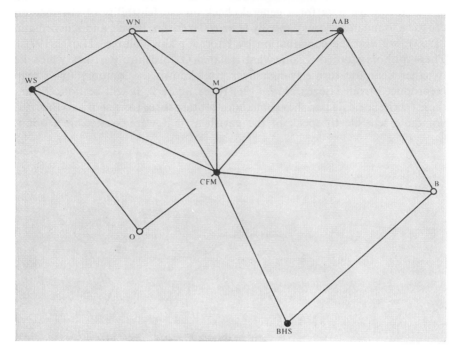

Figure 3. The Otmoor parishes. Contiguity graph

   BHS: Beckley, Horton, and Studley
   CFM: Charlton, Fencott, and Murcott
     O: Oddington
     M: Merton
   WS: Weston-on-the-Green
   WN: Wendlebury
  AAB: Ambrosden, Arncott, and Blackthorn
    B: Boarstall

Parishes which enjoy a common boundary have been linked in figure 3 by solid segments, while those which meet merely at a single point are linked by a broken segment. Other things being equal, one would expect more mixing and so more intermarriage between persons resident in parishes so linked, than between persons from unlinked parishes. Conversely, if we could construct a standardized intermarriage rate between parishes for some period of time prior to the large-scale mobility characterizing the present world, we might hope to be able to use it as a measure of similarity from which the map of the parishes could be reconstructed. We shall now attempt to carry this program out in detail, as a test of our general method.

4. From Hiorns *et al.* (1969) we know the numbers of marriages within and between the 8 parishes (and also the numbers of marriages between a member of one of the 8 parishes and the 'outside world', OW) for the whole of the (unequal) periods prior to 1850 covered by the surviving parish registers. The legal compulsion to register marriages started in England in 1538, but

unfortunately the rule was not universally observed until much later. Even when the rule was observed, the early registers may not be available because of loss, and while in the case of lost registers the gap can often be made good by referring to the Bishop's transcripts (copies of the registers held at the archdiaconal or episcopal level) the earliest date from which marriage records in some form exist varies considerably from one parish to another. A further difficulty, familiar to genealogists, is the paucity or even total absence of records during the Commonwealth (the period from the execution of Charles I in 1649 to the restoration of Charles II in 1660). It follows that any process of 'standardization' we adopt *must* take into account the fact that the records cover periods of time of differing lengths in various parishes.

Some sort of mathematical model for the intermarriage process seems essential before a standardization procedure can be constructed. There is no point in trying to be very sophisticated about this, and we therefore put forward and shall use the simplest such model that could possibly be devised, without of course any wish to imply that it should be used uncritically in other contexts.

Let M_{ij} be the number of marriages registered in parish P_i between persons resident in the distinct parishes P_i and P_j. Let M_{ii} be the number of marriages registered in parish P_i between two persons who were both resident in the parish. Let M_i be the total number of all marriages registered in parish P_i. Let N_i be the size (average population size during the period) of parish P_i, and let T_i be the effective length of the period covered by the registers surviving in parish P_i.

We shall suppose that the marriage is governed statistically by the following very crude formulae:

$$M_i = r_i N_i T_i, \tag{1}$$
$$M_{ij} = \rho_{ij} N_i N_j T_i \qquad (i \neq j), \tag{2}$$
$$M_{ii} = \rho_i N_i^2 T_i . \tag{3}$$

Here r_i, ρ_i, and ρ_{ij} are marriage rates corrected both for population size and length of period of record. There is of course a latent assumption of temporal homogeneity here which is quite unrealistic, but possibly just acceptable for the present purpose, at any rate for the period (roughly 1600 to 1850) with which we are dealing.

Now the Ms [given in table 1, reproduced from Hiorns *et al.* (1969)] are the observed variables. The Ns are not observable, and it would be unwise to treat the Ts as observable because of the uncertainty of non-registration during the Commonwealth (for example). We must therefore eliminate the unknowns N_i and T_i in forming standardized intermarriage indices out of the Ms. There is only one way to do this, and that is to compute the ratios,

$$L_{ij} = \frac{M_{ij} M_j}{M_i M_{jj}} = \frac{\rho_{ij} r_j}{\rho_j r_i} . \tag{4}$$

There are now two possibilities. First, we may suppose that r_i and ρ_i do not depend on the parish P_i; in that case L_{ij} can be accepted as a standardized index of inter-marriage from parish P_j to parish P_i (marriage registered in the latter). It is convenient to use an index depending symmetrically on i and

P_i \ P_j	BHS	CFM	O	M	WS	WN	AAB	B	OW	Total, M_i
BHS	303	10	—	—	—	—	4	6	104	427
CFM	6	297	8	8	1	3	10	3	109	445
O	3	20	132	1	3	2	1	—	54	216
M	—	12	1	82	3	2	7	—	32	139
WS	—	2	1	2	260	2	4	—	78	349
WN	—	6	2	4	3	98	5	—	89	207
AAB	3	5	4	5	—	4	432	3	168	624
B	3	—	—	1	2	—	4	115	65	190

Table 1. Numbers of marriages registered in parish P_i where one of the persons married was resident in a different parish P_j (or in the 'outside world', OW). The number of marriages in which both persons were resident in parish P_i is shown on the main diagonal of the table. The number to the extreme right of the ith row gives the total number M_i of marriages registered in P_i. [Data for the period up to the year 1850. Source: Hiorns *et al.* (1969)]

----

j, and so we could define the 'intermarital' similarity of P_i and P_j to be

$$S_{ij}^{(1)} = L_{ij} + L_{ji} \quad . \tag{5}$$

An alternative possibility is to take the geometric mean of L_{ij} and L_{ji}, so obtaining

$$S_{ij}^{(2)} = \sqrt{(L_{ij}L_{ji})} = \sqrt{\left(\frac{\rho_{ij}\rho_{ji}}{\rho_j \rho_i}\right)} \tag{6}$$

as a second index of 'intermarital' similarity.

To begin with I worked with $S^{(1)}$, principally because many more of the values of $S^{(2)}$ were equal to zero. At a later stage it was thought preferable to work with $S^{(2)}$. This second index has one very attractive feature; it does not require the rather dubious assumption of the equality of the r_is. This is of importance because the value of M_i (and also of r_i) must be influenced by the $P_i \times$ OW marriages, and the number of these must in turn be influenced by the distance from the city of Oxford (which lies immediately to the south-west of Otmoor). We shall therefore present analyses based on each index in turn.

In table 2 the pairs P_i/P_j (first column) are arranged in order of increasing 'similarity' in the sense of the measure $S^{(1)}$ (second column); the third column contains the corresponding value of $S^{(2)}$. It is interesting to examine this table in relation to figure 3. An asterisk (*) before the names of the parishes indicates that they do *not* come into geographical contact at any point. The concentration of the asterisks towards the top of the table is very marked, and shows clearly that $S^{(1)}$ does contain some topographical information. It will also be seen that $S^{(2)}$ is very nearly, but not quite, a monotonic function of $S^{(1)}$, so that it too contains topographical information.

Parishes	Value of $S^{(1)}$	Value of $S^{(2)}$
* BHS/M	0·000	0·000
* BHS/WS	0·000	0·000
* BHS/WN	0·000	0·000
* O/B	0·000	0·000
* WN/B	0·000	0·000
* M/B	0·009	0·000
CFM/B	0·011	0·000
CFM/WS	0·012	0·005
* WS/B	0·014	0·000
* WS/AAB	0·017	0·000
* O/AAB	0·017	0·008
* BHS/O	0·020	0·000
* O/M	0·020	0·010
* BHS/AAB	0·020	0·010
O/WS	0·023	0·009
WS/WN	0·032	0·015
* O/WN	0·035	0·018
AAB/B	0·038	0·016
* M/WS	0·039	0·017
CFM/AAB	0·044	0·020
BHS/B	0·045	0·023
WN/AAB	0·048	0·022
BHS/CFM	0·054	0·026
CFM/WN	0·058	0·025
M/WN	0·063	0·032
M/AAB	0·086	0·031
CFM/M	0·160	0·063
CFM/O	0·168	0·064

Table 2. Parish-to-parish contact, and the similarity measures based on intermarriage rates. (The asterisk indicates that the two parishes have no geographical contact.)

5. We shall now report the results of a MDSCAL map-construction analysis using the *first* measure of similarity, $S^{(1)}$.

The numerical details are set out in table 3 and require some preliminary explanation. Ideally, as was first pointed out to me by Mr A. D. McLaren, a MDSCAL analysis should be carried out in a *minimum* of $k+1$ dimensions, when a k-dimensional structure is being looked for. This means that an initial 3-dimensional analysis is appropriate in the present case. If the 3-dimensional 'map' turns out to be reasonably 'flat', more precisely, if the smallest eigenvalue of the covariance matrix of the 3-dimensional array of points is sufficiently less than the other two eigenvalues, then orthogonal projection parallel to the corresponding eigenvector will yield a two-dimensional configuration which can be taken to be the starting point of the final 2-dimensional MDSCAL analysis.

A program package was therefore constructed, consisting of the following components in the order shown:

(1) construction of a random 3-dimensional configuration;

(2) a MDSCAL analysis (50 or 100 iterations) transforming this into a low-stress 3-dimensional configuration;

(3) a principal components analysis of the 3-dimensional configuration with which stage (2) terminated, and the identification of the eigenvector with least eigenvalue;

(4) projection of the final 3-dimensional configuration parallel to this eigenvector onto the plane containing the two principal components, so yielding an initial 2-dimensional configuration;

(5) a MDSCAL analysis (50 iterations) starting with this 2-dimensional configuration and yielding a low-stress 2-dimensional configuration;

(6) automatic drawing of the latter.

At an earlier stage of the investigation the above (strictly the only proper) procedure was not followed, and instead of this a series of 100-iteration MDSCAL analyses were run directly in 2 dimensions, using a series of random initial 2-dimensional configurations. The first (top) section of table 3 refers to this work. The first column gives the number of iterations, the second gives the five digits of the random number used to initiate the randomizing mechanism, the third (and fifth) column is irrelevant, while the fourth column gives the final stress σ and the final number of blocks β, and an asterisk attached to the stress value indicates that equilibrium had not been reached after the stated number of iterations.

The second (middle) section of table 3 refers to a pilot version of the 3-first-then-2 analysis. Here the third column lists σ and β for the preliminary 3-dimensional analysis, but the later columns present 2-dimensional solutions obtained *not* by a principal components analysis, but instead solutions ob-

Iterations	Randomizer	$\sigma : \beta$ (3D)	$\sigma : \beta$ (2D)	Eigenvalues
100	55048	...	0·1490 : 5	...
100	49230	...	0·1929 : 4	...
100	64901	...	0·1727 : 4	...
100	72964	...	0·1574 : 3	...
100	10983	...	0·1977 : 2	...
100	94895	...	0·1179 : 9	...
100	56194	...	0·2843* : 2	...
100	68551	0·0455 : 7	0·1179 : 9	...
			0·1490 : 5	...
			0·1179 : 9	...
100	68551	0·0455 : 7	0·1179 : 9	11, 7·1, 4·8
50	48938	0·1705* : 2	0·2715 : 3	8·5, 7·5, 7·0
50	57896	0·0430* : 7	0·1179 : 9	11, 7·2, 4·9
50	97293	0·1081* : 4	0·1179* : 9	13, 6·3, 3·5

Table 3. Analyses using the first similarity measure, $S^{(1)}$

tained by projecting the 3-dimensional solution onto each one of the three coordinate planes in turn, and taking the 2-dimensional configuration so obtained to initiate MDSCAL in 2 dimensions.

The third (bottom) section of table 3 gives the results of using the program package listed above; note that for the first run the values of the randomizing digits are the same as those for the pilot run in the middle section of the table. There is now a further column at the extreme right; this lists the approximate magnitudes of the three eigenvalues found in stage 3. These have been listed because a clear gap between the smallest eigenvalue and the other two is desirable, and some of the analyses are much better than the others in this respect.

Examination of table 3 shows that one (the smallest) value of the final stress, 0·1179, occurs again and again, and that it is always associated with the largest recorded final number of blocks, 9. The next smallest final stress, 0·1490, occurs twice, and is associated with the next largest final number of blocks, 5. All other stress values occur once only, and are larger than these two, and are associated with a smaller final number of blocks. It is a useful feature of such analyses that (*with given similarity data*) equal final stress values usually correspond to identical final configurations (up to a random rotation and reflection), and this rule of thumb turns out not to be broken here. Thus it will suffice to present just the two configurations associated respectively with $\sigma = 0·1179$, $\beta = 9$, and with $\sigma = 0·1490$, $\beta = 5$. It seems likely that the first of these gives a global minimum to the stress, but of course one cannot be certain of that. The other (at most a local) minimum is worth examining also, because it is the next best on both counts (that is, in respect both of the values of σ and β) and because it has occurred twice. These two configurations are shown in figure 4.

On comparing figure 4 with figure 3 it will be seen that the 'second best' computer configuration ($\sigma = 0·1490$, $\beta = 5$) compares very well with the actual geographical configuration, while the 'best' computer configuration ($\sigma = 0·1179$, $\beta = 9$) differs from it chiefly in the placing of the single parish w s. To assist the comparison we have drawn again on figure 4 the 'contiguity links' shown in figure 3.

6. Let us turn now to the second measure of similarity, $S^{(2)}$. From table 2 it will be seen that there is now a substantial number of tied similarities (10 are now equal to zero, whereas previously only 5 were equal to zero). Those familiar with the details of the MDSCAL algorithm will recall that there are two possible treatments of ties (object-pairs having identical similarities). What Kruskal calls the 'secondary treatment of ties' (which is what we have used so far) requires pairs having equal similarities to be given, so far as possible, equal distances in the map. The 'primary treatment of ties', however, imposes no such strict requirement, and this is a good reason for preferring it. We may expect the difference between the two treatments to show up most sharply when $S^{(2)}$ is used, and accordingly we have here carried out sixteen analyses, using four different values of the randomizer, each randomizer-value being used once with the primary and once with the secondary treatment of ties, at each dimension level. The results are shown in table 4.

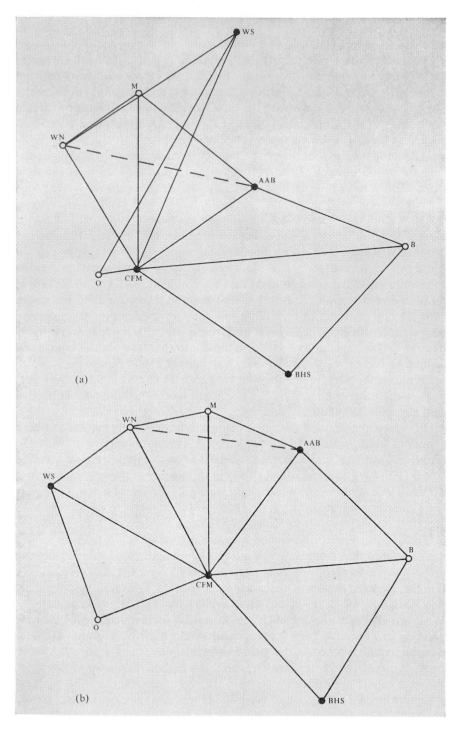

Figure 4. Computer maps of Otmoor: (a) $S^{(1)}$, $\sigma=0\cdot1179$; (b), $S^{(1)}$, $\sigma=0\cdot1490$

Iterations	Randomizer	$T : \sigma : \beta$ (3D)	$T : \sigma : \beta$ (2D)	Eigenvalues
50/50	68551	P 0·0218* : 15	P 0·0449 : 12	14, 5·4, 4·0
50/50	44450	P 0·0000 : 28	P 0·0449 : 11	17, 4·6, 1·5
50/50	65661	P 0·0349* : 10	P 0·0711 : 11	16, 4·2, 3·2
50/50	71310	P 0·0020* : 14	P 0·0451* : 12	14, 4·8, 4·4
50/50	68551	S 0·0674* : 6	P 0·0362* : 16	12, 5·9, 5·0
50/50	44450	S 0·0790 : 5	P 0·0449* : 12	11, 6·1, 5·7
50/50	65661	S 0·0994 : 4	P 0·0348* : 13	13, 6·1, 4·2
50/50	71310	S 0·0790* : 5	P 0·0449* : 12	11, 6·1, 5·7
50/50	68551	S 0·0674* : 6	S 0·1291 : 5	12, 5·9, 5·0
50/50	44450	S 0·0790 : 5	S 0·1291 : 5	11, 6·1, 5·7
50/50	65661	S 0·0994 : 4	S 0·1531* : 4	13, 6·1, 4·2
50/50	71310	S 0·0790* : 5	S 0·1291 : 5	11, 6·1, 5·7
50/50	68551	P 0·0218* : 15	S 0·1291 : 5	14, 5·4, 4·0
50/50	44450	P 0·0000 : 28	S 0·1291 : 5	17, 4·6, 1·5
50/50	65661	P 0·0349* : 10	S 0·1564 : 4	16, 4·2, 3·2
50/50	71310	P 0·0020* : 14	S 0·1291* : 5	14, 4·8, 4·4

Table 4. Analyses using the second similarity measure, $S^{(2)}$; (the columns headed T show the treatment of ties—P for primary, S for secondary)

Notice that stress values with the 'primary' treatment in two dimensions should be compared only among themselves (and so not with those in the analyses summarized in table 3); stress values with the secondary treatment in two dimensions, however, can be compared with those occurring in table 3.

To facilitate the latter comparison, we have used in the $S^{(2)}$-analyses one value of the randomizer (68551) also used in the $S^{(1)}$-analyses.

If we first examine the eight analyses in which the *secondary* treatment of ties was used at the 2-dimensional stage, it will be seen that a configuration with $\sigma = 0·1291$, $\beta = 5$, was obtained six times (these values of σ and β being optimal within this set of experiments). The next smallest value of σ in this group was $\sigma = 0·1531$ (with $\beta = 4$). These two configurations are shown in figure 5. In each case the map compares very well with the true map (figure 3) apart from the location of the parish ws.

If we turn to the eight analyses in which the *primary* treatment of ties was used at the 2-dimensional stage, we find that the best solution is one with $\sigma = 0·0348$, $\beta = 13$ (another solution with $\sigma = 0·0362$, $\beta = 16$ giving essentially the same configuration), while the next best solution ($\sigma = 0·0449$, $\beta = 11$ or 12) was obtained on five occasions. Here the two configurations are shown in figure 6. The configuration $\sigma = 0·0449$ is once again quite good apart from the customary anomalous behaviour of the parish ws, while the configuration $\sigma = 0·0348$ is almost identical with the true configuration (figure 3). In particular the parish M now lies inside the triangle CFM–AAB–WN, as it should do, instead of outside that triangle as was the case in the $S^{(1)}$-configuration with $\sigma = 0·1490$.

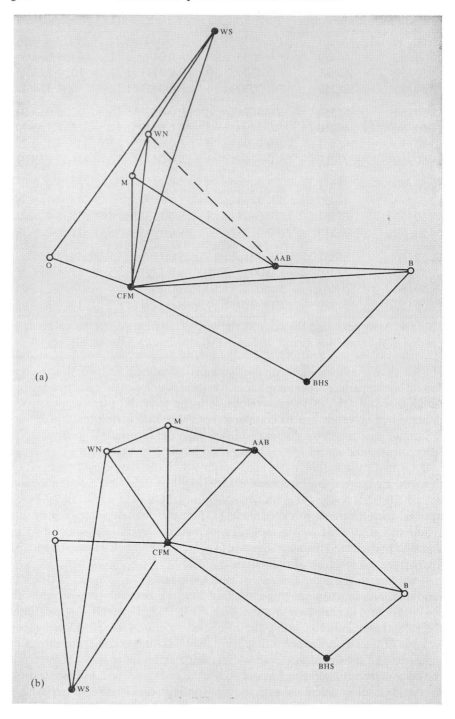

Figure 5. Computer maps of Otmoor: (a) $S^{(2)}$, $\sigma = 0.1291$, S_3S_2; (b) $S^{(2)}$, $\sigma = 0.1531^*$, S_3S_2

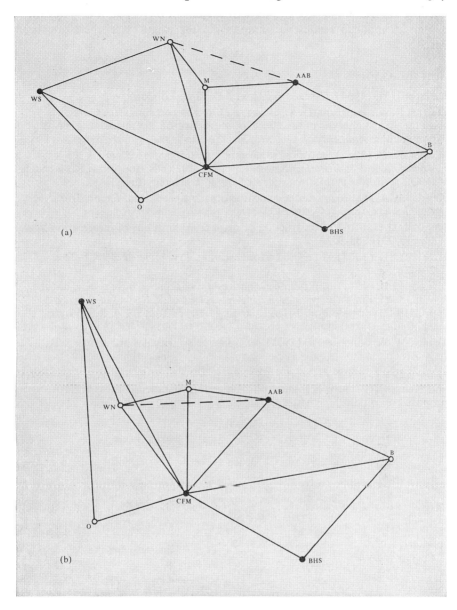

Figure 6. Computer maps of Otmoor: (a) $S^{(2)}$, $\sigma=0\cdot0348^*$, S_3P_2; (b) $S^{(2)}$, $\sigma=0\cdot0449$, P_3P_2

Thus bearing in mind that there are solid reasons for preferring $S^{(2)}$ to $S^{(1)}$, and that, as $S^{(2)}$ involves a large number of ties, the treatment P is then decidedly preferable to the treatment S, we can say that the configuration using treatment P and similarity matrix $S^{(2)}$ having minimum stress gave an almost perfect reconstruction of the map of Otmoor, and that this computed configuration is the one we should in any case have chosen had we known nothing about the true geographical arrangement of the Otmoor parishes.

Our attempt 'to reconstruct maps from marriages' has, therefore, been successful.

BIBLIOGRAPHY

Beresford, M. (1954) *The Lost Villages of England.* London.

Hiorns, R.W., Harrison, G.A., Boyce, A.J. & Küchemann, C.F. (1969) A mathematical analysis of the effects of movement on the relatedness between populations. *Ann. Human Genetics*, **32**, 237–50.

Hiorns, R.W. (1971) Statistical studies in migration. *Mathematics in the Archaeological & Historical Sciences*, pp. 291–302 (eds Hodson, F.R., Kendall, D.G., & Tăutu, P.). Edinburgh: Edinburgh University Press.

Kendall, D.G. (1970) A mathematical approach to seriation. *Philos. Trans. Royal Soc. London (A)*, **269**, 125–34.

Kendall, D.G. (1971) Construction of maps from 'odd bits of information'. *Nature*, **231**, 158–9.

Kruskal, J.B. (1964) Multi-dimensional scaling. *Psychometrika*, **29**, 1–27 & 28–42.

Kruskal, J.B. (1971) Multi-dimensional scaling in archaeology; time is not the only dimension. *Mathematics in the Archaeological & Historical Sciences*, pp. 119–32 (eds Hodson, F.R., Kendall, D.G., & Tăutu, P.). Edinburgh: Edinburgh University Press.

Tobler, W. & Wineberg, S. (1971) A Cappadocian speculation. *Nature*, **231**, 39–41.

[*Note added in proof*: the reader may care to refer to Tobler & Wineberg (1971) and Kendall (1971) for accounts of investigations parallel to those tentatively proposed on p. 306.]

Parish Register Studies

Mark H. Skolnick, A. Moroni, C. Cannings, and L. L. Cavalli-Sforza
The reconstruction of genealogies from parish books

It is well known that demographic knowledge is essential to an understanding of genetic and evolutionary problems. Migration rates, population size, and age structure are examples of demographic observations that are basic for a description of the genetic structure of populations. Age specific mortality and fertility rates, and distributions of progeny sizes are similarly important for the measurement of natural selection.

We are interested, in addition, in the inheritance of some important characters such as fertility, longevity, and twinning which are, themselves, demographic in nature. They require study over several generations, and on a sufficient scale for a complete picture of their inheritance to emerge.

Finally, the socio-economic changes of the last centuries have deeply affected all demographic values and, with them, the trends and rates of biological evolution in man. For these reasons, it is useful for the geneticist to make recourse to demographic records of the past, when they are available.

An important source of demographic information which occasionally dates back as far as the late Middle Ages is parish books of baptisms, deaths, and marriages. They have been kept for the last few centuries more or less regularly and in a more or less standard form wherever Christian communities have existed. In the Roman Catholic Church, parish books antedating the Council of Trento, that is, before 1545, are rare. It was this Council which prescribed that every parish priest keep such records, and gave rules for their keeping. Abidance by the rules spread slowly, especially to the more remote parishes. For instance, in a highly rural part of the diocese of Parma, where we have been working, the first records date back to 1535. They were initially written in Italian or even in local dialect, then towards the end of the sixteenth century statements were increasingly made in an almost standard form and written in Latin. With time, there was an increase in the detail of records; thus, until the eighteenth century only the Christian name of the mother of each baptized child was on the records, but later the mother's maiden name was also given. Records are fairly complete, though occasional gaps are seen. The records of different parishes do not all start at the same time. Some parishes were founded later, some were fused with others, and occasionally books or parts of them (usually the earliest) have been lost. Figure 1 gives an idea of the state of parish books in part of the area in which we have been working (*see also* Moroni 1960). Photographs of parish book records of various centuries are given in the paper by Barrai *et al.* (1965).

The area which we have selected for study covers the upper part of the Parma Valley and of one adjoining valley. It belongs to the Parma diocese and corresponds to the 'comuni' (the smallest administrative divisions of the State) of Corniglio, Monchio, Palanzano. It involves 40 parishes and, today, approximately 13,000 people. It was chosen for study because, at the same time, an extensive investigation of genetic markers and of population structure was undertaken there (Cavalli-Sforza 1962, Conterio 1962, Conterio and Cavalli-Sforza 1962, Cavalli-Sforza, Barrai, and Edwards 1964, Cavalli-Sforza, Kimura, and Barrai 1966, Cavalli-Sforza and Zei 1967, Cavalli-Sforza 1969a, b).

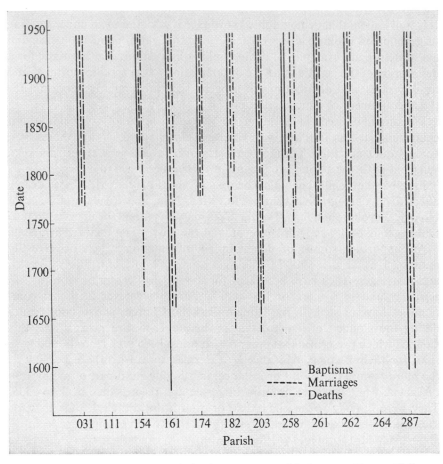

Figure 1. Available parish records in the commune of Palanzano, Parma Valley, Italy. Note that in parish 258 the records have double lines, indicating that the Vatican records of parish books erroneously overlapped dates

A first trial to use parish book registers from this area was made for a small parish, Riana, of 145 inhabitants (Cavalli-Sforza 1957). Record linking was done by hand, first by reconstructing sibships from baptisms (through names of father and mother), then linking baptisms to deaths and to marriages, finally linking parents' names on the baptism records with earlier births. Genealogies thus reconstructed were used, among other things, to compute the 'fitness' of a marriage as the number of children from that marriage that survived and married in the same parish.

Trials to automate the record linking procedure were then made. Cards were punched from the data of the 40 parishes of the area already mentioned according to the plan given in detail by Barrai, Cavalli-Sforza, and Moroni (1965). Attempts to use a mechanical card-sorter and an early computer were futile because of the time involved in the operation (Cavalli-Sforza 1960). Partial success was met when a computer equipped with magnetic tape became available. Programs for linking birth and death records were, however, prepared and tested successfully on one family surname (Barrai, Cavalli-Sforza, and Moroni 1965). This program and one for linking siblings were then used on the whole batch of data, producing, among other things, birth interval distributions as a function of birth order and family size, as well as progeny size distributions (Barrai, Cavalli-Sforza, and Moroni 1969). It became increasingly clear, however, that the data at hand could not be efficiently analyzed with a computer using tapes and of the size then available. When a new computer with disc memory (IBM 360/44) was installed at the University of Pavia efforts were renewed. Because of the impossibility of translating magnetic tapes used in the earlier computer, the record linking work had to be started from the original punched cards. This had, however, the advantage of permitting changes in the general strategy, based in part on the earlier experience.

In the earlier attempts to link parish records with a computer, the absence of disk drives giving rapid access to all of the data at any point in the processing made it necessary to rewind a tape every time data from another portion of the data set was required. Data had therefore to be ordered before entering the computer and reference to distant areas of the data set avoided. As much linking as possible had to be done at each stage. The limited speed of access to files on tape as well as the limited size of the memory made it necessary to divide the work into discrete segments, each of which had to be completed before the next stage was initiated. Thus the births were linked to the deaths, and the linked birth–death records were linked to the marriages. The sibling linkages were created using the baptism files alone, and in all of the above linkages ambiguities that arose had to be resolved as they were encountered. Because of the small computer memory no recall or reference to past linking decisions or information on relatives could be used in making linkages. The following method is an attempt to link parish records by utilizing the data more completely.

This report deals with the present state of the work, and in particular with the method of reconstructing genealogies and progeny distributions.

AMBIGUITIES AND UNCERTAINTY IN LINKING

There are many ways in which uncertainty in the process of linking arises. The most difficult cases are those where in one parish, at about the same time, two males with the same name and surname marry two females with the same name and surname. How does one assign the children to the two sets of parents? If there are two baptism records which could link to the same death record, on what criteria does one decide which baptism record to link to the death record? Apart from such extreme cases of isonymy, the

21

most common causes of ambiguity and uncertainty are gaps, omissions, and errors. In addition to the variable availability of the data, there appear to be a number of death records missing, since the total number of deaths is about half as large as that of births. This may be due partly to the fact that in some places death books start later and in part to emigration not compensated by immigration. Uncertainty in linking is also due to omissions of mothers' maiden names in earlier books, or the frequent omission of some of the names of the baptized person, his father or his mother. In other cases the names are poor identifiers, especially in the earlier period where the second, or third name of many males and females was Maria.

In addition to the possibility of an error in the spelling of a name when the record was written, one must deal with the evolution of names and surnames themselves, and the alternate spellings that exist for many names due to the existence of similar but not identical forms for one surname in Italian, Latin, and even dialect. Thus it is easy for variable spellings of the same surname to arise. To deal with this difficulty the names were coded numerically, and alternate spellings of the same name were given the same code. This procedure has two disadvantages. Sets of spellings may overlap; thus A can be an alternate spelling for B and C, but B and C may be unrelated. In addition one loses some of the information, and it may be that the alternate spellings of a name actually distinguish two families. As an example, one person was recorded in the baptism records with the surname Berini, and in the death records with the surname Bernini. A name such as Abati could change to Abate, Abbate, Abbati, Abatti, Abbiati, or Abiatti. This name is also evolutionarily related to names such as Bati, Biati, and more distantly to names such as Frati. In such cases the computer could resolve the ambiguities only if all the information were coded phonetically, and the computer were programed to search for likely phonetic alterations.

Another problem is introduced by inversion of name order. A person baptized Giovanni Carlo Matteo Abati, may prefer to call himself Matteo, and may be registered as Matteo Abati in the death records. Or the first and second names may be merged into a name such as Giancarlo which, although related to both Giovanni and Carlo, would not be coded the same as either of them and would thus make linking using numerical codes very difficult. Again a phonetic coding would be necessary to make the proper linkages.

The approach that we have adopted in dealing with these complications is one of making at the beginning only unambiguous linkages, marking the points of ambiguity, and storing appropriate information on the ambiguity. One can then construct family groupings and parental relations to aid in the resolution of the more difficult cases. Children which certainly have the same parents are linked as siblings. Baptism, death, and marriage records which positively refer to the same person are linked. An attempt to construct family genealogies is done to aid in uncertain linkages. As there is very little migration (*see* Cavalli-Sforza 1963), and in most cases children are born in the same parish as their parents (especially their fathers) the first stages of linking are done within the parish. Marriages between parishes are the greatest cause of migration in this area and they form the most likely links between the parishes. Thus the linking of a birth record of one parish to the death record of another is done only when there is supporting evidence for the migration. This supporting evidence would be an interparish marriage, or the presence of close relatives in the parish to which migration occurred. Support for migration without an interparish marriage could consist of the birth or death of one's children in the second parish. The more distant two parishes are from each other, the more supporting evidence one wants to have before linking records. Thus it became clear that one needs at least a rough genealogy for each parish before attempting to resolve ambiguities within the parish and link records between parishes. In this paper we shall explain the method of constructing these rough genealogies, and we shall then examine the resultant family size distributions.

CONSTRUCTING GENEALOGIES WITHIN THE PARISH

With ideal data, genealogies could be constructed from baptism records by themselves. Because each baptism record provides pointers to the father and the mother, one can trace a family line as far as the records permit. The method is divided into three discrete stages. The first stage links all of the children with identical information on fathers' and mothers' names into a single sibling group. The sibships thus formed give the distributions shown in figure 2. We shall refer to them as sibships obtained by the strict criterion just mentioned. This distribution forms a lower bound on the number of large families and an upper bound on the number of small families since in many cases two or three of the families formed by the strict criterion should be joined under one sibship. It is interesting to note the large family size indicated by these data for the 19th century. This suggests that at the onset of the demographic transition, with a fall in the death rate, and with child spacing patterns as yet unchanged, fertility actually increases since a reduction in the death rate of parents would cause an increase in the mean reproductive period.

Century	No. of Sibships	Mean	Variance
16th	897	1·9715	2·4590
17th	3545	2·7005	4·8668
18th	4626	2·9078	5·4698
19th	7608	3·3865	7·2504
20th	7144	2·5105	4·5960

Table 1. Sibship size distribution by the strict criterion

Table 1 lists the means and variances by century for this method of estimating family size distributions. A comparison with results obtained on the same material by the earlier linking procedure (Barrai, Cavalli-Sforza, and Moroni 1969) shows a parallel trend. All means are lower here however, (except for twentieth-century data), not surprisingly so, because of the strictness of the criterion employed. Moreover these data refer only to siblings born in the same parish, while those of Barrai *et al.* were obtained from linkage over the whole area.

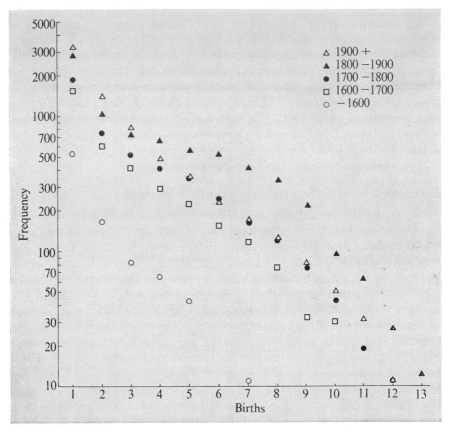

Figure 2. Sibship size distribution by the strict criterion. Absolute frequency of births per family, first approximation

The second stage consists of finding the most probable father and the most probable mother for each of the sibling groups. This is done by looking for the parent in the baptism records whose baptism record is closest to thirty years earlier from the baptism record of the first child. Since the most probable parent is not certain, an alternate parent file is created and stored for use in future resolution of the genealogies. It is at this stage that the strictness of the sibling linkage is compensated for, because more than one group of siblings can have the same most probable father, and the siblings are temporarily linked to him. This process however results in over-estimation of family size, that is, baptisms which are not really children of the same family may have the same most probable father. Therefore a third stage consists in examining the mothers' surname and names. Where there was no blatant conflict between the mothers' names, the children were considered to be of the same family, and where there was a conflict of coding the children were split into several families.

A fourth stage which has not yet been carried out could consist of resolving conflicts on the basis of likelihood ratios computed from ages, as well as from additional data provided by the marriage or death records, and so on.

Number	111211	111211	111212	111211	111213
Father's first name	Petri	Petri	Petri	Petri	Petri
Father's second name	Joannis		Joannis	Joannis	Joannis
Mother's surname	Simonettis	Simonettis	Simonettis	Simonettis	Simonettis
Mother's first name	Domenica	Domenica	Domenica	Domenica	Domenica
Mother's second name	Maria	Maria	Maria		Maria

Table 2. An example of omissions in baptism records of mother's and father's names

Table 2 shows three sibling groups who all had the same most probable father. They were different sibling groups under the strict criterion because in one case the second name of the father is omitted, and in another case the second name of the mother was omitted. Thus they might be children of different marriages. As there is no direct conflict in the name data, but only missing information, for the following family size analysis they are considered as one family.

It is possible to create male descent lines at the same time as one searches for fathers of sibling groups. By searching from the oldest records to the youngest one can carry all of the previously found information to successive generations.

More explicitly, when a baptism record cannot be linked to an already existing tree, a new tree is begun, and the father on the baptism record is considered to be the original ancestor of the tree. For the nth tree, the code for the original ancestor is $(n, 1)$. The code for his k_1th child is $(n, 1, k_1)$. The k_2th child of $(n, 1, k_1)$ is $(n, 1, k_1, k_2)$, and so on. Thus, for example, the array $(n, 1, k_1, k_2 \ldots k_{L-1}, k_L)$ represents the k_Lth child of $(n, 1, k_1, k_2 \ldots k_{L-1})$, and the set of subarrays $(n, 1)$, $(n, 1, k_1)$, $(n, 2, k_1, k_2)$, $(n, 1, k_1, k_2, k_3)$, ..., $(n, 1, k_1, \ldots k_{L-1})$ represent the set of male ancestors linking that individual directly to $(n, 1)$.

Figure 3 illustrates a tree with the nodes numbered. Males are represented by wide lines, females by thin lines. This sample tree is in agreement with the custom that during the earlier centuries the first sons inherited the land, and therefore had a higher chance of having children in the parish.

Once male descent lines within a parish have been reconstructed it is a simple matter to build pedigrees and complete genealogies. The backbone of a pedigree consists of the ancestral array of a person's male descent group. One then attaches the ancestral portion of the male descent groups of all wives of ancestors in the original male descent group. The pedigree is completed by repeating the procedure $n-1$ times, n being the maximum number of generations present in the enlarged descent line. This process will result in attaching 2^n ancestor arrays, where n is the number of generations. The number of ancestors is $2^{n+1}-2$. Using arrays thus saves 2^n-2 searches. Similarly, genealogies can be constructed by attaching the progeny portion of the male descent groups of the husbands of the females belonging to the original male descent group, and iterating as above.

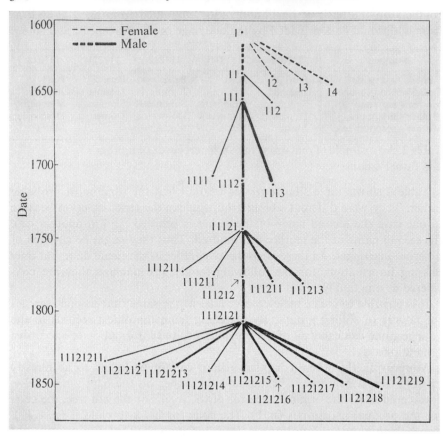

Figure 3. A method of construction of male descent lines: Original ancestor, Petro Potori from the parish of Agna, Parma Valley, Italy

Several interesting observations can be made from figure 4, which shows an example of a 13-generation tree. Even though the tree is continued only by male descendants born in the parish, it spans a 400-year time period and 13 generations. The left branch and the center branch disappeared in the parish after 5 and 6 generations respectively, and one sees that the progeny of the right-hand branch became more numerous and filled in the gap left by their dying or migrating cousins. Mixing of the generations can also be seen, as the earliest offspring of the sixth generation of the right-hand branch were born before the last of the fifth generation of the center branch.

CHILDREN EVER BORN TO FATHERS BORN IN THE PARISH

Trees thus constructed and corrected permit one to obtain a 'family size' distribution of particular interest for genetic problems. This can be described as the distribution of progeny born in the parish to people born in the parish. As the distribution represents the rate of increase per generation, it offers interesting ways to compute 'fitness' for genetic purposes and its variation, as well as the distribution of the number of descendants after any number of

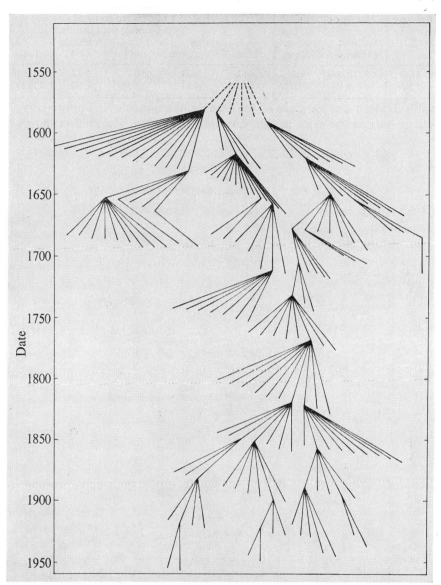

Figure 4. A male descent line of 13 generations: Original ancestor, Peregrino Ferrari from the parish of Bosco, Parma Valley, Italy

generations. These theoretical distributions, predicted on the assumption of no inheritance of fertility, might then be compared to observed distributions. A very sensitive test of inheritance of fertility might be provided in this way.

Means and variances of the distributions thus obtained are given in table 3. Consideration was limited to the eighteenth and nineteenth centuries which include most of the data. Means have changed with respect to those given in table 1 but it is impossible to make an accurate comparison since the century refers in table 3 to the birthdate of the fathers, rather than of the first child.

| Century | Number of fathers | | Number of children in family | | | | |
| | Without children | With one or more children | All families | | Families with children | | |
			Mean	Variance	Mean (M)	Variance (V)	Total
18th	1778	965	1·52	7·24	4·32	8·47	4166
19th	4719	3083	1·55	6·83	3·93	7·90	12131

Table 3. Mean and variance of the number of children ever born to fathers born in the same parish. Complete family size distribution shown

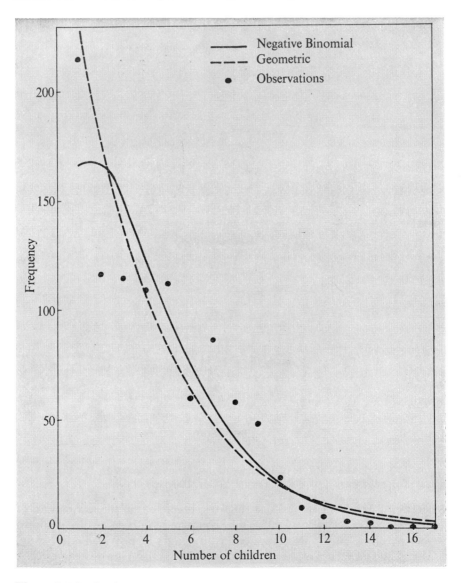

Figure 5. Distribution of the number of children ever born to fathers born in the same parish, for fathers born in the eighteenth century, Parma Valley, Italy. Also shown are the geometric and negative binomial distributions fitted by ML

The overall increase of the means in table 3 (computed on families with at least one child) is due to the relaxation of the strict criterion and to other factors, such as the elimination of families which immigrated after having begun the reproductive process. In addition, the frequency of individuals who contribute no children is now available. The mean 'family' size obtained taking account also of individuals with zero children is more meaningful from the point of view of net reproduction rates.

The distributions of 1, 2, ... r, ... children are given graphically in figures 5 and 6, along with theoretical curves fitted by the process described below. Since the zero term includes unmarried males, it has been truncated, and all fitted distributions are correspondingly truncated.

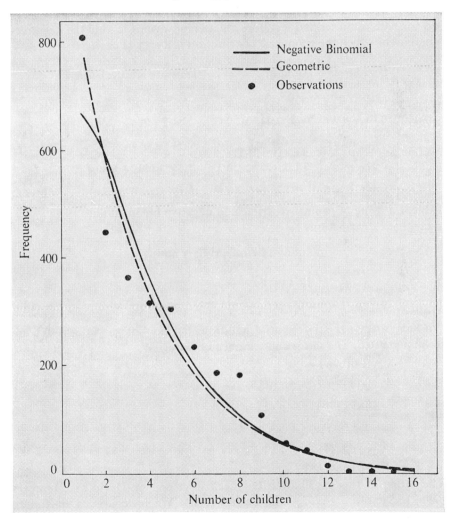

Figure 6. Distributions of the number of children ever born to fathers born in the same parish, for fathers born in the nineteenth century, Parma Valley, Italy. Also shown are the geometric and negative binomial distributions fitted by ML

FITTING OF GEOMETRIC AND NEGATIVE BINOMIAL DISTRIBUTIONS

The geometric distribution was fitted by Lotka (1939) to the US White American data of 1920, of type equivalent to those of figures 5 and 6, with partial success. This distribution is especially attractive because the convolutions of its probability-generating function are easy to specify (*see* Lotka 1939, Harris 1963), and our later work will be concerned with number of descendants and with the survival of family names over many generations.

Suppose that m is the mean and v the variance of the observed distribution. Then, if the probability of a family of size r is

$$P_r = p(1-p)^{r-1}, \quad r = 1, 2, \ldots, \infty ; \quad 0 < p \leq 1$$

(the geometric distribution) the maximum likelihood estimate of p is given by $\hat{p} = 1/m$. Values for p and χ^2 are given in table 4. The fit is extremely bad for both centuries and therefore an attempt was made to fit the negative-binomial of which the geometric distribution is a special case.

Century	Logarithmic estimate		Geometric estimate		Truncated negative binomial					
					Max. likelihood estimates			Moment estimates		
	p	χ^2	p	χ^2	p	k	χ^2	p	k	χ^2
18th	0·10	471	0·23	115	0·37	2·2	98	0·56	3·08	154
		17		17	±	±	16			16
		d. of f.		d. of f.	0·02	0·24	d. of f.			d. of f.
19th	0·09	866	0·26	252	0·33	1·65	223	0·40	2·35	288
		16		16	±	±	15			15
		d. of f.		d. of f.	0·01	0·11	d. of f.			d. of f.

Table 4. Fitting of geometric, truncated negative binomial and logarithmic distributions

The probability of a family of r offspring is now

$$P_r = \frac{\binom{r+k-1}{k-1} p^k (1-p)^r}{(1-p^k)} \quad r = 1, 2, \ldots \quad (0 < p < 1).$$

We have written this in factorial notation, but non-integer values of k are to be permitted. The mean and variance of r are

$$m = \frac{k(1-p)}{p(1-p^k)}$$

and

$$v = \frac{k(1-p)}{p^2(1-p^k)} - \frac{k^2 p^k (1-p)^2}{p^2(1-p^k)^2}$$

or

$$\frac{m}{p} - m^2 p^k .$$

The fitting of this distribution has been discussed by David and Johnson (1952), Sampford (1955) and Brass (1958). We have used a maximum likelihood estimation procedure which also permits computer plots to be made of the likelihood surface. In addition, fitting by moments was carried out. Results are shown in table 4 together with the value of χ^2 for goodness of fit. The fit is extremely poor.

We have also obtained an estimate p for the logarithmic series distribution (the limiting form of the negative binomial distribution when $k \to 0$), $P_r = -(1-p)^r/r \log p$ (Fisher, Corbet, and Williams 1943). The maximum likelihood estimate $\hat{p}$ is found by solving

$$m = \frac{-(1-p)}{p \log p} \text{ numerically} \quad .$$

The fit is again poor.

Figure 7 shows the log likelihood surface for the nineteenth century. The four pairs of estimates (logarithmic, geometric, negative binomial, by maximum likelihood and by moments) have been plotted on the surface.

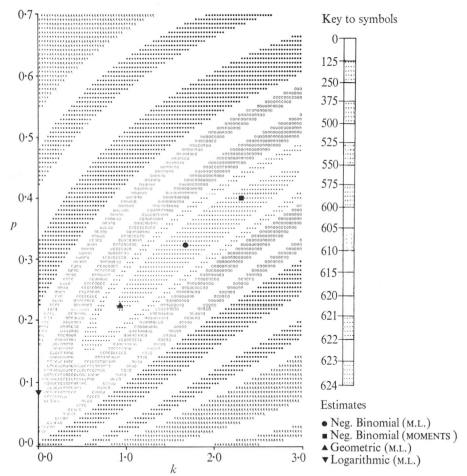

Figure 7. Computer plot of likelihood surface showing maximum likelihood estimates of logarithmic, geometric and truncated negative binomial distributions, and moment estimates for truncated negative binomial distributions

The total change of the log likelihood for the range of parameters plotted has been divided into 624 equal segments and each band in the diagram represents the number of these segments indicated in the key.

The poor fits obtained in the above cases are due in part to the inappropriateness of the models used (*see* following section). There is also a further problem associated with this kind of data. In sampling a population, chance deficiencies in observations of one class will be spread at random over the other classes. Here however a family of size 4 would be more likely to be misclassified as a family of size 3 or 5 and this will produce slight correlations between neighbours. As the linkage becomes more and more accurate it is to be hoped that these correlations will be minimized. It remains to be seen whether the above functions will then fit the data more adequately.

DISCUSSION OF THE STOCHASTIC PROCESS UNDERLYING THE PROGENY SIZE DISTRIBUTIONS

The occurrence of birth during the reproductive period may be treated as a stochastic process. Clearly an inappropriate stochastic process will lead to poor fit between the observed and expected values.

The assumption of fixed reproductive period and independent births leads naturally to a Poisson distribution of family size. Fisher (1958) observed that the mean and variance of the completed-family size distribution of women who survived 20–25 years after marriage were significantly different (they should be equal for a Poisson distribution). This difference he attributed to variation in female fertility. A modification to the distribution can be made to accommodate this variability by letting the parameter λ of the Poisson distribution $(\lambda t)^r e^{-\lambda t}/r!$ have a Gamma distribution with probability element

$$\frac{\lambda^{k-1} e^{-\lambda} d\lambda}{\Gamma(k)} \qquad (\lambda \, \varepsilon \, [0, \infty]) \quad .$$

This then leads to a negative-binomial distribution for r given by

$$\frac{\Gamma(k+r)}{\Gamma(k)r!} \left(\frac{t}{t+1}\right)^r \left(\frac{1}{t+1}\right)^k \qquad r = 0, 1, 2, \ldots \quad .$$

Writing $1/(t+1)=p$ reduces it to the form of the negative-binomial which we have fitted (though we have truncated the zero term).

However, as has been pointed out by Brass (1957), the process under consideration is not a point process. The period of gestation, and indeed possibly a further period corresponding to failure to ovulate if the mother is nursing, are effectively blank periods with respect to reproduction. If α is the length of this blank period then the probability of r or less births in time t is

$$W(r, t) = \sum_{j=0}^{r} \exp(-\lambda(t-r\alpha)) \frac{\lambda^j (t-r\alpha)^j}{j!} \qquad (t \geqslant r\alpha) \quad ,$$
$$=1 \qquad (t \leqslant r\alpha) \quad .$$

As before, this can be modified by allowing λ to take a Gamma distribution to give

$$W^*(r, t) = \sum_{j=0}^{r} \frac{\Gamma(k+j)}{\Gamma(k)j!} \left(\frac{t-r\alpha}{t+1-r\alpha}\right)^j \left(\frac{1}{t+1-r\alpha}\right)^k \qquad (t \geqslant r\alpha) \quad ,$$
$$=1 \qquad (t \leqslant r\alpha) \quad .$$

(Dandekar 1955). As Brass (1957) has pointed out, this distribution and its truncated form are difficult to fit but we shall endeavor to develop methods for fitting in the near future.

In fact the term $r\alpha$ appearing here is simply the total time spent in blank periods for the first r births, and the assumption of fixed α can be relaxed by replacing $r\alpha$ by $\sum_{i=1}^{r} \alpha_i$. Thus one might take some account of the variation of birth interval with parity. These birth intervals have been estimated for the present set of data by Barrai, Cavalli-Sforza, and Moroni (1969).

CONCLUSIONS AND SUMMARY

A new method of record linking by computer has been tried on a set of data from the parish books of the Upper Parma Valley, Italy. Genealogies have been produced which, in some cases, span over 13 generations. Male descent lines have been constructed and it has been shown how to obtain complete pedigrees by our coding procedure. The general principles underlying the method are described. Distribution of progeny sizes, and in particular of the number of children ever born to a father born in the same parish, were obtained. These data are especially relevant to the problem of genetic fitness, and that of the extinction of surnames. They were poorly fitted by the logarithmic, the geometric and the negative-binomial distributions. The reasons for the poor fit and possible alternatives are discussed.

ACKNOWLEDGMENTS

This research has been supported in part by a grant from the United States Atomic Energy Commission. The work done by M. H. Skolnick was partial fulfillment of PhD thesis requirements while the author was at the Istituto di Genetica, Università di Pavia.

REFERENCES

Barrai, I., Cavalli-Sforza, L. L. & Moroni, A. (1965) Record linkage from parish books. *Mathematics and Computer Science in Biology and Medicine*, pp. 51 60. Medical Research Council.

Barrai, I., Cavalli-Sforza, L. L. & Moroni, A. (1969) Demography and genealogy (Part I) family reconstitution by computer. *World Conference on Records and Genealogical Seminar*. Salt Lake City, Utah. 5–8 August 1969.

Brass, W. (1957) Models of birth distributions in human populations. *Internationella Statistiska Instututet*, *30th Session*, Stockholm.

Brass, W. (1958) Simplified methods of fitting the truncated negative binomial distribution. *Biometrika*, **45**, 59–68.

Cavalli-Sforza, L. L. (1957) Some notes on the breeding patterns of human populations. *Acta genet. et statist. Med.*, **6**, 395–9.

Cavalli-Sforza, L. L. (1960) Demographic attacks on genetic problems. *Int. Symp. Demo. & Genet.*, *Ginevra*, pp. 221–33.

Cavalli-Sforza, L. L. (1962) Indagine speciale su alcune caratteristiche genetiche della populazione italiana. *Note e Relazioni n.* 17. Istituto Centrale di Statistica.

Cavalli-Sforza, L. L. (1963) The distribution of migration distances; models, and application to genetics. *Entretiens de Monaco en Sciences Humaines.* Première session 24–29 May, 1962. *Human Displacements*, pp. 139–58.

Cavalli-Sforza, L.L. (1969a) Human Diversity. *Proc. XII Internat. Congr. Genetics, Tokyo (Japan)*, 1968. **3**, 405–16.

Cavalli-Sforza, L.L. (1969b) Genetic drift in an Italian population. *Sci. Amer.*, **22**, 30–7.

Cavalli-Sforza, L.L., Barrai, I. & Edwards, A.W.F. (1964) Analysis of human evolution under random genetic drift. *Cold Spring Harbor Symposia on Quantitative Biology*, **24**, 9–20.

Cavalli-Sforza, L.L., Kimura, M. & Barrai, I. (1966) The probability of consanguineous marriages. *Genetics*, **54**, 37–60.

Cavalli-Sforza, L.L. & Zei, G. (1967) Experiments with an artificial population. *Proc. Intern. Congr. Human Genetics*, pp. 473–8.

Conterio, F. (1962) I gruppi sanguigni della Val Parma. *L'Ateneo Parmense*, **33**, suppl. 2.

Conterio, F. & Cavalli-Sforza, L.L. (1962) Fluttuazione de frequenze geniche nella populazione della Val Parma. *L'Ateneo Parmense*, **33**, suppl. 2.

Dandekar, V.M. (1955) Certain modified forms of binomial and Poisson distributions. *Sankhya*, **15**, 237.

David, F.N. & Johnson, N.L. (1952) The truncated Poisson. *Biometrics*, **8**, 275–85.

Fisher, R.A. (1958) *Genetical Theory of Natural Selection.* (2nd ed.) Dover Publ.

Fisher, R.A., Corbet, A.S. & Williams, C.B. (1943) The relation between the number of species and the number of individuals in a random sample of an animal population. *J. Anim. Ecol.*, **12**, 42–58.

Harris, T.E. (1963) *The theory of Branching Processes.* New Jersey: Prentice-Hall.

Keyfitz, N. (1968) *Introduction to the Mathematics of Population.* Addison Wesley Press.

Lotka, A.J. (1939) *Théorie Analytique des Associations Biologiques.* Paris: Hermann.

Moroni, A. (1960) Sources, reliability and usefulness of consanguinity data with special reference to Catholic records. *International Symposium of Demography and Genetics*, UN, WHO, *The Use of Vital and Health Statistics for Genetic and Radiation Studies, Geneva.*

Sampford, M.R. (1955) The truncated negative binomial distribution. *Biometrika*, **42**, 69.

Population Genetics

Kenneth K. Kidd and L. L. Cavalli-Sforza
Number of characters examined and error in
reconstruction of evolutionary trees

Recently, attention has been focused on the possibility of reconstructing evolutionary histories and interrelationships among populations on the basis of genetic data obtained on present day populations [*see*, for example, Cavalli-Sforza and Edwards (1967), A. W. F. Edwards (1971), and K. K. Kidd (1971)]. Various methods have been proposed for such phylogenetic analysis, none of which is perfect. The best method theoretically—maximum likelihood—has been shown by Edwards (1970) to be inapplicable in practice. Thus, we must rely on less exact methods, and there is no estimate of the error involved.

It is intuitively evident that the number of characters used will influence the error, but there has been no previous quantitative investigation of their effect. Because of the practical problems involved in collecting data, it is important to know which method and what minimum number of characters will yield a sufficiently high probability of reconstructing the correct tree. We have therefore undertaken a simulation study which could answer this and some of the other problems that affect the error involved in estimating phylogenetic relationships.

Early unpublished work by one of us (L.C.S.) with David Gomberg, simulating the simplest tree—two splits yielding three populations—had already shown a great effect of the times of the splits on the error. Other work (Kidd 1969, Kidd and Sgaramella-Zonta 1971) showed that the different methods can give different results on real data. Our simulation study is designed to consider: (1) the effect of the number of characters; (2) the efficiency of the various methods; (3) the effects of deviations from the standard evolutionary model (considered to be Brownian motion for differentiation of characters and a Yule branching process for the splitting of populations), such as (a) branching not according to a Yule process, (b) non-constant evolutionary rates, (c) non-independence of descendants after their separation, and (d) fusion or hybridization of populations; (4) the importance of the times of the splits; and (5) the accuracy of estimation of the lengths of the segments by the various methods. In this report we present the results obtained for problems (1), (2), and (4), above, on the basis of the analysis of 6,800 simulated trees of four populations each.

THE SIMULATION PROCESS

In this paper we examine the results of simulating trees leading to four populations. There are three possible forms for *unrooted* trees with four branches, leading to populations A, B, C, D, as shown in figure 1. If the trees are *rooted*, the number of different forms is 15, as can be obtained by introducing the root, that is, the first split or branching, in any one segment of the three forms.

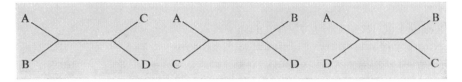

Figure 1

For the purpose of our analysis it is sufficient to consider two different forms (indicated as topologies 1 and 2 in figure 2), which represent, respectively, three and twelve of the possible fifteen rooted trees of four populations. In order to examine the effect of splitting time on estimation, various trees of either topology were examined, according to a set of splitting times chosen arbitrarily and given in figure 2. The number of independent characters used were $n = 3, 5, 10, 20, 50, 100$. Almost all sets of tree parameters (form and splitting times, as given in figure 2) were examined for these character numbers, except a few for which no simulation was run with 100 characters. Each character was simulated by a normal variate having mean zero (at the beginning) and variance one. In practice, every one of the four populations was considered as a 'particle', all four originating from one original particle splitting three times while undergoing Brownian motion in the n-dimensional character space. The position of each particle with respect to every dimension (=character) was computed on the basis of a random normal independent deviate having mean equal to the position (character value) of the particle at the last split, and variance equal to the time elapsed since the last split.

Having generated character values for the populations, we then calculated the distances between populations (in the n-dimensional character space) as well as the correlation coefficients between populations. Standardization of each character to the same mean and variance was not done, but all characters of the four populations had expected zero mean and equal variance.

THE RECONSTRUCTION OF TREES

Using the distance or correlation matrix, we reconstructed trees using various methods which are given below. With methods which can evaluate only unrooted trees, the three possible unrooted trees were tested, and the tree fitting best by the criterion employed was compared to the true tree used to generate the data. The frequency of correct results was scored in (at least) 100 independent simulations of each of the 11 sets of tree parameters given in figure 2 for each of the various numbers of characters tested. With methods yielding 'rooted trees' (that is, methods (4) and (5) given below) the tree inferred was tested for correspondence with the correct rooted tree. Five of the fifteen possible rooted trees are equivalent to the correct unrooted tree and the inferred tree was also checked for correspondence with these trees.

Thus, a frequency of correct unrooted solutions and a frequency of correct rooted solutions were calculated.

Methods (1) (Σe^2) *and* (2) (*LS length*). These are both based on least squares solution of the additive tree. The additive model and the use of least squares to solve it have been extensively discussed by Cavalli-Sforza and Edwards (1967) and by Kidd (1969) and Kidd and Sgaramella-Zonta (1971). There are at least two statistics by which trees solved with least squares can be compared. The least squares value that is minimized in this method may be used as a measure of the degree to which the solution deviates from strict additivity; the tree with the lowest value is the most nearly additive, and hence best by this criterion. Kidd and Sgaramella-Zonta (1971) proposed that the solution which requires the minimum amount of evolution, measured as the sum of the absolute values of the segments obtained by least squares fitting of the additive tree, is the best estimate of the correct tree. By each of these two statistics, called Σe^2 [method (1)] and *LS* length [method (2)] respectively, we selected a 'best' tree from the three least squares solutions of a distance matrix.

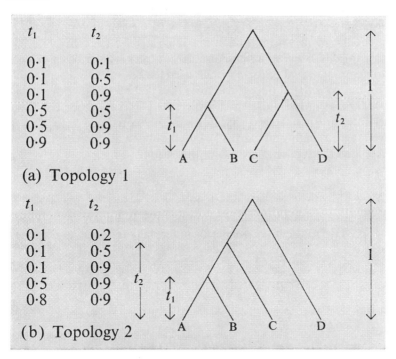

Figure 2. The two topologies and the splitting times studied for each

Method 3 (MP). This method uses the minimum path method (Edwards and Cavalli-Sforza 1963, Cavalli-Sforza and Edwards 1967, Kidd and Sgaramella-Zonta 1971) which finds by successive approximations the minimum length of 'string' needed to connect the populations in the character space according to a specified tree structure. We adapted the original program by Edwards for this study. The statistic for comparing trees, called *MP* length, is the

22

quantity that is minimized, that is, the sum of the segment lengths. The unrooted tree that has minimum 'string' (smallest MP length) is considered the best of the three.

Method 4 (CA). This method uses the cluster analysis method developed by Edwards and Cavalli-Sforza (1965) for inferring rooted trees and is based on an extension to n-dimensions of the analysis of variance. The populations are divided into two groups such that the variance between the groups is maximized. This is used to infer the first split in the tree (the root). Each of those two groups is divided, in turn, into two groups in the same way, and the process continued on subsequent groups until all groups are of size one. The method was used to compare the seven possible first splits. The one with greatest variance between the two groups was chosen. If one cluster contained three populations, it was similarly divided.

Method 5 (CC). This method uses correlation coefficients. It has been shown (Felsenstein, cited by Edwards 1970) that, if r is the correlation coefficient between two populations for the characters considered, $1-r$ is proportional to the time elapsed since separation of the two populations. We have used correlation coefficients to construct rooted trees by testing all possible splits, as in cluster analysis, and choosing the split with the minimum average of correlation coefficients between populations separated by the split.

Other ways of constructing and/or evaluating trees on the basis of continuous variates exist. Cavalli-Sforza (1966) used the Σe^2 value to discriminate among trees, but considered only those trees that had no negative segments. Fitch and Margoliash (1967) used a statistic called '$\%SD$'. Since Kidd and Sgaramella-Zonta (1971) showed that Σe^2 is highly correlated with '$\%SD$' and that LS length is highly similar to Σe^2 used only on all-positive trees, we have not included these other statistics in this study.

RESULTS

As mentioned already, for each topology, set of times, and number of characters, we have repeated the generation of trees and analyses 100 times. Tables 1–4 (pp. 341–5) present these experimental results as frequency of experi-

Method	χ^2	d.f.	Probability %
Σe^2	3·448	6	70–80
LS length	1·396	6	95–98
MP length	1·893	6	90–95
CA (rooted)	7·243	6	20–30
CA (unrooted)	5·367	6	30–50
CC (rooted)	9·390	6	10–20
CC (unrooted)	10·799	6	5–10

Table 5. Repeatability of simulation. For the tree parameters $t_1 = 0.1$, $t_2 = 0.2$, topology 2, two complete series of simulations were run for all character values. Chi squares were calculated for each set of characters and summed separately for each statistic

ments in which the right tree was inferred from the data. In order to test for reproducibility, in the case of one particular set of the parameters, the experiment was repeated for all numbers of characters. Table 5 gives the χ^2 values for repeatability for each of the five methods. Each χ^2 is the sum of six independent chi squares with one degree of freedom, testing the agreement between frequencies of correct answers in the two repeat runs for each number of characters. None is significant.

It is quite clear that with increasing number of characters the frequency of correct tree diagnosis increases regularly. On the other hand, splitting times also affect the error of inference very deeply. The earlier the splitting, the more difficult becomes correct diagnosis. With late splittings (for example, $t_1 = t_2 = 0.1$ with topology 1) the frequency of correct inference is above 95% already, with five characters or less. But, with the same topology, and early splittings ($t_1 = t_2 = 0.9$) even with 100 characters this frequency is only about twice the probability of a correct random choice ($1/3$) for unrooted topologies. These results are clear, irrespective of the method of inference used.

Coming to the comparison between methods, one finds significant differences between those five that were employed. χ^2 values between the frequencies of correct answers by the various methods, summed over all 68 experiments listed in tables 1–2, give a very highly significant value ($\chi^2 = 756.5$ with 282 d.f.). The total frequency of correct answers is highest, for unrooted trees, with cluster analysis (80.3% of correct diagnosis on 6,800 trees examined). The next best two methods are LS length and correlation coefficients (with respectively 78.9 and 78.6% of right answers). Minimum path gives 76.9% and Σe^2 71.5%. Even omitting the last method, which turned out to be by far the least efficient, the comparison between the other methods still shows a significant heterogeneity ($\chi^2 = 387.5$ with 204 d.f.).

In the analysis of rooted trees (tables 3 and 4) cluster analysis proves on average superior to correlation coefficients. Here, naturally, the frequency of correct diagnoses is constantly smaller than for unrooted trees, as the choice is, in fact, between fifteen trees and the probability of a random correct choice is $1/15$ for rooted trees versus $1/3$ for unrooted trees.

It is also clear, however, that the superiority of one method over the other depends on the particular tree examined. Thus, comparing results on the different topologies one can notice that the best-fitting method is not necessarily the same for topologies 1 and 2. Tables 6 and 7 show two particularly striking examples. Here, 'superiority' of a method over another is induced from direct comparison of the frequency of correct inference for a given tree. These observations show, therefore, that there is no universally best method among those employed, but at least three among them, LS length, cluster analysis, and correlation coefficients, lend themselves almost equally well to the analysis of unrooted trees, and the latter two to that of rooted trees.

The overall probability of error by these methods depends, of course, on the prior distribution of trees. Those selected here for experimental purposes do not lend themselves to compute it. Another program suitable for handling a larger number of populations is now being used, also with this purpose in mind.

		Topologies		Total
		1	2	
Number of trees in which the	LS	15	5	20
method found superior is	CA	5	24	29
	Total	20	29	49

Table 6. Comparison of results obtained by LS length and CA (cluster analysis) with the two topologies (unrooted trees). $\chi_{(1)} = 16{\cdot}35$, $P < 0{\cdot}001$

		Topologies		Total
		1	2	
Number of trees in which the	CA	31	11	42
method found superior is	CC	0	20	20
	Total	31	31	62

Table 7. Comparison of results obtained by cluster analysis (CA) and correlation coefficients (CC) with the two topologies (rooted trees). $\chi_{(1)} = 26{\cdot}65$, $P < 0{\cdot}001$ (with Yates correction).

CONCLUSIONS AND SUMMARY

A simulation experiment was run to compare methods of reconstructing trees and estimating the error involved as a function of the number of independent characters. The test was made on trees leading to four populations by three branchings using various numbers of characters varying from 3 to 100 and a variety of branching times. The probability of correct answers increased regularly with increasing number of characters, but depended also to a large extent on the times at which branching occurred. With late branchings the probability is about 100% with few characters, but with early branching even 100 characters did not give a satisfactory error probability. Thus, it is impossible to give a simple rule for the minimum number of characters required.

Of the five methods used, one based on least squares was much worse than the others, but the other four gave almost indistinguishable results. However, some proved superior in certain conditions, others in other conditions. The following methods can be recommended as having almost the same efficiency: for both rooted and unrooted trees, two methods of cluster analysis (as specified in the text), one based on analysis of variance (CA) and one, somewhat less satisfactory, based on correlation coefficients (CC); for unrooted trees, solution by least squares with ranking of trees by one particular statistic (LS length), and also, though least efficient, the method of minimum path (MP).

This research has been supported in part from a grant of the United States Atomic Energy Commission. Kenneth Kidd is a United States National Institutes of Health post-doctoral fellow.

Times		Method	Number of characters					
t_1	t_2		3	5	10	20	50	100
0·1	0·1	1	0·95	1·00	1·00	1·00	1·00	1·00
		2	0·96	1·00	1·00	1·00	1·00	1·00
		3	0·96	1·00	1·00	1·00	1·00	1·00
		4	0·96	1·00	1·00	1·00	1·00	1·00
		5	0·82	0·99	1·00	1·00	1·00	1·00
0·1	0·5	1	0·82	0·91	1·00	1·00	1·00	—
		2	0·89	0·97	1·00	1·00	1·00	—
		3	0·88	0·97	1·00	1·00	1·00	—
		4	0·88	0·96	1·00	1·00	1·00	—
		5	0·74	0·91	0·99	1·00	1·00	—
0·1	0·9	1	0·80	0·82	0·99	1·00	1·00	1·00
		2	0·89	0·92	1·00	1·00	1·00	1·00
		3	0·85	0·88	1·00	1·00	1·00	1·00
		4	0·86	0·99	0·99	1·00	1·00	1·00
		5	0·66	0·96	1·00	1·00	1·00	1·00
0·5	0·5	1	0·63	0·67	0·88	0·95	0·99	—
		2	0·74	0·79	0·92	1·00	1·00	—
		3	0·74	0·79	0·92	1·00	1·00	—
		4	0·65	0·74	0·88	0·99	1·00	—
		5	0·59	0·69	0·84	0·99	1·00	—
0·5	0·9	1	0·40	0·50	0·61	0·71	0·86	0·96
		2	0·48	0·60	0·76	0·85	0·97	1·00
		3	0·48	0·59	0·76	0·84	0·97	1·00
		4	0·44	0·61	0·69	0·87	0·98	1·00
		5	0·51	0·59	0·75	0·88	0·99	1·00
0·9	0·9	1	0·27	0·40	0·34	0·40	0·37	0·48
		2	0·28	0·42	0·41	0·47	0·53	0·72
		3	0·29	0·42	0·42	0·49	0·52	0·72
		4	0·35	0·39	0·32	0·42	0·46	0·63
		5	0·34	0·43	0·32	0·46	0·47	0·66

Table 1. The frequency of correct inference of a topology 1 tree by unrooted methods. The times given are splitting times as specified in figure 2 for topology 1. The methods of analysis are described in the text

Times		Method	Number of characters											
t_1	t_2		3		5		10		20		50		100	
0·1	0·2	1	0·42	0·45	0·44	0·43	0·52	0·49	0·61	0·71	0·76	0·79	0·93	0·90
		2	0·52	0·49	0·58	0·51	0·65	0·66	0·82	0·84	0·92	0·91	0·98	0·98
		3	0·44	0·44	0·55	0·49	0·57	0·53	0·71	0·75	0·85	0·82	0·96	0·95
		4	0·64	0·59	0·64	0·63	0·79	0·80	0·87	0·95	0·99	1·00	1·00	1·00
		5	0·46	0·38	0·56	0·50	0·73	0·75	0·82	0·94	0·98	1·00	1·00	1·00
0·1	0·5	1	0·60		0·74		0·80		0·97		0·99		—	
		2	0·75		0·84		0·92		0·99		1·00		—	
		3	0·67		0·76		0·83		0·97		0·99		—	
		4	0·78		0·94		0·99		1·00		1·00		—	
		5	0·68		0·91		0·98		1·00		1·00		—	
0·1	0·9	1	0·64		0·83		0·95		0·98		1·00		—	
		2	0·74		0·85		0·98		1·00		1·00		—	
		3	0·68		0·80		0·94		0·99		1·00		—	
		4	0·85		0·92		0·98		1·00		1·00		—	
		5	0·74		0·89		0·97		1·00		1·00		—	

0·5	0·9	1	0·41	0·46	0·54	0·62	0·81	0·87
		2	0·49	0·54	0·69	0·70	0·95	0·96
		3	0·48	0·55	0·70	0·68	0·95	0·94
		4	0·50	0·54	0·64	0·88	0·97	1·00
		5	0·49	0·54	0·71	0·83	1·00	1·00
0·8	0·9	1	0·42	0·36	0·44	0·26	0·32	0·46
		2	0·44	0·39	0·44	0·41	0·53	0·60
		3	0·43	0·40	0·44	0·41	0·51	0·60
		4	0·42	0·40	0·35	0·37	0·52	0·63
		5	0·45	0·40	0·41	0·45	0·61	0·65

Table 2. The frequency of correct inference of a topology 2 tree by unrooted methods. The times given are splitting times as specified in figure 2 for topology 2. The methods of analysis are described in the text.

Times		Method	Number of characters					
t_1	t_2		3	5	10	20	50	100
0·1	0·1	4	0·92	1·00	1·00	1·00	1·00	1·00
		5	0·53	0·86	0·98	1·00	1·00	1·00
0·1	0·5	4	0·56	0·81	0·86	0·97	1·00	—
		5	0·33	0·57	0·68	0·90	0·99	—
0·1	0·9	4	0·45	0·47	0·61	0·74	0·91	0·98
		5	0·21	0·28	0·31	0·33	0·43	0·53
0·5	0·5	4	0·49	0·60	0·74	0·97	1·00	—
		5	0·23	0·34	0·54	0·82	0·99	—
0·5	0·9	4	0·27	0·34	0·48	0·60	0·69	0·88
		5	0·17	0·26	0·29	0·37	0·49	0·58
0·9	0·9	4	0·11	0·23	0·15	0·31	0·28	0·46
		5	0·09	0·14	0·13	0·16	0·16	0·32

Table 3. The frequency of correct inference of a topology 1 tree by rooted methods. The times given are splitting times as specified in figure 2 for topology 1. The methods of analysis are described in the text

Times t_1	t_2	Method	Number of characters 3	5	10	20	50	100
0·1	0·2	4	0·53 0·46	0·55 0·57	0·76 0·80	0·86 0·95	0·99 1·00	1·00 1·00
		5	0·30 0·31	0·49 0·44	0·72 0·73	0·82 0·94	0·98 1·00	1·00 1·00
0·1	0·5	4	0·38	0·51	0·71	0·85	0·95	—
		5	0·32	0·55	0·81	0·94	0·99	—
0·1	0·9	4	0·24	0·29	0·28	0·28	0·26	—
		5	0·38	0·36	0·39	0·48	0·67	—
0·5	0·9	4	0·11	0·14	0·16	0·26	0·48	0·38
		5	0·17	0·22	0·29	0·42	0·65	0·71
0·8	0·9	4	0·08	0·05	0·10	0·06	0·21	0·32
		5	0·11	0·12	0·17	0·13	0·39	0·42

Table 4. The frequency of correct inference of a topology 2 tree by rooted methods. The times given are splitting times as specified in figure 2 for topology 2. The methods of analysis are described in the text

REFERENCES

Cavalli-Sforza, L.L. (1966) Population structure and human evolution. *Proc. Roy. Soc.*, **194**, 362–9.

Cavalli-Sforza, L.L. & Edwards, A.W.F. (1967) Phylogenetic analysis: models and estimation procedures. *Amer. J. hum. Genet.*, **9**, 234–57; also *Evolution*, **21**, 550–70.

Edwards, A.W.F. (1970) Estimation of the branch points of a branching diffusion process. *J. Roy. stat. Soc. B*, **32**, 155–74.

Edwards, A.W.F. (1971) Mathematical approaches to the study of human evolution. *Mathematics in the Archaeological & Historical Sciences*, pp. 347–55 (eds Hodson, F.R., Kendall, D.G., & Tăutu, P.). Edinburgh: Edinburgh University Press.

Edwards, A.W.F. & Cavalli-Sforza, L.L. (1963) The reconstruction of evolution. *Ann. hum. Genet.*, **27**, 105 (abstract).

Edwards, A.W.F. & Cavalli-Sforza, L.L. (1965) A method for cluster analysis. *Biometrics*, **21**, 362–75.

Fitch, W.M. & Margoliash, E. (1967) Construction of phylogenetic trees. *Science*, **155**, 279–84.

Kidd, K.K. (1969) *Phylogenetic analysis of cattle breeds*. Ph D Thesis, University of Wisconsin, Madison, Wisconsin.

Kidd, K.K. (1971) Application to man and cattle of methods of reconstructing evolutionary histories. *Mathematics in the Archaeological & Historical Sciences*, pp. 356–60 (eds Hodson, F.R., Kendall, D.G. & Tăutu, P.). Edinburgh: Edinburgh University Press.

Kidd, K.K. & Sgaramella-Zonta, Laura (1971) Phylogenetic analysis: Concepts and methods. *Amer. J. hum Genet.*, **23**, 235–52.

Population Genetics

Anthony W. F. Edwards
Mathematical approaches to the study of human evolution

Those of us who are more mathematician than archaeologist or historian have been asked to address mainly those in the latter disciplines, and I am therefore going to take the opportunity to discuss developments in my own field, human genetics, in rather general terms, paying particular attention to the logic of our procedures and to techniques for pictorial representation of our results. In fact it is a moot point as to whether I am more mathematician than historian, for my training is in genetics, and my particular interest the reconstruction of the recent genetic history of man, recent, that is, in biological rather than historical terms. But modern work in this field incorporates a large mathematical element, and has benefited greatly from the consequent increase in objectivity and clarity. My own experience has convinced me that in those subjects which hitherto have not had much mathematical content, progress will best be made by scholars learning some of the mathematical techniques for themselves, rather than by expecting their mathematical colleagues to apply these techniques for them in an advisory capacity. There is, in my view, a real danger in the latter course that techniques which are logically quite inappropriate will be applied. This is especially true in statistics, where the logical foundations are still in dispute. For example, the over-enthusiastic application in human genetics of some standard statistical methods, now seen to be inappropriate, led to some quite unwarranted conclusions about genetic linkage—the occurrence on the same chromosome of genes for specific characters. Conferences such as the present one are of great value in bridging the gap between mathematics and other disciplines, but I hope that archaeologists and historians will apply to mathematical techniques the same critical judgment that they employ in their own fields, and that this conference is providing some of the understanding without which that judgment cannot be made. In biology there is no sadder sight than young men pouring their hard-won observations into voracious computers which obey commands and produce yards of printed output beyond the young biologists' capacity to understand and interpret. The new technology must be treated as an aid to, not a substitute for, thought.

DEVELOPMENT OF STUDIES OF THE PHYLOGENY OF MAN

The Darwinian view of the evolution of man presents us with the hypothesis that all the races of man are descended from a common ancestor, and that the genetic differences which distinguish them have arisen by the progressive accumulation of different genes, or of the same genes in different frequencies, through the influence of four agents. First, mutation has given rise to new gene variants. Some, such as the mutant for albinism, are probably very old, since they are not confined to our own species; others, such as some blood-group genes, seem to exist only in man, but are common in all races; others exist in some races of man, but not in all, such as the B blood-group gene, which was probably absent in pre-Columbian American Indians; and yet others are confined to single families, such as some haemoglobin variants. Secondly, natural selection has influenced the frequency of occurrence of the various genes, eliminating some, making others universal, and establishing polymorphisms for others, in which two or more allelic variants are maintained within a population. Thirdly, the vagaries of Mendelian segregation ensure that the genes present in one generation are but a sample of the genes of the previous generation, so that sometimes genes will be lost altogether, and invariably polymorphic genes will change their frequencies from generation to generation. And fourthly, the migration of man throughout the world has led to a 'world trade' in genes.

The great genetic variety of man, therefore, may be ascribed to forces about which we now have considerable knowledge. Mutation provides the raw material; natural selection, acting with different intensities at different times and places, provides a major diversifying force, aided by the statistical processes of genetics which ensure that, even without selection, no generation is like its predecessor; and migration provides the movement of genes, and ensures that populations once similar in their genetic composition can evolve in different ways, separated by distance or other isolating factors.

This genetic diversity exists in parallel with cultural diversity, and much of what we know about the development of man into separate races has been contributed by research in the fields of history, archaeology, and social anthropology, particularly linguistics. Cultural evolution parallels biological evolution, and indeed the two are interdependent: some cultural traits may have quite specific genetic determinants, and certainly some cultural traditions, such as infanticide, leave their mark on the genetic complement of a population.

A further large contribution to our knowledge has been made by physical anthropologists, working with physical characteristics, either qualitatively or, in the tradition of the early biometricians, quantitatively, but without specific reference to the underlying genetic determinants. It is when we turn to the utilization of genetic information that we find a pressing need for a mathematical treatment. Cultural and, to some extent, physical similarity between races or populations may be intuitively appraised, but what do we mean by genetic similarity? Is a population which carries only the O blood-group gene more similar to one that carries only B than it is to one that is half A and half B? Is a gene frequency difference at the Rhesus locus as informative as a similar difference at the ABO locus? Are gene frequency differences between two small populations as informative as similar differences between large populations? A framework for answering such questions must be established if we are to do justice to the ever-increasing quantity of data that is being collected about the presence and frequency of genes in populations. Certainly, some progress can be made without such a framework, for the frequencies can be regarded as population characteristics in the same way as any other character, cultural or biological, and the pioneering work of Dr Arthur Mourant in synthesizing the information from the blood groups, published in 1954 in his book *The Distribution of the Human Blood Groups* amply demonstrates this. As Dr Mourant points out in his introduction, the great advantage in using blood group information lies in the accuracy with which the observed blood group—or 'phenotype'—reflects the genetic determinants, and he correctly insists in using gene frequencies, rather than phenotype frequencies, as the relevant characteristics. But in other respects he and his predecessors made comparisons between populations which were essentially qualitative rather than quantitative.

My specific interest is in the differentiation of our species into the races that inhabit the earth today. One of the lessons of modern taxonomy is that the precise definition of any unit of sub-specific classification, such as a race, is virtually impossible; nevertheless, one needs terms to describe, in a general way, the level of classification at which one is working. I shall use 'race' to mean the smallest subdivision of our species to which an individual can be ascribed, with a small probability of error, on the basis of his biological characteristics. Though I am of Welsh stock, I have frequently been mistaken for a German, and sometimes for an Italian, but never for a Swede, an Eskimo, or a Pygmy. I think you can see the level of subspeciation at which I am aiming.

Our knowledge of the differences between the races of man, in the form in which they existed before the large-scale migrations of historic times, is very good, thanks to the efforts of anthropologists and, latterly, geneticists. But our knowledge of how these differences arose, or even when they arose, is very sketchy, in spite of the determined efforts of generations of archaeologists and palaeontologists. It is not that they have dug up insufficient cultural and fossil remains, but that the results of their labours do not fit easily into any simple pattern for human evolution. It is not clear whether the present races of man all descend from a single race which existed 30,000 years ago or one which existed 100,000 years ago. Presumably if we go back far enough we will encounter some group, ancestral to us all, which was sufficiently homogeneous to merit the title of a race, but we may have to travel very far indeed. I do not wish to discuss the controversy here, but merely to point out that a fresh approach to the problem of the phylogeny of man, using data which is independent of that used so far, is most welcome.

DATA

The data to which I refer are, of course, the frequencies of genes around the world. There are now some sixty polymorphic loci, that is, loci in which two or more different genes are represented with appreciable frequency in the species as a whole, that have been sufficiently well studied to be able to provide useful information on racial differences. They include the many blood-group systems, the red-cell enzymes, and serum groups and enzymes, but in practice only the major blood-group systems need be considered because insufficient information is, as yet, available about the frequencies of other genes on a world-wide basis. But the principles I shall discuss hold for all the systems.

The longest-known blood-group system, ABO, was discovered by Land-steiner in 1900, and, in 1919, the Hirszfelds showed that the genes responsible differed in frequency from race to race. Since then a large amount of information about gene-frequencies in this and other blood-groups has been collected. Samples of blood are taken from a group of people, and the blood-group phenotypes determined by serological techniques. The frequencies of the various phenotypes are then used to estimate the gene frequencies in the population to which the group of people tested belong. There are difficulties in this process of statistical estimation: the group may not be representative of the population, or may not consist of people who are not closely related; dominance in the genetic system may introduce further uncertainty in the estimates. At the serological level, some tests may be unreliable. But by and large it is possible to obtain estimates of gene frequencies whose uncertainty is small compared with the differences between races, and we therefore neglect this small uncertainty. For this neglect to be unimportant we have to ensure adequate sample sizes, but this is not a problem at the level at which we are working.

On the basis of this information, gene-frequency maps may be drawn, as given in Dr Mourant's book, showing the world or regional variation in the incidence of the various genes. Thus, in the ABO system, we see that A is relatively frequent in the aboriginal populations of Canada and North-West United States, in Lapland, and in Australia, whilst B is common in Asia. O makes up the difference, and is virtually universal in South America.

How did these differences arise? What phylogenetic history do they reflect? We must answer the first question before we can answer the second, but unfortunately no clear answer is possible. We know, in general terms, that the differences must have arisen through the four agencies already mentioned: mutation, selection, random genetic drift, and migration. We have practically no direct evidence about mutation and selection, but we may cautiously assume that the occurrence of the same gene in different races is due to common ancestry rather than independent mutation, and that subsequently mutation pressure has been relatively unimportant. Further, any selection that there may have been will have led to small rates of change, differing in rate and direction, depending on the time, the place, and the blood-group system. By an application of the Central Limit Theorem, such selective forces will lead to an essentially random movement of gene frequencies if enough genetic systems are considered simultaneously, as shown by Kimura. They will thus closely simulate, and may be considered part of, the random changes in gene frequencies due to the vagaries of Mendelian segregation, called 'random genetic drift'. The general picture, therefore, is one of gene frequencies changing in a random fashion, and Kimura has shown that the characteristic dispersion matrix may be expected to be approximately proportional to the dispersion matrix of the multinomial distribution, which I will give later.

The fourth agency of change, migration, has been instrumental in leading to the observed distribution of gene frequencies, but it is largely this migration we want to learn something about, and therefore we do not regard the present geographic distribution of the races of man as primary information. On the other hand, we must make some assumption about the nature of past migrations, for if these caused different races to meet and interbreed, rather than always to diverge, it will influence our conclusions. In order to make as simple (and therefore as tractable) a model for evolutionary divergence as possible, we will assume that significant interbreeding has not taken place between races during the period of interest, and that the process of differentiation has been one of a race splitting into two groups, each then travelling its own genetic route independently, the process being repeated again and again. Thus the overall picture is one of an evolutionary tree, and if one can imagine this placed in a Euclidean space whose metric represents overall differences in gene frequencies, each branch of the tree will represent a random walk of a population, twisting, turning, and splitting, until finally arriving at its present position. Our problem is to infer the shape and dimensions of this tree given only the positions of the tips of its branches, representing our knowledge of world gene-frequencies.

It is, of course, too simple a model for evolutionary divergence. But every statistical inference is conditional on a model, implicit if not explicit, and no model is true in an absolute sense. We must not ask 'Is it true?', but 'Is it good enough for present purposes?'. I think the above model is, at least for a first attempt. If the attempt fails, then the model may have to be reconsidered.

METHODS: A MEASURE OF GENETIC DISTANCE

I now come to the first aspect of the methodology specially created for this problem which might be of general interest. Considering a single population and a single genetic locus with k alleles, we picture it, according to the above model, as pursuing a random-walk in a space indexed by the frequencies of the genes at that locus. Since the frequencies of the genes at a locus must sum to unity, if we use Cartesian coordinates for the k gene frequencies p_i, $i=1$, ... k, the space of possible points must be the hyperplane $\sum_{i=1}^{k} p_i = 1$, which is a flat Euclidean space of $k-1$ dimensions. Indeed, since no gene frequency can be negative, it is a simplex. For $k=3$ this simplex is an equilateral triangle, and we may think of the perpendiculars from a point to the three sides as equal to the three gene frequencies provided we scale the triangle to have unit height.

A typical population is wandering round the simplex with dispersion matrix whose (i,j)th element is $-p_i p_j t/2n$ for $i \neq j$ and $p_i^2 t/2n$ for $i=j$, where t is the time elapsed, and n is the size of the population. This result is approximate, requiring that t, in generations, be small compared with n, and is due to Kimura. The random walk has zero mathematical drift, the expected position in the next generation equalling the actual position in the preceding generation. Since the variances are functions of the gene frequencies, the simplex space is not isotropic for the random walk. Near the boundaries the random walk is slow in contrast to the central regions; it is also then asymmetric, preferring particular directions. If a stochastic distance is to have any useful meaning, it must clearly be measured in a space which is isotropic for the random walk, for otherwise the same distance will have different meaning in different parts of the space, or in different directions. In an isotropic space, the meaning to be attributed to a particular distance anywhere is that there is a certain probability that this distance will be traversed by a point undergoing the random walk, in a given time.

Isotropy will be achieved if we can find a transformation of the p_i so that the transformed variables have a distribution in the simplex which exhibits circular symmetry. Since the dispersion matrix of the p_i is proportional to the corresponding multinomial dispersion matrix, we can use the general form of the transformation which Fisher suggested for the binomial distribution:

$$\sin^2 \theta_i = p_i, \text{ for all } i.$$

This transformation is equivalent to the plotting of the square roots of the gene frequencies, $\sqrt{p_i}$, along k Cartesian axes, and the resulting population space is the $(1/2)^k$th part of the surface of the unit hypersphere in k dimensions.

It is easy to show that the dispersion matrix for the θ_i has (i, j)th element $-\tan \theta_i \tan \theta_j \, t/8n$ for $i \neq j$ and $t/8n$ for $i=j$. Bhattacharyya showed that the resulting distribution is approximately normal, circularly symmetrical, and with variance $t/8n$, which is precisely what we want. There has been some misunderstanding, even in statistical circles, of the fact that θ_i and θ_j are not independent variables, being correlated with coefficient $-\tan \theta_i \tan \theta_j$. The space in which the normal approximation holds is a curved space with $k-1$ degrees of freedom, but is conveniently indexed by the k variables θ_i. Indeed, $\cos (\pi/2 - \theta_i)$ is the ith direction cosine of the population with respect to the k original Cartesian axes. If the distribution really is circularly symmetrical in the spherical $(k-1)$-space, then the correlation between θ_i and θ_j will be given by $\cos \phi$, where ϕ is the angle between the great circles joining the population to the ith and jth vertices of the space. These great circle arcs are, from the direction cosines, of length $\pi/2 - \theta_i$ and $\pi/2 - \theta_j$, and since the length of the great circle arc joining any two vertices is $\pi/2$, we have to solve a spherical triangle with these sides, for the angle ϕ opposite the side of length $\pi/2$. Applying the cosine rule of spherical trigonometry we immediately find $\cos \phi = -\tan \theta_i \tan \theta_j$, the required result.

Hence, however we care to index the space, it is asymptotically isotropic for the random walk, whose distribution is everywhere the same and everywhere circularly symmetrical, just as required. As Bhattacharyya observed, the distance between two points representing populations with gene frequencies p_i and p_i' is α, where

$$\cos \alpha = \sum_{i=1}^{k} \sqrt{(p_i p_i')} \ .$$

I think this formula deserves to be more widely known, for it is relevant as a measure of distance wherever we have a random walk, amongst proportions, which is characterized by a dispersion matrix proportional to that of the multinomial distribution.

Unfortunately those same statisticians who have been unable to understand that the circular symmetry in the space of $k-1$ degrees of freedom is quite unaffected by the fact that k interdependent coordinates are used, have also misunderstood another point: the above transformation is designed to place the populations in an isotropic space, it being assumed that the population gene frequencies are sufficiently well known for their sampling errors of estimation to be quite uninteresting compared with the differences between populations. It is in no way intended to standardize these sampling errors, though incidentally it will do so if all the samples are the same size and are multinomial (as is the case only when there is no dominance).

Our task is still not quite finished, because the random walk is now taking place on the surface of a hypersphere, and if we wish to combine the information from several gene loci, this fact raises a difficulty. Furthermore, many computer programs rely on the points being in Euclidean space, so we take the final step of projecting the $(1/2)^k$th part of the hypersphere into a Euclidean space of $k-1$ dimensions. Circular symmetry is preserved at the expense of some marginal scale distortion if we use the multi-dimensional orthomorphic zenithal projection, sometimes known as the stereographic projection. Omitting the details, the new Cartesian coordinates are

$$y_i = \frac{2(\sqrt{p_i} + \sqrt{(1/k)})}{1 + \sum \sqrt{(p_i/k)}} - \frac{1}{\sqrt{k}}, \quad \text{all } i,$$

and populations thus displayed lie in a Euclidean space of $k-1$ dimensions, since $\sum y_i = \sqrt{k}$. Of course the overall scale factor is arbitrary, and it is convenient to adjust it so that the distance in the centre of the space is in gene substitutions. The distance between two populations is then

$$E = \frac{4\sqrt{2}}{\pi} \sqrt{\left\{ \frac{1 - \sum \sqrt{(p_i p_i')}}{(1 + \sum \sqrt{(p_i/k)})(1 + \sum \sqrt{(p_i'/k)})} \right\}}$$

gene substitutions. Being a distance in a Euclidean space, distances from different loci may be combined by Pythagoras' rule.

METHODS: ESTIMATING THE PHYLOGENETIC TREE

Collecting the available data from every locus for each population or race, we can now represent it as an array of points in a Euclidean space which is as near isotropic as we can make it with respect to the random walk implicit in our model. Indeed, using Bhattacharyya's result about the approximate normality of the distribution characterizing the random walk, the evolution of a population appears as a Brownian motion in the space. On the simplest possible model for population splitting, that in which in every small time interval there is a constant probability of each population dividing into two, the stochastic building of the tree will be characterized by a Yule process.

Our problem, then, is to infer the tree size and shape from a knowledge of the present population positions, on the assumption that the present positions have arisen according to a Brownian motion/Yule process. It turns out to be quite a difficult problem, and the mathematical intricacies required so far are nothing compared to those now needed. I venture to suggest that this problem is the fundamental problem of statistical inference in cases where a tree-structure is admitted, for the Brownian motion/Yule process is the simplest model we can contemplate.

23

I have made two attempts to solve the problem. The first, suggested in 1963, was purely intuitive. If we collapse the actual, but unknown, evolutionary tree in the time direction, obtaining its projection on to the space of present populations, we could start by trying to estimate this projection. Observing that the straight line between two points was the maximum-likelihood estimate of the path traversed by a randomly-walking point that visited both, I conjectured that the maximum-likelihood estimate of the projected tree was the shortest tree uniting all the population points. Since distance in the space represents an amount of evolution, this method was called the 'Method of Minimum Evolution'. Computer programs were written to seek the minimum-length tree, since no algorithm is known which finds it with certainty, and in actual application the method has proved quite successful. A great advantage of the metric tree representation is that, without changing the lengths of the branches, the tree can be dragged out of the multi-dimensional space and flattened out on a piece of paper. The disadvantage of the method of minimum evolution is that I now know the conjecture on which it was based to be false, and it does not give any estimates of the times of the nodes, nor even of the root of the tree, though Haigh's method can be adapted here. But it is simple, easy to visualize, and intuitively quite sensible; and though I hardly dare mention it in view of my earlier comments, it is fun.

The second attempt to solve the problem involved a frontal attack using standard statistical estimation theory. I say 'standard', though in fact it soon became apparent that one had to use methods which were anything but standard. Last year I gave an account of what I believe to be the outline of the correct solution, but it is far too complex to put into practice. But one thing did become apparent in the hours of computing I spent trying to forge a solution: though we may be able to estimate the form of the tree, and even the positions of its nodes, the times of the nodes can be estimated only with such vagueness that they are hardly worth bothering with. And that means that we might as well return to the method of minimum evolution, which tells us the form of the tree and the node positions.

In the absence of a full solution to the Brownian motion/Yule model, a solution which is a little more firmly based than the method of minimum evolution would indeed be welcome. Professor Whittle has made some most interesting suggestions as to how this might be achieved, by picturing the process reversed in time. But for the present I think the method of minimum evolution is likely to be the commonest method, at least in human genetics, and I suggest it to you as a not unreasonable way of obtaining some idea of the tree structure of points in a Euclidean space—the second aspect of the methodology of my particular problem which might be of general interest.

CONCLUSION

I should like to conclude by returning to the philosophical implications of our activities. Computers ready-programmed with the most sophisticated multivariate statistical analyses are becoming commonplace, and the pressure to use the standard programs is increasing. I can foresee a time when a PhD student with a batch of multivariate data who declines to use one of these omnivorous programs will be regarded as rather odd, not to say a nuisance, like people who ride bicycles in cities. Now the only sure way to decide what form of analysis is appropriate is, in my view, to commit yourself to a specific model according to which you think the observations might have been generated. Merely to define the properties which you wish the solution to have is not good enough for critical work unless you can explain why you want those properties. I am myself guilty of having invented one such method of cluster analysis; others have invented other methods which use other criteria, but the argument over which criteria are best cannot be resolved without a model for the process of dispersion. We are in a characteristic phase in the development of a statistical technique. For centuries, I suppose, people used the arithmetic mean of observations, but not until Gauss was there a satisfactory justification of this procedure, which of course simultaneously explained why, on some models, other procedures might be better. For several decades estimation was undertaken by the method of moments, until Fisher pointed out that on most models you should really do something quite different. Nowadays we train armies of young statisticians to think that estimators should be unbiased, a well-defined property which in fact turns out to be quite irrelevant on a deep analysis.

In developing our methods, it is vital that we nourish that intellectual variability in approach without which, as every biologist knows, evolution cannot proceed. The computer represents the gravest threat yet to that variability, and at the same time as we enjoy the tremendous advances in calculating power that it provides, we must consciously strive to defend our subjects from the dead hand of automation and the narrow logic of programmers.

BIBLIOGRAPHY

Details of the methods are most fully described in:

Cavalli Sforza, L.L. & Edwards, A.W.F. (1967) Phylogenetic analysis: Models and estimation procedures. *Evolution*, **21**, 550–70; *Amer. J. Hum. Genet.* (supp.), **19**, 233–57.

Full references are given in the above paper. For recent work on maximum-likelihood estimation applied to this problem, consult:

Edwards, A.W.F. (1970) Estimation of the branch points of a branching diffusion process (with discussion). *J. Roy. statist. Soc.*, B. **32**, 155–74.

For recent work on measures of genetic distance, consult:

Edwards, A.W.F. (1971) Distances between populations on the basis of gene frequencies. *Biometrics*. In press.

Edwards, A.W.F. & Cavalli-Sforza, L.L. (1971) Affinity as revealed by differences in gene frequencies. In *The Assessment of Biological Affinity and Distance between Human Populations*. To be published by Oxford University Press.

A recent reference not given in any of the above is:

Haigh, J. (1970) The recovery of the root of a tree. *J. Appl. Prob.* **7**, 79–88.

Population Genetics

Kenneth K. Kidd
Applications to man and cattle of
methods of reconstructing evolutionary histories

The methods of phylogenetic analysis developed by Cavalli-Sforza and Edwards (1967) are based on gene frequency differences among populations. They have since been amplified (Kidd and Sgaramella-Zonta 1971) and further applied to studies of man (Ward and Neel 1970, Friedlaender *et al.* 1971) and cattle (Kidd 1969, Kidd and Sgaramella-Zonta 1970). One basic assumption of the methods is that evolution has produced the separate populations by a simple dichotomous branching process. In the two studies of primitive human populations the bifurcating trees produced by the analyses cannot be true representations of evolutionary relationships because of the complicated patterns of migration and hybridization among populations. Nevertheless, the 'phylogenetic' trees were good graphic representations of the genetic relationships of the populations and, as such, useful. Such 'phylogenetic' trees, based on immunogenetic data, showed generally high agreement with linguistic, geographic, and anthropometric distances in the study of Melanesian populations on Bougainville (Friedlaender *et al.* 1971).

In the studies of cattle breeds it was possible to reduce the effects of hybridization by selecting breeds that have had long, distinct genetic histories. We showed that the reconstructed phylogenetic trees were in good general agreement with available historical data on the cattle breeds. For example, Icelandic cattle always grouped with Norwegian cattle, while Jersey and American Longhorn were distinct from each other as well as from all Scandinavian and Low Countries breeds. Figure 1 shows a phylogenetic tree for nine cattle breeds drawn on a map of Europe. While there is reason to believe that this tree is a reasonable estimate of the true phylogenetic relationships of these breeds, such a representation cannot at present be considered to represent migrational paths. It is simply a graphic illustration allowing one to see both the genetic and geographic relationships of these breeds.

Additional data are now being collected to extend the studies to other breeds and to improve the probability of reconstructing the correct tree (*see* Kidd and Cavalli-Sforza 1971). With the data now available, however, it is possible to make a first approximate estimate of when various breeds separated.

Cavalli-Sforza (1969) showed that under random genetic drift the kinship coefficient, f_θ, between populations was related to time of separation in the following way

$$f_\theta = 1 - e^{-t/2N}$$

where N is the effective population size. A time estimate may thereby be

obtained as
$$t = -2N \log (1 - f_\theta) \quad .$$
Because we do not yet have estimates of the effective population sizes for cattle breeds over the last 3–4,000 years, we are forced to calculate only relative time estimates assuming the effective population sizes to be equal, that is, $t_r = -\log (1 - f_\theta)$.

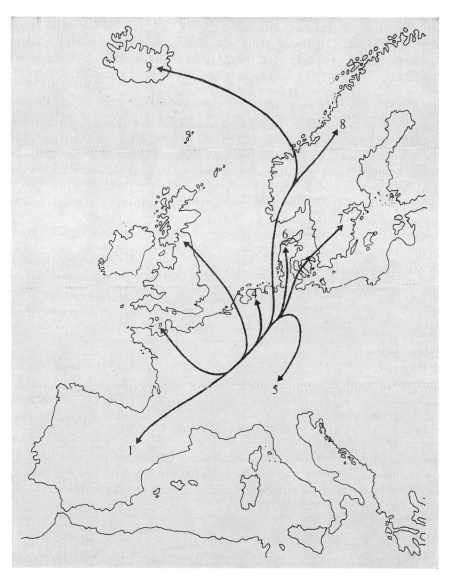

Figure 1. A graphic representation of a phylogenetic tree for nine cattle breeds. Kidd (1969) discusses the analyses and data that produced this tree. In this representation the topological relationships are preserved but the segments are not drawn to scale. The breeds indicated are (1) American Longhorn, (2) Jersey, (3) Ayrshire, (4) Holstein-Friesian, (5) Brown Swiss, (6) Red Danish, (7) Polled Swedish, (8) Trønder, and (9) Icelandic

The kinship coefficient, f_θ, is related to the genetic distance G (Kidd 1969) by the following formula

$$f_\theta = \frac{G^2\pi^2}{2\sum_i (k_i - 1)}$$

where summation is over loci and k_i is the number of alleles at each locus. Thus G-values previously calculated can be used to estimate relative times of separation. By using the historically known isolation of Icelandic cattle almost 1,000 years ago with their probable common origin with modern Norwegian breeds (Braend *et al.* 1962; Kidd 1969), it is possible to convert the relative time estimates into estimates of the actual times of separation.

ANALYSIS

The data given in Kidd (1969) was based on 6 loci. Five loci had two alleles each; the B blood-group locus had a total of 157 distinct alleles in the study. For the B-locus it would be better to use the effective number of alleles than the actual number, but it was difficult to estimate for all breeds. Since there are usually only four or five alleles at even moderate frequency (10–30%), two approximations of the effective number of alleles were used for the analyses: $k_B = 6$ (low) and $k_B = 11$ (high).

Figure 2 shows the phylogenetic tree extracted from the results in Kidd (1969) and the average squared genetic distance separating the two groups at each split. The time estimates are given in table 1.

Comparison	$\bar{G}^2$	First estimate $-\log(1-f_\theta)$	Approximate times	Second estimate $-\log(1-f_\theta)$	Approximate times
Norwegian–Icelandic	0·52	0·297	1,000	0·188	1,000
Norse–Swedish	0·61	0·358	1,205	0·224	1,191
Scandinavian–others	1·21	0·909	3,060	0·509	2,707

Table 1. Time estimates for Breed Separation. [Times are given in years before present. The first and second estimates are based on low and high estimates of the effective number of alleles at the B blood group locus (*see* text)]

DISCUSSION

There are several reasons for considering these time estimates to be very inexact. The assumption of equal effective population sizes is almost certainly not correct, but is necessary since there are no estimates of the effective sizes of the various breeds throughout the past 3,000 years. By using historical data on the individual breeds, it may be possible to estimate these more accurately in the future. The effective number of alleles at the B locus may also be estimated more accurately and will probably be found to vary among the breeds. Variation among populations in both effective population size and effective number of alleles will affect both the relative and absolute time values.

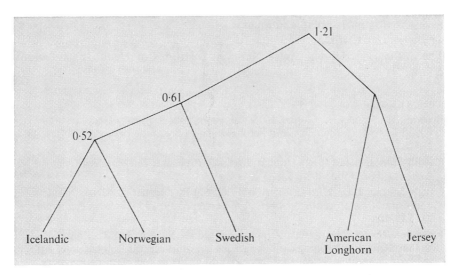

Figure 2. The phylogenetic relationships used to calculate time estimates. The values given at three splits are the average G^2 values across those splits calculated from data in Kidd (1969). Norwegian cattle are represented by four native breeds, Swedish cattle by the Polled Swedish breed, and non-Scandinavian breeds by Jersey and American Longhorn (of Spanish origin). The tree is not drawn to scale

There is one reason, however, for thinking that the time values given here are underestimates. Icelandic cattle have been through one bottleneck in addition to whatever founder effect occurred at the time of colonization. Thus it is possible that relative to the other breeds Icelandic cattle have had a smaller effective population size. This would lead to an underestimate of the other times based on the Icelandic–Norwegian separation having taken place 1,000 years ago.

Though they are probably underestimates, these approximate time values nevertheless seem to be of the correct order of magnitude. When better genetic data and better estimates of the effective population sizes are available, such time estimates should be more accurate and may be valuable to the historian interested in human population movements and the cultural archaeologist studying the domestication of cattle.

SUMMARY

Methods of phylogenetic analysis have been applied to human populations and to cattle populations. The results are encouraging, as when the reconstructed evolutionary trees for cattle breeds of western European origin confirmed the common origin of Icelandic and modern Norwegian cattle. If one assumes, from historical records, that this common origin dates from 1,000 years ago, additional analyses indicate that ancestral Swedish cattle separated from the Norwegian stock at least 1,200 years ago and that these Scandinavian cattle have been separated from Jersey and Spanish cattle for perhaps 3,000 years. Such time estimates are only rough first approximations; additional data and refined estimates of population size will be necessary for more reliable estimates.

ACKNOWLEDGMENT

The author is a United States National Institutes of Health post-doctoral fellow.

REFERENCES

Braend, M., Rendel, J., Gahne, B. & Adalsteinsson, S. (1962) Genetic studies on blood groups, transferrins, and hemoglobins in Icelandic cattle. *Hereditas*, **48**, 264–83.

Cavalli-Sforza, L.L. (1969) Human diversity. *Proc. XII International Congress of Genetics, Vol. 3*, pp. 405–16.

Cavalli-Sforza, L.L. & Edwards, A.W.F. (1967) Phylogenetic analysis: models and estimation procedures. *Amer. J. hum. Genet.*, **9**, 234–57; Also *Evolution*, **21**, 550–70.

Friedlaender, J.S., Sgaramella-Zonta, L., Kidd, K.K., Lai, L.Y.C., Clark, P. & Walsh, R.J. (1971) Biological divergences in south-central Bougainville. An analysis of serological gene frequencies and anthropometric measurements utilizing tree models, and a comparison of these variables with linguistic, geographic, and migrational 'distances'. *Amer. J. hum. Genet.*, **23**, 253–70.

Kidd, K.K. (1969) *Phylogenetic analysis of cattle breeds*. PhD thesis. University of Wisconsin, Madison, Wisconsin.

Kidd, K.K. & Cavalli-Sforza, L.L. (1971) Number of characters examined and error in reconstruction of evolutionary trees. *Mathematics in the Archaeological & Historical Sciences*, pp. 335–46 (eds Hodson, F.R., Kendall, D.G. & Tăutu, P.). Edinburgh: Edinburgh University Press.

Kidd, K.K. & Sgaramella-Zonta, L. (1970) Relationships of domestic cattle breeds. *XII Int. Conf. on Animal Blood Groups and Biochemical Polymorphisms Proc.* July 1970, Budapest, Hungary. In press.

Kidd, K.K. & Sgaramella-Zonta, L.A. (1971) Phylogenetic analysis: concepts and methods. *Amer. J. hum. Genet.*, **23**, 235–52.

Ward, R.H. & Neel, J.V. (1970) Gene frequencies and micro-differentiation among the Makiritare Indians. IV. A comparison of a genetic network with ethnohistory and migration matrices; a new index of genetic migration. *Amer. J. hum. Genet.*, **22**, 538–61.

Linguistics

Joseph B. Kruskal, Isidore Dyen, and Paul Black
The vocabulary method of reconstructing language trees:
innovations and large-scale applications

Language Families

Language is man's greatest cultural invention. The history of man's languages is always fascinating. Some parts of this history are obvious to the most casual investigator. That French, Romanian, Italian, Spanish, and Portuguese have a common origin in Latin has always been known to many speakers of these languages. The common Germanic origin of English, German, Swedish, Danish, Norwegian, and Dutch is equally familiar. However it was a truly remarkable discovery that these two groups of languages have descended from a common language spoken long before, and that from this earlier language come also the Slavic languages (such as Russian, Polish, and Bulgarian), the Baltic languages (such as Lithuanian), the Indic languages (including Sanskrit and its many modern descendants such as Hindi, Punjabi, and Romany), the Iranian languages (such as Persian and Kurdish), the Celtic languages (such as Welsh), and many other languages, such as Greek and Albanian.

One of the great achievements of the nineteenth century was a reasonably clear history for this family of languages, as well as reconstruction of much of the grammar and more than a thousand items of proto-Indo-European, the hypothesized common ancestor, which is believed to have been spoken about four and a half thousand years ago. Since that time, many other language families, such as Dravidian and Algonquian, have been studied by the same methods, with gratifying results.

Methods of Analysis

Despite their great success the traditional methods of language history have some limitations. First, a very large amount of information about the languages is required to perform such an analysis. Second, the effort to carry out the reconstruction is very great. Third, the exact relationship between the major branches may be difficult to decide. Fourth, little can be discovered about the dates at which various branches have split apart.

Suppose we wish to analyze a family, such as the Austronesian (also called Malayo-Polynesian), about which the information is inadequate to perform a traditional analysis. Is there any hope? If we insist on all that the traditional analysis yields, namely a family tree, *plus* a detailed history for a large number of words and grammatical constructions, *plus* reconstruction of large parts of the proto-language, the answer must surely be 'no'. If on the other hand we are willing to settle merely for a family tree, and give up the other results, the answer may quite reasonably be 'yes'.

In 1952 Morris Swadesh introduced a new method for studying language history based on vocabulary alone. This method is much faster and requires much less information than the traditional methods. For this reason, it can be applied more widely and to less deeply studied families. To be sure, it yields much less information than the traditional methods, as indicated above: this is only natural. However it offers the hope of yielding information which the traditional method does not yield, namely, approximate dates at which language separations took place, based on purely linguistic evidence.

This method has been widely applied [for example, see the bibliography in Dell Hymes (1960)]. Other important developments, including new advances in the methodology itself, have been published in many articles, including Lees (1953), Carroll and Dyen (1962), Dyen, James, and Cole (1967), and Sankoff (1970).

These new methods have received considerable criticism within linguistics. Some of this we accept as well considered, particularly with regard to the question of dates, since improvement of the dating methods is truly needed, and since a really convincing demonstration of their validity has yet to be given. However we feel that some of the criticism is based on less justifiable grounds, such as unreasoning resistance to the use of quantitative methods in linguistics, and a failure properly to understand such quantitative methods.

Purposes and Results

One purpose of this paper is to describe some important technical improvements and extensions, both in the theory and in the computer methodology, which we have introduced into the vocabulary method of language classification and dating. A second purpose is to describe the application of these methods to large-scale data on Malayo-Polynesian, Philippine, Indo-European, and Cushitic languages. A third purpose is to present some very interesting by-products of these massive analyses.

As far as language classification alone is concerned, we consider our results and methods valid and satisfactory. The critical test, of course, is provided by the Indo-European data, where our results can be compared with well-established facts. On the other hand, even though the *classification* which emerges from the Indo-European data seems quite satisfactory, the tentative *dating* results which emerge are definitely not (though far from absurd): this clearly reveals that our innovations have not yet been perfected.

Due to a technical distinction (whose importance we did not realize right away) between the Malayo-Polynesian (MP) analysis and the other three analyses, we still hope that the MP dates may be valid, though of course this still remains to be proved. We believe that a certain approximation (described later) is one of the primary causes of the difficulty in the Indo-European dates, and there are substantial reasons for believing this has a far less serious effect on the MP dates. We hope that future improvements will permit our dating methodology to pass the crucial test of giving historically satisfactory dates for Indo-European. Such success would give at least presumptive validity to the dates in other families.

THE BASIC VOCABULARY METHOD

The basic vocabulary method, as introduced by Swadesh, is based on a list of about 100 or 200 'basic' meanings, such as 'eye', 'hand', '1', '2', '3', 'mother', 'to fly', and so on. (These meanings are chosen to occur in almost every language, and to have little cultural content.) For each meaning on the list, the usual everyday word for that meaning is determined in each language being studied. Then each pair of languages is compared, as shown in table 1, meaning by meaning. For each pair of meanings, the comparison is scored as + if the corresponding words in the two languages are *cognate* (for example, English *hand* and German *Hand*,) and as − if they are not cognate (for example, English *hand* and French *main*). The pattern of + and − values for each pair of languages constitutes the entire comparison for the basic vocabulary method: nothing else is used.

Meaning	English	German		French	Romanian	
all	all	alle	+	tout	tot	+
and	and	und	+	et	iar	−
animal	animal	Tier	−	bête	animal	−
ashes	ashes	Aschen	+	cendres	cenuşă	+
back	back	Rücken	−	dos	spate, dos	+
bad	bad	schlecht	−	mauvais	rău	−
bark	bark	Rinde	−	écorce	scoartă	+
bird	bird	Vogel	−	oiseau	pasăre	−

Table 1. Swadesh comparison of languages

Most earlier work has relied entirely on the percentage of + values for each pair of languages, that is, the percentage of meanings for which the corresponding words are cognate. This is called the lexico-statistical percentage. However, the method of this paper makes full use (for the first time) of the entire pattern of + and − values.

COGNATION

If we consider a single meaning with a language, two different kinds of change occur in the everyday word used for that meaning. One kind is a gradual change of sound which occurs *within* a continuing language (for example, from Latin *manus* to French *main*, and Latin *caput* to Spanish *cabeza*): this is called regular phonetic change. The other kind is complete replacement of one word by another (for example, Old French *novante* (later *nonante*) by French *quatre-vingt-dix*, and Latin *caput* by French *tête*). We use the word *replacement* only for the latter kind of change.

Words are called *cognate* if they come from a common source by regular phonetic change: note that this implies that each word has been used continuously in its own language since the time of the common source. Thus English *mother*, French *mère*, German *Mutter*, and Russian Мать are all cognate, and their common source is the Indo-European **māter*. However, English *flower* is not cognate to French *fleur* in the technical sense. Instead they are connected by borrowing. In fact, the Indo-European *bhlōw* led to Old French *flo(u)r*, which led to French *fleur*, all by regular phonetic change. The Old French word was borrowed into the English lexicon (presumably in the centuries immediately after 1066), a process which naturally involves *non*-regular phonetic change. Subsequently, the borrowed word replaced an earlier word for the meaning 'flower'. (The earlier word may well have come from the Old English *blōstma*, which *is* cognate to *fleur*, and gives rise to the modern English *blossom* by regular phonetic change.)

Figure 1

The determination of cognation and borrowing is of course a difficult matter. Since it is a major topic in linguistics, we do not have the space to say very much about it here. However, a few brief remarks are vital. First, some errors are inevitable, particularly since the situations we are most interested in are ones in which the languages have not been very fully studied. Our attitude toward such errors, and toward certain other difficulties, is discussed later. Second, though the determination is based primarily on the correspondence between the sounds of the two words in question, to the extent feasible this is interpreted in the light of other available information. Third, the determination is based entirely on the skill and expert knowledge of the linguist making the determination, though he does have some objective principles to help him. Fourth, the fact that these determinations are being made for words *with the same meaning* is of vital practical importance. There is an unacceptably high probability that a given word in one language will quite by chance be matched by a similar-sounding word in another language. However, the probability that the similar-sounding word will by chance also have the same meaning as the given word is very low.

Fifth, the ease with which borrowing can be distinguished from cognation depends heavily on the type of borrowing. In one type, the words in languages A and B are similar because they both result from borrowing from a language C which is very different from A and B (generally from a different family). In the other type either language C is similar to A and B, or the borrowing was directly between A and B. The former type is easier to detect, and has relatively often been noted in the Malayo-Polynesian and Philippine data. The latter type can only be detected with great effort, and has not been systematically pursued in the same data. The problem of undetected borrowings of this type has been discussed by Dyen.

LIST OF MEANINGS

Ideally, we would like (1) the meanings in the list to be very stable, (2) the meanings to be easily 'glossed', and (3) the list to be as long as feasible. A meaning is called stable if a replacement of the word for that meaning occurs relatively seldom. We need stable meanings because we wish to study distantly related languages. To gloss a meaning is to supply a word which has that meaning. A meaning is easily glossed if most languages have a single dominant word whose meaning is the one desired. While this property is obviously desirable, even the best constructed list cannot be perfect in this respect. Meanings such as 'brother' and 'sister', for example, which in English seem basic, have no exact counterparts in Hungarian and Chinese (which instead have single everyday words for 'sibling', 'older brother', 'younger brother', and so on). A sufficiently long list is necessary for statistical accuracy. This is our primary protection against the inevitable random errors in determining cognation. Also, since word replacement is best thought of as a random process (*see later* for a fuller discussion), statistical accuracy would be needed even if there were no errors in determining cognation.

Swadesh originally constructed a list of 215 meanings. Due to the difficulty of glossing which he experienced with several of these meanings, he modified the list to one of 200. Still later, he formed a shorter list of 100. See table 2 for a brief summary of the lists we used.

	Meanings M	Lists L	List-pairs L_2^*
Malayo-Polynesian (MP)	196 (5)**	371	68,635
Philippine (PH)	196	107	5,671
Indo-European (IE)	200	95	4,465
Cushitic (CU)	100	63	1,953

Table 2. The four families, $(*L_2 = L(L-1)/2$; **see text* for explanation)

Our analysis of the Indo-European data is based on the entire list of 200. In the Malayo-Polynesian and Philippine data, three of these meanings offer severe difficulty of glossing ('ice', 'freeze', and 'snow' due to the warm climate in the South Pacific). The demonstrative 'that' was dropped for a different reason. Thus the analyses of these two data sets are based on 196 meanings. Of course, many other meanings cause milder difficulty, and might well have been replaced by better meanings. However, there were several practical advantages in not changing the list. The Cushitic data were collected quite quickly, and use only the 100 meaning list.

Our experience suggests that with a list substantially shorter than 200, the picture of language relationships begins to get quite blurred. Probably it would be well to consider increasing the length of the list, say up to 400 or 500. While it is possible to use still longer lists, such as that over 1000 used by Sankoff for Indo-European (1969, 1970), collection difficulties will probably restrict such long lists to special situations like Sankoff's for the time being.

It should also be noted that glossability and stability of meanings inevitably varies from family to family (and from language to language). We believe that it is natural and appropriate to adapt the list to the family being studied. Of course, this slightly complicates the comparison of analyses from different families, but the problem is a minor one.

SOME LINGUISTIC DIFFICULTIES

There are several linguistic difficulties and criticisms which can be raised. Many of these can be described under the broad heading of 'measurement difficulties', if we realize that the word-lists are the means we use to measure the relationships between languages. A given meaning may be represented by two words (for example, English *big* and *large*); different sources may provide different words for the same meaning; the language may contain no single common word for the meaning (for example, Hungarian and Chinese for 'brother', English for 'younger brother'); *parts* of words may be cognate (for example, English *fireplace* and German *Feuerstätte* 'fireplace'); for closely related dialects, the distinction between cognation and borrowing is extremely fine; the cognation judgments will doubtless contain definite errors; and so forth.

All these problems are real, require practical consideration, and reduce the accuracy of our measurements. But as we now explain, they need not destroy the meaningfulness of our measurements.

There is no 'perfect' word-list for a language, nor can we expect that cognation judgments will be 'perfect'. Thus we must always expect that different investigators collecting independent word-lists and making independent cognation judgments will arrive at somewhat different divergence times. However, we *can* hope that the divergence times they get will not differ too much. [Of course, lists specially made up to cause difficulty may cause extra large deviations.] The same situation exists for all measurements, from the ultra-precisely measured speed of light, to the Gross National Product or an Intelligence Quotient, whose very definitions are vague and arbitrary. Because different investigators get different values, the measurement is considered known only to a certain degree of accuracy, which may be 1 part in a million, 1 part in 10, or even less accurate. We already know a good deal about the degree of accuracy of the lexico-statistical percentages, and somewhat less about estimated divergence times. An adequately long list of meanings is the key to achieving accuracy in this sense, for it provides the necessary statistical reliability so that individual errors are diluted or cancelled out.

A separate difficulty is whether our so-called 'divergence times' have any connection with historical reality. The only way we can ever find out is by testing our divergence times against as many other kinds of evidence as possible. The most notable test available, of course, is the comparison for Indo-European languages against historical records and the classical linguistic evidence. The same validity problem 'Does this measure what we want it to measure?' exists in all measurement situations. (It is particularly acute for IQ, which is nevertheless of some value.) As the philosophy of science has made clear, the only assurance available in any science is comparison with other kinds of evidence. There is no absolute yardstick, only the approximate agreement of many fallible yardsticks.

A third difficulty is that the circumstances of word replacement are so diverse that an all-encompassing theory seems out of the question. Fortunately, we do not need such a theory, any more than the health-insurance actuary needs an all-encompassing theory of what causes disease. He needs to know only the overall frequency of various treatments, and we need to know only the over-all frequency of certain word-replacements.

Work by Sankoff (1969, 1970, 1971a, 1971b) has thrown considerable light on the effect of certain linguistic difficulties. For example, he has studied (both mathematically and by computer simulation) a model which explicitly allows for the many-to-many relationship between words and meanings. While accepting a single word for a meaning may distort the truth, his work supports the idea that this distortion creates no basic problem, but merely shows up in the measurement error.

THREE BASIC ASSUMPTIONS

The statistical aspects of our work rest on three basic assumptions. Each is subject to valid criticisms, which we mention. Like other scientific assumptions (for example, Newton's law of gravity, $F = km_1m_2/r^2$), these assumptions are not entirely correct. The deviations may even be substantial.

However, our assumptions are good enough so that we can learn a good deal. With the aid of what we learn, we will be able to improve the assumptions. Use of partly true ideas as a tool for further learning is the classic method in science.

Assumption 1: Tree structure. We assume that the modern languages being compared arose from successive separations, which can be thought of as a family tree, and that after a separation development occurs independently in the separate branches (*see* figure 2).

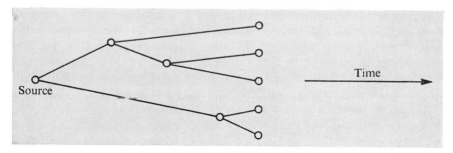

Figure 2

Conceptually, one major criticism may be made of this assumption. The separation process, in which a single relatively homogeneous speech community separates into two speech communities with independent development, does not usually occur at a sharp instant of time, but rather occurs over a considerable period, during which development is neither fully shared nor fully independent. In other words, dialects continue to influence each other even after they have begun to diverge, provided their speakers maintain some degree of intercommunication. At the practical level, however, the main difficulty with this assumption, fortunately not too serious, is the appearance in the data of certain clear though minor violations of tree structure.

Assumption 2: Exponential probability. We regard replacement of words as a random process (just as the health insurance actuary regards disease, and the physicist regards radioactive decay and other phenomena of quantum physics). In addition, we assume that the process is statistically (=probabilistically=stochastically) independent for distinct branches of the tree, and for distinct meanings (even on a single branch). Finally, for a single meaning, following any single language in the tree for a time period t, we assume that the probability of non-replacement is given by $p=e^{-rt}$, where r is some constant (*see* figure 3). Note that the formula e^{-rt} arises from the Poisson process, which is based on simple plausible assumptions, and which is widely used to model both physical and social phenomena (such as radioactive decay, people making telephone calls, and so on).

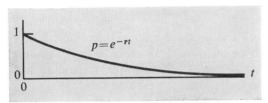

Figure 3

We feel that this assumption, though surely not perfect, is least in need of refinement. The most likely place where refinement might be needed would be in the matter of independence among distinct branches for a single meaning, where refinement would accompany a refinement of the tree structure assumption to allow for influence among nearby branches.

Assumption 3: Meaning determines replacement rate r. We refer to the constant r in $p=e^{-rt}$ as the replacement rate. (This is a good name, for small $r\leftrightarrow$ slow replacement, and large $r\leftrightarrow$rapid replacement.) We assume that r depends only on the meaning (within a single language family). There is abundant evidence to show that r does depend on meaning. Even though Swadesh limited his list of meanings quite successfully to those with small values of r, it is clear that r varies substantially within his list.

Almost all previous work has ignored the variation of r within the list, though Dyen (1960) contains a brief discussion of this phenomenon. However in 1962 Joos pointed out, and in 1966 van der Merwe explained in detail, that this variation can have a substantial effect on dating language separation (a fact which is thoroughly familiar in the field of radio-active decay). In 1967 Dyen, James, and Cole did the first work allowing for such variation of r. However they grouped the meanings into 9 groups, and allowed only one value of r for each meaning. Their paper is the direct forerunner of this paper which goes further by allowing a separate value of r for every meaning. We believe that this may permit better time estimates, as well as allowing study of the rates themselves.

The most significant criticism of this assumption is that replacement rates vary somewhat, even for a single meaning [as was allowed for in principle by Dyen (1960)]. They were larger in Anglo-Saxon after 1066, and smaller in Icelandic for hundreds of years. However, when attention is limited to 200 basic meanings, the effect is smaller than one might think. (Swadesh indicated that English received replacements from Norman French for only about 12 meanings in his list of 200, while English and modern French have roughly 50 meanings for which their words are cognate.) While these variations will undoubtedly create distortions, there are possibilities for estimating and accommodating such variations when a large family of related languages is being compared. We hope to introduce such refinements in the future.

THE FOUR LANGUAGE FAMILIES

We have studied four language families. *See* table 2 for a brief summary. By far the largest set of data pertains to Malayo-Polynesian (Austronesian) languages, and includes 371 word-lists. Of these, 18 are now known not to be from Malayo-Polynesian languages, despite their geographical provenance. (We refer to word-lists rather than languages or dialects, since this is what the data actually are. Also, this avoids difficult judgments as to which word-lists are from the same languages or dialects as other word-lists. It should be noted, however, that in many cases different word-lists do come from the same dialect or language). Further information about this data and an extensive classification of these languages based on lexico-statistical analysis appears in Dyen (1965).

The second set of data pertains to 107 Philippine word-lists. Approximately 40 of these word-lists are also among the 371 Malay-Polynesian lists. The third set of data consists of 95 Indo-European word lists. It should be noted that although these data cover all major branches of Indo-European tolerably well, some branches (such as Slavic and Greek) are covered especially heavily. In a substantial number of cases, the same dialect is represented by two (or even more) word-lists, taken from different sources or prepared by different experts. Finally, the fourth set of data are 63 Cushitic word-lists.

For Malayo-Polynesian, Philippine, and Indo-European, the lists were assembled and the cognation judgments made by Dyen. (Of course, in the case of Indo-European these judgments are based heavily on standard sources, with only occasional controversial cases being re-judged.) In the case of Cushitic, the lists were assembled and the cognation judgments made by Black. It should be noted that the Cushitic data was prepared very rapidly, and should be regarded as only preliminary.

All analyses were done on the four languages separately. Families were never combined.

COGNATION JUDGMENTS AND THE DATA BASE

For each language family, the *linguistic* data base consists of the word-lists which have been collected for that family, plus any additional information which is useful in making the cognation judgments. However since the statistical methods are applied only to the cognation judgments, it is the table, or matrix, of such judgments which forms the *statistical* data base.

Table 3 shows a tiny example of such a table of cognation judgments, for 4 languages and 3 meanings. Figure 4 shows such a table in general. The table has one row for each meaning m, and one column for each *pair* (i, j) of languages. The cell value f_{mij} in row m and column (i, j) indicates one of

| Meanings | The word forms: Lists | | | |
	English	German	French	Russian
Mother	Mother	Mutter	Mère	Матъ
Father	Father	Vater	Père	Отец
Hand	Hand	Hand	Main	Pyka

| | The cognacy determinations: List-pairs | | | | | |
	E G	E F	E R	G F	G R	F R
Mother	1	1	1	1	1	1
Father	1	1	0	1	0	0
Hand	1	0	0	0	0	0

Table 3. An illustration of the data: 3 meanings, $M=3$; 4 lists, $L=4$; 6 list-pairs, $L_2=6$. In the cognacy determinations, 1 is cognate, 0 non-cognate, ? cannot decide

three possibilities for meaning m and languages i and j: cognate (indicated by 1), not cognate (indicated by 0), or no decision (indicated by ?). (Most often no decision comes about because no word for meaning m has been recorded in one of the languages. Occasionally it results from a decision that the case is doubtful.)

Suppose there are M meanings and L languages. Then there are $L_2 = L(L-1)/2$ language pairs, so the cognacy table contains M rows, L_2 columns, hence $M \times L_2$ cells. The values of these numbers are shown in table 2. It is apparent from the very large values why sophisticated computer processing is essential for this work.

In the occasional cases where two or more words are indicated for the single meaning in one or both word-lists involved, the highest cognation level found between the two languages has been recorded. This is not necessarily the best thing to do, but reflects a decision made very early which would have been extremely difficult to modify.

Even with the aid of high-speed computers, used in a sophisticated way, Malayo-Polynesian was too large to handle exactly as we have described. Hence for these data the meanings were grouped into 5 homogeneous groups, based on crude estimates of r (the groups contained 12, 34, 40, 60, and 50 meanings), and the matrix of cognation judgments was reduced to 5 rows. Each cell value is the fraction cognate among that group of meanings for languages i and j, ignoring cells marked?. (Note that the PH, IE, and CU tables may be considered to fit this description, if we consider each row as a group with just one meaning in it.)

(In the actual development, the work on Malayo-Polynesian was done first, and represented a direct extension of the work by Dyen, James, and Cole, with the purpose of treating *all* pairs of languages where they had treated a small sample of 46 pairs. The work on the other families represented a further extension to separate replacement rates for each meaning, which was practical because L_2 is so much smaller in these cases.)

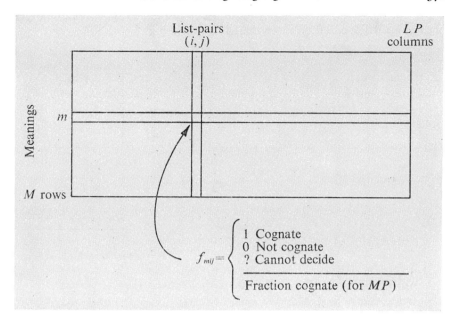

Figure 4. The cognacy determinations

BEST-FITTING TREE AND THE TWO-STAGE APPROACH

What we would like to do is find the *best-fitting* tree in some sense (where the tree includes a date for each separation). In principle, this is possible, since we have a fully-defined statistical model. For example, it makes sense to talk of the maximum likelihood tree (with dates). In practice, the problem is too hard: we simply could not carry out the necessary computations (though we have realistic hope of coming close to this goal in the future).

Instead, we have used a two-stage procedure. (Even this involves massive calculations.) In the first stage, we *ignore* the tree structure, and use the cognation table to determine the separation times t_{ij} between language pairs, and the replacement rates r_m simultaneously, by a maximum likelihood procedure which would be correct if there were no connection between the language pairs (except that they share common values for the replacement rates). In the second stage, we use the times t_{ij} to estimate the tree.

For the MP case, this procedure is modified in an important way. The cognation table is first reduced to five rows, as described above, before the maximum likelihood calculation ignoring tree structure is carried out. The last stage is the same. (*See* figure 5 for a summary diagram.)

Compare both of these procedures with the procedure previously used by Dyen. This procedure immediately reduces the table all the way down to one row, whose entries then consist of the lexico-statistical percentages. These percentages are then directly used to form a tree (with percentage levels instead of dates at the nodes). [Alternatively, the percentages can be transformed to times, and the tree (with dates) made from the times. However, if the percentages were transformed into times by a simple exponential relationship, as is traditional, these dates would be fully subject to the distortion discussed earlier. Sankoff uses a modified exponential relation-ship in his work based on more than 1,000 meanings.]

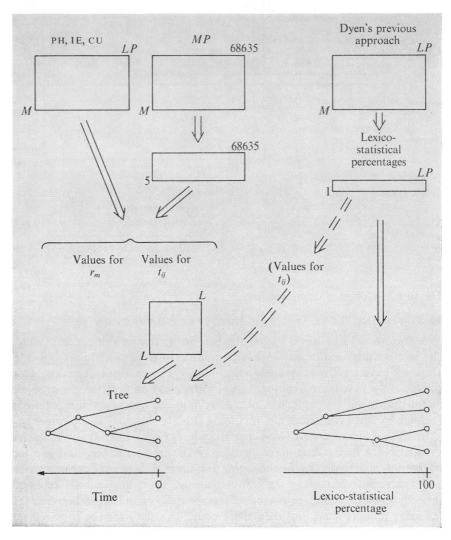

Figure 5. Two-stage approach

As remarked before, we now know that our Indo-European dates are not satisfactory (even though the classification yielded is). It seems to us that the primary difficulty in our dating must be in our first stage. In particular, our present way of fitting times and replacement rates without taking into account the tree structure is just not good enough. Whether we should attempt to bring in the tree structure, or improve this stage by some other method, is difficult to decide.

FIRST STAGE

Our first stage is based on maximum likelihood. In brief, we formulate the likelihood (=probability) that the actual data would occur by chance for any given set of replacement rates r_m and divergence times t_{ij}, and then (by extensive numerical calculation) find the values of all r_m and all t_{ij} which make this likelihood a maximum. (For further discussion of maximum likelihood in general, consult a statistics text.) However, in formulating the likelihood, we ignore the tree structure. This formulation is the key approximation which made it practical (though still difficult) to find the maximum, but which we consider to be the greatest cause of nonsatisfactory dates for Indo-European.

For the meaning m to be truly cognate in languages i and j, no replacement can have occurred in either language. Our assumptions lead directly to the probability of this event being

$$p_{mij}=e^{-2r_mt_{ij}} \ .$$

Recall that this cognation is indicated by $f_{mij}=1$, the reverse by $f_{mij}=0$, and no decision by $f_{mij}=?$. Then the likelihood (=probability) of observing the actual value of f_{mij} is

$$L_{mij}=\begin{cases} p_{mij} \\ 1-p_{mij} \quad \text{if} \quad f_{mij}= \\ \text{undefined} \end{cases} \begin{cases} 1 \\ 0 \\ ? \end{cases}$$

Since replacements of distinct meanings have (quite reasonably) been assumed independent, the likelihood of observing the entire ij column of the cognation table is given by

$$L_{*ij}=\{\text{product of } L_{mij} \text{ for all } m \text{ except those for which } f_{mij}= ?\}.$$

At this point we ignore the relationship among the language pairs, and treat the columns of the cognation table as independent. This leads to the likelihood of observing the entire cognation table as

$$L=\text{product of all the } L_{*ij} \ .$$

(This step is the key approximation.) L depends ultimately on the replacement rates r_m and the divergence times t_{ij}, and it is these which are varied so as to give L its maximum possible value.

The key approximation is not so wild as it might at first appear. Notice that if the replacement rates r_m are treated as fixed known numbers, then maximizing L comes to the same thing as obtaining each time t_{ij} separately without reference to the others by maximizing each L_{*ij} separately (this does not involve us in the key approximation). Thus it is only through inducing wrong values of the rates r_m that the approximation introduces error. However we have two reasons for thinking that the rates we have found make some sense. First, as we discuss in detail later, there is a very meaningful degree of agreement between the rates for the MP, IE, and CU sets of data. Since these sets of data are entirely separate, and the analyses are entirely separate, this gives evidence that the rates from all three sets of data make some sense. The second reason involves some special analysis of the MP data, which we now describe.

When we first set out to do the MP analysis (long before doing the other three analyses), we were acutely aware of the problem of dependence among the 68,635 columns of the cognation table. Consequently, even before doing the main maximum likelihood analysis, we did 16 small analyses of the same type, each based on a sample of columns from the cognacy table (but using all rows). The number of columns used ranged from 39 up to 1,714. Of the samples, 14 were randomly chosen from all columns, and 2 were systematically chosen. The analyses were done exactly the same way as the large one: however, for the random samples it is clear that the problem of dependency among the columns is not serious. The results of these analyses agreed with each other and with the subsequent large analysis satisfactorily, based on statistical analysis which allowed for the larger variability of results based on smaller samples.

Thus for the MP case we have clear evidence that the key approximation is fairly accurate. The methodology for the other cases differs somewhat, so that this evidence suggests that the key approximation is *reasonable*, but not necessarily *accurate*, in the other cases. While the use of individual rates in itself permits greater accuracy, it fails to provide insulation against the inaccuracy which may be introduced by the key approximation.

SECOND STAGE

The times t_{ij} may be arranged into a square matrix (using $t_{ii}=0$ and $t_{ji}=t_{ij}$). To form a tree from such 'dyadic' data is, of course, one of the basic problems in classification theory. There are many methods and computer programs for this purpose, though none of them are entirely appropriate for our situation. So far we have not seriously attacked this problem using times. (However, in earlier work Dyen has made serious analyses of a similar nature, based on lexico-statistical percentages rather than times.)

We have, however, fed the MP times into what is perhaps the most widely-known method of clustering, the pair-group method. (This method has been independently invented and published by Sokal and Sneath, by Chrystal and Ward, by Cronbach and Gleser, and by S.C. Johnson (1967), among others. We used Johnson's program.) This method has several versions, according to how the dissimilarity for a newly formed cluster is calculated from the dissimilarities of the two smaller clusters making it up. We used the version in which the new dissimilarity is formed by averaging the old dissimilarities, weighted according to the number of single elements each old cluster contains.

Actually, we applied this method twice. The first application was to the times t_{ij} themselves, slightly modified however. A very few times yielded by the maximum likelihood method are infinite, because there are no cognates at all for the language-pair (recall that the MP data contain 18 lists now known not to be MP). These infinite values had to be replaced by finite values, a little larger than the largest observed times.

The maximum likelihood calculation of the t_{ij} values yielded as a by-product a crude estimate of s_{ij}, the standard deviation of t_{ij}. When the s_{ij} are plotted against the t_{ij}, a tight relationship is found (s_{ij} increases some-what faster than proportional to t_{ij}, and a quadratic function appears to fit well). Thus it was easy to form a variance-stabilizing transformation f [*see* Bartlett (1947), Kruskal (1968), and many statistics texts]. Intuitively, it seems desirable to use $t'_{ij}=f(t_{ij})$ rather than t_{ij} in the clustering program, since the t'_{ij} have approximately constant standard deviation (this is what the variance-stabilizing transformation achieves). Incidentally, this also takes care of the infinite times very elegantly, since $f(\infty)$ is finite.

When the two clusterings, based on t_{ij} and t'_{ij} are compared, they are found to be almost identical. Thus even though the transformation f is strongly curved, it hardly affects the clustering. (For those familiar with these clustering methods, this is only to be expected.)

BY-PRODUCT RESULTS

The most interesting by-product of this work is shown in figure 6, which is the scatter diagram of lexico-statistical percentages *versus* times for the Malayo-Polynesian data. It displays a heavy band of 68,635 points, each of which represents a pair of languages. The vertical coordinate shows the percentage P_{ij} on a logarithm scale, while the horizontal coordinate shows the time t_{ij} (from Stage 1). If P_{ij} were approximately equal to $e^{-Rt_{ij}}$, as supposed in most previous work using the vocabulary method, then the band would show a straight-line relationship. In fact it is clearly curved, demonstrating the effect discussed by Joos and van der Merwe (and due to the variation of r among meanings).

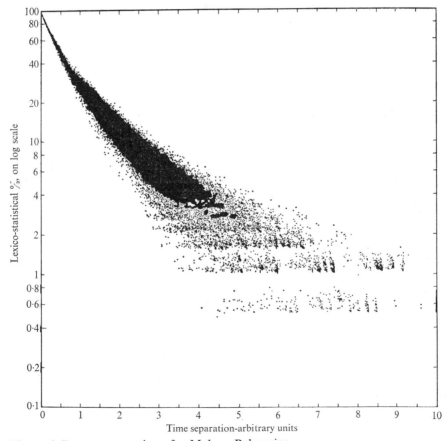

Figure 6. Percentages *v.* times for Malayo-Polynesian

This diagram can be used to estimate time of divergence from the lexico-statistical percentage P for a given pair of languages, which are known to be Malayo-Polynesian, without the error due to the usual exponential assumption. It is necessary only to draw a horizontal line corresponding to the P value, and note the interval where this line crosses the heavy band. The time of divergence is presumably in this interval. For example, $P = 40\%$ corresponds to the interval from 0·55 to 0·7, and $P = 20\%$ corresponds to (1·1, 1·7). The fact that the estimate is only to within an interval is a realistic reflection of the fact that precise times are not assignable, and the width of the interval may give some idea of the degree of uncertainty.

Note that as P decreases and t increases, the size of the interval increases. Furthermore, the size increases *faster* than proportional to t. This is clearly appropriate.

In 1964 Dyen compared the stability of 196 meanings in different language families, and showed conclusively that there is a relationship, that is, meanings more stable in Malayo-Polynesian tend to be more stable in 4 other families. He used not individual replacement rates for this purpose, of course, since they were not then available, but a simpler measure of stability, which he handled in a very robust way.

Now that individual replacement rates for each meaning have been estimated for three language families (Indo-European, Philippine, and Cushitic), it is natural to compare these values between families with similar purpose. To do this, we plotted three scatter diagrams, one for PH $v.$ IE (196 points), one for CU $v.$ IE (94 points), and one for CU $v.$ PH (94 points). Each point represents a meaning, and its coordinates are the replacement rates r in two families. Although none of these diagrams reveal a strong relationship, and the associated correlation coefficients are as small as 0·32 (*see below*), the probability of a correlation as large as any one of these values occurring by chance if there were no systematic relationship is absurdly small (the least significant case has probability 2 in 10,000).

However the distribution of replacement rates in each family tends to be rather skew towards the larger values. This is undesirable both because it may distort the significance levels from the cited values somewhat, and because it causes too many points to pile up in one area of the plot for easy examination. Consequently we made similar plots using e^{-r} instead of r. This takes out most of the skewing, and seems a natural transformation in this situation. (Figure 7 shows this diagram for IE $v.$ PH. Each meaning is plotted by the English word used to indicate it.) This increases all the correlation values, two substantially, as shown in table 4.

		IE–PH	IE–CU	PH–CU
	n	196	94	94
Correlation	r	0·32	0·43	0·40
based on	e^{-r}	0·44	0·52	0·42

Table 4

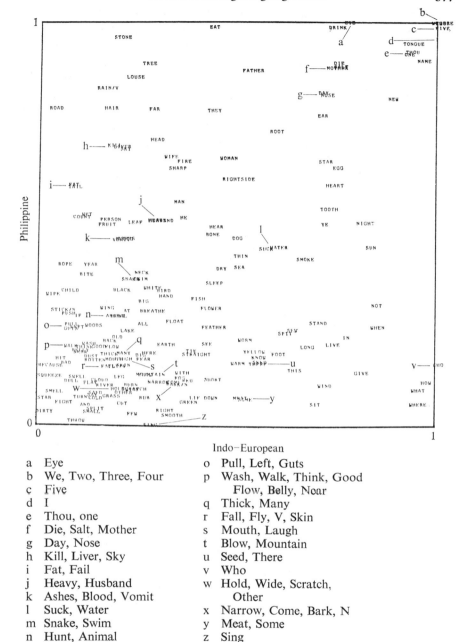

Figure 7. Scatter diagram of transformed rates for Philippine *versus* Indo-European

a	Eye	o	Pull, Left, Guts
b	We, Two, Three, Four	p	Wash, Walk, Think, Good
c	Five		Flow, Belly, Near
d	I	q	Thick, Many
e	Thou, one	r	Fall, Fly, V, Skin
f	Die, Salt, Mother	s	Mouth, Laugh
g	Day, Nose	t	Blow, Mountain
h	Kill, Liver, Sky	u	Seed, There
i	Fat, Fail	v	Who
j	Heavy, Husband	w	Hold, Wide, Scratch,
k	Ashes, Blood, Vomit		Other
l	Suck, Water	x	Narrow, Come, Bark, N
m	Snake, Swim	y	Meat, Some
n	Hunt, Animal	z	Sing

THE ARBITRARY TIME UNIT FOR
MALAYO-POLYNESIAN IS ABOUT 3,500 YEARS

The vocabulary method of estimating times can only determine them relative to one another, unless additional information is used. (To see how this works in our model, suppose times t_{ij} and rates r_m have been determined. For any positive multiplier k, define new times and rates by $t'_{ij}=kt_{ij}$ and $r'_m=r_m/k$ for all ij and m. Then $r'_m t'_{ij}=r_m t_{ij}$ so $p'_{mij}=p_{mij}$, hence the new times and rates are necessarily just as plausible as the original ones.)

For this reason, our Stage 1 divergence times have all been expressed in terms of an arbitrary unit. Comparing figure 6 with Lees' (1953) data on 13 language pairs of known historical relationship, we find that a value very close to 3,500 years for this unit optimizes the agreement. Although Lees data are mostly for IE languages, and none for MP languages, we feel justified in using them this way because figure 6 is not sensitive to individual replacement rates, only to the distribution of replacement rates. Sankoff (1970) shows that the distributions for IE and for MP are very similar. (In making the comparison, it is necessary to recall that Lees' pairs each consist of a mother and a daughter language, while our pairs each consist of sister languages, which affects the times by a factor of 2.)

Superficially, figure 6 *seems* to suggest that we are seriously estimating divergence times of 35,000 years and more. This is, of course, absurd, since even if such enormous divergence times exist within the MP data, we obviously cannot handle such large values on the present foundation. This observation may appear to some people to discredit the whole approach.

There are two reasons why this criticism is not valid. First, the estimated divergence times cannot be considered valid unless both the languages are known by other means to be Malayo-Polynesian, and these data contain 18 languages which are now known not to be MP. Thus $18 \times (371 - 18) + 18 \times 17/2 = 6,507$ of the 68,635 t_{ij} are not to be used, and these surely include a great many of the very large values.

Second, every statistical estimate has some degree of uncertainty. In this case, the uncertainty of the larger divergence times is very great. Thus an enormous estimate like 35,000 years really means no more than that the true divergence time is larger than some value such as 5,000 or 10,000 (these numbers are purely hypothetical).

For pairs whose lexico-statistical percentage is less than 10% or 15%, all we can really say is that the divergence time is large. This still leaves estimated divergence times as large as (say) 8,000 years which we consider meaningful (subject to the qualifications mentioned elsewhere in this paper), though with a region of uncertainty that might be as wide as 6,000 to 12,000, or even wider. Regardless of the individual divergence times, however, it does seem abundantly clear that the Malayo-Polynesian protolanguage must be far older than the Indo-European protolanguage.

SUMMARY

We have reviewed the theoretical basis of the vocabulary method of dating language separation. We have introduced several innovations into the theory, such as permitting each meaning to have its own replacement rate, and using the maximum likelihood method to estimate simultaneously the time separations and the replacement rates for a family of languages. We have devised numerical methods and written computer programs which are efficient enough to make the massive calculations feasible (a substantial piece of work).

We have not yet reached definitive conclusions concerning the separation times for any family. (To reach definitive conclusions for such large-scale data requires a lot of work, especially when novel methods of analysis must be devised.) However, the first stage of our methodology, which estimates separation times and replacement rates, has been applied to four language families. It seems reasonable to believe that the times for Malayo-Polynesian may be approximately correct, subject to certain limitations (*see below*). Due to the use of individual rather than group replacement rates, which caused trouble in the key approximation, the separation times for the other three families are not yet acceptable. The second stage of our methodology, which yields a tree with times at the nodes, has been carried out only in a very preliminary way by using a simple published method, without adequate adaptation to our special circumstances.

While the Malayo-Polynesian separation times may well be close to correct, it is important to understand the limitations. First, the 3,500 year figure for the arbitrary time unit is only approximate, since it is based on a small set of data. Second, the statistical variability of large estimated times is greater than the statistical variability of small estimated times. Moreover, the increase is faster than proportional. Hence the large time estimates are extremely uncertain. Third, we will no doubt find a few time estimates which are seriously in error when we use the computer to do thorough systematic checking and intercomparison, which all large bodies of data need. Fourth, we will no doubt systematically modify the dates to some extent when we use statistical methods to detect and correct for undetected borrowing.

We have produced some valuable by-products. One is a scatter diagram which shows the relationship between lexico-statistical percentage (based on 196 meanings) and time separation. Though made for Malayo-Polynesian, it is probably also applicable to other language families. Another by-product is proof that replacement rates for individual meanings tend to be the same from family to family. This is based on direct comparison of rates among three families, and corroborates an earlier proof by Dyen, using a different technique.

In conclusion, we have introduced some innovations into the theory, made substantial computational progress, and produced some valuable by-products. We are still analyzing the data, have some tentative separation times, and hope in the future to reach definitive values for several families.

REFERENCES

Bartlett, M.S. (1947) The use of transformations. *Biometrics*, **3**, 39–52.

Carroll, J. & Dyen, I. (1962) High-speed computation of lexicostatistical indices. *Language*, **38**, 274–8.

Dyen, Isidore (1960) Printed remarks appended to Hymes (1960).

Dyen, Isidore (1964) On the validity of comparative lexico statistics. *Proceedings of the Ninth International Congress of Linguistics, Cambridge, Mass., 1962* (ed. Lunt, H.G.). The Hague: Mouton.

Dyen, Isidore (1965) A lexicostatistical classification of the Austronesian languages. *Int. J. Amer. Linguistics*, Supplement to volume 31, No. 1.

Dyen, I., James, A.T. & Cole, J.W.L. (1967) Language divergence and estimated word retention rate. *Language*, **43**, 150–71.

Hymes, D.H. (1960) Lexicostatistics so far. *Current Anthropology*, **1**, 3–44 & 338–45.

Johnson, S.C. (1967) Hierarchical clustering schemes. *Psychometrika*, **32**, 241–54.

Joos, M. (1964) Glottochronology with retention-rate inhomogeneity. (abstract) *Proceedings of the Ninth International Congress of Linguists, Cambridge, Mass.,* 1962 (edt. Lunt, H.G.). The Hague: Mouton.

Kruskal, J.B. (1968) Statistical analysis: Transformations of data. *International Encyclopedia of the Social Sciences*. The MacMillan Company & The Free Press.

Lees, B. (1953) The basis of glottochronology. *Language*, **29**, 113–27.

Sankoff, D. (1969) *Historical linguistics as stochastic process*. Doctoral thesis. McGill University.

Sankoff, D. (1970) On the rate of replacement of word-meaning relationships. *Language*, **46**, 564–9.

Sankoff, D. (1971a) Mathematical developments in lexicostatistic theory. *Current Trends in Linguistics*, vol. 11 (ed. Sebeck, T.).

Sankoff, D. (1971b) Stochastic models for glottochronology. *Mathematics in the Archaeological & Historical Sciences*, pp. 381–6 (eds Hodson, F.R., Kendall, D.G. & Tăutu, P.). Edinburgh: Edinburgh University Press.

Swadesh, M. (1952) Lexico-statistic dating of prehistoric ethnic contacts. *Proc. Amer. phil. Soc.*, **96**, 452–63.

van der Merwe, N.J. (1966) New mathematics for glottochronology. *Current Anthropology*, **7**, 485–500.

Linguistics

David Sankoff
Stochastic models for glottochronology

Glottochronology, or the dating of linguistic events from lexical cognation data, is based on stochastic models of word turnover. Two words are cognate if they are the same, or if one was derived from the other, or if both derived from the same word by a series of phonological changes. The formalizations of these models postulate the sudden replacement of one word for a meaning by another, non-cognate, word. By suitably parametrizing the theory, one can simulate replacement rate variation according to meaning or time; accidental or false cognation; borrowing; drift; or other relevant phenomena. These developments are surveyed in a forthcoming review. In the present discussion I will describe a more realistic gradual turnover process and its properties. For expository purposes we will start with the simplest one-parameter model, although the generalizations carry through to the fully parametrized versions. I shall not dwell on glottochronologic procedures, but will show as my main result that a more realistic model does not in any way weaken or destroy the mathematical foundation of glottochronology.

The turnover process to be described resembles historical processes other than linguistic. The crucial elements are one or more identifiable types of site or position, and a set of associations at each such type which changes gradually over time. I hope this conference suggests possible applications of these resemblances.

POISSON REPLACEMENT

In linguistics, the 'types of positions' are just meanings in a fixed test-list, which are identifiable by translation into some reference language, pictorial elicitation, and so on. The associations are just the words elicited to express the meanings. In the original model for glottochronology, it is assumed that, in every language, there is one word which best corresponds to each of the meanings. This word runs a risk $\lambda \Delta t$ of being suddenly replaced by some non-cognate word, in a short time interval of length Δt (Poisson replacement). Figure 1 schematizes the replacement of a word A by word B and then the replacement of B by C. It can be proved that for any time interval of length t, the probability that the word for a meaning remains unreplaced in the interval is $e^{-\lambda t}$. This function is plotted in figure 2. Suppose there are N meanings on the test-list (usually 100 or 200). An assumption of glottochronology is that their lexical manifestations turn over independently. Table 1 illustrates the evolution of a hypothetical language in terms of lexical retention for 10 meanings at four successive points in time. It can be shown that the expected proportion of words which remain unreplaced after a time interval t is exactly $e^{-\lambda t}$ (independent of N), the function plotted in

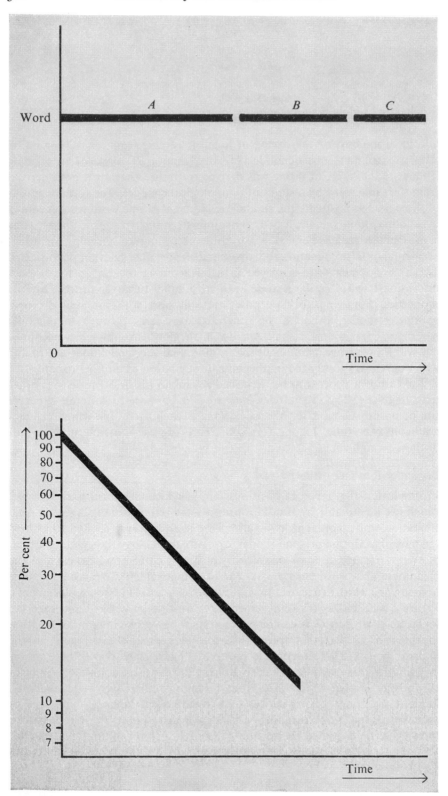

Time	0	1	2	3
Meaning	Word	Word	Word	Word
1	1	1	1	New word
2	2	2	New word	New word
3	3	New word	New word	New word
4	4	4	4	4
5	5	5	New word	New word
6	6	6	6	New word
7	7	New word	New word	New word
8	8	8	8	New word
9	9	9	9	9
10	10	10	10	New word
Per cent unreplaced	100	80	40	20

Table 1. Effect of replacement on test-list

figure 2. Let M/N be the proportion of words unreplaced after an interval of length t. Then $\hat{t} = -\lambda^{-1} \log_e (M/N)$ is the maximum likelihood estimator of t. It can be used to estimate the time interval between two sets of lexical data in a language. Note that, mathematically, this is completely analogous to C_{14} dating. By the same reasoning, $\hat{t} = -(1/2\lambda) \log_e (M/N)$ can be used to estimate the date of split of two languages which once had a common history, where M/N is the proportion of test-list meanings which have cognate lexical realizations in the two languages.

GRADUAL REPLACEMENT

While the sudden, or Poisson, replacement process may be a convenient mathematical simplification when dealing with long time intervals, it is not a very realistic model of historical turnover (except for radioactive decay). Associations tend to change gradually—if word A expresses a given meaning at some time, at a later time word B may take on that meaning occasionally, still later it may be used just as frequently as A, and finally B may displace A entirely. Instead of figure 1, a typical pattern might be as in figure 3.

This type of turnover may be formalized as follows. For some fixed meaning let $F_t(I)$ be the proportion of the instances where the meaning is expressed such that word I expresses it. Then $\sum_I F_t(I) = 1$, for all t. Let n be some positive integer and $\varepsilon = 1/n$. For any $F_t(I) > 0$, in the small interval of time between t and $t + \Delta t$, let $\beta \Delta t$ be the probability that $F_t(I)$ increases by ε and $\beta \Delta t$ the probability that $F_t(I)$ decreases by ε. As in figure 3, there are still sudden changes, but this is not serious as they can be of arbitrarily small

Figure 1. (facing, top) Sample of Poisson replacement process

Figure 2. (facing, bottom) Expected change in lexicostatistic index. The graph shows, on a logarithmic scale, the probability that a word remains unreplaced, *or* the expected percentage of words unreplaced

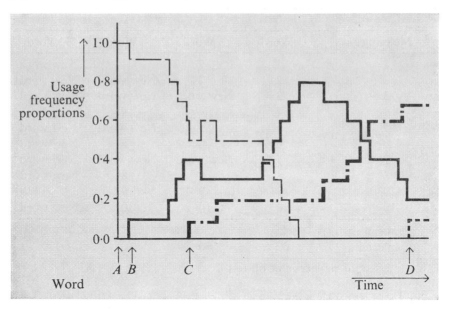

Figure 3. Sample of turnover process

magnitude. If $F_t(I)$ increases then for some J (chosen at random), $F_t(J)$ must simultaneously decrease by the same amount so that $\sum_I F_t(I)=1$.

Further we allow the possibility that at some time s in the interval between t and $t+\Delta t$ a new word K can start to take on the meaning. We assume the probability of this event is $\alpha\Delta t$ and that the initial value of $F_s(K)=\varepsilon$. Again for some other I, $F_t(I)$ drops by ε at s to compensate (I chosen at random with probability $F_t(I)$). Finally if for any I, $F_t(I)$ becomes zero, the word I is considered obsolete for that meaning and $F_t(I)$ remains at zero forever.

A New Index of Lexical Divergence

Using this model of gradual turnover in comparing the lexical manifestations of a meaning at two points in time, it no longer suffices to see whether two words are cognate or not. We must have some quantitative way of comparing a number of words at time zero with some other set of words at a later time t. I have found that an indicator which most naturally generalizes the single cognation judgment is

$$1-\tfrac{1}{2}\sum_I |F_o(I)-F_t(I)| \quad .$$

Sample calculations are given in table 2.

What can we expect of this index as a function of time? As is easily seen for very large β and very small β, and as [I have recently shown] it is approximately true for intermediate values, the expectation of this indicator after a time interval of length t is just $e^{-\lambda t}$, where $\lambda=\alpha\varepsilon$. Once again this is just the function plotted in figure 2. This result is remarkable in that it is independent of β. (The variability of the stochastic process, however, will depend on β.)

One other question one might ask is what could we expect if, instead of using the new indicator, we chose as the appropriate word at a point in time

Time	0	10	20
Frequency Proportions	A 0·9	A 0·5	
	B 0·1	B 0·3	B 0·8
		C 0·2	C 0·2

(new) lexicostatistic index	For $t=10$	For $t=20$
$1-\frac{1}{2}\sum_I \lvert F_0(I)-F_t(I)\rvert$	$1-\frac{1}{2}(0\cdot4+0\cdot2+0\cdot2)$ $=0\cdot6$	$1-\frac{1}{2}(0\cdot9+0\cdot7+0\cdot2)$ $=0\cdot1$

Table 2. Calculation of new index

the one with the highest usage frequency proportion $F_t(I)$? (The sample process in figure 3 would produce the data in figure 1, with this procedure.) Computer simulation experiments suggest the same result—the expected proportion of most frequent words at time zero being the most frequent at time t follows an exponential law as in figure 2. No proof is available for this.

CONCLUSIONS

What are the implications of these results for glottochronology? The theory and techniques based on Poisson turnover can be replaced by those based on a more realistic model. The important thing is that the original model is not discarded; it predicts the same expected pattern of evolution as the new model. The latter may be considered a more detailed version of the former. Furthermore, if reality is in fact closely modelled by a gradual turnover process, but a linguistic fieldworker uses techniques based only on Poisson turnover, he can expect valid, if not as accurate, results.

BIBLIOGRAPHY

The development of glottochronology can be traced through the following articles.
Swadesh, M. (1950) Salish internal relationships. *Int. J. Amer. Linguistics*, **16**, 157–67.
Swadesh, M. (1952) Lexico-statistic dating of prehistoric ethnic contacts. *Proc. Amer. phil. Soc.*, **96**, 452–63.
Lees, R.B. (1953) The basis of glottochronology. *Language*, **29**, 113–27.
Swadesh, M. (1955) Towards greater accuracy in lexicostatistic dating. *Int. J. Amer. Linguistics*, **21**, 121–37.
Hymes, D. (1960) Lexicostatistics so far. *Current Anthropology*, **1**, 3–43; 338–45. (*See especially* Comment by Dyen).
Bergsland, K., Vogt, H. (1962) On the validity of glottochronology. *Current Anthropology*, **3**, 115–58.
Dyen, I. (1964) On the validity of comparative lexicostatistics. *Proceedings of the Ninth International Congress of Linguistics*, pp. 238–52 (ed. Lunt, H.). The Hague.

Dyen, I., James, A.T. & Cole, J.W.L. (1967) Language divergence and estimated word retention rate. *Language*, **43,** 150–71.

Brainerd, B. (1970) A stochastic process related to language change. *J. appl. Prob.*, **7,** 69–78.

Sankoff, D. (1970) On the rate of replacement of word-meaning relationships. *Language*, **46.**

Sankoff, D. (forthcoming) Mathematical developments in lexicostatistic theory. *Current Trends in Linguistics*, vol. 11 (ed Sebeck, T.).

Sankoff, D. (in preparation) Turnover processes.

Filiation of Manuscripts

Peter Buneman
The recovery of trees from measures of dissimilarity

The problem of inferring an evolutionary tree from a set of measurements is one that crops up in various fields, such as biology, palaeography, and archaeology. For example, amino-acid sequences of the same protein extracted from different organisms can be determined, and one can attempt, from the dissimilarities between these sequences, to construct a phylogenetic tree of these organisms. A similar situation occurs when one has a set of manuscripts all directly or indirectly copied from a common original manuscript. One seeks to reconstruct a family tree or 'stemma' of these documents from the errors that the various scribes made in copying one document from another. A frequent starting point in the solution of such a problem is the measurement of a dissimilarity coefficient (DC) between every pair of objects, and to this end one might, for example, count the number of sites at which two protein sequences differ. Similarly, one might count the number of places at which two manuscripts differ. A DC computed from morphological data for taxonomic purposes could also be used.

The object of this paper is to show that there is a method for inferring a tree from a DC which has properties that may make it rather more attractive than other currently available methods. Sokal and Sneath (1963) and Jardine and Sibson (1971) have given detailed accounts of the measurement of DCs and we shall not discuss this further, except to state that there are circumstances in which the measurement of a DC in the manner outlined above for protein chains or manuscripts can obscure useful information provided by the raw data. Thus the methods discussed here, involving DCs, are not the only ones that might be employed nor are they necessarily the best, but it is felt that they might provide a valuable starting point for closer examination of the data. This may be of special use in the reconstruction of a stemma where, for example, the techniques indicated by Maas (1958) for this purpose are impractical for all but a small number of manuscripts.

If we are given a tree, which may be thought of informally as a collection of nodes and links, the assignment of a length to each link will make each node a certain distance from any other node. This distance is the total length of the path between the two nodes, and we shall call such a measure of distance (which is itself a DC) an *additive tree metric*. A DC is not, in general, an additive tree metric: we shall see later that to be so it must satisfy a specific condition. Our problem then, is to find a transformation from the given DC to an additive tree metric. Cavalli-Sforza and Edwards (1967) and Eck and Dayhoff (1966) among others have described methods for finding the *nearest* additive tree metric to a DC. A dissimilarity or *stress* can be defined between two DCs in a number of ways. Subject to this definition, the nearest additive tree metric (we shall call it Δ_N) is that which minimizes the stress between it and the given DC. To find Δ_N reliably is usually an impossible task: it could involve a search through all the enormous number of possible configurations for the tree and for each configuration optimizing the link lengths. The methods invented for finding Δ_N operate by making a good guess at an initial configuration and then optimizing for a limited type of perturbation of that configuration. Such methods can still be lengthy, and there is no guarantee that they will not get trapped in a local, but not absolute, minimum for the stress. Another objection to Δ_N, given that it can be found, is that it will usually produce a detailed tree even from a DC which does not at all resemble an additive tree metric. In the absence of any theory as to why the data should give a tree, Δ_N may be misleading.

It will help our purposes to give a slightly unusual definition of a tree; and this is done in the next section. Observe that we are not seeking a tree which directly relates the given objects: we may want to reconstruct 'missing' nodes. Moreover we cannot hope to find a root to the tree on the basis of a DC nor can we necessarily find it even from examination of the raw data. What we shall do, therefore, is to define a tree in terms of its links. We can then show that a dissimilarity coefficient will produce a set of links and an additive tree metric, Δ_d. The relative merits of Δ_N and Δ_d are examined in the last section. The mathematics that follows is all very straightforward, but for any graph theoretical terms whose meaning is not obvious the reader is referred to Harary (1969).

TREES DEFINED BY THEIR LINKS

We shall call the finite set of objects on which the given DC has been measured the *base set*. A link in a tree divides the nodes of the tree into two complementary subsets, and by analogy with this we shall define a *split* of the base set to be a pair of non-empty complementary subsets. Thus if S is the base set, σ is a split if $\sigma = \{S^0, S^1\}$ where $S = S^0 \cup S^1$, and $S^0 \cap S^1$ is empty. If two members A and B of S lie in different members of σ, we shall say that σ *separates* A from B. Suppose that $\sigma_1 = \{S_1^0, S_1^1\}$ and $\sigma_2 = \{S_2^0, S_2^1\}$ are two splits; they are *compatible* if at least one of the intersections $S_1^0 \cap S_2^0$, $S_1^0 \cap S_2^1$, $S_1^1 \cap S_2^0$, $S_1^1 \cap S_2^1$ is empty. If two such intersections were empty the splits would be identical and, of course, any split is compatible with itself.

A *tree* on S can now be defined as a set of distinct, pairwise compatible splits of S. From now on, unless explicitly stated otherwise, we shall use the word 'tree' in this sense. Suppose that $T = \{\sigma_1, \sigma_2, ..., \sigma_n\}$ is a tree. A *node* of T is a set $\{S_1^{i_1}, S_2^{i_2}, ..., S_n^{i_n}\}$ where $S_k^{i_k} \in \sigma_k$, and each of the intersections $S_k^{i_k} \cap S_m^{i_m}$ is non-empty. Nodes exist; we can, for example, choose from each split that member which contains some given member of S. $\mathcal{N}(T)$ will be used to designate the set of nodes of T. Two nodes are *linked* by σ_k if they are, in some order,

$$\{S_1^{i_1}, ..., S_k^0, ..., S_n^{i_n}\}$$
and $\quad \{S_1^{i_1}, ..., S_k^1, ..., S_n^{i_n}\} \quad .$

That is to say that two nodes are linked by a split if they differ just on that split. We can now show that this set of nodes and links constitutes a graph-theoretic tree.

Lemma 1

Let N and M be two nodes of T; then there is a path from N to M.

This means we can find a sequence of nodes $N_1, N_2, \ldots N_p$ such that $N = N_1$, $M = N_p$ and N_k is linked to N_{k+1} for $1 \leqslant k < p$. Suppose, for convenience, that N and M differ on $\sigma_1 \ldots \sigma_k$ so that they can be expressed:

$$M = \{ S_1^{i_1}, \ldots, S_k^{i_k}, S_{k+1}^{i_{k+1}}, \ldots, S_n^{i_n} \}$$
$$N = \{ S_1^{j_1}, \ldots, S_k^{j_k}, S_{k+1}^{i_{k+1}}, \ldots, S_n^{i_n} \}$$

where $i_1 \neq j_1$, and so on. Of the k members of N which do not agree with the corresponding members of M there must be a minimal one (under set inclusion). Suppose that it is $S_k^{j_k}$. Since it is minimal, its complement $\bar{S}_k^{i_k}$ must intersect $S_1^{j_1}, \ldots, S_{k-1}^{j_{k-1}}$. But $S_k^{i_k}$ also intersects $S_{k+1}^{i_{k+1}}, \ldots, S_n^{i_n}$ because M is a node. Therefore

$$N_2 = \{ S_1^{j_1}, \ldots, S_{k-1}^{j_{k-1}}, S_k^{i_k}, \ldots, S_n^{i_n} \}$$

is a node and is linked by σ_k to N. Repeating this process we reduce, at each step, the number of disagreements with M and thus get a path from N to M.

Lemma 2

$$|\mathcal{N}(T)| = |T| + 1 \quad .$$

The proof is by induction on $|T|$ and the result is trivial when T contains just one split. Let N and M be two nodes linked by some member σ of T. The previous lemma assures us that such nodes exist. There can be only one pair of nodes linked by σ, for were there another such pair we would get a violation of compatibility. Removing σ from T therefore reduces the number of nodes by just one; and this gives the inductive step.

Lemma 3

$\mathcal{N}(T)$, linked by T, is a graph-theoretic tree.

It is connected by lemma 1 and has the right Euler number by lemma 2.

The remaining results in this section are given without proof, which is in all cases easy.

Lemma 4

The (graph theoretic) degree of a node is the number of minimal members it contains. A terminal node has one minimal member.

The *support* of a node is the intersection of its members and a *latent* node is one whose support is empty. A tree is *maximal* if there are no splits, compatible with all its members, which it does not contain.

Lemma 5

A terminal node has non-empty support. A latent node has degree greater than two. The nodes of non-empty support partition the base set.

Lemma 6

$|\mathcal{N}(T)| \leqslant 2(|S| - 1)$. Equality obtains iff T is maximal.

Lemma 7

A tree is maximal iff every terminal node has support containing just one member of S and every other node is latent and of degree three.

It may be of value to interpret briefly these preliminary results in terms of the reconstruction of a stemma. The surviving manuscripts constitute the base set. We can infer the former existence of a missing manuscript only when we have two manuscripts, with some common ancestor, neither of which has been copied from the other. Bearing in mind that we do not necessarily know the root of the stemma, this corresponds to the statement that a latent node must have degree at least three. Moreover we cannot hope to postulate the former existence of manuscripts which have not been copied from, so that each terminal node of the stemma must have a surviving manuscript in its support. It is also desirable, when the data is not adequate to discriminate them, to allow two or more manuscripts to lie at the same node in the stemma; and so we do not insist that there should be a separate node for each member of the base set. A parallel interpretation holds for the reconstruction of phylogenetic trees. This definition of a tree, in terms of compatible splits, is also of use when constructing a stemma, not from a DC but from the actual variations between texts. In an ideal situation each scribal error would give rise to a split, though in practice the problem is very much complicated by some errors obscuring others.

ADDITIVE TREE METRICS

The given dissimilarity coefficient, d, is a function which associates with each pair of points in the base set S a positive real number. It satisfies

$$d(A, A) = 0$$
$$d(A, B) \geqslant 0$$
$$d(A, B) = d(B, A)$$

for all members of A, B of S. Any split σ of S defines an elementary DC, δ_σ, by

$$\delta_\sigma(A, B) = 1 \text{ if } \sigma \text{ separates } A \text{ from } B$$
$$\delta_\sigma(A, B) = 0 \text{ otherwise.}$$

δ_σ, since it satisfies the triangle inequality, is a pseudometric, and it follows that any positive linear combination $\Sigma \alpha_\sigma \delta_\sigma$ of these elementary DCs is also a pseudometric. If the splits of such a sum are restricted to being the splits of a tree T, then we can define an *additive tree metric* by:

$$\Delta(A, B) = \sum_{\sigma \in T} \alpha_\sigma \delta_\sigma(A, B) \quad (\alpha_\sigma > 0) \quad .$$

[An additive tree metric is strictly speaking only a pseudo-metric for it allows distinct members of S to be zero distance apart.]

An additive tree metric on S will define a metric Δ^* on $\mathcal{N}(T)$ by:

$$\Delta^*(N, M) = \sum_{\sigma \in T} \alpha_\sigma \delta_\sigma^*(N, M)$$

where　　$\delta_\delta^*(N, M) = 1$ if σ is a link in the path from N to M;
　　　　　　　$= 0$ otherwise.

Δ^* and Δ, while they are not the same thing (one is defined on S, the other on $\mathcal{N}(T)$), are such that Δ^* defines Δ for $\Delta(A, B) = \Delta^*(N, M)$ whenever A and B are in the respective supports of N and M. Δ^* corresponds to the informal definition of an additive tree metric given in the introduction but Δ as defined is more convenient for our purposes. We now show how a dissimilarity coefficient naturally gives us an additive tree metric. Suppose that d is a DC on S and $\sigma = \{S^0, S^1\}$ is a split. We define

$$\mu_\sigma = \tfrac{1}{2} \min (d(A, C) + d(B, D) - d(A, B) - d(C, D))$$

for A, B in S^0 and C, D in S^1.

Lemma 8

If σ_1 and σ_2 are splits such that $\mu_{\sigma_1} > 0$ and $\mu_{\sigma_2} > 0$ then σ_1 and σ_2 are compatible.

If σ_1 and σ_2 were not compatible then we could choose A, B, C, D so that σ_1 separates A and B from C and D, and so that σ_2 separates A and C from B and D. The quantity $d(A, C)+d(B, D)-d(A, B)-d(C, D)$ would have to be strictly positive since $\mu_{\delta_1}>0$, but since $\mu_{\delta_2}>0$ it would also have to be strictly negative.

From d we can derive $T_d=\{\sigma:\mu_\sigma>0\}$ and lemma 8 ensures that T_d is a tree. Consequently we can define an additive tree metric Δ_d by:

$$\Delta_d=\sum_{\sigma\in T_d}\mu_\sigma\delta_\sigma\ .$$

Lemma 9

$$\Delta_d\leqslant d\ .$$

For any pair of members A, B of S there is by lemma 1 a path N_1, N_2, ... N_p such that A is in the support of N_1, B is in the support of N_p, and N_k is linked to N_{k+1} by σ_k for $1\leqslant k<p$. For each σ_k we may suppose that $\sigma_k=\{S_k^0, S_k^1\}$ with $A\in S_k^0$ and $B\in S_k^1$. Then we can choose, for each k, $1<k<p$, a member P_k of S such that P_k lies in $S_k^0\cap S_{k-1}^1$. We can do this because S_k^0 and S_{k-1}^1 are both members of the node N_k and therefore have a non-empty intersection. Thus σ_k separates A from P_{k+1} for $1\leqslant k<p-1$ and it separates B from P_k for $1<k\leqslant p-1$; so that

$$\mu_{\sigma_1}\leqslant\tfrac{1}{2}(d(A, B)+d(A, P_2)-d(B, P_2)),$$
$$\mu_{\sigma_2}\leqslant\tfrac{1}{2}(d(A, P_3)+d(B, P_2)-d(A, P_2)-d(B, P_3)),$$
$$\mu_{\sigma_3}\leqslant\tfrac{1}{2}(d(A, P_4)+d(B, P_3)-d(A, P_3)-d(B, P_4)),$$

$$\cdot$$
$$\cdot$$
$$\cdot$$

$$\mu_{\sigma_{p-1}}\leqslant\tfrac{1}{2}(d(A, B)+d(B, P_{d-1})-d(A, P_{-1}))\ .$$

Adding these we find that $d(A, B)\geqslant\sum_1^{p-1}\mu_{\sigma_k}$. We have considered all those splits in T_d which separate A from B and so the result is proved.

Theorem 1

If T_1 and T_2 are trees and $\sum_{\sigma\in T_1}\alpha_\sigma\delta_\sigma-\sum_{\sigma\in T_2}\beta_\sigma\delta_\sigma$ where $\alpha_\sigma>0$ and $\beta_\sigma>0$, then $T_1=T_2$ and $\alpha_\sigma=\beta_\sigma$.

This means that an additive tree metric specifies a unique tree. Let $d=\sum_{\sigma\in T_1}\alpha_\sigma\delta_\sigma$. If A, B, C, D are chosen so that some split in T_1 separates A and B from C and D then the quantity

$$\tfrac{1}{2}(d(A, C)+d(B, D)-d(A, B)-d(C, D))$$

is, by the compatibility of splits in T_1, the sum of the α_σ for exactly those splits which separate A and B from C and D. From this we deduce that for all splits σ of T_1, $\mu_\sigma\geqslant\alpha_\sigma$ and hence $T_1\subseteq T_d$. If the inclusion were strict we would have $\Delta_d>d$ contrary to the previous lemma. If then any of the inequalities $\mu_\sigma>\alpha_\sigma$ were strict we would similarly violate that lemma. We conclude that $T_1=T_d=T_2$ and $\alpha_\sigma=\mu_\sigma=\beta_\sigma$.

A necessary and sufficient condition that d is an additive tree metric is now given. It is that for all members A, B, C, D of S,

$$d(A, B)+d(C, D)\leqslant\max\ (d(A, C)+d(B, D), d(B, C)+d(A, D))$$

and we shall refer to it as the *four-point condition*. Before proving this assertion we can make some elementary observations about the four-point condition.

If we put $C = D$ in the expression above, it reduces to the triangle inequality, so that a DC which satisfies the four-point condition is necessarily a pseudo-metric. Each sum in this expression corresponds to one of the three distinct ways of partitioning a set of four members into two subsets each of two members. Notice that the four-point condition is equivalent to the condition that two of these sums are equal and not less than the third. It is apparent that there is a resemblance in form between the four-point condition and the ultrametric inequality $[d(A, B) \leqslant \max(d(A, C), d(B, C))]$; and we note the following result, which can be proved in various ways:

Lemma 10

An ultrametric satisfies the four-point condition.

We now prove our assertion that the four-point condition is necessary and sufficient for a DC to be an additive tree metric.

Theorem 2

$\Delta_d = d$ iff d satisfies the four-point condition.

To establish this we shall first show that Δ_d itself satisfies the four-point condition. The converse is proved by showing that the four-point condition implies that $\Delta_d \geqslant d$; and this, in view of lemma 9, is all that is needed.

Consider four points and the way in which the splits of T_d can separate them. If σ separates A and B from C and D, then, by compatibility, no split of T_d can separate A and C from B and D nor can it separate A and D from B and C. We can write: λ_{AB} for the sum of the μ_σ for which σ separates A and B from C and D; λ_A for the sum of the μ_σ for which σ separates A from B, C and D; and λ_B, λ_C and λ_D similarly. Then $\Delta_d(A, B) + \Delta_d(C, D) = \lambda_A + \lambda_B + \lambda_C + \lambda_D$ and $\Delta_d(A, C) + \Delta_d(B, D) = \Delta_d(B, C) + \Delta_d(A, D) = \lambda_A + \lambda_B + \lambda_C + \lambda_D + \lambda_{AB}$ and the four-point condition is satisfied.

For the converse, take any two members A and B of S and define a function f on S by:

$$f(X) = d(A, X) - d(B, X) \quad .$$

d is necessarily a pseudo-metric and so for all X in S $-d(A, B) \leqslant f(X) \leqslant d(A, B)$. Suppose that α and α' are real numbers within this range such that $\alpha' > \alpha$ and for no X does $f(X)$ lie between α and α'. Then the pair of subsets,

$$\{X : f(X) \geqslant \alpha'\} \quad \text{and} \quad \{X : f(X) \leqslant \alpha\}$$

forms a split. We shall show that for this split $\mu_\sigma \geqslant \frac{1}{2}(\alpha' - \alpha)$. By the definition of μ_σ there are members X, Y, Z, T of S such that $\mu_\sigma = \frac{1}{2}(d(X, Z) + d(Y, T) - d(X, Y) - d(Z, T))$ and such that X and Y are separated by this split from Z and T. We can assume for convenience that $f(X) \leqslant f(Y) \leqslant \alpha < \alpha' \leqslant f(Z) \leqslant f(T)$. Thus, for example, $d(X, A) + d(Z, B) < d(X, B) + d(Z, A)$ and by applying the four-point condition:

$$d(X, Z) = d(X, B) + d(Z, A) - d(A, B) \quad .$$

By further applications of the four-point condition we find:

$$d(Y, T) = d(Y, B) + d(T, A) - d(A, B) \quad ,$$
$$d(X, Y) \leqslant d(X, B) + d(Y, A) - d(A, B) \quad ,$$
$$d(Z, T) \leqslant d(Z, B) + d(T, A) - d(A, B) \quad .$$

Combining these last four expressions gives:

$$\mu_\sigma \geqslant \frac{1}{2}(f(Z) - f(Y)) \geqslant \frac{1}{2}(\alpha' - \alpha) \quad .$$

Now let $\alpha_1, \alpha_2, \ldots \alpha_p$ be the values of $f(X)$ arranged in ascending order so that $\alpha_1 = -d(A, B) = f(A)$ and $\alpha_p = d(A, B) = f(B)$. Each pair α_i, α_{i+1} gives us a split σ_i in the manner just indicated and $\mu_{\sigma_i} \geqslant \frac{1}{2}(\alpha_{i+1} - \alpha_i)$. Since each σ_i separates A from B, we get:

$$\Delta_d(A, B) \geqslant \sum_{i=1}^{p-1} \mu_{\sigma_i} \geqslant \frac{1}{2} \sum_{i=1}^{p-1} (\alpha_{i+1} - \alpha_i) = d(A, B)$$

which is what we wanted to prove.

To summarize: we have defined the transformation $d \to \Delta_d$; we have shown that it defines a unique tree and preserves an additive tree metric; we have also established a necessary and sufficient condition for a DC to be an additive tree metric. One further observation will be of use to us in the discussion that follows. The transformation $d \to \Delta_d$ is continuous with respect to the natural topology on the set of DCs. Informally this means that, given reasonable definition of stress between DCs, any sufficiently small perturbation of d will result in a small perturbation of Δ_d.

DISCUSSION

Δ_N was described in the introduction as the nearest additive tree metric to d for some given definition of stress. We now turn to a practical comparison of the two transformations $d \to \Delta_d$ and $d \to \Delta_N$. Any discussion of why a particular set of data should give rise to an additive tree metric has been deliberately avoided. The justification would usually be given by some theory such as a postulate about evolutionary rates. Such a theory might also be adequate to determine how to recover the additive tree metric, but it is felt that none of the existing theories which presently figure in any of the situations mentioned is sufficient to do this. We therefore list some criticisms of Δ_N and Δ_d which may be of value in deciding which is best suited to a particular situation.

(1) Δ_N is not well defined. There may be two additive tree metrics equally near to d.

(2) There is no practical algorithm which reliably finds Δ_N on a large base set.

(3) The transformation $d \to \Delta_N$ is not continuous.

(4) Δ_d can give uninteresting trees from a DC which does not resemble an additive tree metric.

The first of these is not a pedantic quibble. DCs constructed, for example, from amino acid sequences can take on small integral values, and it is quite possible to find two additive tree metrics equally close to this DC. As for the second point: we have seen some of the difficulties involved in finding Δ_N; these do not apply to Δ_d. It happens that there is a reasonably fast algorithm for finding Δ_d which does not involve a search through all the possible splits of S, and it is hoped to publish details of this algorithm and its implementation shortly. Whether or not the third criticism is important depends on one's prior assumptions of what form the result can take. If there are no such assumptions then it certainly is important; but there may be circumstances where, because of some appreciation of the data, one can reject alternative trees that can result from small perturbations of the original DC. Nevertheless, it is felt that continuity is a desirable property of any transformation from a

DC to an additive tree metric. The fourth criticism is very much bound up with the third. The possibility of getting uninteresting trees (that is, trees with few splits) is the price paid for continuity. A detailed tree produced by Δ_N would usually be of value either because the stress with the original DC is very low or because, having produced it, one can find some other justification for its form. In the absence of any such justification, an intricate tree may be more misleading than helpful. Moreover if Δ_N does give very low stress with d, Δ_d will do so also for much less computation.

The first and third of these criticisms are the same as those made by Jardine, Jardine, and Sibson (1967) with respect to certain methods in cluster analysis. We have also noticed a correspondence between the four-point condition and the ultrametric inequality, which is central to nearly all types of cluster analysis. These similarities are not all fortuitous. There is an extension of the theory contained in this paper which embraces both. Loosely speaking, this extension involves an asymmetry in the definition of a split and asymmetry in the derivation of a DC from a split. In the limit of lop-sidedness, one component of each split gets entirely neglected and the other turns into one of Jardine's ball clusters (Jardine 1969). The four-point condition, or rather its extension, turns into the ultrametric inequality. The case we have dealt with is the symmetrical case in this extended theory and it may be that the intermediate cases will prove of some value as well.

Computing a DC is not the only way open to us for finding a tree. For protein chains one can avoid a DC and define a set of splits in terms of the amino-acid sequences themselves; and these splits turn out to be compatible. The same thing can be done with manuscripts or for any data in which one has recorded a set of discrete attribute values for the given objects. Trees constructed in this way can be more representative of the raw data since, as we have noted, a DC can obscure useful information. One way of seeing this is that a DC is calculated on the properties of *pairs* of objects, while compatible splits can be defined by properties of objects taken *four* at a time. It is not surprising that by avoiding a DC, one can build trees which give much better descriptions of the data. Finding trees, and possibly clusters, from raw attribute data is something that deserves further investigation.

ACKNOWLEDGMENTS

The author wishes to express his gratitude to Professor H.C.Longuet-Higgins, FRS, for his good advice and constant encouragement. He would also like to thank Professor A.McIntosh, Mr C.Stephenson, Dr N.Jardine, and Dr R.Sibson for many useful discussions. This work was supported by a grant from the Royal Society.

REFERENCES

Cavalli-Sforza, L.L. & Edwards, A.W.F. (1967) *Am. J. hum. Genet.*, **19**, 233–57.
Eck, R.V. & Dayhoff, M.O. (1966) *Atlas of Protein Sequence and Structure*
        1966, pp. 164–9. Nat. biomed. res. Found.
Harary, F. (1969) *Graph Theory*. New York: Addison-Wesley.
Jardine, N. (1969) *Nature*, **244**, 185.
Jardine, C.J., Jardine, N. & Sibson, R. (1967) *Mathematical Biosciences*, **1**, 173–9.

Jardine, N. & Sibson, R. (1971) *Mathematical Taxonomy*. New York: Wiley.

Maas, P. (1958) *Textual Criticism* (tr. Flower, B.). Oxford University Press.

Sokal, R.R. & Sneath, P.H.A. (1963) *Principles of Numerical Taxonomy*. W.H. Freeman.

Filiation of Manuscripts

John Haigh
The manuscript linkage problem

We have N manuscripts, all of the same work but with various errors and alterations produced when the copying was done. The problem is to decide, as well as possible, the original version of this work, and to deduce the relationships of the scripts we have to this original version and to each other.

Of course, in general this task is impossible; the scripts we have may be only a minute fraction of the scripts produced; for two identical scripts, it may be quite impossible to differentiate between them; and it will be impossible to justify any of the assumptions we may be forced to make about the manner in which the copying was done.

The approach of this paper is to suggest a model of the copying process, to derive various consequences of the model, and then to fit the manuscripts together as consistent with the model as possible. Several papers at this conference have suggested that, if a model is to be employed, it should be as simple as possible, advice with which I concur. The model I suggest is that, when k scripts are present and another copy is to be made, one of these k scripts is taken at random and then copied. Our N scripts are the ones we have traced among those that have survived.

There are serious objections to the model: we do not allow conflation of sources; the scripts are forced to fit together on a (mathematical) tree; we do not allow several scripts to be copied simultaneously; earlier, more reliable versions may be more likely to be copied than those just made. However, the model is sufficiently non-trivial to be interesting, and serves well to illustrate the possibilities of this approach—postulate a model, derive consequences, fit the observations as consistently with the consequences as possible—in the general fields of history and social phenomena.

Quentin (1925) devised a method to construct a tree consistent with the discrepancies between scripts. Given three distinct scripts A, B, and C, look at the places where A and C agree, but B disagrees; if there are several such places, say that ABC is a *forbidden triad*, and reject any tree connecting our scripts in which the path from A to C contains B. The logic of this can easily be seen; if the path from A to C contains B, the relative positions of the scripts are as shown in figure 1(a) or (b).

If figure 1(a) represents the true state of affairs (with ABC a forbidden triad) then the same errors have been made independently in the copyings of A from B, and C from B; if figure 1(b) represents the true state of affairs, errors and alterations made when B was copied from A have been 'corrected' in the path from B to C *without reference* to A. Quentin finds as many forbidden triads as he can, and aims to construct a tree consistent with them. His

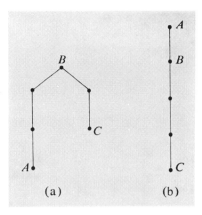

Figure 1

task is not easy—there are N^{N-2} possible ways of drawing and labelling a tree with N points—and, even if this Herculean task is successfully achieved, there is no way of telling, *from the discrepancies between scripts*, which of the points we should choose to be the root!

[I find it helpful to look on the tree constructed by Quentin as a set of beads (the scripts) joined by pieces of string (the links); by suspending the tree from any one of these beads, we have a rooted tree consistent with our information on the scripts—our problem is to decide which bead to suspend from.]

This decision is taken by our idea of fitting the scripts together so as to be as consistent with our supposed model as possible. If the scripts are linked together as we have found, which point should we select as root so as to maximize the likelihood of obtaining the tree we have? My work (1970) shows that this task can always be performed, giving a unique point when N is odd, but possibly two points of equal likelihood when N is even. The algorithm is particularly easy to perform, and is as follows:

(1) select an arbitrary point as preliminary root;

(2) counting each point as being below itself, count the number of points below each point—this attaches an integer to each point in the tree;

(3) write out this sequence of integers in descending order $(y_1, y_2, ..., y_N)$ [Clearly $y_1 = N$ and $y_N = 1$];

(4) choose a point P labelled y_m, where

$$y_m \geqslant N/2 > y_{m+1} \quad .$$

This P is the maximum likelihood choice as root.

Illustration

The sequence in figure 2 is $(21, 12, 7, 7, 4, ...)$ and so, since $12 \geqslant 21/2 > 7$, the point labelled 12 is the so-called maximum likelihood root; whatever point had been selected as 'preliminary root', we would have obtained this point as the solution.

It is easy to give a method of selecting a root, but it is essential to answer the question: 'How good is your method?' In my 1970 paper I gave formulae

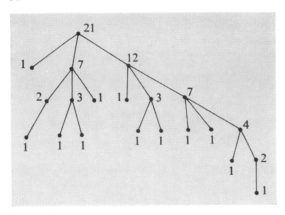

Figure 2

for deducing the probability of the point selected being really the kth point which arose, and the probability of the point selected really belonging to the rth generation below the true root (both probabilities being calculated, of course, on the basis of the model of the copying process). Their asymptotic values (that is, for large N) reproduced from Haigh (1970) are shown here in tables 1 and 2.

k	A_k	k	A_k	k	A_k
1	0·30685	4	0·09852	7	0·01362
2	0·30685	5	0·05164	8	0·00693
3	0·18185	6	0·02664	9	0·00351
				$\sum_{k=10}^{\infty} A_k = 0·00357$	

Table 1. Asymptotic values A_k of the probability that the point selected really is the kth script that arose

r	B_r	r	B_r
0	0·30685	3	0·99038
1	0·75977	4	0·99867
2	0·94450	5	0·99985

Table 2. Asymptotic values B_r of the probability that the point selected belongs really to, at worst, the rth generation below the genuine original script

It is submitted that these probabilities are encouragingly high; their practical use is limited severely by the assumptions under which they were derived, but the facts that, even with an enormous number of scripts present, we shall select the *true* root 31% of the time, and a script not more than two copyings away from the true original 94% of the time, lead one to suggest that this general approach may lead to usable and useful results. Opportunities to try out the method in practice are limited by the lack of fully

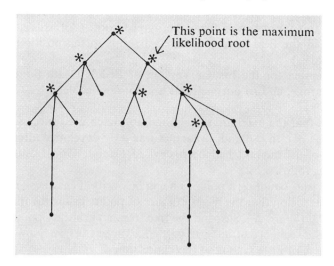

Figure 3. The reconstructed family tree of Caedmon's Hymn (Dobbie 1937)

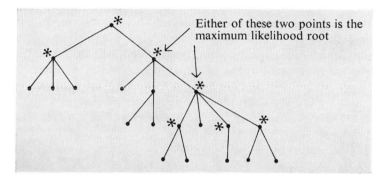

Figure 4. The reconstructed family tree of the Continental Version of Bede's Death Song (Dobbie 1937)

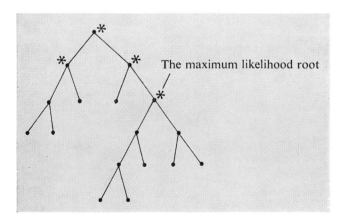

Figure 5. The stemma of Cicero's Letters to Atticus (Shackleton Bailey 1965)

agreed stemma of scripts, but the three illustrations given in figures 3, 4, and 5 all give results not too far removed from the agreed root. (An asterisk denotes that workers in the field have postulated a script in this position, this script now being lost.)

Note. The 'agreed' stemma for the Insular Version of Bede's Death Song shows alarming conflations, and so our methods are not applicable.

ADDENDUM

It is not at all obvious that the maximum likelihood approach used successfully in this work is the one to use and, in fact, it was only developed after a heuristic 'goodness-of-fit' method had been devised (Haigh 1968). This latter method works as follows.

In the reconstructed tree, counting a point as being below itself (as above), it is easy to show by induction that the mean number of points below the ith point which arose is N/i $[1 \leqslant i \leqslant N]$. Suspend the tree from an arbitrary point as above, and obtain the sequence of integers $(y_1, y_2, \dots y_N)$ as before. Now, recalling the χ^2 goodness-of-fit test, look at the expression

$$\sum_i \frac{(y_i - N/i)^2}{N/i}$$

and choose that point as root which minimizes this expression. In my doctoral thesis (Haigh 1968) I showed that we always get at least two (adjacent) points which give equal minima; one of them will always be the maximum likelihood root found by the principal method described here.

REFERENCES

Dobbie, E.K. (1937) *The manuscripts of Caedmon's Hymn and Bede's Death Song.* New York: Columbia.

Haigh, J. (1968) *Ph.D. thesis,* Cambridge University.

Haigh, J. (1970) The recovery of the root of a tree. *J. appl. Probab.,* **7,** 79–88.

Quentin, D.H. (1925) *Essaies de Critique Textuelle (Ecdotique).* Paris: Picard.

Shackleton Bailey, D.R. (1965) *Cicero's letters to Atticus, Vol. 1.* Cambridge: Cambridge University Press.

Filiation of Manuscripts

Sorin Cristian Niţă
Establishing the linkage of different variants of a Romanian chronicle

We shall try to show in this paper how the linkage can be established of the different copies which still exist of an old Romanian chronicle, namely, *The History of Romania*, 1290–1690 (Cantacusino's Chronicle), and how one can automate some operations which otherwise involve a great deal of work.

As we know, an important stage in textual criticism is the establishment of the genealogical tree for the transmission of the text, called by philologists 'the stemma of the manuscripts'. Mathematicians have observed that this stemma is a graph, in which the manuscripts are the vertices and the genealogical relations are the edges of the graph. When there is no confluence, this graph is a tree, whose root is the original text. A graph presents two principal aspects: *linkage*, which in our case indicates that it is possible to pass from one manuscript to another by a series of intermediate manuscripts, and *orientation*, which comprises the choice of an origin, and of a 'sense'. Because the linkage characterizes an independent orientation structure it can be found independently. It is not necessary to know the ultimate ancestor of the existing manuscripts in order to reconstitute the linkage, which can be constructed with different origins; if the origin is the real historical ancestor the genealogy will be called 'absolute' or 'real', and if we consider an arbitrary manuscript as origin, then the genealogy is 'relative' to this manuscript.

Because of these considerations we will be concerned only with the establishment of the linkage of the manuscripts, without being interested in the problem of finding the true genealogy. This last is a task for a specialist—a historian or philologist—taking into account, for instance, data which concern the external history of the text. The genealogy is established by orienting the graph of the linkage. The ultimate ancestor then follows implicitly from this.

In our study we use 'the method of common errors', as it is systematized and presented in Froger's works (1952, 1968).

Using the method to get a critical edition of the work *Graduel Roman*, he observed that the procedures had a logically complete structure, and so he proposed to treat the problem using a computer. A group of mathematicians from the Bull Company created a program for the Gamma ET computer, verifying in this way both the hypotheses, and Froger's hand-calculations.

From among the different variants of the method, we use the indirect method of 'groups of fictitious mistakes', because it requires no familiarity with the principles of textual criticism, but only an appreciation of the logic of the method.

The method of common errors is based on an analysis of clerical mistakes.

Let us study the copying mechanism in relation to a simple example (*see* figure 1). Suppose that two copies X, Y were made from an original manuscript O, and that from X two other copies A, B were made, from Y three copies C, D, E were made, and finally from E the copies F, G were made.

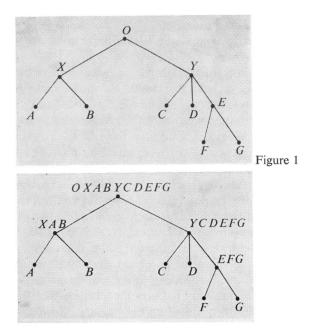

Figure 1

Figure 2

In general, the clerks made mistakes, either involuntary (carelessness) or voluntary (the desire to correct the source). These mistakes, except for rare anomalies, will be transmitted to the successor-manuscripts. The more distant from the original a manuscript is, the more different it will be, containing both its own peculiar mistakes and also the mistakes of all intermediate manuscripts between it and the original. So in our example manuscript F contains its own mistakes to which are added the mistakes of the manuscripts E and Y. Normally the peculiar mistakes of a manuscript will also be found in all its descendants. If we insert in the graph of figure 1 at every vertex not only the respective manuscript but also all of its descendants, we obtain a graph of *groups* of manuscripts which, in certain places of the text, called 'variant places', present the same variables from the original (figure 2).

Each group of *manuscripts* includes all inferior groups connected with it (for example, $YCDEFG \supset C$, D, EFG, F, and G); on the other hand the group of *mistakes* associated with a group of manuscripts Z includes all the groups of mistakes associated with all the groups of manuscripts that are 'superior' to this group of manuscripts Z and connected with it. This is what happens in the case of a normal transmission in which there is no contamination, random coincidence (two clerks making the same mistake at the same place), or parallel mistakes (a clerk making a mistake in exactly the same place as one in which the model he is following already has a mistake, and so on).

We have described the real situation, starting with the structure and deducing the consequences. In practice the problem is the reverse one, that is, starting from the consequences, the structure is deduced; that is, starting from the groups of manuscripts with a common group of mistakes, the genealogy of the manuscripts is deduced. Because we do not know the original manuscript we shall deal with the case of a *relative* genealogy, choosing an arbitrary manuscript, called the basic manuscript, with which we shall work as if it were the original manuscript. We shall obtain the genealogical graph relative to this manuscript, but this graph will be, at the same time, the graph of the real linkage of the manuscripts. It will then remain for us (or others) to orient the graph in order to obtain the real (absolute) genealogy.

The principle of the method is as follows. In one way or another the basic manuscript is chosen, for instance, because it is among the most complete manuscripts, or because it does not have fortuitous gaps, and so on. After that, each other existing manuscript is compared with this basic manuscript. The result will be a list, for each manuscript, containing the addresses of the variant places (the places in the text where there are differences between this and the basic manuscript) and the respective variants. In the next stage, from these $n-1$ lists (n being the number of existing manuscripts) a list is made containing all the variant places, the corresponding variants, and the groups of the manuscripts which contains those variants.

In the study of the chronicle we did not go through these stages because we used the critical edition of the chronicle by C. Grecescu and D. Simonescu published in 1960, an edition which transcribes a manuscript (which can be considered as the basic manuscript) and which then gives in the footnotes a critical apparatus which can be identified with the lists we have just spoken about.

From the lists (critical apparatus) we tabulate the variant places with only *two* variants, each of which defines a group of manuscripts, one of which contains the basic manuscript. The cases in which there are more than two variants in the same place are caused by rare anomalies in the transmission of the text and will therefore be left aside.

From the last list, the one which contains the variant places with only two variants, we find the groups of manuscripts which contain the variant differing from the basic manuscript. After this we compute how many times each group appears in the list and so obtain another list containing the groups of manuscripts and the 'weights' of each of these groups.

For this phase of the investigation we write a program in FORTRAN IV for the computer IBM-360, which counts the weights of the groups of manuscripts and arranges the groups in descending order of weights.

As will be seen, the method is called the indirect method of fictitious mistakes, because the groups depend on the differences from an arbitrary manuscript (the basic manuscript) and not from the original one.

We shall now apply the method to Cantacusino's Chronicle. We studied the critical edition of the work in three places, using 25 pages from the 195 pages of the whole work.

To establish the linkage, only the groups with large weights are considered; those with small weights are doubtful—they can be due to fortuitous coincidences (two or more clerks making, by chance, the same mistake in the same place). Because of this the small-weight groups are left on one side for the moment, and the graph of the linkage is constructed from the large-weight groups only; if some small-weight groups do not present contradictions they can be introduced at a later stage.

In the critical edition, manuscript V was transcribed from page 1 to 188 and manuscript K^1 from page 188 to the end (page 195).

We observed that in pages 6 through 10 in the critical apparatus only the manuscripts A, K, C, and L appear. For this section of the text the computer yielded table 1. We considered next pages 1–5, which contain in addition manuscript O. From the data of this text we obtained table 2. In the text from pages 106–115 manuscript G also appeared (whence table 3).

AK	83	AC	3
CL	13	AL	3
CK	6	ACK	2
ACL	5	KL	2
AKL	5	$ACKL$	1
CKL	4		

Table 1

AK	20	AL	5	$ACKLO$	2
CL	10	AO	4	ACK	2
AKO	9	$ACKL$	3	CO	2
ACL	7	$CKLO$	3	KO	2
AKL	7	KL	3	$AKLO$	1
CK	6	AC	3	LO	1
CKL	5				

Table 2

AK	20	GK	3	$ACGK$	1
$AGKO$	9	$ACGKO$	2	$AGKL$	1
CL	9	$ACKL$	2	AGK	1
GO	5	$AKLO$	2	CGL	1
$ACGKLO$	4	$CGKL$	2	CKL	1
AKL	4	ACK	2	CLO	1
ALO	4	ACL	2	GKL	1
AKO	3	AC	2	KLO	1
AO	3	CG	2	AG	1
CK	3	AL	2	KL	1
CO	3	$ACGKL$	1	LO	1

Table 3

In these three tables the manuscript groups, together with the weights, are given. We mention that we did not include in the tables the groups formed by a single manuscript.

Considering at first the most heavily weighted groups and then some less heavily weighted groups, not in contradiction with the former, and working with the inclusions of the manuscript groups, we were led to the linkage graphs of the manuscript groups shown in figures 3 to 5.

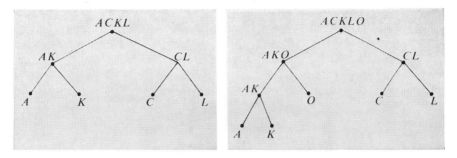

Figure 3   Figure 4

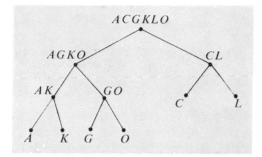

Figure 5

It is to be observed that these graphs do not contradict one another, and that their information-content increases as new manuscripts are introduced. The graph in figure 3 is a subgraph of that in figure 5. We now subtract from every group all the manuscripts which appear in the descendant groups linked to it; this is the reverse of the step in which we passed from figure 1 to figure 2. When nothing remains in a group, it means that we have found a *lost* manuscript. We indicate the lost manuscripts by new letters. The graphs obtained are those in figure 6–8.

We add the basic manuscript *V* as ultimate ancestor of the linkage (figures 9–11).

We have now obtained the linkage graphs for the respective manuscripts. The problem which is posed now is how to orient these graphs and so obtain the genealogy. We are not here primarily concerned with this, but in the preface to the critical edition the stemma of the manuscripts is given (*see* figure 12), so in this we had the possibility of a check.

In this stemma the indices have two different meanings: those which

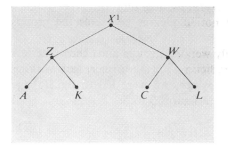

Figure 6

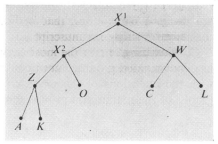

Figure 7

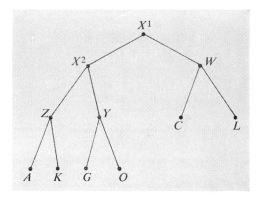

Figure 8

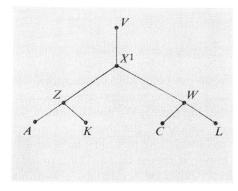

Figure 9

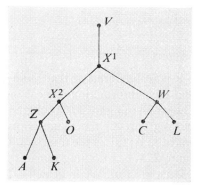

Figure 10

correspond to X each denote a separate manuscript, but the rest of the indices represent the number of the manuscripts in the corresponding group, for example, in the group A^3 there are three manuscripts A^0, A^1, A^2.

From among the three graphs of the linkage which we have obtained, we will orient only that in figure 11, which is the most complete. The orientation is achieved by taking into account the stemma from figure 12. In this way we obtain the genealogical graph in figure 13.

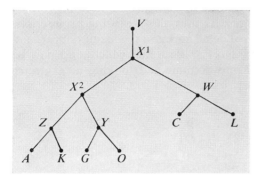

Figure 11

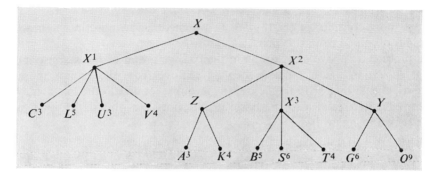

Figure 12

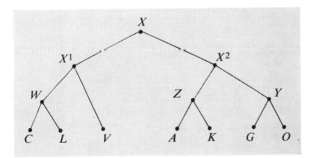

Figure 13

It was necessary to suppose the existence of a lost manuscript (X) without which, with the method used, we could not complete the tree. The 'common mistakes' method can find the lost manuscript only in the centre of a 'star' (the manuscripts from which at least two copies were made). The mistakes of a lost manuscript in the centre of a segment appear to be due to its immediate descendant and do not appear in the linkage.

Coming back to our original problem, we observe that the graph in figure 13 is almost identical with a part of the graph in figure 12. It coincides only with a part of the latter because the graph in figure 13 uses only seven existing manuscripts and that in figure 12 uses all 48 existing manuscripts. In the graph in figure 13 an additional detail appears: the manuscripts C and L have a common immediate 'lost' ancestor W, a fact which must now be verified, taking more manuscripts into account and looking at a greater section of the text.

BG	18	A^1B	4
A^1BG	7	GK	3
A^1BGK	4	A^1BK	3
A^1GK	4	A^1G	2
A^1K	4	BGK	1

Table 4

Let us now consider pages 189–93, in which other manuscripts appear. Table 4 is obtained from this text.

We proceed as above and so obtain the linkage graph of the manuscript groups shown in figure 14, and then we remove from the groups those manuscripts that appear in the descending groups; let us add the lost manuscripts (figure 15) and also the basic manuscript. We obtain the linkage graph shown in figure 16.

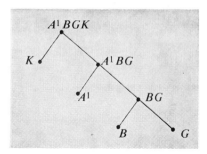

Figure 14   Figure 15

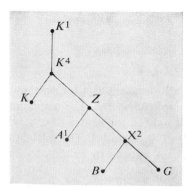

Figure 16

We orient this last graph with the help of the stemma in figure 12. In this way we obtain the oriented graph in figure 17, which is almost identical with another part of the graph in figure 12.

[K^1 is a 'basic manuscript' (the 'relative ancestor'), K^4 is the 'non-existent ancestor', and K is a putative manuscript.]

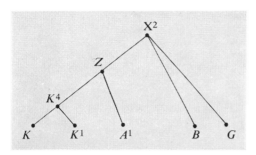

Figure 17

We consider that the establishment of the linkage of the manuscripts by the method explained here can be a valuable help to those who have to do with the editing of such texts.

REFERENCES

Froger, D.J. (1952) La critique textuelle et la méthode des groupes fautifs. *Cahiers de lexicologie*, **3**.

Froger, D.J. (1968) *La critique des textes et son automatisation*. Paris: Dunod.

Evolutionary tree structures in historical and other contexts

Discussion and comments

A. W. F. Edwards. Since I find the method of maximum likelihood intrinsically more compelling than any arguments involving the probability of obtaining the 'right' answer, I should like to express my confidence in the maximum likelihood solution by comparing the likelihood of the *ml* node with that of the other nodes, so as to rank the nodes in order of likelihood. Can one do this in Dr Haigh's problem?

J. Haigh (in reply). Yes. The answer will depend on the shape, and not just the size of the tree, and is obtained by enumerating, for each of the N nodes, the number of ways of consistently labelling the tree when that node is chosen as root and labelled 1. (A *consistent* labelling is one in which the point labelled i is not an ancestor of the point labelled j whenever $i > j$.) For example, for the three possible shapes of tree when $N = 5$, the enumerations are given in the figure. The maximum likelihood nodes are marked $+$, and the enumerations are exactly the relative likelihoods. Unfortunately, this computational task has to be performed *ab initio* any time these relative likelihoods need to be calculated.

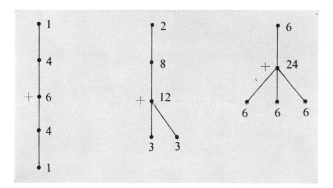

G. Granasztoi. J'ai une objection à faire concernant la méthode présentée par L. L. Cavalli-Sforza et ses collègues. Avec cette méthode—recherches généalogiques basées sur des registres paroissiaux—ils proposent de donner le nombre de la population de telle ou telle localité. Mon objection consiste en une remarque: cette méthode ne tient pas compte des migrations, qui sont très fréquentes dans les couches pauvres d'une population. M. Cavalli-Sforza m'a répondu là-dessus et a déclaré que ce phenomène (la migration) n'existe pas dans les localités examinées par lui. A mon avis, dans ce cas il travaille dans des circonstances très nuisible pour ces recherches, mais la méthode proposée n'est guère utilisable que dans un nombre assez restreint des cas.

J. Haigh. Mr Skolnick has information on the distribution of family size at birth, or at baptism; does he also have information on the size of families whose members are at the reproductive ages, for this is more important in studying consanguinuity and genealogy?

R. W. Hiorns. The problem (which arises in Professor Kendall's paper) of upper and lower triangles of a matrix providing separate information concerning similarity measures reminds me of the recent approaches of L. A. Goodman in assessing the information in a social mobility matrix. The highly sophisticated statistical techniques he has devised separate the diagonal, upper and lower triangles by considering a partition of χ^2 into components representing upward, downward, and diagonal mobility, and the interactions between them. This technique is known, I believe, as 'ransacking' a matrix, and clearly this might provide a preliminary analysis before applying INSCAL or similar techniques.

T. H. Hollingsworth. In England a recent study (see *Population Studies* 1971) has shown that about 30 per cent of persons in a London parish around 1600 AD cannot have survived to baptism. This figure assumes that burials were completely registered, and would be even higher if they were incomplete.

Although this is an urban parish, high literary and living standards and the absence of nonconformity at this date might have led one to expect a better result. Moreover, there were none of the long journeys to make to the parish church for a baptism which must often have reduced the completeness of the record in rural parishes.

Miscellaneous Applications

Archaeology

History

Discussion and Comments

Archaeology

Sylviu Comănescu and Corneliu N. Mateescu
Measurement and presentation of archaeological features excavated below ground: principles and practice

As with other categories of 'monuments', archaeological structures beneath ground level (grain pits, wells, cisterns, hypogea) are of importance for reconstructing the past. Nevertheless, until recently research in this sphere has been neglected [as regards grain pits valuable information is available in the works of Latin authors (Varr., *De agr.*, I, **57**, 63; Col., *De re rust.*, I, 6; Plin., *Nat. Hist.*, XVIII, 30)]. However, with the increase in archaeological excavation and the improvement in methods of investigation, it has become necessary for field observations on such 'monuments', made during excavation, to be accurately recorded.

For more than ten years we have been concerned with the shapes of grain pits in the Vădastra settlement (in the Oltenian Plain, 14 km north west of Corabia, a small port on the Danube) where these 'monuments' were used from the Neolithic age up to the beginning of this century. In this time, we have succeeded in developing a simple and easily managed device which enables researchers to make accurate measurements during archaeological excavations, to determine and record subterranean 'monuments' used for storage (Comănescu and Mateescu 1971).

The spatial determination and, subsequently, the geometrical representation of these 'monuments' require, first of all, visual reconstruction, as well as definition from a geometrical point of view of the surface that limits the 'monument'. For this, the space defined by the structure must be emptied. Since it is impracticable to measure all the points that define the shape of the structure, an approximation is made, where the real surface is replaced by a reasonably similar one. We may consider this as a topographical surface, to which all the familiar geometrical properties apply.

In order to define the geometrical shape of the 'monument', its volume is intersected by a number of horizontal planes, the number being adjusted to the irregularity of the structure and to the precision which we wish to obtain. The intersecting curves—closed horizontal curves—are taken at depths measured from a reference level, and give the basic geometric elements of the surface. The surface between two consecutive curves is represented by the surface generated by a straight line following these two curves and remaining constantly perpendicular to one of them.

In accordance with these principles, we have endeavoured to make the necessary measurements by the simplest possible means: a vertical reference axis is placed inside the space to be measured and the depths of the various horizontal planes are taken from it (for the sake of simplicity the planes are taken at equal distances from one another). In order to determine the intersection curve for each of the planes, a number of points on the curve are chosen, and their position in the plane is determined by a system of polar coordinates taken from the axis. The angle of the polar radius is measured from an arbitrary reference point; in fact, for simplicity, a limited number of polar directions are chosen and the 360° of the circumference are divided up into the same number of equal parts.

The device for measuring these elements is made up of the following components.

(a) A wooden ruler having a square section of 4 cm and 2·50 m length (figure 1). The lower end of the ruler is provided with a pointed metallic shoe which can be thrust vertically into the ground down to the 0 cm mark. At the upper end, a metallic anchoring point is fixed in the ruler's axis. The ruler is graduated on two sides at intervals of 10 cm, from the bottom to the top. The metallic point is also used as a topographic marker for locating the plane of the volume under consideration. The ruler provides the vertical mathematical axis on which the depth measurements will be made.

(b) A small circular wooden platform, 40 cm in diameter with a square hole in the centre 4·1 cm square, so that it can move up and down the graduated ruler. On the surface of the platform are traced 8 polar directions with an angle of 45° between them, numbered from 1 to 8 (or more if more precision is required). Along each of these directions two reference marks are made: the first at 10 cm from the polar reference point (the vertical axis), the second on the circumference. The platform can be fixed on the ruler at any multiple of 5 cm by a pin pushed into holes specially cut in the ruler. The platform gives the horizontal intersection planes. With its help the lengths of the various polar directions of the points of every intersection curve can be measured.

(c) A common metal tape, graduated in centimetres, but with measurements starting at 10 cm instead of 0 cm, so that a direct reading of measurements can be made.

(d) A plummet for fixing the ruler vertically. A water level may also be used for this purpose.

The equipment is used as follows: the ruler is pushed down to the 0 cm mark approximately in the centre of the basal level, and is anchored in a vertical position by fastening to four stakes the metallic point of the upper end (which should be level with the ground surface). The vertical position is checked by the plummet on two adjacent sides of the ruler. Then the exact position of the metallic point is established in plane and height, so fixing the position of the 'monument' within the relevant archaeological complex. The platform is lifted up to the metallic point and the orientation angle of polar direction 1 is determined.

Once the device is set up, the measuring proper can begin. The platform is lowered and fixed at the 0 cm mark. The end of the tape is fixed to the 10 cm reference mark along the first polar direction and aligned against the mark on the circumference of the platform. It is stretched to the wall of the pit and the distance is read at an appropriate scale. The 8 or 16 polar directions

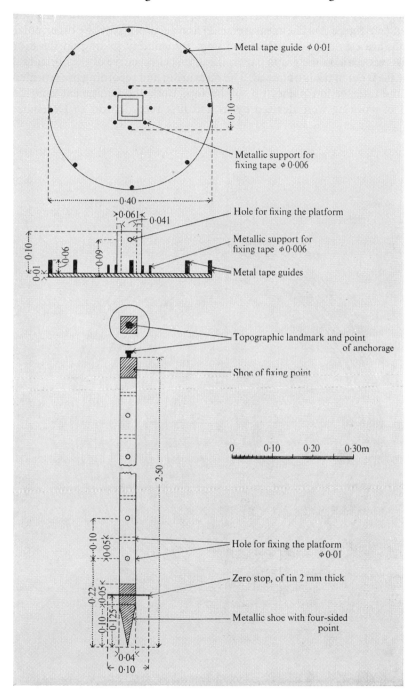

Figure 1. Device for measuring an archaeological 'monument' excavated below ground level.

27

have previously been drawn on graph paper and the measurements are recorded (*see* figure 2). The measurements and recording for the other polar directions are carried out in the same way. By suitably joining up the 8 or 16 points recorded on the graph paper, the intersection curve of the horizontal plane at the 0 cm mark is obtained. The measuring and recording are repeated for all the intersection planes up to the top. Both the equipment and the method of working were devised by us and first recorded on 16 December 1966.

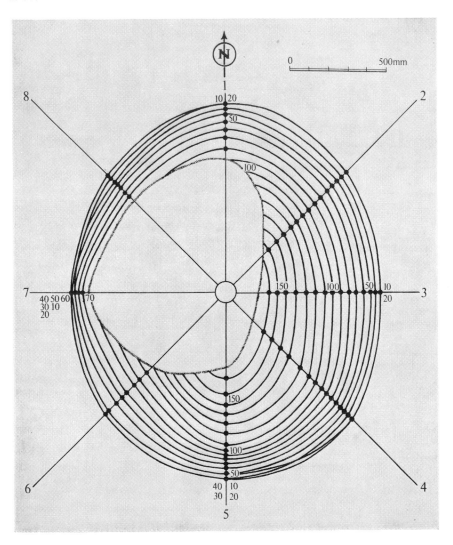

Figure 2. Recording the measurements of a grain pit belonging to the Middle Neolithic period, at Vădastra (excavations, Corneliu N. Mateescu, 1969)

The final result is therefore a topographic plane with depth level curves at equal distances of 5 or 10 cm on which mathematical calculations, characteristics of topographic planes, can be made, namely:

a graphic and analytic representation of any vertical profiles in order to study the characteristic shapes of these 'monuments';

a graphical and analytical determination of the volume excavated;

a graphical representation of certain intersection curves of the pit under consideration;

the recovery of features destroyed in the course of time (by a comparison with similar forms);

the drawing of perspective representation of the 'monument';

the execution of spatial mock-ups.

The precision of the results obtained depends on the recording scale and the scale of the topographic plan.

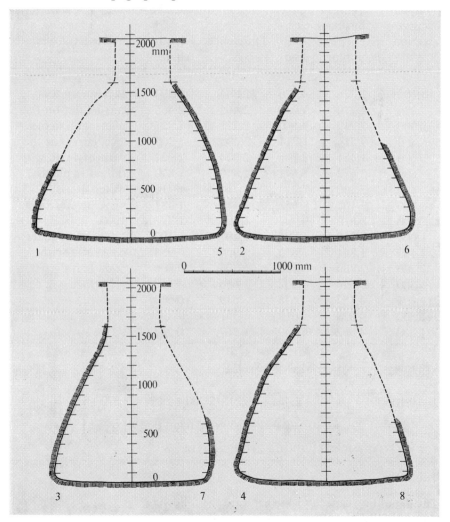

Figure 3. The grain pit of Vădastra with profiles

Next, we show the numerical and graphical results of the volumetric determination carried out for the grain pit (*see* figures 3 and 2) of the middle Neolithic period at Vădastra.

The pit (reconstituted in the drawing) has been represented spatially in the topographic plan at a scale of 1:10, with equidistant depth level curves of 10 cm.

For archaeological studies, determination of the grain storage volume has been recommended. Using the method of elementary volumes, the total space in the pit from the base up to the lower part of the neck was divided into 16 elementary volumes defined by the horizontal sectioning planes and the wall of the pit. The surfaces of the sections that limit the elementary volumes were determined with the planimeter, and by simple arithmetic (see table 1) the volume of the pit was found to equal 2·114 cubic metres.

Depth curve section mm	Average reading of planimeter		Difference Δ	Surface of section sq. m.	Observations
	Beginning	End			
0	—	—	—	—	—
100	2,376	4,770	2,394	2·394	Planimetry was
200	4,770	7,235	2,465	2·465	carried out on the
300	7,219	9,540	2,221	2·221	plane with depth
400	9,514	11,714	2,200	2·200	level curves at the
500	1,681	3,705	2,024	2·024	scale of 1:10, with
600	3,672	5,542	1,870	1·870	the polar plani-
700	5,500	7,214	1,714	1·714	meter 'Reiss'
800	7,165	8,652	1,487	1·487	nr. 4336–37/350/
900	8,610	9,907	1,297	1·297	1000.
1,000	789	1,896	1,107	1·107	The planimeter
1,100	1,861	2,815	954	0·954	constant for the
1,200	2,780	3,586	806	0·806	scale 1:10c=0·001
1,300	3,546	4,202	656	0·656	Surface=Δ. c.
1,400	4,157	4,676	519	0·519	
1,500	4,628	5,019	391	0·391	
1,600	4,982	5,249	267	0·267	

$$\text{Volume} = i\left(\frac{S_1 + S_{16}}{2} + S_2 + \ldots + S_{15}\right)$$

$$V = 0\cdot10\left(\frac{2\cdot394 + 0\cdot267}{2} + 2\cdot465 + 2\cdot221 + 2\cdot200 + 2\cdot024 + 1\cdot870 + 1\cdot714 + 1\cdot487 + 1\cdot297 + 1\cdot107 + 0\cdot954 + 0\cdot806 + 0\cdot656 + 0\cdot519 + 0\cdot391\right)$$

$$V = 10(1\cdot331 + 19\cdot811) = 0\cdot10 \times 21\cdot142 = 2\cdot114 \text{ cm}$$

Table 1

The depositing capacity was therefore the following:
approximately 1·6 tons of corn of a volumetric weight between 0·7–0·8 tons per cubic metre;
about 1·5 tons of barley of a volumetric weight of approximately 0·69 tons per cubic metre.

Archaeological excavations at Vădastra, especially in the last 15 years, have produced numerous grain pits of different periods. Studied year after year, the determination and spatial representation of the better preserved pits have contributed to our knowledge of the typology of these 'monuments' as well as to the estimation of their grain storage capacity. A comparative study of the grain pits is impossible for the time being, since there arc only approximate details for other settlements.

Grain pits, like other subterranean 'monuments' excavated for use, could, if studied over wider areas, lead to ethnological and statistic-economic conclusions. Thereby they could help to correct errors found in some historical works or, generally speaking, they could contribute to our knowledge of certain aspects of life in past times.

REFERENCE

Comănescu, S. & Mateescu, C. N. (1971) Bestimmung und Darstellung im Raum der 'Getreidegruben' (Anhand einer Gruben von Vădastra). *Zephyrus*, **21** (in press).

Archaeology

James Doran
Computer analysis of data from the la Tène cemetery at Münsingen-Rain

In this paper I shall review computer analyses of data drawn from the la Tène cemetery site of Münsingen-Rain, and then discuss how such work might best be extended. The paper is part of a joint evaluation, by Dr F. R. Hodson of the London University Institute of Archaeology and myself, of the scope for further computer work based on this site. During the course of my discussion I shall very briefly describe the form and results of a previously unpublished computer chronological seriation experiment using Münsingen data, and some details of this experiment are given in an appendix.

The arguments in favour of using mathematical and computer methods in archaeological work have often been stated: perhaps their most often mentioned virtue is their objectivity—what is done is done publicly and repeatably, be it good or bad. A little less often mentioned is the better understanding which almost always follows any attempt to integrate such methods with some particular aspect or application of archaeological inference, whether or not the attempt itself is judged a success. Insight into the nature of archaeological inference will not create evidence where there is none, but it may well prevent the misuse of the evidence that does exist.

THE LA TÈNE CEMETERY OF MÜNSINGEN-RAIN

That part of European Iron Age culture designated 'la Tène' extends in time very roughly from 500 BC to the birth of Christ, and in space, at its widest extent, from Spain through central Europe to the Balkans and the Ukraine. It is characterized in the first instance by a distinctive art style, but also by abundant material evidence of a relatively homogeneous though, of course, evolving technology and cultural tradition. There is no doubt that the archaeological la Tène culture corresponds more or less closely to the peoples known to history as the Celts (Rowlett 1968).

The chronology of the la Tène is not well understood (Hodson 1964). One approach to refining the present rather uncertain division of the period into five phases (ia, ib, ic, ii, iii) is to seek one localized sequence of la Tène material which spans the entire time period, and which can be used as a yardstick to which all else can be referred. The cemetery site of Münsingen-Rain, near Berne in Switzerland, is of fundamental importance because it provides just such a sequence of la Tène material (Hodson 1968).

The cemetery consists of about two hundred graves distributed along a gravel ridge. The graves typically contain inhumations, many of the skeletons being well preserved. Associated grave goods are typically jewellery (fibulae, torcs, rings) and weapons (swords, spearheads) in bronze and iron. The graves vary greatly in the richness of the grave goods they contain. In a few cases there are multiple burials.

The evidence provided by the site may be grouped as follows:

(a) the location, orientation and form of the graves;

(b) the sex and age of the burial where known;

(c) the location of each skeleton within its grave, and the location of the associated grave goods with respect to the skeleton;

(d) the details of the grave goods themselves; and

(e) some miscellaneous facts, such as signs of disease, or the remains of planking in a grave.

The roughly linear arrangement of the graves immediately suggests that the cemetery might have been systematically built up from one extremity to the other. Closer examination, taking into account what is known of the evolution of la Tène material from elsewhere, strongly supports this hypothesis, indicating which end of the cemetery is early and which late, and that the time span must be almost that of the la Tène culture itself.

In a most careful study of the evidence, Hodson (1968) has constructed a detailed relative chronology for the site. It is this solid conventional study which is the background to the experimental computer work to which I now turn.

Automatic Classification of the Münsingen Fibulae

There are about 350 bronze fibulae (brooches) from Münsingen. Any traditional study of these fibulae would certainly commence by grouping them, partly on the basis of general la Tène typology, partly on the basis of a comparative examination of the objects themselves. For the purpose of his study of the relative chronology of the cemetery, Hodson recognized over thirty types of fibulae.

A number of computer experiments have been performed to explore how far this grouping procedure can be paralleled by automatic methods (Hodson, Sneath, and Doran 1966, Hodson, 1969, 1970, 1971). Two stages can be distinguished:

(a) a descriptive stage in which the form and decoration of each fibula is coded for machine usage; and

(b) a computational stage in which an algorithm is employed which gives effect to some precise definition of what constitutes a good classification.

Stage (b) itself often splits into two parts, the first concerned with the calculation of numerical measures of similarity or dissimilarity between pairs of fibulae, and the second with the classification algorithm proper.

Details of these experiments are given in the papers cited. Typically only subsets of the fibulae have been used. The results of the experiments can be summarized briefly as follows. Sensible classifications are often obtained, judged by what is known about the fibulae and the site. However, no new insights have been obtained. Further, a general difficulty is encountered: there is no fully convincing way of deciding which of the range of automatic classification procedures available is the most appropriate in this context. This is important since the classifications yielded by these procedures differ markedly.

CHRONOLOGICAL SERIATION

At the heart of the task of constructing a relative chronology for the Münsingen cemetery is the task of putting the individual graves into chronological sequence. Following Kendall, this subsidiary task can be simplified and given a mathematical form as follows. Define an *abundance matrix* to be a matrix whose rows correspond in some specified way to graves, and whose columns correspond to types of object. Every entry in the matrix is an integer which gives the number of objects of the corresponding type found in the corresponding grave. The task is then to so reorder the rows of the matrix that the corresponding grave sequence is the true chronological sequence. Obviously this requires one or more assumptions linking types to time. Kendall (1963, 1969, 1970, 1971), in a most important series of papers, has discussed the theoretical and practical aspects of this problem. He has demonstrated experimentally that his HORSHU method (making use of non-metric multi-dimensional scaling) generates a sequence for the graves close to that obtained by Hodson (which I shall call the 'Hodson sequence') in his conventional study. Sibson (1971) has also obtained good results with the Münsingen data using a careful refinement of the Hole and Shaw (1967) approach to chronological seriation.

I shall now describe briefly my own computer seriation experiment with the Münsingen data. The first step, as is common, is to reduce the abundance matrix to a binary *incidence matrix* by replacing any non-zero entry by unity. Following an early discussion by Kendall (1963), I then distinguish two problems:

(1) the essentially archaeological problem of finding a numerical measure of the extent to which a particular grave sequence is chronologically accurate; and

(2) the purely computational problem of finding the grave sequence for which the measure yields the best score.

My solution to the first problem has been to make use of what Kendall has called the 'Concentration Principle'—that grave sequence is to be preferred for which the total spread of non-zero entries along the columns is least. More precisely, we minimize

$$\sum_{i=1}^{i=n} R_i$$

where n is the number of columns, and where R_i is the number of rows between the first and last entry inclusive in the column i. Of course, there is no guarantee that this measure is indeed minimized when the graves are in true chronological sequence. However it is intuitively attractive and has proved useful in the past (*see* Kendall 1963).

The second, computational, problem is a much more familiar one. The task of finding that member of some large set (for example, a set of permutations) which scores best on some criterion is common in operations research applications of computers and elsewhere. Roughly speaking, if we insist on finding the *best* member of the set, then the computation required is likely to be very long. However if we are prepared to accept something which may fall a little short of the best, then the computation becomes much shorter.

Lin (1970) gives a good introduction to the relevant literature. Archaeologists such as Hole and Shaw (1967) have used particular forms of the latter, heuristic, approach. They have searched for good orderings of pottery assemblages by using a comparatively small set of modifying permutations iteratively to improve some initial ordering. I have employed an algorithm of this type, with one special heuristic, to sort (directly) the rows of the Münsingen incidence matrix.

My results can be summarized thus:

(1) the criterion as defined above does seem to have chronological significance, since the Hodson grave sequence has a very low (good) criterion score indeed; and

(2) starting from a randomly generated and high scoring sequence, the program has found a sequence very similar to the Hodson sequence and with a very slightly lower score.

More details of this experiment are given in an appendix to this paper.

The general conclusion to be drawn from all these experiments seems to be that the several approaches to chronologically seriating the Münsingen graves are all effective as measured by the yardstick of the Hodson sequence. This is not too surprising, as far as the computational problem is concerned, given that Goldmann has successfully seriated a data set an order of magnitude larger (Goldmann 1971).

Some Limitations of the Münsingen Experiments

Computer work using Münsingen data may be assigned two broad objectives:

(a) to discover which mathematical and computer methods are effective in this particular context; and

(b) to discover more about the cemetery itself.

Virtually no progress has been made towards the second, more ambitious, objective. It is possible, but by no means certain, that this is because there is little more to be discovered. All the conclusions that may soundly be drawn from the Münsingen evidence may already have been drawn.

On the other hand, considerable progress has clearly been made towards the first objective. However it is not difficult to point to areas where further exploration seems desirable. As regards the classification experiments:

(1) a better understanding is needed of how to describe complex decorated objects for computer work;

(2) more of the Münsingen fibulae need to be considered, and other grave objects beside the fibulae; and

(3) some way must be found of integrating the classification process into a wider computer study of the cemetery (*compare* Doran 1970).

It seems possible that work on point (3) may help resolve the difficulty of deciding how to choose between alternative automatic classification procedures.

The Münsingen seriation experiments seem incomplete in that:

(1) they depend upon uncertain and somewhat artificial assumptions;

(2) they make use of a subjectively defined typology which is open to dispute, and which by its nature fails to capture all the available evidence;

(3) they make no use of the differing properties of the types, for example, no use is made of Hodson's attempt to separate highly specific types from the less specific; and

(4) they ignore the other categories of evidence available, such as the location and orientation of the graves.

The second part of point (2) needs some expansion. Evidence is almost inevitably lost when a non-overlapping set of types is employed since it will commonly happen that objects assigned to different types have in common one or more features of potential chronological or cultural significance. Thus at Münsingen a finger ring and a fibula may well have a decorative motif in common. A rather different loss of evidence occurs when a disjoint typology is imposed upon a body of material which is in fact the outcome of steady evolution. To some extent this may be happening at Münsingen.

It may reasonably be argued that since the computer seriation results agree well with the Hodson sequence, the deficiencies I have mentioned cannot be important. However these deficiencies also apply in large measure to the conventional arguments leading to the Hodson sequence itself. Further, even if it turns out that these deficiencies are unimportant at Münsingen, they may well be significant elsewhere. Thus further investigation is surely justified.

DATA AND DESCRIPTIONS

In order to investigate in practice the issues raised in the previous section, one thing seems clear: the first step must be to code as data for computer analysis much more of the evidence from Münsingen. The task of compiling such an archaeological data bank has been much discussed (*see*, for example, Chenhall 1967).

The most difficult problem is that much of the evidence resides in the form and decoration of the grave objects: the torcs, the finger rings, and so on. How can this information be captured symbolically?

This problem was encountered, for the fibulae alone, for the purposes of the automatic classification experiments previously described. However, there the aim was to formulate descriptions in such a way that a particular similarity coefficient, the Simple Matching Coefficient, might be used (Hodson, Sneath, and Doran 1966). This simplifying restriction no longer applies: a 'general purpose' description is needed.

Much attention has been given to such general problems of description by Gardin and his colleagues (Gardin 1967, also Borillo 1970) and the reader is referred to their work for a full examination of the difficulties both practical and theoretical. Here I shall merely indicate what seems the best approach to the Münsingen material.

In general, a descriptive procedure, or *code*, must satisfy the following requirements:

(1) it must unambiguously associate with each of the objects involved a formal description capable of expression as a computer data structure (using arrays, lists, strings, records, and so on);

(2) these formal descriptions must be such that with each of the potentially

important observations or comparisons which we might choose to make upon one or more of the objects, we can associate a (practicable) computer procedure which, applied to the corresponding descriptions, will give an answer equivalent to that obtained from the observation or comparison; and

(3) the formal descriptions must not *in toto* exceed the computer storage capacity available.

In addition the code should, as far as possible, be compatible with codes devised for other comparable material.

In practice a balance must be struck between requirements (2) and (3). This will involve an assessment of which of the innumerable observations and comparisons available are potentially the most useful. Some such exercise of judgment seems quite unavoidable.

For the Münsingen grave objects these principles suggest the following steps:

(a) define a few broad categories of object (fibulae, rings, swords, and so on);

(b) for each category of object define a hierarchical decomposition of the object into parts (for example, a fibula consists of coils + bow + foot + pin, and so on);

(c) define a set of decorative and structural motifs (for example 'diamond', 'split leaf' and 'tapering segment') noting instances where one motif is part of another, or where two motifs can reasonably be said to be similar; and

(d) for each part of each object, take characterizing measurements and record the structural and decorative motifs present.

Of course, this plan of campaign involves a great deal of detailed work, and this is in progress.

The reader may feel unhappy about the large subjective element apparent in (c) above, especially the reference to the similarity of *motifs*. My feeling is that intuitively assigned similarity relationships, crude but realistic, make better sense than a mathematically pleasing but unrealistic policy of treating all motifs as independent and equal. Of course, if we find that our conclusions depend critically upon uncertain intuitive judgments, then these conclusions must also be regarded as uncertain.

FUTURE COMPUTER ANALYSES

Assuming that the approach described in the last section does lead to an acceptable Münsingen 'data bank', what kinds of computer analysis might reasonably be explored? I shall indicate three general possibilities.

First, a variety of small-scale and comparatively simple operations should be facilitated. These include ways of selecting desired subsets of the data, ways of presenting data by means of histograms, distribution maps, and the like, and the simple calculations leading to such things as correlation coefficients and similarity measures. The usefulness of such capabilities should not be underestimated, especially when there is access to a fully interactive computer system. Under such conditions, having the machine generate a distribution map of a particular type of fibula, say, would take at most a matter of minutes.

The second possibility is to try to link together the two classes of experiment already performed. That is, automatic classification techniques might be used to define types which would immediately be fed as input to a seriation procedure. The set of types would then be an internal variable of the compound algorithm. Much of the interest would lie in a study of how far the generated grave sequence changed with changes in the type set involved.

Thirdly, and most ambitiously, there is the possibility of bringing into a computer analysis some of the categories of evidence from Münsingen which have not yet been drawn upon for such work. For example, one might wish to work towards a relative chronology for the graves, taking account of their locations, or taking account of the possibility that the set of object types represented in a grave may be partially a reflection of the sex and age of the person buried as well as of the actual date of burial [compare the discussion of Münsingen by Schaaff (1966)]. Clearly such aspirations soon force consideration of cultural dimensions other than that of time, and this is surely all to the good.

Even at this very early stage of consideration two problems loom unpleasantly large: the difficulty of deciding the relative weights to be given to different categories of evidence, and the computational problem of handling ever more intricate and ill-structured situations. The former problem suggests a continuous and flexible interaction between archaeologist and computer, and the latter an ever increasing reliance on the heuristic search procedures and hypothesis-generating techniques being developed by computer scientists (Banerji and Mesarovic 1970, Doran, 1970).

APPENDIX: SOME DETAILS OF THE
CHRONOLOGICAL SERIATION EXPERIMENT

The 63×69 *incidence matrix* for this experiment was derived from the corresponding chart in the Münsingen monograph (Hodson 1968, pl. 123) by:
(1) omitting graves 190 and 193;
(2) omitting types 26, 59, 72, and 73;
(3) omitting all question marks; and
(4) interpreting any non-empty cell as a '1' and an empty cell as a '0'.

The *computer program*, written in Atlas ALGOL with ABL subroutines, will accept any binary (incidence) matrix and will attempt to find that ordering of the rows of the matrix which minimizes the criterion

$$\sum_{\text{cols}} R$$

defined in the main body of the paper. It proceeds by:
(a) iteratively checking every possible transposition of an adjacent pair of rows, making those transpositions which reduce the criterion score, and when no further improvement can be effected in this way
(b) iteratively checking each possible permutation of each set of four adjacent rows for an improvement. Again, where an improvement can be made, it is.

During stage (b) the program employs the following *special heuristic*. Repeatedly it 'shrinks' the original matrix and then re-expands it to its full size. This the program does by amalgamating sets of adjacent rows (not columns). For example, the full-size matrix has in this case 63 rows. If the appropriate control parameter is set at 3, then the first row of the shrunken matrix will be formed from the current first, second, and third rows of the full-size matrix, the second row of the shrunken matrix will be formed from the current fourth, fifth, and sixth rows of the full-size matrix, and so on. When rows are combined in this way a '1' is placed in the new row whenever a '1' occurs in the corresponding location of one or more of the original rows. When the shrunken matrix has been sorted [as in (b) above] then the full-size matrix is reconstructed preserving, of course, the new ordering of (in the example) the triads of rows. In practice this device does much to prevent the search being trapped in uninteresting 'local' criterion minima.

The *results* (to date) of the experiment are as follows. The criterion score of the Hodson sequence is 525. The program, given this sequence as input, generated a sequence with score 492. Successively given as input four randomly generated sequences with scores 2,143; 2,234; 2,514; and 2,291, it generated sequences with scores 616, 684, 512, and 658 respectively. Each of these four trials took about five minutes on an ICL Atlas (at Chilton). The Hodson sequence (score 525) is:

13	32	7	9	16	23	44	12	8a	8b
6	31	51	40	48	46	62	91	49	80
107	50	68	61	152	121	90	79	84	102
136	138	94	106	135	140	134	81	130	145
132	157	158	75	149	119	171	170	101	161
168	166	178	184	164	181	180	182	211	212
207	210	214							

The lowest scoring sequence generated entirely by the program (score 512) is:

13	7	32	170	44	16	9	23	8a	12
31	6	8b	51	40	62	48	80	49	46
91	107	79	136	50	121	61	68	84	152
90	102	135	138	94	106	134	140	210	207
81	130	145	132	157	158	75	149	119	171
161	101	214	212	168	178	184	164	181	166
180	211	182							

In each sequence the figures given are the published grave numbers. The sequences should be read by rows from top to bottom, scanning each row from left to right.

The following *comments* are important.

(1) The program always had difficulty in placing the very late graves 212, 207, 210, 214. If the sequence exhibited above is 'corrected' by placing these graves at the appropriate extreme (an obvious improvement to make when the corresponding matrix is inspected) then a criterion score of 483 is obtained.

(2) The most striking difference between the Hodson sequence and the exhibited program sequence is the difference in position of grave 170. This occurs because the program makes no use of the type weighting used by Hodson.

(3) The criterion scores quoted above should be compared with that of 593 given by Kendall's sequence $\hat{r}$ (see pp. 215–52) having in mind the slightly different grave and type sets used by him.

ACKNOWLEDGMENTS

Many of the ideas and attitudes which I have presented in this paper have developed in the course of conversations with Dr F.R.Hodson of the London University Institute of Archaeology. It should not be assumed, however, that he would agree with all that I have written. He has also, of course, been the channel through which I have learned about the Münsingen cemetery. I also gratefully acknowledge financial support from the UK Science Research Council.

REFERENCES

Banerji, R. & Mesarovic, M.D. (eds) (1970) *Theoretical Approaches to Non-Numerical Problem Solving*. Berlin: Springer-Verlag.

Borillo, M. (1970) La vérification des hypothèses en archéologie: deux pas vers une méthode. *Archéologie et Calculateurs: Problèmes Sémiologiques et Mathematiques*. Paris: CNRS.

Chenhall, R.G. (1967) The description of archaeological data in computer language. *Amer. Antiquity*, **32**, 161–7.

Doran, J.E. (1970) Archaeological reasoning and machine reasoning. *Archéologie et Calculateurs: Problèmes Sémiologiques et Mathématiques*. Paris: CNRS.

Gardin, J.C. (1967) Methods for the descriptive analysis of archaeological material. *Amer. Antiquity*, **32**, 13–30.

Goldmann, K. (1971) Some archaeological criteria for chronological seriation. *Mathematics in the Archaeological & Historical Sciences*, pp. 202–8 (eds Hodson, F.R., Kendall, D.G. & Tăutu, P.). Edinburgh University Press.

Hodson, F.R. (1964) La Tène chronology. *Bull., Inst. Archaeol., University of London*, **4**, 123–41.

Hodson, F.R. (1968) *The La Tène Cemetery at Münsingen-Rain*. Berne: Stämpfli.

Hodson, F.R. (1969) Searching for structure within multivariate archaeological data. *World Archaeology*, **1**, 90–105.

Hodson, F.R. (1970) Cluster analysis and archaeology: some new developments and applications. *World Archaeology*, **3**, 299–320.

Hodson, F.R. (1971) Numerical typology in archaeology. *Mathematics in the Archaeological & Historical Sciences*, pp. 30–45 (eds Hodson, F.R., Kendall, D.G. & Tăutu, P.). Edinburgh: Edinburgh University Press.

Hodson, F.R., Sneath, P.H.A. & Doran, J.E. (1966) Some experiments in the numerical analysis of archaeological data. *Biometrika*, **53**, 311–24.

Hole, F. & Shaw, M. (1967) Computer analysis of chronological seriation. *Rice Univ. Studies*, **53**, (3). Houston: Rice University Press.

Kendall, D.G. (1963) A statistical approach to Flinders Petrie's sequence-dating. *Bull. I.S.I.*, 34*th Session, Ottawa*, 657–80.

Kendall, D.G. (1969) Some problems and methods in statistical archaeology. *World Archaeology*, **1**, 68–76.

Kendall, D.G. (1970) A mathematical approach to seriation. *Phil. Trans. Roy. Soc. Lond. A.*, **269**, 125–35.

Kendall, D.G. (1971) Seriation from abundance matrices. *Mathematics in the Archaeological & Historical Sciences*, pp. 215–52 (eds Hodson, F.R., Kendall, D.G., & Tăutu, P.). Edinburgh: Edinburgh University Press.

Lin, S. (1970) Heuristic techniques for solving large combinatorial problems on a computer. *Theoretical Approaches to Non-Numerical Problem Solving* (eds Banerji, R. & Mesarovic, M.D.) pp. 410–18. Berlin: Springer-Verlag.

Rowlett, R.M. (1968) The Iron Age north of the Alps. *Science*, **161**, 123–34.

Schaaff, U. (1966) Zur Belegung latènezeitlicher Friedhöfe der Schweiz. *Jahrbuch des Römisch-Germanischen Zentralmuseums Mainz*, **13**, 49–59.

Sibson, R. (1971) Some thoughts on sequencing methods. *Mathematics in the Archaeological & Historical Sciences*, pp. 263–6 (eds Hodson, F.R., Kendall, D.G. & Tăutu, P.). Edinburgh: Edinburgh University Press.

Archaeology

Albert Hesse
The measurement of ancient bricks and its archaeological interest

The purpose of this short note is to stress three interesting aspects of the systematic measurement of bricks in ancient buildings. The collected data result from two experiments, the first on the Egyptian site of Mirgissa (Sudanese Nubia) (*see* Hesse 1970), the second in Susa (Iran), on Achemenid palaces. Although limited, these tests have been successful and, when complementary data are collected, should lead to the formulation of a technical, chronological and metrological brick theory, based on more reliable information than the few measurements made, and summarily published by previous authors.

The bricks considered here are made in a mould composed of a frame lying on a horizontal surface. Since the bricks are laid in the building in the same orientation, the measurement of their length and width is straightforward on eroded surfaces of walls. The thickness e, often imprecise for technical reasons connected with the manufacturing process, is a very scattered variable and is of little interest in our investigation. Readings are taken on samples of 100 bricks collected at random, as far as possible, on the whole of one building or on different areas of the same monument. Then the widths l and the lengths L are plotted on rectangular coordinates so as to constitute a random set of points representing the relevant sample.

At present, the main results have been obtained on Mirgissa and their first interest is to point out the well-known relationship between the dimensions $(L=2\ l=4\ e)$ which stretches the random set of points along a straight line through the origin of the coordinates. This representation allows comparison of the quality of manufacture of the bricks, which varies widely from one building to another: thus the Christian settlement, which is very well built, gives a close set of points without any noticeable stretch, whereas the large fortress of the Middle Kingdom indicates, for several areas of sampling, a greater dispersion of the measurements. On the next fortress in Dabenarti island the set of points no longer shows any general shape and the points gather in different groups most probably corresponding to several moulds, or even several workshops, as can be seen for instance on the main fortress, where the stretched set of points is sometimes divided into two clearly separated parts.

The second interest of these data lies in the chronological information they can provide, as some remarks on the contemporaneity or non-contemporaneity can be made on the random set of points representation, which is clearer than the simple and usual histogram of marginal distributions: as a matter of fact, it is obvious that there is no relationship at all between the two fortresses, while a certain kind of connection must be imagined between the main upper fortress and the lower fortifications with round bastions, which could very probably be due to a re-use of the bricks. Re-use, on the contrary, must be ruled out in the case of the Christian building.

These comparisons, of course, are fairly subjective and would certainly be improved by a more rigorous treatment of the data, by statistical analysis of the means, variance and correlation, if more information on different sites is collected. The mutual relationships between the different sets of points can already be investigated in a more synthetic way by plotting all their characteristics on a single graph: each sample is represented by a circle with radius proportional to the coefficient of correlation between the values of L and l; the coordinates of the centre correspond to the mean values of the marginal distributions and, at this same point, a cross represents the standard deviations on the scale of the axis of coordinates. Previous remarks are obviously confirmed (*see* figure 1): the unique situation of Dabenarti's fortress and the homogeneous construction of Mirgissa's (except for the outer wall; this is better built, with somewhat larger, and less dispersed dimensions of bricks, and could belong to a second phase of building). This summary of the statistical characteristics of the samples under investigation also sets apart two other structures and emphasizes their very similar characteristics (mainly a very low coefficient of correlation and close positions on the graph): a small external fort (M IV) and the large north gate of the upper fortress (sample MF 9); thus both may be interpreted as complementary fortifications, which may have been built later in the Middle Kingdom.

The third interest in measuring the dimensions of the building materials also relates to chronology, but is concerned with the history of metrology. One may expect, indeed, to be able to estimate the length of the Egyptian cubit at different periods from a great number of bricks measured in a similar manner on several buildings of known date (if we take into account the important fact that the great royal cubit, which was exactly divided into seven palms, corresponds to the length $L+l+e=7e$, centring around 50 or 55 cm).

In this connection, the following results have been obtained in Susa, on square bricks: on the one hand, all the bricks of the palace of Darius I are of exactly the same size including the foundations of the Apadana, even though this was later rebuilt by Artaxerxes II; this suggests that the rebuilding was in fact limited to the upper parts of the Apadana without alteration of the original plan. On the other hand, a similar investigation was carried out on the remains of a second palace, recently discovered down the tell in the plain of Chaour: the elements of two different pavements, one with large bricks (average size: 470 mm), the other with small bricks (average size: 320 mm) have been measured. Each of these classes is a good bit smaller in size than the classes of the corresponding pavements in Darius' palace, but with the same ratio, varying around 0·945 (provisional result). This not only eliminates the hypothesis of contemporary construction or even of re-use of the bricks, but also suggests the possibility of a variation of the length unit during the period investigated (from Darius I up to the end of the Achemenid period) (Hesse 1971).

28

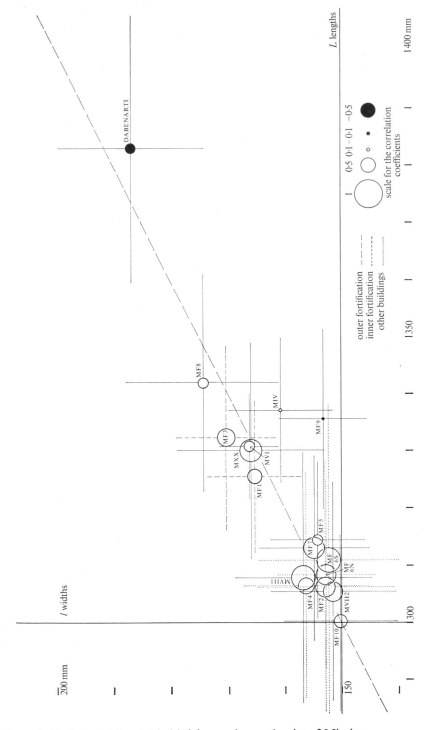

Figure 1. Statistical data of dried brick samples on the site of Mirgissa

REFERENCES

Hesse, A. (1970) Essai technochronologique sur la dimension des briques de construction. *Mirgissa I*, pp. 102–14 (ed. Vercoutter, J.). Paris: Geuthner.

Hesse, A. (1971) Metrologie statistique d'elements architecturaux des palais achemenides de Suse (briques et bases carrées). In preparation.

Archaeology

Albert Hesse

Tentative interpretation of the surface distribution of remains on the upper fort of Mirgissa (Sudanese Nubia)

On the surface of the fortress, twenty-six thousand objects (mainly sherds) have been collected and typologically classified. The distributions of the whole collection and of each class have been studied in order to test their possible correspondence with the contents of the archaeological levels underneath, and possibly to reveal identical or different distributions of classes by means of convenient indices.

This experiment deals with a collection of surface finds made before excavation of the great Middle Kingdom fortress. The whole set of objects (mainly pottery sherds) is of size X (approximately twenty-six thousand), and has been collected on a regular grid of $N=110$ squares of 10 m by 10 m. In each of the squares (A, 1), (A, 2), ..., (B, 1), (B, 2), ..., (i, j), ..., the x_{ij} objects collected have been assigned to about $n=70$ typological classes and subclasses. Each class k is represented in a given square by, say, a_{ij}^k finds, with a total number A^k for the whole surface (*see* figures 1 and 2). So we have the relations:

$$X = \sum_{ij} x_{ij} = \sum_{ij}\left(\sum_{1}^{n} a_{ij}^k\right)$$

and
$$\sum_{ij} a_{ij}^k = A^k \;.$$

Because of impending flooding from the rising waters of the Aswan dam, the first aim of this survey was to identify significant groupings of remains of particular interest, on which an emergency excavation could then take place at once. The second purpose was a tentative testing of the identity of distribution of several classes of known and unknown types of material so as to point out certain kinds of relationship between them, or, on the contrary, to differentiate them by the dissimilarity of their distributions. First of all it was necessary to take into account the general distribution of all the remains on the surface. As a matter of fact, the map of the x_{ij} reveals the prevailing effects of the following sedimentary factors (*see* figure 2).

(1) Concentrations of sherds in areas where the walls have been almost completely eroded, or where the Nubians have dug deep hollows while searching for the rich sediments of the occupation levels.

(2) The comparative absence of sherds where buildings have not been extensively damaged; also on the lee-side of fortifications where the strata are hidden by thick deposits of sand, and on modern paths. An empirical formula can be established as follows. Let

$$x'_{ij} = (X/N - 400(h - 0{\cdot}5) + 40\,c)(1 - 0{\cdot}7\,p)(1 - 0{\cdot}9\,s),$$

where, in each square, h in metres represents the average height of the walls as revealed by later excavations; c the number of obvious diggings; and p and s the percentage of surface occupied by paths and sand respectively. The coefficients of this formula are rough estimates, and could be improved, but this would not be of much interest because of their specificity for this site. Nevertheless they are accurate enough for our present purposes, for the coefficient of correlation between the pairs constituted by the *calculated* x'_{ij} and the *actually collected* x_{ij} reaches the value 0·665, highly significant, at 99%, of a strong dependence of the general distribution of the remains on a set of selected and weighted variables (threshold at 99% = 0·25).

Figure 1. Pottery sherds on the surface of Mirgissa fort

It is quite obvious that all these factors, which are subsequent to the deposition of the remains in their original layers, will essentially influence their presence or absence on the surface, and will tend to mask any intrinsic chronological, technological, cultural, or even sedimentary features of the distributions for the different classes.

This result is particularly clear for large collections of objects made up of several classes; for instance, the map of the wheel-made pottery rims is not appreciably differentiated from the map of the hand-made pottery rims (both

| A | B | C | D | E | F | G | H | I | J | K |

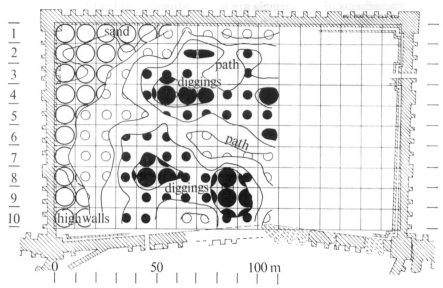

Figure 2. Total distribution of remains on the surface of the fort (the circles represent the empty squares and the black dots the areas of concentration)

classes contain 6–7000 items), and both look like the general distribution.

The first method one can think of consists of expressing the value of a_{ij}^k, as a proportion of the total contents of the square (i, j). This procedure by itself allows a clear differentiation of the hand-made rims by emphasizing in this category two clear concentrations, whereas the first (wheel-made) category, which is made up of many rather small classes of very different types of pottery, gives after correction a quite uniform map. Moreover this comparison gives a first indication of the importance of the hand-made group considered as a whole, in which we shall be interested below (*see* figure 3).

The index can conveniently be taken in the following form

$$\alpha_{ij} = \frac{a_{ij}^k}{x_{ij}} \frac{X}{A^k} \quad .$$

Thus we have here the ratio of the *actual* number of objects of a given class to the expected number in the square, assuming a random distribution.

Assuming, as a first approximation, that the sortings were non-exhaustive and independent, the following indices have also been employed:

P_{ij}; the probability of coming across a_{ij}^k elements of the given class when sorting x_{ij} objects according to the binomial or Poisson law;

$$e_{ij} = a_{ij}^k - x_{ij} \frac{A^k}{X} \quad \text{(deviation from the expected value);}$$

$$d_{ij} = \frac{a_{ij}^k}{x_{ij}} - \frac{A^k}{X} \quad \text{(difference between the actual proportion in the square and the expected proportion).}$$

It has appeared from these trials that the index P_{ij} is of interest in the search for significant concentrations or absences. Nevertheless it turned out that the concentrations actually noticed in the distribution of some classes did *not* reflect the situation of the underlying strata. In fact, on the one hand these concentrations are not exclusive and the irregularity of the sedimentation could make areas other than the expected one rich in remains of the same class. On the other hand, the following concentrations were obvious even from raw counts of material: bread moulds in squares B, C−7, 8 [we write F8 for square (F, 8), and so on], seal stamps in F8, F9 and glazed sherds in I, J–9, 10 accompanied by the 'supervisor of the copper workers' seal and the bottom of a crucible bearing traces of this metal. However, they involved difficulties of archaeological interpretation during excavation and generally did not correspond to the expected finds (respectively bakeries, library, smelting furnace, …). Such apparent discrepancies are also a feature of some other types of investigation which may happen to draw attention to factors which would not be noticed in a traditional excavation.

The index e_{ij} seemed to be best for comparing the superficial distributions of the different classes. Its use rests upon the following assumption: if several objects have been used simultaneously in the same place and thus belong to the same level, they should go through the same transformations and be affected in the same way by successive removals and depositions (without any consideration of the fragility, shape or weight of the sherds). So the objects reach the surface under the same conditions and, thereby, the superficial distribution should be similar, except for a proportionality factor and random variation. This condition is obviously necessary but not sufficient. If we now calculate the coefficient of correlation between typical values of the frequency of the classes in the squares, it should be significantly positive for remains chronologically, technologically, or culturally connected; equal to zero for independent remains; negative in the case of remains that might be mutually exclusive. One can imagine more complex cases, but their interpretation would certainly be less obvious.

A test of the efficiency of the indices just described was made on two types of remains; first, on fragments of large jars bearing a cartouche of the New Kingdom (a comparison between the distribution of handles with the distribution of rims and bases) secondly, on sherds of small hemispherical bowls of the Middle Kingdom and of the stands on which they originally stood (*see* figure 4).

The correlation reaches a significant positive value between the raw counts a_{ij}^k for remains of the same period but this result can be due to the influence of the general distribution on all the classes. The use of the α_{ij} reduces considerably the value of the coefficient of correlation, owing to the fact that the representative points of pairs, in which one of the values equals zero, are stretched along the axes of coordinates. Between the P_{ij} the correlation is strongly positive on account of the important disturbance produced by the weakly filled squares. For e_{ij}, the value is still highly significant, but considerably weaker for d_{ij} for reasons similar to those suggested in connection with α_{ij}.

|A|B|C|D|E|F|G|H|I|J|K| ↗N

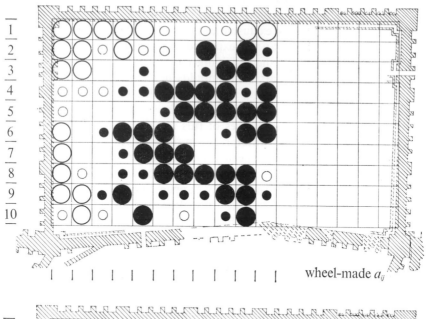

wheel-made a_{ij}

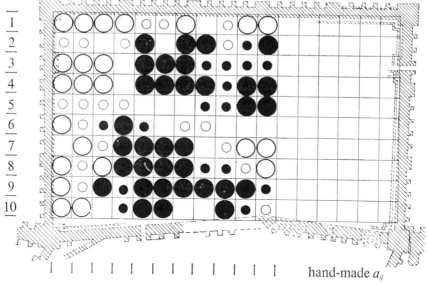

hand-made a_{ij}

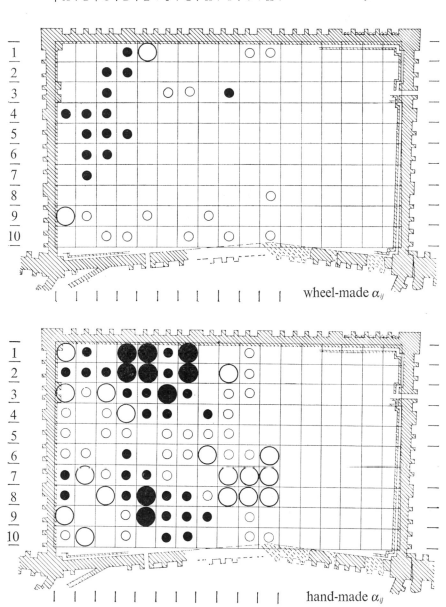

Figure 3. Comparison of the hand-made and wheel-made pottery distributions: raw numbers on the left, index α_{ij} on the right

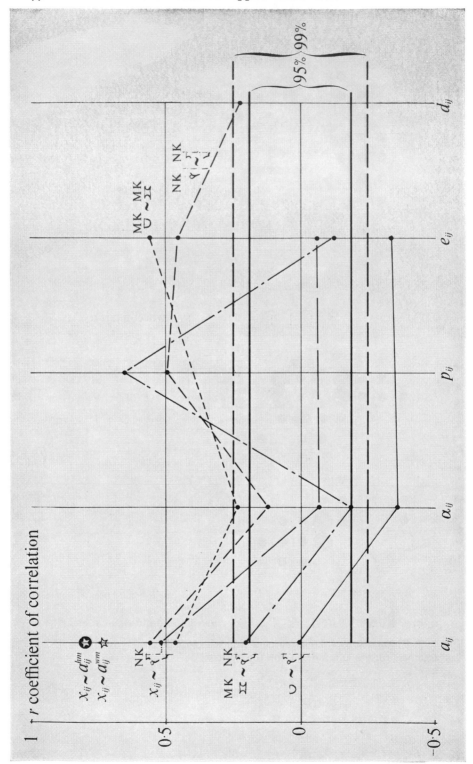

Figure 4. Values of the coefficient of correlation between New Kingdom and Middle Kingdom remains for different indices

If we now compare the whole of the New Kingdom remains (handles, rims, and bases) with the total distribution represented by x_{ij}, and consider equivalent indices (ratio to the average X/N and deviation from the same), we can see that the correlation, which was positive for the raw counts a_{ij}^k and x_{ij}, almost falls to zero when calculated on those two indices. This demonstrates the independence between the features they represent and the general distribution of the remains.

Moreover, the comparison of the same New Kingdom sherds with the small Middle Kingdom bowls, and then with their corresponding stands, indicates that the correlation which was weakly positive on the raw counts falls down to significant negative values—under the threshold at 99%— when it is calculated using the α_{ij} or the e_{ij} (but not the P_{ij}, since the contribution of the probabilities near to 1—produced by the almost empty squares— always makes a positive correlation certain). As, on the other hand, the reduction of the coefficient of correlation when using the α_{ij} is a consequence of the same disturbing effect of the empty squares, the use of the index e_{ij} (deviation from the most probable value) is revealed as the most powerful test to differentiate or identify typical features of the distributions.

The occurrence of a negative value of the coefficient of correlation requires a sedimentological explanation, for it corresponds to a mutual exclusion between the Middle Kingdom and the New Kingdom sherds. One can indeed guess that only the remains belonging to a thin, late layer of the New Kingdom should be visible on the surface; the Middle Kingdom objects of the thick underlying layer which result from a long occupation could only appear through the agency of holes dug through the upper layer. Consequently it could happen that the redeposition of old sediments on the surface would partially mask the recent ones, so that Middle and New Kingdom sherds would not coexist in the same squares. In fact, the Middle Kingdom remains do present a significant positive correlation (0·5) with the number of hollows plotted in the square, while the New Kingdom sherds give a very weak value which turns negative if we leave out of account the marginal areas of the fort, where the prevailing sedimentary factor is not the digging. Thus the hypothesis has been verified.

Finally, the index e_{ij} was used in a tentative investigation of differences of distribution in the homogeneous-looking group of hand-made pottery. Here this group is composed, on the one hand, of sherds belonging to the 'Kerma' culture, which is quite well known, on the other hand of a quantity of remains related to the so-called 'Pangrave' culture. A typological and technological investigation of the decoration patterns allowed us to distinguish, very roughly, at least three classes in the subgroup so far considered as homogeneous by many writers: basket impressions (most probably in close connection with the 'Kerma'); incised triangles or various types of crossed lines; and stamped herring-bone patterns. As a result of this investigation a relationship is suggested between the first two types by a strong positive value of the coefficient of correlation calculated on the e_{ij} of their distributions, whereas the group with herring-bone patterns is clearly differentiated from the other two classes by negative values, among which one at least is significant

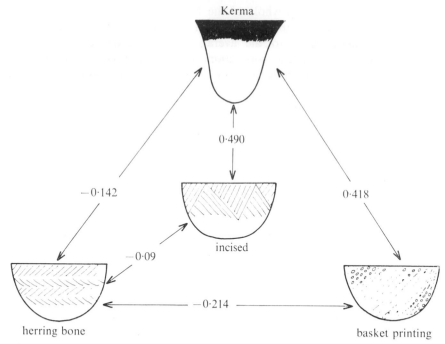

Figure 5. Values of the coefficient of correlation for e_{ij}
between several hand-made pottery classes

(the relationship between herring-bone patterns and basket impressions)
[*see* figure 5].

This method is obviously not beyond criticism, because all of the theoretical
assumptions are not fully justified, but mainly also because the coefficient
of correlation between squares of which the contents are not independent is
not powerful enough an index to take into account, for instance, the fact that
significant concentrations may occur in neighbouring squares and not
elsewhere (this is relevant to the regionalized variables theory and, in this
respect, only conjectural considerations on the general aspect of the distribution maps have been introduced here).

Nevertheless we may suggest that, suitably developed, this kind of treatment
of the data could produce interesting results for surface collections. This
approach has been neglected, most probably on account of the disappointing
indications given by the concentrations of material, but we consider that a
better knowledge of the mutual relations of the objects could be obtained
before excavation and with little damage to sites, if some sort of distance
were defined and introduced into the classifications of the different types.

Finally, if such a method were perfected, it could also be useful in the
interpretation of occupation levels in prehistoric and archaeological excavations, and in comparing the geographical distributions of remains collected
under similar conditions.

Archaeology

Richard E. M. Moore
A relationship observed between mosaic units and
the sizes of Roman mosaic stones

Geometric patterns in ancient Greek and Roman floor mosaics tend to be of certain particular sizes (Moore 1964). More than 89 per cent of 310,000 pattern dimensions measured on such floors lie within 4 mm of eleven alternative sizes: 12, 24, 36, 60, 96, 156, 216, 251, 407, 658, and 1,065 mm respectively (Moore 1966a, 1969). It has been postulated (Moore 1968c) that these eleven 'mosaic units' were the units marked on the rulers which the ancient literature states (Moore 1968a) that floor-mosaicists used. The question arises: to what extent are these eleven standard pattern sizes related to the various different sizes of mosaic stones?

First we must consider the possibility that mosaic stone sizes might be unrelated to the pattern sizes which they form. There are basically two ways in which this might occur: either if occasional stones were specially cut to suit, in order to force the pattern to come wherever the mosaicists pleased, regardless of the sizes of the usual stones; or, instead of using special stones, if stones were simply spaced out leaving gaps wherever discrepancies between the stones and the intended patterns arose. In the case of Classical floor mosaics [excluding *emblemata* (Moore 1966a)] there is apparently no evidence for, and much evidence against (Moore 1966b, 1968a) normal use of either special stones or special spacing.

The difference in appearance between a mosaic in which stones used are of special sizes to suit the pattern, and one where stones are not selected for size, is really quite obvious. For example, figure 1(b) shows a tracing of the stones in part of a *modern* mosaic (East part of Colonnade, Guy's Hospital, London) in which I have marked a stone of special size with a small arrow. Had this stone been of more normal size, it would have distorted the adjacent strip of pattern of stippled stones. In contrast, this is just what has happened in figure 1(a), which is a tracing of part of an *ancient* mosaic (West end of *Caserma dei Vigili*, Ostia Antica, Italy). Lack of stones of special sizes results in erratic rims to the patterns. I find such effects to be quite general in Roman floor mosaics, and frequent in Greek floor mosaics. Although the rim of a pattern in an ancient floor mosaic is normally not straight, I find the lack of straightness to be normally significantly less than half the mean size of a stone—which would be the theoretical maximum lack of straightness if there was no relation between stone sizes and pattern sizes: for if there was no relation, the mosaicist could work to an accuracy of only the nearest single stone. That the rims are far less erratic than this suggests that stone sizes and typical pattern sizes are probably related in general.

The component stones of classical mosaics are almost always arrayed in

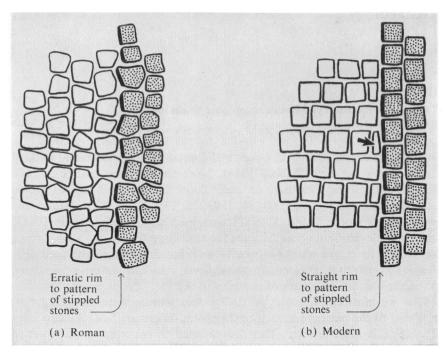

Figure 1

rows (Moore 1964); this was apparently done for a practical reason (Moore 1969). Measurement of more than 30,000 stones has shown (Moore 1966a, 1966b) that their dimensions measured across these rows tend to be more constant than their dimensions measured along the rows [a reason has been offered for this by Moore (1969)]. Thus, in a square pattern, such as shown in figure 2 (in which we have two equal pattern dimensions—the length and breadth of the square of black stones), the pattern dimension along the length of the rows is often not composed of the same number of stones in each row, whereas the pattern dimension measured across the rows is composed (by virtue of the rows) of a constant number of stones throughout the pattern. There is thus a greater relationship between the pattern dimension and the dimensions of stones measured transversely across the rows, than exists in the other direction.

In this direction, along the lengths of the rows, a tendency has been suggested (Moore 1964) and found (Moore 1968b), and confirmed by others (for example, Herrisman 1969), for stones in adjacent rows periodically to lie in alignment laterally through the rows, at intervals corresponding to the typical pattern dimensions (mosaic units). However, this connection between pattern sizes and the dimensions of stones is not simple (Moore 1966b).

A similar phenomenon has been shown (Moore 1969) across the rows themselves, that is, a tendency for periodically straighter rows. The latter occur at the same intervals at which stones tend to align. Both these sets of distances coincide with the typical pattern sizes—the eleven mosaic units. I have suggested (Moore 1966a) that the ancients hit upon the alignment

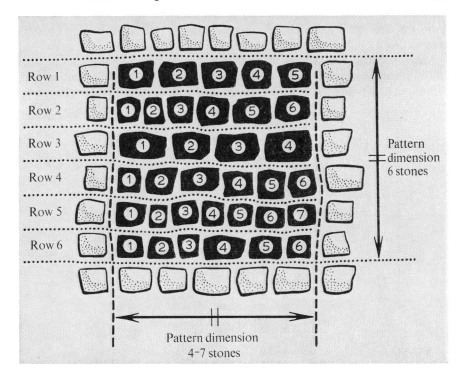

Figure 2

phenomenon empirically, and employed it by making their patterns of sizes at which alignments tend to occur, thus producing smoother edges to the patterns for no extra effort. I find that this also happens in the case of children who have made mosaics for me, using stones removed from ancient mosaics. In addition, it has been suggested (Ledin 1969) that the ancients might have used mosaic units for aesthetic reasons, but this seems improbable (Moore 1970).

It is the purpose of this paper to consider the dimensions of stones measured transversely across their rows, these being generally their most constant dimensions (ignoring their vertical thickness), and their dimensions generally most directly related to the sizes of patterns, in relation to mosaic units. The present thickness of the stones is less than it was originally not only because of wear, but because of the final grinding process of the mosaicists (Moore 1968a). Fortunately, the thickness of stones does not play a direct part in the dimensions of patterns.

Measuring the transverse dimensions of many stones in a region of a mosaic, I find nearly always a distinct modal value. In some mosaics, stones of two or more sizes exist, the modal transverse dimension of one size being clearly different from that of the other. The two sizes of stone usually occur in different regions of the mosaic. Normally, any change to bigger stones is encountered as one moves towards the periphery of a mosaic. [I am concerned here simply with the actual mosaic, and do not include data on the *testae*, each often more than four times the top surface area of a mosaic stone

(Moore 1968a), which are frequently found packed around a mosaic making good the discrepancy between the mosaic and the walls of the room (Moore 1966a, 1966b).]

Measuring the dimensions of mosaic stones as row-widths in more than 130 different mosaics, I find a distinct tendency for a set of alternative sizes for stones (*see* figure 3): 2, 4, 6, 8, 10, 12, and 18 mm respectively. The modal

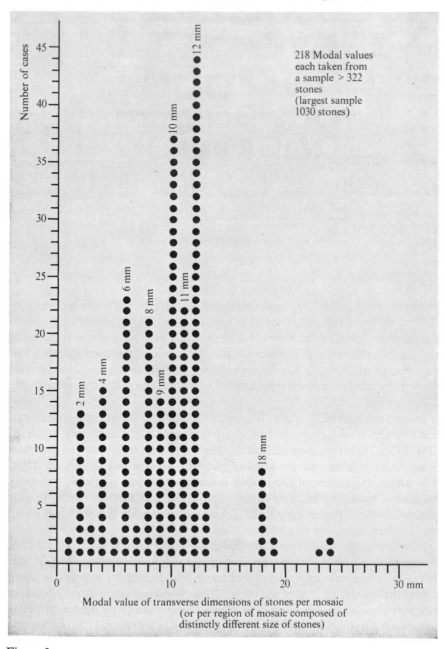

Figure 3

size of stones in one mosaic is sometimes very similar to that of another, but so many stones in the second mosaic are just slightly bigger than those in the first (and I find the same two sizes occurring in other mosaics) that I count these as being two separate sizes. This is the case with two further apparent alternative sizes for stones: 9 and 11 mm (*see* figure 3) which differ only slightly from the near values of 8, 10, and 12 mm.

If observed stone dimensions are not sorted into transverse and longitudinal lengths, the greater variation in longitudinal lengths clouds this tendency for transverse dimensions to fall into a discrete set of alternatives. Stone dimensions have been published by others (for example, Blake 1930, Levi 1947, Becatti 1953), but the distinction between transverse and longitudinal dimensions is not made. However, on converting the published data to frequency distribution form, I find that their data are not statistically significantly different from the distribution that I find when adding to my distribution for transverse lengths (*see* figure 3) my data on longitudinal lengths.

Supposing that this phenomenon of a set of different sizes for the transverse dimensions of stones was originally intentional, that is, that mosaicists had a set of alternative 'standard' sizes for the widths of mosaic stones, it is conceivable, especially when two or more standard sizes are used in the same mosaic, that mosaicists would decide to make patterns of dimensions that could be composed of whole numbers of two or more standard sizes of stone (in some mosaics, three or more standard sizes occur; they are almost never mixed, but used in different, often adjacent, regions of the mosaic).

For example, if stones of 12 mm and 8 mm be used, patterns of width 96 mm would have the advantage of being able to be formed of whole numbers of either size of stone, either eight stones of 12 mm or twelve stones of 8 mm. The fact that there are four more junctions between stones when there are twelve stones instead of eight will not inherently tend to cause the result to measure more than 96 mm, for adjacent stones in ancient mosaics are normally in contact (Moore 1966a, 1968a) and the cement does not normally play a part in the packing. Packing cleaned loose stones taken from ancient mosaics led to results (Moore 1968b) mensurally identical to packing effects observed in intact ancient mosaics (Moore 1968b). Thus I deduce that presence, or absence, of cement between the stones normally makes little or no difference to the result from the point of view of the dimensions of patterns. In cases where I have removed the cement in mosaics, I find that adjacent stones normally have at least one point of mutual contact, and the cement can be regarded as simply occupying interstices remaining between the close-packed stones.

The method of multiplying two values together to obtain a third, common to both, occurs (in other contexts) in the ancient literature, for example, *de Architectura, lib.* III.

If stones of each different standard size are laid out in adjacent lines, the stones in any one line being all of the same size [*see* figure 4(a)], we see that a favourable size for patterns would be 72 mm, for this can be made of seven of the nine different standard sizes. The number of different standard sizes

29

which lie in phase in this way, as the lines lengthen (up to 200 mm) is shown in figure 4(b).

Taking stones in five or more lines in phase to be significant (that is, just over half the total nine lines), I obtain a set of favourable pattern sizes [see figure 4(c)] as follows: 24, 36, 48, 60, 72, 90, 96, 108, 120, 132, 144, 168, 180, 192, and 198 mm respectively.

At first sight there seems no particular rhyme to this set of values, but closer inspection reveals that more than half (that is, eight) of these fifteen favourable pattern sizes can be yielded by a set of values formed by repeatedly setting down a length of 24 mm [figure 4(d)]. Moreover, three of the remaining seven dimensions can be similarly yielded by a length of 36 mm [figure 4(e)]. The other two values yielded by 36 mm each fit a favourable pattern size too, but these are also fitted by multiples of the length 24 mm.

Of the fifteen favourable pattern sizes, eight coincide with the eight integral multiples of a length of 24 mm, and five coincide with the five multiples of 36 mm. In similar fashion [figure 4(f)], three coincide with the three integral multiples of a length of 60 mm. All but three (see figure 4) of the fifteen favourable pattern sizes can be generated by these three lengths: 24, 36, and 60 mm. (These three lengths themselves exhibit an interrelationship, for $24 + 36 = 60$.)

Whilst it is true that, of the three values yielded by 60 mm, two are also yielded by 24 or 36 mm, the length 60 mm comes into its own when patterns bigger than 200 mm length are considered. For, continuing this analysis up to 1,100 mm, I find a total of seventy-eight favourable pattern sizes. All but twelve of them can be similarly generated by these three lengths, forty-five by each whole multiple of 24 mm, a further fifteen by whole multiples of 36 mm, and an additional six by whole multiples of 60 mm. Every whole multiple of each of these three basic lengths coincides with a favourable pattern size.

In the analysis up to 1,100 mm, every occasion where two or more of the three sets of lengths yielded by 24, 36, and 60 mm happen to be in step themselves, is matched by an unusually high number (at least six) of the nine standard sizes of stone also falling into phase. The very favourable pattern size of 360 mm (at which eight of the nine standard sizes of stone are in phase) is matched by the occasion where all three of the basic lengths fall in step: 15×24 mm $= 10 \times 36$ mm $= 6 \times 60$ mm $= 360$ mm.

The following situation exists:
(a) ancient floor mosaic geometric patterns tend to be of eleven particular sizes (mosaic units);
(b) the dimensions of mosaic stones most related to mosaic pattern sizes are their dimensions transverse to the rows of stones;
(c) these transverse dimensions exhibit nine 'standard sizes';
(d) there are seventy-eight pattern sizes, each of which can be made from whole numbers of at least five of these nine alternative standard sizes of stone;
(e) sixty-six of these seventy-eight 'favourable pattern sizes' have in common the property of being whole multiples of either 24, 36, or 60 mm respectively;
(f) these three 'basic lengths' coincide with three of the eleven mosaic units: mosaic units 24, 36, and 60 mm.

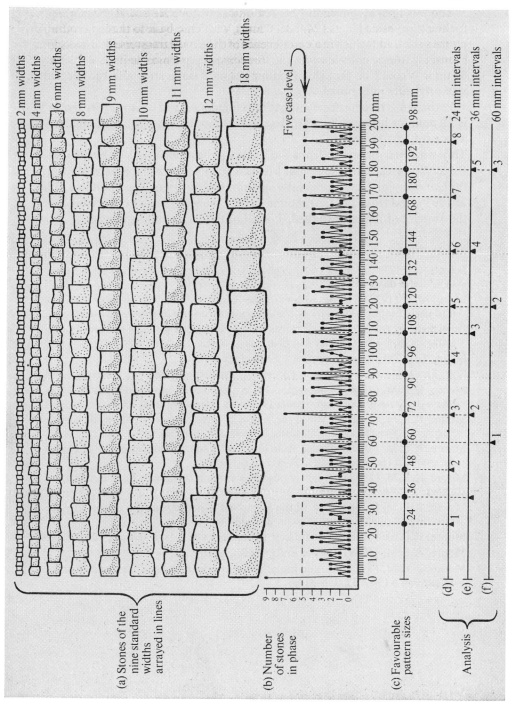

(a) Stones of the nine standard widths arrayed in lines

2 mm widths
4 mm widths
6 mm widths
8 mm widths
9 mm widths
10 mm widths
11 mm widths
12 mm widths
18 mm widths

Five case level

(b) Number of stones in phase

(c) Favourable pattern sizes

Analysis

(d) 24 mm intervals
(e) 36 mm intervals
(f) 60 mm intervals

Figure 4

There is thus a connection between mosaic stone sizes and mosaic units, for the three basic lengths (24, 36, 60 mm), which are basic to the favourable pattern sizes, and which are a consequence of the typical transverse dimensions of mosaic stones, coincide with the three consecutive mosaic units 24, 36, and 60 mm. It could be that this relation between stone sizes and mosaic units was originally intentional.

Perhaps it is also no accident that the commonest size of stone (*see* figure 3) is 12 mm, for it coincides with the smallest mosaic unit—also 12 mm.

ACKNOWLEDGMENTS

This work has benefited from the great encouragement given by Professor Roger Warwick, Guy's Hospital Medical School. Awards from the Worshipful Company of Goldsmiths (1962), from University College London (1962 & 1963), and from the Leverhulme Trust (1966–68) have helped to increase the amount of material studied. For all of this, I am most grateful.

REFERENCES

Becatti, G. (1953) *Scavi di Ostia* ,Vol. 4. Rome: Istituto Poligrafico dello Stato, la Libreria dello Stato.

Blake, M.E. (1930) The pavements of the Roman buildings of the Republic and early Empire. *Memoirs of the American Academy in Rome*, **8**, 7–159.

Herrisman, L. (1969) Il y avait un secret mathématique dans les mosaiques antiques. *Science et la Vie*, **116** (No. 626), 60–5.

Ledin, G. (1969) Mosaic numbers. *Science*, **163**, 704–5.

Levi, D. (1947) *Antioch Mosaic Pavements*. Princeton: Princeton University Press.

Moore, R.E.M. (1964) Some factors governing ancient mosaic design. *Bulletin of the Institute of Classical Studies* (London University), **11**, 87–91.

Moore, R.E.M. (1966a) Pattern formation in aggregations of entities of varied size and shapes as seen in mosaics. *Nature*, **209**, 128–32.

Moore, R.E.M. (1966b) Order as an apparently spontaneous product of chaos. *Intermedica* (Summer issue), 31–41.

Moore, R.E.M. (1968a) A newly observed stratum in Roman floor mosaics. *Amer. J. Archaeol.*, **72**, 57–68.

Moore, R.E.M. (1968b) Test of the alignment hypothesis as the reason for the mosaic unit phenomenon. *Nature*, **217**, 482–4.

Moore, R.E.M. (1968c) Mosaic unit ruler: does one exist? *Science*, **161**, 1358–9.

Moore, R.E.M. (1969) Mosaic units. *Archaeometry*, **11**, 145–58.

Moore, R.E.M. (1970) Mosaic units: pattern sizes in ancient mosaics. *Fibonacci Quarterly*, **8** (No. 3), 281–310.

Archaeology

Clive Orton
On the statistical sorting and reconstruction of
the pottery from a Romano-British kiln site

The Romano–British kiln site at Highgate Wood, London, which lies about five miles NNW of the Roman city of London, was discovered in 1962 during an archaeological field survey of the open spaces of north London (Brown and Sheldon 1969a). Excavation commenced in 1966 and has continued to date. A number of kilns and a large quantity of pottery (over two tons) have been discovered, much of the pottery being wasters from the kilns themselves. Some 20 per cent of the pottery has been examined by adult students at the City Literary Institute, and Brown and Sheldon have reported on the progress made in sorting and classifying it (1969b). A further report on the excavations has been made (Brown and Sheldon 1970), and a detailed report on two groups of pottery is in press (Sheldon *et al.*, 1970). Of particular interest in studying the production from the kilns is the material from a large dump of waster sherds, and from some pits which were thought to be dug originally to provide clay and later filled with wasters. A report of a preliminary statistical investigation has been made (Orton 1970).

Aims

The task of the statistician in this situation is to construct a statistical description of the production of the kilns, which task is being undertaken in the 'SHERD' (Sorting Highgate Excavations Roman Debris) project during the year 1970–71. The aim of this paper is to describe the background to the project by stating the archaeological problems in mathematical terms. Various suggestions for their solution will be put forward, but their validity and usefulness will depend on the outcome of the project. If the project is successful it is hoped that a general program will be available for use in similar situations: if it fails, it is hoped that this statement of the problems involved will interest other statisticians and lead to their eventual solution.

Theory and Models

1. *Notation and Definitions.* All the pottery excavated from one level or feature in a trench is referred to as a 'lot'. There are L lots under examination and they are referred to by the suffix j. The rim sherds have been classified into k_1 'rim categories', the base sherds into k_2 'base categories', and the decorated sherds into k_3 'categories of decoration'. These categories are referred to by the suffices i or h. The number of rim sherds of a given category in a given lot is called x (with the appropriate suffices), similarly y is used for base sherds and z for decorated sherds. In counting the classified sherds, if there were more than one rim sherd from the same vessel in the same lot,

they were counted as one rim, and similarly for base or decorated sherds. The diameters of rim and base sherds were measured and classified into T_1 rim size groups and T_2 base size groups, for which suffices t and s are used. The number of rims in a size group is called N (with appropriate suffices) and the number of bases M.

A related pair of rim and base categories, with any associated category of decoration, is called a vessel form.

2. *Relationships between Rim and Base Categories.* We start with a very simple model (much simpler than the real situation) and progress to more complex and realistic models.

Suppose that each vessel in each lot is represented by one rim and one base (as defined above). The number of rims of each form in each lot is x_{ji} and the corresponding number of bases is y_{jh}. Suppose further that of all the vessels with rim category i, a proportion p_{ih} had base category h. Since the vessels have all (or almost all) been broken, these values p are unknown, and must be estimated in order to reconstruct the forms of vessels produced. The relationship between the xs and ys can be written as

$$y_{jh} = \sum_{i=1}^{k_1} p_{ih} x_{ji}, \quad \text{for all } j \text{ and all } h.$$

In other words, the number of bases of category h equals the sum of the numbers of rims of each category multiplied by the proportion of rims of that category which belong to the same vessel form as bases of category h.

We can express all these equations in one matrix equation,

$$\begin{pmatrix} y_{1,1} & \cdots & y_{1,k_2} \\ \vdots & & \vdots \\ y_{L,1} & \cdots & y_{L,k_2} \end{pmatrix} = \begin{pmatrix} x_{1,1} & \cdots & x_{1,k_1} \\ \vdots & & \vdots \\ x_{L,1} & \cdots & x_{L,k_1} \end{pmatrix} \begin{pmatrix} p_{1,1} & \cdots & p_{1,k_2} \\ \vdots & & \vdots \\ p_{k_1,1} & \cdots & p_{k_1,k_2} \end{pmatrix}$$

or simply as $Y = XP$

To solve for P we write $X'Y = X'XP$ and so $P = (X'X)^{-1} X'Y$, assuming $X'X$ to be nonsingular.

This equation for P is formally identical to that for estimating regression coefficients in multiple linear regression, and suggests that multiple regression may be a useful technique in more realistic models. An important point to note is that the 'constant term' of the usual regression equations must be identically zero; if there are no rims then there are no vessels and no bases.

A quick examination of the data shows how this model breaks down; even after allowing for more than one rim or base belonging to the same vessel, our counts gave about three times as many rims as bases. Clearly, we could not identify all the rim sherds from the same vessel, and so were over-counting the number of rims. For bases, which are generally smaller and less likely to break into many pieces, over-counting did not exist to the same extent, if at all. The problem is probably more difficult because the vessels are wasters, so that sherds from opposite sides of a distorted rim may not look alike, or even have the same diameter.

Whatever the causes, a more complicated model is needed to allow for the over-counting. We retain the underlying equation $Y = XP$ as an equation about vessels represented, rather than sherds present. For example, Y_{jh} now stands for the number of vessels with base category h represented in lot j, and to make the distinction between vessels and sherds we replace the small y (for sherds) with a capital Y (for vessels). In the earlier model, we could have written

$$y_{jh} = Y_{jh} \quad \text{and}$$
$$x_{ji} = X_{ji}$$

but we now know these equations to be inadequate. Instead we write

$$y_{jh} = g_h Y_{jh} + \varepsilon_{jh} \quad \text{and}$$
$$x_{ji} = f_i X_{ji} + \delta_{ji}$$

where f and g represent the 'brokenness' of the different rim and base categories, and δ and ε are error terms. If we suppose that for each vessel represented in a lot, the number of rims and bases to which it gives rise are Poisson variables with means f_i, g_h respectively, then to the above equations we can add

$$E(\varepsilon_{jh}) = E(\delta_{ji}) = 0$$
$$\text{var}(\varepsilon_{jh}) = g_h Y_{jh},$$
$$\text{var}(\delta_{ji}) = f_i X_{ji}, \quad \text{and}$$
$$\text{cov}(\varepsilon_{jh}, \varepsilon_{j'h'}) = \text{cov}(\delta_{ji}, \delta_{j'i'}) = 0$$

when $j \neq j'$ or $h \neq h'$, and $j \neq j'$ or $i \neq i'$.

These equations give a complete model of the situation, but whether they fit it adequately remains to be seen. There are also the k_1 constraints

$$\sum_{h=1}^{k_2} p_{ih} = 1 \quad \text{for all } i,$$

since the proportion of vessels with a rim of a given category which have a base of some category must be unity. Also, all the p_{ih}, g_n, and f_i must be greater than or equal to zero.

We must now consider the possibility of using multiple linear regression in this model to estimate the p_{ih}. One reason for doubt is that the 'independent' variables, the X_i, are likely to be correlated with each other from lot to lot since, in general, a lot with a large number of rims of one category will also have large numbers of rims of all the other categories. One could avoid this difficulty by replacing X_{ji} by

$$\tilde{X}_{ji} = X_{ji} \bigg/ \sum_{i=1}^{k_1} X_{ji}$$

that is, by expressing the X_{ji} as proportions of all rims in their lot, and similarly for the bases. Some straightforward algebra shows that

if $\quad Y = XP$

then $\quad \tilde{Y} = \tilde{X} P$

though of course the error structure is changed. It might be useful to employ the proportion-equations to eliminate insignificant coefficients in the regression, and to use the actual numbers to estimate the remaining coefficients. Again, experiments will be carried out to discover the best method.

Having regressed the numbers of bases on the numbers of rims we obtain the estimated regression coefficients a_{ih}, giving the matrix equation

$$y = xa \quad .$$

The problem is now to relate this to the underlying equation

$$Y = XP$$

in order to estimate the p_{ih}. In the matrix notation,

$$E(y)=gY,$$

where g is the matrix

$$\begin{pmatrix} g_1 & 0 & \ldots\ldots & 0 \\ 0 & g_2 & 0\ldots & 0 \\ \vdots & & & \vdots \\ 0 & & \ldots\ldots\ldots & g_{k_2} \end{pmatrix}$$

and similarly $E(x)=fX$. So we can write $g^{-1}E(y)=f^{-1}E(x)P$ which suggests that P can be estimated by $\hat{P}$, given by the equations

$$g^{-1}E(x)a=f^{-1}E(x)\hat{P} \quad \text{for all matrices } x,$$

that is, $\hat{P}=fg^{-1}a$

or $\hat{p}_{ih}=f_i g_h^{-1} a_{ih}$ for all i and h,

giving $k_1 k_2$ equations. There are also the k_1 constraints

$$\sum_{h=1}^{k_2} \hat{p}_{ih}=1,$$

giving in all $k_1 k_2 + k_1$ equations in $k_1 k_2$ (the p_{ih})$+k_1$(the f_i)$+k_2$(the g_h) unknowns. The situation is therefore indeterminate, requiring k_2 more equations. It is tempting to obtain them by writing

$$X=\bar{P}Y$$

and imposing the k_2 constraints

$$\sum_{i=1}^{k_1} \bar{p}_{hi}=1$$

as an obvious inverse relationship between bases and rims. However, this approach is not sound, as an application of Bayes' theorem shows. We denote by A_i the property that a vessel has the ith rim category, and by B_h the property that a vessel has the hth base category. Denoting by $P(A_i)$ the proportion of vessels with the ith rim category and by $P(A_i|B_h)$ the proportion of vessels with the hth base category which have the ith rim category, we have

$$P(A_i|B_h)=\frac{P(A_i)P(B_h|A_i)}{\sum_i P(A_i)P(B_h|A_i)}$$

or, in the original notation

$$\bar{p}_{hi}=\frac{P(A_i)P_{ih}}{\sum_i P(A_i)P_{ih}} \quad .$$

Therefore the matrix expressing the inverse relationship is not obtained by inverting the original matrix P, but also depends on the relative proportions of the various rim categories. Our approach to the relationships between the rims and bases is therefore not symmetric, as the rims are treated to some extent as 'independent' and the bases as 'dependent'. This seems reasonable in this case, as the rims are far more indicative of the general vessel shape than are the bases but the opposite could be true in other cases.

We are still left with more unknowns than equations. Some of the equations will be immediately solvable; for example, if a_{ih} is zero then p_{ih} must also be zero, and if for some h all the p_{ih} except one are zero, that one p_{ih} must have a value of unity. We may be able to assign values to some f_i or g_h by using archaeological knowledge, and some values will have to be left as ratios—if all vessels with rim category i have base category h then we can find only the ratio f_i/g_h, and never the individual values. Practical experience is needed to see how serious the problem really is.

Alternatively one could perhaps base a model on the idea of $k_1 k_2$ different vessel forms (every possible combination of rim and base), some of which actually exist and some of which are purely notional. One would say that the (i, h)th form constituted a proportion p_{jih} of the vessels of the jth lot, where p_{jih} was either identically zero or had some distribution with mean p_{ih}, and would attempt to find the values of the p_{ih}, perhaps by maximum likelihood methods.

Categories of Decoration. The next stage of the project, as envisaged, is to regress the numbers of sherds with different sorts of decoration on both the rim and base categories, and so to find the forms of vessels with which they are associated. The method should in general follow the lines laid down above; difficulties may arise where one sherd exhibits more than one form of decoration.

Relationships between Sizes of Rims and Bases. The theory of this aspect of the problem is, at the time of writing, less developed. The general ideas can best be appreciated by considering the case where there is a unique relationship between a particular rim category (say i) and a particular base category (say h), that is, where all the rims of category i are thought to belong to the same vessel form as all the bases of the category h, and vice versa. This we call a $(1, 1)$ relationship between categories i and h.

If we think of all the vessels of the form defined by these two categories, we can see that there is likely to be some relationship between the diameters of rim and base. For example, if all the vessels were of the same shape and differed only in size, the rim diameter would be some multiple of the base diameter, whatever the size of the vessel. Of course such an exact relationship is unlikely to occur, but it seems reasonable to assume that, within a form, the base diameter increases as the rim diameter increases. Mathematically, we say that the base diameter (r) and rim diameter (q) are related by the equation

$$r = h(q)$$

where h is a monotone increasing function. We shall be interested in finding out what we can about h.

Given the complete vessels, it would be a simple matter to plot r against q and examine the function h. However, we have only the measured diameters of individual rims or bases. From these we can construct cumulative density functions $F_j(q)$ and $G_j(r)$ for each lot, such that $F_j(q)$ is the proportion of rims (of the appropriate category) which have a diameter less than or equal to q, and similarly for G_j (Orton 1970). Using the simplest model of the relationship between rim and base categories—that each vessel in a lot is represented by just one rim and one base—we can transform the equation

$$r = h(q)$$

which relates to one complete vessel, to the new equation

$$F_j(q) = G_j(h(r)) \quad ,$$

which relates to all the relevant rims and bases in each lot.

To relate this equation to the sherds as actually measured, we need to make some assumptions about the f_i and g_h above. There is no reason to suppose *a priori* that either f_i or g_h is independent of diameter, and if, for example, f_i increased with diameter while g_h did not, any estimate of the function h would be distorted. The simplest assumption necessary for us to proceed appears to be that the ratio f_i/g_h is independent of vessel size, which is convenient because in the $(1, 1)$ case we know only f_i/g_h and not the separate values.

In the general case, it is cumbersome to deal with the large numbers of distributions F_{ji} and G_{jh} involved. At least in the first instance, I propose to simplify the situation by (1) assuming that the function h is linear, and (2) by ignoring the within-lot information (the shapes of the distributions) and attempting to find h by using the between-lot information (the variation between the means of the distributions in each lot). Having estimated h for each vessel form, we can use the within-lot data to test the fit of the estimated values, and perhaps to improve them. It appears that multiple regression methods, possibly weighted, will be of use in obtaining the preliminary estimates of the functions h.

Reconstruction of the Forms. To summarize, we hope by this stage to have established the existence of a number of vessel forms, defined by a rim category and base category pair, and possibly associated with some categories of decoration. For each such form, there should be a linear relationship between rim and base diameters. Clearly our final ambition must be to reconstruct each form over a typical range of sizes.

The first step would be to divide each form into size-groupings, and, for each grouping, to collect a 'family' of base profiles and a 'family' of rim profiles from the drawings made of the sherds. The problem is then to relate corresponding members of the two families by extrapolating their profiles, and trying to obtain a complete smooth profile by adjusting the distance between rim and base (that is, the height of the vessel). These ideas are, at the time of writing, purely hypothetical.

CONCLUSION

It is important to remember that this paper is tentative in nature. Its purpose is to restate an archaeological problem in more mathematical terms, rather than to present solutions to the problem. I hope that statistical methods will be useful in this problem of describing the production from a group of kilns, but experimental analyses on the lines described above will be needed to tell if this is so. The project is expected to end in July 1971, when the computing facilities expire. It is hoped that a report on the progress made, whether successful or not, will appear as soon as possible afterwards.

ACKNOWLEDGMENTS
Thanks are due to A. E. Brown and H. L. Sheldon for allowing me to use data from their excavations, and to the adult students at the City Literary Institute who have sorted, measured, and drawn much of the pottery. The computer terminal and computer time are supplied by Honeywell Information Systems Ltd (formerly GEIS Ltd), in association with *New Scientist* magazine.

REFERENCES

Brown, A.E. & Sheldon, H.L. (1969a, b). Excavations in Highgate Wood 1966–68, parts 1 and 2. *The London Archaeologist*, **1**.

Brown, A.E. & Sheldon, H.L. (1970) Excavations in Highgate Wood 1969. *The London Archaeologist*, **2**.

Orton, C.R. (1970) The production of pottery from a Romano-British kiln site: a statistical investigation. *World Archaeology*, **1**, 343–58.

Sheldon, H.L. *et al* (1970) *A Kiln and Pit Group from Highgate Wood, Excavated in 1968*. London: City Literary Institute.

Archaeology

Henrieta Todorová-Simeonová
Typological processing of the finds from the Tell Goljamo Deltschevo

The large scale of archaeological field investigations carried out after World War II, and the huge quantity of archaeological finds and observations accumulated in this connection, exact ever greater requirements from the methods of treating and processing this material.

The opportunities which the classical investigatory methods of archaeology offer, in this respect, are simply insufficient. It must also be borne in mind that the development of the methods of a given science ought to proceed hand in hand with the development of the science itself. This applies all the more to archaeology, which is in itself a relatively 'new' science, operating with flexible methods.

The enormous progress in methods of field investigation, especially in prehistory, and the gradual transition to exploring greater complexes and areas, necessitate a further improvement in methods of treating and processing excavated material, so that the maximum amount of information is obtained. This necessity is conditioned by the fact that archaeological finds from contemporary excavations greatly surpass, both in quality and in quantity, the finds from older explorations. We must admit the need to add new, modern investigatory techniques to the traditional ones, without in the least abandoning the latter. Undoubtedly, the new, modern devices permit a more intensive processing of finds and a reduction of the interval between excavation of a given site and its publication. Up to now, this interval has varied, with few exceptions, from 10 to 20 years.

The extreme necessity of improving laboratory processing of material is very clear when referring to the prehistoric Gumelniţa culture, which dates back to the late aeneolothic (chalcolithic), and has been known to science for nearly 70 years. Material from this culture can be discovered on the surface of most Tells, in both Bulgaria and Romania, which are the subject of constant investigations in both countries. The chronological limits of this culture are well known; several local variants can be observed in its vast distribution: in Mutenia, in north-east Bulgaria, and on the Black Sea coast. The characteristic elements of this culture, namely, its graphite ornament, specific shapes, idols, architecture, metallurgy, and so on, have been known for many years. New settlements belonging to this culture are excavated, new finds are acquired, but for many years we have not been able to make any progress in its scientific interpretation. The complex inner dynamics of the development of this culture remain obscure, in spite of the huge quantity of finds. Its separate phases and stages of development remain more or less theoretical. This applies mostly to the subphases: we lack a clear formulation of the typological content of the phases. Nowadays there are as many opinions as authors who have tackled this problem. The main shortcoming of the attempts to subdivide this culture into phases which have been published so far is the impossibility of reflecting the inner evolution of the culture within the framework of traditional typological tables. This is due to the fact that the dynamics of the development of the various ceramic shapes is diverse. Fine ceramics change most quickly, but here we can also find some shapes that are shortlived and others which survive with modifications through several phases or subphases. The most sensitive shapes and ornaments are at the same time the most precise chronological indicators. Ceramic kitchenware represents a rather conservative element, which changes little within the framework of a whole culture; there are cases when we find it passing through two chronologically consecutive cultures or appearing unchanged in two contemporary cultures. Its importance from a scientific point of view is different: it is of no use for chronology, but at the same time, it is an indispensable indicator of the cultural and genetic relations between separate chronological complexes.

At present we lack a satisfactory system capable of embracing and reflecting the above-mentioned problems. Progress in the investigation and exploration of the Gumelniţa culture, therefore, is directly connected with the problem of creating, with the help of mathematics, a universal and all-embracing system, within the framework of which we can place the whole complex of archaeological finds of that culture, and which would allow the thorough processing of that complex by means of a computer.

Further development in investigating the Gumelniţa culture is therefore a matter of system and statistics.

But one must not assume that no statistics have been used so far in investigating this culture. On the contrary—the fragments, shapes, ornaments, and so on, are counted everywhere. Unfortunately, all previous statistical experiments have been based upon individually-selected criteria, which, at best, are valid only for a given site. This is why they are being constantly changed.

It is possible that these statistics may meet the demands and requirements of individual investigators or research workers, but they can, by no means, meet requirements for investigating the culture as a whole, because they do not operate with comparable categories. When comparing the complexes of finds, we usually operate with analogies. Within the limits of the area of a given culture, however, the latter are quite a regular phenomenon. In the end, they can only confirm the well-known fact that two sites (for example, Tell-Rousse and Tell-Hîrşova) belong to one and the same culture.

Nowadays, conclusions and inferences at such a level can gratify no-one. If we wish to solve successfully the complex problems of the origin, development, and decline of a given prehistoric culture, it is necessary to build up a universal system of accounting for the finds. This must be built up so as to take into consideration (and conform to) new achievements in the field of mathematics, and it must allow the processing of enormous amounts of material by computer. This is the only way which can lead to any progress in investigating the Gumelniţa culture. This consideration was the sole reason which compelled us to resort to the help of technology in processing the finds from Tell Goljamo Deltschevo (Varna district).

The Tell Goljamo Deltschevo is situated some 60 km (by air) west of the Kamchia River mouth in the Black Sea. It lies on the left bank of the Luda Kamchia River at the foothills of Kamchiiska Stara Planina, and represents the last link, towards this mountain, in the system of Tells following the course of the Kamchia River. This mound belongs to the group of mounds with an average height over 5 m and consists of 16 cultural horizons dating back to the early neolithic Ţonevo culture, the early aeneolithic Sava culture, the transitional Varna-stage and the late aeneolithic Kodjadermen-Gumelniţa culture. In 1968 and 1969 the entire area of the Tell was thoroughly investigated down to its very foundations, since the site is to be inundated by water from the Ţonevo Dam. The cemetery near the mound was examined as well. All the finds are kept at the museum in the town of Varna and will soon be published.

A comparatively simple, but at the same time, an all-embracing and extensive system was elaborated with the valuable help of Mr V. Stavrev, an engineer. The entire material was classified within the framework of this same system.

The general model of the system is shown in figure 1. It is divided into 3 parts according to the level of the information obtained, namely: constant information; partially variable information; and variable information.

The *constant* part of the model contains the following data: no. (number) of the model (2 columns); name of the institute (3 columns); name of the site (4 columns), according to the nomenclature of the sites; state (2 columns); district (2 columns), according to the corresponding nomenclature as well.

The *partially constant* part of the model includes all data, which remain constant within the framework of a definite group of archaeological finds, namely: (1) the date when the excavations were made; (2) plansquare (horizontal location); (3) depth; (4) horizon; and (5) location (house no., tomb no., pit no., and so on).

The next category—that of the *variable* information—has the purpose of supplying a most detailed and extensive characterization of each separate find. Here, we are aiming to avoid any summing up of the criteria, since the appraisal and estimation *at the level of the detail, which is deliberate and intentional for pre-historic man,* only can render that completeness, which is of utmost importance for vivid description and for painting the entire picture. Unpremeditated detail, however (for example—the shades and nuances in colouring the vessels and the thickness of the fragments, and so on), are not taken into account from a statistical point of view. The whole complex of finds is divided into 9 large groups: (1) ceramics, (2) stone, (3) flint, (4) horn, (5) bone, (6) metal, (7) mussels, clams, and so on, (8) art, (9) architecture and cemeteries.

Here we shall devote our attention to the system for the classification of ceramics only, because it is at once the most complex and the most necessary system, since the processing of a mass of ceramics is the most labour-consuming and the most complex of processes in investigating a given site. *Ceramics* are divided into 8 classes, namely: (1) fine ceramics, (2) ceramic kitchenware, (3) pots and lids, (4) cult vessels, (5) small vessels, (6) articles used in farming, (7) models and patterns, (8) other.

Within the limits of each class, ceramics are further divided into *types* (figure 2).

After this, an account of the specific shape of the vessel is given, with the help of a detailed nomenclature of the shapes (figure 3). The nomenclature in this system is able to embrace all shapes, known so far (in the first two numbers), and their variants (in the following two numbers). The fifth number gives the dimensions of the vessel—small, medium, large. Thus we give an account of all fragments which belong to definite shapes, and this fact can be determined with certainty.

The classification of the ornament of the Gumelniţa culture is very complex, since we usually find several different ornaments on one and the same vessel. In the first place, the classification was carried out on the basis of the technology of the ornament, namely: (1) drawn, (2) grooved, (3) concave, (4) relief, (5) cannelure (fluting), (6) with a surface made rough and uneven, (7) ornaments made by pricking (impressed), (8) bud-shaped ornaments.

The ornament is subdivided into types within the framework of each of the classes (figure 4).

The most frequent combinations found in each separate type of ornament are reflected in the two following columns (figure 1). The pattern is examined according to a detailed nomenclature of patterns, worked out on the same principle as for the nomenclature of forms.

Those fragments of ceramics, where there is no proof of their belonging to any definite form, are examined in the next column of the model—under the heading 'Fragments', which consist of the following columns:

1. *Mouth of the vessel.* Here we examine the slope of the mouth of the vessel: (a) with a vertical slope, (b) with a mouth sloping inwards at an angle of 72°, (c) with a mouth sloping inwards at an angle of 45°, (d) with a mouth sloping outwards at an angle of 72°, (e) with a mouth sloping outwards at an angle of 45°, (f) a circle, (g) with a mouth bending inwards, (h) with a mouth bending outwards, (i) with a mouth made thicker.

2. *Belly of the vessel.* (a) slightly bulging, (b) bulging to a great extent, (c) with a cylindrical belt, (d) with a deviation at the shoulders, (e) with a deviation under the belly, (f) with a deviation *under* and *above* the belly, (g) a sharply biconic vessel, (h) a biconic vessel with a rounded break, (i) a rounded biconic vessel.

3. *Base of the vessel.* (a) flat, (b) concave, (c) convex, (d) sharp, (e) with a base made thicker, (f) false, ring-shaped, (g) false, ring-shaped with concavity.

4. *Stand and pedestal.* (a) with a short stand, (b) with a high stand, (c) with a stand and a foot, (d) with a stand sloping at an angle, (e) a short ring-shaped pedestal, (f) with a high cylindrical pedestal, (g) with a pedestal with protruding walls, (h) bell-shaped pedestal, (i) a pedestal with a widened flare.

5. *Spout of the vessel.* (a) with a hole in the walls, (b) with a hole at the edge

of the mouth, (c) short spout, (d) long spout, (e, f, g, h, i).

We give an account of the handles by a more detailed classification since they are very important from a chronological, cultural, and typological point of view.

In this case the first column determines the place of the handle: (1) at the edge of the mouth, (2) at the neck, (3) at the shoulder, (4) at the belly, (5) in the lower part of the vessel, (6) on a pedestal, (7) on a lid, (8) on a handle, (9) in the inside of the vessel. We give as well an account of the cross-section of the handle in the next column, that is: (1) circular, (2) ellipse, (3) square, (4) ribbed (with edges), (5) band-shaped, (6) bud-shaped, (7) cord-shaped, (8) tongue-shaped. The section includes the shapes of handles known so far: (1) vertical, (2) vertical, arched (for lids on top of the lid), (3) vertical, with breaks (for the lid front), (4) vertical, high, (5) vertical with an excrescence, (6) vertical, nearly straight (for a lid—rectangular), (7) false, (8) horizontal, (9) horizontal, with an excrescence.

The bud-shaped handles of the lids are classified in an additional column: (1) short, cylindrical, (2) false, flat, (3) false, of the base type, (4) high, cylindrical, (5) high, cylindrical with a cone, (6) high, cylindrical with a small cupola, (7) of the 'Spantov' type, (8) biconical, sharp, (9) biconical, rounded.

With a view to expanding this elaborate system in relation to other prehistoric cultures, we envisage a classification of cultures in three columns. The latter comprises in chronological order the neolithic, the aeneolithic, the Bronze Age, and the Hallstatt, all the prehistoric cultures known so far in south-east Europe. Sufficient place is left for the inclusion of groups of cultures and cultures discovered subsequently. Naturally, all exceptional and non-standard shapes are located and described separately, and are not included in our system.

After appropriate modifications to suit the methods of an archaeological excavation, the system described can be applied directly in field investigation without any need for long preliminary training of the executive personnel. Moreover, it is not necessary to process all the squares (1 square $= 2 \cdot 5 \times 2 \cdot 5$ m) in the horizontal network of squares in this way, in order to have a clear and detailed description of the site. 40 or 50 squares, stratigraphically pure and intact (which of course must be proved conclusively), alongside the control over the results obtained from another 12–24 squares (also stratigraphically pure and intact), following immediately, will be quite sufficient.

During the first two years of our activity, we have been able to obtain our first results, using the system just described. Thus, for example, we have been able to determine in detail the distribution of the separate shapes and forms in the various horizons, which gave us the possibility of establishing the precise typological content of each separate horizon; the evolution of a given shape from the moment it appeared for the first time in the mound, till the period of its decline.

An unquestionable hiatus was discerned, which lasted too briefly to leave any traces at all in the ground. Nevertheless, it was sufficiently long to interrupt the development of definite forms.

These observations made it possible to determine the separate phases and subphases to which the occupations of the Tell belong. It is worth noting that with the help of the system described, we can fix scientifically shorter periods of time. This fact has given to prehistory the opportunity of operating with a much more detailed relative chronology in future.

At present, our modest attempt is confined to processing the finds from one site. Nevertheless, the system proposed can embrace with any alterations all the finds from the Gumelniţa culture, published up to now in the relevant literature or kept in various museums. A generalizing treatment of this culture as a whole, taking into consideration its separate stages of development and its local manifestations, will be undertaken after the completion of this work.

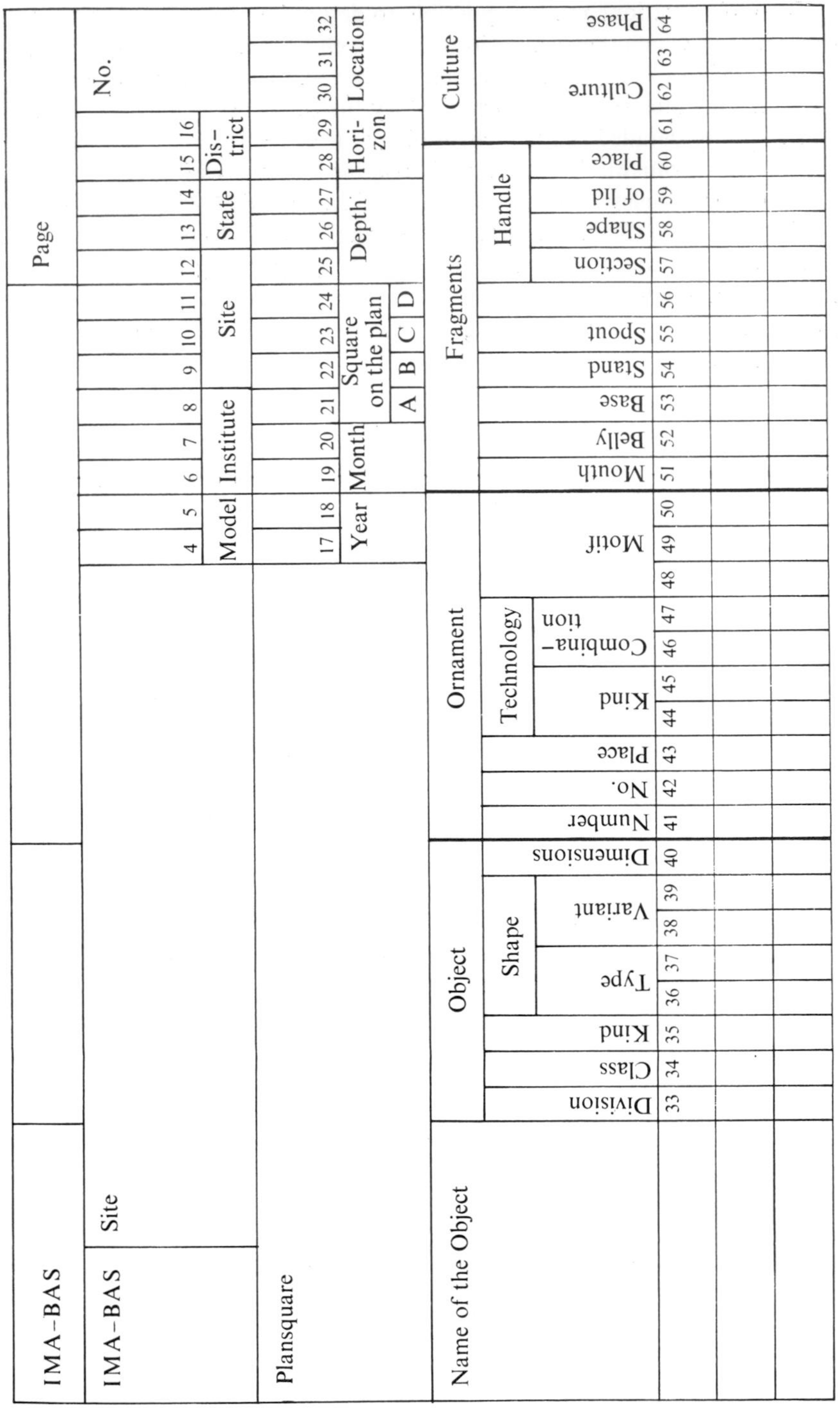

Page

No.

Culture   Phase   64

Culture   61 62 63

Model   4 5

Institute   6 7 8

Site   9 10 11

State   12 13 14

District   15 16

Year   17 18

Month   19 20

21

Square on the plan   A B C D   22 23 24

Depth   25 26 27

Horizon   28 29

Location   30 31 32

Fragments

Handle   Place   60

Handle   of lid   59

Handle   Shape   58

Section   57

56

Spout   55

Stand   54

Base   53

Belly   52

Mouth   51

Ornament

Motif   48 49 50

Technology   Combination   46 47

Technology   Kind   44 45

Place   43

No.   42

Number   41

Object

Dimensions   40

Shape   Variant   38 39

Shape   Type   36 37

Kind   35

Class   34

Division   33

IMA–BAS

IMA–BAS   Site

Plansquare

Name of the Object

Figure 1. General model of the system

Ceramics

	Fine 1	Kitchenware 2	Pct and lid 3	Cult vessels 4	Small vessels 5	Used in farming 6	Models 7	Other 8	9
0									
1	Dish	Earthen pan	Lid	Anthropo-morphic lid	Dish	Spindle whorl	of house	Marble vessels	
2	Plate	Plate	Cover	Zoomorphic lid	Plate	Weight	of oven	Non-fired vessel	
3	Bowl	Strainer	Base	Anthropo-morphic vessel	Bowl	Knitting on the bottom	of fortification		
4	Cup	Spoon	Pitt	Zoomorphic vessel	Cup	'Falus'	of instrument		
5	Vase	Pot	Amphora	Altar	Vase	Tile	of table		
6	Jug	Jug	Box	Ring	Pot	Potta	of chair		
7			Support	Drum	Support	Funnel	of horn		
8			Sponge	Sign		Pintadera	Fronton plate		
9									

Figure 2. Classification of the ceramics

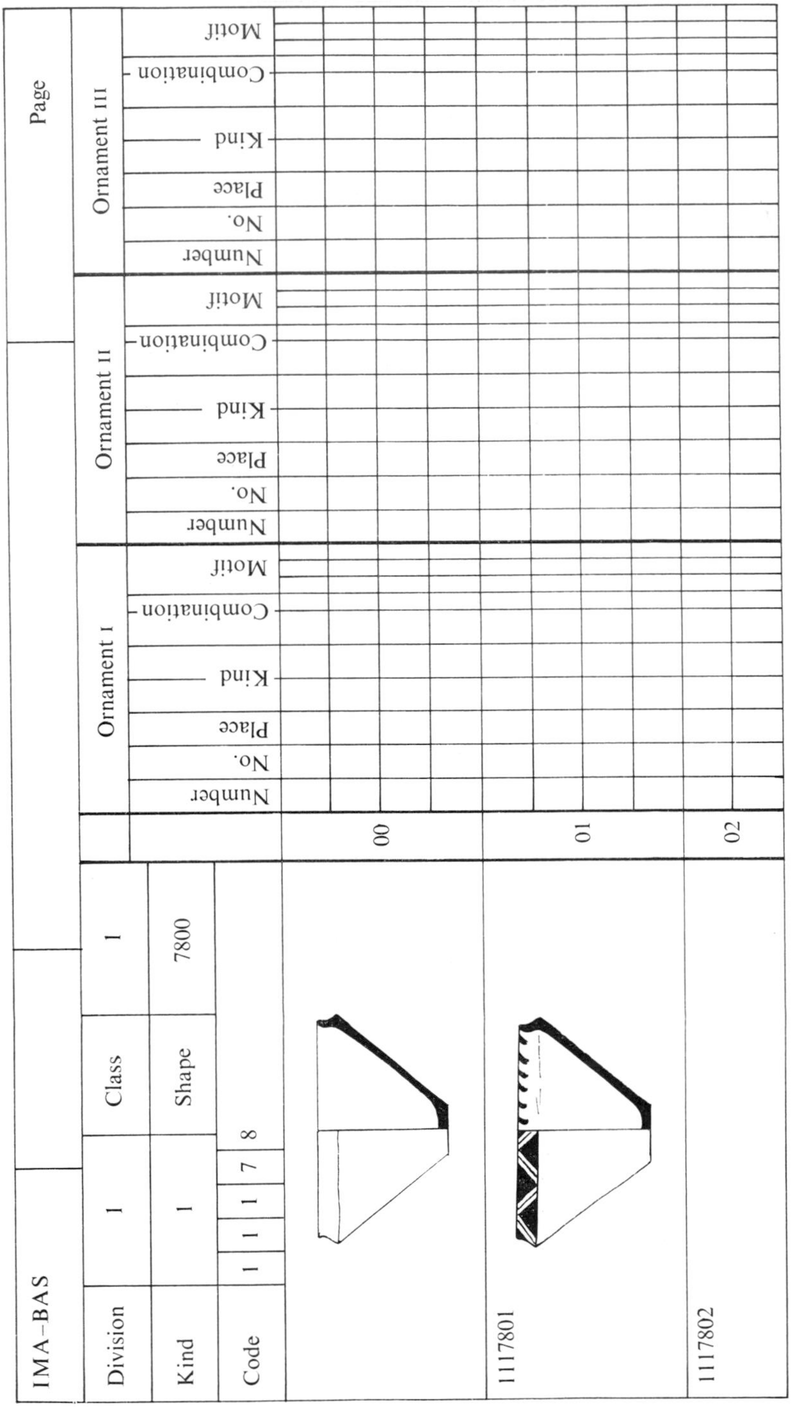

IMA–BAS

Division	Kind	Code		Class Shape 7800		Number No. Place Kind Combination Motif (Ornament I)	Number No. Place Kind Combination Motif (Ornament II)	Number No. Place Kind Combination Motif (Ornament III)
1	1	1 1 1 7 8	00					
			01					
			02					

1117801

1117802

Page

Figure 3. Nomenclature of the shapes

Ceramics Ornament–Technology									
0	Drawn 1	Grooved 2	Concave 3	Relief 4	Cannelure 5	Crude and uneven 6	Impressed 7	Bud-shaped 8	9
0									
1	Graphite	Notch	Cord	Stuck-on	Ribs	Poly-chrome	Separate impressions	Cone-like	
2	Red ochre	'Sava type'	Furrows	Pressed by fingers	Wide cannelures	Poly-chrome with notches	Impressions on the whole surface	Cylindrical	
3	White ochre	Channel	Stamp	Pressed by an instrument	Ordinary cannelures	Non-organized barbotine	Row of nail impressions	Flat	
4	Yellow ochre	Net	Fingers under the mouth arranged in a row	Wide notches	False cannelures	Barbotine put on top by the fingers	Impressions in several rows	Concave	
5	White paint	Grooved at an angle	Fingers under arranged in 2–3 rows	'Ezerovo' type	Pleats	Barbotine put on top by means of a rag	Impressions on the whole surface	Double	
6	Red paint	Narrow notches	Little pits	Relief grooved	Relief edge	Scratched by a wide edge	Row of shell impressions	Disjoined	
7	Brown paint	Ladder of 'Maritsa' type	'Hamangia' type			Uneven	Impressions on the whole surface	False Buckel	
8	Gray paint	Wide ladder				Barbotine put on top by fingernails	Holes made by piercing		
9	Bi-chrome and poly-chrome					'Hedgehog' type			

Figure 4. Classification of the ornaments, according to their technology

Archaeology

John D. Wilcock
Non-statistical applications of the computer in archaeology

This paper describes an overall computer-aided system for the use of archaeologists employing plain-language keywords to control information retrieval, graphics, and ancillary techniques such as routine reduction of instrument survey readings, objective classification of profiles, and statistical studies of the data.

The majority of papers at this conference have dealt with statistical applications in archaeology, where mathematical techniques are employed in the empirical study of archaeological data as phenomena with observable regularities. Inevitably, the computer has been pressed into the service of mathematicians and statisticians with an interest in archaeology. But it is a fact that the majority of present-day computer applications in business and industry are essentially non-statistical, and many are even non-numerical. It would therefore seem profitable to explore archaeology for non-statistical and non-numerical problems to which computer science may be applied. This seems likely to be an expanding field.

This paper describes applications of the computer in information retrieval, instrument surveys, graphics and the objective classification of artifacts by pattern recognition techniques.

INFORMATION RETRIEVAL

It is becoming very common in these days of the high-speed digital computer for large files of information to be stored on computer media for subsequent analysis. A file of data covering a well-defined topic is called a *data base*, which may then be used as input for an *Information Retrieval* exercise; information relevant to a particular query or set of queries is located and retrieved. The results are usually printed by computer and are then directly available for reference or reproduction by offset-litho printing.

Ideally, records should be made in plain language with as little contraction, stylization, or coding as possible. To have to refer to a code book every time a request is codified or results have to be interpreted is annoying and time-consuming. A request may be formulated from a set of plain-language descriptive terms (called *descriptors*) and it is usual to combine these descriptors by logical operators, for example, logical AND (.), OR (+), NOT (−), ANY n OF ($n/(t+t+t$, and so on)), where n is an integer less than the number of terms t combined by logical operators OR (+).

In order to set up a system using information retrieval, cataloguing terms must be chosen and a thesaurus of words compiled so that the terms and the words embrace all facets of the information to be stored. The terms and the words may be expanded and amended once the system is in operation, but a determined attempt must be made to compile a comprehensive list of possible cataloguing terms at the outset, since it would be very wasteful of time and money to have to go back through thousands of records already compiled to insert omitted information. A thesaurus is necessary, for if all possible terms were allowed, a variety of descriptive terms could be used by different cataloguers and in different retrieval requests to describe the same concept. Added to each record is a unique accession number.

For example, consider an archaeological cave record retrieval request containing the following descriptors:

1. Iron Age
2. Roman
3. Hyena remains
4. Bronze brooch
5. Cave entrance facing south
6. More than 200 m above sea level
7. Less than 10 Km from main land route
8. Less than 5 Km from navigable water.

Suppose the logical function is:

$$(1+2) \cdot -3 \cdot 4 \cdot 2/(5+6+(7+8))* \quad .$$

This particular logical function means that the request is for any cave records satisfying the following:

the date must be Iron Age or Roman;

there must not be hyena remains;

there must be a bronze brooch among the finds;

and at least two of the following must be satisfied:

(a) cave mouth facing south;

(b) cave mouth higher than 200 m above present sea level;

(c) *either* less than 10 Km from a main land route,

     or less than 5 Km from navigable water.

When these descriptors are compared with the filed records, those records satisfying the request will be printed out. A very large data base can be scanned in a matter of minutes. The complexity of the logical functions which can be used is unrestricted, and there may be numerical comparisons as well as presence/absence checks; the compiler program scans the function until some terminator (*in the expression above) is encountered, then sets up the appropriate logical checks to be carried out on each record. The descriptors may be given numerical identifiers as in the example above, or they may be described explicitly in plain language in the logical expression. The printed output of the information retrieval scheme is controlled by parameters, and the printing format may be changed from run to run. A common printing format will be standard A4-size numbered pages for direct offset-litho reproduction.

It is useful to have the facility of printing the whole of the current thesaurus of terms, and also accumulated counts of the frequency of use of descriptors in the matching of records. Descriptors which are infrequently used might be deleted from the system with advantage, and those descriptors which are widely used can be redefined in greater detail.

Three main types of archaeological data file may be distinguished: the large body of specialist data; the museum collection and accession record; and the excavation record.

The large body of specialist data may contain all known information on a well-defined topic, for example, Roman inscriptions, prehistoric carvings, cave deposits, clay pipes, pottery types, and so on. The result of a search carried out on such a file is usually the identification and output of items satisfying certain criteria (see example given above). Research workers may make requests for searches on a file, and may often create their own computer input documents using plain-language keywords to specify the criteria and control the search.

Museum collections may be catalogued and held on computer files, and it is best if these are stored centrally at the computer site rather than at the museum, since this simplifies the processing of requests from other museum workers. This need not be any disadvantage, since the records may be amended and added to by remote operation using a teletype at the museum and the British Post Office Datel system (or equivalent service in other countries), as illustrated in figure 1. The cataloguing of archaeological data has received some attention internationally during the past five years. A good survey of the most important work has been made by Ellin (1968a). Good descriptive articles are given by Chenhall (1967, 1968), Cowgill (1967), and Gardin

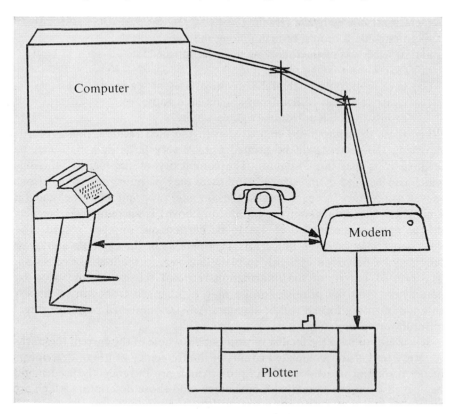

Figure 1. PO Datel system

(1967). Two ambitious projects are already being conducted by consortia of museums. The first, in the USA, is sponsored by a consortium of 25 museums (known as the Museum Computer Network). This project anticipates the eventual recording of all museum records in the USA within a single integrated system. Any museum's records could then be accessed by any worker, and by using multi-access techniques and data transmission by ordinary telephone line the central records could be accessed from hundreds of kilometres away, as shown in figure 1. The task is therefore to make all the museum records compatible (Ellin 1968a,b). The British project is being conducted under the direction of the Museums Association, and is again concerned with the formulation of a single interdisciplinary system for all museums in Britain. The organizing body is known as the Information Retrieval Group of the Museums Association, or IRGMA. Draft proposals were published in 1969 (Lewis *et al.* 1969) and the system is at present engaged in extensive field trials. The main workers in Britain concerned with information retrieval for extensive collections have been Cutbill (Sedgwick Museum of Geology, Cambridge), Lewis (Sheffield City Museum), Perring (The Nature Conservancy, Monk's Wood Experimental Station) and Roads (Imperial War Museum). There has been work from an early date by Lewis (1965, 1967).

The excavation record has not received much attention yet as a computer application. Orton (1970) has described the statistical analysis of pottery finds at the Highgate Wood excavations, and further work on this material is proceeding apace by multi-access computer using remote teletype, as shown in figure 1. Experimental work on excavation files has been carried out at the University of Keele. The typical excavation file will contain 3-dimensional coordinates in the metric system (to the nearest cm or mm, as applicable, if possible linked to the National Grid) for all important finds and features of buried constructions, and so on. It may also contain an objective description of all finds (not only measurements, but actual profiles held in numerical form, and even pictures of finds held numerically or by reference to photographs filed on aperture cards). These records are invaluable in the subsequent preparation of diagrams, lists of finds, tables showing correspondence between artifact types and layers, and so on, for the final publication. The process of publication may often be speeded up by the mechanization of these operations on the computer.

ROUTINE REDUCTION OF INSTRUMENT SURVEY READINGS

During the past ten years archaeologists have been turning to the use of geophysical instruments in the exploration of sites before excavations begin. Such instruments detect any changes in the physical properties of the subsoil attributable to archaeological features. For example, the resistivity meter measures the electrical conductivity of the ground by passing an electric current between probes inserted in the earth. Buried stonework has a high electrical resistance compared with the surrounding earth, so wall foundations are readily detected as an anomaly. Another group of instruments, the proton gradiometers and magnetometers, measure the earth's magnetic field with a high degree of sensitivity. They employ a principle of operation based on the free precession of protons in a magnetic field. The basic field is modified on an archaeological site by buried pits and ditches and particularly large changes are caused by structures which have been burnt or fired (for example, kilns and hearths), called thermoremnant features. The proton magneto-meter and gradiometer are essentially passive in principle, since they measure a magnetic field which already exists. Instruments of a third group actively inject signals into the earth and measure the returning signal. These are the pulsed magnetic induction meter and the soil conductivity meter ('Banjo'). The results are broadly similar to those produced by the previously mentioned magnetic instruments.

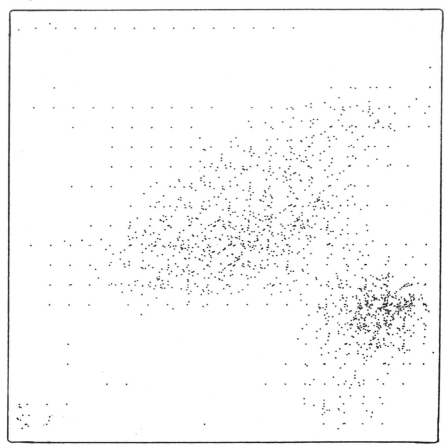

Figure 2. South Cadbury 1969, square 10

Geophysical surveys aimed at the exhaustive exploration of an area must be systematic; in general, readings are taken at the intersection points of a rectangular grid of 1m spacing, or less, superimposed on the main site grid. Hundreds of thousands of readings are often taken in this way on a large site. Having obtained the readings, usually in numerical form (although systems are now available for the automatic recording of results on magnetic tape for later analysis by pen recorder, and on punched paper tape for computer analysis), the results must be plotted using various pictorial conventions to give the archaeological feature map. A typical dot-density plot is shown in figure 2, being part of the survey of South Cadbury described by Wilcock (1969a,b, 1970). A great deal of labour is involved in the production of these feature maps by hand. The job is tedious, prone to error, and takes several days. It is an ideal application for the digital computer. Moreover, the use of the computer allows us to enhance artificially the contrast of the diagrams by numerical manipulation or filtering, something which we could never do by hand because of the large number of calculations involved. If data collection for instrument surveys is not automatic, it is an advantage if the readings are entered on special forms which can be used as direct source documents for punch operatives. A specially-designed form for this purpose is described by Wilcock (1969b). Routine reduction of instrument survey readings is an obvious application for the computer.

GRAPHICS FOR ARCHAEOLOGISTS

In order that we may get the computer to draw diagrams, it is necessary, first of all, to understand the capabilities and limitations of the graphics devices which may be attached to the computer. Typical graph plotters are illustrated in figures 3 and 4. The drum plotter usually has a paper width of less than 1m, but the flat-bed plotter may be several metres in length and breadth. Each has a pen-carriage which may carry up to four pens with different colours of inks. The diagram is built up by lowering and raising the pens as required, and by moving the pens across the paper on the pen-carriage and along the paper (either by moving the paper itself on a drum, as in the drum plotter, or by moving the pen-carriage itself, as in the flat-bed plotter). In either case the pen may reach any point on the paper, but it usually does so in increments of 0·01 cm along 8 vectors at 100 increments per second, so 'straight' lines are in reality rather zig-zag, as shown in figure 5. More advanced plotters use 24 vectors and more than one increment size, but even with these increased speeds it takes several minutes to draw a diagram on one of these devices.

Automatic drafting machines also operate on plotter principles, but the 'pen' in this case is a beam of light controlled both in size and intensity, and the plotting medium is a photographic plate.

Alternatively we may draw our diagram on the face of a cathode ray tube using a beam of electrons. This draws the whole diagram in a fraction of a second, but to obtain a permanent print it is necessary to photograph the tube face, or transfer the whole diagram to a plotter as described above. The cathode ray tube has several other attachments, such as a typewriter keyboard, function switches and 'light pen' (*see* figure 6). The software is manipulated to draw and label the desired diagrams using the keyboard, function switches, and light pen. The diagrams may generally be moved laterally on the tube face, rotated in pseudo-3-dimensional perspective, and so on. 'Light Buttons' are groups of characters or small symbols which are often displayed along the bottom of the screen, and are a software analogue of the hardware function switches. These light buttons may be detected by the photosensitive light pen and transformed into orders to the computer. In the same way the light pen may be used to specify the position of a point, and to draw a line on the tube face. A further use of light buttons is to store replicas of frequently-used

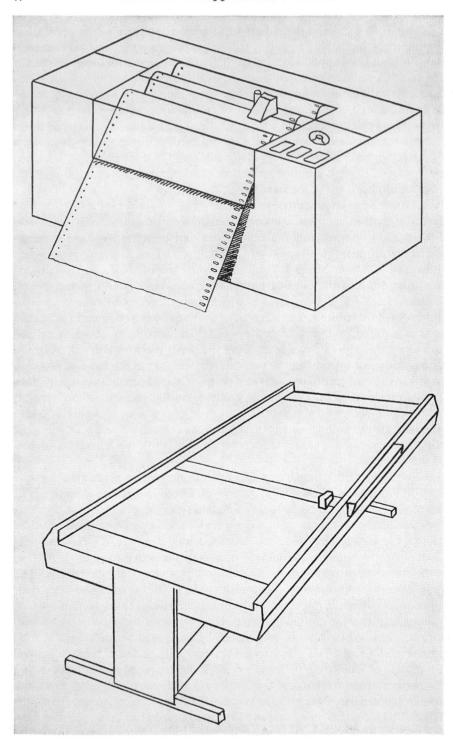

Figure 3 (top). Drum plotter   Figure 4 (bottom). Flat-bed plotter

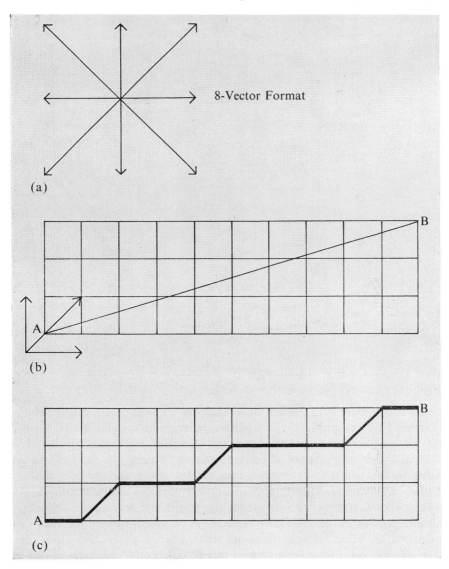

Figure 5. Plotting with the 8-vector format

symbols; for example, the archaeologist may frequently require symbols for small finds of various types, grid intersection points, and so on.

A further versatile device is the microfilm printer/plotter, which can produce several permanent diagrams per second on microfilm using conventional optical techniques or direct dry-silver electron beam recording.

Ideally the archaeologist would like to control these devices using plain-language keywords submitted to the computer either by typing them in, or by punching them on cards, paper tape, and so on. Graphics languages used in industry at present do this to a limited extent, for example, the EXAPT language for machine-tool control by computer (Opitz and Simon 1967)

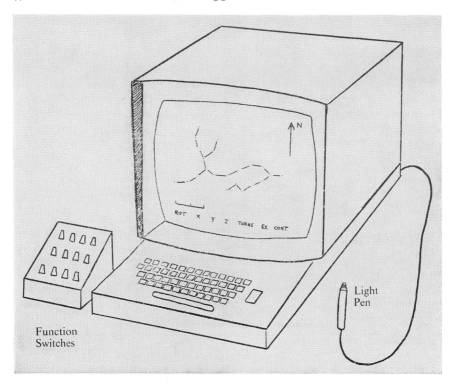

Figure 6. Line-drawing display 'graphoscope'

and the 3G Gerber Graphics Generator for automatic drafting machines (Gerber 1969). A graphical picture-drawing language has also been described by Notley (1970). A graphics language especially for archaeologists is at present under development at the University of Keele. Desired features are not only the ability to draw lines, arcs, circles, site grids, symbols, shading within a defined boundary, and so on, but scaling, rotation, translation, mirror effects, perspective views from any height and bearing, and labelling. Small pictures of actual artifacts may be included in their actual find positions on plans. Hidden lines are deleted from perspective views, and stereoscopic views may be generated as two perspective views from slightly different angles plotted in two different colours, to be viewed with coloured lenses.

Actual profiles of artifacts may be input to such a system using the D-Mac Pencil Follower (figure 7). A lens with crosswires is moved along the required line on the diagram mounted on the table of the device, and a string of coordinates is punched on paper tape ready for input to the computer. Once in the computer in numerical form, the profile may be scaled, rotated and positioned in whatever manner required, and also stored on magnetic tape.

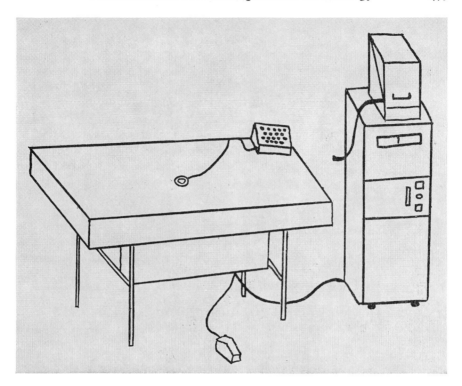

Figure 7. Device for producing paper-tape records of positional information

OBJECTIVE CLASSIFICATION OF ARTIFACTS BY PATTERN
RECOGNITION TECHNIQUES

Picture processing by computer has been treated by Rosenfeld (1969a,b) and others. Pattern recognition has been treated by many workers, among them Rutovitz (1966). The aim in the archaeological context is to classify, for example, pottery profiles, according to their objective features (*see* Gardin 1967); the resulting objective classification will depend upon the content of the data base. The technique as formulated at the University of Keele uses input from the D-Mac Pencil Follower and has similar features to pattern recognition; starting with an arbitrary number of classes of profiles, the classes are subdivided or amalgamated as necessary to produce the final objective classification.

THE COMBINED SCHEME

All the above techniques may be used in a combined scheme and then become even more powerful. Information retrieval files may carry graphics data. The graphics language may obtain parameters from the information retrieval feature, generate site plans, sections, histograms, diagrams, graphs and tables, and so on, which may be recorded permanently on plotter or microfilm, or added to the information retrieval files. Outline maps of any desired area of the world may be stored on files, and called for plotting whenever required. These maps are drawn complete with scales, north points, and titles, generated from computer input, and may be plotted to any paper size ready for direct

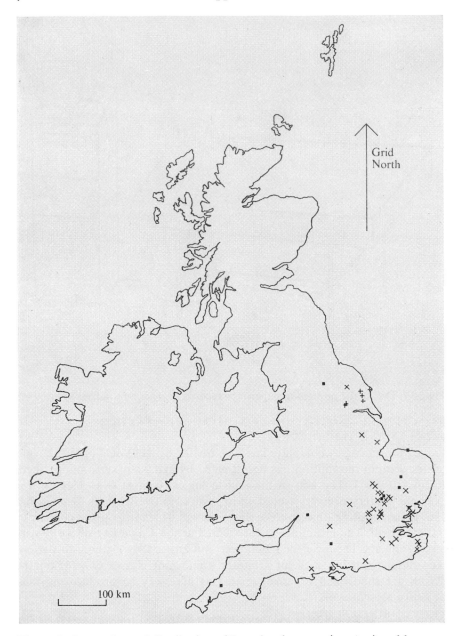

Figure 8. Comparison of distribution of Iron Age barrows (squares) and barrow groups (+) with Roman barrows and Mausolea (×)

offset-litho printing. Locations of interest (for example, those sites obtained from the information retrieval files satisfying certain criteria) may be plotted on the map as grid references (a typical map is given in figure 8). Survey data may be reduced to maps to guide the excavator, and the finds from the excavation recorded in the information retrieval scheme. Objective classifications may be formulated and used as the basis for future classification. Of course, statistical programs may also be called to operate on the data from the information retrieval scheme, and here we may perhaps see statistics in its true perspective as just one of several tools in the workshop of the computer-equipped archaeologist.

REFERENCES

Chenhall, R.G. (1967) The description of archaeological data in computer language. *Amer. Antiquity*, **32**, 161–7.

Chenhall, R.G. (1968) The impact of computers on archaeological theory. *Computers & Humanities*, **3**, 15–24.

Cowgill, G.L. (1967) Computer applications in archaeology. *Computers & Humanities*, **2**, 17–23.

Ellin, E. (1968a) An international survey of museum computer activity. *Computers & Humanities*, **3**, 65–86.

Ellin, E. (1968b) Information systems and the humanities: a new Renaissance. *Metropolitan Museum Conference on Computers and their Potential Applications in Museums*. New York, 1968.

Ellin, E. (1968c) *Report of the Museum Computer Network Project*. New York, 1968.

Gardin, J-C. (1967) Methods for the descriptive analysis of archaeological material. *Amer. Antiquity*, **32**, 13–30.

Gerber Scientific Instrument Company. (1969) Gerber Graphics Generator Program (3G). Prepared for The Gerber Scientific Instrument Company, Hartford, Connecticut by Applied Programming Technology Corporation, Sudbury, Massachusetts, USA.

Lewis, G.D. (1965) Obtaining information from museum collections and thoughts on a national museum index. *Museums J.*, **65**, 12–22.

Lewis, G.D. *et al.* (1967) Information retrieval for museums. *Museums J.*, **67**, 88–120.

Lewis, G.D. *et al.* (1969) *Draft Proposals for an Interdisciplinary Museum Cataloguing System*. Information Retrieval Group of the Museums Association, London. 23 April 1969.

Notley, M.G. (1970) A graphical picture drawing language. *Comput. Bull.*, **14**, 68–74.

Opitz, H. & Simon, W. (1967) *EXAPT 1 and EXAPT 2 Part Programmer Reference Manuals*. Aachen: Verein zur Förderung des Exapt-Programmier systems e.V.

Orton, C.R. (1970) The production of pottery from a Romano-British kiln site: a statistical investigation. *World Archaeol.*, **1**, 343–58.

Rosenfeld, A. (1969a) Picture processing by computer. *Computing Surveys*, **1**, 147–76.

Rosenfeld, A. (1969b) *Picture Processing by Computer*. New York & London: Academic Press.

Rutovitz, D. (1966) Pattern recognition. *J. Roy. statist. Soc. Brit.*, **28**, 504–30.

Wilcock, J.D. (1969a) Computers and Camelot. South Cadbury, an exercise in computer archaeology. *Spectrum (British Science News)* **60**, 7–9. London: HMSO.

Wilcock, J.D. (1969b) Computer analysis of proton magnetometer readings from South Cadbury 1968 — A long-distance exercise. *Prospezioni Archeologiche*, **4**, 85–93.

Wilcock, J.D. (1970) Prospecting at South Cadbury: an exercise in computer archaeology. *Science & Archaeology*, **1**, 9–11.

History

Valeriu Bulgaru
The theory of historical series formulated by A.D.Xenopol as a
mathematical approach to history

The aim of this first Anglo-Romanian Conference on 'mathematics in archaeological and historical sciences', is to contribute to the solution of the mathematical problems raised by the modern treatment of the various fields of
archaeology and history. In this connection it is appropriate to describe a
theory formulated at the end of the nineteenth century by the Romanian
scientist Alexander D. Xenopol (1847–1920), who considered the 'series of
causal succession' as the basis of historical science itself.

Although the themes of the Conference suggest a more limited and therefore a more cautious approach to mathematical applications in history, I
nevertheless hope that the current extent and complexity of historical
information, as well as developments in the technology for processing
information in all sciences, today favours a confrontation between historical
thought and the methods and instruments of modern mathematics.

Under these circumstances, history—as well as the other social sciences
which have previously been the object of increasingly thorough mathematical
elaboration (political economy, then sociology, linguistics, etc.)—will have
to formulate its own theory which should clearly express its *structure model*,
that is susceptible to modern information techniques and to the processing
of historical material by mathematical methods. For, in our opinion, if the
social sciences are to use certain mathematical procedures which depend on
the elaboration of a *mathematical model* of the relations and structures
included in the representation, analysis, or forecast, the characteristics of
these relations or of these structures must be previously established in the
most accurate and correct manner. Without this, the use of any mathematical
instrument, no matter how thoroughly it has been thought out, is bound to
remain purely formal, and the results of its application may be in practice
erroneous and devoid of significance. That is why the structure model of
history by the 'series of succession with causal linkage' elaborated by A. D.
Xenopol at the end of last century could be taken into account when
debating the contribution of mathematics in up to date historical research.
It is also the moment to determine at which stages in the scientific treatment
of history the contribution of mathematical methods would become possible,
useful, and even necessary.

We have already stressed that any mathematical approach in the field of
social sciences should be previously supported by a 'specific model' of the
structures and relations we wish to analyze or to express by means of the
mathematical instrument. If the political history of nations cannot be treated
exclusively on the basis of quantitative data, which provide the statistical

basis of economic or demographic history, it can nevertheless be considered from the point of view of relations ordered according to causal succession where the direction, the aims and the intensity of the acting forces can be represented by characteristics or properly assigned values—and thus be the object of mathematical procedures of comparative estimation (Onicescu 1970). In this connection it could be useful to recall the Romanian historian's theory of the 'series of causal successions' during these discussions.

Xenopol, professor of history at the Iasi University from 1883, member of the Romanian Academy from 1895, author of numerous scientific works— among them a *History of the Romanians in the Dacia of Trajan* (the first volumes of which, with a foreword by Alfred Rambaud, were issued in French in 1896), published in Paris in 1899 an important work on the *Fundamental principles of history* (Xenopol 1899). A few years later this was revised and completed under the title of the *Theory of History* (Xenopol 1908). As collaborator in the great French collection of universal history run by Lavisse and Rambaud, Xenopol was invited in 1901 to present his theories at the Institut de France—where, a few years later, he was elected corresponding member of the Academy of Moral and Political Sciences. In his time he was invited to give lectures at the Sorbonne as accepted professor on the *Theory of History* (Xenopol 1907). His fame within European historical science of his time was strongly related to the elaboration and documentation of this theory which we will present in its essential features at the very beginning of our study.

XENOPOL'S THEORY OF HISTORY

Xenopol justifies the necessity for research on the fundamentals of history by the fact that 'in spite of all the seriousness and depth which our colleagues have devoted to their studies, our science has not yet established its theory and its system' (Xenopol 1899). He sets himself the task of proving that 'history is a science in the full meaning of the word, possessing its general elements and a system of classifiable, true facts'. On the other hand, he recognizes that it can formulate only abstract laws on the manifestation of the forces contributing to its formation and 'no laws on the manifestation of the phenomena themselves', which would enable us to 'forecast facts concealed in the bosom of the future'. Likewise, 'the abstract laws of the sequence of historical facts originate only *series of phenomena or events* which are always unique and characteristic' (Xenopol 1908). This is the leading thought in his work. He considers that he has found the 'organizing principle of the science of history in the *historical series*, equivalent to that of a law for the sciences of repetition'. Although, in order to establish these 'great truths', he had had, by thorough researches, 'to create quite a system of principles related to the science of history', he considered that he had succeeded in 'setting an unequivocal basis to the theory of this science, which is after all only one of the two modes of conceiving the world: the successive mode versus the repetitive mode' (Xenopol 1908).

The general frameworks within which the successive facts of all sorts may be included, and consequently also the facts of history, are the series in which the individual facts of the development are linked (Xenopol 1906a). In these successive linkages we find the 'system of classifiable truths constituting the science'. Obviously, the smaller series are included in the larger ones. But this stacking of truths, superposed one upon the other, form a perfect 'scientific system', similar to the system of laws 'containing truths hierarchically arranged' (Xenopol 1906a).

The stuff history is made of is the 'historical fact'. According to Xenopol, 'to be historical, i.e. to serve as a basis to development, a fact should assume a social character; it should extend over a more or less numerous group of individuals'. 'In order that a fact, individual by its origin, may acquire a historical value, it should act upon the more or less deep masses of humanity or it should represent, under an individual appearance, interests or facts which are general' (Xenopol 1899). On the other hand, any historical fact, be it elementary or complicated, results from the action of a force, or of the combination of several forces through certain circumstances. But there is one more agent—chance—which is, however, no force, but only the fortuitous encounter of the action of several forces which, while able to originate facts and to interfere also in the development of the historical series, could not determine their formation (Xenopol 1908).

In order to acquire an exact understanding of the progress of history, Xenopol looks for the 'generalities of the succession' not in space but in time. For 'each series of successive phenomena finally leads to a result *into which it embodies itself*', each historical fact being always, by its general bearing, the result of a previous development. Thus, the final fact represents the condensed series, as the law of repetition represents the generalized fact. Each fact is the result of a series and each series should result in a historical fact. But, in order to realize the succession of the facts of history, we should study the linkage of these facts in the historical series. In each historical series we always find at work a whole complex of forces. In their action these forces are favoured or hindered, reciprocally or separately, so that the succession of the phenomena forming the historical series is the result of the qualitatively and quantitatively variously combined action of all these united forces, upon ever changing conditions (Xenopol 1908).

However, these successive linkages show a certain regularity which is revealed in the historical series by consistency in the development of the facts constituting them. Although the mode of action of the force, and consequently of the laws by which it manifests itself, is the same—even if it is embodied in continuously changing circumstances—it is only natural that the results of this action should vary continuously. Thus, the regularities of the succession will never have a universal character for the same order of phenomena. Each regularity will set up a particular historical series. Therefore, the sequence of regularities expressed by the historical series can only serve, in the context of forecasting 'to give a hint as to the direction which the future facts, *in themselves unknown*, will follow in their development' (Xenopol 1899).

Concerning the various modes of production of the historical series, by the action of principal or secondary forces, Xenopol suggests that they be classified in three categories: 1. Those which are due to the repetition of the action of the same force, without causal relation between the facts which constitute them; 2. Those which are due to this repetition, with causal linkage between the facts; 3. Those which are primarily due to the causal linkage of the facts, with the eventual repetition of the action of one force (Xenopol 1908).

CAUSALITIES, REGULARITIES, AND DYNAMICS

We have already stressed that, in the mind of Xenopol, the general element which gives history its scientific character is represented by the historical series constituted by a linkage of successive, and therefore dissimilar facts, interrelated by the bond of causality. 'It is this bond alone which draws the facts out of their isolation and makes of them a whole which acquires a more general character than the events of which they are made and which are subordinated to them' (Xenopol 1908). Thus the sequence of historical facts is always determined by the causality itself when the causes are due to chance. On the other hand, in this succession of cause to effect, series do not repeat themselves in time, they continue. So, we could not forecast the future phenomena of development, we could only have a glimpse of the direction that series will follow in the future (ibid). The French historian Gabriel Monod also agrees with this general theory; at the beginning of the twentieth century he wrote: 'History is an uninterrupted chain of causes and effects, and these causes which act upon human evolution present themselves in the shape of series, acting in parallel' (Monod 1910).

After the characteristics of the causality and regularity of the historical series, we will examine the even more important characteristics of its dynamism. In this respect, Xenopol considers that the historian must choose, in the period preceding the one we are concerned with, the series which will prolong their development in the period we have in view, in order to relate the future evolution to the one which has preceded it. Thus, 'instead of a static account of the basis upon which the historical structure we want to build should be erected, we will proceed to a dynamic account of the historical series which have acted and act upon the group of human beings concerned' (Xenopol 1906a). We can illustrate this part of his thesis by taking as an example the historical series expressing the principal aspects of the history of the Romanians since the nineteenth century, and which he had laid out as a web for the political action of Prince Alexander Ioan Cuza, whose double election in 1859 to the thrones of Moldavia and Walachia, against the will of most of the great European powers, had initiated the first union and consequently the independence of the Romanian State.

According to Xenopol, thirteen main series of facts continue to develop during this reign. First, the great series of the regeneration of the Romanian people and the series of the increase of French influence. As regards the events determined by the Prince's action in the international context, they group themselves in eight other series particular to this period, beginning with those concerning the restoration of the country's autonomy, and ending with the series of the deposition of the Prince and the accession of the foreign dynasty.

In the account given of this reign, the historian had first focused his attention 'upon a historical series foreign to the Romanian people, but which —being connected through a chance contact with the historical series of the *Romanian regeneration*—gave to the latter considerable support and transported, into the political arena, aspirations which the Romanians had until then barely dared to formulate (and with what precautions) and only in the field of ideas. This foreign series belongs to the history of France. It is partly due to the individual initiative of Napoleon III whom another historical series had made master of the destinies of France. In this series, the Crimean war which ended for France with the Treaty of Paris in 1856, was 'a simple accident for the historical development of the great Latin people but which had for the Romanians incalculable consequences from which finally sprang the actual condition of their country: the union, the foreign dynasty, independence . . .' (Xenopol 1906b). It was the same with the Italian War (1859) which enabled victorious France to make Austria recognize the double election of Prince Cuza, which in fact achieved the first stage of the unity of the Romanian Principalities.

In what concerns the great series of the *French influence*, its beginning was well marked from the middle of the eighteenth century by the introduction of French as a diplomatic language and the activity of the French secretaries around the Phanariot princes. Throughout the whole development of ideological and cultural relations, of the political currents born from the great French revolution of 1789, this series politically succeeded through the brilliant intervention of Napoleon III keeping, even after the fall of the second French empire and the accession to the throne of the Hohenzollerns in Romania, a deep influence on the culture and aspirations of the Romanian people: 'This series of the French influence constitutes an uninterrupted causal linkage, continued from fact to fact with a mathematical rigour, but without figures' (Xenopol 1913).

THE MATHEMATICAL OPTION IN HISTORICAL RESEARCH

So we have come, by the words in which the Romanian scientist expressed himself, to the problem we are concerned with to-day—the relations between mathematics and history. In our opinion, it is a question of trying to unite historical theory to mathematical thinking, to confront the dynamic presentation in time of a field of events constituted by the historical series with the logic of mathematical reasoning, with symbols, with the instruments and the procedures of its calculations and its representations.

But, first of all, is this cooperation—not to say collusion—possible, useful or necessary? This question should not be put to mathematics. The penetration of its methods into the fundamentals, and in the up-to-date application of so many sciences, should exempt it from wanting to play any new part. It is to history and historians that we have to put it—for it is in the very conditions of contemporary research and historical synthesis that the elements and dimensions of the problem should be found. We have already stated this at the beginning of this study, stressing the absolute necessity of establishing previously, through theory, the structural models of the various fields of history which are able to represent in the most complete, correct and significant way the ordering and relations of its scientific system. Therefore, it is the orientation and the quality of these 'specific history models' themselves that should show us, by their structure and dynamism, how relevant they are to up-to-date mathematical models, under existing conditions of scientific research.

Already, at the end of last century, while approaching the theory of history and attempting to constitute its 'scientific character' through the historical series, Xenopol drew attention to the 'severe dangers threatening the research worker because of the accumulation of works in each field of study making very difficult and nearly impossible knowledge of all that has been written on a subject'. He drew from this the very modern conclusion of 'the risk of sinking under the too heavy burden of knowledge *assembled by time*'. The enormous bulk of information—books, studies, articles, documents—which our century has since poured forth in the field of historical knowledge, could not be met by the old techniques of chronology and classification. But the discovery of the electronic computer and the perfecting of this cybernetic application for the collecting, storage and elaborate retrieval of documentation, should allow historical science to-day to stand up to the vertiginous flow of information rising up from all continents, in space and time. In order to determine the requirements and resources of the computer in the service of historical researches, we have to establish a programme, a language and finally a mathematical transposition, necessary for the elaborate processing of information by the machine. In our opinion, this would be the first logical and useful step in a mathematical approach to history.

On the other hand, historical science implies, besides information and its criticism, several—essentially successive—phases of historical exposition and interpretation, in time and space, of comparison and synthesis and finally of a certain forecasting, concerning at least the direction and intensity of the great current historical movements. If the 'historical series' is circumscribed in time not only by the chronology of its dates, but also—and mainly—by the dynamics of its facts, the historian will have to make a reasoned selection of them in order to set out fully the sense, energy and finality of the given series. Once the specific model of this 'historical subassembly' has been judiciously and correctly established by the historian himself—who has also to assign the orders of succession, relation and even value to the elements and ratios of the structure under study—and if the multitude of these 'subassemblies' and of their particular characteristics requires in the trials of comparative synthesis a treatment which not only exceeds the means of representation of statistics, of historical geography and even of up-to-date graphical plotting—then it will be inevitable to resort to the mathematicians in order to make clear and to simplify the problems by means of the most adequate mathematical instruments. At this second level, which can be usefully attained only if it corresponds to an obvious requirement of comparative analysis and historical synthesis, the utilization of mathematical methods becomes compulsory. These are the only ones able to solve in the shortest possible time and with the highest accuracy (clearly in the spirit of the historical structure problem previously established, and according to the programme processed by the computer) the bulk of data and hypotheses covering the objectives of research. The selection of the mathematical procedures will only have to follow upon the structure and conditions of the relevant historical model and the solution required from it. Until this structure is established in a validly coherent and verifiable manner, it seems to us untimely to make a choice or even to discuss, comparatively, the possibilities of applying such mathematical methods. That is why the theory of historical succession series with causal links, formulated previously by Xenopol, could serve as a starting basis to actual discussions of a mathematical approach to history, not only in relation to its information technique, but also for some important fundamental problems.

One of the hardest of these is forecasting. But, considering the dynamic character of the historical series, the latter is better suited than other theoretical series, if not to predict, at least to supply a hint of the actual direction and intensity of the forces and great currents of history. Although Xenopol himself puts us on our guard about the changing situations and the effects of chance which very often hinder the regularity of the historical series—it appears nevertheless that its development has not been interrupted; indeed the contrary is the case. On the other hand, the fortuitous element which was considered in the past as being above human knowledge is nowadays encompassed, due to the enormous advance of modern mathematics in computation systems in the science of probability. The contribution of mathematics to the approach to the third stage of historical research is obvious—and we will be able to select from among the most complex and most versatile procedures of probability calculations.

But, should we, to this end, abandon the traditional method for the study or the account of history, and compel the historian—like the economist, or even the linguist or the sociologist of to-day—to integrate himself in the mathematical option? This subject has recently been opened to discussion. Without further persisting in the old methods of the 'current language', the problem was to find if another representation—somewhat different from the language of mathematical symbols—would not be not only necessary, but also sufficient for the documentation, analysis and systematization, and finally for the complete study of modern history. The graphical method suggested by M. Jacques Bertin has been considered, as well as the discussion about the merits of graphics or of mathematics in relation to a preference for the processing of information (Bertin 1969).

Without going into the details of this method described in a recent book about graphic semiology (Bertin 1965), we have to remember that the graphical system by which it was considered possible to represent—and thence to give a solution to numerous problems, including those of historical order— implies 'its own means and laws, which are therefore different from the laws of other systems', among which are those of 'language and mathematics', the graphical representation being the 'transcription into the graphical system of the signs of thought, of information' (Bertin 1965, 1969).

However, we will add that mathematical representation (which gives at the same time a code of visual signals which are its own, but also a code for structure relations expressed in highly elaborated formulas) has a much deeper bearing on the human mind, because it defines properties and ratios which exceed the possibilities of graphic construction, without considering additionally the electronic processing of information which implies necessarily a mathematical computer programming apparatus. It would be enough to mention at the same time that, in the Soviet Union, electronic computers have been used in studies upon the rural life in Russia in the nineteenth century (Kovalcenko *et al.* 1965) and that a recent book, treating the mathematical analysis of social facts—the sequence of which is very similar to historical facts—comes necessarily to the conclusion that 'the determination of causal structures requires that mathematical formalism be used' (Boudon 1967). R. Boudon writes on this subject that in sociological research 'as in any other science', mathematical formalism 'takes the shape of an essential heuristic function: that of relieving intuition when it is incapable of perceiving all the consequences of a group of propositions' (Padioleau 1969).

In order to analyze sociological eventualities, it has been necessary to establish in what measure a dependent variable is explained by a series of independent variables. To this end, it has been considered that a causal order can be represented in the shape of a system of recurrent equations and that it can be mathematically demonstrated that the coefficient of the equation can be interpreted as metrical values, estimating the intensity of the reciprocal effects (*ibid*). Causality, the essential element in a scientific theory of history based on the structure model of the 'sequence series', thus assesses its actuality and its importance for the mathematical approach of sociological relations which, precisely in this field, are most related to the dynamics of historical fact.

But the essence of the historical series itself seems to become clear again. We find a striking example in the 'similarity of the successions of historical situations', the theme of an important chapter in the book of Bertin, already mentioned. He recalls having built a whole series of graphical messages, 'as for instance, to allow the visual recall of this succession of historical situations'. The listing of some of this 'succession of historical situations', as well as their structure and their content, unmistakably resemble Xenopol's historical series (Bertin 1965).

But this similarity does not stop only at the methodology of general constructions. For the history of France, in particular in series 3 (restoration of order) and 4 (French preponderance)—according to Jacques Bertin—one can find the same methodology and, almost word for word, the same facts, with the same causal succession linkage as the one laid out by Xenopol in the *French influence* series and especially in that of the 'political action of Napoleon III'. This almost perfect similarity confirms, in our opinion, the consistency and actuality of the theory of historical series, formulated with an extreme accuracy from the very beginning of the twentieth century by the Romanian historian A. D. Xenopol, as well as its capacity to serve the new techniques of scientific research.

ACTUALIZATION OF HISTORICAL SERIES

However, we have to stress that at that time, a certain 'mathematization' in the social sciences had already started. First in political economy (Cournot

1838, Jevons 1871, Karl Menger and particularly the work of Walras 1900). The final edition of Walras' capital work on the fundamental principles of mathematical economy was being published at about the same time as 'The fundamental principles of history' of Alexander Xenopol. In sociology, an essay of the Romanian mathematician Spiru Haret on mathematical representations, especially of mechanical order, for the study of the 'social problem', was soon to appear (Haret 1910). But these new procedures, most promising for scientific research, are not explicitly reflected in the work of Xenopol. Striving to determine the objectives and structures of the 'Historical series of causal succession' as a basis for his theory and his method, he did not contribute to the progress of research in this other field where his logical mind—formed also by certain mathematical studies—would have allowed him to approach successfully the new scientific methods of the present century.

However, by constructing a theory of the 'historical series' he had already succeeded not only in defining a logical structure for the systematization and the development of historical facts, but also in determining a typology of the linking of these facts, which is nearly identical to the system suggested nowadays in France for the graphical expression of historical knowledge. The 'historical succession series', by its logic of causality, certainly constitutes a 'structure model' for the actual treatment of the development of historical science, in its ensemble of problems, times and geographical spaces.

This model, specific to history itself, could be called in to support an information system for the collecting and cybernetic synthesis (by means of programming) of different historical data. In a second, more thorough stage of the mathematically based electronic processing of general and special information, the model (or the collection of models of the parallel or convergent 'historical series') could lead to some comparative static and dynamic analysis of the historical facts—within the frame of countries and continents—as well as to their integration in the models of evolution and structure at world level. There we would also find the thought of Xenopol who already saw, in the final development of his system 'a universal series which should relate and include all these partial series in its immense bosom'.

Thus, at the current stage of development, when an increasing range of information is being processed electronically, the 'historical series', because of its own structure, could serve as an approach to the mathematization of history and as a methodological basis of what could be called *historiometry*.

REFERENCES

Bertin, J. (1965) *Sémiologie graphique. Les diagrammes—Les réseaux—Les cartes.* Paris: Gauthier–Villars.

Bertin, J. (1969) Graphique et mathématique. Généralisation du traitement graphique de l'information. *Annales Economies Société Civilisation,* **24,** 70–101.

Boudon, R. (1967) *L'analyse mathématique des faits sociaux.* Paris: Plon.

Cournot, A. A. (1838) *Récherches sur les principes mathématiques de la théorie des richesses.* Paris.

Haret, Sp. C. (1910) *Mécanique sociale.* Paris: Gauthier–Villars.

Jevons, S. (1871) *The Theory of Political Economy.* London: Macmillan.

Kovalcenko, I. D. et Ustinov, V. A. (1965) Les calculateurs électroniques appliqués aux études historiques (la vie rurale en Russie au XIX-ième siècle). *Annales Economies Société Civilisation*, **20**, 1128–49.

Menger, K. (1888) Zur Theorie des Kapitals. *Jahrbücher für Nazionaloekonomie und Statistik*, **17**.

Monod, G. (1908) *De la méthode dans les sciences* (volume collectif), pp. 324–44. Paris.

Onicescu, O. (1970) Procedee de estimare comparativă a unor obiecte purtătoare de mai multe caracteristici. *Revista de statistică*, **4**. Bucureşti.

Padioleau, J. G. (1969) L'analyse mathématique des faits sociaux. *Annales Economies Société Civilisation*, **24**, 947–8.

Walras, L. (1900) *Eléments d'économie politique pure*. Edition définitive, Paris-Lausanne.

Xenopol, A. D. (1896) *Histoire des Roumains de la Dacia-Trajana depuis les origines jusqu' à l'Union des Principautés en 1859*. Avec une préface par Alfred Rambaud. Paris: Ernest Leroux.

Xenopol, A. D. (1899) *Les principes fondamentaux de l'histoire*. Paris: Ernest Leroux.

Xenopol, A. D. (1906a) La notion de valeur en histoire. *Revue de Synthèse historique*. Paris.

Xenopol, A. D. (1906b) Le règne du prince Alexandre Jean (Cuza) traité d'après la méthode des séries historiques. *Revue de synthèse historique*. Paris.

Xenopol, A. D. (1907) *La théorie de l'histoire*. Cours professé à la Sorbonne 1907–1908. Iasi.

Xenopol, A. D. (1908) *La théorie de l'histoire*. Deuxième édition des principes fondamentaux de l'histoire. Paris: Ernest Leroux.

Xenopol, A. D. (1910) De la méthode dans les sciences et dans l'histoire. *Revue Internationale de l'Enseignement*. Paris.

Xenopol, A. D. (1913) La causalité dans la série historique. *Revue de synthèse historique*. Paris.

History

Thomas H. Hollingsworth
Mathematical methods with historical data: a note of caution

In this paper, we consider the purposes of certain types of historical research and how far the powerful methods of mathematics are applicable to them. In particular, the use of cluster analysis on the data of old censuses is discussed, with an illustration of methods not using a computer. We conclude with suggestions that may lead to useful results.

INTRODUCTION

Whereas all the various sciences attempt to learn about the real world, mathematics is really a branch of philosophy which tries to co-ordinate the findings of the sciences and to help in the interpretation of data. Amongst sciences, however, there is a sharp distinction between the experimental sciences and the historical sciences. When the data that can be used are not selected by the observer but are whatever happens to be available, extra difficulties of interpretation arise. The risk of selectivity in the observations through an unsuspected cause cannot be ignored, and errors of observation are all the worse in that every piece of data is unique and so no replication is possible, and spoiled observations cannot be remade.

Nevertheless, in at least one such 'historical' science, astronomy, mathematical methods of great complexity have been used with striking success, and for a very long time. We are now at the threshold of a new era in inquiry, when some analogous advance in archaeology and in history in general may be anticipated.

The first stage, of course, is to collect data. If we have a body of knowledge to rely upon, it is fairly easy to guess what to observe, and indeed how to measure it. The main difficulty is to be sure what is relevant and what is not. At an early stage in the development of a science, all the information must be collected that tradition or hunch suggests may matter and which at the same time we are capable of measuring. This last often excludes many interesting phenomena if the research is historical in character, since presumably much of the evidence is lost.

The second stage through which the discipline must pass is that of classification. The analogy with biology is obvious here, and the influence of taxonomy on cluster analysis is clear. But while the biologist wishes to perfect his classifications by the use of numerical methods, and the archaeologist to confirm his suspicions by clustering his artifacts with the help of a computer, the social historian is hard pressed to produce even a working outline of social classes at a distant date, since our knowledge of class structure in the present is largely intuitive and not empirical. If we can successfully classify people in some way, we shall have a grouping that moreover has a precise meaning; one set of individuals will differ from another according to objective criteria. However, we can remark even here that a classification into r clusters rarely means much to us in practice if $r > 10$. The mind is not comfortable with too many classes and generally simplifies them into about 4 or 5 only.

The third stage to which a science must aspire if it is to be more than mere amateur fact-hunting is the formulation of laws. These need be no more than a concise way of summarizing the facts that have been discovered. They will have predictive value in a non-historical science, but if we are interested in phenomena that change at a relatively fast rate we shall need super-laws to explain them, and sub-laws to explain the phenomena of any one epoch. The associations found by classifying the data are the basis of what laws we find. We want, in fact, both to get clusters of data and to discover which characteristics really determine the clustering.

Although the older sciences have not obviously passed through these stages, they are logically necessary, and we can hope to follow this sequence in the newer sciences, so as to develop them most quickly. For instance, three statistical techniques, that all attempt much the same thing, have appeared: factor analysis, chiefly used in psychology; principal components, widely used in industry; and cluster analysis, which has come to the fore through biologists' use of it in taxonomy. The widespread availability of electronic computers has enormously increased the possibilities of applying such methods in all problems of classification, which in turn is the basis of the laws that we hope to discover in these new sciences. The first two are strongly related, and the object of all three is to discover what interrelations are in a set of data consisting of n objects, each with k observable characteristics. The choice of both n and k can, however, be rather arbitrary, depending on a balance of zeal between collection and analysis of data.

Mathematicians are tempted to simplify scientific research to the point where all sciences are the same, and all are applications of the same statistical methods. One has often heard the terms 'plots' and 'treatments', for instance, used in an analysis of variance where there are really neither plots nor treatments present. This is to be deplored, since the differences between sciences are in some ways very important. Sociology, archaeology, demography, medicine, and astronomy, for instance, may all seem to raise problems of cluster analysis, but the same computer program may not do for all of them. We need to ponder our preconceptions about the nature of the observations and our expectations of them before choosing a line of attack.

The main difficulty in working with a census, which is always historical data in the sense that getting any further data on the same population is impracticable, is in fact to cluster the data before any analysis is begun. It is all very well to deal with 200 individuals, each having been measured for a dozen characteristics; this is meaningless compared with a census of several million people, each measurable for a large number of characteristics. It would take all the statisticians in the world to consider the tables that a computer might produce of cross-classifications, even without any further analysis at all. It is not at all obvious what characteristics should be studied, nor even how many. Is it true that the more we study the better (provided our computer can cope with them)? Moreover, characters of the population are really non-numeric. Occupation, for instance, is normally available in several hundred different headings. Geographical location is best given as a pair of co-ordinates, producing further difficulties in analysis. The correct classifications to group the data in, however, are exactly the problem, yet we do not want to see a dendrogram of the millions of individuals in order to see how they interrelate, supposing that a computer could draw it for us. A small scale analysis of not too many characteristics is less likely to go wrong. There are many historical censuses that could be analyzed along the lines we describe, and not only from the nineteenth and twentieth centuries. For Tuscany in the fifteenth century, for instance, some kind of cluster analysis might lead to a deeper understanding of the social structure than is at present possible.

ILLUSTRATION OF USING HAND-METHODS OF CLUSTERING

A study is now in progress of the population of the county of Ayrshire in Scotland at the 1951 census. Using a 10% sample of householders from just this one county, we still have some 8,000 records. This means that the mere tabulation of the data is a major problem. As a preliminary study, we tried to classify the occupations according to similarity in the distribution of number of children. Only those whose wives were present and under the age of 50 at the time of the 1951 census were included in this family size data, but the total number of cases was still almost 4,000. The object was to study social variables in terms of demographic variables instead of the other way round. In order to simplify matters, some initial grouping of occupations from the original list was also inevitable. It was done intuitively, but we were still left with 75 groups instead of the 5 or 13 that the British census normally was using at that time in its official tabulations. Since we had no clear understanding of the problems that would be involved, we began by clustering by hand methods, using only 40 of the occupational groups in the first instance. Ayrshire was chosen because it embraces a wide range of occupational types, with some farming, fishing, mining, manufacturing, commerce, and so on. It is probably the most representative county in the whole of Scotland in this sense.

Since the techniques were developed before we had heard much of the more general interest in cluster analysis, they may show how one tries to operate when there is the opportunity to control every stage of the analysis. A computer may lead to exciting new groupings, but if they are *too* new, one might suspect the technique, while if they are too familiar one has not achieved very much. We therefore believe that simple hand calculations are preferable whenever practicable. The first step was to calculate the proportions of each occupational group that had 0, 1, 2, or 3 children. This accounted for about 90% of most of the groups, and if the four were treated as independent factors it seemed likely that most of the family size patterns would be reflected by them.

It would take too long to describe the process in full detail, but the main stages were as follows. First, the two most important factors of the four were guessed to be the percentages with 0 and with 1 children. The whole 40 observed groups were split into quintiles according to each factor, thus ignoring possible influences of non-uniformity of the frequency distributions. In the absence of all prior expectations, this seems a fair thing to do. The 40 occupational groups only used 22 of the 25 provisional classes generated, and 10 of the classes each contained only a single occupational group. The second stage was to assign each of the 10 single groups to one or another of the 12 larger classes. The order in which they were considered depended on their position in the two-way table. As a criterion of closeness, the sum of the moduli of the distances from the mean of a class along each of the four axes was taken. This distance metric has the effect of not giving as much weight to the more remote points in a single dimension as the more usual square root of the sum of squares would give. Since all the observations were, in fact, proportions of the same populations, this seemed realistic as well as simpler to calculate. We thus had 12 provisional clusters.

The third stage was to determine which point lay farthest from the centre of each cluster in turn, observing the same ordering as before. This outlier was then tested against all the other clusters, although for several of them the test was only formally necessary. If it lay nearer the centre of some other cluster than it did to the rest of its own cluster, it was transferred. In the case of two-member clusters, if either member (both were treated as outliers) became attached to another cluster during this process, the remaining member was immediately assigned to its nearest neighbouring cluster. The reason for this was merely that the clustering was for convenience of further analysis, and remote outliers, which might strictly require a cluster of their own consisting of only one member, had to be discouraged to the point of their absolute prevention. A final pattern of 4 wild cases and 36 regular ones was not wanted.

One cluster of the 12 disappeared at this third stage, but since the original grouping had been in terms of only two factors and not the full four, a considerable amount of re-allocation took place. Repeating the process, a fourth stage affected only 3 of the 11 clusters at all, however. It would possibly have been sensible to examine all the members of a cluster as well as the outliers in stages three and four, but the main job of getting roughly the best clusters in 4 dimensions was surely now done. The fifth stage was to calculate all the distances between the means of clusters (in practice, only 20 of the 55 pairs really needed any serious examination) and to merge that pair of clusters whose means were closest. The combined group was immediately tested for its outlier, which proved to be nearer another cluster mean than to the combined cluster mean in which it had found itself. The new outlier, of the reduced cluster, however, was evidently a true member of it. Again, it would have been conceivable to apply the process to all the existing clusters in turn, since they now had a somewhat different set of neighbouring clusters that might possibly steal their outliers.

In practice, since there were still 10 clusters and the whole object was to reduce their number to about five—purely because the mind can readily grasp only about five different entities at once—the sixth stage was to merge the two clusters that were now closest. None of the members of the combined cluster proved better placed in any other cluster. Repeating the process once again, we reduced the number of clusters to 8 at the seventh stage, of which the latest merger produced a cluster of as many as 12 individuals. However, one of these 12 at once joined a different cluster.

Intuition now told us to go through the clusters again, as the eighth stage of the analysis, having first arranged them in order of their size on the first factor, childlessness. We allowed the whole cluster to be examined, and not merely the ostensible black sheep of the cluster, and also reconsidered a cluster as soon as it had lost one member to see if any more members should be removed. The result was remarkable. The first cluster chosen, a 3-member one, lost all its members in turn to the same cluster. The second, a 4-member cluster, similarly lost all its members—although to a different cluster. This reduced the number of clusters to only 6, and one of the four not yet affected lost three of its four members to one of the remaining three. The last member of this cluster, however, did not go the way of the rest but joined one of the only 2 clusters not already altered at this eighth stage. Two further transfers were quickly spotted, and having now achieved five clusters, we though it worthwhile to examine them to see if they made any intuitive sense. Random variation in the fairly small numbers of members in each occupational group must prevent very neat relationships from appearing, but it was hoped that we would have a pattern that made some kind of sense.

The first cluster comprised only 5 members: building labourers, navvies, charwomen, manufacturing labourers, and general labourers. This was highly distinctive, since none of the other 35 occupational groups could be called labourers. The remaining four clusters did not conform so well to our preconceptions about social groups. If we designate the labourers as cluster A, being the most fertile, then cluster B (the next most fertile) consisted of 12 occupational groups: industrial managers, steam engine men, rail traffic men, carriers, busmen, small commercial men, food sellers (not elsewhere specified), butchers, roundsmen, storemen, low grade workers, and unspecified occupations. Cluster C, with almost the same level of fertility as cluster B, but fewer childless families, consisted of five groups: carpenters, transport managers, lorry drivers, chemists, tobacconists, and miscellaneous service workers. Cluster D comprised 9 groups: bakers, painters, restaurateurs, members of learned professions, teachers, scientists, policemen and firemen, general domestics and cost clerks. Cluster E comprised 8 groups: woodworkers (excluding carpenters), building foremen, skilled building workers, administrators, commercial travellers, grocers, shopkeepers (not elsewhere specified), engineers, and clerks (not elsewhere specified).

Many of these clusterings will be attributable to different ages of their members, different ages at marriage, and different proportions with wives under 50 at the time of the census. However, D seemed to include people with certain special skills, whereas E, although also clearly skilled, perhaps comprised people with talents at dealing with others rather than technical qualifications. The large B was more industrial or commercial than the others (the main industrial occupations were, however, amongst the 35 occupational groups that were not included in this preliminary analysis), and c had a touch of the individual worker about it.

This is obviously only a preliminary analysis. It is important that the occupational groups used should be roughly equal in size, or else the effect of sample errors will mean that more weight in a cluster should be given to some of the groups. The next step will be to extend the analysis to the whole range of occupations. After that, the other factors influencing fertility should be looked at. The ultimate objective is to determine which groups of occupations make best sense in analyzing the characteristics of the population. The study should clearly be extended to other dates and to larger parts of the country also. It is by building up our knowledge of empirical social structure rather than by trying to find it by a single grand computer program that we are most likely to avoid making serious errors on the way.

An interesting approach would be to subcluster any persistent clusters that appeared regularly. We might produce 5 clusters as above from 4 characteristics, and then analyze each cluster using 4 other characteristics. This strictly requires, however, both a clustering of the observations and a grouping of the characteristics, because there are clearly many ways in which the sets of 4 characteristics might be chosen. Yet only by such an approach can we hope to unravel such complex situations as undoubtedly commonly exist. It is analogous to interaction effects, which a global method might easily miss.

DISCUSSION

The main limitations of the purely mathematical approach can be listed. First, too much data (as from a census) can easily strain computer capacity. We do not know how many objects need to be studied in order to show us new laws, nor how many of their characteristics to try to study. Second, the trees that a taxonomist would draw of the relationships between genera and species are probably meaningless in a sociological example. The existing social classes did not obviously evolve from single classes in the past, but are the results of extinctions and mergers of older classes, as new distinctions between persons have become important. Third, the main need for classification is less ambitious than the ultimate goal of understanding the very structure of our material. Instead, we are chiefly concerned with tidying the data up to make it more palpable. Fourth, numerical methods are not very helpful in dealing with qualitative factors—such as occupation—where literally hundreds of possibilities can occur. Although this problem can be solved in mathematical terms it is by no means peripheral in social analysis and any computer program for a cluster analysis that cannot deal with several dozens of non-numerical possibilities for a factor might as well not be used for the kind of problem we have in mind. Moreover, we can easily invent new possible factors that might prove important. Fifth, there is always a serious risk in historical work that a large number of observations may be missing, and that others may be mistaken. How many can be missing before it matters? What happens if further objects are subsequently discovered?

32

For instance, the archaeologist may not be sure what has been stolen and what has been twisted or faded before his spade found a group of objects. A large proportion of such cases is not usually considered in mathematical statistics, but some such non-random errors are always probable in historical science. Demographic equivalents would be people excluded from a census (such as fugitives from justice or recent immigrants) and ages given wrong through bias and exaggeration. We cannot be sure that the surviving records are in any sense the key to the totality from which they came. If cluster analysis were a wholly satisfactory technique, it might lead to a detection of all outliers that were sufficiently remarkable, but we have no agreement on how important it is that difficult cases should be correctly classified. Sixth, as our illustration has shown, there is no obvious method of producing clusters. In our illustration, we have not assumed a Euclidean distance function. Even if distance is agreed upon, should one try to assign an individual to the nearest cluster at the expense of getting all clusters equally compact? The latter will mean that at the centre of a multivariate distribution there will often be a rather large cluster, with smaller ones at the edges. The former, however, means that no tree is possible because as one reduces from r clusters to $r-1$ some of the new cluster will generally have to be hived off to other clusters. Seventh, the significance tests for cluster analysis that are beginning to be developed overlook the question of what they are for. Just as in geometry we like to draw a two-dimensional diagram, so we are constrained possibly by the fact that four—or five—colours are needed to distinguish areas on an ordinary map to want four or five groups, whether they are 'significant' or not.

CONCLUSIONS

We suggest that the same set of data should, for the time being, be subjected to as many different approaches as practicable. We should then be able to assess which methods lead to support for, or disagreement with, existing knowledge—bearing in mind the possibility that existing knowledge is sometimes very inadequately based. We should also see which methods lead to unsuspected relationships, since only they can have real value. We could try, for instance, separating the data into two parts (sex springs to the social scientist's mind as an obvious division), and see whether similar sub-clustering is suitable for each or not.

The likelihood is that different approaches will prove to suit different subjects. This will be inconvenient for everyone, as it will almost certainly mean that we all have to do our own work and cannot draw very much on someone else's theory. But if this is inevitable, it is at least better than blindly following a technique devised to solve a different problem than one's own. The purpose of the intended classification must be clarified at the outset; in particular we should be sure whether we want knowledge in general, simplicity of description, or help towards the formulation of new hypotheses.

We believe that mathematics is often too powerful for the data as existing. This is often the difficulty in econometrics, for instance; and factor analysis implies that our original conceptions of psychological factors are so far wrong that at best we can only explain the unknown in terms of unfamiliarly located transformations of the basic data. Cluster analysis, properly used, could avoid these difficulties. At the same time, we still have to ensure that the data are not seriously in error.

History

J. Kahk
Computer analysis of socio-economic development in Estonia in the
first half of the nineteenth century

The introduction of Marxist methods into the social sciences can be regarded
as a turning point in their development and relations to natural sciences.
Marx and Engels were convinced that the social processes can be studied
with the same materialistic methods as the processes taking place in nature.
Describing his method of study, Marx (*Das Kapital*, **I**, 10) wrote that from
his standpoint 'the evolution of the economic formation of society is viewed
as a process of natural history . . .'. In the course of their researches into
many aspects of socio-economic development, Marx and Engels considered
the statistical material at their disposal as a succession of figures, and eagerly
followed the connections that revealed themselves between these. Marx,
Engels, and Lenin emphasized that in society we have to deal with a rapidly
and radically changing community—with a phenomenon that makes the
study of social processes extremely complicated. In spite of that, some
methods used in the study of more complicated phenomena of nature can
be used to a certain degree in analyzing social phenomena as well.

History is an excellent field for comparative mathematical analysis. An
historian works all the time in three-dimensional space: he can compare
processes in different geographical settings (a horizontal section) and
compare the events of the near and remote past (a vertical section).

In our day, computers make it possible for a group of research workers
(or even one person) to grasp and analyze the entire available material
(going into the most minute detail) over a wide field of historical events,
despite great difficulties in putting all the theoretical possibilities into practice.
First of all, it is essential to find means of rationalizing the stage of collecting
the material, which at present consumes about 90 per cent of the time
devoted to research. It would be absurd to try to measure quantitatively all
phenomena in social life.

The first half of the nineteenth century, and especially its second quarter,
in the history of tzarist Russia, and particularly of Estonia, offers many
interesting aspects as a period when an out-of-date system of feudal agriculture had to retreat before the modern capitalist system (which, in the
Baltic area, retained many of its feudal traits until the October Revolution).
At the same time it is one of the first periods from which we have enough
statistical data to undertake detailed mathematical analysis, using computers.
In this period of transition the pace and direction of many social processes
undergo a change. With the help of correlation and regression analysis we
can study these changes.

Using the program developed by the Institute of Cybernetics of Estonia, we have calculated the linear equations of general trends of the production of grain and potatoes in Estonia for the last decades of feudal and the first decades of capitalist formation (1840–1880). It has become evident that production of crops for the market soared. In Northern Estonia the potato was used as raw material in the vodka distilleries owned by the landlords. (The equations for the trend-lines of the net-product of potatoes on the landlords acreage for 1842–1859, $y = 217 + 1.6x$ and for 1860–1880 $y = 430 + 42x$; on the peasants acreage, $y = 104 + 1.9x$ and $y = 252 + 21x$ respectively).

In the manorial system (*Gutswirtschaft*), which was typical in the Baltic provinces, one can establish a difference between two conflicting factors in the development of peasant farms: economic growth and the pressure exerted by various feudal obligations, first of all, in the form of obligatory serf labour. One of the most interesting theoretical problems of the last decades of the feudal system (the first half of the nineteenth century) concerns the relationship between these two factors: were they in balance, or were the forces of oppression and economic decline prevailing? In the first case, that is, if the two factors were balanced—there should be a clear correlation between the indices of economic growth and feudal obligations. To find an answer to this question we have carried out a computer analysis of various data from the period concerned.

Using the mean data of South Estonia (Ligi 1968) from the end of the seventeenth century until the beginning of the nineteenth, relating to man-labour (X_1) and draught-animals (X_2) on peasant farms, and to the extension of manor-fields (z) in respective estates, we come to the conclusion that there existed quite a strong correlation between z and X_1

$$z = 1.289 X_1 - 42.261 \qquad R(z : X_1) = 0.967 \ .$$

The correlation between the indices that show how the peasants' farms were provided with draught-animals (X_2) and those of the general amount of feudal obligations [natural and labour] (y) in respective estates was somewhat weaker, but still exists.

$$y = 4.744 X_2 + 17.174 \qquad R(y : X_2) = 0.605$$

In all those analyses we used mean and summarized data and, as has already been pointed out, this could have given us exaggeratedly strong correlations (Blalook 1964). On the other hand, using concrete data concerning individual peasant farms, we come to the conclusion, as far as we could ascertain it for North Estonia at the end of the seventeenth and the beginning of the nineteenth century (Kahk 1962), that the correlation between the available amount of draught-animals on peasant holdings and the general amount of labour obligations (y) was quite weak: for the end of the seventeenth century

$$y = 57.815 X_2 + 123.416 \qquad R(y : X_2) = 0.343;$$

for the beginning of the nineteenth century

$$y = 49.853 X_2 + 330.831 \qquad R(y : X_2) = 0.387 \ .$$

We have therefore formed quite an interesting hypothesis. The impression that the growth of feudal obligations during the eighteenth century was balanced and supported by the process of economic growth of peasant holding is only an abstract of principal tendencies. In real life one cannot see such a correlation and balance, since a majority of peasants was suffering from disproportionately high obligations, whereas, at the same time, others had temporarily and casually achieved a better balance between the economic strength of their households and the pressure of feudal obligations. The general tendencies show the abstract arising from the impoverishment of the majority and the relatively good standing of the minority.

In carrying out these analyses, we used a computer program worked out at the Institute of Cybernetics, which gave us not only linear equations, but also equations of higher degrees. Since they did not give us stronger correlations or a clearer picture of relationship, we have limited ourselves to the use of linear equations.

We were able to collect data from the eighteen-forties about the yields of rye in the fields of 130 landlords and in those of their peasant-tenants. As a rule, the fertility was higher on the lands of the landlords—about 4·5, whereas on those of the peasants it was from 2·5 to 3·5. But more detailed analysis suggested that these arithmetical means do not reflect a prevailing and functional relationship between the yields: it cannot be said that the latter are always significantly higher than the former; the one cannot be determined by the other. When we analyzed the collected data, using regression analysis by computer, we concluded that the correlation between the two rows was quite weak, as was the regression equation (Kahk 1969).

In our opinion, the mathematical results justify a conclusion (albeit hypothetical): in modern agriculture, where advantages of scale have been clearly established, one naturally expects that higher yields in larger farms, as compared with the yields in small holdings, show up as a general relationship, in a form of high correlation. The weak coefficients of correlation, on the contrary, demonstrate that the higher yields of the landlords' fields are of feudal origin; they prove that the best soils were in the hands of the feudals, but, at the same time, their yields as well as those of the peasants' fields, depended on such irregular factors as the climate and the structure of the soils.

To strengthen this hypothesis we have to find comparative data from the period of capitalism. Unfortunately we could not find such data about individual estates of Estonia, but we were able to analyze the mean data about the yields on landlords' and peasants' fields in different provinces of the Russian empire. We carried out comparative correlation analyses, with the data from 1842–1850, of 43 provinces (collected and published by I. Kovalchenko) and from 1881–1896 about 35 provinces (Kovalchenko 1959), and established that in the first case the correlation coefficient was 0·44, and in the second case 0·86. The coefficient was strengthened by using the mean (and not the individual data), but nevertheless it was much stronger in the period of capitalism.

As a general result of feudal oppression part of the peasant holdings suffered economic decline, and were abandoned by their tenants. Until recently we had no sufficiently reliable statistical data about the number of abandoned peasant holdings in Estonia in the first half of the nineteenth century. We made an attempt to get this information from the taxroll of

1816 and 1850, with entries by name, not only of all peasants living on *estate* lands, but also of the peasant holdings where they were living. As we had no hope of studying twice over (for 1816 and 1850) the data of all (approximately 6,000) holdings in 600 baronial estates, we carried out a process of random sampling, based on a table of random numbers. Two samples (42 and 49 estates) gave us identical results, but with excessive ranges of error. Therefore we took a third larger sample of 95 manors and, as a result, came to the conclusion that, with a 95 per cent probability, the proportion of abandoned peasant holdings in North Estonia increased during the first half of the nineteenth century, but not to a very great extent; (in 1816, the abandoned holdings were 8–14 per cent of the total, and in 1850—15–21). At the same time, as a result of a general but slow growth of population, the number of peasant holdings did not decrease (in 1816, in the 95 manors of the sample, there were 3,358 holdings where peasants were living, and in 1850 their number was 3,389).

We can assume that even in the second quarter of the nineteenth century there existed distinct elements of the future national market, although the process of its formation was not yet finished. To study this problem we had at our hands the data of prices of rye and vodka published in Tallinn and Riga soon after the end of the eighteenth century. The local paper of a relatively small inland town (Tartu) published vodka prices from 1811 and prices of different crops from 1835 on, but, as was clearly stated in the paper, these were not local prices, but the prices of Riga and Tallinn. In another small town, Pärnu (a seaport), some information about the prices of different kinds of pastry, meat, and products of vodka-distillation was published from 1831. Even the character of these publications speaks of the strong influence of larger towns on small ones, in the sense of price formation. It does not mean, of course, that there existed no local prices in small towns. From 1843 we have some interesting data about the weekly prices of different crops of all the towns and districts of South-Estonia. We carried out a correlation analysis with these data. As we had data on prices from 20 places (the minimum limit of significant correlation was 0·4227) we established that, for the sale of rye, significant correlation existed between all places (great and small towns and rural districts) with the exception of only two isolated and far-situated areas—the isle of Saaremaa and district and town of Wŏru. Therefore we came to the conclusion that the rye-market of Southern Estonia represented in the eighteen-forties a relatively complete unit except for some distant areas.

Analyzing the above-mentioned data on prices published in local papers, we tried to compare the character of correlational relationship in the period of domination of feudal relations (1835–1849) and the period of bourgeois reforms and capitalist development (1850–1861). When we turn our attention to the correlation coefficients demonstrating the relationship between one particular price and all the other prices in common, we see that it did not increase in the second half of the nineteenth century (compared with the first half) as it was sufficiently strong already (about 0·8 – 0·9). But in studying the order of relationship of different prices (which of them were most closely related), we notice an interesting development. Until 1850 the most closely related prices were those of rye in Riga and of bread (made of rye) in Pärnu; and the price of rye in Tallinn and liqueur made of rye in Pärnu. After 1850 the most closely related prices were the prices of rye in Riga and Tallinn and the prices of vodka in Riga and Tallinn.

From all this we can conclude that in the last decades of the first half of the nineteenth century the dominant correlation is between the prices of raw material and products (rye and bread); and in the beginning of the second half of the nineteenth century the correlation is between the market prices of the same article in different places. The development of capitalist relations reveals itself in the broadening of area of prices regulated by the same general trends.

These first examples of computer research carried out in the field of the socio-economic development of the first half of the nineteenth century in Estonia demonstrate, in our opinion, the possibility of analyzing the relevant processes in a more complex and profound way.

REFERENCES

Blalook, H. M. jr. (1964) Causal inferences in non-experimental research.

Iyenk, A. & Oper, U. (1966) Regressional analysis—Programs for *Minsk-2* digital computer, No. 2: Mathematical statistics programs I, Tallin 1966, pp. 23–66.

Kahk, J. (1969) Die Krise der feudalen Landwirtschaft in Estland (Das zweite Viertol des 19. Jahrhunderts), *Tallinn*, pp. 204–8.

Kahk, Yu. & Ligi, Kh. (1962) On the question of the economic position and feudal duties/obligations of peasants in the Estland province in the 18th c. (Experimental application of computers in historical research). *Year-book on the agrarian history of Eastern Europe*, pp. 43–58. Minsk.

Kovalchenko, I. D. (1959) On the question of the position of landowners' peasants/privately owned peasants and the state of farming in European Russia in the 40's and 50's of the 19th c., 'Higher Educational Papers— Historical Sciences', 1959, No. 2; —, On the question of the state of land-cwners' farming before the abolition of serfdom in Russia, 'Year-book on the agrarian history of Eastern Europe, 1959'; P. D. Dolgorukov and I. I. Petrunkevich, *The agrarian question*, Vol. 2, Moscow, 1907.

History

Vasile Liveanu, L. Asănăchescu, C. Lulea, V. Medeleanu, C. Moţei
Coefficients of correlation in historical research

In the present paper, without presuming to solve the problem, I wish to discuss our work at the *N. Iorga Institute* of Bucharest on 'Factors determining the variation in rent paid by the peasants to the big landowners in Romania at the beginning of the 20th century'. The work is being carried out in collaboration with two documentalists, V. Medeleanu and C. Moţei, and with two mathematicians from the Computation Centre of Bucharest University, C. Lulea and L. Asănăchescu. The initiative and direction of this study were undertaken by Vasile Liveanu, as was the writing of this paper.

As a historian, I am addressing myself first of all to mathematicians, not only because this was the motivation of the conference, but, particularly, because a confrontation of opinions on the way historians use coefficients of correlation seems to be topical. The analysis of correlations represents one of the main directions of applying mathematics to history, as shown also by the International Congress of Historians held this year in Moscow (Andrae & Lundkrist 1970; Deopik 1970). Nevertheless some mathematicians, as well as specialists in political sciences (Tufte 1969), seem more or less to contest the importance of coefficients of correlation in the study of social, and hence historical, phenomena.

It is not my purpose to deny the limitations of correlation coefficients. I agree that these coefficients are not *absolute* indicators, that one must examine them together with other indicators; and first of all with scatter diagrams. It was François Pottier, of the Paris *Centre d'Etudes Sociologiques*, who drew my attention to the importance of scatter diagrams in the interpretation of correlation coefficients and who arranged the plotting by computer of the scatter diagrams needed for my problem. All that I intend to point out is that, despite their limits, correlation coefficients *are* important for historical research.

The basic problem of any historical work is the selection of facts whose connexions are to be studied. Often, traditional methods do not allow the historian to consider the totality of existing information. The authors who have dealt with the considerable increase of the rent paid by peasants to big landowners in Romania in the 1870–1906 period attributed this increase to different factors: population increase, increase of the number of landless peasants, leaseholders' cupidity etc.

At the beginning of the 20th century in Romanian agriculture, wage labour coexisted with the 'tithe labour system'. This system, used in Romania and other East European countries, is one in which the peasants had not enough land and the landlords had few agricultural implements. The peasants took land on lease, cultivated it with their own implements, and paid to the landlords a rent in kind and in labour (rarely a quitrent). It is the total amount of these various forms of rent per acre which considerably increased after 1870.

Research workers took account of some aspects of the problem, but they could not use the whole amount of available data on agrarian statistics, since that amount could not be covered and handled by traditional methods. (These traditional methods are usually based on the cursory comparison of columns of figures or on the comparison of a very small number of ratios.) The computation of coefficients of correlation by means of computers permits the analysis of relationships between a great number of variables, making use of a huge amount of information.

In social sciences, causal inferences are usually based on the method of concomitant variations. When facts may be quantified, a measure of those variations is given by coefficients of correlation.

Of course, high coefficients of correlation do not always indicate causal relationships. Only on the basis of the *totality* of the available information, quantified and non-quantified, is it possible to infer from a correlation that a causal relationship exists. Nevertheless, in the totality of information about the relationships between variables, the correlation coefficient is an important and sometimes a decisive element.

We have, therefore, undertaken to compute the coefficients of correlation between rent variation and the variation in 84 other variables, representing different economic, demographic, and cultural factors. The variables were calculated for all the 32 counties of Romania in the year 1906. The correlation computing has represented, in this case, the testing of at least 83 hypotheses on the existence of an important causal dependency between the amount of the rent and each of the 83 variables under consideration. We refer only to the equivalent in money of the work done by the tenant for the fulfilment of the obligations included in the lease-contract. We refer to the amount of rent per hectare. The computing of the amount of rent on the basis of 'current labour prices', as in our study, has some shortcomings—but it is sufficiently adequate for our purpose here, which is to examine the utility of correlation coefficients in researching on causal historical relationships. On the other hand, the coefficients of correlation between the *amount* of rent and the other variables mentioned in this paper are in concordance with the correlation coefficients between these same variables and the *rate* of rent (ratio of the total product taken by the proprietary to the total product left to the tenant).

The computation permitted us, first, to rule out certain hypotheses; and it revealed the absence of any significant correlation between rent and many of the variables initially taken into consideration. Some instances are given in table 1.

The absence of a significant correlation refutes the hypotheses of causal dependencies between the amount of rent and the variables mentioned in table 1.

The coefficients of correlation obtained repudiated the hypothesis of an important causal influence of the variables X_2, X_3, X_4, X_5 on X_1. Particularly

	Amount of the rent (X_1)	
	Linear correlation coefficient	Non-linear[1] correlation coefficient
$X_2 =$ Wheat production per ha. (in farms over 100 ha.)	0·054	0·278
$X_3 = \dfrac{\text{Cultivated surface of the farms of over 100 ha.}}{\text{Total surface of the properties of over 100 ha.}}$	0·043	0·262
$X_4 = \dfrac{\text{Surface of the estates of over 100 ha.}}{\text{Number of families without land}}$	0·257	0·283
$X_5 = \dfrac{\text{Surface of the estates of over 100 ha.}}{\text{Rural population}}$	0·252	0·196

[1] Polynomial correlation up to 5th degree calculated; the calculus requires verification.

Table 1

interesting—and surprising, hence new, for the scholar—is the absence of a significant correlation between the amount of rent (X_1) and the variable X_4 (*see* table 1). However it is possible that this absence merely shows the failure of the social investigation which, in 1905, collected the data about the number of peasant families without land. Thus, coefficients of correlation may be used for testing the data about the past (*see* Muller 1969). But our interest in this paper is the usefulness of the correlation coefficient for research into *causes* in history.

An objection may be raised from the very beginning and is indeed raised by some mathematicians: if a polynomial of a sufficiently high degree is considered, it is always possible to obtain a close fit of the data by a regression curve and to find a significant non-linear coefficient of correlation. Hence, according to some mathematicians, the absence of a polynomial correlation of a sufficiently high degree between two variables does not prove anything.

When examining this question, account must be taken, however, that it is the *historical* significance of mathematical relations, i.e. of coefficients of correlation, which interests historical research and that this significance depends not only on quantified information but on the totality of information including non-quantified information.

We shall now illustrate the way we carried out our research in order to test the influence of an economic demographic factor. We have calculated the coefficient of linear correlation between rent (variable X_1) and the ratio of the surface of the estates to the rural population (variable X_5). The coefficient of linear correlation is 0·252 not significantly different from 0 and the coefficient of nonlinear correlation is 0·196 (polynomials up to the fifth degree were taken into account).

The scatter-diagram has the distribution shown in figure 1.

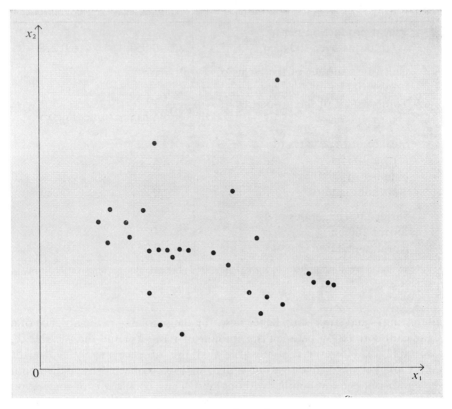

Figure 1. x_1=the amount of rent; x_2=surface of estates over 50 ha/rural population

In this case, a curve which should fit the data well would have too many bends or in any case it would imply that according to the regression equation, a high number of different values of X_5 *necessarily* correspond to the same values of X_1. This seems to be the expression of an absence of a *real* historical relationship between the variation of X_5 and that of X_1. Available information on the nature of the two variables does not allow us to admit that the density of rural population per hectare of estate might have an influence on rent, liable to be described by a polynomial of the fifth degree or more.

Of course, in some cases the relationships between two variables may be different in different fields, or at different levels, as an expression of the fact that to the same cau e (=variations of the independent variable) may correspond different effects (=variations of the dependent variables). It is possible that in historical reality an increase in variable *A* in certain fields or between certain limits determined an increase in variable *B*, and an increase of variable *A* in other fields or between other limits determined a *decrease* in variable *B* so that the same value of *A* had *different* effects in different fields and corresponded to *different* values of *B*.

One may suppose this is our case with X_1 (amount of the rent) and X_5 (ratio of the surface of the estates to the rural population). But the existing information does not allow us to distinguish such groups of counties, or such levels in the variation of either of the two variables, which could permit us to assign to the variable X_5 a causal influence on X_1 (or to X_1 a causal influence on X_5) with different effects in different groups of Romanian counties (or with different effects between different levels of the variable's variation).

Sometimes the shape of the scatter diagram suggests a necessity to compute correlation coefficients of higher degree. Between the amount of the rent (X_1) and the percentage of the estates surface in the county's total surface the coefficient of linear correlation is -0.085, and of non-linear correlation is 0.750.

Because our research is not finished we cannot present a conclusive interpretation of this high coefficient of non-linear correlation, but we have formulated a working-hypothesis which must be verified.

In the first part of the scatter diagram are located 16 counties in which the competition between peasants was weak and in the second part are located the counties in which the competition between peasants was intense. We will clarify our idea. The coefficient of linear correlation between the amount of the rent (X_1) and the percentage of peasants' ploughs in the total number of county's ploughs (X_7) is 0.642. The percentage of the peasants' ploughs was an indicator of the competition between peasants. Where peasants had more ploughs, they could demand more land on lease, the competition between them was greater, and the rent rose; where the level of the variable X_7 was lower, the competition between peasants was less intense.

The coefficient of linear correlation between the amount of the rent and the ratio of the number of owners of more than 100 ha to the number of peasants without landed property (X_8) was -0.461. Where the number of the landlords was small, the competition between landlords was also small and the rent higher. Where the number of peasants without landed property was higher, the competition between peasants was higher and the rent also higher. Where the level of the variable X_8 was higher the competition between peasants was weaker.

In the 16 counties located in the second part of the scatter diagram, the level of X_7 (the percentage of peasants with ploughs) was high, and the level of

$$X_8 = \frac{\text{Number of owners of over 100 ha}}{\text{Number of peasants without landed property}}$$

was low. In *all* these 16 counties the level of the X_7 was higher than the mean and in 14 counties the level of the X_7 was near the maximum; in only one of these counties was the level of X_8 over the mean. Hence in these counties the competition between peasants was intense. In 13 of these 16 counties the rent was *over* the mean; in eight counties the rent was near the maximum.

In the 16 counties located in the first part of the scatter diagram the level of X_7 was low, and the level of X_8 was relatively high. Out of these 16 counties, only seven had the level of the variable X_7 over the mean (only 4 had the level of X_7 near the maximum); in six of these counties the level of X_7 was over the mean. Hence in the counties located in the first part of the scatter diagram the competition between peasants seems to have been much weaker than in the counties located in the second part. In these counties the rent was low—it was *under* the mean in *all* these 16 counties. Such being the case, our hypothesis is:

1. In the counties with intense competition between the peasants— represented in the second part of the scatter diagram—the increase of the percentage of the surface of the estates (the decrease of the surface of peasants' land) became a 'tool of pressure' in the hands of the landlords. In these counties, the greater the percentage of the surface of the estates was, the greater was also the pressure of the landlords, and hence the greater was also the rent.

2. In the counties with weak competition between peasants, represented in the first part of the scatter diagram, the landlords could not use the increase of the percentage of the surface of their estates (that is the decrease in the percentage of the surface of peasants land) as a 'tool of pressure' against the peasants. In these counties, where the percentage of the surface of the estates was greater, the competition between landlords was also greater and hence the rent was lower.

Thus, we suggest it is possible to distinguish two groups of counties, accounting for the different behaviour of the variable X_6 in these two different groups. This hypothesis is a preliminary one and may be rejected by further advances in our work. We offer it only to instance the kind of case in which the non-linear correlation seems to have a historical sense as an indicator of a historical causal relationship. Only when the totality of information allows us to assign a meaning to the different 'behaviours' of a variable in different fields, may the non-linear coefficient of correlation have historical significance.

We may assert that for any of the variables supposed to causally influence rent variation, a nonlinear correlation implying that data are fitted by a polynomial of a higher degree than 5 is not to be accounted for by the characteristics of the counties or by the real nature of variables under consideration.

In the section on curvilinear regression and correlation, a classical hand-book points out: 'So long as the equation had been derived merely by the "cut and dry" method described, it would have no logical meaning beyond serving as a simple device for estimating values of the one variable from known values of the other and would throw no particular light upon the real or inherent nature of the relation ... Merely because a given equation *can* reproduce a certain relation, is no proof that it really "expresses" the nature of the relation. To establish this, we need a logical explanation which leads to the given equation, which in turn does closely fit the central tendency of the observed data.' Parabolas of a degree greater than four are rarely useful 'as the greater the number of terms, the greater the tendency becomes for the curve "to wiggle".' (Fox and Esekiel 1959).

From a philosophical point of view the possibility of always finding a high coefficient of correlation between two variables, if a polynomial of a sufficiently high degree is taken into account, may be considered as an expression of the fact that there always exist certain relationships between two phenomena, processes, or objects. But some relationships are strong and others very weak. The historian retains only the first kind of relationships. The coefficients of correlation offer to historians an objective criterion for the selection of the important, *influencing* relationships, for the selection of the variables with strong influence on the historical process.

But we do not aim at generalizing from our experience. We maintain only that our experience suggests that, though there is always a possibility of fitting the data by a polynomial of sufficiently high degree, the absence of a significant linear correlation or of a non-linear correlation of a low degree between historical variables allows us to infer the absence of a real relation between the two variables. (In our experiment we did not transform variables. The logarithmic transformation of a variable and in general variable transformations in order to compute correlations is admissible only when a real historical significance may be attributed to this transformation.)

It is worth mentioning the use we made for historical interpretation of the correlation coefficients and for the formulation of the hypothesis concerning the variable X_6 of a 'visual matrix' constructed in J. Bertin's *Laboratoire de Cartographie* with the help of Bertin and Gronoff. The methods of the construction of such a matrix were presented in the paper of our colleague Dinu Teodorescu. Offering a comprehensive image of *all* the quantified information about *each* county, this matrix helps to grasp, behind the correlation coefficients, meanings which, otherwise, could perhaps remain hidden from the historian.

The ruling out of some hypotheses is a considerable help offered by correlation analysis in selecting historical facts submitted to causal analysis. On the other hand, the *presence* of some significant correlations may *confirm* a series of hypotheses on causal relations between historical variables, showing that these hypotheses—constructed on the basis of logical, qualitative analysis of the historical material—are consistent with the results of quantitative analysis.

For instance, the computing of correlation coefficients confirmed our hypothesis about the influence of the variable X_8 on the amount of rent: this supposed, and hence predicted, a significant correlation coefficient between these two variables, and such a coefficient was really found. Of course, later information may contradict the facts implied (predicted) by the given hypothesis and thus refute it.

The advantages of correlation analysis are far from confined only to the confirmation or refutation of some causal hypotheses, constructed before the carrying out of correlation analysis. The results of correlation analyses may suggest new ideas. Thus, the strong correlation coefficient between the amount of rent and the percentage of peasants' ploughs suggested computing the coefficient of linear correlation between the amount of rent and the ratio of the number of peasants' ploughs to the surface of peasants' properties:

$$X_9 = \frac{\text{Number of ploughs of owners under 100 ha}}{\text{Total surface of properties under 100 ha}} \, .$$

X_9 is an indicator of the peasants' potential to take on lease alien land. (The statistics of agricultural implements indicate only two categories of farmers: big owners (over 100 ha) and small owners (under 100 ha). The number of owners with 50–100 ha, their land and implements were in fact of very little importance.) The coefficient of linear correlation with X_1 is 0·496. It is a proof that the development of peasants' implements contributed to an increase in rent.

The correlation analysis can reveal the existence between historical variables of relationships other than previously supposed. Because some sources related the peasants opinion that the landlords increased the surface directly cultivated by themselves in order to exert pressure on the tenants and to impose on them a greater rent—we expected to find a positive correlation coefficient between the amount of the rent and the ratio of the number of landlords' ploughs to the total surface of the estates (X_{9bis}).

$$X_{9bis} = \frac{\text{Number of ploughs of the owners of over 100 ha}}{\text{Total surface of the properties of over 100 ha}}.$$

The coefficient of linear correlation between X_{9bis} and the amount of rent is $-0·597$. The historical sense of this coefficient is clear: where the rent was low, the landlords were interested in the extension of the surface directly cultivated by themselves, and bought more ploughs. Where the rent was high, the landlords were less interested in the direct cultivation of their land, and they bought fewer ploughs. The extension of the big owners' land that was cultivated with wage labour (that is with their own ploughs) was a reaction of the big owners in the places where the rent was small.

This throws a new light on agriculture based on the 'tithe system': the rent was the mobile, and in a sense, the 'regulator' element of the production, and the variation of the amount of rent was an important factor in the extension of wage labour. A high rent hindered this extension. One may say that this is only logical and could have been asserted without any computation. But without computation, to such logical arguments it would have been possible to oppose others just as logical and the problem would have remained unsolved. Only computation could take into account the *totality* of the quantitative relationships between X_1 and X_4 and render evident the above relationship.

More particularly, the results of correlation analysis permit us to establish a hierarchy of causal influences, quite impossible with traditional means.

We wished to verify, for instance, whether the amount of rent was influenced to a greater extent by the *number* of peasants without land property or by the number of peasants with lots of 5–10 ha, or by the number of peasants with 0·1–5 ha, or by the sum of persons belonging to these two categories. Table 2 is eloquent.

Of the categories included in table 2, the peasants without land property represent the category whose correlation with the amount of rent is strongest.

As social life and history are characterized by processes with numerous interacting factors, historians are interested in calculating multiple and partial correlations.

The multiple correlation points out the result of the interaction of several

Independent variables	Rent amount (X_1)
$X_8 = \dfrac{\text{Number of owners of over 100 ha}}{\text{Number of peasants without landed property}}$	$-0\cdot461$
$X_{10} = \dfrac{\text{Number of owners of over 100 ha}}{\text{Number of owners of } 0\cdot1\text{–}5 \text{ ha}}$	$-0\cdot316$
$X_{11} = \dfrac{\text{Number of owners of over 100 ha}}{\text{Number of owners of } 5\text{–}10 \text{ ha}}$	$0\cdot300$
$X_{12} = \dfrac{\text{Number of owners of over 100 ha}}{\text{Number of owners of } 0\cdot1\text{–}10 \text{ ha}}$	$0\cdot314$
$X_{13} = \dfrac{\text{Number of owners of over 100 ha}}{\text{Number of owners } 0\cdot1\text{–}5 \text{ ha} + \text{Numb. p.w.l.}[1]}$	$-0\cdot364$
$X_{14} = \dfrac{\text{Number of owners of over 100 ha}}{\text{Number of owners } 0\cdot1\text{–}10 \text{ ha} + \text{Numb. p.w.l.}}$	$-0\cdot360$
$X_{15} = \dfrac{\text{Number of owners of over 100 ha}}{\text{Number of owners } 5\text{–}10 \text{ ha} + \text{Numb. p.w.l.}}$	$-0\cdot337$

[1] Numb. p.w.l. = number of peasants without land.

Table 2. Coefficients of linear correlation

factors and the coefficient of partial correlation and beta coefficients provide an objective criterion for establishing the hierarchy of the influence of different factors, within their interaction. We are now testing causal models by calculating multiple and partial correlations.

Because the number of Romanian counties in 1906 was 32, we thought of constructing a causal model—a multiple regression equation with no more than 16 variables. The analysis of the coefficients of correlation suggests so far that the number of variables we must retain for our model is smaller. It seems that 80 per cent of the variance of the amount of rent (calculated on the basis of the regular price of the labour requested by the fulfilment of the obligations included in lease contracts) was explained by: (1) the ratio of the peasants' ploughs to the surface of their land (as suggested, an indicator of the peasants potential to take land on lease); (2) the ratio of the number of the landlords to the number of peasants without landed property (as suggested, an indicator of the intensity of the concurrence on the market of land leasing); (3) the ratio of the surface taken on lease by the peasants to the total number of tenants (an indicator of the ratio of offer to demand on the land leasing market); (4) the ratio of the surface of the estates and the number of proprietaries with 2–5 ha (an indicator of ratio of important portions of offer and demand on the land leasing market); (5–8) Other variables, less important. After the construction of the regression equation, the partial correlation coefficients and beta coefficients will allow us to put the variables included in the causal model (regression equation) in an objective order according to the importance of their causal influence.

33

It is important to emphasize that historians are interested not in rigorously exact coefficients, but in '*l'ordre* de grandeur' of the coefficients, which is sufficient for ordering the historical variables according to the intensity of their causal influence in the given process.

One may say that the causal model of rent variations constructed by our computing of regression and correlation may not be a perfect, definitive one. But it will be better than any of the 'models', constructed with traditional methods. For the 'traditional models' cannot handle so many variables (initially more than 80). Even the few variables considered in such traditional models are selected on criteria much more uncertain (and subjective) than the correlation coefficient, which offers an *objective* criterion for the selection of the variables involved in a given process and for their ordering according to the importance of their causal influence. On the other hand, the coefficient of multiple determination (R_2) indicates clearly the proportion of the variance explained, and hence the proportion of the variance unexplained by the variables involved in our causal models—and the different statistical tests show clearly the limits of confidence of the computed coefficients. The *limits* of the computed models are non-equivocal, which is not the case of the traditional methods.

We wished to point out by the present communication that: (1) correlation analysis may refute some causal hypotheses; it may show that other causal hypotheses are compatible with known data; it may help in establishing the hierarchy of causal influences; (2) mathematical theory may help the historian in finding certain mathematical relations which cannot be grasped by traditional methods. Mathematics cannot be absent from the methodology of historical research. However, establishing the historical significance of some mathematical relations is not the work of mathematical theory but of historical theory, of historical conceptions, which combine quantitative and qualitative analysis, at least at the present stage of development of science.

It might be said that correlation analysis does not exclude the uncertainty of some results of historical analysis. This is quite right. Yet, the application of mathematics to history, whenever possible, without representing a transition from absolute uncertainty to absolute certainty, results in reduced uncertainty, in a more accurate approximation of reality. Though mathematics does not make history perfect, it contributes to its perfectibility and this is essential.

REFERENCES

Andrae, C.G. & Lundkrist, S. (1970) *The Use of Historical Mass-Data Experiences from a Project on Swedish Popular Movements*. Moscow: Nauka Publishing House.

Deopik, D.V. *et al.* (1970) *Quantitative and Machine Methods of Processing Historical Information*. Moscow: Nauka Publishing House.

Ezekiel, M. & Fox, K.A. (1959) *Methods of Correlation and Regression Analysis: Linear and Curvilinear*. New York: Wiley.

Muller, O. (1969) *Analyse de Séries Météorologiques Anciennes*. Paris: Centre de Calcul de la Maison des Sciences de l'Homme.

Tufte, E.R. (1969) Improving data analysis in political sciences. *World Politics*, **21**, 643, 647–9, 653–4.

History

Mircea Maliţa

A model of Michael the Brave's decision in 1595

Using the method of efficiency developed by Decision Theory (*see* Churchman, Ackoff, and Arnoff 1957, Fishburn 1964), the author attempts to estimate the efficiency of Michael the Brave's decision to rise against the Ottoman Empire on 15 January 1595, and compares the result with the probable efficiency of other courses of action.

THE PROBLEM

At the end of 1594 Wallachia raised the standard of revolt against Ottoman domination by killing the Turkish military officials and creditors found in Bucharest and on Wallachian territory. This action was the signal for war and had a thoroughly deliberate character. In this sense, the Bucharest rising was not an accident, but the outcome of a long-planned decision. It is reasonable to suppose that this action, which we shall call *armed struggle*, was the most suitable response to the question: which is the best way of attaining a finite set of objectives?

A historical analysis points to the following five principal objectives:

O_1: The immediate preservation of the reign.

O_2: Stopping the economic spoliation.

O_3: Obtaining assistance from Christian countries.

O_4: Restoring Wallachia's traditional rights.

O_5: The country's independence from the Ottoman Empire.

In reconstructing the above-mentioned objectives one will notice that they are not exhaustive. Thus, they do not include another possible objective, attested in the chronicles, which was the liberation of Christian subjects south of the Danube.

One essential requirement of the operation of objective definition is that the results of their attainment should be regarded as discrete, non-contradictory, and mutually exclusive phenomena. The first two requirements are easier to fulfil, since we may agree that the results are expressed in definite acts (the conclusion of a formal agreement, a military victory, and so on), but their independence is more difficult since, as a rule, reasoning in decisions follows the path of choosing progressive objectives which condition one another.

In the case under consideration, one may consider that they are relatively independent from the viewpoint of later analysis. Thus, the country's independence is not necessarily linked to outside assistance or to the stability of a certain reign.

In arranging the objectives according to their importance account should be taken of the *hypothesis of the rationality* of the decision factor which is expressed here by its degree of realism. Thus, the priorities are established not according to an ideal scale of values but by the criterion of practical achievement. Michael the Brave did not set himself a broader objective, for example, the restoration of Wallachia's traditional relations with the Porte, characterized by internal autonomy and the payment of a fixed tribute agreed upon on a *contractual basis*, before other objectives, because it was of a longer duration and could not be imagined without the realization of the latter. Certainly this is more important than preserving the throne and it is a broader objective than stopping the economic exploitation. But, despite the fact that it remains an active concept rendering a real aspiration, it has fewer chances of achievement and is placed in a more remote, rather than secondary, position. Michael the Brave considered the maintenance and consolidation of his power to be an immediate objective, and to his mind that was the primary step to be taken, without which the achievement of the others was not only uncertain, but also unlikely.

The rationality hypothesis intervenes in different models with different *nuances*. In this case, it may be defined as:

(a) the ability to distinguish among several attainable objectives;

(b) their hierarchical arrangement;

(c) the ability to compare the efficiency of several *possible* courses of action.

THE UTILITIES

A non-negative value known as utility (λ_j) is associated with each objective O_j, representing the importance attached to it. A vector of utilities is thus formed. To establish the utilities, we shall use the method of successive comparisons (*see* Churchman, Ackoff, and Arnoff 1957).

The first approximation given by the sequence of objectives itself is

$$\lambda_1 = 1 \cdot 0 \quad \lambda_2 = 0 \cdot 9 \quad \lambda_3 = 0 \cdot 8 \quad \lambda_4 = 0 \cdot 7 \quad \lambda_5 = 0 \cdot 6 \quad . \tag{1}$$

Let us now compare the values of the various objectives.

(a) Is λ_1 greater than $\lambda_2 + \lambda_3 + \lambda_4 + \lambda_5$?

Considering that objective O_1 cannot be more important than the certain realization of all the other objectives, among which the last ones are predominant, we have:

$$\lambda_1 < \lambda_2 + \lambda_3 + \lambda_4 + \lambda_5 \quad .$$

(b) Comparison with $\lambda_2 + \lambda_3 + \lambda_4$ leads to a similar conclusion:

$$\lambda_1 < \lambda_2 + \lambda_3 + \lambda_4$$

as it contains λ_4.

(c) But if we ask whether the decision-maker prefers to achieve O_2 and O_3 together rather than O_1 alone, we shall answer

$$\lambda_1 > \lambda_2 + \lambda_3 \quad .$$

This is explained by the absence of the final-settlement objectives O_4 and O_5. Foreign assistance and restoration of the economic power do not exceed in importance the stability of the reign.

We shall consequently rewrite (1):

$$\lambda_1 = 1 \cdot 8 \quad \lambda_2 = 0 \cdot 9 \quad \lambda_3 = 0 \cdot 8 \quad \lambda_4 = 0 \cdot 7 \quad \lambda_5 = 0 \cdot 6 \quad . \tag{2}$$

We continue the comparison between the importance of objective O_2 and that of O_3, O_4 and O_5.

(d) By a similar reasoning, we reach the conclusion

$$\lambda_2 < \lambda_3 + \lambda_4 + \lambda_5,$$

a requirement fulfilled by (2)

(e) We consider, however, that

$$\lambda_2 > \lambda_3 + \lambda_4$$

on account of the fact that domestic economic rehabilitation is more important than O_3 and O_4 taken together, since the result O_4 involves considerable financial burdens, which are absent in the case of total independence O_5. This hypothesis leads to rewriting (2), so that the new condition is met:

$$\lambda_1 = 2\cdot5 \quad \lambda_2 = 1\cdot6 \quad \lambda_3 = 0\cdot8 \quad \lambda_4 = 0\cdot7 \quad \lambda_1 = 0\cdot6 \ . \tag{3}$$

(f) Finally,

$$\lambda_3 < \lambda_4 + \lambda_5,$$

because the simultaneous attainment of objectives O_5 and O_6 surpasses the need of achieving O_3, no matter how important it may be.

We shall normalize (3) through division by the sum of the values, so as to have $\sum\limits_j \lambda_j = 1$:

$$\lambda_1 = 0\cdot403 \quad \lambda_2 = 0\cdot258 \quad \lambda_3 = 0\cdot129 \quad \lambda_4 = 0\cdot113 \quad \lambda_5 = 0\cdot097 \ . \tag{4}$$

THE NEGATIVE EFFECTS

In decision making, account should be taken of side-effects, whose value will be defined in an analogous manner, by negative utilities. One will notice that, in contrast to game theory, the negative utilities are not equal in absolute value to the positive utilities of the objective whose non-fulfilment they represent. In the present problem, namely, failure to attain O_2, that is, continued economic exploitation of the country, represents only the value zero. There are however phenomena, brought about by the choice of a course of action, which affect the efficiency of the latter in the sense of its diminution. We shall refer to these actions as N_k, and to their utilities, which act as restrictive factors, as μ_k ($\mu_k > 0$).

In the present case, we define the following negative effects as:

N_1: Reprisals

N_2: Internal revolt

N_3: Aggravation of dependence

N_4: Deterioration of the economic condition.

We calculate $|\mu_k|$ in a manner similar to that used in calculating λ_j.

In a first approximation, we have:

$$|\mu_1| = 0\cdot9 \quad |\mu_2| = 0\cdot8 \quad |\mu_3| = 0\cdot7 \quad |\mu_4| = 0\cdot6 \ . \tag{5}$$

(a) We question the fact whether N_1 is more serious than all the other effects taken together, which leads us to the relation

$$|\mu_1| < |\mu_2| + |\mu_3| + |\mu_4| \ .$$

(b) The following comparison leads us to

$$|\mu_1| < |\mu_2| + |\mu_3|$$

considering that the effects of reprisals are more serious than N_2 and N_3 taken together.

(c) It will be easily noticed that the position of N_2 in reference to N_3 and N_4 justifies the relation

$$|\mu_2| > |\mu_3| + |\mu_4|$$

which is not satisfied by (5).

We obtain the new approximations

$$|\mu_1| = 1\cdot5 \quad |\mu_2| = 1\cdot4 \quad |\mu_3| = 0\cdot7 \quad |\mu_4| = 0\cdot6 \quad . \tag{6}$$

We then normalize the above:

$$|\mu_1| = 0\cdot357 \quad |\mu_2| = 0\cdot333 \quad |\mu_3| = 0\cdot166 \quad |\mu_4| = 0\cdot144 \quad . \tag{7}$$

ANALYSIS OF ACTION EFFICIENCIES

The total efficiency of an action is defined as

$$E_i = \sum_j e_{ij}\lambda_j + \sum_k \bar{e}_{ik}\mu_k = E_i^+ + E_i^- \tag{8}$$

where e_{ij} is the efficiency of course of action i in relation to objective j, defined in the course of action i. $\bar{e}_{ik}$ is the efficiency of the negative consequences N_k, residing in the probability of their realization.

Michael the Brave chose *armed struggle*. We shall now calculate E_1.

Let us consider that O_1, O_2, O_3 have been fulfilled, and therefore $e_{11} = e_{12} = e_{13} = 1$, whereas O_4 and O_5 have not. Consequently, $e_{14} = e_{15} = 0$.

As regards the negative effects, we may consider that N_1 has actually occurred, whereas N_2, N_3, N_4, despite certain attempts, have not had the expected serious consequences. Therefore, $\bar{e}_{11} = 1$, $\bar{e}_{12} = \bar{e}_{13} = \bar{e}_{14} = 0$.

$$E_1^+ = \sum_j e_{1j}\lambda_j = 1\cdot00 \times 0\cdot403 + 1\cdot00 \times 0\cdot258 + 1\cdot00 \times 0\cdot129 = 0\cdot790$$

$$E_1^- = \sum_k \bar{e}_{1k}\mu_k = 1\cdot00 \times (-0\cdot357) + 0\cdot00 \times (-0\cdot333) +$$

$$0\cdot00 \times (-0\cdot166) + 0\cdot00 \times (-0\cdot144) = -0\cdot357$$

$$E_1 = E_1^+ + E_1^- \simeq 0\cdot443 \quad .$$

We may state that the total efficiency of the course of armed struggle is $0\cdot443$. Without its negative implications, it is considerably greater, namely, $0\cdot790$.

The courses of action that Michael the Brave could contemplate in 1594 were:

(1) an alliance with the Ottoman Empire against the Christian Powers;

(2) compensation in cash;

(3) active diplomacy;

(4) a continuance of the *status quo*.

Historical sources show that none of these was ruled out. Alternative (1) is seen as an active military alliance with the Turks against the Austrians, involving actual participation in the military operations then in progress. Alternative (2) represents not military assistance to the Porte, but an aggregate payment for settlement, which would involve hard bargaining. Alternative (2) is but alternative (3) to which financial means have been added. Alternative (3) differs from alternative (4) by setting in motion all the workings of the Porte's administration and attempting to point out the disadvantages entailed by a continuance of its policy towards Wallachia. It is an attempt at temporization and gradual approach to some O_j. At the same time, inclusion of alternative (4) is not trivial. Not to undertake anything did not mean giving up the objectives, but rather relying on the fact that time would solve everything, the natural course of events being oriented towards the realization of at least a few objectives.

We shall use the same formula (8) for alternative efficiency. In this case, e_{ij} and $\bar{e}_{ik}$ will not be 0 or 1. No alternatives have been chosen, the events have not occurred within their framework. Using the same sources that enabled us to define the objectives O_j and the negative effects N_k, the corresponding values λ_j and μ_k, and the possible alternatives, we can evaluate e_{ij} and $\bar{e}_{ik}$ as the probabilities of realization of the objectives and the negative effects, if the remaining courses of action had been adopted. To diminish the error of this estimation, we shall give the probabilities a minimum and maximum value, and regard the resulting efficiency as varying within a given interval [e_{ij} is the (subjective) probability measuring the realization chance of objective O_j in the course of action i; there are no reasons to regard these events as independent and exhaustive.]

Table 1 represents the probabilities allotted to the events consisting in the realization of the objectives and negative consequences within each course of action.

It will be noticed that the four new courses of action are essentially an offer to the Porte to satisfy the objectives of Wallachia in return for some service in which it is interested.

This service is of a military nature in the war with the Hapsburg Empire ($i=2$), and financial nature ($i=3$), and is also an attempt at persuasion without financial means ($i=4$). Position $i=5$ represents lack of initiative.

We expect e_{ij}, representing the stability of the reign, to be proportional to the size of the service. The other e_{ij} values also appear in a decreasing order. We notice that the chances of gaining independence appear only in the case of using diplomacy, with or without financial means, whereas a military alliance offers greater chances of restoring the country's traditional autonomy.

As regards the negative effects, a punitive invasion appears to stand few chances, if diplomacy is employed, and if the latter is regarded as generating suspicion. There is increased danger of an internal revolt engineered by the Austrians ($i=2$) or the Turks ($i=3, 4$).

The economic condition cannot become worse than in the case of diplomacy without financial means, or passivity. The conclusion of alliances with third parties has maximum negative effects in the case of compensation.

Comparing the efficiencies E_i^+, E_i^-, E_i of the five courses examined here, we are led to certain observations which can be verified intuitively or on the basis of historical texts.

(a) The efficiencies are below 50 per cent, which is characteristic of a critical situation.

(b) The maximum total efficiency is that of the course of *armed struggle*, which proves to be the best alternative in the given situation.

(c) The positive efficiency (considering the negative effects as nil) is high in the maximum estimation of the three courses, excluding inactivity. This indicates that they were all contemplated, which is an attested fact.

(d) The course with the closest efficiency to armed struggle was an alliance with the Turks. It was up to the Porte to secure the Prince against any over-

λ_j, μ_k		O_1 0·403	O_2 0·258	O_3 0·129	O_4 0·113	O_5 0·097	N_1 -0·357	N_2 -0·333	N_3 -0·166	N_4 0·144	E_i^+	E_i^-	E_i
$i=1$ (Armed struggle)		1	1	1	0	0	1	0	0	0	0·790	-0·357	0·443
$i=2$ (Alliance with the Porte)	min	0·6	0·2	0	0·4	0	0	0·2	0	0	0·339	-0·066	0·273
	max	0·8	0·3	0	0·5	0	0	0·3	0	0	0·456	-0·099	0·357
$i=3$ (Compensation)	min	0·5	0·1	0·3	0·1	0·1	0·1	0·3	0·3	0	0·287	-0·185	0·102
	max	0·7	0·2	0·4	0·3	0·2	0·2	0·4	0·5	0	0·439	-0·288	0·151
$i=4$ (Diplomacy)	min	0·3	0	0·2	0·1	0	0·1	0·3	0·1	0	0·158	-0·152	0·006
	max	0·6	0·1	0·5	0·3	0·1	0·2	0·4	0·2	0·2	0·376	-0·266	0·110
$i=5$ (Status quo)	min	0	0	0·1	0·1	0	0	0·1	0	0·1	0·024	-0·047	-0·023
	max	0	0·1	0·1	0·2	0	0	0·2	0	0·2	0·062	-0·095	-0·033

Table 1

throw and the realization of such major objectives as O_4 ($e_{24} > 0$), and the decision would have remained in the balance. Everything the Turks did in the autumn of 1594 was in the opposite direction.

(e) The interval within which the efficiency of diplomacy with financial means ($i = 3$) varies is much narrower than that of diplomacy without financial means ($i = 4$). This may be interpreted as follows: in C_3 the means are prevalent and the variation of the result is minimal; in C_4, it all depends on the quality of diplomacy, which may yield very good or very poor results.

(f) The result $E_4^+ = 0.376$ is surprising for a diplomacy without financial means, but also without negative effects. Michael the Brave perceived the possibilities offered by C_4, which is proved by the resumption of secret negotiations with the Porte.

Adoption of course C_4 from the outset was not possible on account of the low total efficiency, due mainly to the Turks' non-recognition of their partner's actual possibilities.

(g) Inaction does not prove to be neutral in the case of a small positive result or of no result. It is C_5 which is the worst alternative, which is obvious in the face of a steadily deteriorating situation.

LIMITATIONS AND ADVANTAGES

The disadvantages of applying decision theory to historical study lie in the subjective intervention of reconstructing the objectives, the negative effects, and the courses of action. It is obvious that the model involves selection and preference, and can lay no claim to complete accuracy. The greatest such intervention will of necessity occur—leaving the door wide open to arbitrariness—in defining the utilities and the efficiency of various courses of action by the probabilities of achievement of the chosen events. One may object that some preferences or intuitions are rationalized by these very choices.

The contention that this method cannot yet become a working instrument in decision making, or that its prescriptive role is small, cannot be brushed aside as groundless.

To build the mathematical model of a situation does not signify a claim to substitute a new procedure for the existing means of solution, or to proclaim the superiority, of one method. History will not have to be rewritten in terms of decision comparison or game theory, and international relations will continue to be handled on the basis of qualitative reasoning. We do not add 'as successfully as up to now', lest we should seem ironical.

Nevertheless, modelling is of unquestionable value. This lies primarily in the increased insight it provides into the structure of events. The need for systematization, hierarchical arrangement, and measure entailed by a model is also profitable to the student of international relations. The model used thus points out the significance of the objective in relation to motivation, and of action in relation to temporization. In particular, it develops a taste for specifying details whose necessity may have been overlooked by history as written in a qualitative language.

Secondly, such a method is useful in revealing the directions of development of the mathematical instrument, with a view to making it appropriate for wider and more refined applications.

Lastly, it brings about the application of certain concepts, which have already proved their efficiency in various economic and social fields, to an area of research which so far has been but scantily investigated by the contemporary schools of thought.

REFERENCES

Bălcescu, N. (1967) *Romanii supt Mihai-Voievod Viteazul*. Bucureşti: Editura pentru literatură.

Churchman, C.W., Ackoff, R.L. & Arnoff, L.E. (1957) *Introduction to Operations Research*. New York: Wiley.

Constantinescu, M., Daicovicu, C. & Pascu, St. (1969) *Istoria României, Compendiu*. Bucureşti: Edit. Didactică şi Pedagogica.

Fishburn, P.C. (1964) *Decision and Value Theory*. New York, London, Sidney: Wiley.

Iorga, N. (1968) *Istoria lui Mihai Viteazul*. Bucureşti: Edit. Militară.

History

Ion Văduva
On computer generation of conditional data

The problem may be stated as follows: Let $\mathbf{X}=(X_1, \ldots, X_p)'$ be a random vector, whose components X_i, $1 \leqslant i \leqslant p$, are characteristics of some historical items. Assume that there is incomplete information about these items, in the sense that for a given vector we do not know the values of some of its components; the problem is to generate the values of the unknown components, given the values of the known ones.

If the components of $\mathbf{X}$ are rearranged so that the first q components are unknown and the other $p-q$, $(q<p)$, are known, and if we denote $\mathbf{X}^{(1)}=(X_1, \ldots, X_q)'$, $\mathbf{X}^{(2)}=(W_1, \ldots, W_{p-q})'$, $W_i=X_{q+i}$, $1 \leqslant i \leqslant p-q$, then the problem reduces to the computer generation of $\mathbf{X}^{(1)}$ given $\mathbf{X}^{(2)}$.

For a complete formulation of the problem, further hypotheses are necessary. For instance, one may assume that the distribution of the random vector $\mathbf{X}$ is definitely known; in this case it is possible to derive the conditional distribution of $\mathbf{X}^{(1)}$ given that $\mathbf{X}^{(2)}=\mathbf{x}^{(2)}$. The problem will then consist of generating a sampling value of $\mathbf{X}^{(1)}$, given that $\mathbf{X}^{(2)}=\mathbf{x}^{(2)}$.

Throughout this paper we shall assume that $\mathbf{X}$ has a multivariate normal distribution $N(\boldsymbol{\mu}, \Sigma)$, where $\boldsymbol{\mu}$ is the 'mean' vector and Σ is the variance-covariance matrix; both $\boldsymbol{\mu}$ and Σ are supposed to be known.

THE MATHEMATICAL BACKGROUND

In order to derive the conditional distribution of $\mathbf{X}^{(1)}$ given that $\mathbf{X}^{(2)}=\mathbf{x}^{(2)}$, the following theorem (*see* Anderson 1958, para. 2.4) is necessary.

Theorem 1

Let $\mathbf{X}^{(1)}$ be a q-variate random vector and $\mathbf{X}^{(2)}$ a r-variate random vector $(p=r+q)$. If $\mathbf{X}^{(1)}$ and $\mathbf{X}^{(2)}$ are stochastically independent and $\mathbf{X}^{(1)} \sim N(\boldsymbol{\mu}^{(1)}, \Sigma_{11})$, $\mathbf{X}^{(2)} \sim N(\boldsymbol{\mu}^{(2)}, \Sigma_{22})$ then the random vector $\mathbf{X}=\begin{pmatrix}\mathbf{X}^{(1)} \\ \mathbf{X}^{(2)}\end{pmatrix}$ has the distribution $N(\boldsymbol{\mu}, \Sigma)$, where

$$\boldsymbol{\mu}=\begin{pmatrix}\boldsymbol{\mu}^{(1)} \\ \boldsymbol{\mu}^{(2)}\end{pmatrix}, \quad \Sigma=\begin{pmatrix}\Sigma_{11} & 0 \\ 0 & \Sigma_{22}\end{pmatrix} . \tag{1}$$

Reciprocally, if $\mathbf{X}$ is a $N(\boldsymbol{\mu}, \Sigma)$ random vector such that Σ is given by eq. (1), then $\mathbf{X}^{(1)}$ and $\mathbf{X}^{(2)}$ are independent.

[The abbreviation $\mathbf{X} \sim N(\boldsymbol{\mu}, \Sigma)$ means that the random vector $\mathbf{X}$ has a normal $N(\boldsymbol{\mu}, \Sigma)$ distribution, where $\boldsymbol{\mu}$ is the mean vector and Σ is the variance-covariance matrix.]

The proof of this theorem is immediate; we shall use it to derive the conditional distribution of $\mathbf{X}^{(1)}$ given that $\mathbf{X}^{(2)}=\mathbf{x}^{(2)}$. The following theorem specifies this distribution.

Theorem 2

Let $\mathbf{X}$ be a $N(\boldsymbol{\mu}, \Sigma)$ random vector with det $\Sigma \neq 0$ (where 'det' denotes 'determinant of'), and

$$\mathbf{X} = \begin{pmatrix} \mathbf{X}^{(1)} \\ \mathbf{X}^{(2)} \end{pmatrix}, \qquad \boldsymbol{\mu} = \begin{pmatrix} \boldsymbol{\mu}^{(1)} \\ \boldsymbol{\mu}^{(2)} \end{pmatrix}, \qquad \Sigma = \begin{pmatrix} \Sigma_{11} & \Sigma_{12} \\ \Sigma_{21} & \Sigma_{22} \end{pmatrix} \tag{2}$$

where $\mathbf{X}^{(1)}, \boldsymbol{\mu}^{(1)}$ are q-variate vectors, $\mathbf{X}^{(2)}, \boldsymbol{\mu}^{(2)}$ are r-variate vectors, $(r+q=p)$ and $\Sigma_{11}, \Sigma_{12}, \Sigma_{21}, \Sigma_{22}$ are respectively $q \times q, q \times r, r \times q, r \times r$ matrices. Then $\mathbf{X}^{(1)} \sim N(\boldsymbol{\mu}^{(1)}, \Sigma_{11})$, $\mathbf{X}^{(2)} \sim N(\boldsymbol{\mu}^{(2)}, \Sigma_{22})$ and the conditional distribution of $\mathbf{X}^{(1)}$ given that $\mathbf{X}^{(2)} = \mathbf{x}^{(2)}$ is

$$N(\boldsymbol{\mu}_*^{(1)}, \Sigma_{11}^*)$$

with $\quad \boldsymbol{\mu}_*^{(1)} = \boldsymbol{\mu}^{(1)} + \Sigma_{12} \Sigma_{22}^{-1}(\mathbf{X}^{(2)} - \boldsymbol{\mu}^{(2)})$

$$\Sigma_{11}^* = \Sigma_{11} - \Sigma_{12} \Sigma_{22}^{-1} \Sigma_{21} \quad . \tag{3}$$

Proof. Since, when $\mathbf{X}^{(1)}$ and $\mathbf{X}^{(2)}$ are independent, the conditional distribution of $\mathbf{X}^{(1)}$ given that $\mathbf{X}^{(2)} = \mathbf{x}^{(2)}$ is the distribution of $\mathbf{X}^{(1)}$, it follows that the only case to be considered is when $\mathbf{X}^{(1)}$ and $\mathbf{X}^{(2)}$ are stochastically dependent, that is,

$$\Sigma_{12} \neq 0, \qquad \Sigma_{21} \neq 0;$$

(of course $\Sigma_{21}' = \Sigma_{12}$). Therefore, assuming $\mathbf{X}^{(1)}$ and $\mathbf{X}^{(2)}$ are dependent, let us choose a transform

$$\mathbf{Y}^{(1)} = \mathbf{X}^{(1)} + T\mathbf{X}^{(2)} \tag{4}$$
$$\mathbf{Y}^{(2)} = \mathbf{X}^{(2)}$$

where T is a $q \times r$ matrix, such that the components of $\mathbf{Y}^{(1)}$ and $\mathbf{Y}^{(2)}$ be uncorrelated, that is,

$$\mathrm{Cov}(\mathbf{Y}^{(1)}, \mathbf{Y}^{(2)'}) = 0 \quad . \tag{5}$$

Since we may assume that Σ_{22} is non-singular, and since also

$$\mathrm{Cov}(\mathbf{Y}^{(1)}, \mathbf{Y}^{(2)'}) = \Sigma_{12} + T\Sigma_{22},$$

it follows that

$$T = -\Sigma_{12} \Sigma_{22}^{-1} \quad .$$

Hence, the required transform is

$$\mathbf{Y}^{(1)} = \mathbf{X}^{(1)} - \Sigma_{12} \Sigma_{22}^{-1} \mathbf{X}^{(2)}, \tag{6}$$

and consequently the mean vector and the variance-covariance matrix of $\mathbf{Y}^{(1)}$ are respectively

$$E[\mathbf{Y}^{(1)}] = \boldsymbol{\mu}^{(1)} - \Sigma_{12} \Sigma_{22}^{-1} \boldsymbol{\mu}^{(2)}$$
$$\mathrm{Cov}[\mathbf{Y}^{(1)}, \mathbf{Y}^{(1)}] = \Sigma_{11} - \Sigma_{12} \Sigma_{22}^{-1} \Sigma_{22} \quad . \tag{7}$$

Let us denote by $f(\mathbf{X}; \boldsymbol{\mu}, \Sigma)$ the probability density function of the distribution $N(\boldsymbol{\mu}, \Sigma)$, that is,

$$f(\mathbf{X}; \boldsymbol{\mu}, \Sigma) = \frac{1}{(2\pi)^{p/2} \sqrt{\det \Sigma}} e^{-\frac{1}{2}(\mathbf{X}-\boldsymbol{\mu})'\Sigma^{-1}(\mathbf{X}-\boldsymbol{\mu})} \quad .$$

It follows that $\mathbf{Y}^{(1)}$ and $\mathbf{Y}^{(2)}$ have respectively the probability density functions

$$f(\mathbf{Y}^{(1)}; \boldsymbol{\mu}^{(1)} - \Sigma_{12} \Sigma_{22}^{-1} \boldsymbol{\mu}^{(2)}, \Sigma_{11} - \Sigma_{12} \Sigma_{22}^{-1} \Sigma_{21})$$

and

$$f(\mathbf{Y}^{(2)}; \boldsymbol{\mu}^{(2)}, \Sigma_{22})$$

and hence, the probability density function of $\mathbf{Y} = \begin{pmatrix} \mathbf{Y}^{(1)} \\ \mathbf{Y}^{(2)} \end{pmatrix}$ is

$$f(\mathbf{Y}^{(1)}; \boldsymbol{\mu}^{(1)} - \Sigma_{12}\Sigma_{22}^{-1}\boldsymbol{\mu}^{(2)}, \Sigma_{11} - \Sigma_{12}\Sigma_{22}^{-1}\Sigma_{21}) f(\mathbf{Y}^{(2)}; \boldsymbol{\mu}^{(2)}, \Sigma_{22})$$

and according to eq. (6), this density becomes

$$f(\mathbf{X}^{(1)} - \Sigma_{12}\Sigma_{22}^{-1}\mathbf{X}^{(2)}; \boldsymbol{\mu}^{(1)} - \Sigma_{12}\Sigma_{22}^{-1}\boldsymbol{\mu}^{(2)}, \Sigma_{11} - \Sigma_{12}\Sigma_{22}^{-1}\Sigma_{21}) f(\mathbf{X}^{(2)};$$
$$\boldsymbol{\mu}^{(2)}, \Sigma_{22}) \quad . \quad (8)$$

(Note that the jacobian of our transformation is 1!) From eq. (8), it follows that the probability density function of $\mathbf{X}^{(1)}$ given that $\mathbf{X}^{(2)} = \mathbf{x}^{(2)}$ is

$$f(\mathbf{X}^{(1)}; \boldsymbol{\mu}^{(1)} + \Sigma_{12}\Sigma_{22}^{-1}(\mathbf{x}^{(2)} - \boldsymbol{\mu}^{(2)}), \Sigma_{11} - \Sigma_{12}\Sigma_{22}^{-1}\Sigma_{21})$$

and the proof is complete.

In order to generate sampling values on $\mathbf{X}^{(1)}$ given that $\mathbf{X}^{(2)} = \mathbf{x}^{(2)}$, it is necessary to derive a technique for generating sampling values for a normal random vector $N(\boldsymbol{\mu}, \Sigma)$, when $\boldsymbol{\mu}$ and Σ are known and Σ is a non-singular matrix.

Computer generation of a normal random vector can be based on the following theorem (*see* Naylor *et al.* 1966, p. 98).

Theorem 3

Let $\mathbf{U}$ be an $N(\mathbf{O}, I)$ random vector where I is the unit matrix of order $q \times q$ and $\mathbf{X} \sim N(\boldsymbol{\mu}, \Sigma)$; here $\boldsymbol{\mu}$ and Σ are known and Σ is a $q \times q$ non-singular matrix. Let C be a matrix satisfying the condition $C'C = \Sigma$. Then the random vector $\mathbf{Y} = \boldsymbol{\mu} + C\mathbf{U}$ is a $N(\boldsymbol{\mu}, \Sigma)$ random vector.

Proof. It is known (*see*, for instance, Anderson 1958, appendix 2, consequence 4), that for a given symmetrical positive definite matrix Σ, there is a lower triangular matrix C, such that $CC' = \Sigma$. The elements of this matrix (*see* Naylor *et al.* 1966, p. 98) are

$$c_{i1} = \frac{\sigma_{i1}}{\sqrt{\sigma_{11}}}, \qquad 1 \leqslant i \leqslant q$$

$$c_{ii} = \sqrt{\left(\sigma_{ii} - \sum_{k=1}^{i-1} c_{ik}^2\right)}, \qquad 1 \leqslant i \leqslant q$$

$$c_{ij} = \frac{\sigma_{ij} - \sum_{k=1}^{j-1} c_{ik}c_{jk}}{c_{jj}}, \qquad 1 < j < i \leqslant q$$

$$c_{ij} = 0, \qquad 1 < i < j \leqslant q, \qquad \Sigma = (\sigma_{ij}) \quad .$$

(9)

The vector $\mathbf{Y}$ has the mean value $E(\mathbf{Y}) = \boldsymbol{\mu}$, and the covariance matrix

$$\mathrm{Cov}(\mathbf{Y}, \mathbf{Y}') = CIC' = CC' = \Sigma$$

which completes the proof.

The generation of $\mathbf{X}^{(1)}$ given that $\mathbf{X}^{(2)} = \mathbf{x}^{(2)}$ may be done taking $\boldsymbol{\mu} = \boldsymbol{\mu}_*^{(1)}$ $\Sigma = \Sigma_{11}^*$ (*see* theorem 2).

The calculations required may be systematized into the following algorithms.

Algorithm 1 (Compute matrix C)

  0. Specify elements of Σ (input).

  1. Partition matrix Σ to obtain matrices $\Sigma_{11}, \Sigma_{12}, \Sigma_{22}$ and Σ_{21}, (*see* theorem 2).

  2. Compute $\Sigma_{11}^* = \Sigma_{11} - \Sigma_{12}\Sigma_{22}^{-1}\Sigma_{21}$.

  3. Compute the elements of matrix C according to eq. (9)*. (The star marks the end of the algorithm).

Algorithm 2 (Generation of the random vector $N(\boldsymbol{\mu}, \Sigma)$).

  0. Specify elements of C (input) produced by the algorithm 1.

1. Generate q random variates $N(0, 1)$. [For generating a random variate $N(0, 1)$ *see*, for instance, Box and Muller (1958)].
2. Denote **U** the p-variate vector generated in the preceding step and compute $\mathbf{Y} = \boldsymbol{\mu} + C\mathbf{U}$. (According to theorem 3, **Y** is the required vector).*

Algorithm 3 (Generation of $\mathbf{X}^{(1)}$ given that $\mathbf{X}^{(2)} = \mathbf{x}^{(2)}$).

0. Specify elements of C, $T = -\Sigma_{12}\Sigma_{22}^{-1}$, $\boldsymbol{\mu}^{(1)}$, $\boldsymbol{\mu}^{(2)}$ and $\mathbf{x}^{(2)}$.
1. Compute $\boldsymbol{\mu}_*^{(1)}$ and Σ_{11}^* according to eq. (3).
2. Generate a random vector $N(\boldsymbol{\mu}_*^{(1)}, \Sigma_{11}^*)$. (*See* algorithm 2).

Performing n times the algorithm 3 we can produce a sample of size n on the random vector $\mathbf{X}^{(1)}$ given that $\mathbf{X}^{(2)} = \mathbf{x}^{(2)}$.

Practical Considerations

In order to validate the described procedure for generating $\mathbf{X}^{(1)}$ given that $\mathbf{X}^{(2)} = \mathbf{x}^{(2)}$, a FORTRAN program was written and some runs were performed on the IBM 360/30 at the Computer Center of the University of Bucharest.

The components of **X** were some characteristics of the main estates of Romania during the year 1905. Since for some estates the data were incomplete, the problem was to fill up the list of data, by generating the unknown characteristics. The test was also intended to compare real and simulated data for those estates with complete information; the computer run gave quite satisfactory agreement between real and simulated data. However, the generated data have only a statistical value.

Because of the complicated calculations involved, the computer program was split down into several FORTRAN subroutines. These subroutines themselves use some other subroutines from the 'System/360 Scientific Subroutine Package, (360A–CM–03x), Version III', published by the IBM Corporation.

The practical work has drawn attention to some critical features of the procedure presented here; they will be underlined in the following.

(1) Because of rounding errors, the matrix Σ_{11}^* may be singular and non-symmetrical; in this case the procedure does not work.

(2) Sometimes the simulated data may fall outside of their practical range (for instance they may be negative, while they ought to be positive). In this case the procedure must be reviewed to produce numbers in the required range.

(3) In some cases it may happen that, as we consider different sampling values of **X**, each time a fresh set of components is unknown. In such a situation, a special routine for rearranging the components of each sampled vector **X** and for defining $\mathbf{X}^{(1)}$ and $\mathbf{X}^{(2)}$ must be built up. The vector $\mathbf{X}^{(1)}$ will contain the (sometimes) unknown q components and $\mathbf{X}^{(2)}$ the (always) known $p - q$ components of the sampled vector. Furthermore, rows and columns of the matrix Σ must be permuted according to the corresponding movements performed on the components of **X**. Finally, the matrix Σ will contain on the first q rows and on the first q columns the covariances derived from the components of $\mathbf{X}^{(1)}$ and all other components of **X**.

The mentioned operations on both **X** and Σ may be included in the same routine. This routine must be called before the actual simulation procedure.

REFERENCES

Anderson, T.W. (1958) *An Introduction to Multivariate Statistical Analysis.*

Box, C.E.P. & Muller, M.E. (1958) A note on generation of normal deviates. *Annals of Mathematical Statistics,* **29,** 610–11.

Knuth, D.E. (1969) *The Art of Computer Programming, vol. 2. Seminumerical Algorithms.* New York: Addison-Wesley.

Naylor, Th.H., Balintfy, L., Burdick, D.S. & Chu Kong (1966) *Computer Simulation Techniques.* New York: Wiley.

Văduva, I. (1969) *Computer Generation of Random Variables for Queueing Problems Illustrated by a Machine Interference Problem.* M.Sc. Thesis, University of Manchester, Institute of Science and Technology.

Abstract

Nicolae Oprescu
Some possibilities for using the volume of information in archaeology and history

The author reviews the archaeologists' traditional tasks from the standpoint of data-handling and information theory. Special attention is given to the automatic recording and processing of 'remotely sensed' objects and regions using the whole electro-magnetic spectrum; using emission absorption, and reflection techniques; taking advantage of current techniques associated with the phenomena of polarization, coherence, holography, and so on, and using (a) continuous recording in space and time to achieve maximum reception of information, and (b) computer storage and processing to achieve maximum utilization of the information received, in an acceptable time.

The principles and practice of analysis based on a quantitative measure of information are reviewed, and associated FORTRAN IV algorithms are presented.

The author's approach is illustrated by an account of its application to the site and monuments of Ada Kaleh.

Miscellaneous Applications

Discussion and comments

J. D. Wilcock (addressing R. E. M. Moore). In your printed summary you give a value of 216 mm for a mosaic unit. Would you like to comment on the fact that this unit does not fit into what would otherwise be a perfect Fibonacci series of units?

R. E. M. Moore. If we transform 216 mm in the same way as the other values can be transformed into Fibonacci numbers we get the integer 18, a term in the Lucas series. Thus 216 mm is related to the Fibonacci series. However, alignments occur as a packing phenomenon as frequently at 216 mm as at the other values, thus it is basic. Once alignment is achieved, one might expect the situation to re-cycle and never get beyond the shortest alignment interval. But no alignment is perfect, and which interval occurs apparently depends largely on the degree of imperfection of the preceding alignment. Defining disorder D as

$$\sum_{x=1}^{r} d'_x,$$

where $d' \leqslant d''$, and d' and d'' are the pair of displacements measured along the rows to either end of a stone measured from the end of the nearest-neighbouring stone in an adjacent row, and r is the number of rows, $D_{max} = (L_{max}/2)(r-1)$ where L is the length $|d'-d''|$ of a stone, contrary to the intuitive view that the disorder should continuously increase with growth.

J. D. Wilcock (addressing C. Orton). Are you using information retrieval for the storage of data on pottery rims and bases, and if so what hardware form does this take, and is it by serial or random access?

C. Orton. For the duration of the project (July 1970–July 1971) information retrieval is being used with storage of data on magnetic disc. In the longer term, ordinary card-index methods are in use.

Serial access (BCD) files are in use in the project.

V. Liveanu. The application of mathematics to archaeology is easier than to history because archaeology requests the classification of *objects*. The use of mathematics for relations between objects meets less opposition. But the essential objective is not to pose and solve in mathematical terms questions that can be solved by non-mathematical methods, but to use mathematics for solving problems unresolvable by traditional means. The essential is not to research for mathematical relations between historical facts, but to research for and find the historical sense, the historical signification of such relations. If such mathematical relations between historical facts have not a historical meaning, they are 'spurious relations', artifacts without real historical equivalence, hence of no use or importance for historians. The historical sense of a mathematical relation is a matter of historical theory, of historical conceptions.

Use of models

Use of models

L. L. Cavalli-Sforza
Similarities and dissimilarities of sociocultural and biological evolution

The most exciting mathematical theory ever put forward in biology is that of biological evolution. Its foundations were laid in the twenties by three people, R. A. Fisher, J. B. S. Haldane, and S. Wright. Recent developments in the mathematics of stochastic processes have renewed interest in this field, and the work in it is still very active.

It may seem remarkable that a process like biological evolution is amenable to quantitative study, and that a valid theory can be built on complex phenomena that involve highly complex organisms. The key to success has been largely the isolation of some fundamental 'factors' of evolution which are easily quantified. These theoretical developments have permitted considerable insight into biological evolutionary processes.

No such general theory, apart from a few regarding sectional aspects, seems to be available for the analysis of sociocultural change. If a similar theoretical development were possible, it might prove as powerful as it was for biology in stimulating clear thinking and giving rise to valuable predictions. (In the case of history, when reconstruction of past events and of the forces behind them is an aim, the word 'postdiction' has been suggested for use instead of 'prediction'.) I have been greatly surprised by the existence of considerable similarities (obvious differences notwithstanding) between the evolutionary processes of a biological and a sociocultural nature. This has led me to wonder if some considerations, along the following lines, might be useful in laying down the foundations of a theory of sociocultural change, borrowing, when possible, from the existing body of theories already developed in various fields of biology. As the present conference is mostly concerned with sociocultural change, I thought it might be appropriate to communicate some of these ideas to the audience, and the present paper summarizes and slightly expands a few contributions to the discussion that took place along these lines.

It would be impossible to give, in a short paper, an adequate summary of the mathematical theory of biological evolution. A recent, very authoritative account has just been published (Crow and Kimura 1969). A book to appear (Cavalli-Sforza and Bodmer 1971) analyzes the applications of the theory to human genetics and evolution. I will limit myself here to giving a short list of the major factors and processes of biological evolution, and comparing them with what seem to me the equivalent factors and processes in sociocultural change.

In biological evolution, the source of hereditary variation is *mutation*. The new type originated by mutation (called a mutant) is exposed to the effect of natural selection. If advantageous over the other types already in existence, because of higher fertility, lower mortality, or both, it is expected to be represented in the progeny at a proportionately higher frequency than the old types, and thus progressively increase in frequency, until it may supersede the previous types. If neutral or disadvantageous, it will usually be rejected sooner or later, although it may (very rarely) increase because of chance effects, which will be discussed later.

The equivalent of a mutant, in sociocultural evolution, is a new *idea*. If it turns out to be acceptable and advantageous, it will spread easily. If not, it is likely to be forgotten. But here again the chance element may be important. There are close parallels between mutation and the process giving origin to new ideas, *invention*. Both phenomena are in the nature of rare, discrete changes, which occur almost randomly, but may recur. The similarity seems more remarkable, if one thinks that, both for mutation and invention, it is often difficult to distinguish whether separate occurrences of the same new event are due to independent origins of the same change (that is, to a true recurrence), or to migrants from the first area of origin who promulgate new genes in the one case, and the new notion in the other, even to remote areas. Another similarity: both for mutation and invention the environment, including that around us and that formed by ourselves (the genotypic or cultural background), are important or essential in determining whether a given change will be advantageous or not.

The notion of advantage or disadvantage implicit in the theory of natural selection is clearly applicable to ideas as well as to mutations. As an equivalent of *'fitness'* (in biology the relative number of descendants to which a given hereditary type will be passed in the next generation) one might consider, for cultural evolution, the probability that a given innovation will be accepted by the individual to whom it is presented.

Clearly, however, there is at least one major difference between biological and cultural evolution, and this is the *mechanism of transmission*. Genes are passed from parents to offspring by a very strict mechanism. In organisms reproducing sexually, as Man, every individual has an approximately equal genetic contribution from its father and its mother, and it will pass to its progeny only half of the contribution it receives from each of its two parents, either the paternal or the maternal part.

Because of the mendelian mechanism of transmission, biological inheritance is highly conservative and, ignoring mutation, selection, and statistical sampling of genes, variation is strictly preserved from one generation to the next. New variations are created continuously by mutation, but its rate is exceedingly small and controls only minimally the rate of biological evolution. Rather, it is natural selection which determines the overall rate of change. Even so, usually thousands of generations are necessary before a population experiences an observable change, and millions before the difference is of some magnitude, as, for instance, that between ourselves and the nearest Primates.

The mechanism of cultural transmission is quite different. Parent to child transmission does still play an important role, but not such a rigid one, and in addition, a very large fraction of our knowledge derives from interactions between teacher and pupil, sib and sib, friend and friend. Indirect transmission through books, mass media, and so on, takes an ever-greater share. Today a new notion can be transmitted almost instantaneously to a very large audience. Whether it will be forgotten or accepted depends of course on the notion itself, its persuasive power, and also the way it is imparted; but, potentially, the whole of human beings can be converted to a new idea in a very short time.

Even so, cultural evolution can be slow, sometimes even slower than biological evolution. A group of Pygmies which I have examined shows very little sociological difference from another Pygmy group living a thousand miles away and from which it must have been isolated for a long time. Still, almost half of its genetic background may have been substituted by genes from other neighboring populations that are biologically and culturally quite distinct. Here cultural change has been very slow and the independence of culture from the biological background shows very distinctly (Cavalli-Sforza *et al.* 1969). Probably, the most conservative traits in sociocultural evolution are those that are transmitted early in life and determine an indelible impression.

As was noted by Professor Kendall also, cultural transmission resembles not so much the genetic one, as that of infectious disease, which incidentally has also been the object of intensive mathematical study (*see*, for example, Bailey 1957). If one were to describe mathematically the recent spread of popular games, for example, the yo-yo, one would find that their kinetics can be studied in a way similar to that of epidemics of measles or influenza. The main variables, here again, would be the numbers of contagious, of susceptible, and of immune (isolated or dead) individuals, and the main parameters at play, the rate of infection and the rate of 'removal' (immunity or death in infection, tiredness or a variety of other reactions in sociocultural epidemics).

A further element of similarity between the two types of evolution comes from the role played, in both, by *migration*. Any traveller, be he merchant, sailor, or explorer, spreads new ideas as well as, occasionally, his genes. A person moving elsewhere for reasons of work, marriage, or other, brings with him his genes as well as his customs. Migration must have an almost equal importance in the two types of change.

Finally, the role of chance should be mentioned. In the genetic theory of evolution chance plays an important role. New mutations appear at random in time and space, thus contributing to randomness of biological evolution. In addition, the mechanism of mendelian transmission commonly assigns to each of the two copies of one gene, that of paternal and of maternal origin, an equal probability of being represented in each child. This probability mechanism leaves open the way to sampling accidents. In a population of finite size, as all populations are, the frequency of any one gene in the next generation is a random variable, that is, it is not fixed exactly, but has a probability distribution. Thus, a mutant, even if favorable, could become extinct by chance alone, and inversely, an unfavorable mutant might be fixed in the same way.

The probability of such extreme events is, of course, remote, the more so the larger the size of a population, but the variation due to chance is important because it accumulates over generations, and thus can determine considerable change if given sufficient time. It has received the somewhat confusing name of 'genetic drift'.

It is very likely that similar phenomena play a role in cultural evolution. Just to take an extreme example: many important literary works were lost because none of the manuscripts survived. We know of their existence and perhaps the little and/or fragments of them only because they were cited by other authors. This must have been a function, among other things, of the small number of manuscripts of a particular book. Even in the spread of any innovation, chance must play a role. The two stages through which innovation spreads, (1) the interaction between two or more people who play the active and passive roles in the process, and (2) the acceptance of the innovation by the passive person, have each a probability of occurring. Thus the kinetics of such processes is better given, when possible, by a stochastic rather than by a deterministic treatment.

We are at the moment in the process of investigating in Pavia the kinetics of sociocultural change for some ethnographic characters of African populations. A few existing models of stochastic processes can be applied as such, others require extension or adaptation. Unfortunately, historical data are rarely available and most of the analysis has to be done on the basis of present-day geographic distribution, which narrows considerably the possibilities of analysis. There should, however, be many chances, offered by archaeology, of following an evolutionary process in sufficient detail, to make it possible to investigate the spread of an innovation through both time and space.

One type of cultural evolution in which models undoubtedly near to the genetic ones can be useful is that of language. As noted at this symposium by Dr Sankoff (1971), the equation used in glottochronology to describe the probability of survival of a word, e^{-kt}, or that of its substitution, $1 - e^{-kt}$, where t is time and k a constant (probably characteristic of a given word and language, but taken, in the early work on glottochronology, as a first approximation, as just constant) is similar to equations used in genetic evolutionary theory. But it should be noted that the formally similar equation used by us (Cavalli-Sforza et al. 1969) refers not to a probability of survival or extinction of a gene, but to the variance between gene frequencies of different populations, and is based on a more complex theory. A closer parallel is that of the model and equation first used by Zuckerkandl and Pauling (1965) in molecular evolution, and further studied by Kimura (1968), for the probability of substitution of an aminoacid with another in a protein. It is of interest to remark that this gives, at once, a clear idea of the enormous difference in rates between biological and non-biological evolution. In the former this rate of substitution is found to be of the order of one billion years (expressed as average life of a single aminoacid), that is, roughly one million times higher than the comparable rate for a word substitution in languages. One problem confronting the study of linguistic evolution is that, to date, the values of k in the equation just mentioned cannot be predicted on the basis of *a priori* considerations. In the case of random genetic drift the value of k can be given *a priori* and the data from molecular evolution are surprisingly close to the order of magnitude thus expected, indicating that the role of this factor is hardly negligible (Kimura 1968).

A possible approach for predicting values of k in linguistic evolution may come from some of the following considerations. Sankoff has suggested the study of the frequency of synonyms and how they change with time. This has a close parallel with genetic polymorphism. Genetic theory predicts the behaviour of two or more alleles of one gene under drift and evolutionary processes, such as, for example, mutation or selection. In particular, the expected number of alleles of a given gene existing in a population at equilibrium is given by $1 + 4N_e\mu$ (Kimura and Crow 1964) where N_e is the effective population size (the number of reproducing individuals of a population) and μ the mutation rate. The quantity N_e is equal for all genes. For words, however, it is different; there are some widely used concepts, and for these 'effective population size' must be larger than for the rarer ones. It must be a function of both the number of individuals speaking the language and of the relative use of the concept. In addition, if one looks, for example, at the word 'drunk' in Roget's *Thesaurus*, one is struck by the large number of synonyms in existence (as contrasted, for example, with 'sober'). It is also possible that more commonly used concepts, or those that affect us more deeply (or both) have a higher rate of word invention. This, alone, or a larger 'N_e' for words of common usage, or both, can increase in some predictable way the number of synonyms in existence.

One difficulty in the analysis of cultural change is that it is not always easy to understand how natural selection may operate in each particular case. In some cases it may be easy. If we take the word 'airplane' it is clear why it has an increasing fitness and has come in common usage, and undergone a rapid evolution. We have no doubt that the style of life introduced by the neolithic revolution has, or had, a high fitness. In many other cases the reasons behind the higher 'fitness' of a particular word or of a sociocultural state may be difficult to understand. But the same is often true in biological evolution. Moreover, some types of natural selection, for example, sexual selection, may as in special types of cultural and linguistic change be the expression of 'fashions'. Such fashions may exist, and be equally capricious whether it is the matter of sexual selection for a special type of plumage in birds, or of the popularity of a particular political idea, word, or game. Naturally, capriciousness may be superficial and just hide our lack of understanding.

It is worth commenting on two further points, which have been brought forward in two interesting recent books. One of them is the similar role placed by social hierarchies in both biological and cultural evolution (Mainardi 1968). If an idea is communicated by a person who is high in the social hierarchy it will carry a much greater weight (especially at the beginning), and is much more likely to be adopted by a large number of people than if it is expressed by a person who is lower in the hierarchy. Similarly, if a mutation takes place in a socially dominant male of a mouse colony, it will be transmitted to a larger number of females than if it takes place in a less dominant male, because social dominance gives access to most females of the colony.

Other aspects have been particularly considered by Mather (1964) who has drawn a comparison between genes on one hand and ideas on the other. Professor Mather has stressed the fact that mutation and natural selection do take place not only for genes but also for ideas. His chief preoccupation, however, has been mainly at another level, that of the interaction between the two types of evolution. For instance, certain 'ideas' can confer a higher *biological* fitness to the group that professes them. This is an important concept, but should naturally be recognized as distinct from that of natural selection for ideas themselves. Some of the considerations given in the paper are summarized in table 1.

	Biological evolution	Sociocultural evolution
Process of change (and new type thus formed)	mutation (mutant)	invention (new idea)
Mechanism of transmission	mendelian (rigid, parent to child)	infective (parent or tutor or teacher to child, and so on, and in general anybody infectious to anybody susceptible)
Factors of spread	natural selection (fitness is proportion of representation in progeny)	natural selection (fitness is probability of acceptance by susceptible individual or group)
	migration	migration
Chance	random genetic drift, that is, statistical fluctuation of gene frequencies; and randomness of mutation	stochastic change of frequencies, randomness of invention

Table 1. Similarities and dissimilarities in two types of evolution

ACKNOWLEDGMENT

The work here reported was in part supported by grants from the US AEC.

REFERENCES

Bailey, N.T.J. (1957) *The Mathematical Theory of Epidemics*. London: Griffin.
Cavalli-Sforza, L.L., Zonta, L.A., Nuzzo, F., Bernini, L., De Jong, W.W.W., Meera Khan, P., Ray, A.K., Went, L.N., Siniscalco, M., Nijenhuis, L.E., Van Loghem, E. & Modiano, G. (1969) Studies on African Pygmies. I. A pilot

investigation of Babinga Pygmies in the Central African Republic (with an analysis of genetic distances). *Amer. J. hum. Genet.*, **21**, 252–74.

Cavalli-Sforza, L.L. & Bodmer, W. (1971) *The Genetics of Human Population.* San Francisco: Freeman.

Crow, J.F. & Kimura, M. (1969) *An Introduction to Population Genetics Theory.* New York: Harper and Row.

Kimura, M. (1968) Evolutionary rate at the molecular level. *Nature*, **217**, 624–6.

Kimura, M. & Crow, J.F. (1964) The number of alleles that can be maintained in a finite population. *Genetics*, **19**, 725–38.

Mainardi, D. (1968) La scelta sessuale nell'evoluzione della specie. *Paolo Boringhieri Editore.* Torino.

Mather, K. (1964) *Human Diversity.* Edinburgh: Oliver and Boyd.

Sankoff, D. (1971) Stochastic models for glottochronology. *Mathematics in the Archaeological & Historical Sciences*, pp. 381–6 (eds. Hodson, F.R., Kendall, D.G. & Tăutu, P.). Edinburgh: Edinburgh University Press.

Zuckerkandl, E. & Pauling, L. (1965) Evolutionary divergence and convergence in proteins. *Evolving Genes and Proteins* (eds Bryson, V. & Vogel, H.). New York: Academic Press.

Use of models

Robert M. Loynes
The role of models

Throughout the conference the idea of a model was never far from the surface, and from time to time, notably in one of the organized Round Table Discussions, it became the centre of attention. Yet it is clear that considerable uncertainty about the meaning of the term and about the value of the concept existed, and this essay is written in the hope that it will assist in clarifying matters. Now it is quite plain that, since the discussion of models and their significance represents a large part of the philosophy of science and of scientific method, only a rather limited account can be given here: this will therefore be a personal assessment of some of the more significant points. A longer discussion, with many references, can be found in Chorley and Haggett (1967, chapter 1); their chapter has rather the appearance of propaganda for the use of models, and it is a little difficult to hack a clear path through, but where we do overlap we appear to agree.

There seem to me to be four fundamental questions which must be answered. What is a model? What is a model for? Is a model useful (in individual investigations)? Is a model necessary? These I propose to discuss in turn.

WHAT IS A MODEL?

If one consults a dictionary, or more usefully a philosopher of science, one will obtain a definition, though it may well differ from that given by another source: for example, Braithwaite, as Professor Spaulding reminded us, has defined a model as 'a partially worked-out theory'. Some of these definitions do not seem altogether appropriate, nor to agree with one's intuitive understanding, but this is at least partly due to the fact that, for historical reasons, natural and particularly physical science has received far more attention than any other kind of knowledge. Personally I prefer to define a model as 'a partial representation of reality', as I shall explain below, but the details are not, of course, very important provided it is clear in what sense the word is used.

The most familiar kind of model is the physical miniature, as for example toy cars and trains, and, more seriously, scale models in wind-tunnel experiments. Moving away from the obvious, one recognizes photographs and diagrams as a kind of model, and so one can go on, giving examples of other kinds, and making other distinctions, such as that between static and dynamic models. But this is not the place, and indeed there is no reason, to attempt a classification of models—to construct a model of the set of models, so to speak; it is enough for present purposes to draw the distinction between quantitative (usually mathematical) and qualitative models. Traditionally archaeology has been concerned only with the latter, but, as in all branches of knowledge, more and more stress is being placed on the former. This, incidentally, is a convenient moment to explain why, although there is a school of thought particularly associated with those trained in mathematics or the physical sciences in which the concept of model is considered more or less co-extensive with that of quantitative model, I favour a broader view: it is just that it seems impossible to make a division with any real conviction. Consider, for example, the following rather general verbal model: 'the trade between two communities depends in part on their relative geographical location'. For various reasons this might be made more specific in several stages: from dependence in part, through dependence largely, then mainly, to dependence essentially only; from trade, through amount of trade, then amount of trade in amber, to amount of amber found; from relative geographical location to distance apart. The first stage was a vague verbal model, the last stage in essence a mathematical model of the form $A = f(D)$, A being the amount of amber found, D the distance apart, and f an as yet unknown function: where in this succession should one draw the dividing line?

Having, then, adopted the broad view, it is perhaps worth remarking on the connection between models and theories. Here again there seems to be a divergence between philosophers and logicians on the one hand, and the rest of the world on the other, and my own inclination is to follow the latter. Thus, although models and theories are abstractly the same, their relationships with us and with the facts are different: a model may be inadequate (for a given purpose), but it is not false, and it may be useful on some later occasion, whereas a theory can be false, and if ever proved so will not be considered again as a theory in the same sense. To a great extent, in fact, a theory is about what reality is *really* like, while a model is concerned with how reality behaves—a behaviouristic approach. It would, nevertheless, be pedantic not to describe a model as wrong in at least some cases of extreme inadequacy; the production of a toy boat when asked for a model of a car, for example.

WHAT IS A MODEL FOR?

There are various answers to this question which seem relevant to archaeology, and one which, except in a rather weak sense, is not: prediction. Simplicity seems to be the common theme in all the answers: the creation of order out of chaos, the reduction of highly complex data to a manageable form, and so on. Synthesis, of a mass of unconnected facts into a unified structure, is another answer along the same lines; it seems appropriate here to recall the definition of a model given at the Conference by Professor Olkin, as a set of variables and their interrelationships.

This is perhaps a convenient place at which to make two related points: that there is no such thing as the correct, or the only, model of a given situation, and that it makes no sense to talk of using *all* the information. To take the second point first, though it scarcely needs discussion in a concrete case, to describe even a single artifact completely is impossible: what one does is to describe the *important* or *relevant* features. (What they are important for or relevant to is presumably the use to which the model is to be put.)

The definition of a model as a *partial* representation of reality becomes significant here, for it has often been pointed out that an exact or complete representation requires essentially a second copy, which would be of no use, even if it were conceivable. (There is, of course, a weaker wholly admirable sense in which to interpret 'using all the information': one should not ignore data which do not fit one's ideas.) The other point, that there can be more than one model of (a part of) reality follows from this, for if one cannot achieve an exact and complete description then what is left out must be to some extent arbitrary, and depends on the use to which the model is to be put. It may be, for example, that the broad outline of cultural change in prehistory is fairly well explained by the invasion model, while for a particular group or location more is needed, such as a dash of cultural evolution.

It is, in fact, of some interest to consider why the opposite viewpoint should ever have been adopted. Presumably it is the influence of physical science again, in which one has the feeling that observation has now shown, for example, that the Newtonian theory of gravitation is untrue, but that the relativistic theory of gravitation is still on trial, and may be true. To argue like this, however, is to take too simple a view of matters, for the Newtonian theory remains adequate for all normal purposes, while the relativistic theory only remains tenable if the discrepancies which are called observational errors are ignored, and the attitude implicit in the latter appears itself to arise either from an underlying model in which Nature is simple (compare Jeans' remarks about God being a mathematician) or from an application of Occam's Razor.

IS A MODEL USEFUL?

Since I shall argue later that it is impossible to avoid working within a model, it may seem unnecessary to answer this question; the kind of question that one really wants to ask, however, is a little different, and is whether closely specified or quantitative models are useful. The reply to this can only be that it depends on the circumstances: certainly an insistence on quantitative models will, in many cases, be premature and so prove restrictive and lead to Procrustean thinking. (The choice of the level of detail to be included in a model, and of the particular model, is, now and probably for a long time in the future, an art largely dependent on individual inspiration, although I like to think of statistics as an embryo science of model-building.) One might, incidentally, note the danger in adopting too general a model: if too many features are considered, which are to be related one to another, the model is almost bound to fit, for then situations will remain essentially unique.

This said, what more can be said of the usefulness or otherwise of quantitative models in archaeology? The answer to this is even more a personal guess than the rest of this essay, but it seems to me that one should be optimistic, but cautious: optimistic because experience in other areas of knowledge, especially physical science, has shown that mathematical models have led to progress that could probably have been achieved in no other way; cautious because in constructing a model in an archaeological (as indeed any social scientific) context so much detail has to be omitted that it is not clear whether one can avoid throwing out the baby with the bath water—it is not, in other words, yet obvious whether Nature with human beings included is still simple. There is one apparent side benefit to be derived from an introduction of mathematical or quasi-mathematical models: the increased precision of language. It seems much easier to ignore an author's definition of 'culture', or indeed for an author to avoid having a proper definition, than similarly to maltreat a symbol d. Whether this is inevitable, or is rather a consequence of the fact that a symbol usually stands for a far simpler concept than a word, remains to be seen. If the use of models does prove widely valuable it will reduce the amount of unco-ordinated data, and hence allow greater concentration on its structure, and this should in turn lead to questions of a higher level of abstraction, such as why should a structure occur.

IS A MODEL NECESSARY?

Again one must begin by distinguishing between a general, rather vague model, and a closely specified or mathematical one, for it is impossible to avoid having some kind of model—for example, that fossils occur in accordance with modern beliefs rather than as a direct result of Noah's flood. But such a truism is of little interest, and one is tempted to go immediately to the other end of the scale and ask whether mathematical models are necessary. It is hardly possible to avoid the answer that they are not, but it seems to me that the wrong question has been posed. There has been some controversy, for instance, in statistics as to whether model-building is everything, the opposing view being that exploratory approaches with the lesser aim of 'making sense of the data' are an important component (see, for example, Kendall 1961, 1968, Irwin 1963, Ehrenburg 1968, Yates 1968). If one takes the broad view of models that I have argued above, however, the difference becomes merely one of how precisely the model is specified, and while this may make all the difference to analytical techniques used, there is no need for a different viewpoint to be adopted. This account gives rise to the idea of a hierarchy (or perhaps a more complicated structure) of models possibly applicable to a given situation, and the differences in the method of attack are largely a function of the temperament of the investigator—he can begin either with a model which is more or less bound to be adequate, but does not give rise to precise statements, and proceed to specialize it, or with a quantitative model immediately, which if adequate will allow more progress, but which may prove inadequate and necessitate a new start; the problem of the relationship of graves within a cemetery—whether to work in one dimension (that is, seriate directly) or to allow two or more dimensions initially (as in HORSHU)—is an illustration. For a given degree of specialization of the model, of course, the usual path has to be followed—description followed first by exploration of the data and finally by model-building.

One ought, I suppose, also to observe that in any case the interest in models is a consequence of certain modes of thought. If the individual pieces of information are themselves of interest—for example, in the construction of one's own family tree—then although one can detect the presence of a model there appears to be little point in doing so. Such situations do seem, however, to be rare, and it can be argued that increasing maturity in an individual, and (at least material) advances in civilisation, correspond to the development of ever better models of reality.

35

EPILOGUE

Models and model-building have been implicit in archaeology, and indeed science of any kind, since its beginning, and many of the points made above are obvious; being generalities they are bound to be so. The controversy, such as there is, appears to be due to the enthusiasts for a more explicit role for models, who have sometimes exaggerated the case and produced a natural counter-reaction. The following well-known quotation (Kaplan 1964, p. 288) provides a suitable note on which to end:

'Models are undeniably beautiful, and a man may justly be proud to be seen in their company. But they may have their hidden vices. The question is, after all, not only whether they are good to look at, but whether we can live happily with them.'

REFERENCES

Chorley, R.J. & Haggett, P. (1967) *Models in Geography*. London.

Ehrenburg, A.S.C. (1968) The elements of lawlike relationships. *J. Roy. statist. Soc. A*, **131**, 280.

Irwin, J.O. (1963) The place of mathematics in medical and biological statistics. *J. Roy. statist. Soc. A*, **126**, 1.

Kaplan, A. (1964) *The Conduct of Inquiry*. San Francisco.

Kendall, M.G. (1961) Natural law in the social sciences. *J. Roy. statist. Soc. A*, **124**, 1.

Kendall, M.G. (1968) On the future of statistics—a second look. *J. Roy. statist. Soc. A*, **131**, 182.

Yates, F. (1968) Theory and practice in statistics. *J. Roy. statist. Soc. A*, **131**, 463.

Use of models

Discussion and comments

R. W. Hiorns. In discussion, John Graham has just presented the approach of an archaeological statistician which I would summarize as: observation, model, inference. Although my experience as a statistician has been almost entirely with biologists, I am prompted to suggest that the model should *precede* observation. It is my suspicion that an archaeologist more often than not cannot predetermine to any great extent the type of observation which he makes. This degree of unpredictability is much lower in biological research.

Following from this remark I would like to comment on the attractive analogue presented by Professor Cavalli-Sforza concerning the evolution of populations from the respective points of view of genetic and sociocultural characteristics of populations. Surely, from the observational point of view, the approaches of the geneticist and the archaeologist are rather different and this will limit the usefulness of this analogue.

V. Liveanu. I think it is possible to define a model as a material or ideal construction reproducing in one way or other some features of another object (phenomenon, process). The model can be very simple (a mere hypothesis) or very complex (a theory), non-mathematical or mathematical.

I think that there exists no mathematical history and no mathematical archaeology but only history using mathematics and archaeology using mathematics. By this I wish only to emphasize once more that the meaning of the mathematical relationships discovered between historical phenomena or archaeological objects is not the concern of mathematics, but the concern of history and archaeology and of historical theory, which can use some mathematical concepts as well as non-mathematical ones.

Closing address

Closing address

Carl-Axel Moberg
Archaeological context and mathematical methods

> '*Mathematicians should direct their addresses mainly to the archaeologists and historians,*
> *archaeologists and historians should direct their addresses mainly to the mathematicians.*'

(Instructions for the speakers, Mamaia 1970).

In 1970, we can look back at some seventy-five years of applications of mathematical methods in archaeology—some of them internationally well known, others confined to regional groups of specialists. For a long time, such applications were fortuitous. More significant development has come with the computer age.

Even if the importance of organized meetings should not be exaggerated, a list of meetings illustrates some main trends in the development.

First, papers on mathematical and related methods appeared within conferences with a more general scope:

1950, New York: Conference on archaeological methods. Papers on 'The use of mathematical formulations in archaeological analysis', and 'The use of IBM machines in analyzing anthropological data'. (Brainerd, Thieme, publication ed. Griffin 1951).

1959, Burg Wartenstein: Symposium on the application of quantitative methods in archaeology. Paper on 'Statistical description and comparison of artifact assemblages'. (Spaulding, publication ed. Cook and Heizer 1960).

1963, Moscow: URSS meeting on science in archaeology, section for 'Mathematics and cybernetics'. (Publication ed. Koltchin 1965).

Then, the stage was set for more specialized conferences:

1966, Rome: International symposium on mathematical and computational methods in the social sciences. (Publication: 'Calcul et formalisation' 1968).

1969, Marseilles: International symposium on the application of computers in archaeology. (Publication: 'Archéologie et calculateurs', 1970).

1970, Mamaia: Anglo-Romanian conference on mathematics in the archaeological and historical sciences (this volume).

The following is an attempt to review some tendencies at the Mamaia conference, in an archaeological context. Where are we now? what has been achieved? what is still lacking, or less observed? what may be expected in the future?

The attempted answers to such questions reflect the narrow individual perspective of the observer, necessarily. (For some details, see works listed among the references). Moreover, he will try to use a terminology—a set of concepts—which may be less familiar to many archaeologists than to mathematicians and statisticians for whom these pages are written.

Of course, ideas expressed here are mainly borrowed from papers and argument during the conference. Acknowledgment is due to everyone; but for practical reasons, the full list of participants is not repeated here, and reference to individual contributions is not at all complete.

First, a 'map' of archaeology, from the point of view of methods, and in broad outline.

The purpose of archaeological research is to increase and/or ameliorate knowledge on relations (- - -) in and among structured clusters (-.-.-), the components (. .) of which are human beings (figure 1) and their partners in the natural environment. Emphasis is as much on their ecological out-relations with the environment (figure 2) as on their social, mutual in- and among-group relations (figure 3).

Figure 1   Figure 2

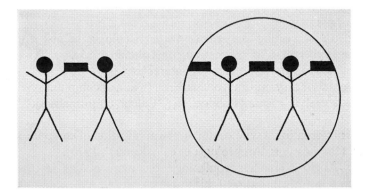

Figure 3   Figure 4

So far (figure 4), archaeology coincides with the social sciences; archaeology belongs to history; both study change with time. However, the components (. .), relations (- - -) and structures (-.-.-) can no more be observed directly. Instead, archaeology has to start with the study of structures (-.-.-) of another kind, the 'finds' in a broad sense. We might call these structures 'archaeograms'—in order to distinguish the subarea of *descriptive* *'archaeography'* from more *interpretative archaeology* in a narrower sense.

The archaeographical structures are believed to show some systematical relationships to human, social structures; this enables some degree of interpretation in terms of social history.

On the archaeographical level, we are observing *components* (..) such as attributes, artifacts, monuments ('features'), closed finds, accumulations, settlements, assemblages, 'complexes', 'culture groups' and so on; and their *relations* (- - -). (NB. 'Components' here means 'structural components'— a structural concept which should not be confused with an entirely different 'component' concept, current in American archaeology).

The components (..) and their relations (- - -) form a complicated and irregular hierarchy of structures (-.-.-). In this hierarchy, lower level structures (-.-.-) become components (..) at higher levels.

Structures are of different size and visibility. There are 'mini'-structures which cannot be observed directly by the archaeologist himself but have to be studied with the aid of natural sciences (for instance radioactivity of C_{14}; chemical composition of metal alloys; and so on).

The opposite upper ends of the hierarchy extend with 'maxi'-structures in direction towards the unattainable (and archaeologically uninteresting) theoretically maximal set of 'all' archaeological 'finds'.

In the middle, between the levels of mini- and maxi-structures are the basic ('midi') structures:
maxi-structures (such as settlements, 'culture groups' and so on)
basic structures (such as artifacts, monuments, refuse, marks) *see* figure 5.
mini-structures (attributes, visible and invisible).
These are basic for *practical* reasons: because they can be observed most directly with comparatively unsophisticated methods and tools.

Figure 5

In the belief of many non-archaeologists and of still not so few archaeologists, two out of four kinds of these structures at one of the several levels are often regarded as the sources of archaeology: (a) *artifacts* and (b) *monuments*. (Compare Clarke 1968).

But archaeology, and especially modern archaeology, uses also the other basic structures: (c) *refuse* without intentional shaping (such as flint waste, offal from butchering, phosphate), and (d) environmental traces, '*marks*', (such as traces of ploughing; or pollen curve 'bends', caused by man) of human activities.

Basic structures (c) and (d) are especially important for the study of man–environment relations, in ecologically oriented archaeology. Already for this reason, artifact and monument studies in a traditional sense, even if still important, have lost not so little of their earlier dominance. But there are deeper reasons, too. The change in archaeological research is somewhat analogous to the change in biosciences, with their extension from an earlier concentration on taxonomical studies, in a contrasting direction toward the levels of subcellular particles and of ecosystems. On the ecosystems level, biology and archaeology are virtually merging now.

Thus, archaeological mini- and maxi-structures are receiving more attention to-day than earlier. On the maxi-structure end, more systematical attention is focussed upon socio-systems than earlier; and, as a consequence, on such archaeographical entities as entire settlements (Chang 1966) viewed as expressions of extinct community systems, and on specialized activity areas within settlements (Binford and Binford 1968).

These developments of the study of maxi-structures have obvious methodological consequences. One, very important, is created by the fact that, on the maxi-levels, relations (- - -) are more complicated than below. On the artifact/monument levels it is often enough to observe simple additive relationships: that components (. .) just belong together in the same structure (-.-.-); for example, attributes in an artifact, or artifacts in a grave inventory. But when the structures are composed of, for instance, grave inventories *and* monuments *and* single artifact finds, one has to account for the fact that such components can be related in different ways, and thus belong to the maxi-structure for different reasons.

Connexion. They may 'belong together', agglomerating in a construction where they once functioned together (as axe+haft; or as building+fields+roads, and so on, of a village). [*See* figure 6(a).]

Inclusion. They may be enclosed as a 'parcel', an archaeological inclusion within some sort of 'envelope' or 'cover' (artificial, as a coffin, or natural as enclosing sediments, for instance within a stratigraphy). [*See* figure 6(b).]

They may form clusters of:

Proximity. 3-dimensional spatial clusters [*see* figure 6(c)].

Similarity. *n*-dimensional similarity clusters sharing (albeit in different proportions) or not-sharing attributes in a narrower or broader sense [*see* figure 6(d)]; or *Synchronism:* one-dimensional chronological clusters [6(e)].

There are gradual transitions from one type of relation to another (as from 'parcel' to spatial cluster).

Further, entities originally belonging together in one construction [figure 6(a)], may be separated and with time [figure 6 (e)] distributed spatially [figure 6(c)] (such as bronze artifacts cast in the same mould; or fragments from the same broken vessel; or products and productional refuse from one and the same piece of raw material, *see* figure 7); this type of complex relation—'affiliation of ex-constructions'—is very important for the discovery of activity subareas in sites and in regions.

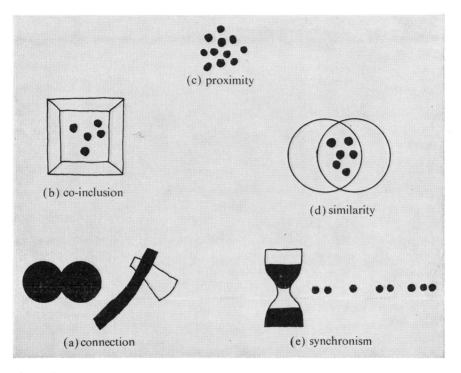

(c) proximity

(b) co-inclusion

(d) similarity

(a) connection

(e) synchronism

Figure 6

Different types of relations may be present simultaneously within the maxi-structure. This threshold of multi-type relations is decisive. Beyond it, the methodological situation for application of mathematical methods changes considerably.

And, last but not least—archaeology is increasingly aware that relations are not only *within* the archaeographical entity, but also with the outside world—linking the archaeographical entity with environment (figure 2). Every single piece of material was once taken out of the environment, with some effect on the ecosystem, which effect has to be taken into account [*see* figure 5(d)].

Spatial, similarity, and chronological relations interact. Thus, the archaeographical entity accessible for immediate observation has properties analogous to those of vectors. Similar complications arise also when structures are described not only in terms of clusters, and so on, but when the results of analysis and ordering take the form of sequences (seriation). Sequences may be determined by interaction of spatial difference, time difference, and sociocultural difference (figure 8, Sibson). For instance, data sampled at different places along a cultural cline seriate, but the sequence should not be mistaken for a chronological one. (Irwin illustrated from Hell Gap how a 'false' seriation might result).

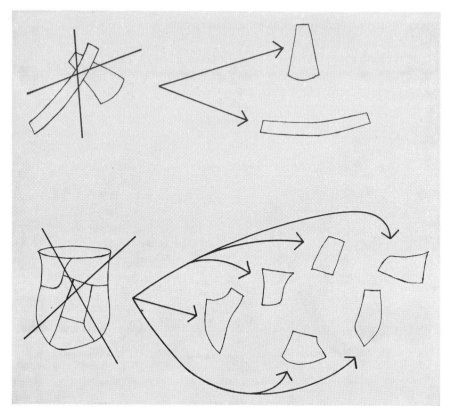

Figure 7

Against the background of this 'conceptual map' of archaeology, the contributions to the Mamaia conference should be plotted. This is helped by the comparatively substantial archaeological exemplification presented (an indication of advance in the bridge-building from methodology to application!)

(1) A first question will concern the archaeographical levels of application.

The silence, mainly, on mini-structures is easy to explain and has good reasons: mathematical methods are already commonplace there, but have to be identical with those of the cooperating natural sciences; thus, there is not the same need for special treatment.

There was a concentration on basic, 'midi' structures; and among these on artifacts (Borillo-Ihm Greek sculptures, Chinese bronzes; Hodson palaeolithic handaxes; Fernandez de la Vega and Landau figurines; Savu Greek vases). Monuments received less attention (Comănescu and Mateescu Vădastra, Moore Roman mosaics). Refuse and marks were treated in part (Irwin Hell Gap), or not at all.

However, interest for maxi-structures was not entirely lacking; but it concentrated close to the artifact level, in contributions on the ordering and so on of grave inventories and hoards (Doran, Kendall, Sibson Münsingen; Goldmann Central European Bronze Age; Kivu-Sculy graves), or on artifact assemblages from sites (Ammerman epipalaeolithic sites in Italy; Borillo-Ihm Deh Luran; Hesse Mirgissa, Kruskal-Wish Amazonas, Orton Highgate, Simeonova Goljamo-Deltschevo); only in a few contributions cemeteries and settlements (Rowlett-Pollnac); analysis of prehistoric landscape (Oprescu Porţile de Fier) and 'culture groups' (Iosifescu and Tăutu Urnfield culture subgroups) were actualized.

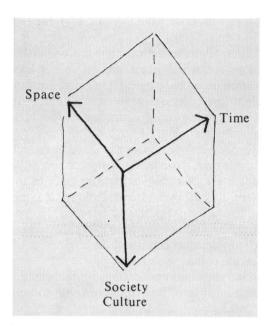

Figure 8. Points of a sequence are within the cube

(2) This takes us close to a second question: which types of relations were studied? For obvious reasons, space-similarity-time relations apply themselves readily to existing mathematical methods for clustering and sequencing-seriation. Among these three directions, the study of spatial relationships already has comparatively well advanced mathematical and statistical tools for locational analysis. Such tools are being used increasingly in archaeology which is oriented toward cultural geography. From the concentration on artifacts of the Mamaia conference it follows that the emphasis was entirely in the second direction, of similarity analysis. But as far as similarity studies have to use spatial models, many contributions were in a broad intersection of locational and similarity analysis.

Obviously, the analysis of *chronological* relations was much in focus. If such relations were not treated so explicitly on their own behalf, this is a natural consequence of the fact that time cannot be observed by the archaeologist himself, but only introduced as extrinsic information (history, C_{14}, geochronology) or inferred from spatial and similarity relations.

The 'ex-construction' relationship mentioned above was actualized in important contributions (Irwin, Hell Gap site; Orton Highgate kilns and dumps).

(3) A third question could concern the complex, more-than-one type relations, such as they appear increasingly in maxi-structures. There were some signs of awareness that such relations exist and create special problems. But the existence of this decisive threshold was more hinted at than thoroughly discussed. Then, finally, on an extreme maxi-structural level, the problems of the ecological aspect of archaeology were touched on, not so much from the archaeological side, but rather by representatives of physical anthropology and of genetics, whose participation was most valuable, not only for this reason.

Further exploration of possibilities of mathematical cooperation on the maxi-structural levels of archaeology seems important. This is so not least because at these levels problematics of archaeological interpretation are actualized more; and this may help to overcome a possibly existing but, if so, certainly erroneous attitude that the application of mathematical methods should be limited to archaeographical description.

It happens that analogies from linguistics appear in archaeological research (Tăutu and Iosifescu). Even if it is true that, if too far fetched, such analogies can be dangerously misleading, there are also obvious positive reasons for investigation in the intersection of linguistics and archaeology. To this writer it seems possible that there is a principal similarity between the type of mathematical problems actualized by multi-type relations within archaeological maxi-structures, and of problems encountered in argument on language structures above the minimal components levels.

An archaeologist's comment on the presented applications of mathematics in historical sciences in a strict sense must be of limited interest. But to him, these applications seemed rather 'archaeological'. In epigraphy, letters and signs were treated as a sort of artifacts and with an archaeological program, mainly for chronological purposes (Ştefan). In linking problems, (Boneva, Buneman, Haigh, and Niţă) manuscripts were treated as complex artifacts, again partly with archaeological programs, and again partly in order to establish chronology, on the basis of a 'genealogical' tree, with concepts not too far from those used by archaeologists when they try to establish the 'genealogy' and chronology of a set of artifacts, but with copying and innovation as factors. So far, the application of mathematical methods in history seemed to be on a very important auxiliary level of establishing good order in a source material.

Other contributions were more concerned with inferential aspects of historical research (Bulgaru). But also the problems discussed there were not too dissimilar from those actualized in contributions on general problems in archaeological research method (Borillo, Manolescu, and Bordenache).

So far, this has been an attempt to 'map' archaeology and 'plot' contributions against this background. Of course the writer is entirely incompetent to even try to 'map' mathematics and statistics for a plotting from the other side of the (more or less) transparent screen between us. He must confine himself to a few and necessarily superficial remarks—mainly a sort of questionnaire.

There were interesting contributions (Lerman) towards answering such vital questions such as

'How does the choice of attributes influence, or is influenced by, the mathematical methods?'

'Which are the archaeological and mathematical effects of different kinds of similarity coefficients?'

But mainly, these types of questions, on work to do before computing, were not so much discussed. If this reflects a situation in the development of methods where these problems can be regarded as mainly solved, then there is no objection. If not, the need for future work in these directions has to be emphasized.

From an archaeologist's point of view, it seems unlikely that they can be thought of as solved. In the majority of procedures, several different attributes as components are merged into one expression: a 'similarity coefficient', a 'correlation coefficient', or a 'subspace of reduced dimensions containing all the necessary information' (Borillo and Ihm). A postulate for such treatment is that the merged components are equally important, presumably. Are they, really? The archaeologists' answer will be 'no', more often than not.

In this situation, it may seem tempting to experiment with weighting of variables (*compare* Maliţa). One can compare the results of alternatives with different weighting of one and the same variable (including the alternatives of giving it maximal weight $=1$ or minimal weight $=0$; by admitting it, or not admitting it). For such situations, techniques enabling systematic comparisons between results of alternative weightings (Wish) are interesting.

For several reasons, tools for comparing procedures are most important: comparisons of the mathematical functioning (as Borillo and Ihm, Edwards, Solomon); and, among these, not least comparisons using measures for comparing the effects of application of different procedures on the same data, or of the same procedures on different data (Gelfand, Gower and Savu). But for the archaeologist, the comparison that has to be made ultimately is the one between the results and the archaeological interpretation (Hodson Münsingen).

For many a good reason, the conference had a marked one-sidedness in the input side of the majority of the procedures presented. This explains the dominance of the matrix as a tool. Here, there is a marked development from a 1959 symposium paper, with emphasis on four-cell tables, and just a final paragraph on matrices—up to the present situation with matrices used to express relations in terms of incidence or abundance, between structures (as, for example, graves) and their components (as, for example, artifacts) —*see* figure 9(a)—then matrices expressing relations among structural components (as, for example, artifact types) in different degrees of similarity, expressed by coefficients [*see* figure 9(b)]; even the use of similarity matrices for similarity between similarities [*see* figure 9(c)] was suggested. The 'best' ordering within the matrices was a dominating goal.

All this will do, as long as relations (- - -) within a structure (-.-.-) are of one and the same type, or when the difference in type between the relations is negligible because of the nature of the problem treated. But what will happen in the more complicated maxi-structural situations mentioned above? Is one to use several sets of matrices simultaneously, one for each type of relation, treating these as different dimensions? (like INDSCAL?) or are there other mathematical tools, more adequate for this sort of problem?

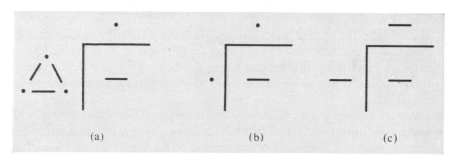

(a)   (b)   (c)

Figure 9

An archaeologist's questionnaire on the applications of mathematics includes also several questions which were discussed, even if no answer or only partial answers could be arrived at.

How far are automatic 'best order' searching methods technically and economically feasible? Beyond which point are step-wise eliminating methods preferable? Or are they the only alternative?

Do non-computer methods of sufficient reliability and facility exist for use in the field or in institutions with limited resources? Or is access to sophisticated computer service a *conditio sine qua non* for the application of methods of sufficient mathematical efficiency and reliability? Obviously, the answers to these questions decide whether the application of mathematical methods is going to be a prerogative for a few centres for archaeological study, with the ultimate perspective that active archaeological research will have to be concentrated into such centres, and 'tactical' archaeology at organizationally and financially undeveloped low levels disappear?

At this point, it seems urgent to inventorize 'manual' procedures, and adequate tools such as, for example, nomograms and visualizing graphical techniques. There is at least one task of increasing importance where 'manual' work is indispensable: in teaching, in order to make the goals and functioning of automatic methods understandable by way of experimenting with smallest scale models.

Can methods be developed which are more suitable than the present ones for the treatment of such incomplete and fragmentary materials as are usually encountered in archaeology? Considerable steps in this direction were demonstrated and welcomed (Borillo and Ihm). The polythetic class is a concept which obviously deserves careful investigation (Lerman).

For an archaeologist of my generation, the mathematical/statistical procedures themselves must remain very much black boxes—because of an insufficient or nonexistent mathematical background. Everything is welcome which can make us understand at least the typology of the 25–30 procedures presented. Discussions gave some impressions that the number may be more apparent than real, because the figure is increased by different sets of terminology for procedures which are mathematically equivalent, or at least so close to each other that they can give archaeologically equivalent results.

Of practical importance, if not more, is the increasing use of graphical representations on the output side. This trend recalls another paragraph in the instructions for speakers: 'it will be essential . . . to use pictorial representation'. Visual representation on computers seems to have possibilities for developing into a most important path for facilitating the difficult intercommunication between mathematicians-statisticians, and archaeologists. But this is true only on condition that these representations will be understood correctly by us archaeologists. We have to learn that a tree does not necessarily symbolize a phylogeny, for example.

Of course, it should be remembered that the conference was planned to concentrate on some principal themes, especially taxonomy-typology, and seriation. A result, in contrast to the dominance of procedures involving measures of similarity (dissimilarity, distance, proximity) was the infrequent use of terminology from, for example: infinitesimal calculus; probability theory (Gower, Sankoff, and Lerman); operations research (Malița); game theory (Oprescu); topology (Moisil); graph theory (Wilkinson); information theory (Oprescu); or simulation (Vaduva).

Finally, some questions which are undoubtedly important for archaeologists were left next to untouched, within a wide range from sampling techniques to hybrid or even pure analogue computers. A main impression is that a positive change is going on, even if slowly, in communication between mathematicians-statisticians, and archaeologists-historians. Difficulties today will be reduced tomorrow, by the coming of a new generation of archaeologists, trained to be better prepared for joint tasks. *Teaching is a key*, to future cooperation.

Will the Mamaia conference indicate the direction for forthcoming developments in the intersection of mathematics with archaeology-history? Or can such development be expected in other directions than those dominating here? If so, will the intersection area be enlarged? and are archaeology-history only the receiving partners? or can they contribute to fertilizing extensions of the contact of mathematics with phenomena of not so much studied classes?

So far, cooperation has resulted in a considerable application of well advanced, and advancing, statistics to traditional archaeology. But the goals of archaeology are broadening, and are getting more diversified. It may be promising to look for applications also of advancing mathematics to advancing archaeology.

REFERENCES

Archéologie et calculateurs (1970) *Problèmes sémiologiques et mathématiques.* Paris: Centre national de la recherche scientifique.

Binford, S.R. & Binford, L.R. (eds) (1968) *New Perspectives in Archeology.* Chicago: Aldine.

Calcul et formalisation dans les sciences de l'homme. (1968) Paris: Centre national de la recherche scientifique.

Chang, K.C. (1966) *Rethinking archaeology.* New York: Random House.

Clarke, D.L. (1968) *Analytical archaeology.* London: Methuen.

Cook, S.F. & Heizer, R.F. (eds) (1960) *The Application of Quantitative Methods in Archaeology.* Viking Fund Publications 28. Chicago: Quadrangle.

Griffin, J.B. (ed) (1951) Essays on archaeological methods. *Anthropological Papers.* Museum of Anthropology, University of Michigan, 8. Ann Arbor: University of Michigan Press.

Koltchin, B.A. (ed) (1965) *Archeologija i estestvennye nauki.* Nauka, Moskva: Akademia nauk SSSR, Institut archeologii.

Moberg, C.A. (1961) Mängder av fornfynd. Kring aktuella tendenser i arkeologisk metodik. Summary. *Acta universitatis Gothoburgensis Göteborgs universitets årsskrift,* **67** (1), 1–31.

Moberg, C.A. (1968) On recent experiments with similarity determination in archaeology. A review article. *Liber Iosepho Kostrzewski octogenario-dicatus,* pp. 578–85. Wroclaw, Warszawa. Krakow: Zakllad narodowy Ossolinskich.

Moberg, C.A. (1969) Introduktion till arkeologi. Stockholm: Natur och kultur.

Moberg, C.A. (1970a) Remarques pragmatiques sur quelques problèmes théoriques dans l'archéologie de la Scandinavie occidentale aux environs de 1300 av. J.-C. *Archéologie et Calculateurs,* pp. 25–43.

Moberg, C.A. (1970b) (Comment on Clarke 1968) *Norwegian archaeological Review,* **3,** 21–4,

List of Participants

Alexandrescu-Dersca-Bulgaru, Matilda-Maria, Institutul de Istorie, Bd Aviatorilor 1, București

Allsworth-Jones, P., Emmanuel College, Cambridge

Ammerman, A.J., Institute of Archaeology, 31–4 Gordon Square, London wc1

Bentzon, M.W., Biostatistical Department, Statens Serum Institut, Amager Bd 80, 2300 Kobenhavn

Boneva, Liliana, Mathematical Institute of Bulgarian Academy of Sciences, Ant. Ivanov 1, Sofia 26, Bulgaria

Bordenache, Gabriela, Institutul de Arheologie, Str. i.c. Frimu 11, București

Borillo, M., Centre d'analyse documentaire pour l'archéologie, 31 Chemin Joseph-Aiguier, 13 Marseille 9

Bulgaru, V., Centrul de Statistică Mathematică, Calea Griviței 21, București 12

Buneman, O.P., Department of Machine Intelligence and Perception, University of Edinburgh, 2 Buccleuch Place, Edinburgh eh8 9lw

Buzatu, G., Institutul de Istorie și Arheologie, Bd K. Marx 15, Iași, Romania

Cavalli-Sforza, L.L., Istituto di Genetica, Via Sant' Epifanio 14, 27100 Pavia

Comănescu, S., Institutul de Arhitectura, Căsuța poștală 223, București

Demonet, M., Sect. Sciences économiques et sociales, Ecole Pratique des Hautes Etudes, 14–16 Butte aux Cailles, Paris 13

Doran, J., Atlas Computer Laboratory, Chilton, Didcot, Berkshire

Driml, M., Ustav teorie informace a automatizace, Vysehradská 49, Praha 2-Nové Mesto, Czechoslovakia

Edwards, A.W.F., Gonville and Caius College, Cambridge

Evnine, Rosaly, 120 Oakwood Court, London w14

Fagarasan, J.T., 977 N. Wilton Pl., 9 Los Angeles, California 90038

Gelfand, A.E., Department of Statistics, University of Connecticut, Storrs, Connecticut 06268

Goldmann, K., Museum für Vor-und Frühgeschichte, Schloss Charlottenburg, 1 Berlin 19

Gower, J.C., Statistics Department, Rothamsted Experimental Station, Harpenden, Herts

Graham, J., Computer Unit, University of Reading, Whiteknights, Reading rg6 2af

Guiașu, S., Institutul de Matematică, Calea Griviței 21, București 12

Haigh, J., University of Sussex, 89 Norwich Drive, Brighton

Hesse, A., Centre de recherches géophysiques, 58 Garchy (Nièvre), France

Hiorns, R.W., Department of Biomathematics, University of Oxford, Pusey Street, Oxford ox1 2tz

Hodson, F.R., Institute of Archaeology, 31–4 Gordon Square, London wc1

Hollingsworth, T.H., University of Glasgow, Adam Smith Street, Glasgow w2

Ihm, P., Institut für Medizinisch-Biologische Statistik und Dokumentation, Cölber Strasse 1, 355 Marburg/Lahn, West Germany

Ioniță, I., Institutul de Istorie și Arheologie, Bd K. Marx 15, Iași, Romania

Iosifescu, M., Centrul de Statistică Matematică, Calea Griviței 21, București 12

Irwin, H.T., Department of Anthropology, Washington State University, Pullman, Washington 99163

Kahk, J., Institute of History of the Academy of Sciences of Estonian ssr, Estonia Bd 7, Tallinn, Estonia ssr

Kendall, D.G., Statistical Laboratory, University of Cambridge, 16 Mill Lane, Cambridge

Kidd, K.K., Istituto di Genetica, Via Sant'Epifanio 14, 27100 Pavia

Kivu-Sculy, Ileana, Facultatea de Matematică-Mecanică, Universitatea București, Str. Academiei 14, București

Kristeva, Maria, Mathematical Institute of Bulgarian Academy of Sciences, Ant. Ivanov 1, Sofia 26, Bulgaria

Kruskal, J., Bell Telephone Laboratories, Murray Hill, New Jersey 07974

Lerman, I.C., Centre de mathématiques appliquées et de calcul, Maison des Sciences de l'Homme, 54 Bd Raspail, Paris

Liveanu, V., Institutul de Istorie, Bd Aviatorilor 1, București

Loynes, R., Department of Probability and Statistics, University of Sheffield, Sheffield s3 7RH

Malița, Mircea, Ministerul Invățămîntului, Str. Spiru Haret 12, București

Manolescu, Mircea, Str. Pictor Stahi 14, București 45

Mateescu, C.N., Institutul de Arheologie, Str. I.C. Frimu 11, București

Matthews, Jane P., Department of Probability and Statistics, University of Sheffield, Sheffield s3 7RH

Mermillod, Bernadette, Institut de Statistique, 16 Bd d'Yvoy, 1211 Genève

Mihoc, G., Centrul de Statistică Matematică, Calea Griviței 21, București 12

Moberg, C.-A., Institutionen för Nordisk Och, Göteborgs Universiteit, Andra Langgatan 29–3 van, s–413 03 Göteborg, Sweden

Moisil, G.C., Institutul de Matematică, Calea Griviței 21, București 12

Moore, R., Anatomy Department, Guy's Hospital Medical School, London SE1

Moroni, A., Department of Genetics, University of Parma, Institute of Zoology, 43100 Parma

Nandris, J.C., Institute of Archaeology, 31–4 Gordon Square, London WC1

Niță, S., Centrul de Calcul al Comitetului de Stat al Planificării, Calea Victoriei 152, București

Nivat, M., 9 rue Portalis, Paris 3

Obretenov, A., Mathematical Institute of Bulgarian Academy of Sciences, Ant. Ivanov 1, Sofia 26, Bulgaria

Olkin, I., Department of Statistics, Stanford University, Stanford, California 94305

Oprescu, N., Institutul de Construcții, Facultatea de Drumuri și Poduri, Bd Lacul Tei 124, București

Orton, C.R., Ministry of Agriculture, Fisheries, & Food, Whitehall Place, London

Parker-Nunley, J., Department of Anthropology, El Centro College, University of Texas, 6626 Santa Anita, Dallas, Texas 75214

Pollnac, R., Department of Anthropology, College of Arts and Sciences, University of Missouri, Columbia, Mo. 65201

Postelnicu, T., Centrul de Statistică Matematică, Calea Griviței 21, București 12

Rao, C.R., Indian Statistical Institute, 538 Yojana Bhavan, Parliament Street, New Delhi 1

Rundfeldt, H., Tierartzliche Hochschule, Bischofsholer Damm 15, 3 Hanover 1

Sâmboan, Anca, Centrul de Statistică Matematică, Calea Griviței 21, București 12

Sankoff, D., Centre de recherches mathématiques, Université de Montréal, c.p. 6128, Montréal 101

Savu, Silvia, Centrul de Statistică Matematică, Calea Griviței 21, București 12

Sibson, R., King's College Research Centre, Cambridge

Skolnick, M., Istituto di Genetica, Via Sant'Epifanio 14, 27100 Pavia

Solomon, H., Statistical Department, Stanford University, Sequoia Hall, Stanford, California 94305

Spaulding, A.C., College of Letters and Science, University of California, Santa Barbara, California 93106

Ștefan, Alexandra, Institutul de Arheologie, Str. I.C. Frimu 11, București

Ştefan, S., Institutul de Arheologie, Str. i.c. Frimu 11, Bucureşti

Tăutu, P., Centrul de Statistică Matematică, Calea Griviţei 21, Bucureşti 12

Todorová-Simeonová, Henrieta, Institute of Archaeology of Bulgarian Academy of Sciences, Bd Stamboliiski 2, Sofia, Bulgaria

Vaduva, I., Centrul de Calcul al Universitatii Bucureşti, Str. Stefan Furtună 125, Bucureşti

Vajda, I., Ustav teorie informace a automatizace, Vysehrdaska 49, Praha 2-Nové Mesto, Czechoslovakia

Vega, Fernandez de la W., Centre d'analyse documentaire pour l'archéologie, 31 Chemin Joseph-Aiguier, 13 Marseille 9

Vogel, W., Institut für Angewandte Mathematik, Lutfridstrasse 8, 53 Bonn

Voinescu, Rodica, Facultatea Matematică-Mecanică, Universitatea Bucureşti, Str. Academiei 14, Bucureşti

Voorrips, A., Institut voor Prae-en Protohistorie, Universiteit von Amsterdam, Nieuwe Prinsengracht 41, Amsterdam

Weerd, M. Derk de, Institut voor Prae-en Protohistorie, Universiteit von Amsterdam, Nieuwe Prinsengracht 41, Amsterdam

Wilcock, J., North Staffordshire Polytechnic, Deaconside, Stafford

Wilkinson, E. M., Statistical Laboratory, University of Cambridge, 16 Mill Lane, Cambridge

Wish, M., Bell Telephone Laboratories, Murray Hill, New Jersey 07974

Zitek, F., Matematický Ustav, Zitná Ulice 25, Praha 1, Czechoslovakia